Contemporary Social Science Curriculum

The Earth, Home of People — Big Book
Families and Their Needs
Communities and Their Needs
People Use the Earth
Regions and Their Needs
This Is Man
MAN AND SOCIETY
Man and Change
Man and His World

PICTURE PACKETS
Families Around the World (series)
Holidays and Special Occasions (series)

Contemporary Social Science Curriculum

AUTHORS

Edna A. Anderson   Associate Professor,
Department of Elementary Education, St. Cloud State College

Norma Jean Anderson   Associate Professor,
Center for Counseling and Human Relations, University of Massachusetts

V. Phillips Weaver   Chairman,
Department of Early Childhood — Elementary Education, University of Maryland

Walter N. Gantt   Associate Professor,
Department of Early Childhood — Elementary Education, University of Maryland

Robert A. Harper   Chairman,
Department of Geography, University of Maryland

Vincent R. Rogers   Chairman,
Department of Elementary Education, University of Connecticut

Herbert J. Bass   Professor of History, Temple University

Kenneth S. Cooper   Professor of History, George Peabody College for Teachers

George H. T. Kimble   Former Chairman,
Department of Geography, Indiana University

CONSULTANTS

James G. Womack, District Superintendent of Schools,
Livingston, Steuben, and Wyoming Counties,
New York

George A. Davis, Former Associate Director of Commission
on Geography of Afro-America

Roy A. Price, Chairman of Interdepartmental Social Science Program,
Maxwell Graduate School of Citizenship and Public Affairs,
Syracuse University

TEACHERS' EDITIONS AUTHORS

Irene Zabawski, Elementary School Teacher,
East Northport, New York, Public Schools

Joseph H. Dempsey, Director of Academic Advancement Program,
Morristown, New Jersey, Public Schools

Gussie M. Robinson, Educational Specialist,
Department of History, Washington, D.C., Public Schools

Sister Mary John Binder, C. S. J., Elementary School Teacher,
Los Angeles Archdiocesan Schools

James O'Hern, Principal, Steele Middle School, Galesburg, Illinois

CRITIC READERS

Bertha Harris, Elementary School Teacher,
Santa Ana Unified School District, Santa Ana, California

Dan Fleming, Assistant Professor,
College of Education, Virginia Polytechnical Institute and State University

Amyan Caporaso, Elementary School Teacher,
Morris Township, New Jersey, Public Schools

Judy Grinwis, Upper-team Teacher,
Tredyffrin-Easttown School District, Berwyn, Pennsylvania

Lewis J. Webster, Coordinator for Closed Circuit Television,
Chicago Public Schools

Thomas Fitzgerald, Elementary School Teacher,
Colorado Academy, Englewood, Colorado

Connie Morgan, Former Elementary School Teacher,
East Islip, New York, Public Schools

Odell Enoch, Geography Teacher, Lawton Public Schools, Lawton, Oklahoma

Charles Lallos, Geography Teacher, Meriden, Connecticut, Public Schools

MAN AND SOCIETY

HERBERT J. BASS
Professor of History
Temple University

End–of–Chapter Material prepared by GEORGE A. DAVIS
Former Associate Director of Commission
on Geography of Afro-America

SILVER BURDETT COMPANY
A Division of General Learning Corporation

MORRISTOWN, NEW JERSEY
PARK RIDGE, ILLINOIS PALO ALTO DALLAS ATLANTA

Page 44: From *Royal Commentaries of the Incas* by Garcilaso de la Vega. Translated by Harold V. Livermore (Austin, Texas: University of Texas Press, 1966) Vol. I, pp. 248, 257, 262, 263, 397. © 1966 University of Texas Press. Page 69: From the Sunday, June 21, 1970 edition of *The New York Times,* Section One, Vol. CXIX, p. 1. © 1970 by The New York Times Company. Reprinted by permission. Pages 84–85: From *Father Henson's Story of His Own Life,* edited by Walter Fisher (New York: Corinth Books, Inc., 1962) Copyright © 1962 Corinth Books Inc. Page 86: From *Judicial Cases Concerning American Slavery,* edited by Helen T. Catterall. Reproduced by the courtesy of the Carnegie Institution of Washington. Pages 96, 97: From *Immigration as a Factor in American History* by Oscar Handlin. (New Jersey: Prentice-Hall, Inc., 1959), pp. 18–19, 21–22. © 1959 by Prentice-Hall, Inc. Pages 97, 98: From *Land of Their Choice* by Theodore Blegen (Minneapolis: University of Minnesota, 1955), pp. 22, 53, 56. © Copyright 1955 by University of Minnesota. Pages 97–98, 195: From *Americans In The Making* by William Smith. Copyright © 1939 by William Smith. Published by D. Appleton Century Co. Reprinted by permission. Pages 109, 426: From *The Mexican Americans of South Texas* by William Madsen, (New York: Holt, Rinehart and Winston, Inc., 1964), pp. 14, 17. © 1964 by Holt, Rinehart and Winston, Inc. Page 111: From *Passage to America* by Katherine B. Shippen, pp. 128–129. Reprinted by permission of McIntosh and Otis, Inc. Pages 118, 411: Poems by Barbara T. Howell. Pages 128, 130: From *The Discovery and Conquest of Mexico 1517–1521,* by Bernal Diaz del Castillo, translated by Alfred Percival Maudslay, M.A., George Routledge & Sons, 'The Broadway Travellers' Series, 1928. Edited from the only exact copy of the original MS (and published in Mexico) by Genaro Garcia. Copyright 1956 by Farrar, Straus & Cudahy. Reprinted by permission of Routledge & Kegan Paul Ltd., and Farrar, Straus & Giroux, Inc. Pages 143, 192: From *A Son of the Middle Border,* by Hamlin Garland (New York: P. F. Collier & Son), Copyright 1914 and 1917 by P. F. Collier & Son; Copyright 1917, 1924 by Hamlin Garland. Pages 167–168: From *The Urban Frontier,* by Richard Wade (Cambridge: Harvard University Press, 1959), pp. 31–32. © 1959 by the President and Fellows of Harvard College. Page 188: From *Harper's Chicago and the World's Fair,* published in 1893 by Harper & Brothers. Pages 193–194: From *Sea Island to City* by Clyde Vernon Kiser (New York: Columbia University Press, 1932). Copyright 1932 by Columbia University Press, pp. 118–119, 121, 137. Page 194: From "Letters of Negro Migrants of 1916–1918" edited by Emmett J. Scott, published in Journal of Negro History, October 1919, Vol. IV, pp. 461–462. Copyright © by The Association for the Study of Negro Life and History, Inc. Page 196: From *Mount Allegro* by Jerre Mangione (New York: Alfred A. Knopf, Inc., 1943). Copyright 1943, 1952 by Jerre Mangione. Reprinted by permission of Alfred A. Knopf, Inc. Pages 212, 213, 407: From *Youth in the Ghetto,* A Study of the Consequences of Powerlessness and a Blueprint for Change, by Harlem Youth Opportunities Unlimited, Inc. © Copyright 1964, by Harlem Youth Opportunities Unlimited, Inc. pp. 314, 315, 317, 318, 322. Page 352: From *A Blind Hog's Acorns* by Carey Pratt McCord (Chicago: Cloud Inc., 1945), p. 4. Reprinted by permission of the author. Page 352: From *Darkness and Daylight, or Lights and Shadows of New York Life,* by Helen Campbell (*The New York Times,* February 16, 1882). Copyright 1882 by The New York Times Company. Reprinted by permission. Page 403: From *The New York Times,* May 22, 1969, p. 87. © 1969 by The New York Times Company. Reprinted by permission.

© 1972 General Learning Corporation. All Rights Reserved. Printed in the United States of America. Published simultaneously in Canada. This publication, or parts thereof, may not be reproduced in any form by photographic, electrostatic, mechanical, or any other method, for any use, including information storage and retrieval, without written permission from the publisher.

CONTENTS

unit one
INVESTIGATING CULTURE

1 THE MEANING OF CULTURE   3

Learning About Culture • People Do Many of the Same Things • Why Different Ways of Living? • Values and Culture • Customs and Culture • Everyone Is Part of a Culture Group • Different Nations, Similar Cultures

2 EARLIEST AMERICANS   21

The Coming of Man to America • The Cultures of the Indians • North American Indians • Many Different Cultures • People of Middle America: The Mayas • The Second Group: The Aztecs • The Third Group: The Incas

3 EUROPEANS AND AFRICANS COME TO THE NEW WORLD   47

Christopher Columbus • Spanish Conquest • Brazil • The Differences in the Cultures • Africans Come to America

4 CULTURE IN SOUTH AMERICA TODAY   63

The Motilones of Venezuela • Culture in Peru Today • An Experiment in Vicos • Culture in Brazil

5 EUROPEANS AND AFRICANS COME TO NORTH AMERICA   75

Europeans Settle North America • Why People Chose to Come • Africans Come to the English Colonies • Europeans and Indians Learn from Each Other • Many Europeans, Many Cultures • Europeans Begin to Become Americans

6 A NATION RICH IN CULTURES   95

How Did Immigrants Learn of America? • The End of a Sad Migration • People from Far and Near • Different Cultures in the New Environment • Preserving Some Ways of Living • Variety Leads to Richness

unit two
INVESTIGATING URBANISM

7 LEARNING ABOUT CITIES   123

Two Cities of America · Tenochtitlán · Tenochtitlán Faces Its Problems · Philadelphia, 1776 · Philadelphia Faces Its Problems · Closer to the Answer · Looking at Farm Life

8 AMERICAN CITIES GROW FROM VILLAGES   147

Studying Location · The Change from Farm Villages · City Problems Change a Way of Living · Safeguarding the People · The Public Health

9 GROWTH OF CITIES, 1800–1900   165

Cities Develop in the West · Cities Grow Along the Great Lakes · Railroads and Cities · Manufacturing Helps Cities Grow · Cities Push Outward

10 LIFE IN THE CITY BY 1900   191

People from the Farms · Southern Black Farmers · People Come from Other Lands · A Changing Way of Life · What the Newcomers Found in Cities · People Describe Slums · Poor Conditions Help Spread Disease

11 CITY LIFE IN OUR TIME   207

People Still Move to Cities · People from the Western Hemisphere · Black Migration Continues · People Leave the City, Too · Megalopolis · Other Kinds of Cities Grow · Los Angeles, a City Made by Climate · Life in Our Cities Today

12 IMPROVING OUR CITIES   231

New Haven Rebuilds Itself · Rebuilding Residential Areas · Our Urban Traffic Problem · Fresno Makes Some Changes · Building New Cities · Steps in Solving Urban Problems · How Would You Decide? · Rebuilding Cities Costs Money

13 CITIES IN SOUTH AMERICA AND CANADA   253

Introducing the South American Continent · Choosing Sites for Cities · Government Cities in South America · Three Important Cities · Some Problems of South American Cities · Cities in Canada

unit three
INVESTIGATING INDUSTRIALISM

14 LEARNING ABOUT INDUSTRIALISM   287

Producing Iron in Colonial Days · Iron and Steel Today · Milling Wheat—Past and Present · The Wheat Industry Today · The Textile Industry · Textile Manufacturing Today

15 MAIN FEATURES OF INDUSTRIALISM — 307

Reasons for the Difference · Machines—Past and Present · New Sources of Power · Raw Materials · Large Factories and Markets · Cultural Values and Industrialism

16 THE UNITED STATES BECOMES AN INDUSTRIAL NATION — 323

Beginnings in England · The Revolution Comes to America · Railroads and Industries · New Sources of Energy · Industrialization Comes to the Farm · Industrialism Continues to Expand

17 INDUSTRIALISM CHANGES OUR WAYS OF LIVING — 345

Industrialism Changes Ways of Working · Some Evils of Industrialism · Early Steps to Control Industrialism · The American Worker in Modern Times · More Effects of Industrialism Today · Problems Still Remain · Pollution Grows Worse · Action Against Pollution

18 WESTERN HEMISPHERE NEIGHBORS INDUSTRIALIZE — 373

The Land of Colombia · Steps Toward Industrialization · Some Problems to Overcome · The Government Takes Important Steps · Education Plays a Big Part · Need for Investments · Industry in Canada

unit four
INVESTIGATING AMERICAN VALUES AND GOVERNMENT

19 EQUALITY — 397

All Men Are Created Equal · Equality for Many, but Not for All · Equality of Opportunity · Equality and Government · An Equal Voice in the Government

20 FREEDOM — 413

People Without Freedom · Freedom Comes to America · Forming a New Government · The Meaning of Freedom Grows · Limiting Freedom to Protect Our Rights

21 DEMOCRACY — 429

Making Laws in a Democracy · How Does Democracy Work? · Making Your Voice Heard · Democracy Needs Laws

22 MAKING A DECISION IN A DEMOCRACY — 443

Bringing Change to Philadelphia · Organizing the Opposition · Reviewing the Decision · Congress Passes a Law · Congress Takes Action

Map Skills 464
Atlas 472
The Constitution of the United States 488
Glossary 492
Index 498

MAPS, CHARTS, AND SPECIAL INTEREST MATERIALS

MAPS

Routes of Early American Indians	23
North American Indians	25
The Mayan and Aztec Empires	35
The Incan Empire	39
Routes of the Spanish Explorers	49
African Homeland of the Slaves	57
Islands in the Caribbean Sea	59
Independence in South America	59
The Motilone Indians	64
The Three Perus	65
European Settlement in Colonial Days, 1650	76
English Settlements, 1650	78
National Groups in English Colonies, 1700	81
The United States, 1783	96
Slaves in the U. S., 1790	99
The Nation Divided, 1861	101
Land Claims in North America, 1750	114
Land Claims in North America, 1763	114
Canada	117
Valley of Mexico	124
Tenochtitlán	126
Colonial Pennsylvania, 1700	133
Philadelphia in 1776	134
Philadelphia and Countryside	138
Colonial Towns and Cities, 1776	148
Colonial Cities, 1776	149
Products of the Colonies, 1776	152
New York in 1776	154
Boston in 1750	156
Charleston in 1776	160
River Valley Cities (Map A)	167
River Valley Cities (Map B)	168
Lake Sites	172
Trade Before the Erie Canal	173
Trade After the Erie Canal	174
Railroads, 1860	176
Towns of the Plains and Mountains	177
Cities of the Plains and Mountains	178
Cities in the U. S., 1870	183
Cities in the U. S., 1900	184
Homelands of the European Immigrants, 1900–1910	195
Concentration of Blacks in an American City	211
Growth of a Black Ghetto	212
Population Growth, 1960–1970	216
The Eastern Megalopolis	218
Renewal in New Haven	236
BART System	240
Renewal in Fresno	244
Landforms of South America	254
Land Use in South America	257
Highways of South America	259
Railroads of South America	259
Population Density in South America	261
Major Cities in South America	262
Brasília	268
Land Use in Canada	278
Population Density in Canada	279
Principal Cities in Canada	281
Iron and Steel Works, 1750	288
Raw Materials for Steel	289
Steel Making in the U. S.	294
The Wheat Industry	300
Steel Making in the Great Lakes Region	332
Petroleum Fields and Pipelines	336
Nuclear Power Plants	341
Colombia	374
Mineral Resources of Colombia	376
Transportation in Colombia	382
Resources of Canada	388
United States Representatives	433
Downtown Philadelphia	444
The Proposed Crosstown Expressway	445
The Redwoods of California	454
The Proposed Redwood National Park	457
The Redwood National Park	458

MAP SKILLS

Directions	464–465
Symbols	466–467
Scale	468
Road Map	469
Contours	470
Latitude and Longitude	471

ATLAS

The World (Political)	472–473
North America (Physical)	474
North America (Political)	475
United States of America (Physical-political)	476–477
South America (Physical)	478
South America (Political)	479
Africa (Physical)	480
Africa (Political)	481
Eurasia (Physical)	482–483
Eurasia (Political)	484–485
Australia and Oceania (Physical-political)	486–487

CHARTS

Who Were the Americans in 1775?	80
National Origin of Immigrants to the U.S., 1820–1968	103
Population of Some Cities, 1800–1860	181
Population of Some Cities, 1870–1900	185
Where the People Lived	208
Immigration from Europe and the Western Hemisphere	209
Black Population in Major Cities, 1960	210
Percent of the Total Black and White Populations Living in Metropolitan Areas and Central Cities	210
Population of the Ten Largest Cities in the U.S., 1950–1970	214
A Plan for Downtown Areas	242
Urban Water Supply in the Americas	274
Production of Coal, Crude Petroleum, and Pig Iron	330
Coal, Iron, and Railroad Track, 1810–1900	334
Farm and Manufacturing Population	335
Man, Animal, and Machine Power	341
Manpower Production Hourly Output	341
Value of Goods and Services	361
Farm and Urban Population	361
Farm Products at Different Altitudes	375
Natural Resources Production	379
Colombian and U.S. Imports and Exports	380
Transportation and Communication in Colombia	382
Separation of Powers	423

SPECIAL INTEREST MATERIALS

Mayan Ideas of Beauty	36
To Help You Read	43
Independence Comes	60
Carnaval	71
A Slave Auction	86
The Great Plains	179
Another Invention Helps Cities	188
How Does Urban Decay Happen?	226–227
Urban Renewal, or Negro Removal?	234
The Recipe for Steel	296

CREDITS

Cover: Plasencia Design Associates
Maps in text and in Map Skills: Lothar Roth
Maps in Atlas: Richard Edes Harrison and Lothar Roth
Graphs and Charts: James Harvin
Unit Openers: Ted Lewin
Special Interest Material Art: Otto van Eersel, except page 296: Eva Cellini

The sources for the illustrations are listed below. Some have been abbreviated as follows: AMNH — American Museum of Natural History; BB — Brown Brothers; C — Culver; WSH — William Sherwood Howe; MK — Monkmeyer Press Photo Service; N-YHS — New-York Historical Society; NYPL, Rare Books — New York Public Library, Rare Book Division, Astor, Lenox and Tilden Foundations; NYPL, Stokes — New York Public Library, I.N. Phelps Stokes Collection, Print Division, Astor, Lenox and Tilden Foundations; PR — Photo Researchers; SA — Shostal Associates; UPI — United Press International. Placement of pictures on each page is indicated as follows: *L.* (left); *R.* (right); *T.* (top); *M.* (middle); *B.* (bottom).

CHAPTER 1: 2 — George Holton, PR. 4 — *T.* WSH; *M.T.* John Dominis for *Life;* *M.B.* and *B.* WSH. 5 — *T.L.* WSH; *T.M.L.* Stephanie Dinkins, PR; *B.M.L.* WSH; *B.L.* Carl Frank; *T.R.* and *T.M.R.* WSH; *B.M.R.* MK; *B.R.* United States Department of Agriculture. 7 — Eric Carle, SA. 9 — WSH. 10 — WSH. 13 — John Lewis Stage, PR. 14 — Pro Pix, MK. 15 — WSH. 16 — *L.* Dmitri Kessel for *Life; M.* WSH; *R.* A. Devaney, Inc. 18 — *L.* Robert Perron; *M.* Dick Hufnagle, MK; *R.* Walter Aguiar.

CHAPTER 2: 20 — WSH. 26 — courtesy AMNH. 27 — *T.* SA; *B.* courtesy AMNH. 29 — Bettmann Archive. 30 — *T.* NYPL, Rare Books. 31 — courtesy AMNH. 32 — *T.* SA; *B.* Bob Westmoreland, SA. 33 — Ray Manley, SA. 35 — Marie Mattson, SA. 38 — Museum fur Volkerkunde, Vienna. 40 — Lee Boltin. 41 — WSH. 42 — WSH. 43 — WSH.

CHAPTER 3: 46 — Rene Burri from Magnum. 51 — Dmitri Kessel for *Life.* 53 — BB. 55 — NYPL, Rare Books. 58 — NYPL, Rare Books.

CHAPTER 4: 62 — Manchete from Pictorial Parade. 66 — WSH. 67 — WSH. 68 — WSH. 69 — Catherine Leroy from Nancy Palmer Agency. 72 — Dmitri Kessel for *Life.*

CHAPTER 5: 77 — Jamestown Foundation. 83 — NYPL, Rare Books. 85 — no credit. 88 — C. 89 — courtesy N-YHS. 90 — no credit. 92 — Ian McLaughlin and American Heritage Publishing Company.

CHAPTER 6: 94 — Horst Schafer from Photo Trends. 98 — Swedish Pioneer Historical Society. 102 — Southern Pacific Railroad. 104 — Allyn Baum, MK. 106 — Allyn Baum from Rapho Guillumette. 108 — Fujihira, MK. 109 — Kenneth Parsons from DeWys. 110 — Russ Kinne, PR. 112 — Mahon, MK. 113 — Hugh Rogers, MK. 115 — Annan Photo Features from Photo Trends.

CHAPTER 7: 122 — Inge Morath from Magnum. 126 — Ray Manley, SA. 127 — Gerster from Rapho Guillumette. 129 — George Holton, PR. 130 — Illustrations from Codex Mendoza, 16th-century early colonial manuscript, Bodleian Library, Oxford. 135 — Herbert Orth. 136 — Herbert Orth, courtesy New York State Historical Association. 139 — NYPL, Stokes. 141 — NYPL, Stokes. 142 — Horace Bristol for *Life.*

CHAPTER 8: 146 — Detail: James B. Marston, Old State House, 1801. oil painting, 37½" × 57¼", courtesy Massachusetts Historical Society. 150 — N-YHS. 151 — From *Lewis Miller, Sketches and Chronicles* published by the Historical Society of York County, in York, Pennsylvania. 153 — NYPL, Stokes. 155 — Clements Kalischer. 158 — NYPL, Stokes. 162 — N-YHS.

CHAPTER 9: 169 — Carnegie Library of Pittsburgh. 171 — Cincinnati Public Library. 175 — C. 182 — Worcester Art Museum. 187 — Library of Congress.

CHAPTER 10: 190 — N-YHS. 192 — BB. 196 — BB. 198 — N-YHS. 201 — Sy Seidman. 202 — C. 204 — Bettmann Archive.

CHAPTER 11: 206 — George Silk. 215 — *L.* Hugh Rogers, MK; *R.* courtesy Publishers Hall Syndicate. 217 — Somerset Valley Industrial Campus. 219 — Florida Development Commission. 220 — Tom McHugh, PR. 222 — *T.* Ralph Morse for *Life; B.* Michael Rougier for *Life.* 223 — *T.* David Krasnor, PR; *B.* Falk, MK. 224 — Art Shay. 225 — Burt Glinn from Magnum. 228 — Sue Johns.

CHAPTER 12: 230 — E.R. Degginger. 233 — Bruce Cunningham-Werdnigg. 235 — Bruce Cunningham-Werdnigg. 238 — Bruce Cunningham-Werdnigg. 239 — courtesy Publishers Hall Syndicate. 243 — Tidyman Studios. 246 — Gulf-Reston, Inc. 248 — Joe Munroe, PR. 250 — Bruce Cunningham-Werdnigg.

CHAPTER 13: 252 — Manchete from Pictorial Parade. 255 through 276 — WSH. 280 — George Hunter, SA.

CHAPTER 14: 286 — Corning Glass Company. 290 — National Park Service. 291 — American Iron and Steel Institute. 293 through 297 — Bethlehem Steel. 299 — Wide World. 301 — T.E. Ibberson Co. 303 — The Wool Bureau. 304 — Leviton of Atlanta, courtesy J.P. Stevens Company.

CHAPTER 15: 306 — Tennessee Valley Authority. 308 — MK. 310 — MK. 313 — Van Bucher, PR. 314 — *T.* Russell Lamb, PR; *B.* Michael Lewi, SA. 315 — Hugh Rogers, MK. 316 — Bethlehem Steel. 318 — Merrimack Valley Textile Company. 319 — Oregon Historical Society. 320 — Bethlehem Steel.

CHAPTER 16: 322 — Charles Rotkin, P.F.I. 327 — Smithsonian Institution. 328 — Gin owned by J.H. Elliott, Sr. and J.H. Elliott, Jr., Atlanta Museum. 329 — BB. 331 — Art D'Arazien, SA. 333 — Lou Moore, SA. 337 — Ford News Bureau. 338 — E.R. Degginger. 339 — United States Department of Agriculture. 340 — International Harvester Company. 342 — Art D'Arazien, SA.

CHAPTER 17: 344 — Benyas-Kaufman from Black Star. 347 — C. 348 — C. 349 — George Eastman House. 350 — George Eastman House. 351 — William Vandivert for *Fortune.* 353 — George Eastman House. 354 — Grant Heilman. 355 — C. 357 — Francis Miller for *Life.* 358 — Farrell Grehen, PR. 360 — Michael Rougier for *Life.* 362 — Ralph Crane for *Life.* 363 — *T.* BB; *B.* National Coal Association. 364 — Burk Uzzle, Magnum. 365 — Robert Blasko, SA. 366 — Rev. James Buckman, SA. 367 — Richard Knapp from Photo Trends. 368 — Tom Morton, SA. 370 — UPI.

CHAPTER 18: 372 — Walter Aguiar. 377 through 387 — William Howe. 391 — Annan Photo Features from Photo Trends.

CHAPTER 19: 396 — Steve Shapiro for *Life.* 398 — Henry Beville. 400 — A. Y. Owen for *Life.* 403 — UPI. 405 — Pat Kirkpatrick, SA. 406 — John Dominis for *Life.* 408 — SA. 410 — A. Devaney.

CHAPTER 20: 412 — R. W. Kelley for *Life.* 415 — Syd Greenburg from D.P.I. 417 — UPI. 418 — courtesy Colonial Williamsburg. 420 — C. 425 — Truman Moore for *Life.*

CHAPTER 21: 428 — Fred Ward, Black Star. 430 — UPI. 431 — New England Mutual Insurance Company. 432 — Bob Peterson for *Life.* 435 — UPI. 437 — Joe Scherschel for *Life.* 438 — Charles Bonnay for *Life.* 440 — UPI.

CHAPTER 22: 442 — Charles Philips for *Life.* 446 — Arthur Tress from Photo Trends. 449 — Venturi and Rauch. 450 — no credit. 453 — David Muench. 460 — Ralph Crane for *Life.*

ATLAS: 466 — Ewing Galloway.

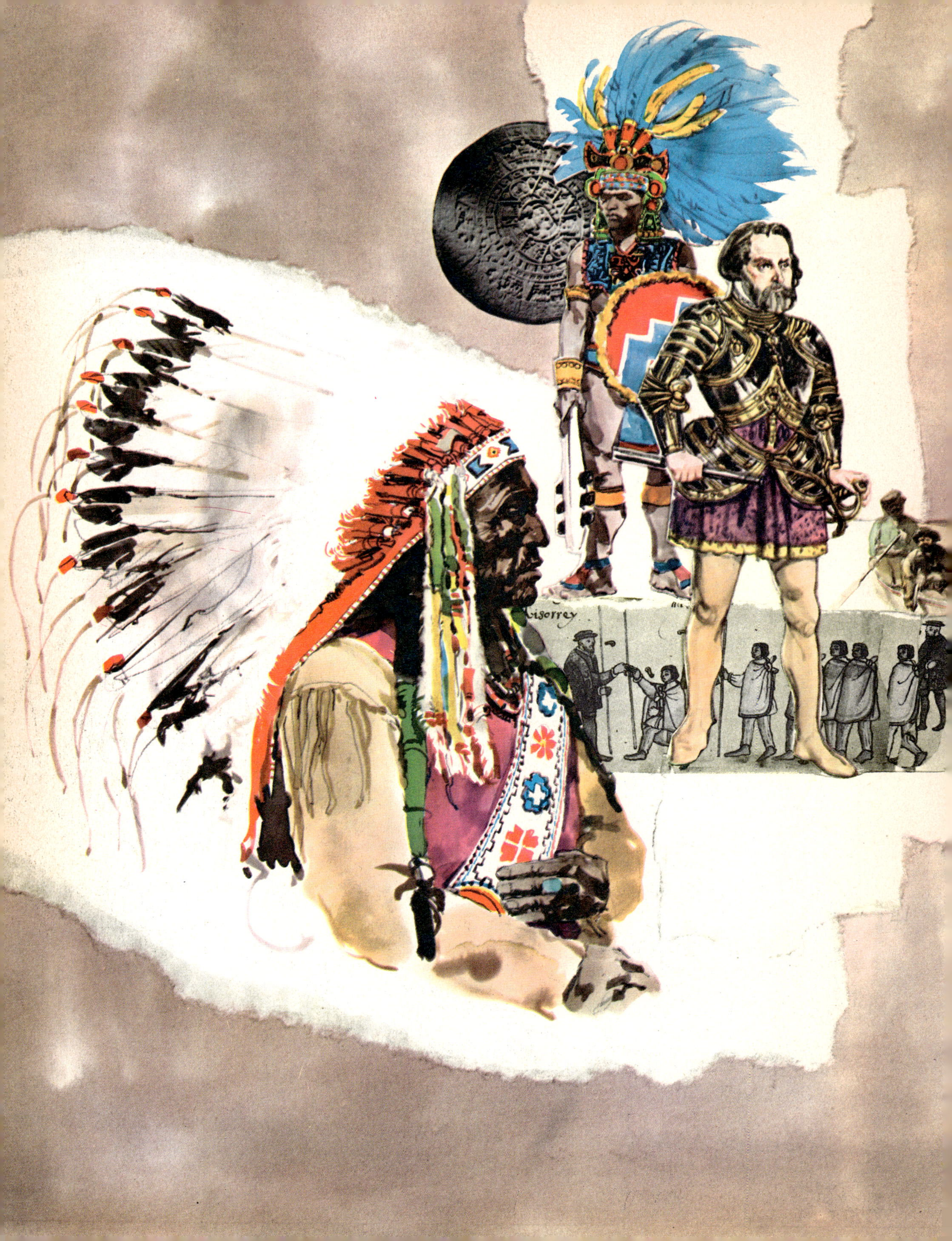

unit one
INVESTIGATING CULTURE

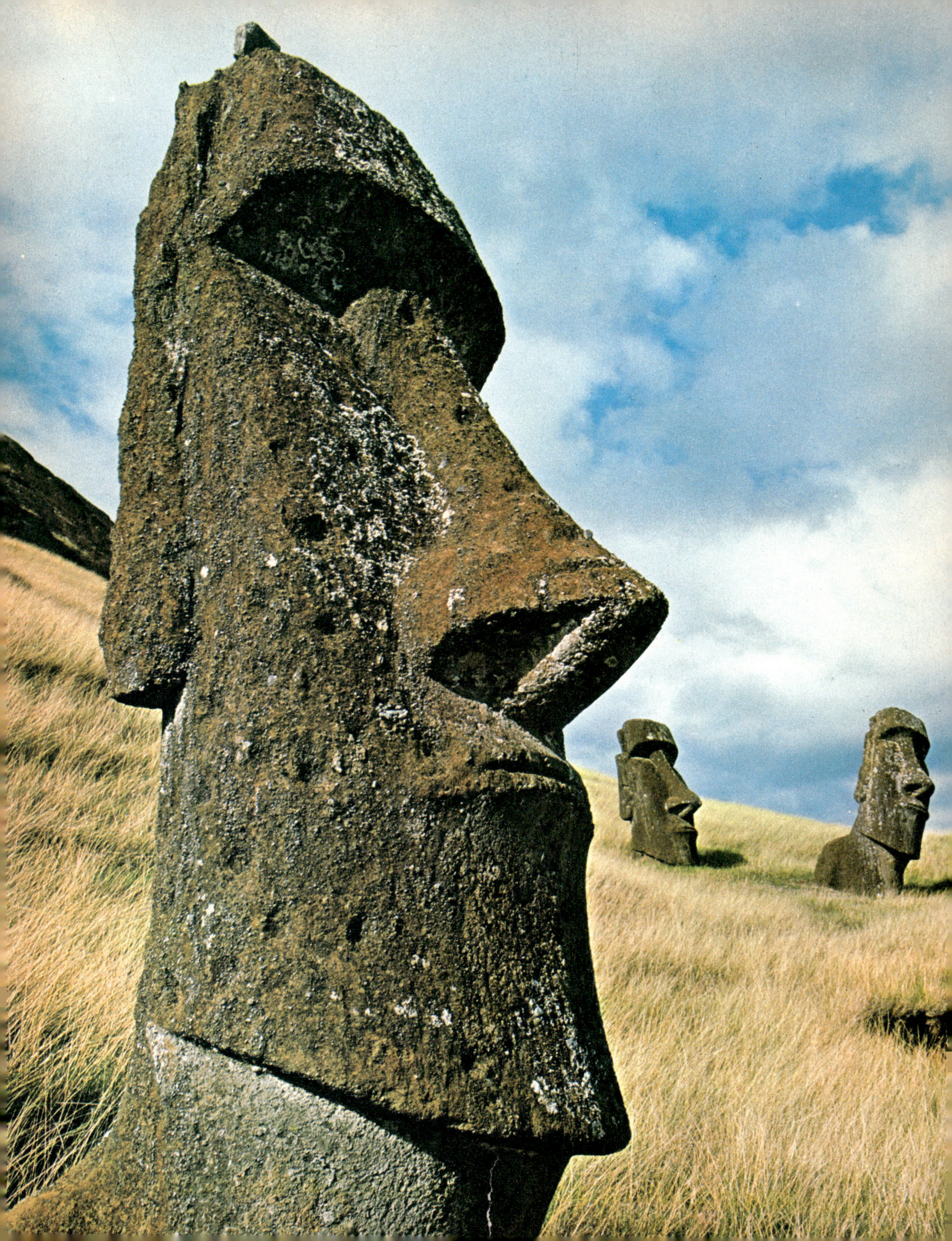

The Meaning of Culture

This chapter is about a small word that stands for a very important idea. The word is *culture*, and we are going to discover what culture is.

You may have heard the word culture before. The word is used in different ways at different times. Sometimes we speak of "cultural activities." By this we mean things like listening to or playing good music, creating or looking at fine art, going to the theater to see plays or to take part in them—things of that sort. We say that people who are interested in these activities are "cultured" people.

In this book we are interested in a special meaning of the word culture. It is the meaning given to it by *social scientists.* Social scientists study the way individuals and groups of people live in society. They try to understand man as he was in the past and as he is now. Their knowledge of man comes from many different subjects—history, geography, government, religion, and even the music, artwork, and writings of different peoples.

You are already familiar with some of the findings of social scientists. Much of the information they have gathered is found in social science books. Now let us try to find out what social scientists mean by culture.

Learning About Culture

To help you understand this meaning of culture, we are first going to study pictures of some of the many people who live in North and South America. The pictures show them doing a variety of things. Of course these are not *all* the people of North and South America, and the pictures do not show all the things the people of these lands do. These pictures were chosen to show you something special about the people in them. We are going to work with these pictures in order to learn something about *all* people. Each picture has a number. Try to decide which pictures seem to belong together. Which of the pictures seem to have something in common?

There is no one right way to group them. You might decide to make two groups, or three or four, or as many as you wish. You can use the same picture in several different groups. Just be sure that in each of your groups, the pictures belong together for some reason; that is, be sure they have something in common. Mark their numbers down in groups; for example, pictures 1, 3, 5, and 6 in one group, pictures 2 and 4 in another group, 1, 2, and 5 in another, and so on. Go ahead and try.

Now let's see how you did with them. How did you put them together? Maybe you decided to put all the pictures with modern machines in one group, and those without machines in

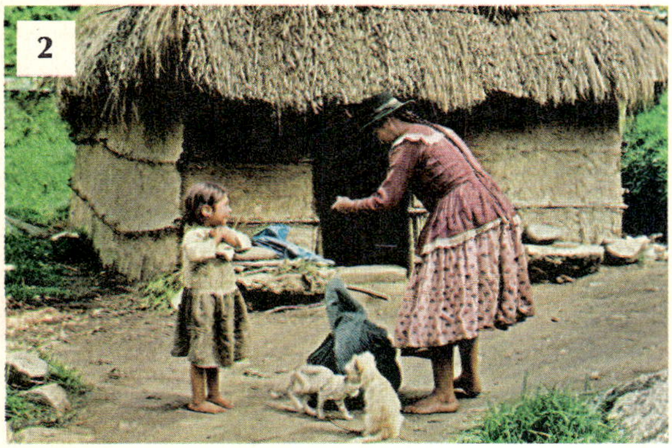
2

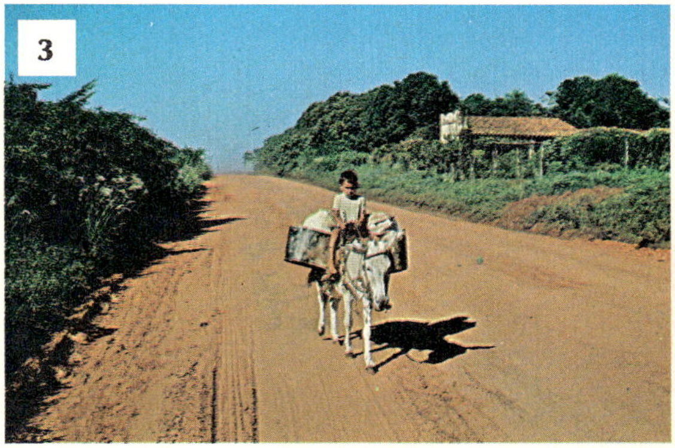
3

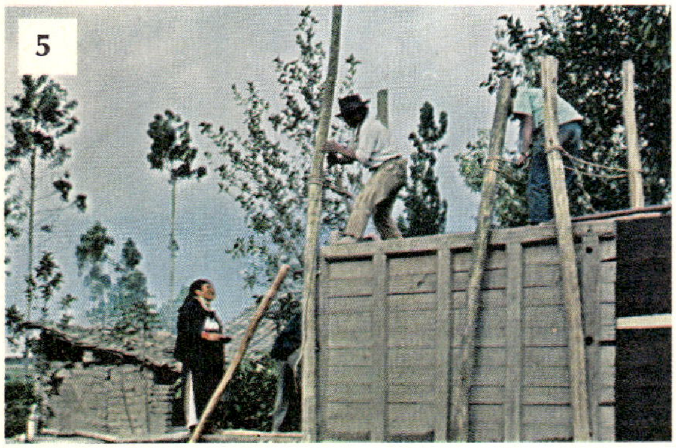
5

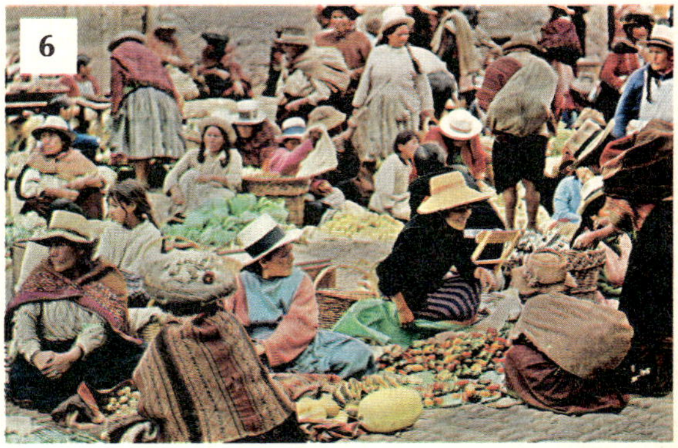
6

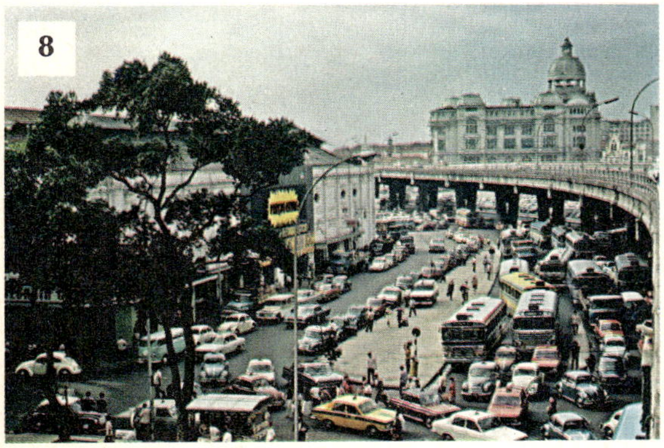
8

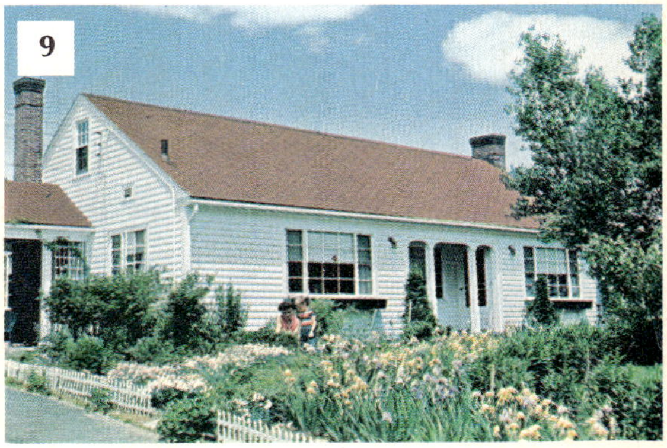
9

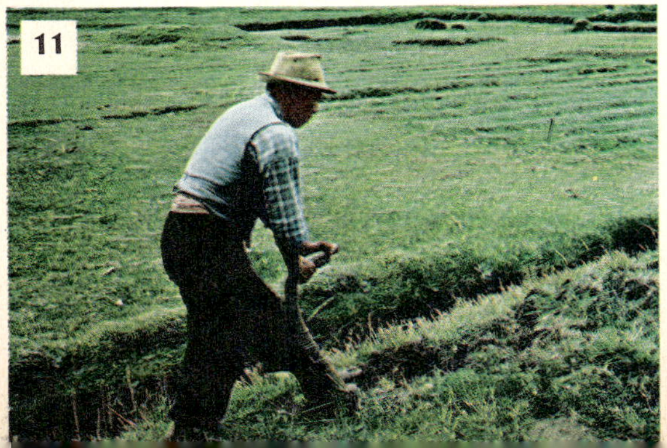
11

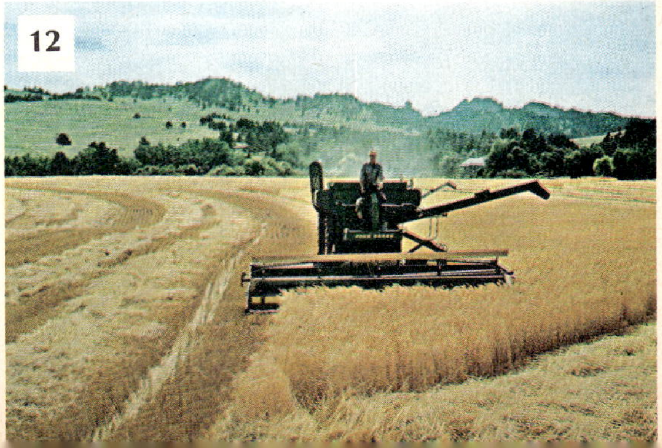
12

another. That would be one way of doing it. Or perhaps you put together pictures 2, 3, and 7 because they all have children in them. That is all right, too. Actually, you could group them in many ways.

Grouping the pictures by activities. One way you might have decided to do this was to put pictures 11 and 12 in one group. If you did not, try it now. What does this group of pictures have in common? Try pictures 4 and 6. Do you see anything they have in common?

As you see, in both of these groups people are engaged in the same kind of activity. Take the first group. Picture 11 shows an Indian who lives in the South American nation of Peru. He lives high in the Andes Mountains, two or three miles above sea level. The land he is farming is rocky, and he does not have any modern tools to help him raise his crops. About the only power he can use besides his own muscle is provided by the llama (lä′ mə). This Indian farmer is quite different from the man on the machine in picture 12. This wheat farmer, who lives in the state of Kansas, is farming on fertile soil. He has all sorts of modern equipment and the latest knowledge about farming to help him. His wheat crop is large because he has planted specially developed seed and has used *fertilizer.* Different as they are, the Peruvian (pə rü′ vē ən) Indian and the Kansas wheat farmer are doing the same kind of thing—they are getting food.

In pictures 4 and 6 you see people who are buying and selling, or trading. The woman in picture 4 can probably drive to a supermarket every day. She is picking out groceries, for which she will pay money. Her way of trading is different from that of the women in picture 6. Once a week they leave their villages to go to the market to sell their wares. They may travel many miles. Because they rarely use money, these women will probably trade their goods for other products instead of for money. Even though the people in these two pictures have very different ways of living, they are engaged in the same kind of activity—trading. Look again at the pictures on pages 4–5 and see if you can make another group in which people are doing the the same kind of thing.

People Do Many of the Same Things

Actually, we could have shown many more pictures of different people in North and South America doing these same things. For example, we could have shown a picture of a Navaho (nav′ ə hō) Indian, who lives in the state of Arizona in the dry American Southwest, farming his parched lands with little more than a hoe and a rake. Or a wheat farmer on the broad prairies of central Canada, moving his

These children are playing games familiar to most American children.

reaper over the golden fields of wheat. Or a farmer in the Imperial Valley of California, irrigating the land from which so many of the vegetables of America come.

Satisfying needs. We could have shown pictures of all those people doing the same thing in many different ways, because people everywhere must have food to live.

Look again at the pictures on pages 4–5 and see which ones show different ways of transporting goods and people. Can you think of other forms of transportation we might have shown people using? Again, you see, we could have shown many pictures of people or goods being moved from one place to another, because people everywhere use some kind of transportation.

We are beginning to discover that all people, no matter who they are or where they live, have much in common and do a great many of the same things.

Of course you know what some of those things are. You know that all people wear clothing, even if they wear very different kinds. People have shelters of some kind. Have you ever heard of people who have no language? Or of people who do not have some kind of religion? All people have ways of teaching their children. Knowing how much fun games are, you will not be surprised to learn that people everywhere play games and have athletic sports. Indians who lived in Mexico long before Columbus came to America used to play a game like basketball. They also painted, carved, and did weaving just as people everywhere have done.

Have you ever wondered about learning manners and obeying rules? Children in every group of people have probably wondered the same thing, for people everywhere have developed manners and rules to live by. They also all have punishments for breaking those rules!

People have all these things in common because they have the same basic needs and they must solve certain problems to satisfy these needs. The biggest problem is how to make a living. We may live in many different surroundings, or *environments* (en vī'-rən mentz)—in the mountains or on flat farmlands, in dry *climates* or rainy ones, in hot lands or cold lands. Wherever we live, we must all learn what we can or cannot do in an environment if we are to survive. We must get food and we must have shelter and clothing even if the clothing is as different as that in pictures 2 and 4.

Man has other needs, too. Man is a group animal—that is, he lives in groups of people. He needs other people, and therefore must develop ways of getting along with them. So he develops rules, laws, and manners. Everywhere, he develops ways of worshipping God, whether he calls Him God, or the Great Spirit, or Nature.

Why Different Ways of Living?

We have seen from our pictures that men living in different lands do many of the same things. The same pictures help us to discover something else just as important.

Take another look at the pictures. You will recall that we agreed that pictures 4 and 6 showed people who had something in common. They are really satisfying a need. Are the people all satisfying the need in the same way?

Do you think the people in picture 2 live in the same way as those in picture 9? What about the people in pictures 6 and 8? How do you think their lives might differ?

We have already stated one important idea about people when we said that they do many of the same things because they have the same needs. Now we can add a second idea. People do many of the same things, but they do them in different ways.

What makes one people's way of living different from another's? Why does the Indian farmer from Peru in picture 11 have a different way of living from that of the Kansas wheat farmer in picture 12?

Tools and knowledge make a difference. One important reason is that he uses very different tools. How is the Indian *cultivating* the soil? Now look at the machine the Kansas wheat farmer is driving. This machine can cut the wheat and *thresh* it, or shake the kernels from the rest of the stalk. In a few seconds it can harvest the wheat grown on a piece of land about the size of your classroom.

This machine and the other machines that the Kansas farmer uses make it possible for him to harvest many times more wheat in one day than the Peruvian farmer can harvest. It is clearly a much better tool than the one being used by the man in picture 11.

What made the threshing machine possible? It required a great deal of scientific knowledge. Think of the many materials in it—steel, aluminum (ə lü′ mə nəm), copper, rubber, and many more. People first had to know about these materials, and then had to have the knowledge to make use of them. The motor alone is a marvel. Not much larger than your desk and chair, it has the pulling power of several hundred horses. There could be no such machine until people had enough knowledge to get the idea for a motor, to build one that could work, and to get energy from gasoline to run it.

There are several reasons why the Kansas farmer's crop is so large. Scientists have learned how to make the soil richer by adding certain chemicals (kem′ ə kelz). They have also produced special seed that grows extra-large wheat kernels. Moreover, they have learned how to control pests and insects that might eat the crop.

Levels of technology. You can see that the Kansas wheat farmer and the Peruvian Indian raise food in different ways because of the scientific knowledge their societies have and the tools and machines they use in their work. These two things—scientific knowledge and tools—are what we mean by the word *technology* (tek nol′ ə jē). We speak of a people's *level of technology* to describe the amount of scientific knowledge and the kinds of tools they have. If the tools are very simple and the people have not learned much

This South American farmer has a gasoline engine to help him. But what can you say of his level of technology?

about science, we say they have a low level of technology. Which of the two farmers in pictures 11 and 12 has a low level of technology? Which has a high level of technology?

Technology affects ways of living. How will their different levels of technology affect the ways of living of the Peruvian farmer and the Kansas farmer? Let us see some of the ways. Which one will raise just enough food for his own family, and which will have more than he needs for his family? What will the latter do with this surplus? How will the amount of wheat each one raises affect his way of living?

A society that has farm machinery like that of the Kansas farmer will have many other machines, which do many different jobs. The Peruvian Indians will have very few machines. Think of your own way of life. Think of just one day in your life—yesterday, for example—from the time you got up until you went to bed. How would your day have been different if you had no more machines and scientific knowledge than the people in pictures 2, 6, and 11?

Values and Culture

Many other things besides technology make up a people's way of life. An important thing is their beliefs about what is good, desirable, and worth holding to. We call these beliefs *values*.

These South American farmers have few tools to help them in their stick farming.

We do things and say things because of our values—even though we may not realize it.

What are values? Let us see what we mean by values. Here are a number of statements. As you read each one, ask yourself, does this mean anything to me? If it does, do I agree with this idea, or do I disagree? Or do I really care about it one way or the other?

1. It is important to work hard so you can make something of yourself.
2. Every person, no matter who he is, should be treated with the same fairness as every other person.

10

3. You should always be a good sport, and never be a bad loser.
4. You should tell the truth at all times.
5. You should never say or do things that might hurt other people's feelings.
6. It is important that you have lots of friends.
7. Having a new car and a big house and being able to buy expensive things are what people should work for.
8. You should always try to help those who are less fortunate than yourself.
9. The most important thing in life is to be happy.
10. You have to look out for yourself in life. If you do not succeed, that is your tough luck. No one can be expected to help the unsuccessful.
11. If a man owns something, he should have the right to do whatever he wants with it. Nobody has the right to tell him how and when to use it.
12. Everyone should have an equal chance to become whatever he wants to be, whether he is born rich or poor.
13. The whole community has a right to tell a man what he is allowed to do with his property, and what he is not allowed to do with it.
14. Stealing is bad.
15. It is right and fair that children who are born poor should expect to remain poor.
16. Learning is very important. Children should go to school and study hard in order to get ahead.
17. Going to war makes a nation strong and great. War brings out the best in people and nations.
18. People should live in peace with each other.

Understanding values. Look at the first statement. Do you agree with it? If you do, we can say that it is one of your values. Of course you may not agree with it. Then it is not one of your values. Now do the same with each statement. Think about what it means, and then decide whether you agree with it or not.

Perhaps you can think of some other values you have—things you believe are good and desirable. You probably can make your own list.

Now compare your feelings about these statements with the feelings of the other students in your classroom. Are there some ideas that nearly all the students feel the same way about? If there are, can we say they are some of the values of your class? Are they values that are shared by the students in your classroom?

Suppose we found that nearly all the students in your whole school shared these values. We might then think of these as the values of your school. What could we say if we found that most people in the nation shared these values?

All groups of people have values shared by most of their members. A club, a community, a church, or a whole society shares many values — things the group believes are good, important, and desirable for the well-being of its members. Shared values make the members of the group feel that they belong together, that they are not just a collection of people who have nothing in common.

Does this mean that every person will agree with every one of the group's values? No; some will disagree with this one or that one, just as some of your classmates probably disagreed with a few. But most people will accept the society's values as their own. For example, in our country almost all of us believe in statement 12 — everyone should have an equal chance to become whatever he wants to be, whether he is born rich or poor. That is one of the values of our society.

Are all values equally important? Now think about some of these values your class has agreed upon. Are they all equally important to you? Are some more important than others? If you had to pick out the three or four most important, which would you say they were? Do you think everyone in your class will choose the same three or four you do?

Do you think it is possible to have two values that might conflict? Think about statements 4 and 5, for example. Can you think of any times when you might have to choose between them because you cannot observe them both? Can you think of any other values that might conflict with each other? When people in the same society have to choose between two values, do you think all of them will agree on which is more important?

How do values affect culture? Now what do values have to do with ways of living? Think of how some of your values affect the way you and your family live. Recall statement 1: It is important to work hard so you can make something of yourself. If you believe in statement 1, will you do different things with your time than if you do not?

Look at statement 7 again: Having a new car and a big house and being able to buy expensive things are what people should work for. Will families who believe in statement 7 live differently from those who do not? In what ways? Do you think it is possible that poor people and rich people might have some different values? Can you think of any?

Suppose most people in your society believed in statement 17: Going to war makes a nation strong and great. That may seem like a strange notion to us, but many societies in the past believed just that. What kinds of things would be taught in schools? What skills would be most admired and imitated? How would people spend their spare time? Who would be the most honored people in the society, the ones children would be taught to look up to? What kind of career would most people train for? What would the government spend money on? Do you think these people would live differently than a society that believes peaceful living is good or a society that feels learning and education are very important things? Do you see why values have a lot to do with a people's way of living?

Customs and Culture

Another reason that ways of living are different is that people's customs differ. *Customs* are practices that are special to one people, or they are special ways of doing things common to many people. Customs include certain celebrations and even everyday occurrences. The passing on of customs from one generation to another is called *tradition* (trə dish′ ən).

Understanding customs. Customs are related to people's ways of thinking, their beliefs, their values, their work, their dealings with each other; in fact, to almost their whole way of life. The customs of a people can be understood only if we know more about their whole way of living.

A very common custom in many countries is the giving of gifts at Christmastime. Another custom is to have a big feast at harvesttime. In the United States we have turned this cus-tom into a holiday. You may be familiar with the custom of shooting off fireworks on the Fourth of July or of throwing rice at a wedding.

People in different countries have special ways of performing a marriage. They have different ways of greeting one another. Some people have certain customs to follow when children reach different age levels, or when they become adults. Often people continue with their customs even though the original meaning is forgotten.

Everyone Is Part of a Culture Group

At the beginning of this chapter, we said you were going to discover what culture is. Well, you have been doing just that as you looked at different

Bursting the piñata at Christmas time is an old Mexican custom. The piñata is filled with candies and toys.

ways of living. For culture, you see, is another word for "way of living." It includes everything that is a part of a way of life. The way people get food, even the way they prepare it and eat it, is part of their culture. So is the way they make a living and the way they buy and sell things. Their technology is part of their culture. Their values and their customs are, too.

You are part of a culture group, just as everyone else is. The kind of dwelling you live in, the language you speak, the holidays you celebrate, the way you worship, and the games you play are all part of your culture. So are your style of dress and the rules you live by. The way you spend your time each day is part of your culture, and it is very different from the way the

Do you think you will ever play among whale bones as these Eskimo children do?

children in the picture on this page spend theirs. In fact, you cannot think of anything you do, or have, or believe that is not part of your culture.

How do we "get" culture? Look back at statement 12 on page 11. Probably your whole class agreed with it, for in our culture nearly everyone shares this value. But did you know there are cultures in the world where the people do *not* share this value? They would say that it makes no sense to them at all. They believe in statement 15. Read that statement again. Do you agree with that?

How can it be that another person would not agree with you that everyone should have the chance to become something, no matter how poor he is? Yet that other person would wonder how *anyone* would not agree with him that people who are born poor should expect to stay that way.

Well, let us think about how that can be. First we have to ask where you got your ideas about statement 12. Can you recall when you first heard the idea? Have you ever heard your parents talk about it? Perhaps you heard it in school. Or maybe you read a story or saw a movie or television show in which a poor boy works very hard and becomes somebody important. You might have met the idea in a dozen different places and a dozen different ways. It became an important value in our culture long before you were born, or your teacher, or the writer of this book. Each culture passes along its values to its young people in countless ways. You were brought up with the idea, just as your teacher and the writer were. You did not even have to think about it. It came as naturally to you as breathing air.

Culture is learned. People are born into a culture. Each person begins to learn his culture in his earliest years, and he learns it from everyone and everything around him. He learns it from his parents, from school, from books, from the radio, television, and movies, from other people he knows or just sees.

It is not just the values of our culture that we learn. We learn everything else about our culture, too—manners, for example, and customs, and behavior. Take manners. What kind of tools do you use when you eat? Where did you learn to eat with a knife and fork? Why don't you use chopsticks? Children in China do. Why don't you just eat with your hands?

Take language. Why do you speak English, and not Portuguese (pôr′ chə-gēz′) as Brazilian (brə zil′ yən) children do? Or behavior. Did you learn you should be polite to others, and should share, and should wait your turn? Where did you learn that?

Maybe a better example is the foods you like. Think of some of your favorite foods. It is hard to believe anyone

Like all children, South American pupils learn much of their culture in school.

in the world would not like them. But did you know that other people have different ideas about what is delicious and that they might not like your special treats at all? Some Mexican children love foods so spicy and hot they would make your eyes water. These children might wonder why you like your special dishes so much. In northern Canada, children cannot imagine people not liking their favorite food—raw fish. If you had been brought up in those lands, you would have learned to eat their foods and would agree they are delicious—and probably would think the special treats you like so much now taste just awful.

You might think fighting is the same everywhere. After all, a fight is a fight. But in Colombia in South America there once lived some Indians who fought very differently from most people. About two hundred years ago a

15

Spanish priest who visited these people wrote the following account of how they fought.

> They do not use bows and arrows, nor any arms, defensive or offensive. Their fights and quarrels are really amusing. Each party to the fight carries a stick of wood to an agreed upon place, where there is a rock or a large tree. They then beat the rock or tree as hard as they can, while at the same time they shout insults at each other. The one who breaks his stick first is the winner, and the other admits that he is braver. Then they embrace and return to their homes in friendship.

Different Nations, Similar Cultures

Look at the three pictures on this page. Would you say that any two of them surely do not belong together? Are there two that do go together? How about the picture to the left and the one in the center?

What was it about these two pictures that made you decide they did not go together? They do not seem to have anything in common, do they? The picture to the left shows a fisherman in Bahia, which is in the northeast corner of Brazil. He is mending his net on shore. The fisherman just does not seem to fit with the man in the center picture. This man lives in an apartment house in Rio de Janeiro (rē′ ō dā zhə nər′ ō) a large city in Brazil. He is a factory manager there.

Of course, we cannot tell from the pictures, but do you have the feeling they probably follow different customs, that they might have some different values? We do know they have a different level of technology.

What other cultural differences might there be between these two persons?

Now look at the pictures in the center and to the right. Do the people in these pictures seem to have much in common? Would you say their levels of technology are alike? What kind of place do they live in? Would you say the way of living of the man in the picture to the right has more in common with that of the man from Rio de Janeiro or with that of the fisherman from Bahia?

The man in the picture to the right lives in San Francisco, California, one of the largest cities in the United States. He is an engineer. Certainly our apartment dweller from Rio de Janeiro seems to have more in common with this man from San Francisco than with the fisherman from Bahia.

But wait. What country is Bahia in? And what country is Rio de Janeiro in? Both the fisherman and the factory manager are Brazilians. They speak the same language, have the same religion, observe the same national holidays, and think of themselves as members of the same nation, Brazil. Is it possible that the way of life of a Brazilian living in Rio de Janeiro might be more like that of an American from San Francisco than like that of his fellow Brazilian from Bahia? But that is what the pictures seem to tell us. That certainly seems puzzling.

Culture is a whole way of living. Actually it will not be too puzzling if you remember that the idea of culture includes the whole way of living—all of man's activities and ways of thinking and behaving. It does not just mean the country he lives in. Of course it includes his language, his religion, and his national customs. But it also includes a great deal more—his values, his manners, the way he makes a living, the way he spends his spare time, and the level of technology he lives with.

Think again about our man from Rio de Janeiro. In some of his activities and thoughts he is very much like the Bahia fisherman. In these same ways he is also very unlike that engineer in San Francisco. But certainly in most other ways he seems to have more in common with the engineer. That is why you decided that the pictures of the man from Rio and the engineer from San Francisco go together, and the pictures of the man from Rio and the fisherman do not.

So you see, culture is not the same as country. People living in the same country *usually* share much the same culture. But they may also have very different ways of living, as we have just seen in the pictures of the two Brazilians. As the pictures of the residents of Rio de Janeiro and San Francisco showed us, it is very possible for people living in *different* countries to have *similar* ways of living.

When you study Unit II of this book, you will see how people who live in big cities have similar ways of living even though the cities are in different countries. Then in Unit III you will see that a high level of technology also creates similar cultures for people in different lands.

As you see, cultures differ from each other, but some are more different than others. Take a look at the pictures on this page. If you were to move from your own community, where do you think you might be most comfortable —with the people in the picture to the left, in the center, or to the right?

Do cultures ever change? What happens when one culture group comes into contact with another? Sometimes each group clings stubbornly to every single bit of its culture. But different cultures often borrow from one another. Not values, or religious beliefs, or customs, usually; those are the parts of culture that people hold on to most firmly. But cultures often borrow ideas and technology from each other. And it is a good thing they do, for without cultural borrowing there would have been very little human progress. Each group would have had to develop ideas themselves to do the things that other groups had already learned to do—like planting seeds, or domesticating (də mes′ tə kāt ing) animals, or making a wheel, or creating an alphabet—or, in our own time, inventing a car or a way to make steel. Without cultural borrowing, you might be reading this in a picture language on a stone tablet—if you were lucky!

18

Working with Concepts and Generalizations

Identifying Concepts

Choose the ending that correctly completes each sentence. Write the answers on paper.

1. The passing on of customs from one generation to another is called (a) habit, (b) tradition, (c) values.
2. Technology means two things: (a) scientific knowledge and tools, (b) values and traditions, (c) customs and beliefs.
3. Culture is another word for a (a) way of worshiping, (b) way of farming, (c) way of living.
4. If a group of people use simple tools and have not learned much about science, we can say they have a low level of (a) learning, (b) customs, (c) technology.
5. Beliefs about what is good, desirable, and worth holding to are called (a) values, (b) culture, (c) customs.
6. Three basic needs of all people are (a) land, tools, and transportation, (b) food, shelter, and clothing, (c) traditions, values, and customs.
7. Your culture is something you have learned from (a) everyone and everything around you, (b) studying other groups of people, (c) your classmates.
8. All people do many of the same things because they (a) have the same basic needs, (b) live in the same kind of environment, (c) have the same values.
9. Cultures often borrow (a) religious beliefs, (b) values and customs, (c) ideas and technology.
10. The values of a group are beliefs held by (a) all members of that group, (b) some members of that group, (c) most members of that group.

Developing Concepts

Write the answers on paper.

1. List three customs that are very special to your family. Tell why each is special. Do you think these customs are special to other families? Are these customs special to your grandparents? your aunts and uncles? your cousins?
2. Draw simple sketches of five different things that are part of your culture. Give each of your sketches a title. Are any of the things you have shown part of the culture of other people? Explain.
3. List five values that are most important to you. Put a star next to each value on your list that is also important to your family. Put an X next to each value on your list that you think is important to many of your friends. Are there any values on your list that are important only to you?
4. Do you live in a country that has a high, or a low, level of technology? How do you know?

Generalizations

Read the generalizations listed below. Using what you have learned, write two examples that show each generalization is true. Write on paper.

1. All people have much in common and do many of the same things.
2. Every culture passes on its values and customs to its children.

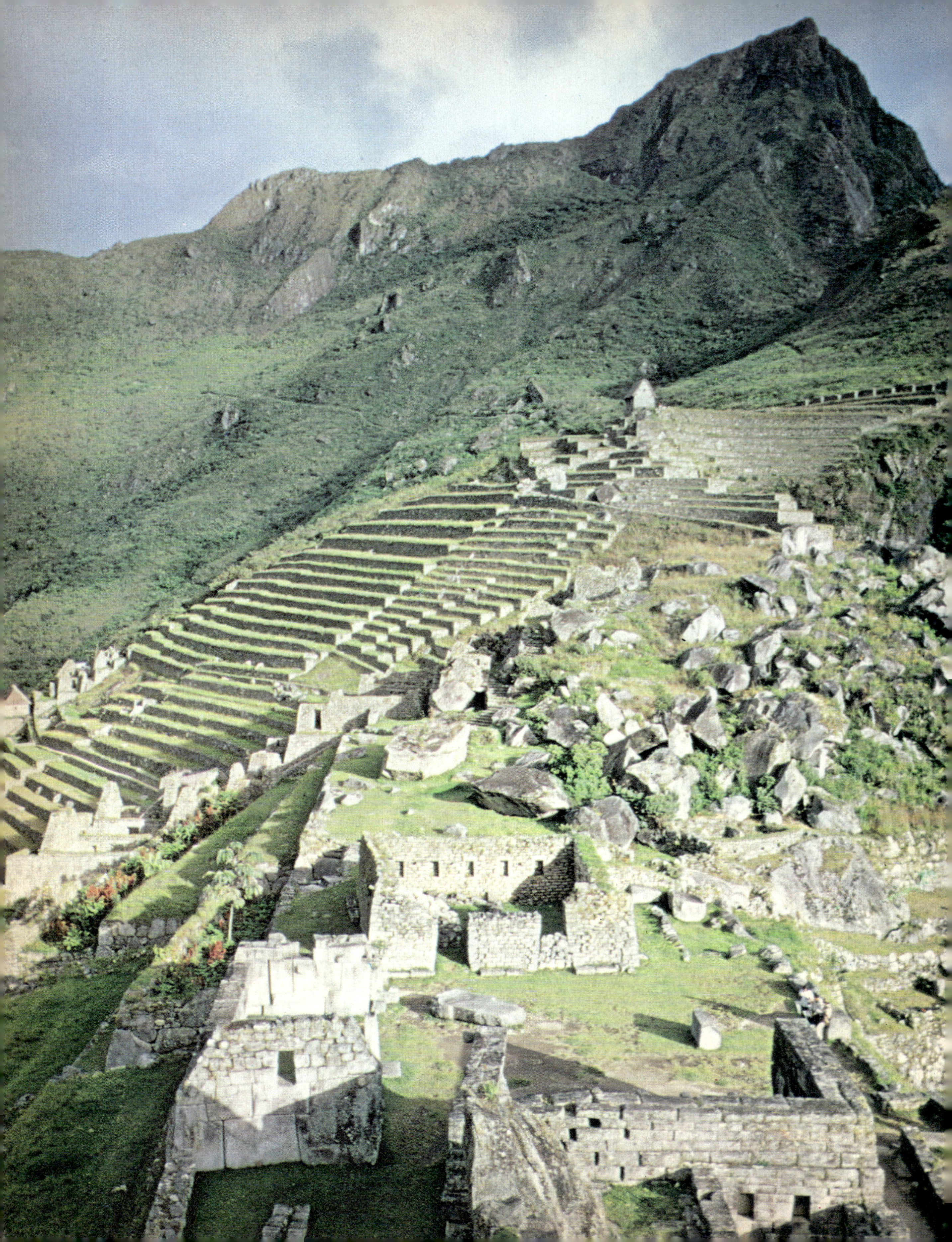

2 Earliest Americans

Where did all the many peoples of America come from? How did it happen that so many peoples with different cultures came to live side by side in these lands?

To learn some of the answers to those questions, we must dig deeply into the past, perhaps twenty thousand years ago. Then North and South America were lands without people. Just as today, they were lands of many types of geography and climate. Temperatures varied from the bitter cold of the Arctic to the heat of the few American *deserts*. There were deserts and rain forests, mountain ranges, and prairies as flat as table tops. Large woolly mammoths the size of elephants roamed the land, and small game ran freely in the forests. But all this no human eye had ever seen. No human had ever set foot upon this land.

At that time the mass of land that we call Europe, Asia, and Africa was thinly populated. There were no nations, no England, France, China, or Japan. However, there were many groups of people on the earth. They lived by hunting animals or gathering wild plants.

The Coming of Man to America

About twenty thousand years ago, they began to come—the first people to see America.

Who were those people? Where did they come from? How did they get here? Why did they come?

How did they get to America? We know where those people came from, and we know what route they took to get here. Look at the map on page 23. Twenty thousand years ago men did not have boats that could make a safe journey across the oceans. Can you think of any way for people to get to America from Asia or Europe or Africa? Is there any place where they would have to cross only a very narrow strip of water to get from one continent to another?

Find the place on the map where the northern part of America seems to touch Asia. Today we call that area the *Bering Strait* (bãr′ ing strāt). It is only fifty-six miles wide. That is not a very long distance to travel by canoe or raft, the kinds of boats ancient peoples probably had. In fact, it is possible that the ancient peoples did not have to use boats at all. They may have walked!

If they came during the long winter, the water was probably frozen into ice thick enough to walk on. Some scientists believe the first people came from Asia during the ice ages. The ice ages were long periods of time when huge *glaciers* (glā′ shərz), or great fields of ice, covered much of the land to the north. At that time the oceans were lower, and the land in the strait was higher than the water on either side of it. So the land formed a sort of bridge over which the wandering Asians walked.

The route. How do we know which route they followed? Do you remember that at the beginning of this chapter we said, "To learn the answers to those questions, we must dig deeply into the past"? Well, that is just what some scientists did. For many years they have been digging into and studying the earth along the route shown on the map. In many places from Alaska southward, scientists have inspected rock formations and layers of rock and soil. They have found that during one of the ice ages there was less ice in Alaska and western Canada than in other parts of the North American continent. That meant the first people to come to America could have migrated south along an ice-free route.

Other scientists have studied the animal life of northeastern Asia and northern America. They have found the animals of both areas very much alike. Could that be a clue to help prove that a land bridge once existed?

Still other scientists have studied the remains of ancient settlements. These experts have special ways of telling the age of ancient objects, especially those of wood, charcoal, or

THE ROUTES OF EARLY AMERICAN INDIANS

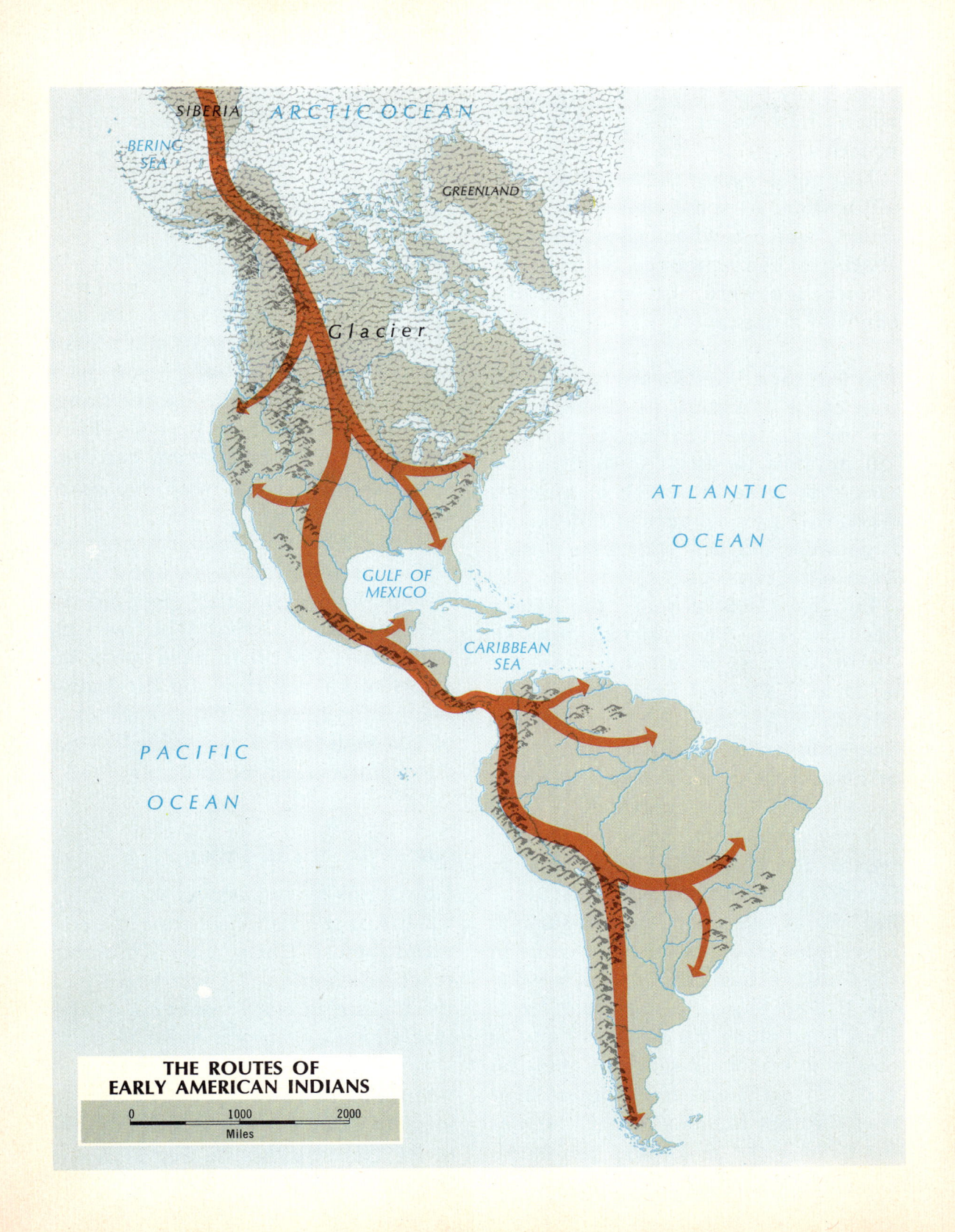

0 — 1000 — 2000
Miles

bone. They have a fairly clear idea of when man began his journey into America.

The objects they have found also tell a story. At some sites there were many stone arrowheads, spear points, shafts, and stone knives. Some of the arrowheads were still stuck in the bones of animals.

Why they came. We can only guess why they came. We know they were hunters in Asia. Hunters have to find and kill animals to survive. Chances are that they were in search of animals when they crossed over to America. It is possible, too, that they were fleeing from some enemies.

For thousands of years, the Asians kept coming. They spread through North America, *Middle America*—that is, Mexico, Central America, and the islands in the Caribbean (kar′ ə bē′ ən) Sea—and on to South America. The arrows on the map show you the directions in which they migrated.

Some groups settled in the eastern part of the United States, in heavily forested areas. Others moved on to the flat plains west of the Mississippi River. Still others made their home in the southwestern part of what is today the United States, a hot desert area. They lived along the seashores and in the mountainous regions of the east and the west. Some groups made their way through Middle America, across the *isthmus* (is′ məs), and into South America. They were the ancestors of the people we call the American Indians.

The Cultures of the Indians

Many of you already have some ideas about the Indian way of life from television, movies, and books. In this chapter you will discover much more about Indians. But before you do, it might be interesting to list the things you now believe about Indian culture. At the end of the chapter you can compare your list with what you know then.

Here are some questions to help you with your list. What do you know about the Indian way of life? How did the Indian make a living? What was his home like? Did all Indians speak the same language? How did the Indian teach his children? What were some of his beliefs and his values? What about his level of technology?

North American Indians

Now let us try to discover more about the life of the Indians during the centuries before Christopher Columbus reached America. We will begin with the Indians of North America. But before starting, you will want to recall a few things you have learned. You will remember that all people have to learn to make a living in their environment. The way they do that is part of their culture. And you will also remember what we said about tools and technology: the more scientific knowledge and the better tools people have, the more they can change their environment and make it work for them. People who lack scientific knowledge and have a low level of technology cannot do very much about their surroundings; they can only move away. If they stay, they have to use the environment the way it is to get their food, clothing, and shelter. In other words, their environment will decide a good deal about their way of life. This could lead to many hardships.

You will need to know some general information about the Indians of North America. Remember, the people who first came to this continent were hunters. But over the centuries most of them somehow learned to farm. Their chief crop was maize (māz), or corn, which they learned to grow in all the climates and soils of North America. It was the Indians of America who first grew this important crop. They taught the rest of the world about it.

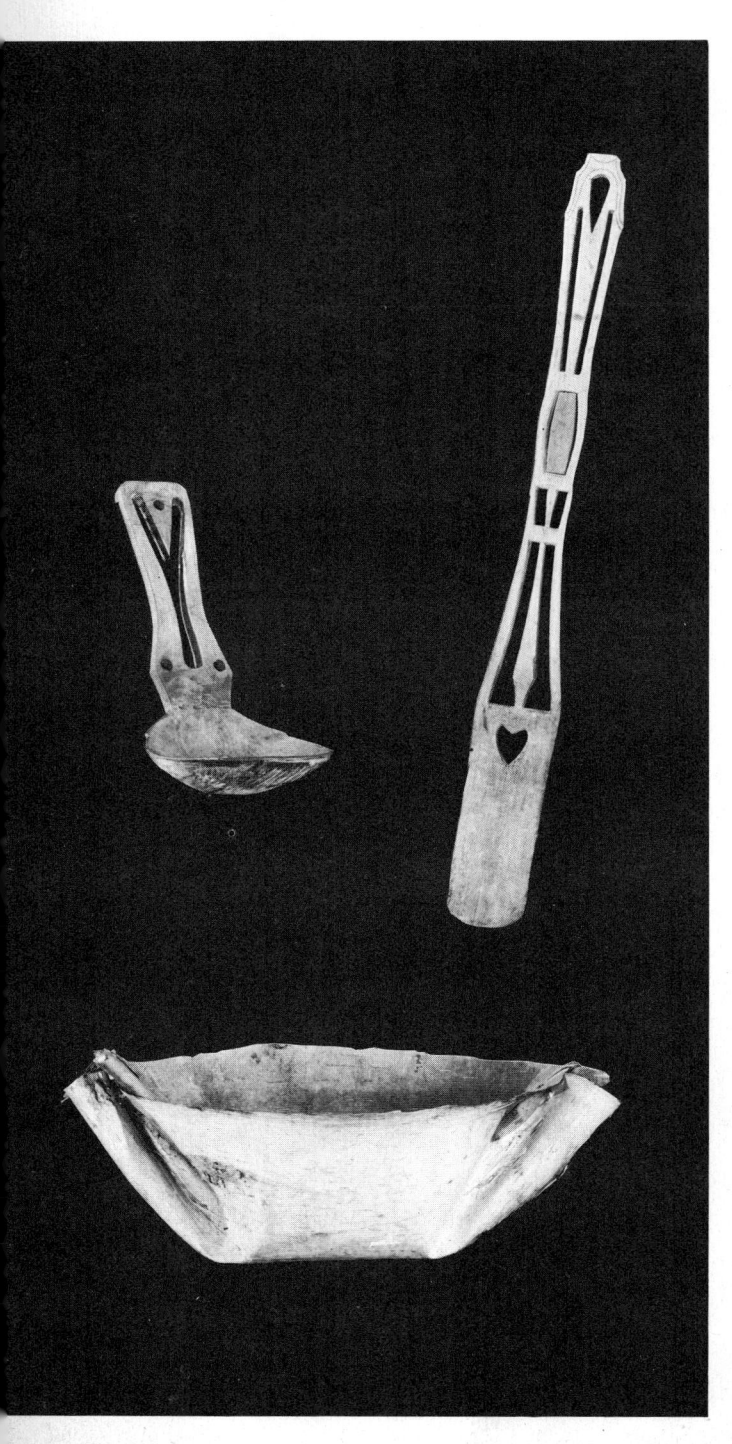

These well-carved tools were used by the Indians in making maple syrup.

Indian technology. North American Indians did not domesticate animals before Europeans brought the horse to America. That means they never had tame animals to provide meat and milk. It also means that Indians had to haul loads over land themselves. This was true of all Indians in North America except one group, who learned to use dogs to pull small loads.

Indians had few tools, and those they did have were made of stone or wood or animal bone. They had not learned to use hard metals, like iron. They did not know about the wheel, which is one of man's most important inventions. That meant there were no carts or wagons. The biggest boats were dugout canoes, used by a few groups that lived near the Pacific Ocean. These were hollowed out of large trees by fire and scraped smooth with dull tools. Most tribes used smaller canoes made of wooden poles from young trees. These were covered with the bark of a birch or an elm tree, or sometimes with a deerskin. Human muscle provided the power to paddle the boats. The Indians never took advantage of the power of wind by using sails.

The North American Indians also lacked an alphabet and a written language. That meant, of course, that they could leave few records for future generations. They could exchange ideas only by word of mouth and could learn things by hearing or by doing.

USING SOURCE MATERIAL
Life in the forest. With this information about the Indian level of technology, you are ready to discover some things about the culture of the Indians. Look at the pictures on this page. They show you the home region of one particular group of Indians. See how much you can find out about their way of life by studying these pictures and using the information you already have. What kind of house would you guess they had? What were the houses made of? Can you tell how they got food? What do you suppose they made their clothing of?

What do the tall green trees tell you? Can you tell anything about the rainfall? What kind of food might be found in this environment? What about the area in the second picture, where there is a clearing in the trees? Why might the Indians have cut down the trees?

Let us see how much you learned about the way of life of the Indians who lived here. These pictures show the forest areas in the northeastern part of what is today the United States. You will find such areas in New York, New Jersey, Pennsylvania, and several other states. This is where the Eastern Woodland Indians lived. Could you tell that these Indians hunted small game and planted crops for food? What in the pictures helped you?

Not all Indians lived in beautiful environments like that shown above. Of course, the beauty had little to do with making a living.

The Indians used their environment as best they could. The picture below shows how they lived and dressed and a few of the goods they produced with their tools.

27

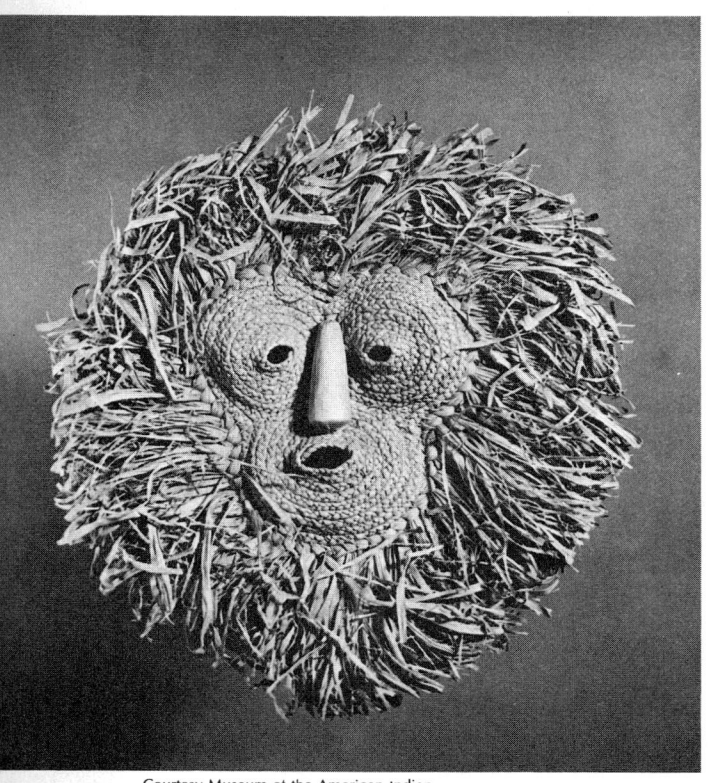

This cornhusk mask is an example of the artwork of the Eastern Woodland Indians. The mask was worn at special ceremonies.

Problem of getting food. The Indians divided up the work of getting their food supplies. Men hunted, and women tended gardens of corn, squash, beans, and pumpkins. To make room for their gardens, they had to chop down large trees, not an easy thing to do with stone tools.

To clear a forest area, the Indians used a method called *slash-and-burn*. They slashed, or cut, a deep ring around a tree trunk, causing the tree to die. Then they set fire to the dead tree. This cleared the land and let the sunshine through. Moreover, the ashes loosened the soil and made it easier to work. The ashes also fertilized the soil for a short time.

Since the tree stumps were much too hard to dig out with their tools, the Indians simply planted around them. They had no plows. They prepared the soil for planting with a digging stick, which was merely a stick with a pointed end. With that and a tool similar to a spade, they loosened the soil, and then planted the seeds. Then they piled the soil into little hills over the seeds. Often, dead fish were mixed into the mounds as fertilizer.

All the Indians of the village farmed the fields together, and they shared equally in the harvest. Most Indians did not have the idea of private ownership of land or food or even homes. They believed in sharing those things among members of the tribe. Tribes also owned hunting grounds and favorite fishing places, which they shared until the tribe moved to another part of the forest.

Hunting and fishing. While the women farmed, the men hunted. Usually they hid near a brook, knowing that the animals would go there to drink. The chief weapon was the bow and arrow, though they used lances for slower animals, and they also set traps. The warriors even used disguises (dis-gīz′ əz) of furs and skins. Besides small game such as rabbits, squirrels, and birds, the Indians hunted deer and bear. Now can you see how they got their clothing?

Eastern Woodland Indians also fished for food. They used nets, spears, bows and arrows, and simple fishhooks. Their small canoes were very light and easy to carry.

Forest homes. What were their homes made of? Remember, these Indians had no domestic animals or wagons or large boats to help them haul heavy loads. Where would they get the materials for building their homes? You were able to answer this question when you saw all the materials of the forest in the pictures. Woodland Indians found full-grown trees too difficult to work with. They cut poles from younger trees, tied them together with vines, and covered them over with bark, branches, and leaves.

These Indians built two kinds of houses. One, a small, single-family house, shaped like a hamburger bun, was called a *wigwam*. The other kind was called a *longhouse,* and looked like a giant loaf of bread. Six or seven families lived in it. Each family had a section of the house, but no one family owned the house. The house was

Eastern Indians often put up stake fences to protect their villages.

These pictures give you a good idea of the environment in which many Indian groups of America lived centuries ago. Study these pictures and then compare them to those on page 27. What differences in environment do you notice?

heated by three or four fires built in a row along the center. The smoke escaped through holes in the roof.

Indian children did not go to school, for there were no schools. They learned from their fathers, mothers, and other relatives, and from the older people in the tribe. They learned by hunting or working alongside them and by watching and listening to them. That was how the Indians passed on their beliefs.

USING SOURCE MATERIAL

Life in the open. Let us see how another group of Indians lived in North America. Look closely at this next set of pictures, showing the environment of these Indians. Again, remember what you know about the Indian level of technology. What can you tell about the culture of these Indians? How did they make a living? What kind of shelter did they have? What food did they eat? What were their clothes made of? What other things can you tell about their life from these pictures?

Let us see how much you discovered. The region pictured above is the *Great Plains,* a large, mostly level area that stretches from the Rocky Mountains almost to the Mississippi River and from central Canada to the Gulf of Mexico. Locate the Great Plains on your map. Look at the pictures again. Would you say there was much rainfall on the Great Plains? Why?

30

The buffalo influences a culture. The many different tribes living here were called the Plains Indians. These Indians were hunters. This was buffalo country, and the buffalo supplied all the essentials of life—food, shelter, and clothing. The Plains Indians became so dependent on the buffalo that they never thought of farming.

From the buffalo came meat for food, bones for tools, sinews (sin′ yüz) for bow strings and snowshoes, dried manure for fuel, intestines (in tes′- tənz) for containers to hold water, and hides for moccasins (mok′ ə sənz), leggings, dresses, and even homes! Of course, just by comparing the environments of the Eastern Woodland Indians and the Plains Indians, you know they would have to make their homes of different materials. The home of the Plains Indians was a *tepee*. A tepee was made by standing ten or twelve limbs of a young willow tree in a circle and tying them together at the top. This frame was then wrapped with buffalo hide. The complete tepee looked something like an upside-down ice-cream cone.

The lack of forest materials was only one reason the Plains Indian made the kind of home he did. Can you discover another? Remember, he made his living mainly by hunting, so his house was light in weight and could be put together and taken apart easily. What would he have to do if the buffalo herd moved on?

Moving day. Moving day was a big chore for the Indians. They used their dogs to help. Two tepee poles were tied to the sides of a dog. The ends of the poles dragged on the ground behind the animal. Across these poles they laid the rest of the folded tepee and any other belongings the family was taking. With this device, called a *travois* (trə voi′), a dog could drag about fifty pounds for five or six miles a day.

The Plains Indians were the only ones in North America who used animal power to help them carry goods, even though the animals were only small dogs. How odd it seems that they depended on the buffalo for everything else in their lives, yet never used these powerful animals to carry their loads. If only someone had had that one idea, it would have made things easier for everyone—including the dogs.

So far we have been able to tell a good deal about the life of some Indians by examining their land. You should be able to compare the two groups we have read about. Which group had a simpler way of living? Which environment offered more ways of making a living?

These were Indians with little scientific knowledge and a low level of technology. What about Indians who had more knowledge and a higher level of technology? Are we able to tell as many things about their culture by examining their environment?

Some of these dwellings were built high above the ground. Built hundreds of years ago, they are still in fair condition.

USING SOURCE MATERIAL

Life on dry lands. Look at the land where the Pueblo (pweb' lō) Indians lived. *Pueblo* is a Spanish word for village. Spanish explorers and settlers gave this name to the Indian tribes about whom you will read.

These pictures show the southwestern part of the United States, where Arizona and New Mexico are today. As you can see, the land is very dry here. Do you think the Pueblo Indians could have made their living by farming? Could they hunt in land like this?

Adapting to the environment. If the Pueblos had no more knowledge than some other Indians, they could not have farmed here. But the Pueblos had the idea of digging *irrigation* ditches from nearby rivers, streams, and ponds to get water to their dry land. They did this especially in times of heavy rainfall to lead the floodwaters to their valleys.

The Pueblos dug long irrigation ditches. One of these ditches was about sixteen miles long and fifteen feet deep. Often these irrigation ditches were linked together in a complicated plan. One series of ditches totaled 150 miles.

So the Pueblo Indians could farm, despite the arid soil. They raised not only corn, squash, and beans for food, but also cotton for clothing. Since animals were scarce, the Pueblos could not depend upon them for clothing as most other North American Indians did. They were expert weavers and made cotton cloth and blankets of beautiful design. They also created very handsome clay pottery.

Unlike the Plains Indians, the Pueblo Indians were farmers and built permanent homes. Looking at the pictures and seeing the materials on hand, you might guess their houses were made of stone, or perhaps dried clay. You would be right. Most were made of a clay material called *adobe* (ə dō′ bē). These Indians, like the others we have studied, did not have any means of transporting heavy loads, like logs, for long distances. But their homes were not the small, simple ones you might suppose. They lived in long, rectangular houses with flat roofs. A Pueblo family lived in one room and stored food in another. One house was built wall to wall with another and sometimes even on the roof of another. The walls of the houses were often a foot or more thick. This kept the homes cool in the summer and warm in the winter.

When finished, the houses sometimes looked like huge apartment dwellings, four or five stories high. One of these buildings housed a thousand families. The Indians used wooden ladders to climb to the upper stories. In case of attack, they protected themselves by climbing to the upper floors and pulling up the ladders.

So you see the Pueblos were able to change their environment and be less dependent upon it. That meant the environment did not affect their culture as much as it did the culture of some other Indian tribes.

Many Different Cultures

The Eastern Woodland, the Plains, and the Pueblo Indians were only three of the large Indian groups living in North America. Many others were spread throughout North America, living in different climates and environments. In fact, there were about six hundred different tribes in North America.

This is pottery made by Pueblo Indians. It was shaped by hand and painted with special designs.

Indian tribes lived on the rocky New England soil and along the New England coast. They lived in the mountains and lowlands of southeastern United States, and in the rolling hills of Michigan, Wisconsin, and Minnesota. There were Indians in the swampy country of Louisiana, on the flat plains and prairies west of the Mississippi River, and along the Pacific coast where the states of Washington and Oregon now are. They built their villages along the lakes and rivers of Canada.

Some made a living from the oceans, some from the forests, and some from the land. Living in different lands and climates and living apart from each other, they developed different cultures.

Why were there differences? Was it just different environment that made their cultures differ? Certainly the environment and the level of technology did affect each Indian culture. But environment and technology do not affect all the important parts of a culture.

Knowing about the environment and the tools of the Eastern Woodland and Plains Indians, for example, did not tell us that the idea of private ownership of land, food, or homes was not a part of their culture. We could discover a little about Indian family life, but not too much. Who disciplined (dis′ ə plīnd) the children? It was not always the parents, but sometimes the mother's brother. That cultural development had nothing to do with tools, land, or climate.

What about other beliefs, values, ideas, and customs? Did the Indian tribes believe wars were good? Did the tribes value peaceful living and getting along with their neighbors? Why did religious ideas differ? Did all tribes speak the same language? These things have little to do with environment or technology. The pictures do not help us learn about these things either. For example, we could not guess by studying the pictures of the environment that there were dozens of different Indian languages.

Now you might want to look at the list you made about Indian culture at the beginning of this chapter. Do you think your discoveries about the North American Indians fit in with what you wrote? Would you make any changes in your description of Indians?

People of Middle America: The Mayas

The Indians of Middle America and South America were similar in many ways to the North American Indians. They used stone or wooden tools and weapons. Most had no domestic animals and made no use of the wheel. They trained their children carefully, but had no alphabet to help them.

Like the Indians of North America, they developed different cultures over the centuries. But unlike their North American relatives, three of these Indian groups made splendid progress in farming, government, and building.

City builders. One of these groups was the *Mayan* (mä′ yən) *Indians.* The Mayas lived in Middle America—in the areas just east and west of the *Yucatán Peninsula* (yü′ kə tan pə nin′-sə lə) and on the peninsula itself. About fifteen hundred years ago, there were very few cities in all of Europe. London, England, and Paris, France, were only small villages. Yet at that time the Mayas had created beautiful, carefully planned cities.

These cities were made up of a number of large courtyards, or open spaces. Temples or public buildings surrounded these courtyards. There were no avenues or streets as we know them. A courtyard simply joined the one next to it. The temples were built of huge stone blocks and were shaped like pyramids. Some were as high as a modern twenty-story building. You can imagine the effort and engineering skill needed to build such a structure if you realize the Mayas had no metal tools to chop the stone into blocks, no wagons and animals to haul the blocks, and no pulleys or other machines to lift them up.

In this case the environment served the Mayas well. Yucatán Peninsula

Mayan artists carved this giant head out of rock hundreds of years ago. You can imagine how difficult it was, since the Mayas had no metal tools to chip the rock.

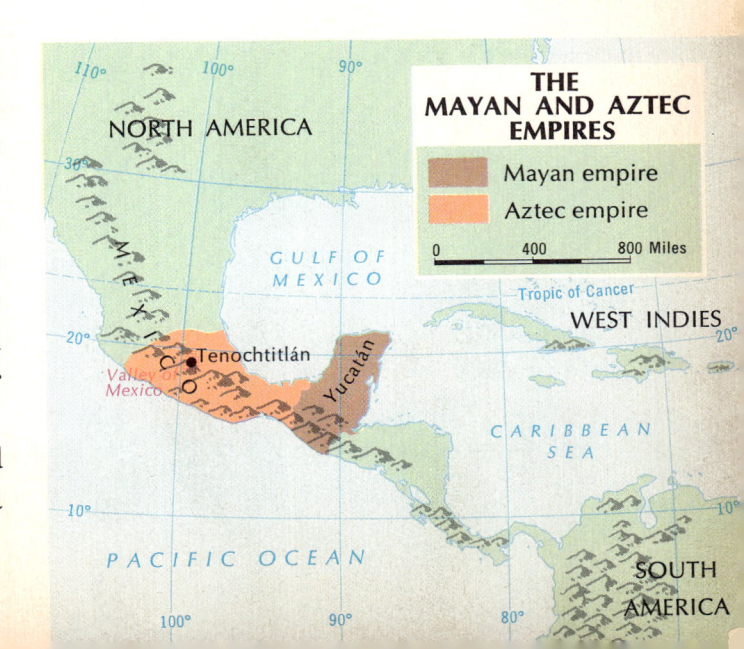

THE MAYAN AND AZTEC EMPIRES

formed the northern portion of their state. There the Mayas found large deposits of limestone. This stone could be easily taken from the ground and shaped into building stones—even with stone and wooden tools. They also discovered beds of limey gravel that could be made into a cement.

An important idea. The Mayas also learned the important idea of the *division of labor*. Instead of everybody doing a little bit of everything, with nobody learning to be especially good at anything, the Mayas *specialized* (spesh′ ə līzd). While most of the common people farmed, some specialized in stonecutting, some in making buildings, some in making pottery.

The nobles and priests did not do even specialized labor. They were the educated class. They learned about arithmetic. Their knowledge helped the Mayas build their huge buildings. They developed an accurate calendar, and learned much about *astronomy* (ə stron′ ə mē). They also invented a kind of picture writing, which was not as useful as an alphabet but which enabled them to record information. The Mayas also produced very fine art.

The Mayas were able to build cities and develop so many skills because of their agriculture. As they increased their knowledge of farming, they were able to improve their crops and grow more food. Fewer people were needed to raise food for the entire group. This

MAYAN IDEAS OF BEAUTY

Ideas of beauty differ from culture to culture. What is beautiful to people of one culture may be ugly to people of another. The Mayas loved colorful clothing, the more colorful the better. They wore clothes made of golden jaguar (jag′ wär) skins, bright-red robes, ornaments made of green jade, brilliant bird feathers, and headdresses with flowers on top, sometimes two or three feet high. Some Mayan leaders even filed their teeth and inlaid them with jewels. The Mayas admired long skulls, so many a mother wrapped her infant's head tightly with cloth and stiff boards to squeeze it into this shape as it grew. Crossed eyes were thought to be especially beautiful, so some parents hung beads from their children's foreheads in order to cross the eyes permanently.

Do these ideas of beauty seem strange to you? Do you think the Mayas would agree with your ideas of beauty? Perhaps some students in your own class have different ideas about beauty than you have.

freed some men to do other things. That is how every *civilization* first developed. Can you see one reason why North American Indians never had cities?

A religious people. The Mayas were very religious people. In all their cities they built stone temples for their religious ceremonies. High priests and their families were held in high honor among the Mayas. It was the priests who decided what temples would be built and what would be offered to the gods. They also announced the times for planting and harvesting.

Mayan religious beliefs were different from most of ours and from those of the North American Indians. They believed their gods demanded human sacrifices, especially when some disaster struck their city. Frequently the victims were taken to the altar in the temple, where priests cut out their hearts to please the gods. Other victims were killed with bow and arrow. At one place, they were first tied and then thrown into a deep well. Sometimes the Mayas used war captives as human sacrifices, but often the Mayas themselves were sacrificed.

Do these religious practices tell us anything about the values of the Mayas? Would you say they believed each human life was important? Can you think of any way these religious beliefs and values might have influenced other parts of their way of life?

The Second Group: The Aztecs

Another important Indian civilization was that of the *Aztecs* (az′ tekz), who lived where Mexico is now. About seven hundred years ago the Aztecs, a tribe of warlike Indians, were looking for a place that could be easily defended. They chose an island in the middle of a lake, on the site of the present Mexico City. There, during the next two hundred years, the Aztecs built a great city, which became the capital of their empire.

City on a lake. This city, called Tenochtitlán (tā näch tē′ tlän), was one of the great cities of the world. Such great cities of today as London, England, and Rome, Italy, were far smaller at that time than Tenochtitlán.

The Aztecs connected their island city to the land around the lake by three large *causeways*, or land bridges. In the city itself were great temples and other public buildings, as well as a large marketplace. There Indians from the city and villages around the lake came every day to sell their wares.

Aztec priests. The priests were the most important group among the Aztecs. They kept track of the many gods to be worshipped, and they conducted the daily religious ceremonies. Their temples and houses were among the grandest in Aztec cities. Visitors to Tenochtitlán would see many priests,

Feather headdresses like this were worn by Aztec priests.

for there were thousands of priests in the city.

Aztec boys who would be priests went to a special school. There they studied the history of the Aztecs, mathematics, and astronomy. Their most difficult task was learning the exact details of the religious ceremonies.

Two great aids. It would have been difficult for the priests to remember all these ceremonies without two important aids. The first was a written language that, like the Mayan system, was based on pictures or symbols. The symbols helped the priests recall the steps and prayers to follow.

The second aid was a calendar. With this the priests could keep track of the days on which each god was to be worshipped. The priests had to know all the details of the calendar and the meaning of the symbols explaining the ceremonies. In fact, the priests made up both the calendar and the written symbol system.

Religious beliefs. The Aztecs believed their gods had to be strong to protect them. Like the Mayas, they believed human blood made the gods stronger. To get victims for the sacrifices, the Aztecs attacked nearby tribes and brought back captives. Because of this practice, the other tribes lived in terror of the Aztecs. If there were no prisoners of war, many Aztecs were willing to sacrifice themselves in order to please the gods.

Military training. All Aztec boys had to attend schools when they reached fifteen years of age. Although other subjects and skills were taught, the boys were especially trained in warfare. They were taught to believe warfare was good, and bravery especially noble. To die in battle was the most honorable way to die. It pleased the gods and assured the warrior of a long and happy life after death.

Trade. Aztec farmers and craftsmen produced more than enough farm products, clay pottery, tools, jewelry, and other fancy objects made of gold and silver. They exchanged many of these products in their own market. But they also sought to trade them for the products of other tribes.

The Aztecs had a well-trained class of merchants, who handled trade with other tribes. The merchants visited villages in search of products the Aztecs needed. They made trade agreements with the other tribes. But the merchants also acted as spies to find out how wealthy and strong the other tribes were.

The trade agreements were followed by conquest by the Aztecs. Then the conquered tribe had to surrender food, clothing, weapons, and anything else the Aztecs wanted. The tribe also had to make regular payments of such products to the Aztecs—much like paying taxes. In this way the Aztecs gained control over a large part of Middle America.

The Third Group: The Incas

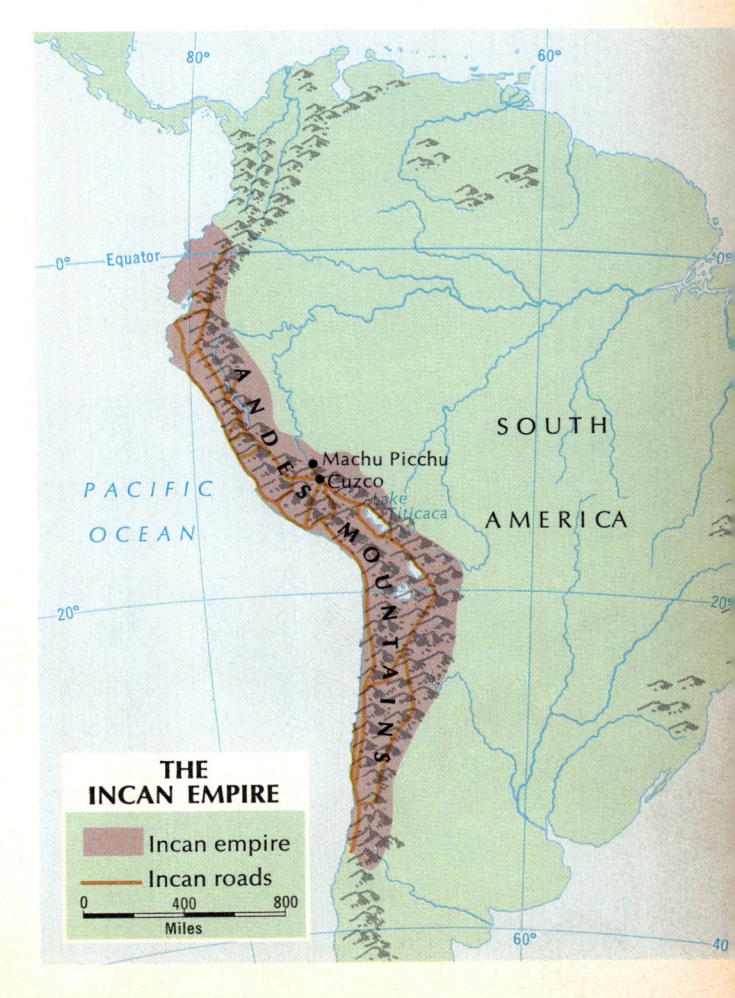

The most remarkable Indian civilization of all was that of the Incas. These people formed an empire in the very mountainous area of South America along the western coast.

A look at the map shows that this area was not a very likely place for a civilization to develop. Part of the *coastal plain* is a desert, and much of the rest gets very little rainfall. Just to the east of this coastal plain rise mountains whose peaks are more than four miles high. Streams flowing down from the mountains provide the only water for the coastal area. To the east of the mountains, the land slopes sharply down into a vast jungle.

The Incan Indians developed a great civilization and built an empire on this land that today includes Peru, and parts of Chile, Ecuador (ek′ wə dôr), and Bolivia.

These beautifully designed cups were used by Incas in their religious ceremonies.
Courtesy Art Institute of Chicago

Solving problems of environment. Like all early civilizations, that of the Incas was based on agriculture. The Incas had to overcome two problems in order to grow a sufficient food supply. In the coastal plain there was not enough water, and in the highlands there was too much. Water was provided for the coastal plain by irrigation. The Incas built ditches that led the water from the mountain streams into the dry areas and made the desert bloom with crops.

The problem in the highlands was also solved. The Indians who lived on the slopes of the mountains found that rainwater would wash the topsoil down the mountainside, leaving only rocks behind. To prevent this, they *terraced* their land by building a series of giant "stairs" into the mountainside. This kept the water from carrying the soil away.

Incas and Aztecs. The Incas were similar to the Aztecs in many ways, especially in their level of technology and in their way of making a living. There were some differences, of course. The Incas did have a few domesticated animals. The most important was the llama, a creature about the size of a small horse and with the appearance of a camel. They used the llama to carry light loads. Another domesticated animal was the alpaca (al pak′ ə), which produced a woollike hair that the Incas wove into

On the mountain slopes above this village near Cuzco, Peru, you can see the terracing that Indian farmers practice today.

cloth. The Incas never developed a written language as the Aztecs did, but they had a way of figuring with numbers. Their art was as fine as that of the Aztecs. They made splendid ornamental pieces and statues out of gold and silver.

Even though the Aztecs and Incas seemed so similar in material culture, an Aztec would have felt very much a stranger if he had suddenly been placed among the Incas. The Incas spoke a different language. They were not nearly so warlike as the Aztecs.

They had a religion, as all peoples do, but their religion did not call for human sacrifices except in times of great danger.

The Incas had schools, although only for the wealthy and important people. At these schools, the students learned about Incan history, religion, and language. They were trained to become government officials who would run the country when they grew older.

How was that different from the Aztec schools? Do you see how the different values of the Incas resulted in a different education for their children?

Empire builders. The Incas built an empire even larger than that of the Aztecs. The Incas did not make war to get human sacrifices. They ruled their empire with kindness instead of with terror. Often the Incas allowed the conquered Indians to keep their own chiefs as long as they obeyed Incan laws. They permitted these people to keep their own religion but insisted that they also worship the Incan Sun God.

On the other hand, the Incas insisted that the conquered people work for the empire. Often they brought the leaders of the conquered people, as well as their sons, to the Incan capital of Cuzco (kü′ skō). There they taught them Incan beliefs and customs. When these leaders returned to their own land, they were to teach their own people Incan ways.

Linking an empire. One of the great accomplishments of the Incas was building roads—over seven thousand miles of them—that reached out to all parts of their empire. The roads, needed only for foot traffic, were about three feet wide and were sometimes paved with stone. Rope bridges, made of braided vines, stretched across the gaps between the mountains, permitting the road to run continuously.

The roads were used by men carrying messages throughout the empire, as well as by men carrying goods. The messages were carried by relay runners. The runners memorized the message and ran a mile or two to the next relay station, where they repeated the message to a waiting runner. With this system, messages could travel about 140 miles a day.

Across such mountains and valleys, the Incas stretched their great road system.

A grand capital. The Incan capital city, Cuzco, was just as splendid as Tenochtitlán, though not so large. A Spaniard, who was one of the first Europeans to see Cuzco, reported that it had fine streets, except that they were narrow. The houses were built of stones, beautifully joined. In the center of the city was a great open area, and along its sides stood religious temples and other huge buildings. The palace of the ruler, who was called *the Inca*, was also here, as were government offices and the homes of the wealthy.

Incan values. Like other Indian peoples in North and South America, the Incas did not value private property as we do today. They believed that the land, even the land on which they lived and farmed, belonged to the whole community and not to one person. Their government planned carefully for the well-being of the people. The Inca divided the land in three parts. One part was set aside as farmland for each family. Larger families received more land, smaller ones less.

A second part of the land was used for the gods. This land supported the priests and paid for religious ceremonies. The third part was set aside for the Inca himself, for his government officials, and for his warriors. The people were responsible for farming all the land—the fields of the gods and of the Inca as well as their own.

When the lands of the Inca produced a surplus, the government stored it up in case of crop failures in future years. The poor were fed from the surplus. The ruler also distributed cotton to the poor so they could make some of their clothing.

The Incas paid taxes by giving their labor. This system was called the *mita* (mē′ tə). Each year, all Incan citizens gave a certain number of days to work in the gold and silver mines, or on public buildings, roads, or irrigation canals. They could also serve as warriors. Of course, they were not treated harshly when they worked. They were simply citizens paying their taxes and would soon go back to their homes when others took their turn.

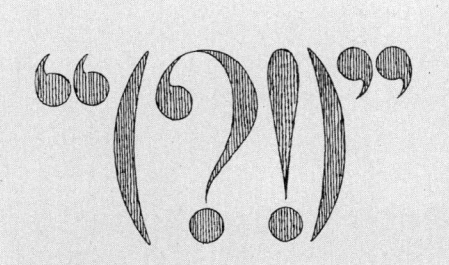

TO HELP YOU READ

There are certain rules to keep in mind when reading a quotation. Words shown within brackets are put in by the editor to make the meaning of the passage clearer. The words that appear within the brackets are not part of the original quotation. If any words are left out of the quotation, the place where they originally appeared is marked by three periods (. . .) known as an ellipsis.

High in the Andes lie the ruins of Machu Picchu, built centuries ago by the Incas.

USING SOURCE MATERIAL

The stories, poems, and songs of a people often give us a clue to their values. So do their laws. Here are some Incan laws, and some sayings of the ruling Inca. What do you think were some of the values of this people?

Anyone who neglected to irrigate his land at the proper time . . . was struck on the back with a stone three or four times in public, or his arms and legs were whipped with osier switches.

No one was to be idle, on account of which even children of five were given very light tasks suitable for their age; and the blind, lame, and dumb were also given various tasks.

All inhabitants of every village were required to assist one another in plowing, sowing, bringing in the harvest, building their houses, and such things. . . .

The blind, dumb, lame, and paralyzed, the aged and infirm . . . who were unable to . . . feed and clothe themselves should be lodged in public houses called "lodging houses" where their needs were supplied free of charge.

He who kills another without authority or due cause condemns himself to death.

Thieves are in no wise to be permitted; they might gain property by honest toil and possess it rightfully, but they prefer to come by it by robbery, so it is only right that thieves should be hanged.

Judges who secretly take gifts from litigants and suitors should be regarded as thieves, and as such punished with death.

Early in this chapter, you made a list of the things you knew about Indians. Now that you have learned more about the Indians of North, Middle, and South America, you might like to compare what you wrote then with what you know now. Do you think the Indians were all alike? Was there one Indian culture, or were there many?

Working with Concepts and Generalizations

Identifying Concepts

Write T if the statement is true; write F if the statement is false. Write the answers on paper.

1. It is believed the first men who came to America traveled from Asia across the Bering Strait.
2. The Mayas were able to carefully plan and construct beautiful cities because they had learned to use metal tools.
3. The buffalo supplied the Plains Indians with all the essentials of life — food, shelter, and clothing.
4. The North American Indians did not have an alphabet or a written language.
5. One of the great accomplishments of the Incas was building roads that reached out to all parts of their empire.
6. Tamed animals provided the North American Indians with meat and milk.
7. Two great Aztec achievements were a written language and a calendar.
8. Most Indians believed in private ownership of land, food, and homes.
9. By digging irrigation ditches, the Pueblo Indians were able to farm, despite the arid soil.
10. The Plains Indians were the only Indians in North America who used animal power to help carry loads.

Developing Concepts

Write the answers on paper.

1. You are the first man to come to America across the Bering Strait. EITHER write a simple description of what you see or draw simple sketches showing what you see.
2. You are a North American Indian. You may be a Plains Indian, an Eastern Woodlands Indian, or a Pueblo Indian. Describe a typical day in your life.
3. You belong to a small Indian tribe in South America. Both the Incas and the Aztecs want to conquer your tribe and rule it. You know that one of them will win. Would you rather be ruled by the Aztecs or by the Incas? Why?
4. You have learned that all people must learn to live in their environment. Make simple sketches showing the different kinds of shelters the North American Indians built. Give each sketch a title, including some information on how the environment influenced the shelter your picture shows.
5. How did the education of Indian children differ from yours? List at least five things you learned to do before you started school. What things on your list do you think Indian children learned to do?

Generalizations

Read the generalizations listed below. Find proof to support each generalization. On paper, tell what the proof is and the page on which you found it.

1. Man has developed a variety of cultures, each influenced by the physical environment.
2. Specialization and division of labor allow man to produce goods faster and in greater quantity.
3. Man is dependent on natural resources for his survival.
4. Much of man's history is contained in the objects and remains he has left behind.
5. Ideas of beauty differ from culture to culture.

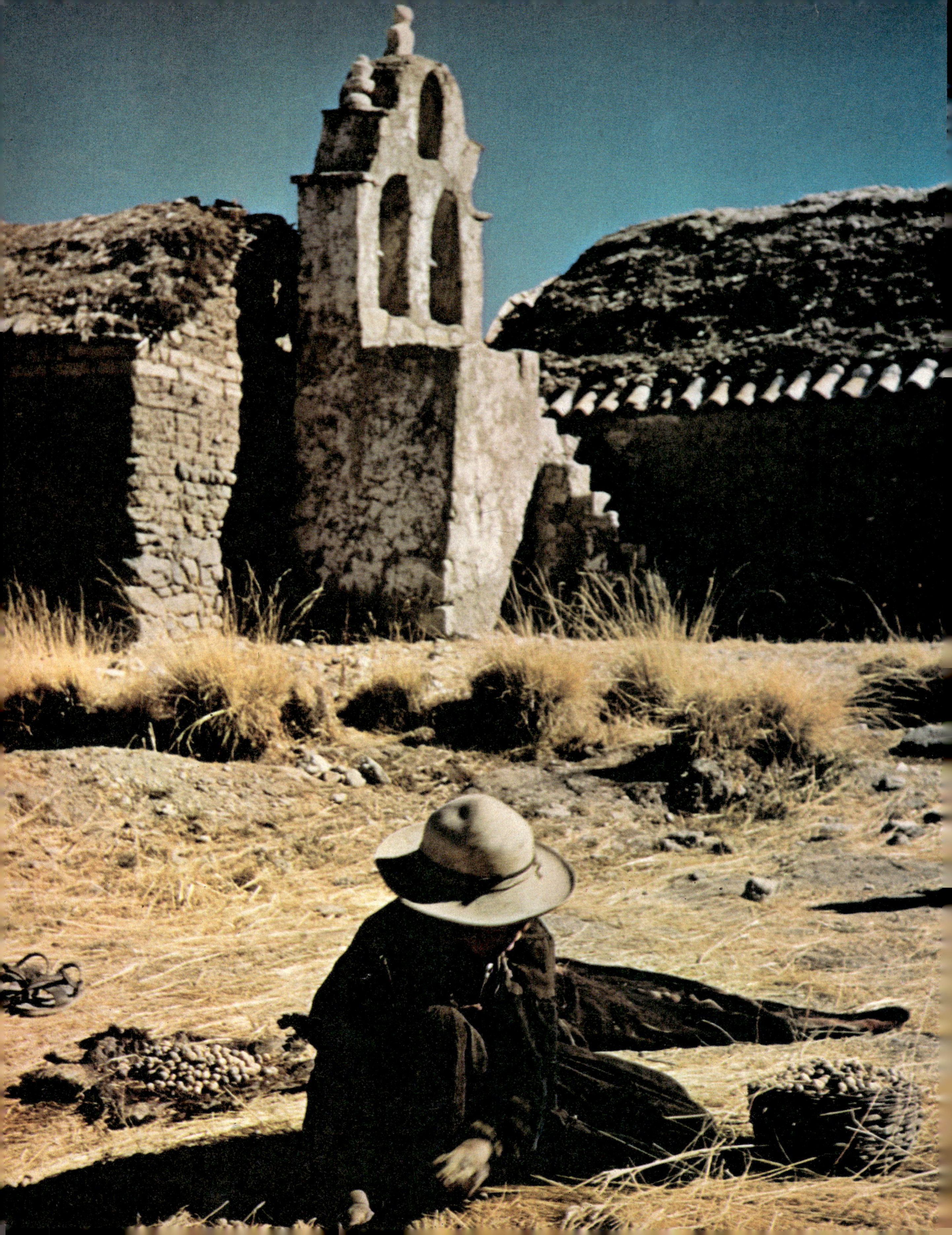

Europeans and Africans Come to the New World

3

For centuries the American Indians lived in this hemisphere unknown to the rest of the world and without knowledge of the rest of the world. Across the Atlantic and Pacific oceans, other civilizations were also developing. But the different worlds were unaware of each other.

Beginning in the fifteenth century, the interests of Europeans led them to look beyond their familiar boundaries. They had developed enough science and skill to satisfy these interests. It was then that the people of the two hemispheres met.

Before very long, peoples from Europe and Africa were living among the early Americans. Why did they come and what did they do when they got here? What effects did the meeting have on each of the peoples? We shall search for the answers to these questions in this chapter.

We will also compare the different ways of living of these peoples. In this way you should be able to develop further your idea of culture.

Christopher Columbus

The man who discovered America was an Italian sailor, Christopher Columbus. He planned to reach the Far East, the *Indies,* by sailing west across the Atlantic Ocean. The idea was not really new when Columbus suggested it. Most people who knew anything about geography agreed that the world was round. Anyone could see that it ought to be possible to reach the East by going west.

A happy error. Most geographers believed there were nearly 11,000 miles between Europe and the Far East. Of course, no one suspected that two huge *continents* (kon′ tə nəntz), or land masses, stood in the way. Columbus, however, believed the world to be much smaller than it really is. He figured that the Far East was only 2,400 miles from Europe. Columbus persuaded the king and queen of Spain to supply him with the ships, men, and money needed to test his theory.

How strangely things worked out. The best geographers of the time were correct, and so they did not try the western route. Columbus was wrong, and he discovered a new world!

After more than two months at sea, Columbus and his men sighted land. The Indies at last, thought Columbus. Of course it was not the Indies at all. Instead, Columbus had discovered land that Europeans did not even know existed.

This was in 1492. Columbus made three more trips in the next ten years. It was several years before he and the Spaniards realized that they had not reached the Indies, but had found a new land.

Spanish Conquest

Within fifty years of the discovery of America, there were few areas in Middle and South America that Spanish explorers had not visited. The map on page 49 shows the routes of these early Spanish adventurers. At first, many were led by a spirit of adventure into these unknown lands. But it was not long before another motive became more important.

The New World had much good farmland, but most of the Spanish who came with Columbus, and those who came after, did not cross three thousand miles of ocean to farm. "I came to get gold, not to till the soil like a peasant," said one Spanish explorer. The Spanish did find gold — more than they ever dreamed existed — when they stumbled upon the Aztec and Incan empires.

Dazzled by the prospect of great wealth, the leaders of the Spanish explorers decided to conquer the Indians and seize their riches. First they defeated the Aztecs. Although there were only a few hundred Spaniards against thousands of Aztec warriors, the Spaniards had the advantage of a higher level of technology. Indian

ROUTES OF THE SPANISH EXPLORERS
- Routes taken by explorers
- Claimed by Spain
- Claimed by Portugal

spears and bows and arrows, made of wood and stone, were no match for the Spaniards' guns. The Spanish also got help from many neighboring Indian tribes who hated the Aztecs and were glad to have the chance to help defeat them.

A few years later, the Spaniards conquered the Incas. Incan Indians were accustomed to letting their ruler, the Inca, make all the decisions. In fact, these Indians believed the royal family was descended from the sun, and they thought of the ruling Inca as a kind of living god. When the Inca was captured and killed by the Spanish, his followers were leaderless and helpless to take the necessary steps to defend themselves. As a result, a handful of Spaniards were able to conquer the entire Incan empire with hardly a struggle.

Slavery for the Indians. The Spanish conquerors, who were called *conquistadores* (kon kwis′ tə dôrz), now expected to collect their reward. They melted down the beautiful artwork that the Aztecs and Incas had made from gold and silver. The Indians had valued these metals in the form of art, but the Spanish were more interested in becoming rich.

The Spaniards planned to become rich not only from the gold and silver but also from the land. To do this, they did not have to take the Indians' land but only their labor. The conquistadores had no intention of doing the hard work of farming and mining themselves. They got the Indians to do it under a plan called the *encomienda* (en kom ē ən′ də) system.

Encomienda comes from the Spanish word meaning "to entrust" or "to put in care of." The Spanish conqueror was "to take care of" the Indians in certain ways. He was supposed to teach the Indians the Spanish religion, Christianity, teach them to be loyal to the Spanish king, and teach them Spanish culture. In return, the Indians were to turn over to the Spanish part of everything they grew on their lands. Of course, no one asked the Indians whether they wanted to learn the Spanish religion and culture or to be loyal to a king they had never heard of.

The encomienda system turned out to be one that allowed the Spanish to take advantage of the Indians. Instead of taking care of the Indians, the Spanish overworked them.

Spanish priests, who were also called missionaries, came to South America with the conquistadores. They established small settlements, called missions, in various parts of the new Spanish empire. They lived among the Indians and taught them the Christian religion and Spanish culture. The missionaries were very disturbed at the terrible treatment of the Indians by the greedy conquistadores, and complained to the Spanish king about it. The king gave orders that the Indians must not be mistreated or made slaves. But the orders did not do much good, for the king was thousands of miles away.

Hardships of the Indians. Many thousands of Indians died because they were forced to work long hours in the fields and mines. Even more died from the diseases the Europeans brought to the New World. These diseases, such as smallpox, the Indians had never known before. Their bodies were not able to resist the unfamiliar germs, and the Indians died in great numbers.

We do not know exactly how many Indians died because we are not sure how many there were to begin with.

This monastery in Bolivia was built by the Spaniards centuries ago. It shows the Spanish style of building at that time.

It was thought there were about nineteen million Indians in Middle and South America when the Europeans came, and another million in North America. But some scholars who have recently studied this subject believe as many as fifty million Indians may have been living on the two continents. We do know that fifty years after the Europeans came, only about seven million Indians were left. That means that at least twelve million Indians died, and possibly as many as forty-three million, which is about the population of Mexico today.

With so many Indians dying and so many fleeing, there soon were not many "to take care of" and the encomienda system began to die out.

Spread of Spanish culture. One hundred years after Columbus discovered the New World, the Spanish had spread throughout all of Middle America and South America except for the part that today is Brazil. In all these places, and in many of the nearby islands, they established *colonies.* This means that they claimed the land for Spain and ruled it for the Spanish king.

In each colony the Spanish were a very small minority. But with their firearms, horses, and military training, they were able to take control and rule

51

over the great majority, the Indians.

Beginning about 1700, the Spanish settlers took most of the land for themselves. The king gave many individuals large pieces of land, which became known as *haciendas* (hä′ sē en′ dəz). The owner, called the hacendado (hä′-sen dä′ dō), could become very rich from this land if he could get someone to work for him. As always, the Spanish turned to the Indians to supply the labor. The hacendado offered them a deal. He would give each Indian a small piece of the hacienda to supply his own family's needs. In return, the Indian had to give several days each week to work on the land the hacendado kept for himself. In addition, the Indian had to give his labor to build all the structures on the hacienda—the chapel, houses, walls, and so forth.

Once the Indians agreed to work on the hacienda, they were almost completely under the control of the hacendado. Most haciendas had a whipping post, and Indians who did not obey the hacendado might be whipped.

Spaniards not only owned most of the land but also ruled the colonies. The settlers kept all the best jobs for themselves. All the main government officials were Spanish. Spanish was the chief, official language. Spanish holidays were observed, and many Spanish customs were followed. If Indians wanted to learn in schools, they had to attend church schools. In these schools, they learned the Spanish religion and the Spanish culture. The Spanish tried to force the Indians to give up their own culture.

Brazil

While the Spanish spread through much of Middle and South America, Spain's European neighbor, Portugal, discovered and settled the area that today is Brazil. The Portuguese soon started several small settlements. Unlike the Spanish, they did not find any great Indian civilizations where they landed. They did not find gold or silver, either. Instead, there were only Indian villages like those of the Eastern Woodland Indians of North America. When they found no precious metals, the Portuguese did not pay much attention to their South American colony, and it grew slowly.

After about fifty years, however, they found that cotton and sugar could be grown there. Both of these products would bring large profits in Europe. More Portuguese came to settle in the colony. They established *plantations*, or large farms, on which they grew sugar, cotton, and later tobacco.

The Portuguese ran their colony much as the Spanish ran theirs, keeping all the best jobs in government for themselves, taking over all the land they wanted, and forcing the Indians to work for them. Like the Spanish, the Portuguese tried to make the Indians adopt their ways of living.

The Differences in the Cultures

The Spanish and Portuguese cultures had a great deal in common with the cultures of other peoples of Europe. In fact, we often speak of a European culture, even though the cultures of European peoples differ from each other in many ways. In what ways did these European cultures differ from Indian cultures?

Differences in technology. One important thing the Europeans brought was a high level of technology. Europeans knew how to use iron. As a result, they could make better tools for building and farming. Indians had stone axes and stone or bone knives for cutting wood. Europeans had steel knives, axes, saws, and hammers. Indian farmers had only a pointed stick to loosen the ground. To cultivate the soil around the plants, they used wooden poles with shells attached. Europeans brought wooden plows to turn up the soil and prepare it for planting, and shovels, hoes, and rakes to help them cultivate plants.

Cortes and his men get their first view of Tenochtitlán.

Europeans knew about the wheel. They had used wheelbarrows, carts, and wagons. They also had pulleys, which saved much labor. Europeans could hardly have made more splendid buildings than the Incas and the Aztecs had made. But with pulleys, wagons, and tools, Europeans could build much faster and with far less human effort.

Use of animals. Europeans had learned to raise animals for food and for the raw material they needed. They brought cows, goats, pigs, chickens, sheep, and ducks to America. These animals gave them a plentiful supply of milk, meat, wool, and hides.

Europeans had also learned to use the muscle power of animals. They used horses, donkeys, and oxen to pull heavy loads and to help them in the fields. The Incas, who used llamas for carrying light packs, and the Plains Indians, who used dogs on moving day, were the only Indians who had used animal muscle power.

The use of tools and animal power allowed a European to farm more land and produce more food than an Indian farmer could. Thus more Europeans were free to do other kinds of work.

The Indians lacked many tools that would have made their lives easier. Yet the Europeans who came both to South America and later to North America often adopted Indian ways. Even Indian foods were a large part of their diet. Potatoes, corn, squash, cacao (kə kā′ ō), manioc (man′ ē ok), pumpkins, and certain kinds of beans are a few examples. Europeans also learned about certain medicines from the Indians.

Division of labor. American Indians knew something about the advantages of division of labor. Some of the Indians of North and South America divided the work among men, women, and children—mostly hunting, farming, and taking care of the household. But they did not divide up the work so that one man might specialize in canoemaking, another in leathermaking, another in hunting or in fishing. When people have very little division of labor, and each family produces most of the goods it needs, we say they have a simple *economy*, or a simple way of making a living.

The Mayas, the Aztecs, and the Incas carried division of labor and specialization further than other Indian groups. This enabled the Mayas, for instance, to develop great skill as builders, weavers, or potters.

Europeans carried the division of labor still further. Carpenters built homes, *blacksmiths* made iron tools, shipwrights built boats, wheelwrights and cartwrights built wagons and carriages. There were skilled workmen who specialized in making barrels, making shoes, or turning iron into armor, guns, pots, and artwork.

Written language. The Europeans also brought an alphabet and a written language to the Americas. Some Indians, chiefly the Mayas and the Aztecs, had developed a picture language. They used pictures to stand for words, objects, and ideas. Some information can be communicated, or made known, through a picture language. But other information cannot be presented well or recorded for future use. This is especially true when it comes to ideas and values, which have no shape or form. For example, how can one draw a picture of the idea of fairness or liberty or truth? These things cannot be drawn. No Indian child was ever able to learn the way you are learning right now, by reading letters that form words that stand for ideas.

Different values and ideas. Many European ideas, beliefs, and values also differed from those of the Indians. The idea of private ownership was an important part of European culture. Indians believed that some things, such as clothing, beds, hammocks, and combs, should be privately owned. However, longhouses and land belonged to gods, who allowed a family, a tribe, or a nation to use them according to its needs. Indians believed in what we might call "use ownership." That is, an Indian and his family "owned" their part of a longhouse or a piece of land as long as they used it. In other words, they owned the right to use it. But when they stopped using it, it was no longer theirs. They could not sell the land or rent it, for it belonged to the whole tribe.

The idea that something as important as land might be owned by a person who did not use it made no sense to the Indians. They could not understand how a person could live in Spain and own land in America. And certainly one could not inherit land just because his father had used it before him.

Mayas kept a simple record of events by using pictures and symbols.

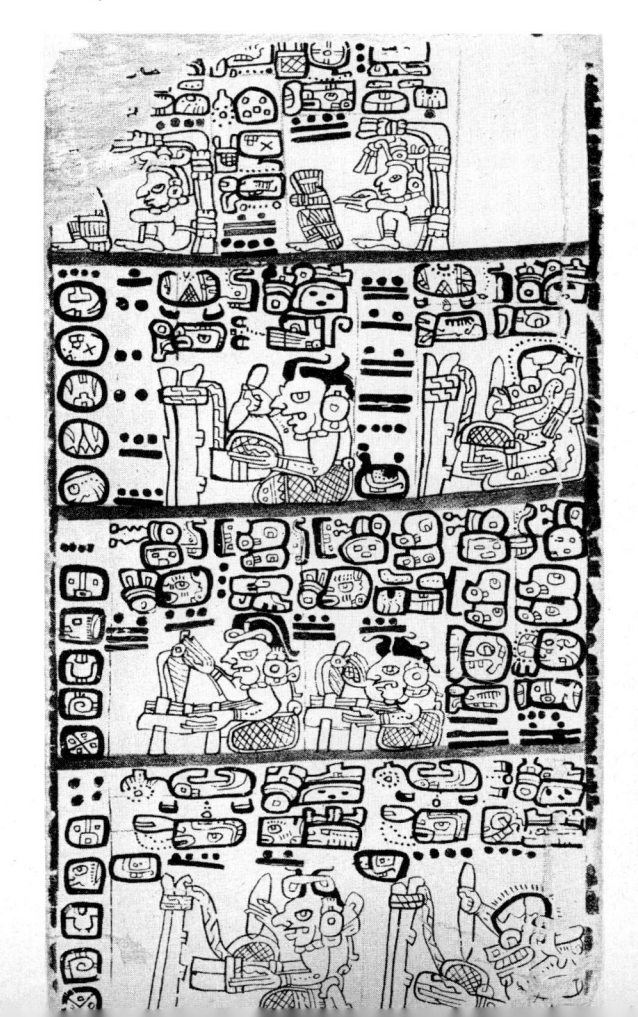

Religious beliefs. There were also many differences between the religious ideas of the Europeans and those of the Indians. One interesting difference concerned the idea of a life after death. The Europeans, who were Christians, believed there was a heaven and hell, and a person went to one place or the other after he died. Which place he went to depended on the kind of person he had been during his lifetime.

Indians also believed in a life after death. But there was no especially wonderful place called heaven nor an especially dreadful one called hell. There was just one place called the "land of the dead," a place very much like their own Indian villages. A person's going there had nothing to do with whether he had been good or bad on earth. Everyone went. Families were reunited there, grandparents and great-great-grandparents all together. To Indians, the Christian idea of an afterlife that rewarded or punished a man for his life on earth did not make any sense. To European Christians, the idea of an afterlife that *did not* reward or punish people made no sense!

There were many, many other ways in which Indian and European cultures differed. The Spanish and Portuguese shared most of their culture with other Europeans. In addition, each of them brought their own special cultural traits. They brought their own languages, for example, and their dress, their holidays and ways of celebrating them, their own customs, and their tastes in food. They also brought their own ideas about what buildings should look like, and how a town should be laid out.

Africans Come to America

The Africans made up the third large group that came to America. They began arriving only a few years after the Europeans did. Very few Africans came to the New World because they wanted to come.

Africans were forced to come to America as slaves. You will remember that the Indians, who had provided the Spanish and Portuguese with labor for their mines and plantations, had died off by the millions. Europeans now looked for another source of labor. They found it in Africa. Soon Portuguese ship captains were bringing thousands of Africans to Middle America and South America and selling them as slaves. Africans who came here were called Negroes, from the Spanish word for black.

Africans were of many cultures. Most Africans who came to America had lived in the western part of Africa. They lived between the Senegal (sen i gôl′) River and Angola, in an area now occupied by such countries as Guinea (gin′ ē), Ghana (gän′ ə), the Ivory Coast, Liberia, and the Republic of the

Congo. You can find this area on the map on this page.

Africans belonged to many different tribes and nations. There were, for example, the Ashanti (ə shant′ ē), the Dahomans (də hō′ mənz), the Congos, the Yorubas (yō′ rủ bäz), and the Angolas (ən gō′ ləz).

African achievements. Some Africans lived in small villages and were organized into tribes or large family groups. Their level of technology was not much higher than that of the Eastern Woodland Indians of North America. Other Africans knew how to use iron to make iron tools, could weave cloth, were good farmers, and had domesticated animals.

Hundreds of years before the European slave traders arrived, there had been great African empires and nations. These were in western Africa in an area near the present countries of Mali, Upper Volta, and Mauritania (môr′ ə tā′ nē ə). These kingdoms were quite advanced and had cities as large as most in Europe at that time. They traded with the Moslem kingdoms of North Africa. They had learned and adopted a written language from the *Moslems*, those people who followed the religious leader Mohammed. Black Africans developed a *literature* and wrote histories of their people. Many had detailed religions and laws. One of their cities, Timbuktu (tim bək tü′), had a population of a hundred thousand. Timbuktu was an important trade center and boasted a fine university. The city is also called Tombouctou.

Slavery. Slavery was not invented by the Portuguese and the Spanish. The practice of slavery was thousands of years old and had existed in many parts of the world. Usually, slavery was connected with war. During wars, the victors took prisoners and made them slaves. African nations and tribes were doing this among themselves in the 1400's. Then Portuguese explorers began sailing along Africa's western coast. Some of these ship captains landed and bought slaves from their African owners in exchange for

AFRICAN HOMELAND OF THE SLAVES
- Land where Africans were seized
- Boundaries of today

0   1500 Miles

57

European goods. They brought the slaves back to Portugal. Arab traders who visited the eastern coast of Africa also bought slaves and carried them to Arabia, Persia, and India.

When the Spanish and Portuguese settlers in America decided to buy African slaves, the evil trade became a big business. Portuguese, Spanish, Dutch, English, and French ship captains hurried to get a share of this profitable but shocking business. The Europeans supplied African chiefs with guns and powder and encouraged them to raid other tribes to capture prisoners and sell them into slavery. Sometimes the European slave traders themselves came upon an unsuspecting group of Africans and kidnapped them. Before long, thousands of Africans were being sold into slavery in the Americas every year.

The horrible passage to America. The slave trade was unbelievably cruel and inhumane (in′ hyü mān′). First the Africans were marched from wherever they were captured to the waiting slave ship. A European slave trader of those days wrote this description of what happened next:

> They were put into a booth, or prison, built for that purpose, near the beach, all of them together; and when the Europeans are to receive them, they are brought out into a large plain, where the surgeons examine every part of every one of them. . . . Such as are allowed good and sound are set on one side, and the others by themselves. . . . Each of the others, which have passed as good, is marked on the breast with a red-hot iron.

Then the slaves, branded and chained together, were packed aboard the slave ships. These ships were specially built to squeeze in several hun-

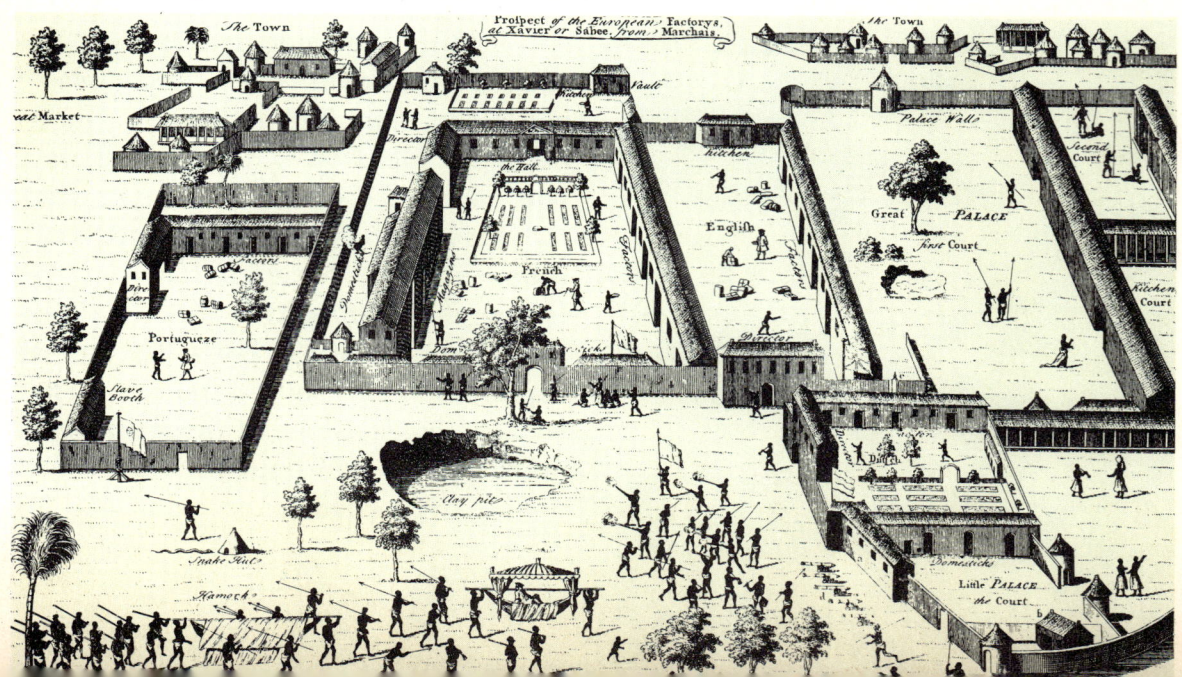

Slaves were brought to centers in Africa for sale to Europeans.

dred slaves. All the slaves entered the hold, which is the area below the ship's deck. There they lay down on the floor, to which their legs and necks were chained. On some ships the space between the floor and ceiling of the hold was only eighteen inches. One slave ship captain wrote this:

> They had not so much room as a man in his coffin, either in length or breadth. It was impossible for them to turn or shift with any degree of ease.

In that position they lay for the voyage, which lasted from six to ten weeks. Sickness often spread rapidly among the slaves, and on every ship a great many of them died.

Another person living at the time wrote this description of the voyage:

> On many of these ships the sense of misery and suffocation was so terrible in the 'tween decks . . . that the slaves not infrequently would go mad before dying or suffocating. In their frenzy some killed others in the hope of procuring more room to breathe. Men strangled those next to them, and women drove nails in each others' brains.

Despite their chains and their weakness, some Africans fought bitterly against becoming slaves. On several slave ships, there were revolts. Without weapons, of course, the revolts did not succeed, and the slaves' bravery was usually rewarded with death. One captain who had put down such a rebellion later reported what happened on his ship. Rather than be slaves, he wrote, many Africans "leaped overboard, and drowned themselves in the ocean."

Many slaves were taken first to the islands owned by Spain in the Caribbean Sea, such as Cuba, Hispaniola (his pən yō′ lə), and Puerto Rico (pwert ə rē′ kō). There they were put to work in the sugar fields. Other slaves were sold to the Portuguese and Spanish in South America. There they were put to work in the mines, the fields, the cities, and the homes of their owners.

The average slave had a short life — about ten years after he came to South America — because he was worked so hard.

More slaves were brought to the Portuguese colony of Brazil than anywhere else in Middle and South America. In fact, 250 years after the founding of Brazil, there were more Africans than Portuguese there. It is certainly true that much of modern Brazil was built by African labor.

INDEPENDENCE COMES

For nearly three hundred years the people of Latin America, that is, Middle and South America, were ruled by Spain and Portugal. During this time, however, important changes took place in Spain and Portugal. These countries did not grow much in population, nor did they increase in strength. In fact, they became weaker.

At the same time, just the opposite changes were taking place in their colonies. Population increased and more goods were produced. The colonists knew they were becoming more powerful and important in the world. They did not like the laws that allowed them to trade only with Spain and Portugal. They also disliked being governed by rulers sent from across the seas.

Then, during the thirty years from 1792 to 1822, Spain and Portugal found themselves losing wars with their European neighbors. The two countries also suffered from revolutions in their lands.

The people of Latin America took advantage of the mother countries' problems and started revolutions themselves. Between 1808 and 1824, all the colonies in Middle and South America, led by men like Simon Bolívar, won their *independence*. Only the islands of Cuba and Puerto Rico remained loyal to Spain.

Independence did not change the lives of most of the people of Latin America. The life of the Indian did not improve. Black slavery continued in many countries. The last South American country to end slavery was Brazil in 1888.

Working with Concepts and Generalizations

Identifying Concepts

Complete each sentence. Write the answers on paper.

1. Many Spaniards came to the New World in search of _____.
2. A few hundred Spaniards were able to defeat thousands of Aztec warriors because the Spaniards had a higher level of _____.
3. The Portuguese discovered and settled in the area that today is _____.
4. Conquistadores was the name given to _____ conquerors.
5. Under the ecomienda system, the Spanish conquerors were to teach the Indians three things: the Spanish religion, which was _____; loyalty to the Spanish _____; and the Spanish _____.
6. Spanish priests were also called _____.
7. Many thousands of Indians died from the _____ the Europeans brought to the New World.
8. The Portuguese established large farms, called _____, on which they grew sugar, cotton, and later, tobacco.
9. Private ownership was an important part of the _____ culture.
10. Africans were forced to come to America as _____.

Developing Concepts

Write the answers on paper.

1. You are a young African prince or princess. Your father is king of a mighty African tribe. You are captured and sold into slavery. You are bound in chains and forced into the hold of a ship bound for America. Write a poem, a song, or a letter expressing how you think a prince or princess might have felt.
2. You have learned that there were many differences between the European cultures and the Indian cultures. Some of these differences are listed below. Choose two of them. Explain how the Indian and European cultures differed in the two areas you have chosen.
   a. Technology
   b. Division of labor
   c. Use of animals
   d. Language
   e. Religious beliefs
3. You know that the Europeans influenced Indian cultures. How did the Indians influence European cultures?
4. How did European ideas about ownership of property differ from those of the Indians? How did this cultural difference affect the life of the Indians in the New World?
5. You are offered the chance to become a millionaire. All you have to do is capture people and sell them into slavery. Will you accept the offer? Explain. How did your values influence the choice you made?

Generalizations

Read the generalizations listed below. Find proof to support each generalization. On paper, tell what the proof is and the page on which you found it.

1. Changes within a culture may be brought about through contact with other cultures.
2. Man's use of natural resources is related to his desires and to his level of technology.

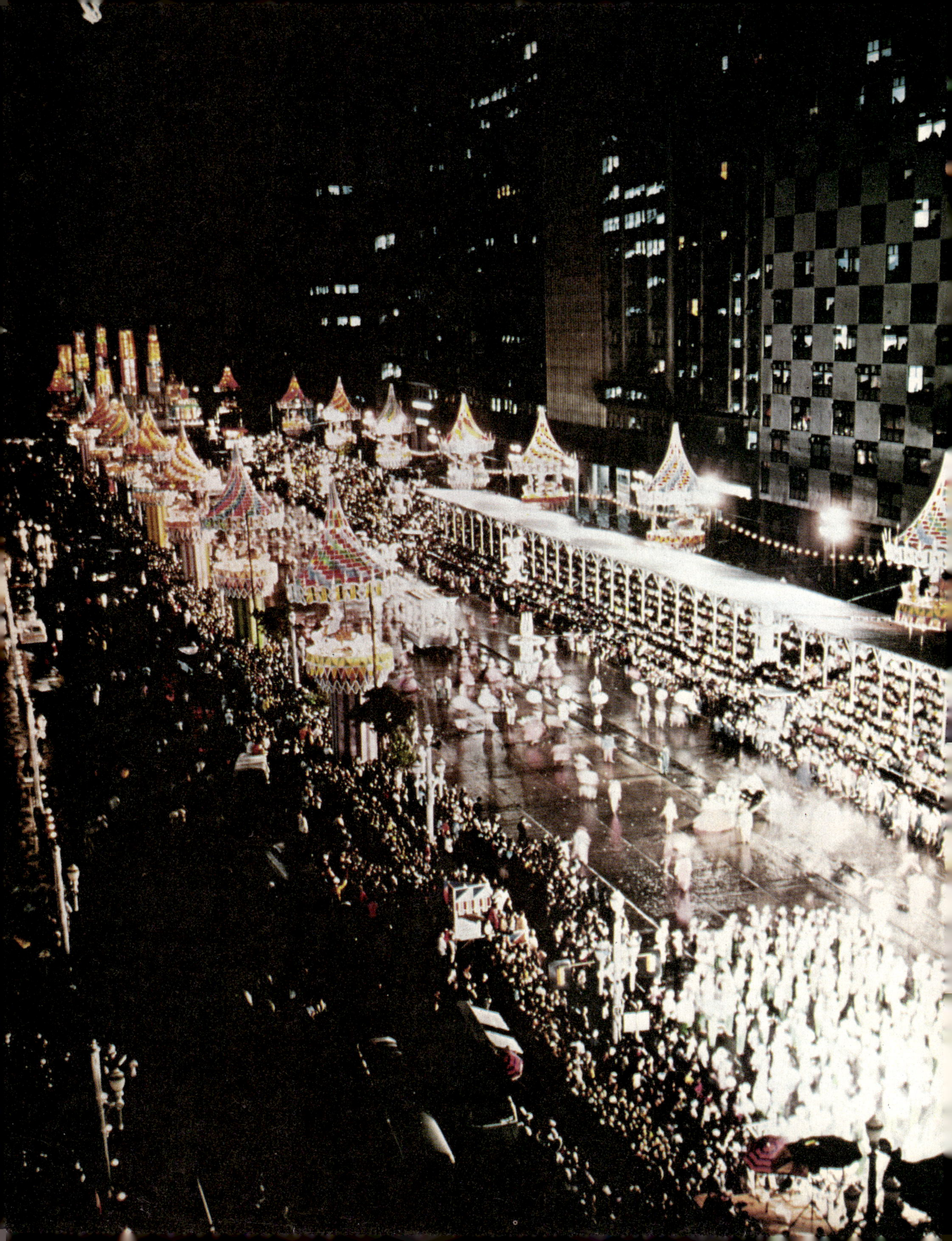

Culture in South America Today

4

Indians, Europeans, Africans—these were the peoples who met in Middle and South America more than four hundred years ago. Later, still other people came. Germans and Italians came to Brazil and Argentina. Japanese came to Brazil and Paraguay (par′ ə gwā). The descendants of these people are our American neighbors today.

What was the result of all these peoples and cultures coming together on one continent? Did the Spanish and the Portuguese succeed in destroying the Indian cultures? Did any of the Indian cultures survive? Did the different cultures borrow from each other when they came into contact? Did they become more alike, or did they remain different, separate cultures? In this chapter we shall study several peoples of South America today, to search for answers to these questions.

The answers to these questions may vary as we study each country. They would probably vary even more if we were to study all the countries of South America. But each answer will help us understand how important culture is to a people and how important the knowledge of different cultures is to us.

The Motilones of Venezuela

On the northern coast of South America lies the nation of Venezuela. Look at the map on this page. It is a modern nation in many ways. Its capital, Caracas, is one of the most beautiful and modern cities on the continent.

In the western part of the country is Lake Maracaibo (mar ə kī′ bō). This is the center of the oil industry that has made Venezuela important throughout the world. Barely a hundred miles to the west of the oil derricks of Lake Maracaibo lies a stretch of jungle that seems to be part of another world. This jungle is inhabited by a group of Indians known as the Motilones.

A culture that did not change. If the ancestors of the Motilones could somehow come back from a thousand years ago, they would notice very few differences in the way their descendants live. The homes of the Motilones are thatch-covered longhouses that look something like giant haystacks. Their tools are very primitive and are made of wood and stone, for these Indians do not know of metal. Bows and arrows and spears are the weapons they use for hunting and fishing. Bananas grow freely, and the Motilones also grow manioc, a plant whose root is something like our sweet potato.

The Motilones have been separated from the rest of the world. Since they have not come into contact with other cultures, they have not been able to borrow ideas and technology. There are a few other places in South America where people like the Motilones live—isolated from other cultures, untouched by modern living. But most groups in South America have come in contact with others. What has happened to them?

Culture in Peru Today

Along the western coast of South America you will find the nation of Peru. The country is divided into three regions that are so different from each other that some people speak of the three Perus. The first is the narrow strip of desert that runs the whole length of the country along the coast. Almost no rain falls here, but some forty small rivers have created oases, where the large cities and towns of the nation are, including the capital city of Lima. To the east of this desert rise the Andes, the highest mountain range in the Western Hemisphere. Here in the second Peru, several miles above the sea, the air is thin and chilly most of the year, and there is very little vegetation. We find the third Peru on the other side of the Andes, where the land slopes down sharply. This part is mostly rain forest, which thins out at higher elevations. It is inhabited by only a small part of the population.

Peru was the home of the Incan civilization, the land that the Spanish conquered. It was in this land that the two great cultures, the Spanish-European and the Incan, met.

As you would expect, each culture borrowed from the other. The Spanish learned about growing corn and other crops from the Indians, and in turn introduced the Indians to many crops grown in Europe. Indians also learned about the wheel, and about making use of the muscle power of domestic animals such as the horse and the ox. Most Indians also adopted the Catholic religion, even though they kept many of their own religious beliefs.

But the cultural borrowing did not last very long. Very soon the two cultures separated. Today, Peru remains a land of two cultures.

Culture of the lowlands. One of those cultures is that of the descendants of the Spanish conquerors. These people live mostly in cities and towns in the coastal desert. Many parts of their culture would be familiar to us in the United States, for they are very modern. These Peruvians wear clothes much like our own. They make many different goods with the aid of machinery, they engage in trade, and they have a great deal of specialization of labor. These Peruvians have a high level of technology. They watch television, eat in restaurants, drive cars, and do all the other things we think of as part of a modern society. Of course,

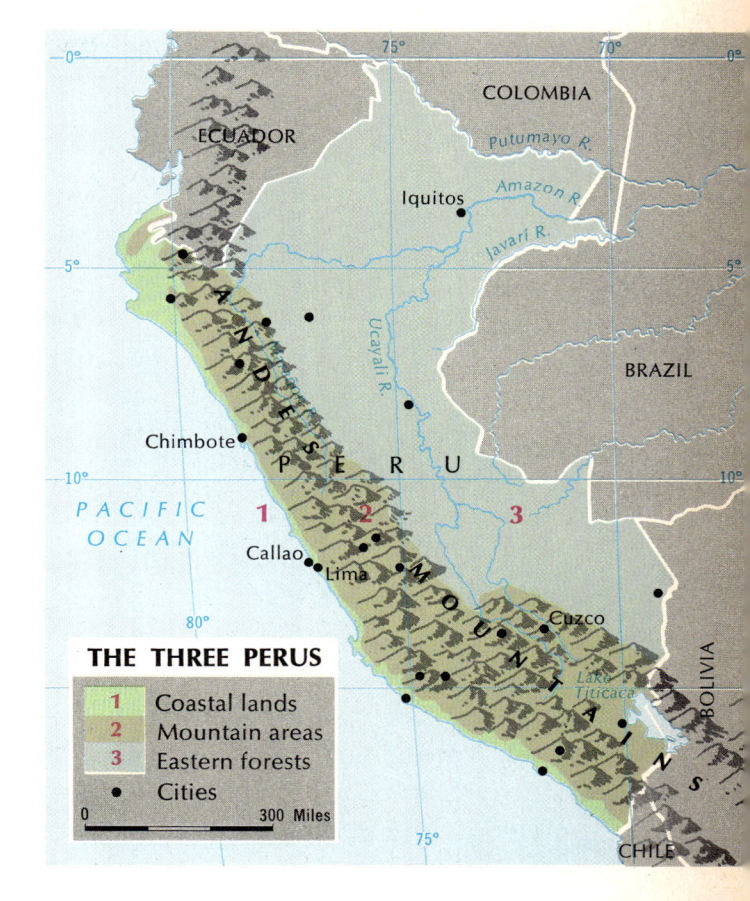

THE THREE PERUS
1 Coastal lands
2 Mountain areas
3 Eastern forests
• Cities

65

This Indian woman is weaving in the same way that her ancestors did years ago.

learning is very important in such a society. Young people attend schools and universities, where they gain the knowledge and skills that lead to new ideas and to better ways of doing and making things.

The language of these Peruvians is the language of their ancestors, Spanish. This is also the official language of the nation. It is the language used in newspapers, schools, government offices, signs, and on the radio.

The original Spanish conquerors were white Europeans, and some of their descendants are white. But even more are part white and part Indian. This is because the early Spanish conquerors did not bring Spanish women with them, but instead married Indian women. Their descendants are called *mestizos* (mes tē′ zōz) or *cholos* (chō′- lōz). Even though they are partly Indian, the mestizos have adopted the modern Peruvian culture as their own.

Indian culture. The second culture of Peru is that of the Indians. Indians make up about half of Peru's population. Although the Spanish tried to destroy the Indians' culture and make them adopt Spanish ways, the Indians resisted. They fled to the highest lands in the mountains where it was possible for man to live. These lands were too harsh and cold for the Spanish, who did not follow them.

The culture of the Indians of Peru today has not changed much from what it was 450 years ago. They have kept themselves separate from the other culture of Peru. Their level of technology is still very low. Their homes are little more than huts, built of stones from the fields. The digging stick is still the main tool they use to farm the rocky mountain soil. Fertilizers, modern farming methods, and machines are unknown to most Peruvian Indians. Theirs is a very simple economy. Nearly all of them farm for a living, and there is almost no division of labor in this work.

In dress, language, values, customs, foods, and many other things, Indian culture is different from the culture of the rest of Peru. Indian women weave the cloth for the blanketlike garments you see in the picture on this page. Very few Indians can either speak or understand Spanish. Their language is an ancient Indian tongue called *Quechua* (kech′ wä). Few of them can read or write this language. Most Indians do not go to schools. The children are needed at home to help raise food for the family. Besides, in the Indian culture, learning new ways of doing things and new ideas is not valued as much as in our own culture.

Indians of Peru are desperately poor. The soil is difficult to farm, and with their low level of technology they cannot make it produce very much. Most of them still live on haciendas, where they must spend nearly half of every week farming the landowner's land without pay. Most of the haciendas are still owned by rich landowners who are descended from the Spanish settlers, although some are now owned by the government of Peru. The few Indians who do own their own land usually have only a tiny patch, barely large enough to make a living.

Most Indians in Peru do not raise enough food to keep them in good health. Hunger and cold are daily companions of the Peruvian Indian. That is why most of them chew coca leaves, which contain a narcotic substance, or drug. This substance is very bad for their health, but it helps them through each day by numbing the pain of hunger and cold.

Two separate peoples. The people of Peru's two cultures neither like nor trust each other. Those who are part of the modern culture say that the Indians are a backward and inferior people. They discriminate (dis krim′ ə nāt) against the Indian, and refuse to accept him as an equal. Indians are hired only for the poorest jobs and are expected to look up to the whites and mestizos almost as their masters.

The whites and mestizos of Peru rule the country, just as they have since the first Spanish conquerors arrived in the early 1500's. They hold all the important government and army

These homes are made of sod squares and covered with a thatched roof. Many Indians cannot afford any other type of house.

The llama is a very important means of transportation for the Indians.

Despite great suffering after the earthquake, these Indians fear outside help.

jobs. They own the stores, the factories, and the banks. They have most of the wealth of the country. They own most of the great haciendas in the countryside, even though they themselves usually live in the cities.

The Indians, on the other hand, do not trust the whites and mestizos and feel hostile toward them. The Indians feel they have always been mistreated by these people—as indeed they have been. They want nothing to do with the people of Peru's other culture and have chosen to live apart from them in their own towns and villages in the mountains. Most spend their entire lives there, never seeing any part of their country beyond the next village. Unable to read or write, they know little of their country outside the village of the hacienda they work on. Many Indians do not even think of their villages as part of a larger nation. They do not think of themselves as Peruvians at all.

A good example of how these Indians feel about people outside their own culture occurred recently. On June 3, 1970, a terrible earthquake struck northern Peru. The hardest hit were Indians living in the Andean foothills. The disaster left thirty thousand people dead, and thousands injured and homeless. The following newspaper story tells what happened when people from other parts of Peru and other countries sent help to these injured and homeless Indians.

LIMA, Peru, June 20—In the bleak, cold Andean highlands of northern Peru, many Indians are still hiding their injured and orphaned, according to missionaries, three weeks after the devastating earthquake there.

Some of the Indians are being hidden because of traditional fear and distrust of Spanish-speaking people, others because of the unusually strong family ties that have helped the Peruvian Indian survive more than four centuries of European domination.

City life brings changes. One important change is taking place in Peru today, just as it is in many other countries of South America. Many people from rural areas are going to the city in search of jobs, so that they can make a better living. In Peru these rural people are the Indians. Once the Indians get to the city, they have to give up many of their ways of living. This is a very hard thing for the Indians to get used to. It is hard for anyone to leave his familiar culture and suddenly have to learn a whole new way of living. They must become accustomed to modern ways. They wear modern dress, learn to ride buses to work, read clocks to tell time, drive trucks and taxis to earn a living, shop in stores, and so on. When they do finally become a part of the other culture of Peru, they are treated somewhat better, for now they are not so different.

An Experiment in Vicos

Even though Peru remains a land of two separate cultures, some attempts are being made today to help the Indians. One important experiment was started about twenty years ago at Vicos (vē′ kōz), a government-owned hacienda high in the mountains. The Peruvian government and an American university, Cornell, cooperated in this work. They sent a team of experts to help the Indians increase their farm production and improve their health and education.

When the experts arrived, they found people suffering from poor diet and from disease. The potato crop was small, not nearly large enough to satisfy the needs of all the Indians who depended on it. There was one school

Spanish-style buildings are a familiar sight in Lima, Peru. Churches in particular reflect Spanish influence.

on the hacienda, an old shack in which a single untrained person served as a teacher. From the entire Indian population on the hacienda, only eighteen children attended the school, and none of them could read or write.

The experts set about trying to introduce the Indians to better methods of farming. They wanted to teach them to use fertilizer, better seed, and better methods of tilling the soil.

At first the Indians resisted. They distrusted these outsiders. Had they not come to take advantage of the Indian or to make him give up his own culture, just as white outsiders had always done in the past? The visiting experts understood. They showed that they respected the Indians. They showed that they did not want to change the Indians' language, beliefs, and customs, but only to help them live healthier and better lives.

Little by little the Indians became less suspicious and less hostile. As they grew to trust the visitors, they were more willing to learn modern technology. They came to see that these newer methods of farming really could work for them.

In a few years the Indians at Vicos were harvesting a potato crop four times as large as they had ever had. They were growing other crops, too, for a more balanced diet. They ate better and even had enough left over to sell outside the hacienda. The people also joined together and built a new schoolhouse. Instead of eighteen children in school there were soon 250, being taught to read and write their native Quechua language by eight well-trained teachers.

Because they have borrowed the technology of another culture, the people of Vicos will live better in the future. At the same time, they will be able to keep the customs, religion, language, and values of their own ancient culture.

Culture in Brazil

In the nation of Brazil the story began much as it did in Peru. The early Portuguese settlers mistreated the Indians, and many Indians died. Then a new group, the Africans, entered the country and brought their cultures with them. Soon there were more Africans than Portuguese.

Brazilian culture. The different groups in Brazil did not try to keep separate from each other. They learned to live with each other and accept each other's ways. As a result, the different cultures that met in Brazil—especially the Portuguese and the African—influenced each other greatly. Today the combination of different cultures has produced a new one that we can call the Brazilian culture.

There is every imaginable shade of skin between white and black in Brazil, for Brazilians of many colors and cultures have intermarried for more than four hundred years. But whatever their skin color, all of them today share the Brazilian culture. So do the millions of recent immigrants from such European countries as Germany and Italy, and from the Asian country of Japan. All have adopted Brazilian ways.

Brazil is a modern nation. Most Brazilians share a high level of technology, although there are still some parts of the country that are backward. No language difference divides the Brazilian people as it does the Peruvians. All speak Portuguese. But an interesting thing has happened to the language over the centuries in Brazil. A great many African words have been added to the Portuguese language.

Brazilians dress the same, eat the same foods, and enjoy the same entertainment. The dancing and music that originally came to Brazil with the Africans has become a part of Brazilian culture for all to enjoy.

Does this mean that there are no differences among Brazilians? Of course not. In parts of Brazil, especially in the northeastern section called Bahia, the population is descended mostly from Africans. Here, there are more things from the African cultures. Portuguese is still the language of these Brazilians, but they use more African words in their spoken language. Dress is

CARNAVAL

One of the best examples of how the Portuguese-European and African cultures have learned from each other and become mixed together is Brazil's great national festival, Carnaval. Carnaval is a gay celebration, with dancing, singing, and entertainment that goes on night and day for a full week.

Where did Carnaval come from? When the Portuguese settled in Brazil, they brought with them their Catholic religion. One of the holidays in that religion is celebrated in the spring, just before Lent and Easter. The religion of the Portuguese was adopted by nearly all the peoples of Brazil, including the people from African cultures. But Africans also added their own ideas of worship and of celebrating religion. To this religious celebration, Africans added dancing, costumes, and music. Gradually this celebration spread out to cover a whole week. The result was Carnaval, which is now both a religious celebration and a colorful festival. It is part Portuguese, part African—and all Brazilian.

mostly modern, but many women wear a turban in the African style. The residents of Bahia worship in ways more like those of their African ancestors than those of the people elsewhere in Brazil. As you may recall from Chapter 1, we said that the life of the Bahia fisherman is very different in some ways from the resident of Rio de Janerio.

In other parts of the country, where European and Japanese immigrants have settled recently, these people still carry on many customs of their fathers and grandfathers. Here and there, German, Italian, and Japanese are still spoken by the immigrants. But their children have learned to speak Portuguese, and they are learning Brazilian ways in the schools. Despite some differences among the people of Brazil, we can still say that Brazilians share a common culture.

Even though Brazilians of all colors have lived together for four hundred years and have borrowed from each other's cultures, the country is not entirely free of *race prejudice* (prej′ ə dis). There is still some prejudice against black people. But this prejudice does not keep whites and blacks from living in the same neighborhoods, going to the same schools, and working together. Brazilians of every color are engaged in trade, manufacturing, medicine, teaching—in fact, just about every job you can think of. Three of Brazil's most famous men are black; one is an artist, another a poet, and the third an engineer. One of the country's recent presidents also was black.

These seven people show us the many faces of Brazil.

Working with Concepts and Generalizations

Identifying Concepts

The statements below are taken from the text. Read each one carefully. Write CB if the statement indicates that cultural borrowing has taken place; write NCB if the statement indicates that no cultural borrowing has taken place. Write the answers on paper.

1. "Their tools are very primitive and are made of wood and stone, for these Indians do not know of metal."
2. "Indians also learned about the wheel, and about making use of the muscle power of domestic animals such as the horse and the ox."
3. "Fertilizers, modern farming methods, and machines are unknown to most Peruvian Indians."
4. "These Peruvians wear clothes much like our own. They make many different goods with the aid of machinery, they engage in trade, and they have a great deal of specialization of labor."
5. "But an interesting thing has happened to the language over the centuries in Brazil. A great many African words have been added to the Portuguese language."

Developing Concepts

Write the answers on paper.

1. You have learned that there are two different cultures in Peru. Which of these cultures would you rather belong to? Why?
2. You are a Peruvian Indian. You have never been outside your village or inside a classroom. EITHER draw a simple sketch showing the games you play, what you see on a village street, or the kind of work your father does, OR write a few paragraphs describing some of these things.
3. You have learned that many different groups of people have come together in Brazil. What has been the result of this mixing of different cultures? Are there any cultural differences among Brazilians today?
4. You are a Peruvian Indian. You are offered a job in a city. You know if you accept the job, you can make a better living. You decide to give it a try. Describe what you see and how you feel on your first day in the city. Will you want to go back to work the next day? Explain.
5. You discover a group of Indians living in a small village in South America. They have a low level of technology. They have not been able to grow enough food to feed themselves. Most of the people in the village are in poor health and very few have ever been to school. You know you can help them but they do not trust you. What will you do to win their confidence? What cultural changes will you encourage them to make? What parts of their culture will you leave unchanged? Why?

Generalizations

Read the generalizations listed below. For each generalization, find three facts in the text that help prove it is true. On paper, write each fact and the page on which you found it.

1. Conflict between groups is often reduced when they understand and appreciate each other's culture.
2. When a culture has no contact or communication with other cultures, there is very little cultural change.

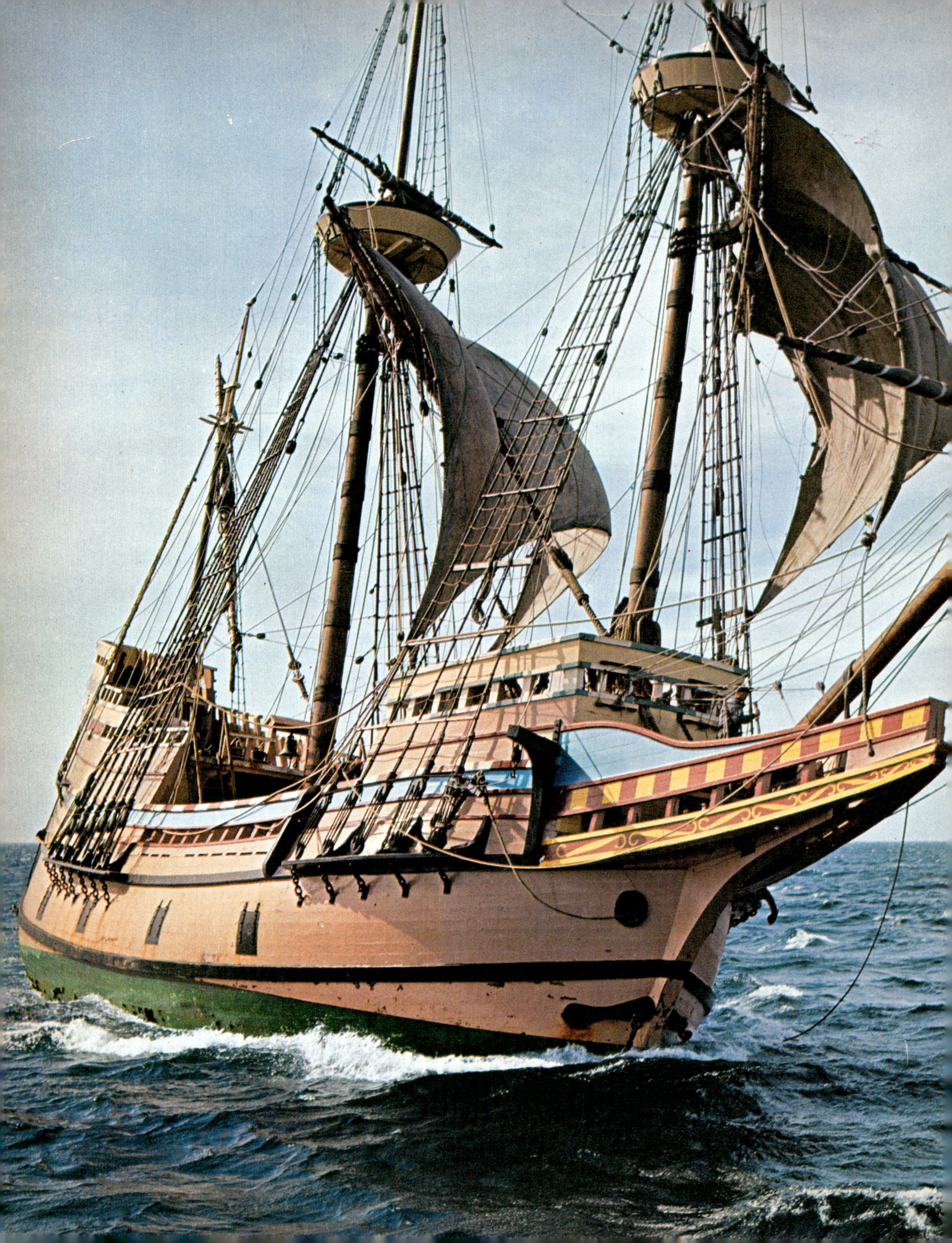

Europeans and Africans Come to North America

5

Explorers reached North America only a few years after Columbus' great discovery. But for a long time after, few Europeans came to the northern continent. The Spanish and Portuguese were well established in Middle and South America before settlers came to North America.

Then, beginning shortly after 1600, many Europeans came and stayed. Most settled along the Atlantic coast. The settlers came from many different countries in Europe. Each year their number increased, and soon little settlements dotted the coast from the St. Lawrence River to Florida.

Why were so many Europeans willing to leave their homes to live in an unknown land? Were their reasons the same as those of the Spanish and Portuguese? Could they solve their problems of living in the same way that they did in Europe? What about new problems that would arise? How would these new problems affect their way of living in the New World? What would happen when these people from different cultures came together in this new land? These are some of the questions we will answer in this chapter.

Courtesy Plimoth Plantation

EUROPEAN SETTLEMENT IN COLONIAL DAYS 1650

Settled areas
0   300 Miles

Europeans Settle North America

The conquests in Middle and South America made Spain the richest nation in Europe, the envy of every European king. Their royal mouths watered at the thought of all the riches to be had in America. They, too, decided to send explorers to win a share of this rich new land. Before long, English, Dutch, French, and Portuguese explorers joined the Spanish in the hunt for the riches.

Each of the explorers claimed that the land he "discovered" belonged to his country and king. The kings in turn announced their claims to the rest of Europe. The idea at the time was that the land belonged to whichever nation discovered it—a sort of "finders-keepers." Of course, the Indians really found it first, but none of the European kings seemed to include them in the contest.

The claiming of land was important, but the claim would not mean very much unless people actually settled on the land. Except for a few tiny Spanish missions in the Southwest, none of the Europeans who came to North America for the first hundred years stayed. Then, early in the 1600's, several European nations succeeded in starting settlements in North America.

French beginnings. In 1608 France set up a colony in *New France* at Quebec (kwi bek'). Like the Spanish, the French wanted to take wealth out of the New World. There was no gold or silver in New France, but there were furs. Most of the French who settled there became trappers, or else traded with the Indians for furs. The king of France also sent whole families to settle on the land. Through hard work, these families built homes for themselves and farmed the land along the St. Lawrence River. French missionaries came to live among the Indians and teach them the Christian religion.

New France grew very slowly. There was plenty of land and the soil was rich. But the growing season was short, and the winters were colder than any the settlers had known in France. Without the help of the Indians, the settlement might have failed. After fifty-five years there were still only about 2,500 Frenchmen living in New France.

Dutch settlements. Holland also founded a settlement in North America. In 1609 an explorer named Henry Hudson discovered the Hudson River and sailed north as far as present-day Albany. Five years later the Dutch started a small trading outpost there.

Jamestown has been rebuilt to show how it looked when settled.

In 1624 they built a fort near the mouth of the Hudson River, on the tip of Manhattan Island. They called this settlement *New Amsterdam,* after the great city in Holland.

Soon New Amsterdam began to look like old Amsterdam, as Dutch-speaking people brought their way of living to the New World.

Not far from New Amsterdam, a small band of Swedish immigrants built several small settlements along the Delaware River. Just as New Amsterdam looked like old Amsterdam, so *New Sweden* looked like old Sweden.

The Swedish settlers built log cabins for their homes, much like those in the northern part of their native land.

The English settlements. England had tried several times to start colonies along the Atlantic coast in the 1580's, but each time the effort ended in failure. Either the settlers gave up and returned home, or they simply disappeared in the strange new land.

The English finally succeeded in starting a colony at Jamestown, Virginia, in 1607. At first it looked as if this colony might fail, just as the others had. The men spent too much time looking for gold and not enough time growing food. They depended on supplies from England. They had made enemies of the Indians living nearby and so received little help from them. The winter of 1609–1610 came to be known as "the starving time." At the start of the winter, there were about five hundred settlers in Jamestown. By spring, only sixty were still alive.

The desperate handful of colonists decided to return to England. They had actually climbed aboard ship and started down the James River, when they met several ships sailing toward them. It was a new supply of colonists and provisions! Jamestown, which was within a few hours of being just another failing colony, was saved.

By this time the colonists had learned that a colony in this part of the New World could survive only through

ENGLISH SETTLEMENTS 1650

78

hard work. Now the settlers raised their own food. They cut lumber and sold it in Europe. Most important, they learned to plant tobacco, a crop that the Indians had raised for many years. They sold their crop in England, where tobacco was in great demand. At last the colony had produced something to bring wealth and encourage more effort.

Plymouth. Thirteen years after English settlers landed at Jamestown, a second English colony was started at Plymouth (plim' əth), near Cape Cod in Massachusetts. The people who settled at Plymouth are called the *Pilgrims.* Unlike so many others who had come to America before them, the Pilgrims came so they could worship as they pleased.

The king of England had insisted that they worship according to the rules of the Church of England. When this small group of men and women refused, he made life so miserable for them that they fled England. First the Pilgrims moved to Holland. After a number of years there, a tiny band of them decided to start a new life in America. In 1620 they set out on their voyage to America.

After landing, the Pilgrims prepared for the winter. They chose a spot for their settlement and put up several houses. Like their houses in England, each building was made of boards cut from logs, and topped with a steep, thatched roof. In these buildings they settled in to wait for spring.

That first winter was a hard one, and there was much suffering from cold, hunger, and disease. By spring, half the colonists were in their graves. With the help of the Indians, who were very friendly, the remainder learned to grow corn and raise enough food for themselves. The Plymouth colony, after a shaky start, had managed to survive.

Why People Chose to Come

By about 1700 most of the colonies on the east coast belonged to England, so it is not surprising that at first nearly all the settlers were English. However many people came from other European countries to live in the English colonies in America.

This is a model of the fort at Plymouth.
Courtesy Plimoth Plantation

The different groups. One of the largest groups was known as the Scotch-Irish. These people had originally lived in Scotland, but had moved to northern Ireland around 1610. Many soon became unhappy there. The Scotch-Irish were Protestants, and they had constant religious arguments and even warfare with the native Irish, who were nearly all Catholics. The English government, which ruled Ireland, also treated them badly. Many Scotch-Irish decided to leave northern Ireland and go to America.

Usually the Scotch-Irish moved directly into the unsettled land just west of the earlier settlements. There, in the silent forests, they carved out small farms. The usual *frontier* home of these people was the log cabin, which colonists had learned about from Swedish settlers living along the Delaware River.

Two other large groups of settlers were the Scots and the Germans. Unlike the Scotch-Irish, these Scots came directly from Scotland, and settled mostly in the towns along the coast. Many of them became merchants. Many of the German-speaking people settled on farms in the rolling farm country of Pennsylvania. They went also to North Carolina, Virginia, and Maryland. In addition to these large groups of settlers, a sprinkling of other Europeans—French, Dutch, Swedes, and Jews from various countries—came to live in the English colonies.

Why did these people decide to leave their own countries to live in American colonies that belonged to another country, England? It could not have been an easy decision for them to make. True, unless the later settlers moved to the frontier, they did not have to face a land quite as unknown as the one the Pilgrims had had to face. Moreover, the Indians were very patient with the settlers. Only when the Indians' hunting grounds were threatened did they defend their rights. Still, even for the settlers who came later, moving to America was difficult.

Reasons for moving to America. The people who went to America did have good reasons for doing so. On the next page you will find some things written

Who Were the Americans in 1775?

English 62%

Africans 20%

Scotch-Irish 7%

Germans 6%

French, Welsh, Dutch, Swedes, Irish, Swiss, Scots   5%

Each symbol represents 125,000 people

80

several hundred years ago in England. As you read them, see if you can find some of the reasons people came to America.

USING SOURCE MATERIAL

The first item is from an English play written in the year 1605—before the first successful English colony at Jamestown was founded. One of the actors in the play, talking about America, says this:

SCAPE. But is there such treasure there, Captain, as I have heard?

SEA. I tell thee, gold is more plentiful there than copper is with us; and for as much red copper as I can bring, I'll have thrice the weight in gold. Why, man, all their dripping-pans and their pots are pure gold; and all the chains with which they chain up their streets are massy gold; all the prisoners they take are fetter'd in gold; and, for rubies and diamonds, they go forth on holidays and gather 'em by the seashore, to hang on their children's coats, and stick in their caps, as commonly as our children wear saffron gilt brooches and groats with holes in 'em.

SCAPE. And is it a pleasant country withal?

SEA. As ever the sun shin'd on; temperate, and full of all sorts of excellent viands: wild boar is as common there as our tamest bacon is here; venison, as mutton. And then you shall live freely there.... Then, for your means to advancement there, it is simple, and not so mix'd. You may be a town leader there, and never one who cleans streets; you may be a nobleman, and never be a servant. You may come . . . to riches and fortune enough.

What does this tell you about the ideas some Englishmen had about America? Do you think Englishmen

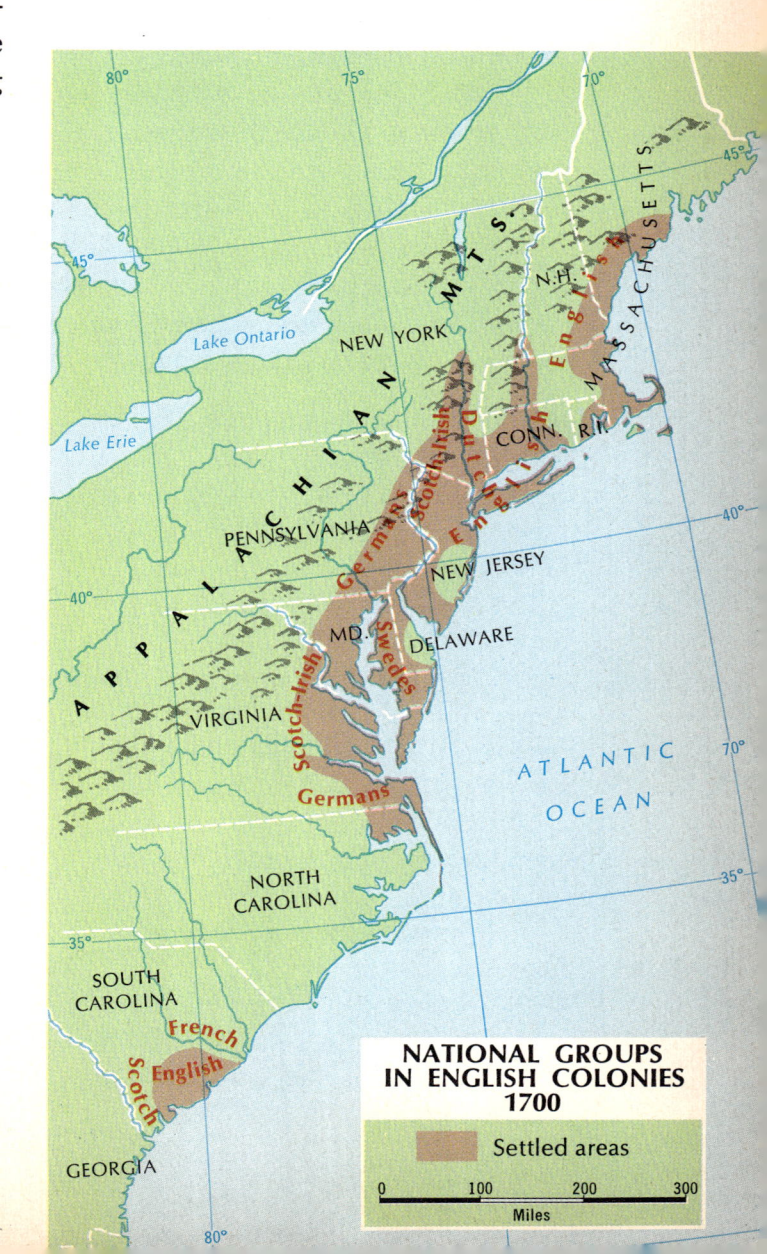

NATIONAL GROUPS IN ENGLISH COLONIES 1700

Settled areas

0   100   200   300
Miles

who heard such things might become interested in America?

The next item comes from a pamphlet written by a man named William Penn. The king of England had given William Penn an enormous piece of land in America. In 1682 the first few settlers went to live in this land called Pennsylvania. A few years later, William Penn wrote a pamphlet describing his new colony. He had many copies of it printed and given to people in England. He also had the pamphlet printed in French, Dutch, and German, and sent hundreds of copies to people in those lands. Here is a part of this pamphlet. We have changed some words to make it easier to read.

The soil has been even richer than we had hoped. Even the poorest places produce large crops of vegetables and grain. We produce from thirty to sixty times as much corn as in England.

The land requires less seed to produce a crop than in England.

We also find that everything that grows well in England grows well in the colony — corn, roots, wheat, barley, rye, oats, buckwheat, peas, beans, cabbages, turnips, carrots, parsnips, cauliflowers, asparagus, onions, garlic, and Irish potatoes. Even Spanish rice grows well there, as do rope and hemp and flax.

Our cattle fatten up for market on weeds, and there is plenty of hay for the winter from our swamps and marshes.

All sorts of English fruits that have been planted take mighty well. Peaches, muskmellons, and watermellon are raised there as easily as pumpkins in England.

Have you figured out why Penn printed so many copies in different languages and gave them away? Do you think everyone who read it would want to go to America?

Here is one more document that can tell us why people were willing to go to the strange land across the ocean. This one was also written by William Penn. It is a part of the main law he wrote for his colony: the Pennsylvania Charter of Privileges (priv′ lij əz). Again, we have shortened Penn's flowery language a bit. This is what the charter said:

Because no people can be truly happy if they cannot follow their own religion and worship as they please, I do hereby grant that no person who lives in this province of Pennsylvania shall ever be persecuted for his religious beliefs. He shall never be forced to attend a church he does not believe in, or to do anything else that is against his religion.

Who do you think might want to move to Penn's colony because of this law? Do you remember which group of colonists had already come to America for a similar reason?

The next document, written more than two hundred years ago, tells a story about a person who did not plan to go to America at all, but wound up there anyway. It is a report about the trial of an Englishman named Henry Justice.

Saturday, May 6, 1736 came on . . . the trial of Henry Justice . . . for stealing out of the library of Trinity College, Cambridge, a Field's Bible . . . [and] several other books of great value . . . the jury found him guilty. [His sentence was that] he must be transported to some one of his Majesty's plantations in America—there to remain seven years—and be put to death if he returned.

Why is Henry Justice going to America? Does this tell us how the court felt about the colonies? Actually, there were several thousand who came to America in this way—though few who were as interested in good books as Henry Justice seems to have been!

People came for other reasons, too. Some had committed crimes and were fleeing from the law. Some owed large debts and were fleeing from those they owed money to. There were even some children who did not come willingly at all. Poor orphans who wandered along the streets of London were regarded by the "better people" of the city as a bother. The city government paid ship

Settlers had to learn to live in peace with the Indians.

captains to pick them up and take them to America.

Indentured servants. Many of the people who wanted to move to the English colonies to better themselves were too poor to pay for the trip. As it happened, there were many American colonists who were anxious to have these newcomers come over. They wanted cheap labor to help on their farms and in their shops and homes. The colonists, the immigrants, and the ship captains struck a bargain. Then they wrote up a contract, or agreement, called an indenture (in den' chər). The colonists would pay the captain for the immigrant's trip to America. In exchange, the immigrant would work for the colonist for four or five years without pay. Persons who sold their future services in exchange for free passage to America were called *indentured servants*. During the period of service, the indentured servant practically belonged to the master. After the time agreed on, he was free. About half of all the people who moved from Europe to the English colonies in America came as indentured servants. Even the children picked up by ship captains were sold as indentured servants.

Africans Come to the English Colonies

Except for people like Henry Justice, the book thief, most Europeans who settled in the English colonies came because they wanted to. The same cannot be said of the Africans. Europeans left their homelands with dreams of a better life in America. Africans were dragged from their native lands, put in chains, and herded onto ships with an unknown destination. For Africans, America did not offer a life of freedom but of slavery.

From servants to slaves. The first Africans to land in North America were brought to Jamestown in 1619—just twelve years after the English started that colony, and a year before the Pilgrims landed at Plymouth. Actually, those first Africans, and some of the others who arrived in those early years, were treated like indentured servants and not slaves. A number of them were freed and given some land after performing five years of service for their owners.

USING SOURCE MATERIAL

Were African indentured servants treated the same as whites? The example below gives you an answer. In the colony of Virginia, three indentured servants were caught after they had run away from their master. A judge found them guilty and gave them this punishment:

The court does therefore order that the said three servants shall receive the punishment of whipping and to have thirty stripes apiece. One called Victor, a Dutchman, the other a Scotchman called James Gregory, shall serve . . . one whole year apiece after the time of their service is expired . . . and after that service . . . to serve the colony for three whole years apiece, and that the third being a Negro named John Punch shall serve his said master . . . for the time of his natural life.

What does the judge's decision tell you about the way indentured servants were treated? Why was John Punch treated differently than the white indentured servants he ran away with? Why did Africans receive worse treatment? The answer is that their language, customs, religion, and appearance were different from the Europeans. As so often happens when one culture meets another, the Europeans decided that *different* meant *inferior*. The culture of the African and the color of his skin set him apart from all others in the colonies.

By the middle of the 1600's most blacks were being held as slaves and not as indentured servants by their masters. Before long several colonies passed laws that *all* Africans were to be servants for life. They were slaves. They belonged to their masters. Not only that, but their children also became slaves.

Treatment of the slaves. By the end of the 1600's, thousands of Africans were being brought to the colonies each year. On arrival they were taken in chains to a market where they were sold to the highest bidder. Most of the slaves went to the southern colonies, where they worked on the tobacco, rice, and cotton plantations. Many

This picture shows some of the horrors of a slave ship. The people had barely enough room to lie down.

worked on smaller farms or in the homes of their masters. Some worked as servants in the growing towns of the northern colonies.

As slaves, Africans had almost no rights. They could not go to school. They were forbidden to learn how to read. They could not leave their plantation without special permission. They could be beaten. They did not even have the right to keep their families together, for their owner could sell any of his slaves at any time.

Not all slaves were treated so badly as the woman whose torment is described in the story "A Slave Auction."

Some masters treated their slaves with kindness. But even when they received good treatment, they were still not free men.

Many slaves fought back. Helped by Northerners, both blacks and whites, thousands of slaves escaped. Some others risked death by starting uprisings against their masters. Many more refused to work, broke their tools, ruined crops, and even burned down the buildings on the farm. But most realized they had little chance to fight their way out of slavery, so they accepted their bitter life while quietly yearning for freedom.

A SLAVE AUCTION

One former slave wrote a description of a slave auction (ôk′ shən), or sale, that he was a part of as a child.

"My brothers and sisters were bid off first, and one by one, while my mother, paralyzed by grief, held me by the hand. Her turn came, and she was bought by Isaac Riley of Montgomery county. Then I was offered to the assembled purchasers. My mother, half distracted with the thought of parting forever from all her children, pushed through the crowd, while the bidding for me was going on, to the spot where Riley was standing. She fell at his feet, and clung to his knees, entreating him in tones that a mother only could command, to buy her baby as well as herself, and spare to her one, at least, of her little ones. Will it, can it be believed that this man, thus appealed to, was capable not merely of turning a deaf ear to her supplication, but of disengaging himself from her with such violent blows and kicks, as to reduce her to the necessity of creeping out of his reach? . . . As she crawled away from the brutal man I heard her sob out, 'Oh, Lord Jesus, how long, how long shall I suffer this way!' I must have been then between five and six years old. I seem to see and hear my poor weeping mother now."

Europeans and Indians Learn from Each Other

The story of North America, in which Indian, European, and African cultures came together, is something like the story of Middle and South America that you read about in Chapter 3. In that chapter you also learned that even though there were differences among the cultures of people from different European nations, there were also many likenesses. Do you remember some of the things that Europeans had in common? Europeans certainly had more in common with each other than they had with the Indians.

You will also remember that the Indians were not all alike. There were many cultural differences among the different Indian peoples. Can you recall some of the differences between the Pueblos and the Aztecs?

But just as the different European cultures had some things in common, so did the different Indian cultures. Do you recall what some of them were? What were their ideas about owning property? What were their ideas about religion and heaven?

When the Europeans and the Indians met in North America, there was some cultural borrowing between them. In the settlement days, this borrowing helped the Europeans to survive. The Indians taught the people of Jamestown and Plymouth special ways of farming in the forest lands. The Europeans learned of food crops they had never grown before. They also profited from the Indians' knowledge and skill in raising tobacco. Europeans adopted Indian methods of tracking and trapping animals. Indians also taught them to prepare the hides for clothing or for building canoes.

The Indians borrowed some things, too. The horse, which later became so important to the Indians who hunted buffalo on the Great Plains, was introduced to America by the Spanish. The Indians also learned to use tools such as metal knives, metal axes, and rifles, although they lacked the knowledge to make such tools themselves.

Different beliefs and values. Except for a few things of this sort, there was not too much cultural borrowing between the European colonists and the Indians. Certainly they did not accept each other's beliefs and values. A good example of the different way the Europeans and Indians could look at the same thing is the *treaties*, or agreements, they made about land. Europeans believed in the private ownership of land. Land was something that could be bought and sold. As Europeans came to America, they tried to buy land from Indians. They would write up a treaty and give the Indians some goods in exchange for the piece of land—perhaps rifles or other supplies.

Gifts often sealed the peace between the English and Indians.

To Europeans the exchange of goods and the signing of the agreement meant, "We are buying the land from you. Now that you accept our goods as payment, we own the land." But you will remember that in Indian culture the idea that land could be privately owned made no sense. To the Indians the exchange of goods meant, "We accept this gift as a sign of your friendship. Now that we are friends, we can all use the land together."

Can you see how this different understanding might make for trouble later on? Each side would believe that it had been honest and good and that the other side had been dishonest and bad.

Many Europeans, Many Cultures

People from the European countries differed in important ways. You know, of course, that the French, the English, the Dutch, and the Germans spoke different languages, and that language is an important part of culture. But there were many other differences as well. They wore different dress and had different customs. They celebrated different holidays and enjoyed different foods. They often had different beliefs about a number of things—like religion. When they came to America, they brought their differences with them.

Old ways in a new land. Think about the kind and the style of homes each group built in America. The Swedes, the English, and the Dutch all settled in areas along the northeastern part of the Atlantic coast, not too far from each other. The climate in which each group lived was very much the same. All of them lived near wooded areas, where they would have the same forest materials to build their homes. Did they, then, all build the same kinds of homes? You can compare their styles by looking at the pictures of homes built by settlers. What kind of homes did the Swedes build? What kind did the Dutch build? What kind did the English build?

Why didn't the English build log cabins? Why didn't the Dutch build homes with thatched roofs as the English did? You know the answer, of course. We might as well ask why the French didn't decide to speak Dutch when they first settled in Quebec. Or why the Dutch, who were Protestants, didn't immediately decide to build a Catholic church when they moved to New Amsterdam.

Each group that came to America brought its own culture with it. The people who moved to America from Europe wanted to live a *better* life, but they certainly did not want to live a *different* life. They wanted to continue their familiar way of living in a new, unfamiliar land. That was why New Amsterdam looked so much like old Amsterdam, and New Sweden looked so much like old Sweden. When Germans moved into the farmlands of Pennsylvania, they spoke German, dressed as they had dressed in Germany, cooked the same way, plowed the fields and farmed in the same way —and raised their children according to the same beliefs.

New Amsterdam resembled a Dutch town.

Change comes slowly. Today we think that these Europeans should have changed their ways right away. Yet it took a long time for them to change. A good example of this is the way English settlers at Jamestown carried their ways of dress to the New World. Jamestown is located near the coast of Virginia on low land between two rivers. In the summer, high temperatures combine with high *humidity* to make many days hot and sticky. Yet even in the hottest weather the English settlers at first dressed just as Englishmen had in the cooler weather of England. They wore heavy clothes and clumsy shoes or high boots. These were perfectly comfortable in England, but hardly suitable for a hot summer day in Jamestown. When they traveled any distance, they also wore, on top of all this, steel armor or at least a steel helmet. Despite the heat, the English settlers at Jamestown continued to wear such clothes for a number of years.

So it was with all the groups of Europeans who came to America. They brought with them their tools, their skills, their different ways of making a living. Each people brought its own ways, and each tried to change the American wilderness into a copy of its own familiar farms, villages, and towns of Europe.

Forcing a culture upon slaves. Of all the people who came to live in the English colonies, only Africans were not free to live as they had done in their native lands. As slaves, they were forced to give up most of their own ways of life and accept the ways their masters forced upon them. The white slave-owner in North America tried to blot out all African culture, just as the Spanish had tried to blot out Indian culture in South America.

They did succeed in blotting out most of the Africans' culture. But some Africans did manage to cling to some of their own ways. Even when they had to learn the English language of their owner, some slaves continued to speak in their own tongues. Even as they learned and accepted the Christian religion of their owners, many also held on to some of their own religious beliefs. They could not cling to their old style of dress or to most of

English clothes did not suit the warm climate.

their customs, but they did manage to continue singing their own music and dancing their own dances.

Europeans Begin to Become Americans

Usually we think of the colonists as very successful people. After all, they managed to survive a dangerous voyage across the ocean and to plant new settlements in a wilderness thousands of miles away from home.

In one very important way the colonists were not successful. They had come to America to live just as they had in Europe. They did not succeed. For as time went on, they found it necessary to change many of their ways. The reason was that their new environment, so different from what they had known in Europe, would simply not let them live in the same old, familiar ways.

Adopting new ways of living. Different climate and different geography forced changes in the way the settlers did many things. For example, think of the Englishmen who went to live in the southern colonies. The growing season for crops in this region was much longer than in England. Even the soil was different. They could grow crops that they had never grown before—crops such as tobacco, cotton, and rice. That meant a very different way of farming.

Forests and wilderness were just as much a part of the American environment as the climate was. They, too, forced some of the farmers in all the colonies to work differently. In England and elsewhere in Europe, the farmer had turned over the soil with the aid of a plow drawn by an animal. Then he raked over the soil to break up the lumps, and planted seed, usually wheat. In America, the European settler found few open spaces where he could start to farm. He first had to chop down the trees and clear a small spot of land where the sunshine could break through—just as the Eastern Woodland Indians had done for thousands of years. His plow and animals were of little use to him as long as there were tree stumps and roots in the ground. So he cultivated the soil by poking holes in it. When he had trouble growing wheat, the crop he was used to growing, he switched over to the Indian crop, corn.

The forests even made a difference in the kind of animals the settlers raised. In England, farmers had raised sheep for their wool and their meat. Mutton was the traditional meat of English farmers. But in America, they soon found that their sheep were easy prey to the animals that inhabited America's forests. They also learned that pigs could be allowed to roam free, feed on acorns in the forest, and protect themselves from most wild animals. So the colonists, especially those living near the frontier, soon switched from raising sheep to raising pigs. Instead of mutton, pork became the main part of their daily diet.

An important failure. So you see, while the colonists labored to change their environment and make it more like England or Germany or France, their environment was also changing them. Try as they might, they could not live in exactly the same way that they had in Europe. They had to adjust their ways of working and living, and even thinking, to the New World. Eventually, those English settlers in Jamestown decided to stop broiling in the hot weather under their heavy clothes, boots, and armor, and changed their dress to suit their new climate.

Today we can be glad that the colonists did not succeed in this way. For it was their failure to continue to live as they had in Europe that created the American nation we know today. Why was this so? Because all the peoples who came here, whether they were French, Dutch, German, English, or whatever, lived in this new environment. All of them had to adjust to it, and as they did, they adopted many of the same ways.

Creating an American way of living. Most of them learned to speak English. All of them lived under the same laws, which they helped to make. They began to learn and borrow from each other. Englishmen and Scotch-Irish and Germans learned that the Swedish log cabin was an ideal home for a frontier life. Soon the log cabin was used by all peoples. Settlers learned that the covered wagon of the Germans was excellent for carrying heavy loads, and soon all people were using it.

As colonists adjusted their ways of living to the same environment, and as they borrowed from each other, their separate cultures changed and became more alike. Soon they began to think of themselves less and less as German or Dutch or English, and more and more as American.

Still, many differences remained — in customs, habits, beliefs, and so on. The old culture of each group did not disappear entirely. But underneath the differences that remained, there was being created something new — an American way of life.

Colonists used Swedish cabins as models.

Working with Concepts and Generalizations

Identifying Concepts

In each sentence below, one word is incorrect. Find the incorrect word. Copy each sentence on paper. In place of the incorrect word, write the correct word.

1. France established the colony of New France at Albany.
2. People who sold their future services in exchange for free passage to America were called transported servants.
3. Most of the slaves went to the French colonies, where they worked on tobacco, rice, and cotton plantations.
4. The Pilgrims came to America so that they could farm as they pleased.
5. William Penn was given an enormous piece of land in America called Virginia.
6. There was no gold or silver in New France, but there were gems.
7. Even when children were treated well by their masters, they were still not free people.
8. The Europeans believed in group ownership of property.
9. The English finally succeeded in starting a colony at Jamestown, Massachusetts, in 1607.
10. The people who settled at Plymouth were called Quakers.

Developing Concepts

Write the answers on paper.

1. You are a member of one of the groups listed below. Choose the group you wish to belong to. Then tell why you came to America and where you settled.
    a. English
    b. Scotch-Irish
    c. Africans
    d. Scots
2. Make simple sketches showing some of the ways the American Indians helped Europeans survive in the New World. This is a chance to SHOW what you have learned. Be as creative as you can!
3. You are an African. After a long, unpleasant voyage across the ocean, you arrive in America. Describe what happens to you on your first day in the New World.
4. You have learned that Europeans wanted to continue their familiar way of living in a new, unfamiliar land. You have also learned that they were not able to do this. Give as many reasons as you can to explain why they failed to live exactly as they had in Europe.
5. You will need to use your imagination to answer these questions. A "new" world has been discovered. American explorers have claimed much of the land there for the United States government. Many Americans are leaving to settle in the new world. What kind of people are going? Why are they going? What part of their culture will they take with them? Will you go? Why?

Generalizations

Read the generalizations below. Each group of words in parentheses can be replaced by one word. On paper, copy each generalization. Put in the correct word. Next, find two facts in the text that support each generalization. Write each fact and the page on which you found it.

1. Man sometimes modifies his (way of living) to meet environmental demands.
2. People are usually unwilling to change their (beliefs about what is good, desirable, and worth holding to).

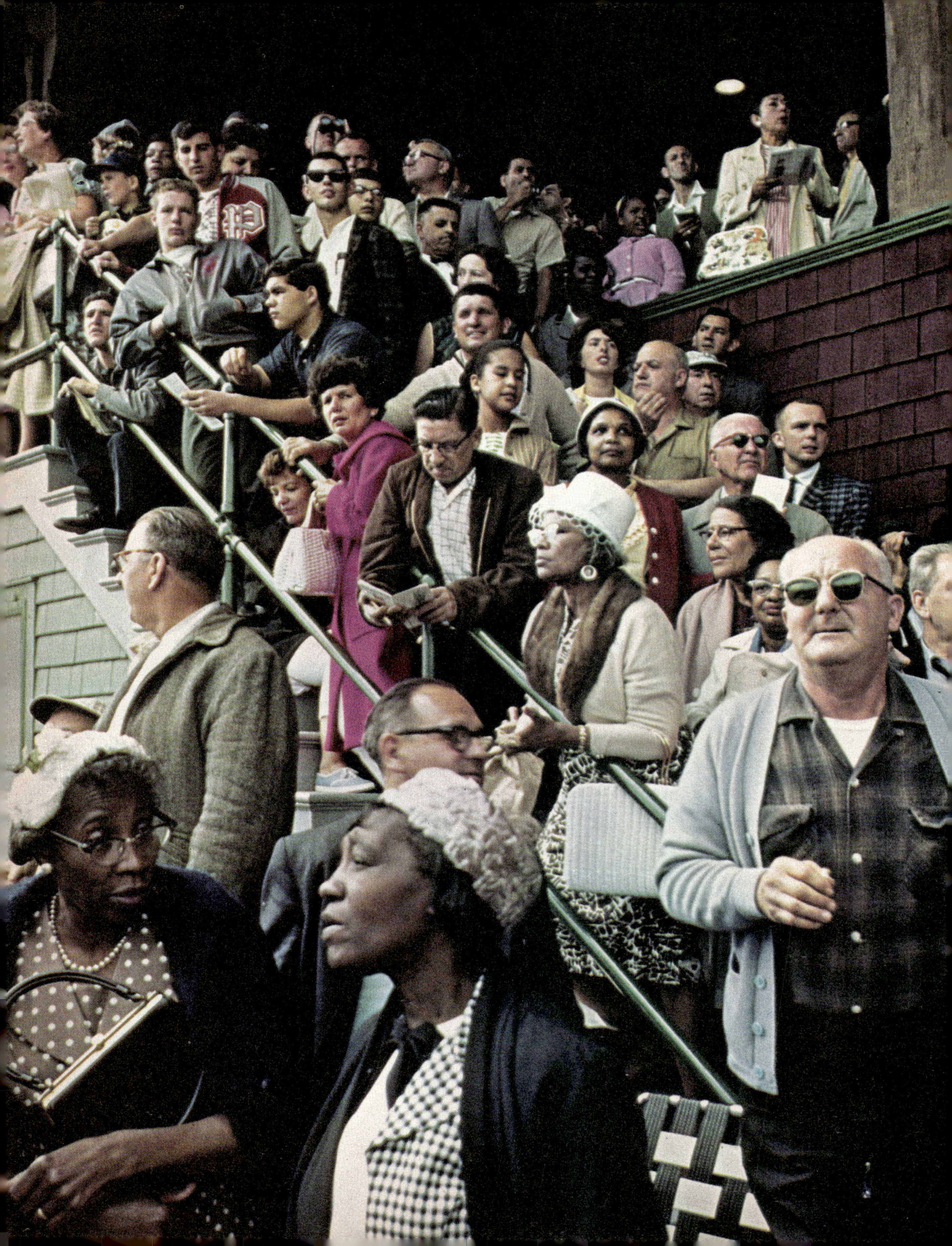

6
A Nation Rich in Cultures

In 1783 the thirteen English colonies in America became the United States of America, an independent nation with boundaries stretching from the Atlantic Ocean to the Mississippi River. The population of the new nation was already over three million. America had come a long way since "the starving time" in Jamestown.

Even then, many Americans predicted that their country would go much farther—that one day its boundaries would stretch to the Pacific Ocean, and that its population would become many times larger.

We know today that these boastful Americans were right. But not even the most hopeful of them dreamed that their country would become a land of more than two hundred million people, as it is today. Many, of course, were born here, but many millions also came from other lands. Why did immigrants continue to come to America, and what lands did they come from? What happened when their cultures met with those of the New World? Did they remain many or become one? In this chapter you will find the answers to these questions.

USING SOURCE MATERIAL

In the middle of the nineteenth century many of the immigrants came to America from Ireland. There was little manufacturing in Ireland and most people lived by farming or grazing. Here is some evidence that will help you find out how conditions in Ireland in 1847 led people to leave.

The first report:

Out of this population of 9,800 souls . . . there are at this moment over 7,000 in the greatest state of misery and distress, out of which 5,000 have not . . . a single meal to provide for their wants tomorrow. This has arisen from the total failure of the potato, upon which the people solely relied, and also, the unproductive nature of the oat crop last harvest, in these districts.

The second report:

I accompanied a Captain of one of her Majesty's steamers. . . . He, too, could scarcely believe the accounts of the famine, until I brought him to their hovels, and showed five or six lying in fever, huddled together on the damp, cold ground, with scarce a wisp of straw under them; and in another cabin, four or five unfortunate beings just risen from fever, crouched over a small pot of seaweed boiling on the fire, that one of them had crawled to the shore, to collect for their dinner.

Such is the mortality, that I do not exaggerate, when I give as my opinion that a third of the population has been already carried away.

What do these two reports tell you had happened in Ireland? If you had been living in Ireland then, do you think you might have wanted to move to America? Actually, as a result of what these reports describe, several million people did leave Ireland for the New World.

The two letters below were written by Polish peasants (pez' əntz) in the early years of the twentieth century. They were written to an organization, called the Protective Association, that provided help to people wanting to move to America.

THE UNITED STATES 1783

96

Here is the first letter:

I have a very great wish to go to America. I want to leave my native country because we are 6 children and we have very little land only about 6 acres and some small farm buildings. . . . Here in our country one must work plenty and wages are very small, just enough to live, so I would like to go in the name of our Lord God; perhaps I would earn more there.

Here is the second letter:

I want to go to America, but I have no means at all because I am poor and have nothing but the ten fingers of my hand, a wife, and 9 children. I have no work at all, although I am strong and healthy and only 45 years old. I cannot earn for my family. . . . I wish to work, not easily only but even hard, but what can I do? I will not go to steal and I have no work.

So I beg the Protective Association to accept me for this journey and not only me, but I should like to take with me two of my children, a boy 16 and a girl 18 years old.

What do those two letters tell you about the life of many Polish peasants? Why would you say they wanted to move to America?

Learning About America

Europeans learned about America in many ways. One very important way was the letters they received from friends and relatives who were already living in America.

USING SOURCE MATERIAL

Here are two letters Norwegian (nôr wē′ jən) immigrants wrote to friends in their hometown in Norway. The letters were printed in the local newspaper there, so many people read them.

It would greatly please me to learn that all of you who are in need and have little chance of supporting yourselves and your families have decided to leave Norway and come to America; for even if many more come, there will still be room here for all.

I am the owner of 160 acres of beautiful land, a cart, three horses and as many other animals as I need. Here you can raise as many cattle as you please. The land everywhere is as good as anyone could wish, for everything sowed or planted yields very rich crops.

A German immigrant wrote this to his parents in 1834:

. . . if you wish to see our whole family living . . . in a country where freedom of speech obtains, where no spies are eavesdropping, . . . if you wish to be really happy and independent then come here and become farmers in the United States.

A man who had been a peasant in Sweden wrote this to a wealthy friend:

If I should go to Sweden now and enter your office, I should hold my cap or hat in hand and bow and scrape and call a plain bookkeeper "my lord," etc., while here in America a worker and an officer are regarded as equals.

Another immigrant wrote this:

All kinds of people from all nations of the world live together here like brothers and sisters.

How do you think the people who received those letters felt? Would all of them be tempted to move to America? Why? How do you think people made their decision to move to America? Do you think they made sudden decisions?

Americans advertise. Letters from relatives were not the only way Europeans and others heard about America. Sometimes American railroad companies and American manufacturers advertised about America in foreign countries. They hired people to go abroad and persuade people to come to America. The railroad companies had just finished building new railroad lines in the West, where not many people were living as yet. They wanted more people to come to America to live, and especially to settle in the West. Can you understand why they would want people to move there? American manufacturers were also looking for people to work in their factories in eastern cities. These people were often unable to pay for the trip to America. American companies agreed to pay their fare for them. In return the immigrants agreed to work for the company for a number of years and so pay back the fare. On this page is a picture of an advertisement used by a company to attract people to move to America.

The immigrants came from all countries in Europe—England, Ireland, Germany, Italy, Russia, Hungary, Poland, Greece, Norway, Czechoslovakia (chek′ ə slō vä′ kē ə), and just about everywhere else. Millions poured into America from these lands in the 1800's and the first ten years of the 1900's — each group with its own language, its own customs, its own tastes and values and special ways.

A Swedish newspaper advertisement offered work building a railroad in Missouri.

Swenskt Arbetskontor.

Önskas genast 500 jernvägsarbetare för en ny jernväg i nordwestra Missouri; godt om stationsarbete till goda priser; också 100 man för "ties"-huggning a 10 cts stycket. Fri resa från Chicago. Stadigt arbete för ett år. För närmare upplysningar wände man sig till

Christian & Ross.
268 South Water St., Rum 11. Chicago.

The End of a Sad Migration

Africa was the continent that gave us the second largest number of our people. Did people continue to come to America from Africa after the United States became an independent nation? Did they still come as slaves?

Steps against slavery. Beginning in 1776, the American colonies fought to become free from England. You will learn more about this war later in this book. During this *Revolutionary* (rev′ ə lü′shə ner′ē) *War* states in the North and South began to take steps against slavery. Many citizens thought it did not make sense to fight a war for independence and freedom for themselves while at the same time freedom was denied to others because their skin was black. As a result, Massachusetts and several other states in the North passed laws to end slavery. By 1800 all the northern states had done so. But most slaves were in the southern states, and unhappily, slavery was not ended there at that time. Even though many Southerners of 1800 believed slavery was wrong, they felt they just could not get along without the slaves, to farm their cotton and tobacco fields and to work in their homes.

Even if slavery was not ended at that time, many felt that the horrible business of the slave trade could be. In 1808 the United States government passed a law that forbade the bringing of slaves into the country. This law was not obeyed, however. Cotton was becoming more important to the South, and plantation owners needed more laborers. As long as people wanted slaves and were willing to pay for them, enough merchants, both northern and southern, and ship captains would gladly break the law to make a profit. Slaves were brought from Africa illegally (i lē′ gəl ē) for another fifty years. The business of bringing Africans to our shores in chains did not finally end until all slavery was ended in the United States in 1865.

Few free black Africans have decided to leave their country and come to America since then. Therefore, today nearly all black Americans, like most white Americans, are descended from people who have been Americans for more than one hundred years. In fact, most are from families that have been here for more than two hundred years, and some have ancestors who were in America more than 350 years ago.

SLAVES IN THE UNITED STATES 1790

Percent of slaves in total population:
- Areas without slaves
- under 10 percent
- 10 to 30 percent
- 30 to 50 percent
- over 50 percent

Slavery divides the nation. Slavery was finally ended in the United States after a bitter struggle. During the first half of the 1800's, northern and southern states disagreed more and more about many things but most of all about slavery.

Actually, three out of every four southern families never even owned slaves. Yet most Southerners had come to accept slavery as part of the South's way of life. In fact, as time went on, more and more white Southerners came to believe slavery was not only necessary, but a really good thing for everybody—even for the slaves! They believed the African, with his different culture and different skin, was inferior to themselves. Certainly, they thought, nothing could be wrong with making such inferior creatures slaves. In return, the white man took care of them, saw that they had food and clothing, and taught them the Christian religion. Many mistakenly thought that blacks were really happy to be slaves.

Not all Southerners agreed with this. Over the years many slaveholders freed their slaves. There were a large number of free blacks in the South living in cities or working on farms. Some owned farms and even held slaves of their own. But most continued to be slaves.

Most people in the northern states felt differently about slavery. Not that they accepted the Negro as an equal—

Families owning slaves in 1860

Number of Families	Number of Slaves
1	1,000 or more
13	500–999
2,300	100–499
8,400	50–99
35,600	20–49
61,700	10–19
89,400	5–9
186,300	1–4

for certainly they did not. Whites in the North looked down on the Negro, just as whites in the South did. Even though the Negro in the North was free, he was discriminated against. Usually he was not allowed to go to the same places or do the same things that whites did. He could not get good jobs, and in many northern states he did not have the same rights as other citizens. Often he was not even permitted to vote.

Abolitionists. Even though most white Northerners did not treat the Negro fairly, they believed it was wrong for one human being to own another. Only a few people insisted that slavery had to be ended in the South right away.

These people were called *abolitionists* (ab′ ə lish′ ə nistz), because they wanted to abolish, or end, slavery right away. A few of them were former slaves who had escaped, but most were white northerners. Not many people listened to them at first, but in time their number grew.

Meanwhile Southerners resented this criticism. They said that if they wanted to have slaves, it was their business and no one else's. Bitter arguments between the North and the South came in the 1850's over whether slavery should be allowed to spread into western lands where people were beginning to settle.

War ends slavery. In 1861 a number of southern states decided to drop out of the United States of America and form their own separate country. Then they would be able to do whatever they wanted about slavery and everything else. The United States government would not allow this, and a long and bloody *civil war* resulted. After four years of fighting, the southern states were defeated, and they became part of the United States again. Slavery was then prohibited in the nation.

People from Far and Near

Europeans and Africans were not the only people who came to America bringing with them their different cultures. Immigrants came also from such Asian lands as Japan and China.

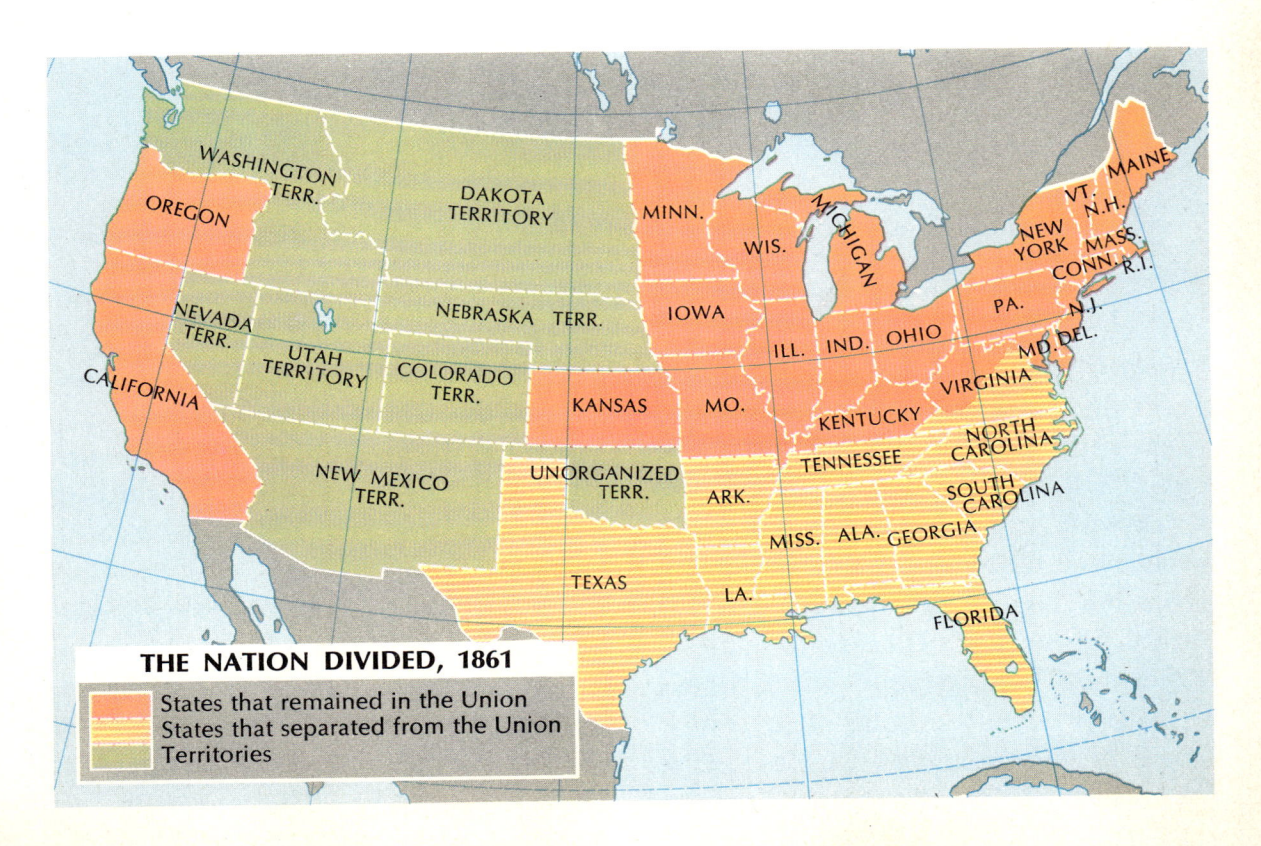

THE NATION DIVIDED, 1861
- States that remained in the Union
- States that separated from the Union
- Territories

Chinese immigrants helped to build the Central Pacific Railroad.

People from Asia. About one hundred years ago, track was being laid for the great railroads that linked the Pacific coast with railroads of the East. The work was very hard, and there was a great need for more laborers. The construction companies decided to hire large numbers of Chinese to come to America. They attracted the Chinese by the promise of jobs. Like many other immigrants, the Chinese were hired to work long hours for very low wages. After the railroads were completed, the Chinese found other jobs, mostly in the western part of the country. Other Chinese came later, settling mostly in the growing cities of the West.

Most of the Japanese who came settled in our western states also. The owners of large farms in California, needing laborers to help them, advertised for workers in Japanese villages. They told of the great advantages of living in California, and urged young people to sign up for a farm job. Many came, not only to California but also to Oregon and Washington. In later years some of the Japanese immigrants moved from the farms to the cities, where they worked at many different jobs.

People from neighboring countries. Immigrants have come to the United States from other lands in the *Western Hemisphere.* Mostly they have come from Mexico, Puerto Rico, and Canada.

During the twentieth century large numbers of Mexicans have come to the United States. At the beginning of the century, some came to escape the hardships of the revolutions that raged in Mexico. But most Mexicans came to find opportunities for making a living. Thousands started new lives in the industrial cities of the Middle West, such as Chicago, Kansas City, and Detroit. Most stayed in the southwestern states of Texas, Arizona, New Mexico, and California. This was the land their ancestors had helped to settle 250 years earlier. Mexicans and *Mexican-Americans* brought the cattle, horses, and sheep that made ranching possible there. To the farmlands of this area, especially in California, they brought the food crops and the fruits that made this section so important.

The Mexican immigrants of the twentieth century helped to build the railroads and the cities of the Southwest. They also worked in the mines, on the farms, and in the orchards of the Southwest. In recent years machines have reduced the need for laborers. This has forced many Mexicans to go to the cities of the West to make their livelihood.

Many Puerto Ricans have come to cities and farms in the Northeast. Unlike other immigrants, these people have come from a land that already belonged to the United States. Puerto Rico, an island in the Caribbean Sea, has belonged to the United States since just before 1900. During the last twenty-five years, large numbers of Puerto Ricans have left the poverty of their native island to seek opportunity here.

National Origin of Immigrants to the United States

Germany	6,896,000
Italy	5,122,000
Great Britain	4,762,000
Ireland	4,711,000
Austria-Hungary	4,292,000
Canada	3,913,000
Russia	3,346,000
Mexico	1,502,000
Sweden	1,265,000
West Indies	980,000

The largest number of immigrants from one country in the Western Hemisphere has come from Canada. Many were from the French-speaking part of Canada. They farmed the land along the Canadian border or worked as lumberjacks in the forests of northern Maine. Many others were attracted to the textile mills of Lewiston, Maine, and Lawrence, Massachusetts. Other Canadians came by the thousands to the cities of the Middle West and California.

All through the 1800's and 1900's, people have come from many lands in Europe, Asia, Africa, and America. They joined those who were already here—the descendants of the early English and Scotch and German settlers, the descendants of the African slaves, and the descendants of America's earliest inhabitants, the Indians.

Different Cultures in the New Environment

Like all other peoples who have moved from one land to another, these immigrants brought their culture with them. They brought many different languages, customs, tastes in food, dress, and values. Many immigrants came from countries that had a different level of technology. Among those who came from Russia, Italy, Mexico, China, and Japan were poor peasants who farmed the way their ancestors had done hundreds of years before.

They knew nothing of the machines that were then being used on America's farms and in her cities, where so many of them settled. Others, however, brought very valuable skills to the United States.

Usually these newcomers to America clustered together in the same parts of the country, or in the same neighborhoods in the cities. For example, many people from Sweden and Norway moved to the states of Minnesota, North Dakota, and South Dakota. In big cities like New York, Chicago, and Philadelphia, and even in many smaller ones, the Irish, Jews, Poles,

Neighborhood stores often supply people with foods special to their culture.

Italians, and other groups each lived in a different section of town. There they tried to preserve the way of living that was familiar to them. In fact, sometimes the sections were called Little Italy, Little Tokyo (tō′ kē ō), or Little Greece. The groups formed their own clubs and spent their time together. They continued to speak their own language. One might wander for many blocks in New York around 1900 without ever hearing a single word of English. Each group even had its own newspaper, printed in its own language, which carried news of special interest to the group.

What has been the result of so many cultures coming together in America? Have all these cultures now melted into one? Is the United States a land of one culture or of many?

Americans share much of the same culture. Certainly we can agree that today's Americans have a great many things in common. For instance, one part of our culture that is shared by all is a high level of technology. The way of living of nearly every American is affected by this technology.

Does this mean that each American knows a great deal of scientific information, and knows all about electricity and motors, and engineering? Some certainly do, but most of us probably do not know very much about these things. Does it mean that all Americans own and use many machines, like cars, washing machines, refrigerators, stoves, television sets? Many do, of course, but there are a great many poor families in our cities and our rural areas that do not. Does it mean that all of us use machines in our work? No, for many Americans still do not.

Even if people do not own machines or use them or know how they work, machines have a lot to do with the way of living in America, because machines do so many things in our country. Trucks bring the food and goods to the stores where people shop; machines produce the goods, can the foods, and bake the bread. Even if people bake their own bread, the flour comes from wheat grown with modern fertilizers and from specially developed seed. The wheat is harvested by a giant machine and ground into flour by a huge machine in a modern mill. Then the flour is shipped to the local store by train and truck.

The high level of technology has a lot to do with the way we earn our living, even if we do not use machines ourselves. For example, do you think many people make a living by weaving clothes on a hand loom or by spearing fish in a stream? Why not? Can you think of other ways in which the high level of technology in America affects the way we all live, even if we do not own or use the machines ourselves? Do you think the way of living of the Peruvian Indian in his village in the

Andes, separated from the rest of his nation, is affected by the machines of Peru in the same way?

People change some of their ways. In other ways, too, Americans share much of the same culture. Just as the earliest people who came to America gradually changed their ways and adjusted to new ways of living, so did the later people. We dress the same way, have many of the same tastes in food, watch the same television shows. We pledge allegiance (ə lē′ jens) to the same flag, feel that we are members of the same country, and celebrate the same national holidays. We play the same games and watch the same sports. We attend the same kinds of schools and study the same things. Although some other languages besides English are spoken, most of us do speak English.

The stores and shops in Spanish Harlem have signs in Spanish to show what goods are for sale.

Certainly, Americans of today have a great deal in common. Culturally, we are the same in many ways.

Preserving Some Ways of Living

Does this mean, then, that no cultural differences remain among the descendants of the Indian, the European, the African, and the Asian? Does the present-day immigrant have the same culture that the grandchildren of the immigrants of fifty years ago have?

Puerto Ricans in New York. Let us visit a section of New York City where some Americans live who have arrived on our shores very recently. The section is called *Spanish Harlem*, and the residents are Puerto Ricans. As we walk down the streets, we see that the signs everywhere are in Spanish—*El Mercado* (el mãr kä′ dō), *Farmacía* (fär mä thi′ ä), *Zapatos* (sä pä′ tōz), *Escuela* (es kü äl′ ə). Farther down the street is a theater where a Spanish-language movie is playing.

Many familiar things. We enter one of the small bodegas, or grocery stores, that we find on almost every block. Inside, near the shelves stocked with the familiar canned goods, is a vegetable bin piled high with yams, a vegetable much like a sweet potato. The yam is a great favorite on the island of Puerto Rico, as it is among those islanders who now live in New York. In the next bin is another food, called plantain (plan′ tən). The plantain looks like a large green banana, but must be cooked before eating. Sometimes plantains are used in place of potatoes. Still another bin contains mangoes, a yellow-speckled, oval-shaped fruit. Like the plantain, the mango is grown in Puerto Rico. Also for sale are other foods that are eaten a great deal on the island—especially *arroz* (ä rôz′), or rice, and *frijoles* (fri hō′ liz), or beans.

On the counter we notice a newspaper called *El Diario-La Prensa* (el di är′ ē ō-lä prän′sə). As you have guessed by now, the newspaper is written in Spanish. It carries all the important news you would find in English-language newspapers, and also has news of special interest to its readers—news of the happenings in Puerto Rican neighborhoods in New York City, and news from the island of Puerto Rico.

If you were to walk down this same street in the evening, you would probably hear music drifting down from the radios and record players in the apartments above. Puerto Ricans are a music-loving people. Their music has a very special sound, created by the soft tones of guitars, gentle drums, and *maracas* (mə rä′ kəz), dried gourds (gôrdz) filled with seeds that rattle when shaken.

Values and customs. As you see, many of the Puerto Ricans living in Spanish

Harlem have kept some of the culture of their native island. If you were to visit longer, you would learn about some values and customs that many Puerto Ricans have also kept.

For example, one of the most important values of Puerto Ricans has to do with family life. They believe all members of a family should remain close all through their lives—not just parents and children, but brothers and sisters, cousins, and aunts and uncles. This means spending time with each other, visiting each other, and helping each other at all times. No matter how poor they may be, most Puerto Ricans are always ready to take in another relative or help bring up the child of a relative.

It is also a custom for close friends to take a very special interest in each other's children. They do many, many things for them, and in fact are called co-parents. Many people might not be so pleased to take on the extra responsibility of caring for the children of others, but among Puerto Ricans it is an honor to be a co-parent.

An especially happy day for Puerto Rican children is January 6, which is Three Kings Day. This day is much like the holiday of Christmas. The night before Three Kings Day, the children make a little path of grass or hay that leads under their bed. According to the custom, the camels or horses on which the three kings ride eat the hay and leave a gift behind. As you might expect, on Three Kings Day, Puerto Rican children are especially happy to have co-parents!

Mexican-Americans in Texas. A visit to Hidalgo County, Texas, would introduce you to another group of Spanish-speaking people. These are Mexican-Americans. Hidalgo County is just across the border from Mexico. The land there is very fertile, and the main occupation is raising cotton, corn, vegetables, and citrus fruits. About three fourths of the population of Hidalgo County is Mexican-American. Most of them have lived there for many years. Some families, in fact, settled there when this land and all the rest of Texas still belonged to Mexico, more than 135 years ago.

Mexican-Americans have strong family ties.

When Mexican-Americans protest, they usually do so as a group. Signs are in Spanish and in English.

Holding onto a way of life. Even though most Mexican-Americans living there were born in the United States, they continue to speak their own language and hold on to many of their own ways. Most of them live apart from the English-speaking residents, whom they call Anglo-Americans, or just Anglos. This is partly because they want to stay separate, and partly because the Anglos have not welcomed them in their own neighborhoods. Mexican-Americans call their section of town *el pueblo mexicano* (mə hē kän′ ō), which means "the Mexican town," or *nuestro lado* (nyü əs′ trō lä′ dō), which means "our side."

Much of Mexican-American culture is similar to Puerto Rican culture. For example, the family is very important. As one grown-up Mexican-American explained:

> I owe everything to my family.... They raised me and taught me all I know. They have protected me and in my parents' home I know I will always find love and understanding. When one has a family, one is never alone nor without help in time of need. God created the family and one way to show respect to him is to respect one's parents.

109

One of the worst things a person can do, Mexican-Americans believe, is hurt his family or bring shame to it. Families are so close that often parents, grandparents, aunts, and uncles live in houses squeezed right next to each other on a small piece of land. Like Puerto Ricans, Mexican-Americans also have co-parents, or *compadres*.

Shopping in the small stores of *el pueblo mexicano* is more pleasant than it is on the Anglo side of town, where people seem to be rushing all the time. Here, shoppers are more relaxed and gay. Shopping is a time when people can visit with each other. Storekeepers and shoppers are never too busy to greet each other and ask about each other's families. It would be considered very impolite and rude not to do so.

Most Mexican-Americans in Hidalgo County believe that Anglos value making money too much. Mexican-Americans enjoy owning cars and refrigerators, but they think that things like enjoying good times together with one's friends and family are more important. Most Mexican-Americans are also very religious.

Of course, there are also many Mexican-Americans who, like the Puerto Ricans, are giving up most of their older ways and adopting the ways of the Anglos. But there are also many other places in southwestern United States where, as in Hidalgo County, Texas, the Spanish-speaking Mexican-

A large paper dragon is a big attraction in the Chinese New Year procession.

Americans continue to keep their culture alive.

Chinatowns. Still another group that has lived in the United States a long time but continues to hold to many of its old ways are Chinese-Americans. In many large cities you will still find a section called *Chinatown*, which looks very different from any other part of the city. Here Chinese is still spoken, and many parts of the Chinese culture are preserved. Here is how one book describes a visit to Chinatown.

> In the shops of Chinatown, either in New York or San Francisco, all sorts of things from China are for sale. There you will find delicate teas, some of them jasmine flavored, great sacks of rice, dried ducks hanging by their necks, square white blocks of bean curd, bean sprouts, and bamboo shoots. . . .
>
> At the time of the Chinese New Year, which is in February, you will see that every man, woman, and child has new clothing, according to the Chinese custom. And down the street at New Year time each year passes a great procession with paper lanterns and an enormous paper dragon held aloft on sticks. It is Chinese tradition to shoot firecrackers at New Year time, to frighten away the evil spirits.

Chinese family life is very close, and there is very great respect for older people. Grandparents and even old people who are not part of the family are listened to very carefully and obeyed.

Variety Leads to Richness

Other groups also cling to parts of their older cultures. Some continue to use their native languages, which they speak in addition to English.

Many places, many languages. In Lewiston, Maine, and in Nashua, New Hampshire, one can often hear the residents speaking the French language of their Canadian parents and grandparents. In many cities you can still hear Italian, Greek, Polish, or Yiddish. The language that is most often spoken, next to English, is Spanish. Spanish is the language not only of the Puerto Ricans, as we have seen, but also of the Cubans who now live in Florida, and of the many Mexican-Americans who live mostly in Texas, New Mexico, Arizona, and California.

There are other cultural differences among Americans, too. For example, Americans have many different religions. They believe different things about God, and worship in different ways. Catholics have different beliefs than Protestants, and even among Protestants there are many different beliefs. Jewish people have still different religious beliefs and customs, and celebrate different religious holidays.

Black culture in America. Many black Americans feel that much of their own culture was taken away from them during slavery. Today they are studying African ways to learn more about the culture of their ancestors. They are very proud of the accomplishments of the ancient African civilizations from which they come, and want to feel a part of them. So they study the history, art, and music of Africa. Some black people have adopted African names and dress, as a symbol that they feel they are a part of the cultures of black Africa.

Not all the differences in the ways of living among Americans are due to the fact that our ancestors came from so many different places. We can also say that city dwellers in America have some different ways of life than people who live on farms have. We shall learn more about this in the next unit. And certainly we can agree that very poor people have some different ways of living than other Americans have.

Cultural pluralism. All these examples show that although the ways of living of Americans are alike in most ways, there are also some differences. This is why some say that America is not a land of one culture but of many. This is what *cultural pluralism* (kul′ chər əl plur′ ə liz əm) means. But others say that in spite of differences in American ways of living, the United States is really a land of only one culture. People who say this believe the many things we have in common with each other are more important than our few differences.

As you see, whether we say that America is a land of one culture, or of many, depends on whether we think our differences are more important than our similarities. Either way, though, we can agree that Americans are a fortunate people, for our differences have added a richness and variety to American life and our similarities have made us a strong, united people.

Many blacks have adopted clothes that reflect African cultures.

On almost any street in any large city in the United States, one passes people of many different cultures.

The Cultures of the People of Canada

Like the United States, Canada has attracted people from many lands. The French, who were the first Europeans to arrive, settled mostly in the part of Canada called Quebec. Later, people from Great Britain came. Some went to Quebec, but most settled in the area that today is called the Maritime Provinces—Newfoundland, New Brunswick, Nova Scotia, and Prince Edward Island. A province in Canada is like a state in the United States.

France and England fought many wars in those early years, and one of them was especially important for the future of Canada. At the end of that war, in 1763, France gave up Canada to England. After that, many more Englishmen came to Canada. As in the early history of the United States, these newcomers often moved into the interior. Many of the English settled in Ontario. Today Ontario is Canada's most populous province.

In our day Canada has become an independent nation, although it still keeps a few ties to England. In the

113

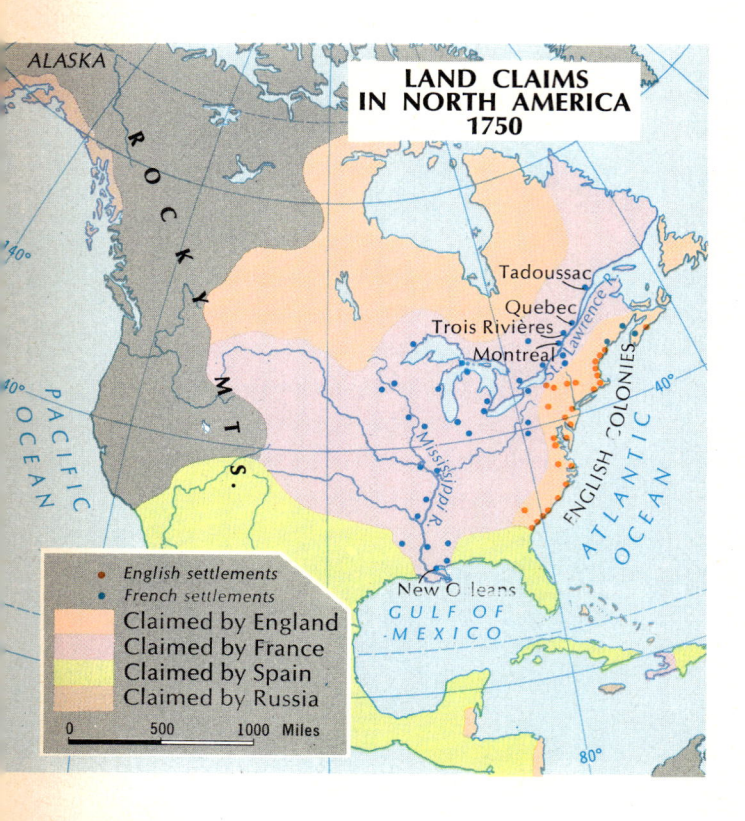

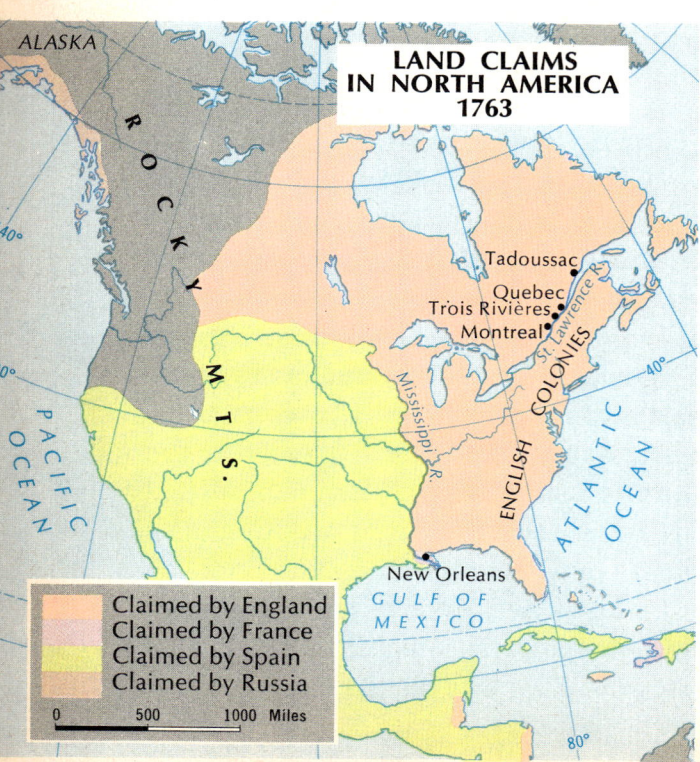

meantime, our northern neighbor has become a home for many other peoples besides the French and English. Canada is a vast land, but much of it is unsettled. For many years the Canadian government has encouraged immigrants to settle there and help build the nation. The government has especially wanted people to settle on the cold but rich farmlands of the western prairies.

As a result, many different peoples now live in Canada. The table on the peoples of Canada shows the makeup of Canada's population.

The many peoples of Canada

British	8,000,000
French	5,500,000
German	1,000,000
Ukrainian	475,000
Italian	450,000
Dutch	430,000
Scandinavian	386,000
Polish	323,000
Jewish	174,000
Russian	119,000

Canada reflects its many cultures. Traveling across the western provinces, a visitor would meet many of the peoples of Canada. Most are descended from English and Scottish settlers. But in one farm community he might find many people who came from Poland, and in another he might meet Swedes or Norwegians who came to make a

The Ice Carnival in Quebec is an old French Canadian custom.

new life in the New World. Some miles away, the sight of a church with an onion-shaped dome would tell him that there is a settlement of Ukrainians, who are members of the Eastern Orthodox Church. In still another town, he would see people from Germany living in their neat homes clustered around their Lutheran church.

In these communities and others, many older people continue to speak their native language and cling to the customs and ways they knew in Europe. But just as in the United States, the children and grandchildren of the immigrants are changing their ways. Children attend English-speaking schools and are growing up learning the ways of the New World. Probably within a few generations the foreign languages now heard in these villages will be spoken by only a few. Does this also mean that none of the Old World customs will remain?

The French Canadians. Next to the English, the largest group of Canadians are the French. Although descendants of the earliest French settlers are now sprinkled throughout Canada, the great majority still live in the province of Quebec. Four out of every five persons in Quebec are French Canadians, and French is their main language. In many villages the entire population is French. English is not even taught in their schools, except as a foreign language!

In these villages French Canadians have preserved their ways. The French farmer lives with his large family in a small white house. The house is one of many set side by side in a row along the riverbank. The farmer and his family work the narrow strip of land, which runs up from the river to the road several hundred yards back. In some farming communities, the houses will be in the center of the village, and each farmer's land stretches outward from the village center like spokes in a wheel.

Modern conveniences have come to many of these farmhouses, but here and there can be seen the outdoor stone ovens in which some continue to bake their bread. French-Canadian families are very close, and even distant cousins are expected to look out for each other. The French family's ties to the church, which is the Roman Catholic Church, are very strong.

As elsewhere in Canada, the people of Quebec Province are moving from the farms to jobs in the cities. This has brought many changes to the French Canadian's way of living, but he still holds proudly to much of his separate culture. In Montreal, the largest city in the province, the street signs, newspapers, and store signs are in French as well as in English.

French Canadians demand equality. Many French Canadians feel that they are discriminated against by the English majority in Canada. They point out that the federal government is run mainly by the English-speaking people, as are most of the nation's businesses. Even in Quebec the best jobs are held by the English, and the main businesses and banks are also run by them. The French are the first to lose their jobs in hard times. They also resent the fact that they must learn English in order to hold many jobs.

Because of this, some French Canadians want to separate Quebec from the rest of Canada and make it an independent nation. But most people in Quebec do not think this is a very good idea. They would be satisfied if they could feel that they were receiving fair treatment and equal opportunities.

The Canadian government has been taking some steps to end this discrimination. More French-speaking people are now being hired for various government jobs. Some private companies are also helping by promoting more French Canadians to higher positions.

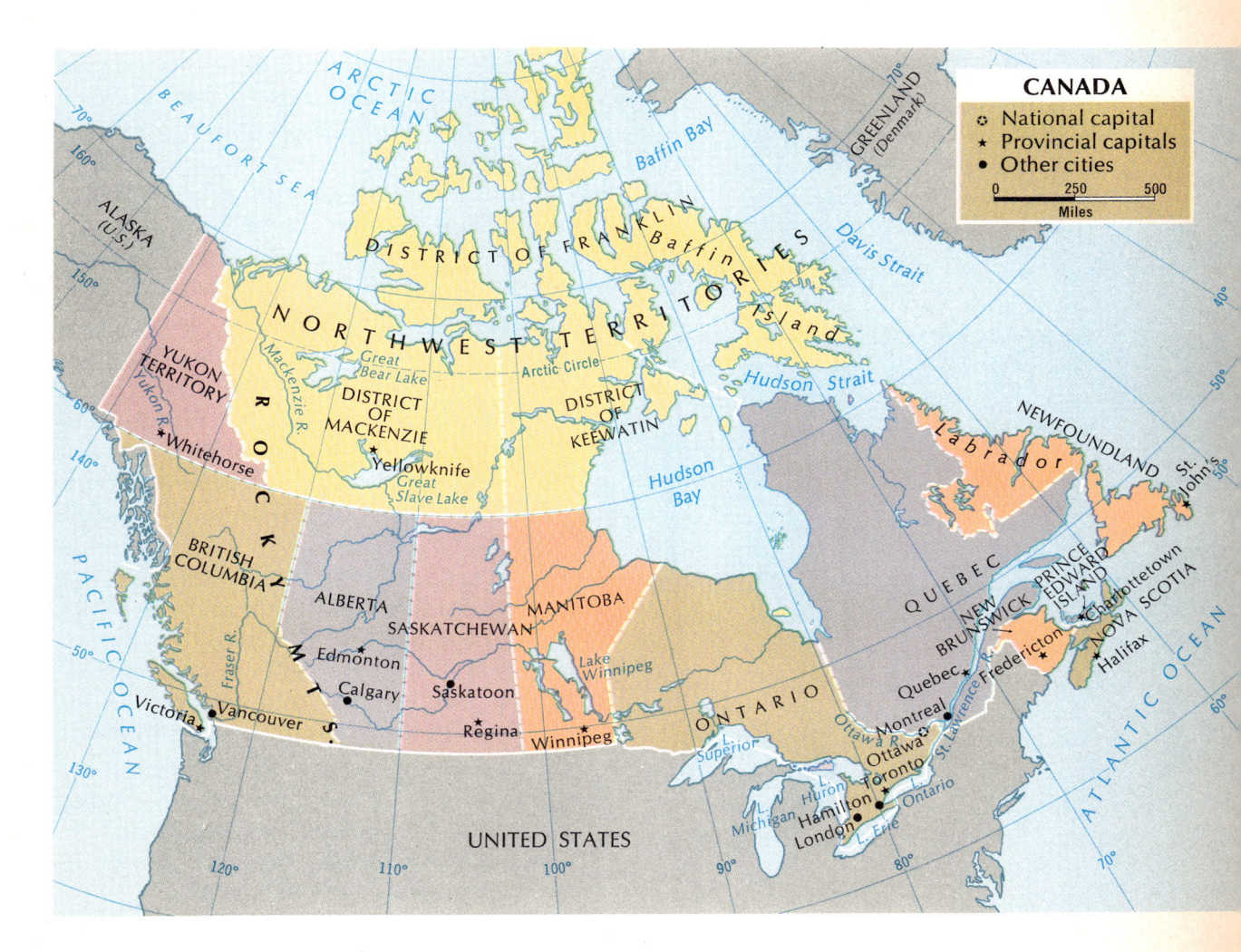

However, the majority of the French Canadians are not simply waiting to be given equality. To obtain their share of the nation's wealth, Quebec's leaders are taking important steps to make their province more modern. They are encouraging more industrialism in order to improve their economic position. They are also making their school system more modern so that it can produce political and economic leaders. In brief the French Canadians are looking more to the future and less to the past.

These recent developments have helped to assure many French Canadians that more steps toward equality will come before long. But feelings between most French Canadians and English Canadians are still not very good. Until these two cultural groups can learn to respect each other more, it will be very difficult for Canada to be a truly united nation.

117

Working with Concepts and Generalizations

Identifying Concepts

Read the poem below. Pick out the words and phrases that tell why people came to America and what they did here. Write the words and phrases on paper. Find as many as you can.

I Am America

I am America.
I welcomed many strangers to my shores.
Some came bound in chains against their will.
Others came to break the chains that bound
  them to hunger and to need.
More followed, drawn by the magic of the stories
  of my wealth.
Still others came in search of freedom and
  equality.
They gave me much, these strangers.
And strangers they were—all with different
  ideas about so many things.
Yet they built great railroads and made rich
  farms.
They settled my empty lands and filled my
  busy factories.
You ask what I gave them in return?
I did not give them wealth or fame, although
  some found both.
I gave them something far more precious.
My gift amounts to just one word—opportunity.
Yet that word carries with it all that I am
  and all that I can be.
For them that seemed enough.
They did the rest.

Developing Concepts

Write the answers on paper.

1. You are president of an American railroad company. You would like to encourage people to live in the western part of the United States. If there are more settlers in the West, your railroad will be used more. Make a poster that will encourage foreigners to leave their homes and settle in the American West.

2. You are a European who has been in America for several months. Write a letter to your relatives in Europe, telling them what it is like to be in America. Tell them what kind of work you are doing and where you are living.

3. The year is 1860. People everywhere are discussing one question: Should slavery be abolished in the United States? You are to answer this question in two ways. First answer it as you think an abolitionist would. Then answer it as you think a southern slaveholder would.

4. Do you think the United States has one culture, or many cultures? After you have made your decision, use the text to find facts to support your answer. Find as many as you can. Write each fact and the page on which you found it.

5. Immigrants from many different countries came to the United States. Choose any three groups mentioned in this chapter and tell why each group decided to come to this country.

Generalizations

The generalization below makes a statement about culture. You are to prove that the generalization is true. Using the text, list the immigrant groups that came to America. List as many as you can. Then, next to each group, list a part of its culture that the group tried to preserve in America.

All immigrants have brought their native culture to their new homeland and have attempted to preserve their culture in the new environment.

Applying Concepts

1. Unless you are a pure-blooded American Indian, you are an immigrant or a descendant of immigrants. Ask your parents and other relatives to help you collect the following information. If you are an American Indian, work with your family to answer as many of these questions as you can. Use the information to write an interesting report to share with the class.
   a. Where did your ancestors (grandparents and great-grandparents) live before they came to America?
   b. When did they arrive in this country?
   c. Why did they come?
   d. How did they feel about living in a new country?
   e. Where did they settle?
   f. What kind of work did they do?
   g. What special customs and traditions did they bring with them to this country?
   h. Does your family practice any of these customs and traditions today? Which ones?

2. Use a reference book or an encyclopedia to help you write a report on slavery in the United States. Your report should include some facts about where slaves lived, how they lived, what their family life was like, the kinds of rights they had, and how they gained their freedom. Perhaps you will want to draw some simple sketches to make your report more interesting.

3. You are to plan an Honor-America Fair for your community. The fair will be held to show how people from many different parts of the world have contributed to the American way of life. You may plan the fair in any of the three ways listed below. You will be able to find the information you need in a reference book or an encyclopedia.
   a. Make a model of the fair. Your model should include several booths to represent a few different groups of people who have come to this country (Italians, Africans, Germans, Irish, Greeks, Chinese, Japanese, Scandinavians, and so forth). Decide what food and souvenirs will be sold at each booth. To represent these items, you may use tiny pieces of cloth, foil, or colored paper. Label each item that is for sale, identifying it by name. Decorate each booth with a model flag of the country the booth represents.
   b. Draw a picture that shows what the fair will look like. Make the drawing large enough to include everything that will be on the fairgrounds. Show the booths that will be built and tell the nations that will be represented. Show some of the different kinds of food and souvenirs that will be sold. Draw models of the national flags that will be displayed at the booths.
   c. Write a description of the fair and the fairgrounds. Tell which groups will be represented. Describe what will be sold and how the booths will be arranged. Tell how you will display the national flags. Perhaps you can find colorful pictures in magazines that show some of your ideas.

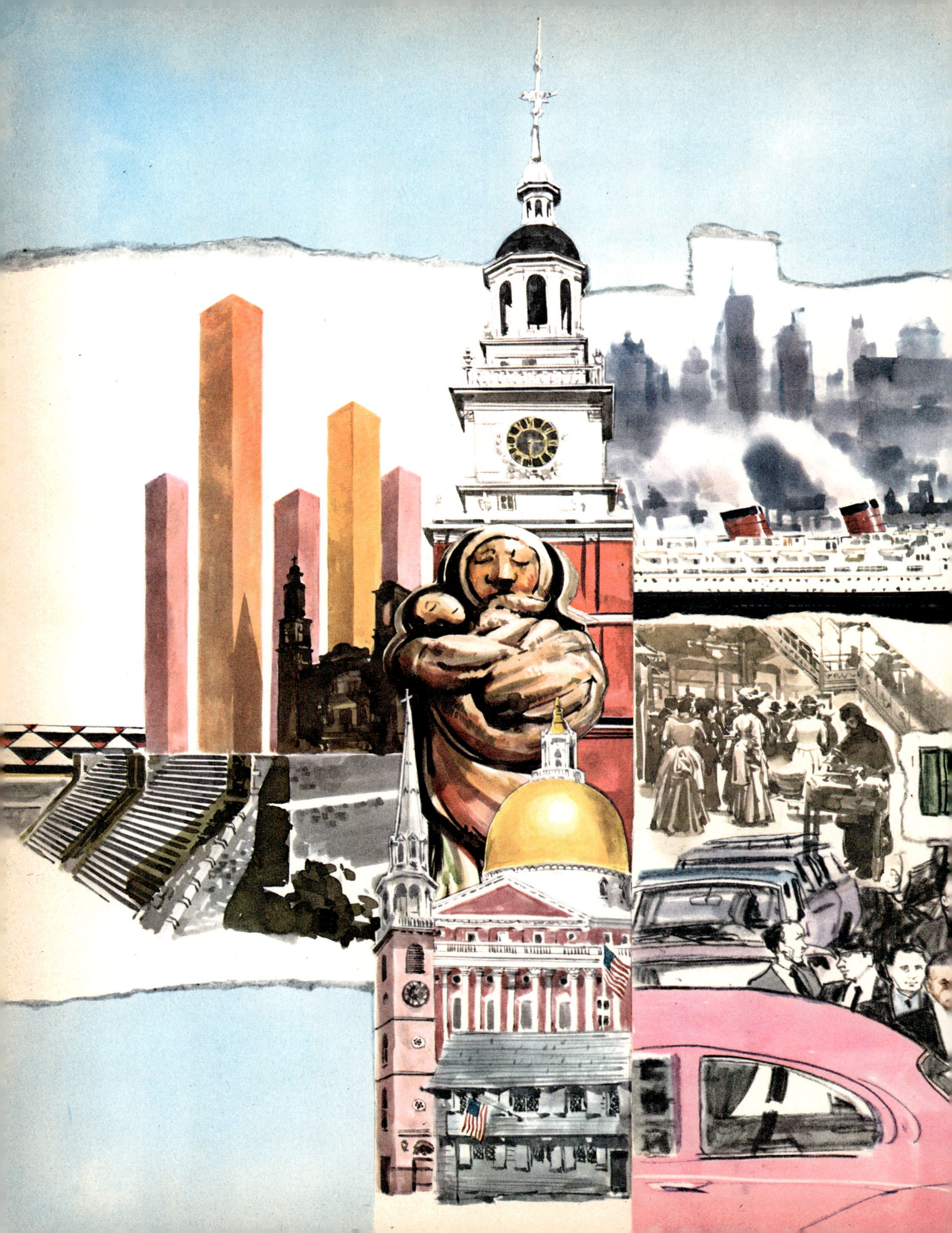

unit two
INVESTIGATING URBANISM

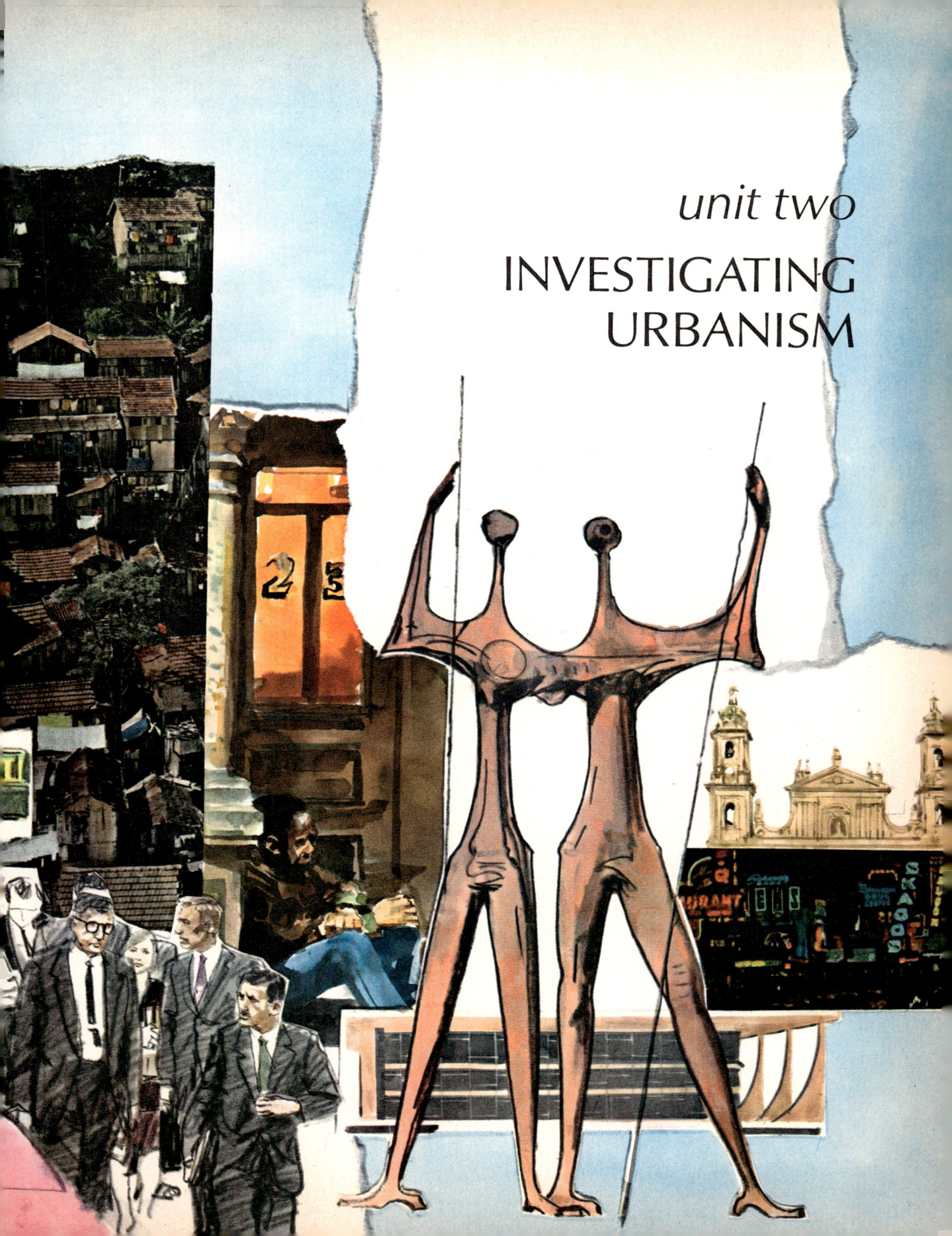

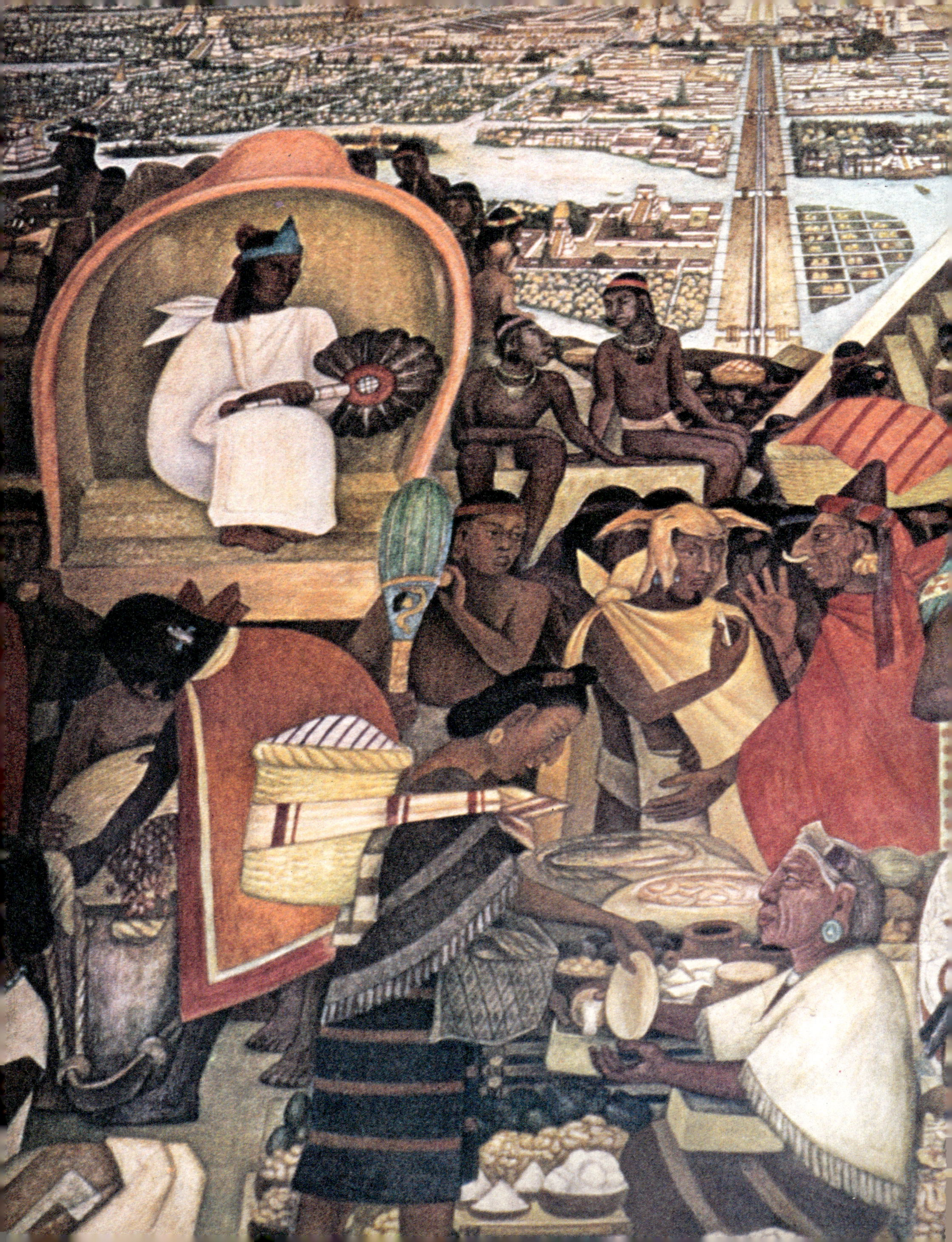

7

Learning About Cities

City is a word that all of you have heard before. Many of you live in or near a city. Those of you who live in a rural or country area may have visited a city on a holiday. So the word city is not new to you. When you think of a city, certain things may come to mind—tall buildings, large factories, many stores, houses crowded together, and plenty of noise. Some will think of traffic, buses, subways, and sidewalks crowded with people. Others may be reminded of their favorite big league baseball or football team.

In this unit you are going to discover much about a city. You will learn how city, or urban, areas are different from rural, or country, areas. In studying about some of the cities of America, you will learn how those cities grew and how special problems arose in city life.

After you have read and studied about some of these things, you will begin to understand why people choose to live in such crowded areas. And it is the people who are most important. It is through their efforts that settlements become cities. The people face the problems of city living and look for solutions to those problems. The activities of the people give life to the cities.

Two Cities of America

In this chapter you are first going to read about two quite different cities of America. One is the ancient capital of the Aztecs, Tenochtitlán. You will see what that Middle American city was like in the year 1521. The other is Philadelphia (fil′ ə del′ fy ə), Pennsylvania, in the year 1776. Different people, different times, and different places—yet both cities. As you read about each one, ask yourself, what do these different cities have in common? If two such different cities have some things in common, you may discover clues as to what *all* cities may have in common.

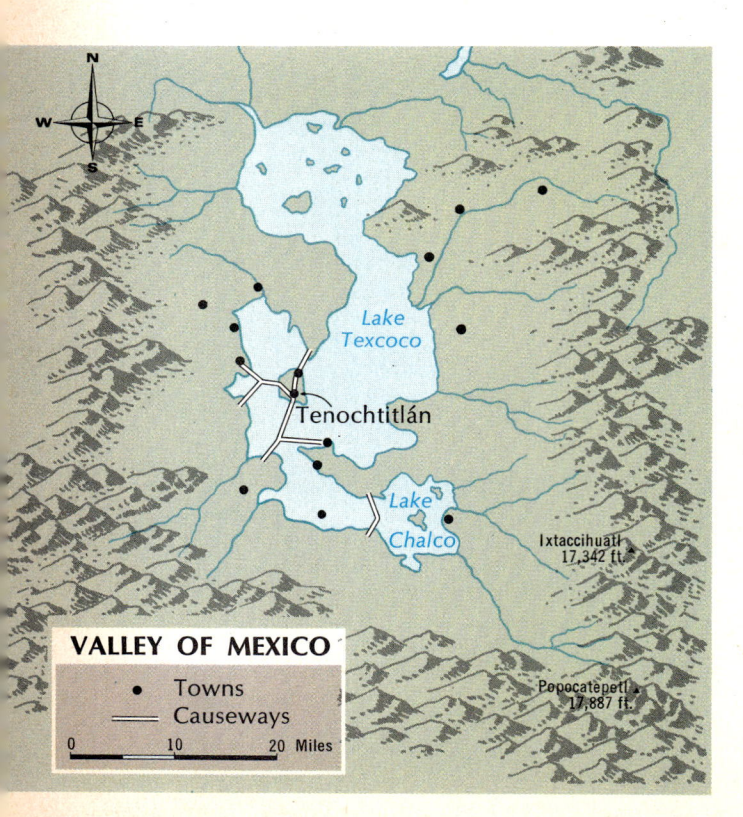

VALLEY OF MEXICO
• Towns
━ Causeways
0   10   20 Miles

Next, as you read about farm life in the last part of the chapter, ask yourself, in what ways do these two cities differ from a farm or a rural area. The answers to these questions will help you learn more about what a city is.

How do we know about Tenochtitlán? One important source of information is the writings of the Spanish conquerors of the Aztecs. Some of these writings have been preserved in libraries.

One book was written by an ordinary soldier named Bernal Diaz (ber näl′ dē′ az), who served under the Spanish commander Hernando Cortes (her nän′ dō kôr tez′). Later in this chapter you will read a description of the capital city from Diaz's book. A Spanish priest named Bernardo Sahagún (ber när′ dō sä hä gun′) wrote another useful book. Father Sahagún spent many years among the Aztecs and tells us much about their centers of worship.

Aztec records. The Aztecs left us some information about Tenochtitlán. You will recall they had developed a kind of picture language, which experts have been able to figure out.

But only a very few of the Aztecs' books and records still exist. After the Aztecs became a great nation, their leader at the time decided to hide the fact that they had once been a small, humble tribe of Indians, who were often defeated in battle. He wanted everyone to think that the Aztecs had always been powerful and victorious. So he ordered all the *historical records* of the early Aztec years destroyed.

When the Spanish came, they destroyed most of the later Aztec records. The Spanish were horrified by the human sacrifices. They were determined to blot out Aztec culture and replace it with their own. One way of doing this was to destroy Aztec temples and build Catholic churches on the same spots. Another way was to erase the Aztecs' memory of their own great past history by destroying their records.

The work of scientists. We also know some things about Tenochtitlán from the work of special scientists called *archaeologists* (är′ kē ol′ ə jistz). Archaeology is the study of man's history through the things people made and left behind. These things are called *artifacts* (är′ tə faktz). They include items as small as stone arrowheads and bone needles, and as large as homes, temples, cemeteries, and, in fact, whole villages and cities. Often these artifacts lie buried beneath layers of sand and earth.

Archaeologists search for artifacts and try to discover their meaning. It sometimes takes years of searching and digging for their efforts to be successful. The archaeologist does not just pick up a shovel and start digging. He first has to decide the kind of thing he hopes to find. Then, using any clues he can get, he has to decide where to look. His knowledge of geography, climate, or rocks will help. He may find clues in old stories repeated by people who live in an area.

Then comes the long, tiring work of digging and examining each shovelful of earth. Sometimes he turns up nothing. Sometimes he makes an important discovery. For example, much of what we know today about the Mayas was discovered by archaeologists. They have also given us some information about Tenochtitlán.

Unfortunately, two things prevented them from telling us much more about this city. One is that the Spanish destroyed so much of Tenochtitlán after they conquered it. The other problem is that most of the evidence that might still be left is buried beneath the shops, homes, and skyscrapers of modern Mexico City. Many of the secrets of Tenochtitlán will remain hidden from us forever.

Tenochtitlán

The city of Tenochtitlán was located on a small island in the middle of a shallow lake in Middle America. Both the lake and the city lay in a *mountain basin,* or valley, about five thousand feet above sea level. High mountains and several *volcano* peaks surround the basin. Many ancient tribes settled in this basin because of the lakes and the rich farmland.

Building a city. The Aztecs first settled on one of two small islands lying close to each other. They made the two into one by dumping rock and earth into the water between the islands. The job took many years to complete.

The island was connected to the mainland around the lake by three large causeways. Causeways are like bridges but are made entirely of land. Aztecs carried earth, lime, and stones from the mainland and dumped them in long, narrow strips until the strips rose to a safe height above the water. Then they paved the surface with a hard cement made of lime, which was plentiful in that area. The completed

The art on the side of this modern building in Mexico City shows Aztec influence.

causeways looked like three long fingers connecting the city to the surrounding countryside. They were not very wide and were used only for foot traffic.

In several places along each causeway, the Aztecs left openings for waterways. These openings served two purposes. First, they permitted canoes to pass from one part of the lake to another. Pedestrians (pə des′ trē ənz) could still use the causeways by covering the openings with removable wooden bridges.

Second, the openings in the causeway provided protection against attacks. If unfriendly Indians tried to invade Tenochtitlán by marching across the causeways, the Aztecs could quickly remove the wooden bridges.

A visitor could enter the city on one of the causeways. Once on the island itself, he would not see many roads. The three important ones were continuations of the causeways and led into the center of the city. Instead of roads, there were *canals* that connected with one another throughout the city. These were more useful to Aztecs than roads. Do you know why?

There were paths alongside many of these canals. People crossed the canals by means of a bridge, which was usually a board or two laid across the water. After crossing over, the person would remove the boards to clear the way for canoe traffic.

Aztec homes. As the visitor entered the city, he would first pass the homes of the poorer farmers on the edges of the island. The walls of their homes were made of adobe, the same clay material used by the Indians of southwestern United States in making their pueblos. The roofs were often made of light branches covered with reeds and grass.

These temple ruins show the vast size of Aztec buildings.

Next to the farmers' homes were their gardens. In the excellent climate of that area they could farm all year round.

Farther along the road the houses became a little larger. Some were made of adobe, but most were made of stone and lime. They were covered by a thin coat of *stucco* (stuk′ ō), or white cement, to make them waterproof. The homes were crowded close together. Land was scarce and these people did not need gardens. Most of them made their living as merchants or skilled workers.

There were expert weavers of cloth and mats, makers of arrows and spears, canoemakers, and goldsmiths, who skillfully changed gold nuggets into beautiful jewelry. There were also feather workers who made the huge, brightly colored feather headdresses and clothing that the Aztecs loved so well. All these craftsmen made their products in their own homes.

As the visitor came closer to the center of the city, the road and the canals became busier. There were people everywhere—on their way to the market, to the temples, or just out to see the sights.

Heart of the city. Soon the visitor arrived at the center of the city. The first thing that caught the eye was the Great Temple. Built on top of a huge pyramid, the Great Temple was the tallest building in the city. Nearby stood many smaller pyramid-temples, as well as the royal palaces. All these buildings were located around two large squares. The public often gathered in these open spaces for the religious ceremonies.

This was the part of the city in which the emperor of the Aztecs lived. Near his palace lived the priests. In this city of very religious Aztecs, the priests were rulers of a sort. They were government officials, whose job it was to look after the well-being of all Aztecs and to keep the nation strong. This they did by pleasing the gods. You may recall how they pleased the gods.

USING SOURCE MATERIAL

Here is how Bernal Diaz described the market in his book. He wrote this account of the marketplace at Tenochtitlán about four hundred years ago.

When we arrived at the great market place, . . . we were astounded at the number of people and the quantity of merchandise that it contained, and at the good order and control that was maintained. . . . Let us begin with the dealers in gold, silver, and precious stones, feathers, mantles, and embroidered goods. . . . Indian slaves both men and women . . . [were] tied to long poles, with collars round their necks. . . . In another part there were skins of tigers and lions, of otters and jackals, deer and other animals. Let us also mention the fruiterers, and the

Aztecs displayed this giant Calendar Stone in a large plaza in Tenochtitlán. The stone was thirteen feet across.

women who cooked food, dough and tripe in their own part of the market; then every sort of pottery made in a thousand different forms from great water jars to little jugs . . . then those who sold honey. . . . and the marketplace with its surrounding arcades was so crowded with people, that one would not have been able to see and inquire about it all in two days.

Suppose you were to describe a shopping center or a busy Main Street near your home. Would your description be very different from that of Diaz? What would your shopping area have in common with the Aztec marketplace?

The market stood beyond the temples and palaces. To this large open area came tradesmen and farmers with goods to sell or exchange. They came not only from Tenochtitlán but from the towns and farms surrounding the lake. Each day there were as many as sixty thousand people crowding into the market—buying, selling, eating the freshly cooked foods, or just looking at the goods.

Trade. Aztecs did not have money as we know it, but they did have a way of expressing how much each item was worth. They used cacao beans and *mantas* (man′ təz), pieces of cloth, for this purpose. Aztecs were very fond of a chocolate drink made from cacao beans, so the beans were of value to them. A manta was worth between

This Aztec drawing shows the different activities in Tenochtitlán.

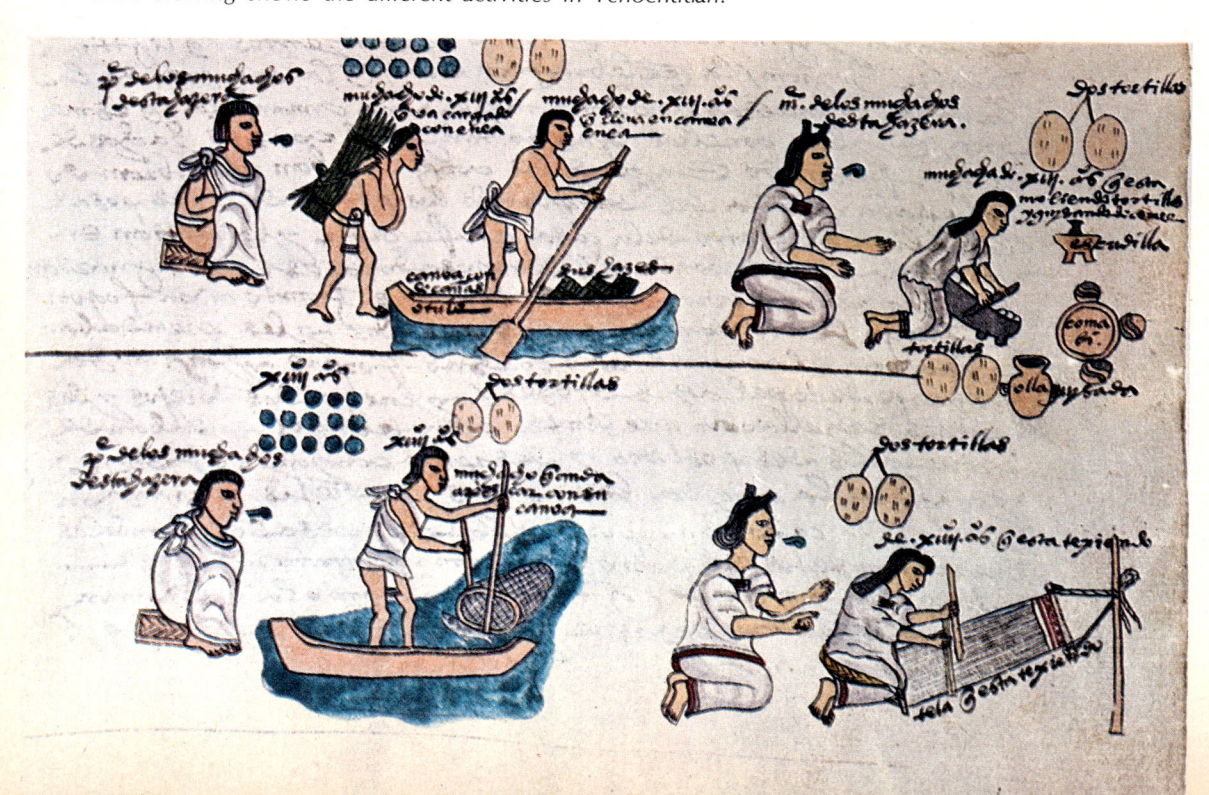

eighty-five and one hundred cacao beans, depending on how large the manta was and whether it was of good or poor quality. Just as we say that an item is worth so many dollars, the Aztecs would say that it was worth so many cacao beans or mantas. A spear, for example, might be valued at three mantas. That did not mean that the seller wanted you to pay him with three pieces of cloth, though. It was just a way of saying how much the spear was worth. The seller would then expect to be paid with some other product—perhaps with corn or fish—that was also worth three mantas. Or, you could pay him with cacao beans.

Aztec warriors patrolled throughout the marketplace. They served as a police force, keeping order and making sure that the laws were obeyed.

Growth of population. The trade of Tenochtitlán made it possible for the city to support its large population. If all the residents had been farmers, they would not have fit on the island. Much of the land would have been used for growing crops. Because people were able to exchange their special skills, such as weaving and canoemaking, for food at the market, it was not necessary for everyone to be a farmer. In fact, as the population grew, it was possible for more and more Aztecs to specialize. A larger number of people could use and pay for the different goods and special services.

Tenochtitlán Faces Its Problems

In the two hundred years after that small band of Aztecs had formed a little village on the island, the population of Tenochtitlán grew enormously. We do not know its exact number. Some social scientists say 80,000. Others think that it may have been 300,000. Since the whole island was only about five square miles, that meant that at least 16,000 people lived in every square mile—and maybe as many as 60,000 did! When many people live on a small area of land, we say that the population is very dense or that the area has a *high population density*. A large population in a small area often creates problems. Certainly this was true in Tenochtitlán.

Making new land. Each year the population increased. Many people from the surrounding countryside came to live in Tenochtitlán. To make room for the growing population, Aztecs filled in the swampy areas at the end of the lake with dirt and rocks brought from the mainland in canoes.

The Aztecs also added to the land space of their island-city in an amazing way. They wove reeds into a sort of huge basket and anchored it to the bottom of the shallow lake just off the shore. Then they lowered small buckets into the lake, scooped up the mud from the bottom, and dumped it into the large basket. They also threw in more reeds and rotting vegetable matter. This would help to make the mud thicker and hold it in. The work took a long time, but after a while the land rose above the level of the water and formed a tiny island called a *chinampa* (chi nam′ pə).

The Indians often planted willow trees at the corners and edges of the chinampa. As root systems formed, they helped to hold the soil in place and helped anchor the floating garden. In a few years the very rich soil of the chinampa could be used for farming. In this way the Aztecs enlarged the land area of the island and were able to provide for a larger population.

Water supply. The crowded conditions of Tenochtitlán created several big problems for the Aztecs. One was the water supply. In earlier days, when Tenochtitlán was a small village, a freshwater spring on the island took care of the needs of the people. Each family helped itself to the springwater.

As the population grew, the spring could no longer supply the needs of the city. The water in the lake did not help, for it was not fit to drink. The Aztecs solved this problem by bringing water into the city from freshwater springs in the hills near the lake. They built an *aqueduct* (ak′ wə dukt), a clay-lined channel that carried the water from the hills to the city. The aqueduct was three miles long. It contained two channels, each about two feet wide. When one channel had to be closed for cleaning or repairs, the water was switched to the second channel. Later the Aztecs built a cement aqueduct.

The aqueducts emptied water into a large *reservoir* (rez′ ər vwär), or manmade lake, in the city. There the fresh water was poured into containers, loaded onto canoes, and transported to all parts of the city. Because of the great building effort by the whole community, the Aztecs had an excellent water supply.

Health. A second problem that resulted from high population density was providing a sanitation system. *Sanitation* means making certain that conditions in the city do not bring on disease. Something had to be done with the garbage and human wastes of the thousands of people living in this small area. There was no place to dispose of wastes on the island.

The Aztecs therefore arranged a system for dealing with the problem. Garbage and wastes were loaded aboard canoes and carried out of the city to the mainland. There the wastes were either dumped or sold as fertilizers. Sometimes they were dropped into the lake.

Keeping streets clean was also a problem. You can imagine the kind of trash and dirt left on the streets each day by the thousands of people who went to the market. The Aztec government had to hire hundreds of people to water the streets and sweep them.

Floods. The location of the Aztec capital caused still another serious problem. The island of Tenochtitlán was not much higher than the level of the lake water. In very rainy seasons, water rose and flooded the city. This was especially serious because the lake water was salty. Floods of salt water ruined the crops on the chinampas. Also, as the population increased, more garbage and wastes were dumped into the lake, which became *polluted*. Floods brought this polluted water right back to the city.

No one person or small group of persons could do much to prevent this flooding, but the government could. One emperor ordered a dike built across the lake. The dike was ten miles long and separated the city from the main part of the lake. It created a sort of enclosed bay near the city. By opening and closing gates in the dike at the right time, the Aztecs prevented much of the flooding.

What makes a city? This, then, was Tenochtitlán. It certainly did not look like Los Angeles, or New York, or even Mexico City, which was built on the same site. Still, Tenochtitlán and large present-day cities have certain things in common. What are some of them? If such different cities have those things in common, is it possible that all cities may be the same in those ways? Will this help us know more about what a city is?

Let's look at another city, built 350 years after Tenochtitlán. Of course the people, their homes, and their buildings will be different. But, again, look for likenesses. They will help you learn more about cities.

Philadelphia, 1776

Philadelphia was founded in 1682 by an Englishman named William Penn. The king of England gave Penn the land in all of present-day Pennsylvania.

William Penn planned a town on the Delaware River, near the point where it meets the Schuylkill (skül' kil) River. This location had a good harbor, and oceangoing ships could sail up the Delaware and dock there.

COLONIAL PENNSYLVANIA 1700

Planning for a city. Much care went into the planning of the town before the first inhabitant even arrived. The whole town would cover about two square miles. Penn hired *surveyors* (sər vā′ ərz) to plan the location of streets. He decided that the streets were to be straight and would crisscross the town like lines on a checkerboard. There were to be nine wide avenues running east and west between the Delaware and the Schuylkill. These main streets would be crossed by twenty-one others, running north and south. Each residential street would be fifty feet wide, and the main market streets would be one hundred feet wide.

The streets closest to the Delaware would be built first, and the earliest settlers would live there. As more people came to Philadelphia, new streets would be built nearer to the Schuylkill.

Penn planned that each house would have a generous lot of land. The house would be placed in the middle of its lot, so that there would be room on every side of the house for gardens, orchards, or just grass. Also, with houses spaced so far apart, fire could not spread from one to another and destroy the town.

Penn decided to have five large open squares in different parts of the town. These would provide space for churches, public buildings, and parks in which the people could stroll about or rest. Penn was familiar with some of the crowded, dingy cities of England. He wanted to build something different in America. Philadelphia, he said, would be a "green country town."

But William Penn's green country town grew much faster than he had expected. By 1776, the year the American colonies declared their independence from England, the population of Philadelphia had reached forty thousand. This was nearly three times larger than it had been only twenty-five years before. Philadelphia was already the largest city in the English colonies. In fact, it was the largest in the entire Western Hemisphere.

The port of Philadelphia was a beehive of activity.

Waterfront. The most important part of the city was its waterfront. Philadelphia was the largest port in all America. Along a distance of three miles, ninety *wharves* (hwôrvz) jutted out from the shoreline into the Delaware River. Ships from England, the West Indies, and other distant points sailed up the river, docked, and unloaded their cargoes—sugar, molasses, hats, glassware, and dozens of other products.

From the docks these goods were taken to huge warehouses. There the wealthy merchants who owned the ships sold the cargoes to the local shopkeepers. Goods produced in the colonies were then loaded aboard the vessels for sale abroad.

The Philadelphia waterfront was a beehive of activity. Men worked as sailors, ropemakers, carpenters, and sailmakers. Coopers made barrels for packing the meat and flour that was loaded aboard the ships. Men found jobs loading and unloading the cargoes, and hauling the goods to local stores.

Philadelphia Faces Its Problems

From the waterfront, the main streets ran to the west. They were splendid, tree-lined streets. At first they were dirt roads, but soon they were paved with cobblestones. The center of the paved street was raised slightly higher than the sides so that the rainwater would run off instead of collecting in pools in the middle of the road. At each side was a gutter that carried the water off and into underground sewers.

At least that was the way it was supposed to work. Unfortunately Philadelphians, like people in other cities of that time, had a bad habit of throwing trash and garbage into the streets. In the country, people buried their garbage or carried it to the edge of the farm. In a crowded city there was not much land near the house for burying garbage, and the edge of the city was far away.

Even when the residents swept the street in front of their houses, as the

The streets of Philadelphia were to be wide and lined with trees.

law required them to do, they often left the garbage in piles in the gutter. In 1776, dirty streets and blocked-up gutters were still a problem in Philadelphia.

Water and light. Every fifty feet or so along the main streets were wells with pumps. The city provided them for anyone who wanted to use them, especially the poor who could not afford to dig their own wells. The *public wells* were also needed for providing water in case of fire.

Most of the city streets also had oil lamps to provide nighttime lighting. At first, Philadelphia had depended on homeowners to hang lanterns in front of the houses to light the streets. Even though many homeowners did cooperate, too many did not. The city then decided to provide the oil streetlamps, which were lit each evening by a night watchman on his rounds. Philadelphia in 1776 was a well-lit city.

A constant stream of traffic went over the streets. People walking to market hurried along the sidewalk. Wagons drawn by teams of horses hauled goods from one part of town to another. The clatter of horses' hooves on the cobblestones and the rumbling of the iron wagon wheels continued from sunup to sundown—and even later on lighted streets.

Housing problems. Lining these main streets and side streets were homes. Some were wooden homes, but most were made of brick. One reason for the brick was that the homes were built close together, and a fire in one could spread to other wooden homes and destroy much of the town.

There was very little space between these homes. William Penn had planned for wide streets with plenty of land for each house. But as people crowded into the city, narrow alleys were cut between the wide streets. New houses used the empty land along the alleys. On many blocks there was no space at all between the brick homes.

Each house was supplied with water from its own well, which was usually in the small backyard. These wells, together with the public wells on the streets, gave Philadelphia a fine water supply at most times. During *droughts* (droutz), or dry spells, however, the water level in the wells fell very low. City leaders worried that there might not be enough water to fight a large fire during a dry spell. They also realized that the population of the city was growing so rapidly that the water supply would not be large enough. They would soon have to find a source outside the city and bring the water in.

Industry and trade. More than half of the city's population were tradesmen and skilled workers. They had been attracted to the city by the opportunity to make a living through their special skills. A large city population needed the services and goods of tailors, carpenters, leathermakers, shipbuilders, shoemakers, and dozens of others. Most of these workers did their work right in their own homes—except, of course, the shipbuilders! The front room on the first floor of a home was often used as a shop.

Most of the shops of the city, though, were in the main market area, on Market Street. Stores of every description could be found there. Some were general stores that carried a variety of goods—mirrors, candles, gloves, pins, wooden dishes, lanterns, fishing lines, bottles, and rat traps. Many stores carried only one special item. In such stores one could select from different kinds of wines, types of writing paper, brands of tea or tobacco, or pieces of glassware. People from all parts of the city and from farms near and far flocked to these stores.

There were food markets as well, some specializing in beef, others in baked goods. When Philadelphia was a smaller town, all the food shops had been located on Market Street. By 1776 there was no longer enough room on Market Street for all the food sellers, and new food markets were opened up on other streets as well.

Trade with the backcountry. Farther to the northwest, beginning at the edge of the city, a long highway extended into the countryside. This dirt road was called the Great Philadelphia Wagon Road. It linked Philadelphia with Lancaster, Pennsylvania, about sixty miles away. Here was some of the richest farmland in the new nation. From Lancaster the road turned toward the south and extended several hundred miles more, into the backcountry of Virginia and North Carolina.

Along this road each day rolled dozens of large covered wagons. They carried the produce from the farms of western Pennsylvania and from other places along the route of the Great Philadelphia Wagon Road—wheat, flour, pork, beef, and butter. They also brought furs from trappers, lumber

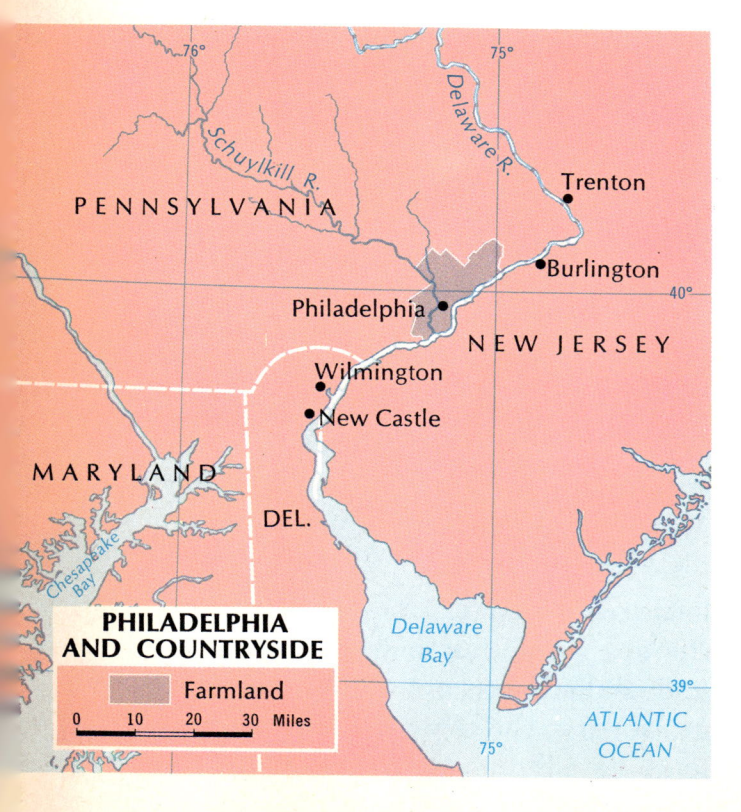

Market Street became the shopping center of Philadelphia.

from woodsmen, and bars of iron made at dozens of little iron forges in the backcountry.

The Great Philadelphia Wagon Road was only one of the roads that connected Philadelphia to the farm country and to cities like New York and Boston. Each year about ten thousand wagons entered Philadelphia by these roads. From parts of New Jersey, Maryland, and Delaware, wagons brought food and *fuel*. They also brought produce to the warehouses at the wharves, where it was sold to merchants.

The wagons carried people, too. Every year thousands of Europeans came to America. Ships brought many of them to Philadelphia. Some settled right in the city, but others, who wanted to farm, boarded the wagons heading for the countryside.

The wagons also brought hundreds into the city from the farm country. Most came to shop or to spend the day in the city. But each year hundreds decided to leave the farm life and move to the city. They were attracted by the jobs, the people, the convenience of the shops, and the excitement of city life.

Social life in the city. There were many forms of entertainment in the city, and many of them continued on into the evening. There were people to spend time with or to visit for a game of cards or an evening of conversation. Many city people enjoyed watching plays at the theater. There were also concerts from time to time.

The favorite form of entertainment for most city dwellers was an evening at the local tavern. Taverns in colonial America were a combination of restaurant, hotel, community center, and meetinghouse all rolled into one. There, friends and strangers gathered to drink beer and cider while exchanging gossip and hearing the latest news of other cities. Often the talk concerned the news of the day as reported in one of the city's seven newspapers.

City services. Philadelphia had many schools in 1776. Most of them were private schools, some of them run by the churches of the city. The children learned to read and write and to do simple arithmetic. Some, mostly the children of the wealthier families, went on to the higher grades, but most went to school for only a few years. Only a very few ever entered the College of Philadelphia, which had opened about twenty years earlier.

Philadelphia could also boast of a new hospital, one of the few in the English colonies. Doctors did not know nearly so much about diseases then as they do now. But at least Philadelphians knew that in their city they could get the best medical care available. Most of the doctors had received their training in other countries. They brought the latest medical knowledge with them when they came to live in Philadelphia.

Even with a hospital and good doctors, the city lived in dread fear of an *epidemic* (ep′ ə dem′ ik)—that is, the spread of a disease to a large number of people in a short time. Smallpox was the most feared disease, for it spread rapidly in cities and was often fatal. Hundreds had died in the smallpox epidemics of 1731 and 1760. The city came to a standstill as people shuttered their windows and stayed off the streets for fear of catching the killing disease.

To the suburbs. As Philadelphia's export and import trade grew, merchants became wealthy. Many built handsome homes in the city, but others built large estates in the *suburbs*, or areas just outside the city. There they sought to escape the crowds, the noise, and the odors of the city.

At first only the wealthy went to the suburbs. But by 1776 Philadelphia's

Philadelphia was proud of its statehouse, which you see above.

growing population was spreading beyond the city's boundaries. Although hundreds of new homes were built in the city each year, the builders could not keep up with the growing population. There was no longer enough room in the city, and some of the population began to spill over into the suburbs. Even so, all the important public buildings remained in the city.

Closer to the Answer

Philadelphia in 1776 and Tenochtitlán in 1521 were two very different cities. Do you remember why we chose these two cities to study? We decided that one way to discover what a city is would be to find out what cities have in common. We picked two cities that were very different. If these two had things in common, there is a good chance that other cities would be alike in the same ways.

For example, you probably noticed that as different as they are, both Tenochtitlán and Philadelphia had a large marketplace where people bought and sold goods. Might this mean that all cities have a marketplace? The two cities also had a large population and heavy traffic. Do all cities have these in common? By now you may have noticed many things that these two different cities have in common. List some of these things.

We have taken our first step in discovering what a city is. Now we can ask our next question, how are cities different from other places? To find the answer to this question, you will have to know something about life in other places. In other words, to know what a city *is*, you have to compare it with something else that a city *is not!*

Looking at Farm Life

One thing that a city definitely *is not* is a farm. So now you are going to read about life on a farm. As you read, remember to ask yourself, how does life in this rural area differ from life in the city?

The farm area you are going to read about is in the midwestern part of the United States. The year is 1875—just one hundred years later than the Philadelphia in our description.

Life on a farm. For a description of what farm living was like, we are going to turn to a famous American author of about sixty years ago named Hamlin Garland. Hamlin Garland was brought up on a farm on the prairies of northern Iowa. In his *autobiography* (ô′ tə bī og′ rə fē), or life story, he recalls the years of his boyhood there.

Looking back forty years later, Hamlin remembered many pleasant things about being a boy on a farm. There was plenty of space—open fields everywhere, with prairie grass as tall as he himself was. The nearest house was a mile away. Snowdrifts piled high in the winter, and there was always ice on the pond. It was a great place to play. Mostly he played with his brother and sisters, for with farmhouses so far apart there were not many other children close by. A few special friends were able to come by from time to time. With his friends and his brother, Hamlin learned much about nature, especially animals.

A treat for a young farm boy was a day in town. How Hamlin looked forward to those special Saturdays when the whole family piled into the wagon and drove the several miles to the village of Osage! Osage had barely twelve hundred inhabitants and a handful of small stores, but to the Garland family it seemed like a very big city indeed. One could get almost anything one needed there—farming supplies, pots and pans, kerosene lamps, or even a

This picture shows some of the loneliness of western farmers.

haircut or a doctor's attention. While the children bought candy and poked around in the other stores, Mrs. Garland shopped for the cloth from which she would make the family's clothes. There was a store that sold ready-made clothes, but those were only for very special occasions. Before returning home, they always spent time with other farm families who had come to town that day.

Farm chores. Life on the farm was not all play, even for young boys. Everyone in the family had daily chores. A young boy's morning chores included splitting logs for the wood stove, milking cows, and taking the animals out to pasture. Then came a hearty breakfast with the whole family and a morning of work in the fields. After the family had finished the noontime meal, all went back to the fields again until supper. Every day someone had to take the garbage out and bury it. And at times a new well had to be dug when the old one ran low.

Although Hamlin's father decided who would do various chores, nature was the real boss on a farm. Sunshine and rain decided whether the fields could be worked each day. Nature's changing seasons decided what kind of work would be done and when. Plowing and planting were done in the spring; cultivating and weeding, in the summer; and harvesting the ripe corn and wheat, in the fall.

While the men worked in the fields, the women worked in the homes. As Hamlin recalled it, even with the help of his sister, his mother's work seemed never to end. From early morning to evening, she cooked, cleaned, and cared for children. The women canned the foods and salted the meat that the family would need throughout the year, for there was no market nearby for daily shopping. Mrs. Garland also wove cotton into cloth for large items like sheets.

A lonely life. In his autobiography, Hamlin recalls the loneliness of farm life. Except for being with the family at mealtimes, a farmer might go many days without seeing another person. Plowing was an especially lonely job, wrote Hamlin.

> It meant moving to and fro hour after hour, day after day, with no one to talk to but the horses. I cheered myself in every imaginable way. I whistled. I sang. I studied the clouds . . . and I counted the prairie chickens.

Evenings were usually spent with the whole family in the living room. No one would have thought of going off to town, for it was too far away. The trip was too difficult on dark nights. Even the neighbors were not close enough for frequent visits. Usually the youngsters read, played a game of cards, or sang together to amuse themselves. But whatever the evening activities, they never lasted very long.

Everyone was too tired and would need a good night's sleep before starting the next morning at five o'clock.

Wintertime, when the fields could not be worked, was a bit easier. Even so, everyone had plenty to do. Hamlin had his daily chores with the animals. When the snowdrifts piled high, he had to shovel a path to the barn. When the weather was clear, Hamlin's father would drive the wagon six or seven miles to the nearest grove of trees. There he would cut wood for the year's fuel supply. On the Iowa prairies, no deliveryman brought fuel to the farmer's door!

Winter also meant a little more time for visiting—unless the family was snowed in. Perhaps once a week or so, during the evenings, Hamlin could look forward to seeing a few of his best friends.

At school. School was another important part of Hamlin's life. The school he attended was a one-room building. The whole school was perhaps the size of your own classroom. With a small population in the area, there were only a few children of each age. All of them, from the youngest to the oldest, were in the same classroom and had the same teacher.

Like so much else in Hamlin's boyhood, the school's schedule (skej′ ŭl) was decided by nature. There was school during the winter months and for part of the summer. During spring planting and fall harvesting, the children were needed on the farms, and the school was closed.

In school, Hamlin began to think about the world outside his prairie home. As he grew older, he longed more and more to see the world and be a part of it. Hamlin did not yet know what kind of work he would do, but one thing he had decided definitely— he would leave farming.

That was a very hard decision to make. It meant leaving his family, for on the prairies farming was the only kind of work. Even in the town of Osage, there would not be much choice of jobs for him. No, he would have to move on to a city. Hamlin Garland eventually moved to Boston.

What the differences tell us. Of course you would never mistake a farm for a city. But as you read about life on the Garland farm in Iowa in 1875, were you able to find any ways in which farm life differed from city living? What were some of them? Does understanding these differences give you a better idea of life in a city?

In this chapter we have concentrated on finding the answers to two questions. We have asked, in what ways are cities *like* each other? We have also asked, in what ways are cities *unlike* other places? Now that you have some of the answers, you have begun to discover what a city really is.

Working with Concepts and Generalizations

Identifying Concepts

Read each statement below. Write T if the statement tells something about the city of Tenochtitlán; write P if the statement tells something about the city of Philadelphia; write B if the statement tells something about both Tenochtitlán and Philadelphia. Write on paper.

1. Many people were able to specialize in certain jobs.
2. The Spaniards destroyed most of the historical records of this city.
3. Wells with pumps were placed every fifty feet along the main street.
4. Many craftsmen made their products in their own homes.
5. We know some things about this city because of the work done by archaeologists.
6. Each year the population increased, as more people moved into the city.
7. Canals were more useful than streets in this city.
8. People often came into the city to buy the goods they needed.
9. Aqueducts were built to carry water from the hills into the city.
10. The most important part of the city was the waterfront.

Developing Concepts

Write the answers on paper.

1. You have always lived on a farm. In 1776 you get a chance to visit Philadelphia for the first time. Describe what you see. How is Philadelphia different from the farm you live on? What things do you like about Philadelphia? What things don't you like? Would you rather stay in Philadelphia or return to your farm? Why?
2. You have learned that disposing of garbage and other wastes was a problem in Philadelphia and in Tenochtitlán. What was done in Tenochtitlán to try to solve the problem? What was done in Philadelphia?
3. The year is A.D. 2500. Archaeologists have uncovered the remains of your school building. What kinds of objects will they find? Will they know that the building they have found was a school building? How will they know? Are there some things in your school that might not last until the year 2500? Which things? Why?
4. How were the Aztecs able to enlarge Tenochtitlán to provide living space for the ever-growing population?
5. You may be a butcher, a baker, or a candlestick maker. You have just moved to the city of Philadelphia. You have set up a shop to sell your wares. Draw a simple sketch showing what your shop looks like. Give the sketch a title, including the name and location of your shop.

Generalizations

An important word is missing from each statement below. When you have filled in the missing word, you will have completed a generalization. The missing words are ones you have learned in this chapter. When your generalizations are complete, find proof to support each one. Tell what the proof is and the page on which you found it.

1. A high _____ density places great demands on available resources.
2. City life enables people to _____ in the work they do and the services they offer.

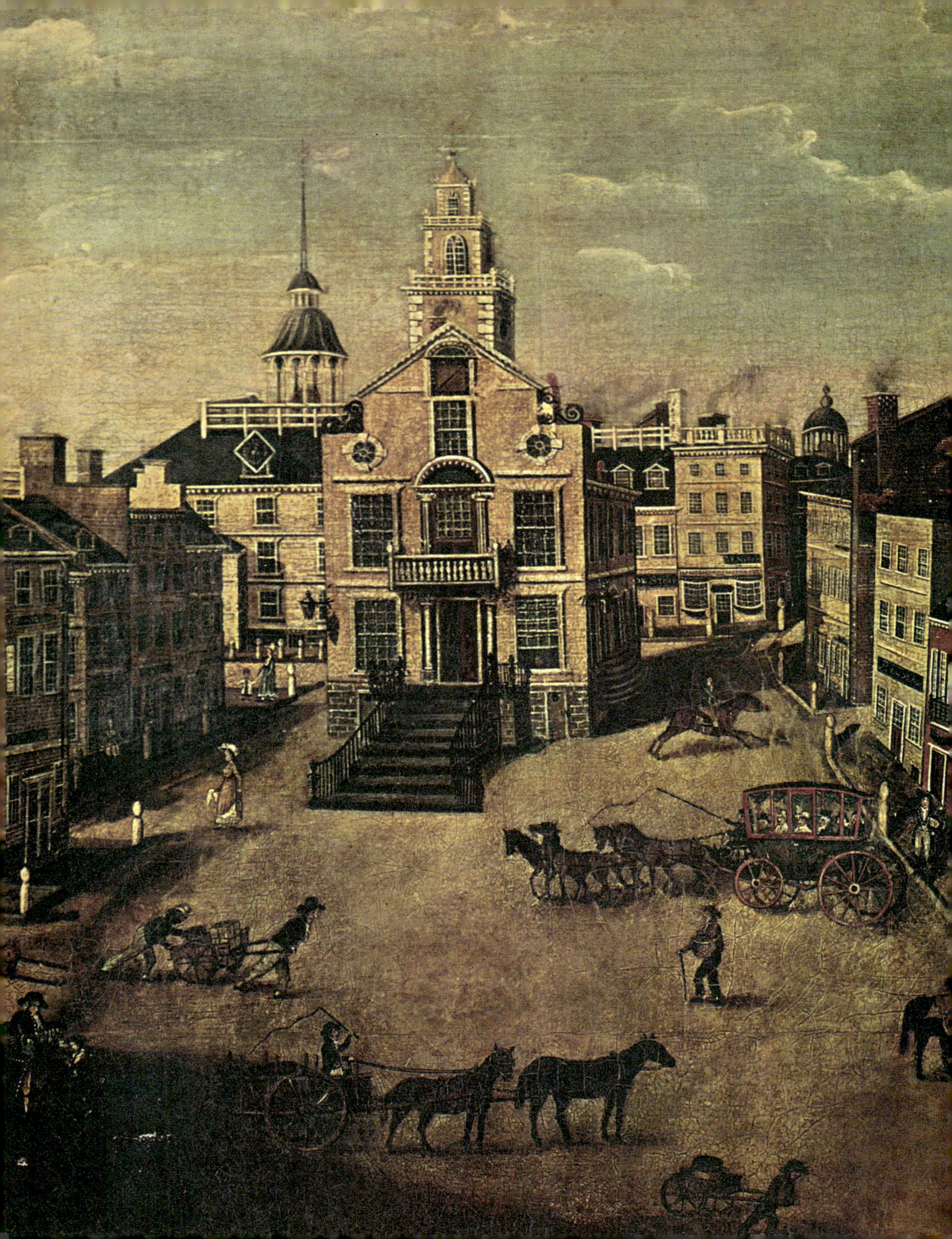

American Cities Grow from Villages

8

Today the United States is a nation of city dwellers. But this was not always the case. For many years after the Europeans arrived, there were no cities in North America. The Spanish built forts in Florida. The French built forts and trading posts in Canada, especially along the St. Lawrence River and the Great Lakes. On the eastern coast, the English started small villages at Jamestown and Plymouth. For a while the Dutch controlled Manhattan Island and much of the Hudson River valley by building a series of forts. But none of these settlements could be called a city.

Villages and towns, however, did spring up in North America. Most of these settlements remained quite small during the colonial period. Some grew larger, and a few grew a great deal larger. By 1776, when the colonists declared their independence, five of these towns had grown into cities. The five were Boston, Massachusetts; New York, New York; Philadelphia, Pennsylvania; Newport, Rhode Island; and Charleston, South Carolina. In this chapter you will be able to add to your understanding of what a city is by studying how these five communities grew from villages to cities.

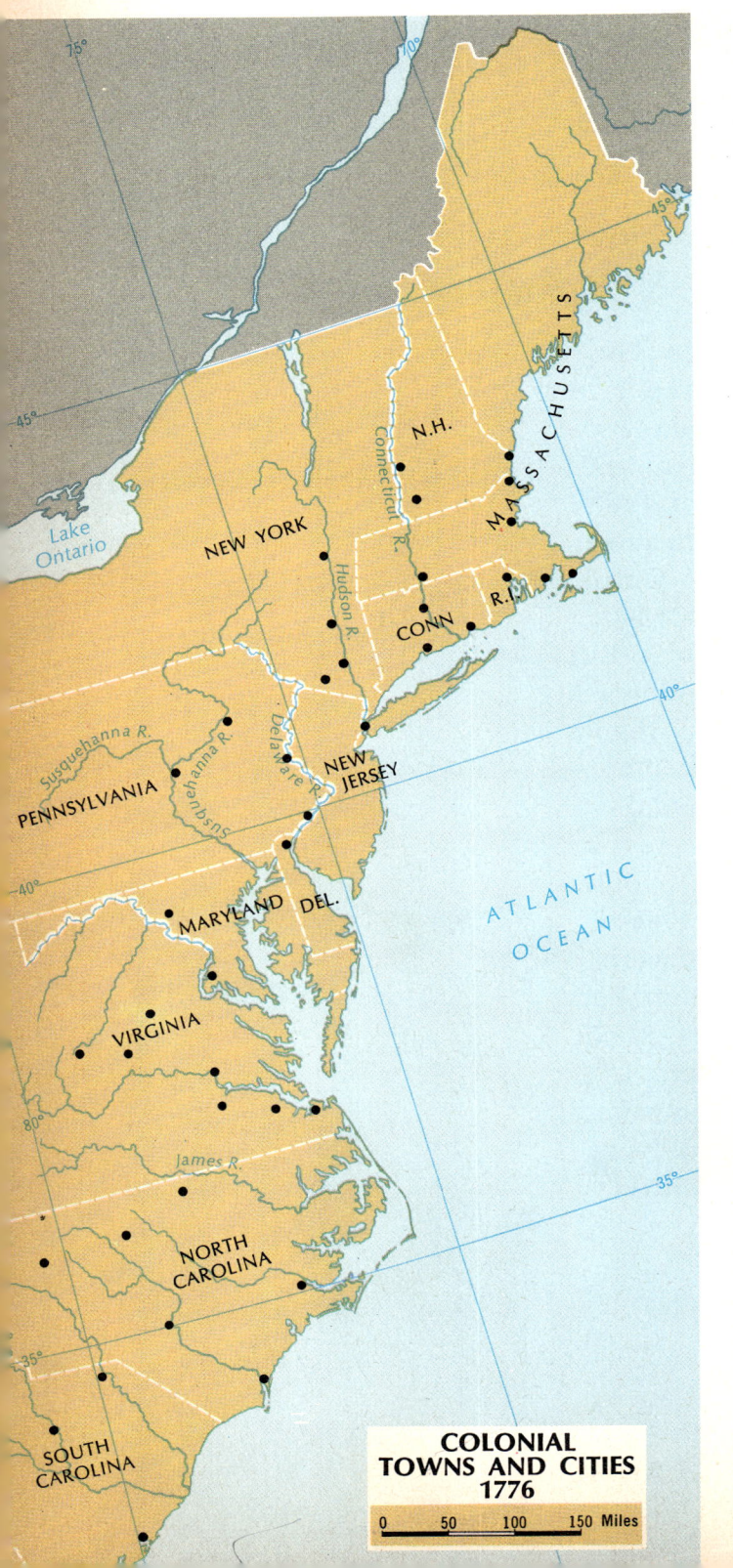

Studying Location

Why did these towns become cities? How did they become cities? Why didn't other towns and villages also become cities?

A part of the answer has to do with their location. Look at the two maps on pages 148 and 149. One shows many of the settlements, large and small, in the mid-1700's, about 150 years after the Europeans came. The second shows the twenty largest settlements at that time. It also shows the five that had become cities.

What do you notice about the location of these settlements? What do you notice about the location of the twenty largest? Do they seem to have anything in common? What about the location of the five cities? Do they have anything in common?

The Change from Farm Villages

Let us see how our five small settlements became cities by 1776. At first most people in the five communities farmed for a living. There were a few skilled workers, like carpenters and blacksmiths, who exchanged their services for food and other goods. Even skilled workers usually did some farming at first. The small population could not provide enough work for them to make a living with their special skills.

Very soon, some of the people became merchants and specialized in *commerce.* That is, they bought and sold large amounts of goods. Many of the goods that people needed for daily living were not available in North America. Merchants bought products like sugar, molasses, cloth, hardware, and other manufactured goods from other lands and brought them to their villages for sale. They also shipped the goods that Americans produced on farms, from forests, and from the ocean to people in other lands.

Commerce and growth. The work of exchanging the goods of America for the goods of other countries quickly became the most important work of the five young towns. Almost like magnets these ports drew the products of nearby villages and farms to their markets. Most villages, even those on the coast, lacked docks, wharves, and warehouses and could not ship goods overseas. Fishermen and lumbermen in Massachusetts sent their goods overseas from Boston. Charleston became the exporting center for rice planters of the Carolinas. Newport unfortunately became a *slave-trade center*. But it also became a chief center for candles made of whale fat. New York and Philadelphia shipped many different products from farmers and merchants far and wide.

Increasing commerce meant more jobs in the seaports for more people. Commerce depended on sailing ships. Sailmakers, ropemakers, carpenters,

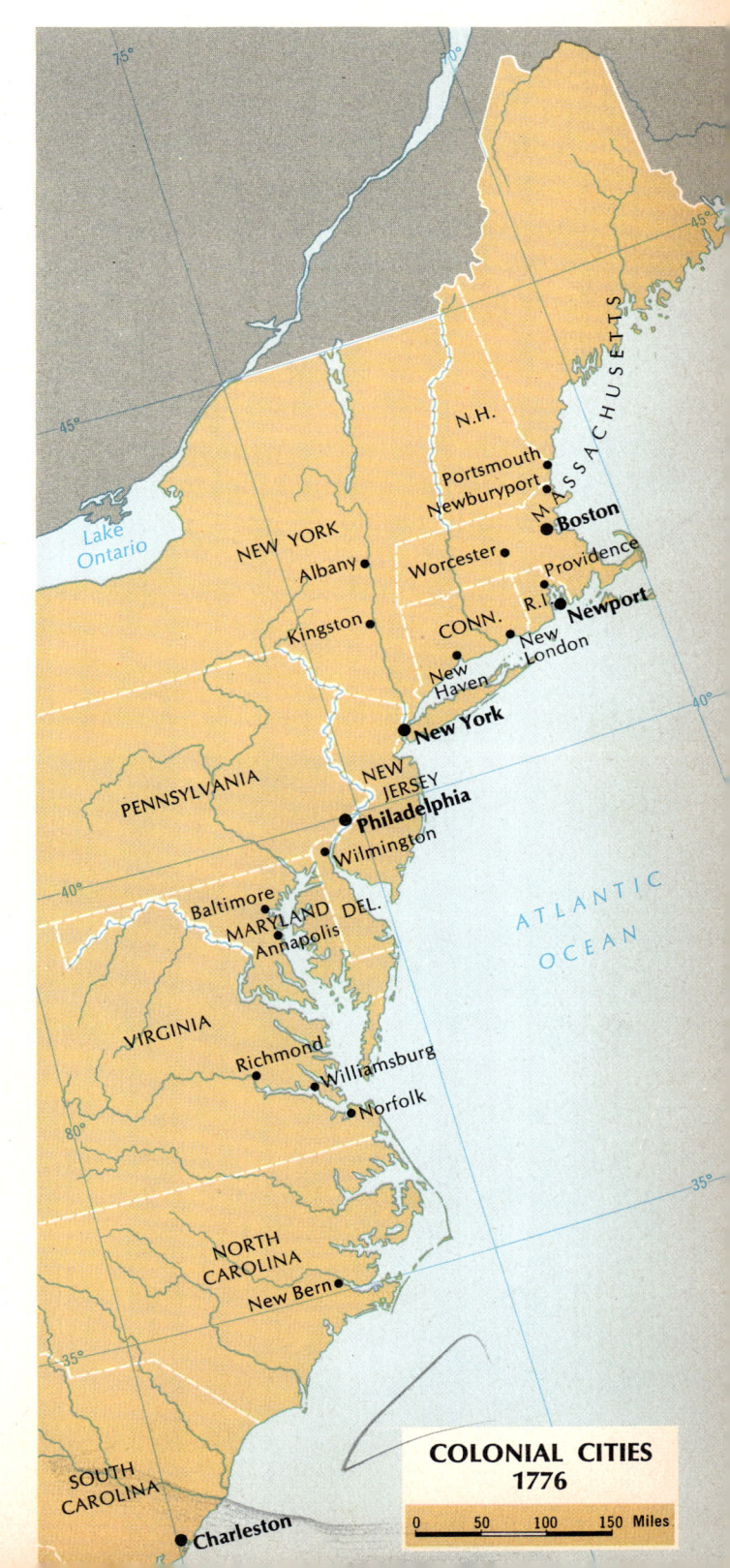

COLONIAL CITIES 1776

and *caulkers* (kô′ kərz), who kept the ships watertight, found steady work. As more ships were needed, they were built by craftsmen called shipwrights.

Other people found jobs preparing America's products for shipment to other lands. Much of the preparation was done in the town. Wheat and corn were turned into flour at a gristmill. Bakers made bread and biscuits for seamen to eat on their long voyages, and for sale in the West Indies. Tanners worked animal hides into leather. Sawmills employed men to cut logs into boards. One of the biggest jobs was that of the *cooper,* who made the barrels in which the fish, salted meat, and flour were packed for shipment.

Men were also needed to load and unload ships, and to work in warehouses. Others found work as drivers of the carts and wagons that hauled goods to and from the docks. Do you see how commerce helped the population to grow?

Specializing helps cities to grow. As commerce increased, the population grew. New industries also began in the town. Skilled workers of all kinds—shoemakers, tailors, glassmakers, bricklayers, and men who specialized

Ships carrying many kinds of goods crowded New York Harbor. New York was soon the busiest port in America.

Carpenters specialized in one product.

in dozens of kinds of work—came to live in these growing communities. In farming areas or small villages, there were not enough people who needed their services. But they were able to make a living at their work in the more populated seaports. In fact, each of the growing towns soon needed the services of several tailors or shoemakers

Soon these skilled workers, or craftsmen, were able to specialize still further. At first, one carpenter might make chairs, tables, cabinets, and many other products made of wood. As town populations increased, there were enough buyers of chairs to support a carpenter who made nothing but chairs. As a result one carpenter might become a chairmaker, another a tablemaker, while a third specialized in cabinets. Instead of each housecarpenter doing all the separate jobs that went into building a house, there soon were roofers, plumbers, painters, plasterers, masons, and glaziers (glā′ zhərz).

No longer did a single blacksmith make all the products out of the different metals himself. Now there were tinsmiths and coppersmiths. The smiths who worked with iron became specialists in iron ornaments, hammers, axes, nails, kettles, pots and pans, and even iron anchors. Specializing permitted the craftsman to concentrate on one single kind of work and to become more highly skilled than ever. As a result he usually provided a job of better quality, and could do it in a shorter time and at lower cost.

Specialization leads to dependence. The more each person specialized in one kind of work, the more he depended on other people to provide the goods and services he needed for his daily living. The blacksmith depended on the carpenter for his shelter, on the tailor and shoemaker for his clothes, and on the baker for his bread. All of them depended on the farmer and the fisherman for their food. In the growing seaport communities, people became very dependent on each other.

Markets spread. Shopkeepers specialized, too. At first there were only a few stores in each town, and each one sold a great variety of items—everything from glass, clothing, and tobacco to candles, kitchen utensils, and tools. As population increased in the five

PRODUCTS OF THE COLONIES 1776

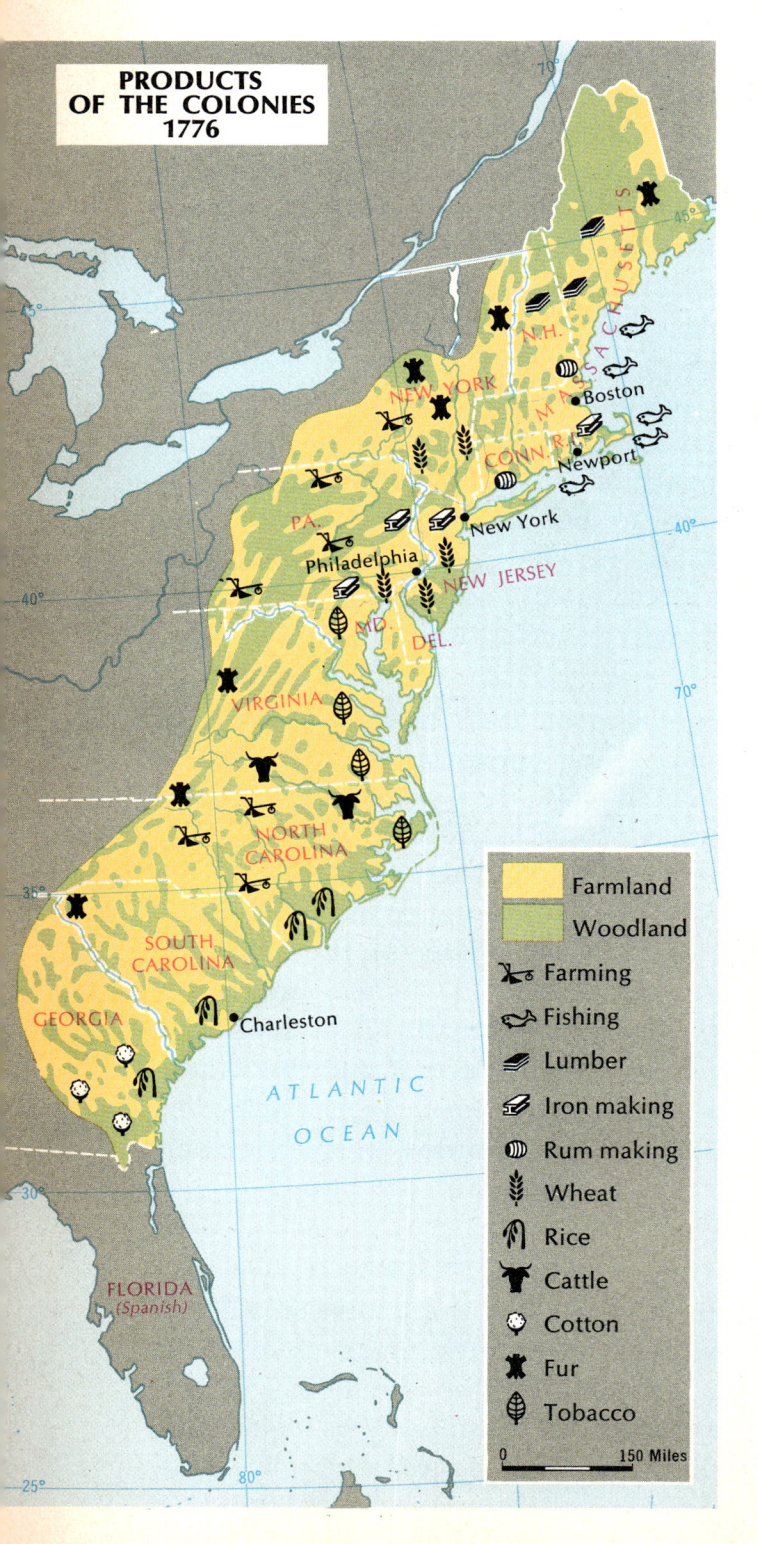

Legend:
- Farmland
- Woodland
- Farming
- Fishing
- Lumber
- Iron making
- Rum making
- Wheat
- Rice
- Cattle
- Cotton
- Fur
- Tobacco

0 — 150 Miles

seaport towns, there were enough buyers of all these goods to support stores that specialized. In the linen stores, tobacco stores, and shops specializing in clothing, shoppers had a greater choice of goods than ever.

The large market area attracted people from miles around for shopping. Farmers came to sell their goods for money and to buy items that were not available at home. They no longer had to make those items or *barter* for them. The larger towns soon became centers for more and more villages and farms around them. This helped the towns grow into cities.

Wealth. The bustling business of New York, Boston, Newport, Charleston, and Philadelphia gave people a great opportunity to make money. A small number of them, mostly merchants and landowners, became quite wealthy. In farm areas and small villages, there were also some people who were somewhat wealthier than others. However, in the five seaports that became cities, the difference between the wealthy and the poor was very great. In time, the wealthy began to live in a separate section of town.

City Problems Change a Way of Living

People who grew up in New York, Boston, Philadelphia, Newport, or Charleston, while these towns were

New York's City Hall was surrounded by homes and shops.

turning into cities, could look back and find that their ways of living had changed. If they had visited friends living on farms, they would be aware of still more changes. The years had made life in a city quite different from life on a farm.

Residents of the growing towns had to find ways to solve many new problems that did not arise on farms and in villages. Even when the problems were the same kind as those that rural people faced, people in towns had to develop very different ways of dealing with them.

Need for roads. One of the problems was the need for roads and streets. Builders had to move lumber and bricks into town or from one part of town to another. Craftsmen needed roads to get raw materials like hides, iron, and wood to their shops. Wagons required roads to haul goods to market or to the docks. As towns spread out, people had to travel farther between their homes and the market. Some traveled by foot and some on horseback; some pushed goods in wheelbarrows and others used horse-drawn carts. All of them needed roads to travel on. Without roads, there could be little exchange of goods and services, and the town could not grow.

Early street building. Early American streets were not like the ones you know today. They were usually very narrow and almost always unpaved. When the people of a village decided to build a street, each resident was expected to pitch in with his own labor, or else hire someone to work in his place. No special skills were needed to make a street. It was simply a matter of clearing away the brush or tree stumps, shoveling dirt, and making the street fairly level. These streets were not very satisfactory. In dry weather, wagons and horses raised clouds of choking dust. In heavy rains, wagons sank to their axles and got stuck in the mud. Pedestrians also used these streets, for there were no sidewalks. Keeping clothes and shoes clean was impossible in almost any weather.

Paving streets. In time most towns decided to pave the streets. At first, towns continued to rely on the local citizens to do the work. In New York each resident was required to give two days of work a year to keep streets in good shape. The system was something like the *mita* of the Incas. This was not very satisfactory. Many people could not be depended on to help, and towns could not be sure that the work would be done on time. Also, paving a street and making it the right height for drainage of rainwater required more skill than most citizens had.

Therefore some town governments began to take on the job of street building. They planned new streets and repaired old ones. City dwellers paid for such services through taxes. By 1776 the five communities had at least their most important streets paved. In fact some visitors from other countries said that Philadelphia was the best-paved city in the world.

Safeguarding the People

Paved or unpaved, streets were not of much use if they were unsafe for pedestrians and riders, or if traffic

Alleys, built of cobblestones, cut through many blocks in the Beacon Hill section of Boston.

could not get through. The communities had to make laws about the use of streets, for the safety of all. In the countryside a man might ride his horse as fast or as carelessly as he wished, and no one would be harmed by his carelessness except himself. But where people lived close together, riders had to be more careful.

The first traffic laws. More than three hundred years ago, Boston passed the first traffic law in the United States. Anyone galloping or riding improperly on the town's streets would be fined. Another law said that horses could not be left alone on the streets, unless they were tied to some place. This was probably the first parking law in America.

Some things never seem to change. Making laws did not solve the traffic problem in those days, any more than it does in ours. People still complained that riders galloped down the streets.

Keeping the streets clean. Keeping the streets clean was another problem of the growing towns. If a farmer decided to throw his garbage out his front door, he was the only one who would be affected. But in a town, throwing out garbage in this way made the streets filthy and caused disease and odors. It also made the streets unsafe for people who had to avoid the piles of rotting garbage.

New York was one of the first to pass a law about this problem, and soon the other towns followed. The New York law said that anyone who threw "any rubbish, filth, oyster shells, dead animals, or anything like it into the streets" would be fined. Every person was required to keep the street clean in front of his own house. One New Yorker discovered a very simple way to do this, but the town officials did not think much of his system, and he was fined. It seems he was keeping his own front clean by throwing his garbage in front of his neighbor's house.

In most towns in America, street cleaning was done not by people but by hogs. They roamed the streets, eating the garbage. But roaming hogs were dangerous, especially to children.

None of the five growing towns we are studying had really solved the problem of garbage disposal by 1776. Boston came closest when it hired carters to scoop up the heaps of garbage and carry them away. This was an early form of our modern, regular garbage collection.

The dangers of fire. The most serious problem the young towns of America faced was fire. Houses in the towns were close together. A fire starting in one house might quickly spread to others, and soon dozens of homes could burn to the ground.

Boston suffered the most severe fires. In 1653 one fire burned nearly fifty buildings. Sixteen years later, another destroyed 150 buildings. That was about one fourth of the whole town. Again, in 1711, a fire broke out and burned more than one hundred homes. New York also had several terrible fires. Although Philadelphia, Charleston, and Newport were not damaged so badly, none of them escaped completely, and the residents lived in constant dread of fires.

To protect the communities, each of the five towns passed laws that were aimed at preventing fires. The biggest cause of fire was a poorly built chimney. In many of the earliest homes, chimneys were made of wood and plaster. Sparks flying up from the fireplace would cause the chimneys to catch fire, and soon a whole block of buildings would be burned. To prevent this, towns passed laws forbidding citizens to make chimneys of wood. They also required that the chimney be cleaned and repaired regularly. Boston and New York even hired inspectors to check all chimneys.

Nighttime was the most dangerous time for fire. On cold nights people burned logs in their fireplaces, and then went to bed. With no one awake to check on the flames, a spark might start a fire that could burn half the town. Again, several of the towns passed laws to protect the community against this. Citizens were not allowed to light fireplaces between nine o'clock in the evening and four o'clock in the morning, no matter what the weather. It was better to have a cold house than no house at all. As you can see, fire was another problem that made it necessary for towns to restrict their citizens.

Fighting fires. Experience had taught the people that in cities special steps had to be taken quickly to keep fires from spreading. In all five seaport towns, each resident was required to help put out fires. First, every household had to have a ladder tall enough to reach the roof, and a pole about twelve feet long with a swab, or a large piece of cloth, wrapped tightly around it. In case of a fire in the chimney or on the roof, the homeowner soaked the swab in water, climbed the

This painting shows how people joined in fighting fires.

ladder, and attempted to beat out the fire.

Householders were also required to have iron hooks with a rope or chain attached. Men threw the hook so that it would catch the edge of a burning wall. Then they pulled until the wall collapsed. In this way they kept the fire from spreading to other buildings.

Bucket brigade. All residents were also required to own a leather bucket or two. At a fire these were filled with water and passed from hand to hand along one line, poured onto the fire, and returned for refilling along a second line. Usually women and children helped on the line with the empty buckets. This was called the *bucket brigade.* It was not a very effective way to fight fires. Frequently the fire was so hot that the brigade could not get close enough to put it out.

Although the town governments owned a few leather buckets, several ladders, and hooks that were used at fires, the main job of putting out the fire belonged to the residents. Late in the 1600's, several of the town governments started to help out by buying machines from England that helped pump water onto the fire. Men dragged these machines to the fire, where the bucket brigade, instead of pouring the water on the fire, poured it into the tub of the engine. The engine did not send the water much farther or higher than a modern garden hose.

Fire companies. One of the big problems during fires in a city was theft. When fire broke out, residents in the neighborhood immediately put all their household goods into the street. That way, if the fire did spread to their house, they would at least save their belongings. But often when they returned from fighting the fire, they found their goods had been stolen. After all, as the population grew larger, not everyone in town could know everybody else, and people were more likely to steal from strangers than from people they knew.

Theft was the main reason why volunteer fire companies were formed. These companies were groups of citizens, numbering about twenty or thirty, who formed a fire-fighting club. Each member of the company was to bring two buckets and two large linen bags to every fire. The bags were used for carrying goods out of the burning buildings and also out of nearby homes. One of the men then stood guard while the others helped put out the fire.

The volunteer companies practiced fire-fighting skills and could be depended on to get to the fire and do the best job possible. Towns soon provided these companies with new equipment, including pumping engines, to help fight fires. In some of the towns the volunteer companies bought the engines themselves. When money was needed for building a storage shed for the engines and hoses, volunteer fire companies usually raised it by asking citizens for contributions.

Water supply. Another problem that people in the five towns had to meet was the need for water. Most families got their water supply by digging wells in their backyards. But there were families that could not afford their own wells. Towns had to take care of this problem.

Private wells could not be counted on to supply enough water for fighting fires. In village days, most of the population had lived close to the river or ocean. There was always plenty of water nearby for fighting fires. As towns grew larger, houses were built a mile or more away from the water. It became impossible to organize a bucket brigade long enough to fight fires in those homes.

To provide water for all and to protect the community against fire, town leaders decided to dig public wells on streets and to equip them with pump handles. By 1776, each of America's five cities had an adequate (ad′ ə kwit) water supply for its people. Many towns followed their example.

CHARLESTON IN 1776

Poor location hurts Charleston. Charleston suffered more than any of the other towns. A smallpox epidemic in 1698 killed more than two hundred residents. The very next year yellow fever struck the town. Here is what one Charleston resident wrote in a letter during the second epidemic: "150 dead in 6 days time.... Shops shut up for 6 weeks; nothing but carrying medicines, digging graves, carting the dead." Just a few years later, Charleston was again hit by outbreaks of yellow fever. Farmers were afraid to enter town. Food became scarce, and trade almost stopped. More than one third of the town's population died in the epidemics.

Charleston's location had much to do with the outbreaks of fever. The city was almost surrounded by water and marshland. The marshes and nearby rice plantations were perfect breeding places for mosquitoes.

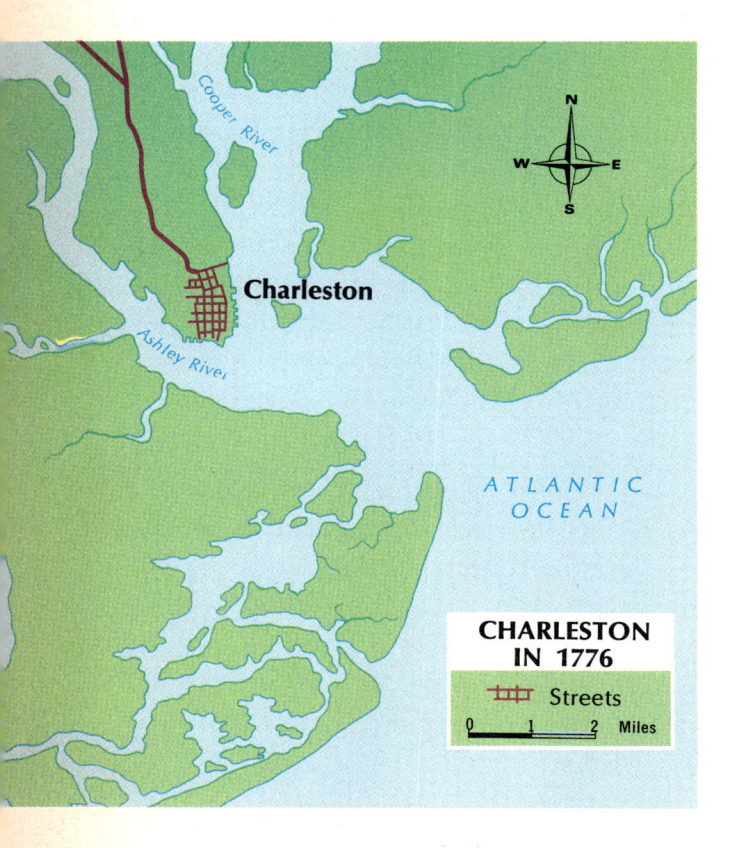

The Public Health

Protecting the health of the community was also a problem for the growing towns. Since people came into daily contact with each other at work, in the market, or simply walking along the streets, disease could spread very quickly.

At one time or another, each of our five seaport towns was struck by a dread disease. Most often it was smallpox, the same disease that had killed so many Indians a few hundred years before. Sometimes it was yellow fever, a disease carried by a certain kind of mosquito (mə skē′ tō).

Steps to control disease. In the 1600's and 1700's, it was not known how people became infected by disease. People then did not know about germs, and certainly they never suspected that yellow fever was carried by a mosquito. It was thought that disease was somehow carried in the air, especially foul-smelling air.

To protect the health of the community, towns passed laws about the disposal of garbage. One of the worst problems arose when butchers threw

160

the unused portions of slaughtered (slô′ tərd) animals into the streets. They soon gave off terrible odors. Towns then required butchers to dispose of these wastes only in places set aside for that purpose. Most of the towns also permitted slaughterhouses to operate only in one small part of town.

Towns had to pass laws about disposing of human wastes, too. In the days before modern plumbing, toilets were located outside of the house. These toilets were simply small wooden buildings that housed an open pit in the ground for human wastes. To protect the community, towns soon required that pits be at least five or six feet deep, and away from public streets or gutters.

None of these attempts at public sanitation were completely successful, and disease continued to strike the towns. But the situation would have been much worse if the towns had not at least made these attempts to protect public health.

One thing that did help the towns in fighting disease was the presence of trained medical doctors. Doctors chose to live where there was a great need for their services, and each large town had a number of them. Some city doctors were beginning to search for ways to fight smallpox.

Crime and police. Growing populations also needed more protection against lawbreakers. Laws were not much good unless people obeyed them. Just as with fire fighting and street building, most towns depended on citizens to provide their services as local policemen. The governments appointed five or ten people to serve for several weeks at a time. Then other citizens would have to take their turns.

Most crimes were committed at night, so the night watch was especially important. Citizens had to take turns doing night watch. The night watchman had a few blocks assigned to him. This area was called his "rounds." During the night he would "walk his rounds," keeping an eye out for thieves and for fire. At the first sign of either, he would shout out an alarm to the sleeping residents. The night watchman also rang a bell every hour and called out the time and the weather. Some of the watchman's duties were to prevent swearing on Sunday, report the names of drunkards, arrest people who smoked outdoors, and report people who threw garbage in the streets.

Most people did not like serving as daytime policemen or night watchmen. They often tried to get out of taking their turns. Walking the dark streets at night, before towns installed street lights, was often dangerous — mostly because of tripping or bumping into things rather than because of criminals. Often citizens did not show up to take their turns. Many of those that did take their turns were not trained for the work. In later times cities realized that they would need to hire specially trained people for police work.

Our cities by 1776. By 1776, when the colonies declared their independence from England, the five towns of Boston, New York, Philadelphia, Newport, and Charleston had become cities. This did not happen in a day, or in a year. The towns had changed gradually (graj′ ủ ə lē), and they had not all grown at the same speed. Philadelphia, which was founded last, grew the fastest. Charleston and Newport grew more slowly than the others. But by 1776, though still quite small when compared to modern cities, they had clearly become cities. Philadelphia, with 40,000 people, was the largest. Then came New York with 25,000, Boston with 15,000, and Charleston and Newport with about 12,000 each.

Why can we call these five communities of 1776 cities? Certainly their age has nothing to do with it. They did not become cities by reaching a certain birthday. Think back to Chapter 7. What did you decide were the special features that made a place a city? Did the five colonial cities have any of these special features? Which ones? Does this explain why we can call them cities?

By 1800 New York was the commercial center of the nation.

Working with Concepts and Generalizations

Identifying Concepts

Use the sketch below to answer these questions. Write the answers on paper.

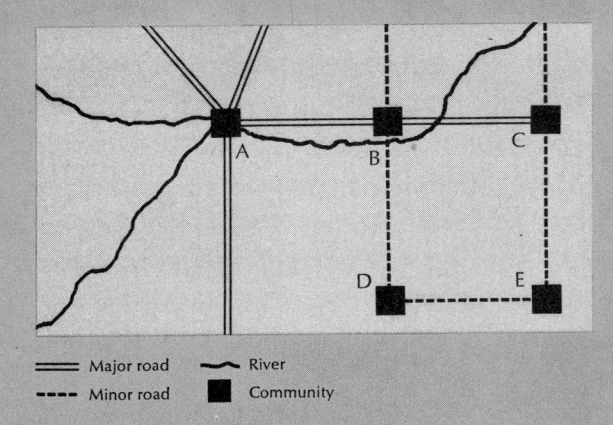

=== Major road ~ River
---- Minor road ■ Community

1. The sketch above shows five communities in the year 1800. Which will grow fastest? Why?
2. Which communities are on a river?
3. Which communities are on a major road?
4. Which communities are on a minor road?
5. Copy the chart below. Fill in the letter of the community that belongs with each set of figures. The first one is done for you.

Community	Population in 1800	Population in 1900
E	500	10,000
	500	100,000
	500	10,000
	500	75,000
	500	50,000

Developing Concepts

Write the answers on paper.

1. Copy the sketch shown on this page. Add one feature that will help Community D grow. Add one feature that will help Community E grow. Explain what each feature will accomplish. Now add one new community to the sketch. Explain why you chose the location.
2. You are a citizen living in Boston in 1773. What are some of your obligations to your community?
3. You finally finish your medical training in 1772. You are now a physician. Where do you intend to settle? Why?
4. You are a citizen attending a town meeting in New York in 1771. What complaints will you bring up at the meeting? Do you think citizens complain about the same things today?
5. You arrive in Philadelphia in 1774. What kinds of jobs are available?

Generalizations

Below are three facts from this chapter. Write one generalization based on these facts. Write on paper.

1. "Almost like magnets these ports (New York, Boston, Philadelphia, Newport, and Charleston) drew the products of nearby villages and farms to their markets."
2. "As commerce increased, the population grew."
3. "As population increased . . . there were enough buyers . . . to support stores that specialized."

My generalization based on these facts is _____

163

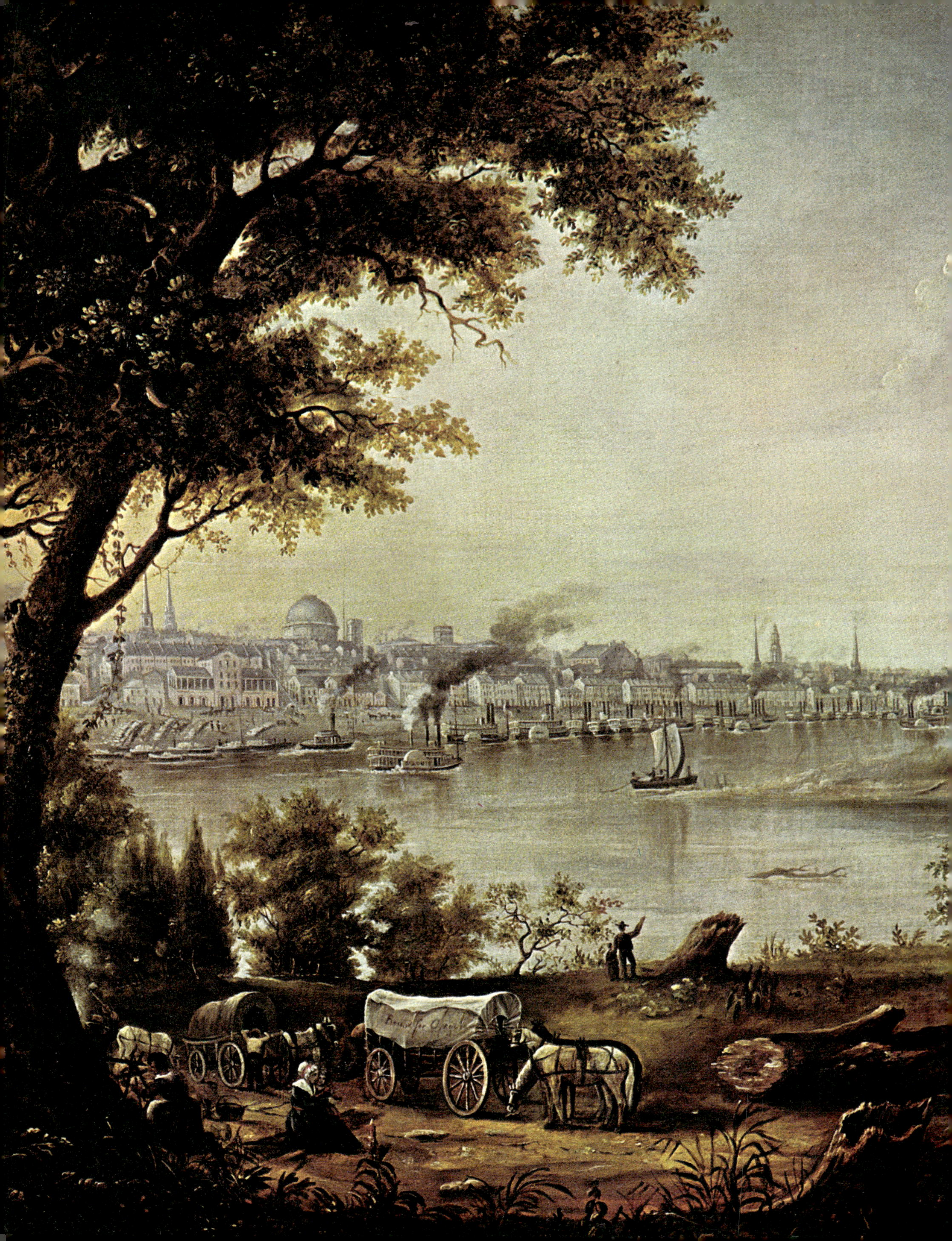

Growth of Cities, 1800–1900

9

As America's population swelled in the century after independence, villages and towns in the East, South, and West grew into bustling cities. So rapidly did some grow that they almost seemed to spring from the soil. Homes, roads, and stores sprouted where a few years before there had been only forest or grassland. By 1900, hundreds of cities had blossomed throughout the nation from the Atlantic to the Pacific Ocean.

Not only were there more cities, but they were also much larger. The small colonial seaport cities of Boston, New York, and Philadelphia grew into large urban centers. In fact, by 1900 America had dozens of cities far larger than Philadelphia, the largest city of 1776. More and more Americans were making their homes in cities.

Most of these new cities were *commercial* (kə mėr′ shəl) *cities*, like the five colonial centers you studied in the last chapter. Later, many became important as manufacturing centers.

Where did these cities grow? Why did they grow where they did? In this chapter you will learn the answers to these questions.

Detail, 170:55, *View of St. Louis, 1846,* Lewis. Courtesy: City Art Museum of Saint Louis

Cities Develop in the West

In the early years of the 1700's a few explorers, hunters, and trappers crossed the Appalachians (ap′ ə lā′-chənz). They returned with reports about the rich land on the other side. The soil was excellent for farming. Farmers would be able to raise more than enough for their families. There was plenty of timber, and herds of buffalo provided a plentiful supply of meat. By the time Americans won their independence from Great Britain, pioneers had begun to settle across the mountains near the Ohio River. This area is known as the Ohio Valley.

Starting inland cities. Farmers were not the only ones to move West. Others went West to start new towns and cities. In fact, very often these people moved to the West before the farmers did. They, too, knew the land was rich. They also knew the population of the United States was increasing rapidly. Very soon, settlers would cross the mountains to farm this fertile area. These farmers would need towns and cities nearby.

The seaport cities on the Atlantic coast were collecting and distributing points, that is, places where European goods were transferred to American soil and American goods were transferred to ships bound for Europe. Inland cities could also be collecting and distributing points. At these places, goods from the western part of America could be gathered for shipment East. Goods from eastern and even European cities could be brought to these places and delivered to people living in the West.

Many of those who wanted to start towns and cities in the West hoped to get rich by speculating (spek′ yə lāt-ing) in land. A *speculator* is a person who buys something cheaply in the hope that he can sell it later for a much higher price. Speculators bought land where they thought a city might develop. Because land was plentiful and not many people wanted it yet, they could buy it cheaply. If the speculators guessed right, a city would develop and their land would become valuable and bring a nice profit.

Where to build towns? Suppose you were a land speculator. What kinds of things would you look for to help you decide where a city might develop?

Page 167 shows you a map of the Ohio and Mississippi river valleys. Study the map, and pick at least seven points where you think cities might grow. Try to recall what it was about the location of the towns of Boston, New York, Philadelphia, Charleston, and Newport that helped them grow into cities. Later on, we will see where some cities actually did grow, and you can compare those places with the ones you chose.

Advertising towns. After speculators bought land, they did not wait around and hope that settlers would come. They tried to get people to move to the sites by advertising or promoting them, just as a manufacturer today advertises his product.

Promoters placed advertisements in the newspapers of larger cities. They usually gave their new town a name like New Athens, New Lisbon, or Palermo (nü ath′ ənz, nü liz′ bən, pə-lėr′ mō), after the name of a famous European city. Why do you think they did that?

Promoters were not at all bashful about telling people what great cities their empty pieces of land were going to become. Here are some of the boasts they made in the advertisements. New Athens, claimed one, was in a "perfect situation, . . . at the confluence [the point where the rivers join] of those majestic rivers, the Mississippi and Missouri, on perhaps the most desirable spot in the known world." Why, a location that good just had to become a great city! Then there was New Lisbon, which was at a fork in the Beaver River in Ohio. An advertisement claimed that there was no better spot in the entire West. Some men bought land at a point where a stream called Swan Creek entered Lake Erie. They called their town Port Lawrence, and advertised that it was certain to become the great collecting and distributing city of the northwest.

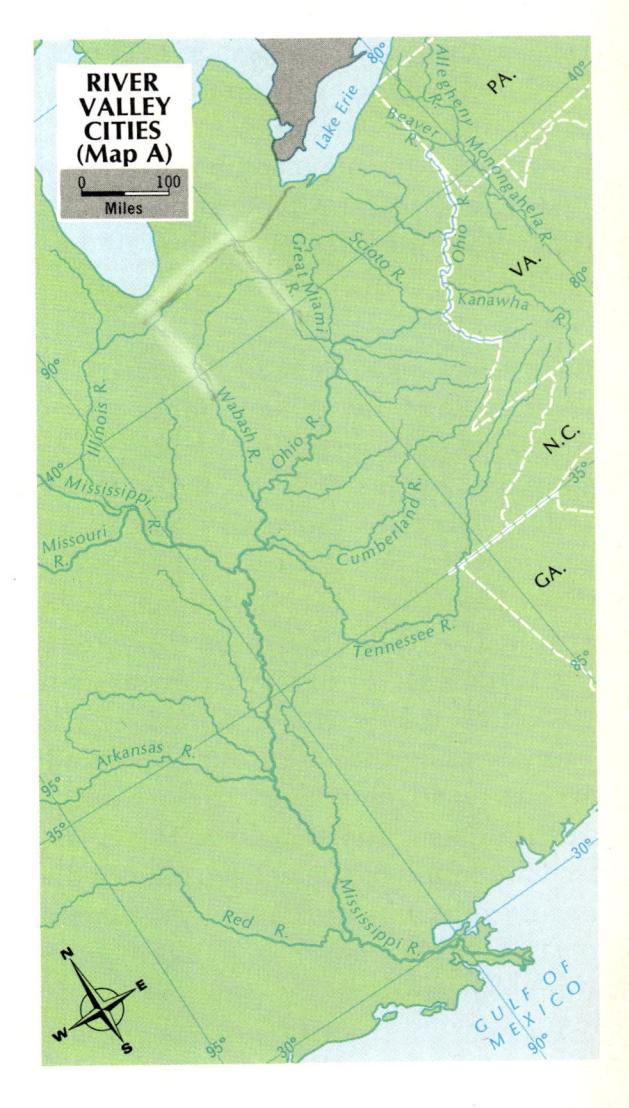

RIVER VALLEY CITIES (Map A)

The biggest, most boastful claims were made by the promoters of a place called Town of America. Town of America was to be located where the Ohio River emptied into the Mississippi River. The farm country nearby was very rich, and it was certain to attract many farmers. In their advertisements, the promoters claimed that of all locations on the entire continent,

167

this spot was most certain to become a very great inland commercial city. This town, they announced, would certainly be among the biggest in America in just a few years. Advertisements like that often persuaded people to buy land.

River valley cities. Several places in the river valleys did become large cities. See if you chose some of these spots for your cities. One of them is St. Louis, which is located four miles south of the point where the Missouri River flows into the Mississippi River. Just a few miles north of this point, the Illinois River joins the Mississippi River. St. Louis was founded by the French when they controlled this land. It was used chiefly as a fur-trading post. Melting snows caused the rivers to flood much of the nearby land in the springtime, but St. Louis was located on land high enough to avoid most of the flooding.

Pittsburgh, Pennsylvania, is another city that grew in the Ohio Valley. Pittsburgh started as a fort at the point where the Allegheny and Monongahela (al ə gā′ nē, mə nän gə hē′ lə) rivers meet to form the Ohio River.

Both St. Louis and Pittsburgh were near fertile land that was soon taken up by farmers. Both of them were also on the main river highways to the West. Pioneers heading toward farmland farther west passed through those cities. Their purchases of food, clothing, wagons, farming tools, horses, and other supplies helped the industries and businesses of Pittsburgh and St. Louis to grow.

The Ohio River is nearly one thousand miles long, and all of it is navigable (nav′ ə gə bəl)—except for one place. There, rapids made the river impossible to navigate most of the year.

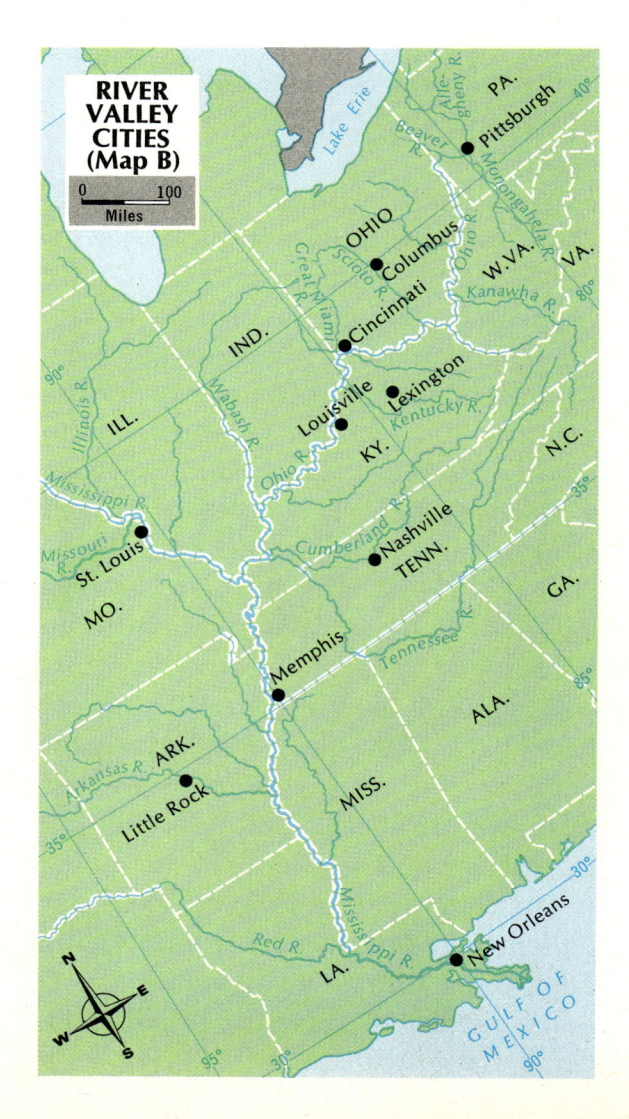

Boatmen had to unload their craft before reaching the rapids, carry their goods by wagon around the rapids, and then reload boats for the rest of the journey south. At this place rose the city of Louisville, Kentucky.

Cincinnati sat between two small rivers that flowed into the Ohio River. Directly across the Ohio from this town, still another river emptied into the Ohio River.

One city, Lexington, Kentucky, was not on a river at all. It was ten miles away from the Ohio, but it stood on one of the main roads that crossed the mountains and connected the Ohio Valley with the cities of the East.

Another important city, New Orleans, had been started in 1718 by the French. It had a fine location on the Mississippi River just one hundred miles north of the Gulf of Mexico. It was already a growing town at the time that New York, Philadelphia, and the eastern seaport communities were becoming cities. At New Orleans, goods were unloaded from the small riverboats and placed in warehouses to await shipment on sailing vessels bound for New York, Philadelphia, Boston, or perhaps even London, England. As more farmers moved into the backcountry and sent their products downriver to New Orleans, the city grew.

Towns that did not become cities. Other locations never became cities in spite of all the advertising of their promoters. For example, there was the

Rivers were natural means of transportation. Towns and cities such as Pittsburgh owed much of their growth to them.

spot where the Ohio and Mississippi rivers meet. Did you choose that for one of your cities? If you did, don't feel too badly. So did many speculators and promoters. That was where Town of America was supposed to become a great city. Nothing ever came of it. What about the point where the Little Miami River meets the Ohio? Or the place where the Great Miami River meets the Ohio? Did you choose either of these? They look like good sites. In fact, towns actually were started in both places. One was named Columbia, and the other, North Bend. Neither of them grew very large. Instead, the city of Cincinnati, which stood between the two river communities, grew.

Why didn't some of these other places become cities? We cannot always be sure of the reasons. Sometimes the actual place was not as good for a commercial city as it appeared to be on the map. In some places the rivers often flooded the land. Another site was perfectly fine, but by the time a town was started, the merchants of a nearby city already had all the business of the farmers in the region.

Probably much depended on the hard work of the people in the town. They had to produce something that people needed. This would help their town become important and grow. Probably luck also played a big part in deciding which spot on the river would become a city of thousands, and which would be a home only for frogs and mosquitoes.

The river cities grow. Rivers are nature's highways. They provide a cheap route for getting farm goods to market. As traffic along the river highways increased, the commercial towns grew. Rafts, flatboats, and keelboats, with their cargoes of goods and passengers, floated downstream from the river towns every day.

But these boats usually were not brought back against the current. Instead, they were broken up at the end of the downstream voyage and used for lumber. Keelboats could make the trip back upstream, but the trip required hard labor by the crew. And it was very slow going. Pushing and towing a boat back upstream from New Orleans to Pittsburgh usually took from four to five months. Struggling against the river currents was not the most pleasant way to spend nearly half a year of one's life. It was much easier to sail around Florida and up the Atlantic coast to Philadelphia and take the wagon road from there to Pittsburgh.

The steamboat. The invention of the *steamboat* changed that. Several inventors built steamboats around 1800, but not many people seemed interested. Then, in 1807, Robert Fulton demonstrated to a crowd of New Yorkers, watching from the banks of the

For years Cincinnati was called the Queen City of the Ohio. The steamboat had much to do with her progress.

Hudson River, that a steam engine could push a boat against the current. It traveled at the amazing rate of five miles an hour! The steamboat was quickly accepted and was soon put to good use.

The steamboat greatly shortened both the downstream and upstream trips on the Ohio and Mississippi rivers. The first steamboat to travel from New Orleans to Louisville made it in twenty-five days. That was about two months less time than the trip had taken before.

As a result, the costs of transporting passengers and goods were lowered. Commerce increased in both directions, and the river towns were well on their way toward becoming booming cities.

Cities Grow Along the Great Lakes

Look at a map of the United States and you will see five large bodies of water to the north. They form a kind of chain along the border between this country and Canada. These are the Great Lakes.

Men built small towns along the shores of the Great Lakes, even before many farmers arrived in the region. These town builders and promoters hoped that their locations would develop into lake ports of great size. Many never did. Remember Port Lawrence, the location that was supposed to become a great city? It did not happen that way. But in time, such cities as Cleveland, Chicago, Detroit, Toledo,

171

and Buffalo did rise on the edge of the lakes.

The Erie Canal. It was the Erie Canal that helped the Great Lakes towns grow into cities. Early in the nineteenth century, New York City, with its magnificent harbor, passed Philadelphia as the largest city in the young nation. Still, New York merchants were anxious to increase their trade.

To provide cheaper transportation for goods and passengers between New York City and the West, the state of New York built the Erie Canal. The canal ran across the state from Buffalo to Albany. From there, boats continued down the Hudson River to New York City.

USING SOURCE MATERIAL

How did the Erie Canal help New York City? Let us see. In 1820 it cost the farmer about $1 to grow a hundred pounds of wheat. He could sell it in any eastern seaport for $1.75. That was a good profit. But the farmer had to pay for shipping the wheat from farm to city. Since transporting wheat by wagon was very expensive, the farmer always tried to save money by shipping to the city closest to him. Look at the map. Would the farmer at point A sell his wheat in New York City, Philadelphia, or Baltimore?

The farmer living near point B had a different situation. He, too,

172

could grow a hundred pounds of wheat for $1, but it would cost him $3 more to ship it by wagon to Albany, and then down the Hudson River to New York City. Do you think this farmer would use his land to raise wheat to sell? Or would he raise just the food his family needed?

The farmer living nearer to point C was able to sell his wheat for a profit, even if he was farther away from New York City than point B. He had another way to get his wheat to market, which was less expensive than by wagon. Can you find it? Using this route, the farmer paid 50¢ for shipping 100 pounds of wheat. Which city did this help to grow?

The completion of the Erie Canal changed all that. It used to take four horses to pull *one* ton of freight by wagon, but the same four horses could tow *one hundred* tons of freight in a canal barge, and do it in half the time. As a result, the cost of shipping a hundred pounds of wheat from Buffalo fell to 30¢. It cost even less from point B, near

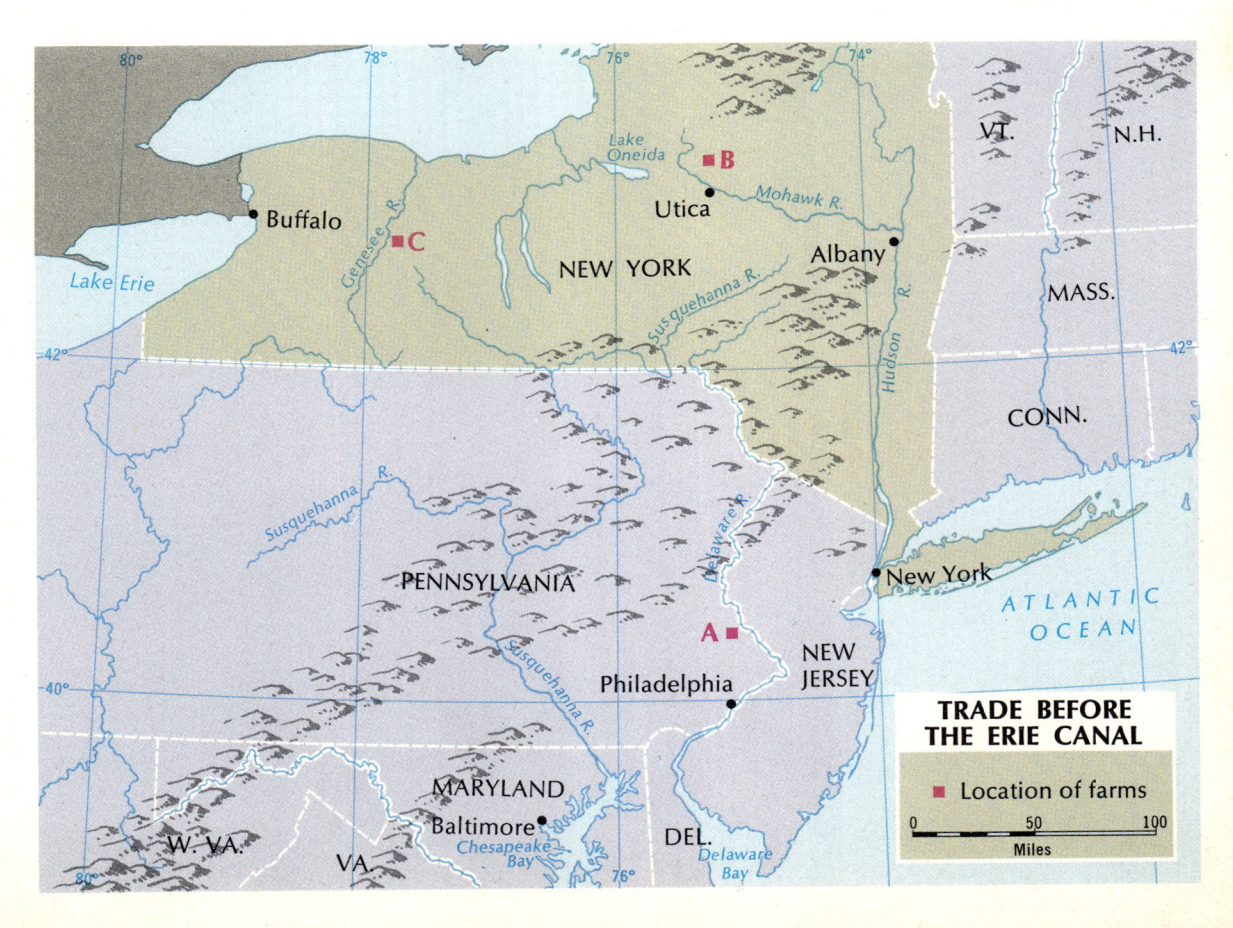

TRADE BEFORE THE ERIE CANAL

■ Location of farms

173

Utica. How do you think the farmer near Utica would use his land then? Why? What route would the wheat farmer near Buffalo use to send his crop to market? Which seaport city would that help to grow?

Helping some lake ports to develop. The Erie Canal helped other cities grow, too. Before the canal was opened, for example, Buffalo had been a small town with a population of about seven hundred. After the canal was completed, the town suddenly became a busy lake port. Buffalo's commerce increased year by year, as ships crossed the lakes to unload their cargo at her docks. Soon Buffalo was shipping millions of barrels of wheat, corn, and flour to New York City. People found employment in loading and unloading canal barges, milling wheat into flour, making barrels, and dozens of other jobs. In a short time, Buffalo was a city of many thousands.

Cleveland, Ohio, is another example of a Great Lakes town that became a big city. As farmers began to settle in the region, the residents of this small village decided to make their town a

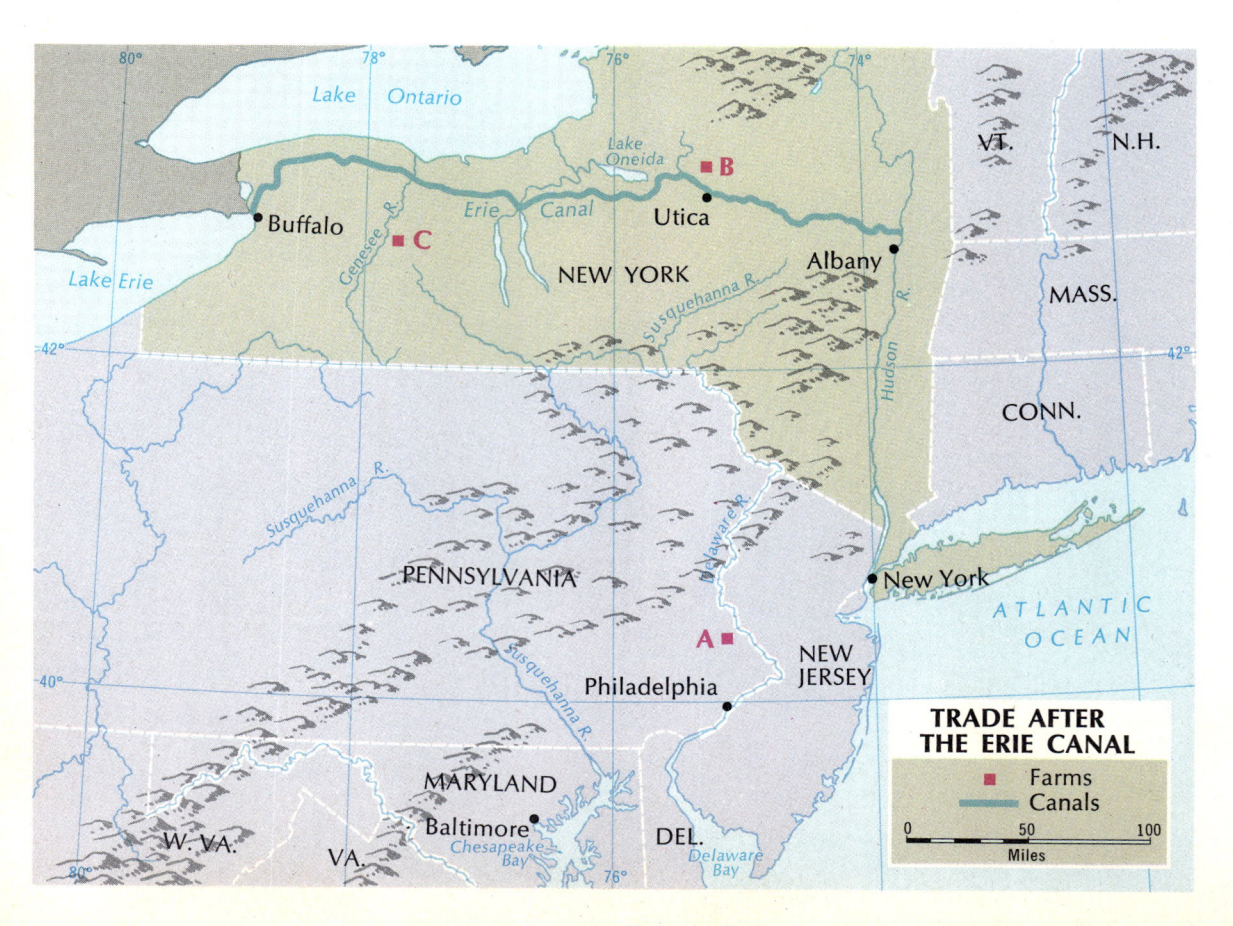

174

marketing center. A road was built from Cleveland to other towns along the Ohio River, where thousands of people had settled. Steamboats began to cross the Great Lakes, stopping at Cleveland. The town's harbor was improved. Despite those efforts, Cleveland still had fewer than a thousand people by 1825.

Then the Erie Canal opened. Cleveland and all the other lake towns were then tied directly to New York City and to Europe by an all-water route. Steamboat traffic on the Great Lakes increased, and the port of Cleveland grew. More and more farmers settled in the area. Cleveland really became a collecting and distributing point. New businesses came, and many new jobs were created. Before long, the town of Cleveland became a city.

The stories of Detroit, Toledo, Milwaukee (mil wô′ kē), and Chicago were all very similar to Cleveland's. Each was only a small community until the Erie Canal made it easier to settle in the West.

Railroads and Cities

Only a few years after the Erie Canal was built, an even more important improvement in transportation came into use in America. This was the railroad.

The railroad had a great many advantages. It could move larger loads than canal boats or steamboats could, and it could move the loads much

Factories lined the Erie Canal at Lockport.

faster. The railroad could be used all year round, including the winter months when canals in the northern states froze over. A canal could be built successfully only on fairly level land. But a railroad could cross hills and valleys, rivers and deserts.

Railroads reach out. It was the merchants of eastern seaport cities who first encouraged the building of railroads into the backcountry. Why do you think they did this?

Railroads soon spread like long fingers from Baltimore, Philadelphia, New York, and Charleston into the farming areas nearby. Two newer seaport cities in the South—Mobile, Alabama, and Savannah, Georgia—also

RAILROADS 1860

tains. In another twenty years, they crossed the Mississippi River. Railroads now connected the East to the cities of the Middle West. They were soon more important highways than the rivers and lakes.

Cities on the plains. As railroads spread farther west, they played the same part in creating cities that harbors, rivers, and lakes had played earlier. There was a big difference, though. Harbors, rivers, and lakes were placed by nature, so that cities only existed where nature allowed them to. Railroads, however, could go almost anywhere that man chose. This meant that cities were now created by man's decisions more than by nature's.

USING SOURCE MATERIAL

On page 177 you will find a map of part of western United States. We will use this map and the one on page 178 to find some reasons why towns were started in this area and why some grew to be large cities.

The map on page 177 shows something about the geography and the resources of the area. The map also shows where towns developed over the past one hundred years or so. Years ago these towns were quite small. Over the years some grew quite rapidly, some slowly, and others not very much. The towns are marked with numerals.

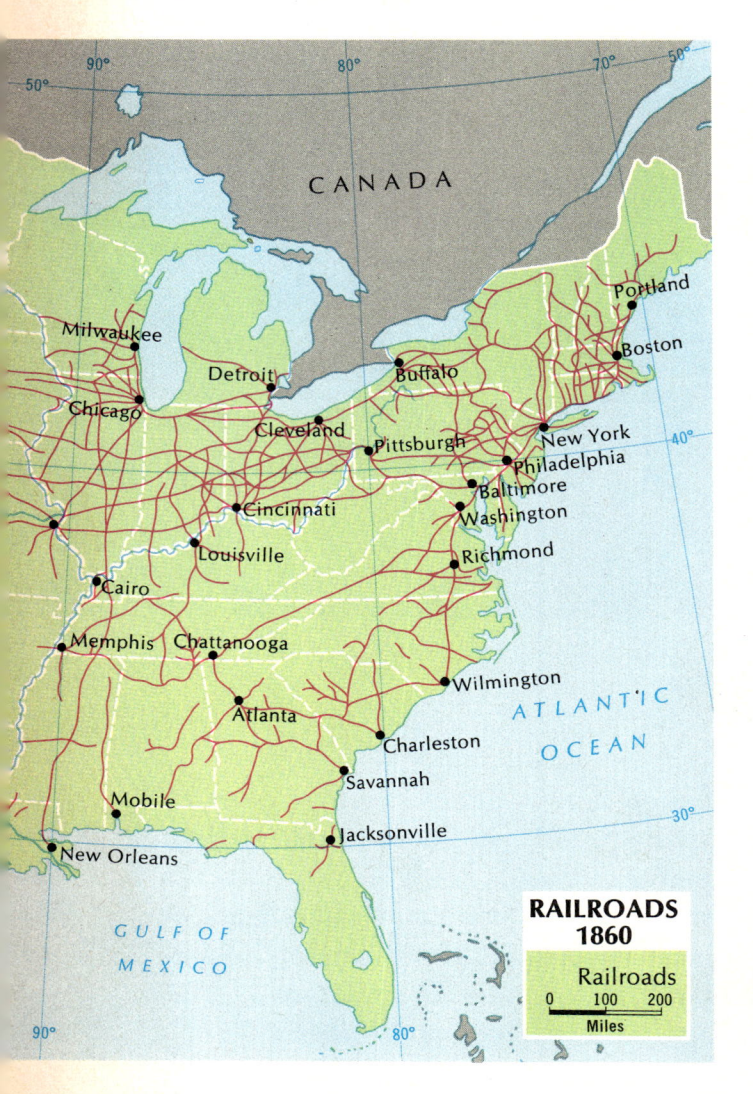

sent railroad tracks into the cotton-growing areas nearby.

Railroad tracks tied cities closer together. The trip from Philadelphia to New York and Boston, which used to take days by horseback, stagecoach, or sailboat, now took only hours by rail.

Each year the railroads pushed farther into the West. By the 1840's, railroads crossed the Appalachian Moun-

Study the map and the location of all the towns. Why do you think these towns are located where they are?

Did you have difficulty in finding a reason for the location of 12, 17, and 19? Certainly this first map does not give us any good reason why these towns started and grew where they did. We shall have to look elsewhere.

Now look at the map on page 178. You will find here the names of those towns that grew into cities. The others are still marked with numerals.

Find locations 12, 17, and 19. What has happened to them? What other information does this map give you? Does this information help to explain why towns 12, 17, and 19 were started in the first place, and why they grew to be large cities? How about 10, 14, and 20?

Denver became a large city. It had a favorable location near minerals and grassland. But take a look at the town marked 11. Does the map give you any reason why Denver became a large city and 11 grew very little?

Probably you decided that the railroad had something to do with the growth of Denver. You were right. But look at your map again. Towns 2, and 9 are also on railroads, but they never became as large as Denver. Can you think of any reasons why some towns on railroads grew into large cities and others did not?

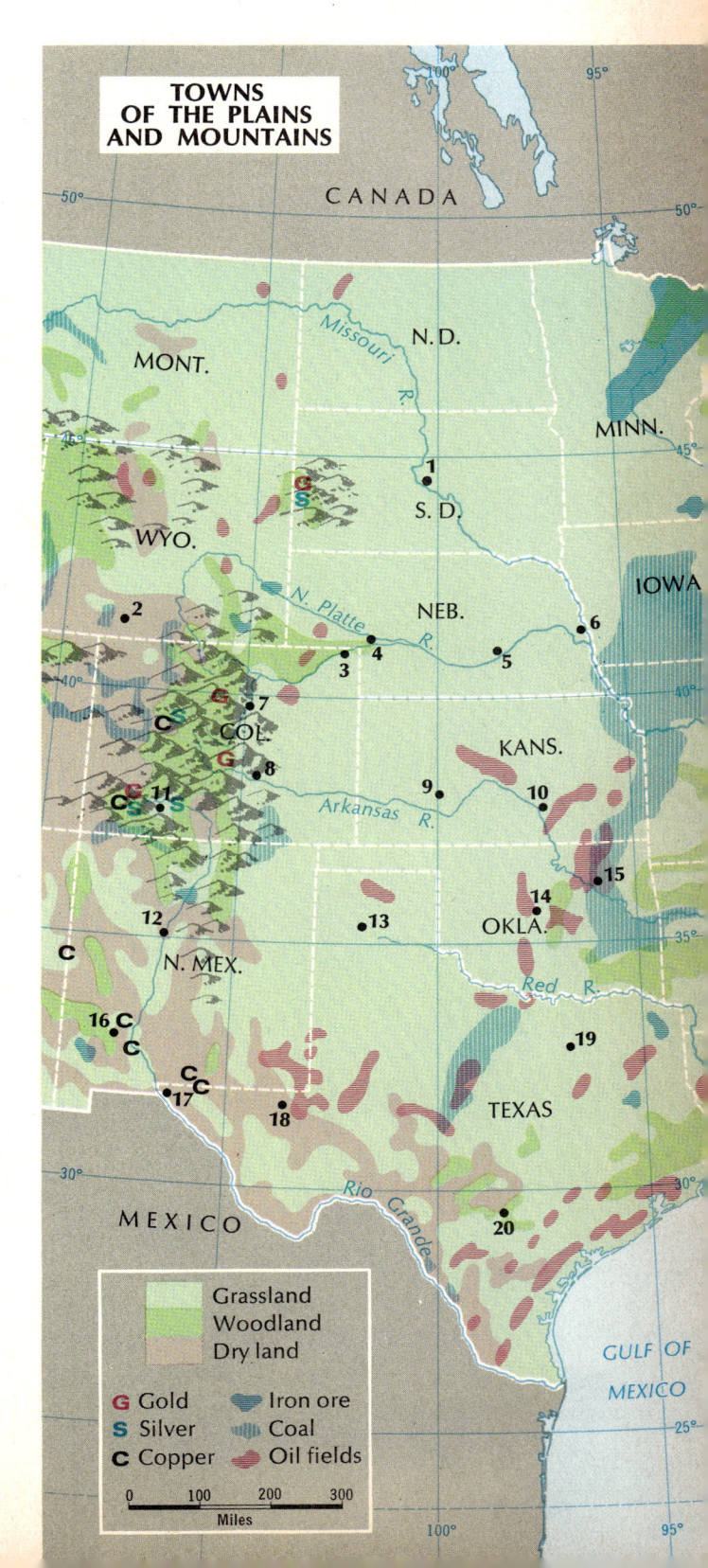

TOWNS OF THE PLAINS AND MOUNTAINS

Legend:
- Grassland
- Woodland
- Dry land
- G Gold
- S Silver
- C Copper
- Iron ore
- Coal
- Oil fields

Scale: 0–300 Miles

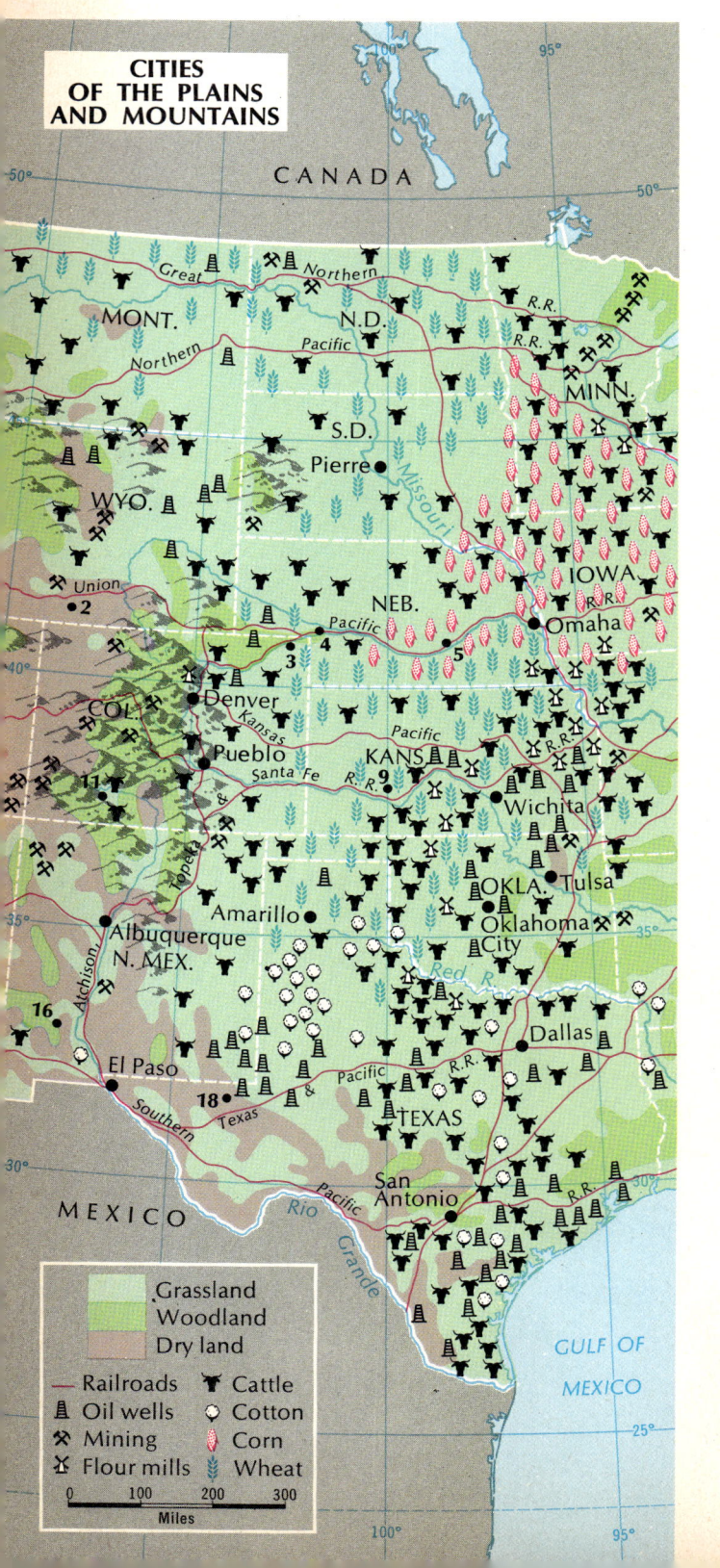

Two cities. Here is an example of how railroads helped cities to grow. Before the railroad came in the 1860's, Kansas City, Missouri, had been a small town of about four thousand people. It was located on a great bend in the Missouri River. Mississippi steamboats stopped here to load and unload goods going east or west. People of Kansas City expected the town to grow but never thought it would become a great city.

Nearby was Leavenworth (lev' ən-wərth), Kansas. Its population was about twice that of Kansas City. Leavenworth was near an army fort, and its merchants sold many goods to soldiers. It was also on the main wagon route to the West and served as a supply center for travelers. Most people at the time thought that Leavenworth would become the largest city in the area.

Leavenworth grew, but it never became a large city. Instead, because of the railroads, Kansas City became the largest in the area. Several companies decided to build their main lines through Kansas City rather than through Leavenworth. Soon railroads connected Kansas City with areas farther west, and with Chicago and St. Louis in the East.

The railroads brought cattle from the Plains to meat-packing plants in Kansas City. Wheat by the carload came to the flour mills. In the twenty years after 1860, the population of the

THE GREAT PLAINS

Find the area on the map marked the Great Plains. As you see, the Great Plains stretch from the Rocky Mountains almost to the Mississippi River. The Plains slope gently to a low point near the great river. The land on the Plains is mostly level, though there are many rolling hills. In an earlier chapter on the Indians, you read about the Great Plains. Do you recall anything about vegetation—grass and trees—on the Plains? What do you know about rainfall there?

West of the Great Plains rise the Rocky Mountains. They form a kind of wall running from southwestern United States through Canada. These mountains and the ranges nearer the coast are the reason the Plains are so dry. Warm, rain-carrying winds from the Pacific Ocean are forced to rise above these mountains. That cools the air and sometimes forces it to give up moisture in the form of rain or snow. When the winds reach the central and southern plains, they are hot and dry. Instead of giving off water, they pick up some water from the land.

Few farmers settled on the Great Plains before 1860. Cattlemen were free to raise large herds, and Indians were free to follow their buffalo. Most of the people going west simply crossed the Great Plains and settled in California and Oregon.

city jumped from 4,000 to 50,000, and by 1900 it reached about 160,000.

Manufacturing Helps Cities Grow

All the earliest cities in the United States, as you have seen, were commercial cities. Trade was the main economic activity—that is, it was the main way of making a living. But in the early 1800's, when sailing ships, steamboats, canals, and railroads were helping older cities grow and creating new ones, another kind of economic activity appeared in America. This activity soon became more important than commerce in the growth of American cities. This activity was *manufacturing*.

Manufacturing for commerce. At first, most of the manufacturing done in cities was connected with commerce, especially the commerce in farm products. This manufacturing was to prepare farm products for shipping. In several seaport cities, like Philadelphia and Baltimore, the milling of

179

Courtesy of the Art Institute of Chicago
Chicago became the railroad center of the United States.

corn and wheat into flour became an important industry. As lands farther west were settled and planted to wheat, the milling was done in nearby cities, like Rochester, Buffalo, Cincinnati, and St. Louis.

Meat was another product that had to be prepared for shipping, and meat-packing became an important industry in several western cities. Cincinnati became famous as a supplier of hog meat. People gave it the nickname of "Porkopolis" (pôr kop′ ə lis) and called it "the pork capital of the world." Later, meat-packing centers arose in the West, closer to the vast cattle herds on the Great Plains.

Factories come to cities. Before long, Americans began to manufacture more goods that were not connected with the trade in grain and meat. For many years, people had made the goods they needed in their own homes. Cotton and woolen textiles, shoes, iron products, watches, guns, and machinery were some of the products that poured out of new factories by the 1840's and 1850's. Factories could sell such goods because the railroad provided fast and cheap transportation. The markets for these goods kept increasing.

Often factories were started in the older commercial seaport cities, like New York, Philadelphia, and Boston. Factories created many thousands of new jobs. People came from the farms and from other countries to take the jobs and live in the city. At the same time, commerce in the port cities was increasing rapidly and providing more jobs. As a result, the population of these older cities grew tremendously in just a short time.

The population table on this page will give you a good idea of how fast some cities were growing, and how large they were becoming. Which city was the largest in 1800? Which was the largest in 1860? Did river cities grow as quickly as ocean ports?

Did you notice any city that did not seem to be growing much at all? What do you think was happening, or not happening, in this city?

Some cities specialize in certain products. Manufacturing sometimes helped to create new cities. Lawrence, Massachusetts, was built entirely for the textile industry. Fall River and Lowell, Massachusetts, changed overnight

The population of some cities from 1800 to 1860

Cities	1800	1820	1840	1860
New York	79,200	152,000	391,100	1,174,800
Philadelphia	41,200	63,800	93,700	565,500
Boston	24,900	43,300	93,400	177,800
Baltimore	26,500	62,700	102,300	212,400
Cincinnati	1,000	9,600	46,300	161,000
St. Louis	1,050	10,000	16,500	160,800
Chicago			4,500	109,300
Charleston	20,500	24,800	29,300	40,500
Newport	6,800	11,800	8,300	9,800

when the textile industry built factories there. Cities became known for the products they manufactured — guns, hats, candles, brassware. Lynn, Massachusetts, became the shoe and boot center of New England. Waltham, Massachusetts, was the center for the manufacture of watches. The leading citizens of Corning, New York, invited glass manufacturers to open a factory in their city. Before long the city was known as "Crystal City." Probably everyone in your class can guess what Hershey, Pennsylvania, became noted for.

Steel was one of the important manufactured products. It helped many cities to grow. The great amount of steel that Pittsburgh produced at the end of the 1800's made that city the industrial center of the nation. In 1865 Birmingham, Alabama, did not exist. By 1900 it was the steel capital of the South. Steel also helped the growth of Great Lakes cities, such as Chicago and Cleveland; Gary, Indiana; and Youngstown, Ohio.

Cities near farming or mining areas specialized in making the tools men needed for those kinds of work. For

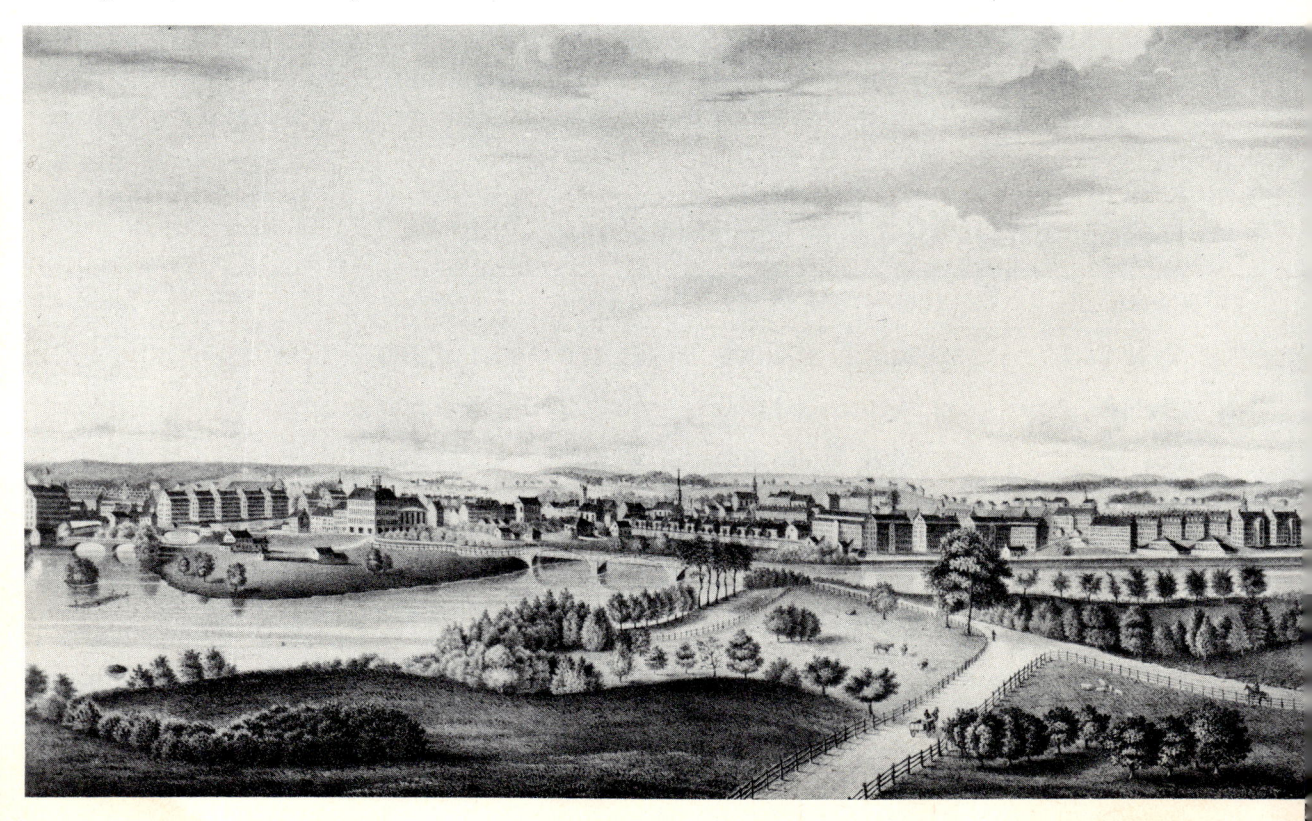

Lowell grew up around its many textile mills.

example, Chicago, which was already a leading commercial and transportation center, became the largest producer of farm machinery. St. Louis, Omaha, and Kansas City, Missouri, also produced farm machinery. After the discovery of oil on the Great Plains, refineries opened in cities in Texas, Oklahoma, and New Mexico. Cities like Houston, Tulsa, and Oklahoma City became oil centers.

Motor city. In 1900 Detroit was a fairly large city of about 250,000. There was a great deal of skilled work going on in Detroit, yet it was a quiet city. Its citizens called Detroit the most beautiful city in America. It was noted for shipbuilding, and for producing ship engines, engine parts, copper goods, stoves, and furniture. Its greatest resource was the skill of its residents.

Then came the automobile. Almost overnight Detroit lost its residential appearance. Sprawling automobile factories were built throughout the city. Many beautiful homes were turned into boardinghouses for the thousands of workers who came to the new plants. By 1920 Detroit was the automobile center of the country. In only ten years its population increased by half a million! Today other cities, like Los Angeles, St. Louis, and Kansas

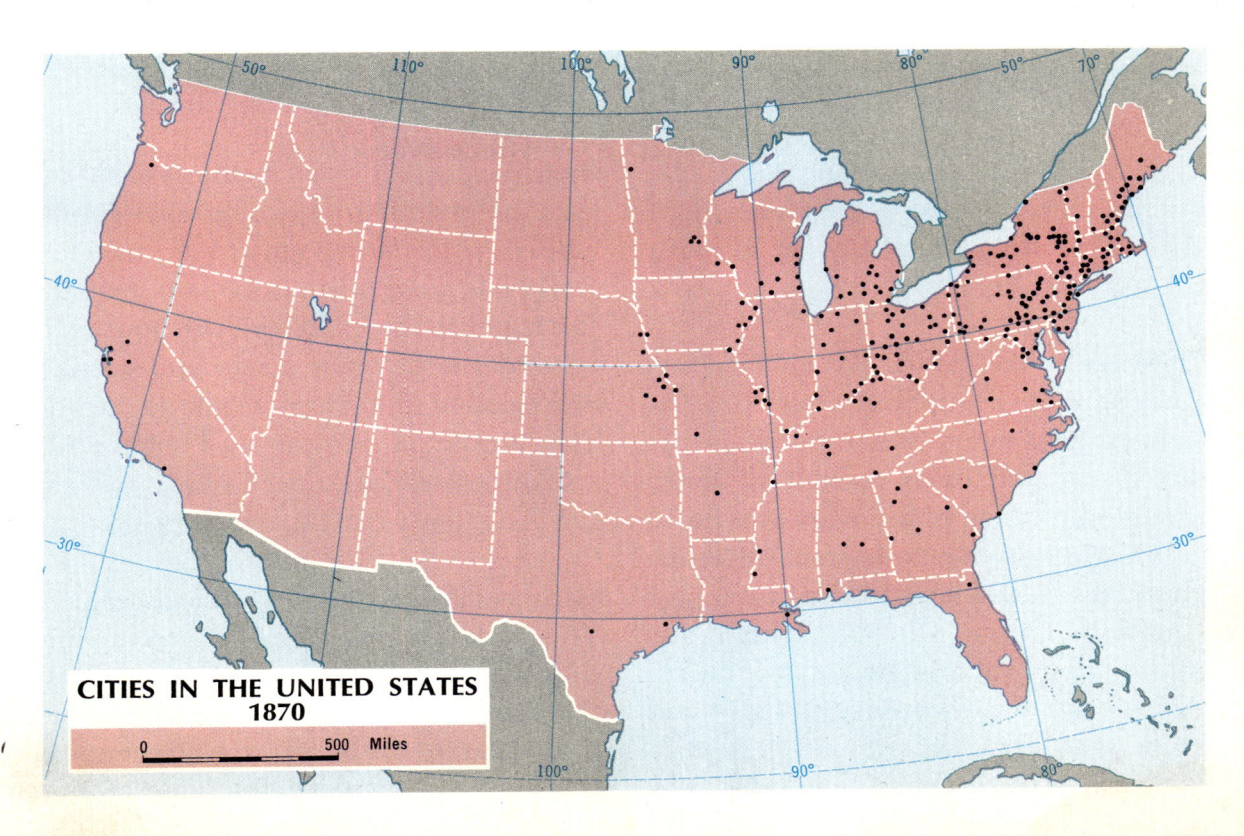

CITIES IN THE UNITED STATES 1870

0 500 Miles

CITIES IN THE UNITED STATES 1900

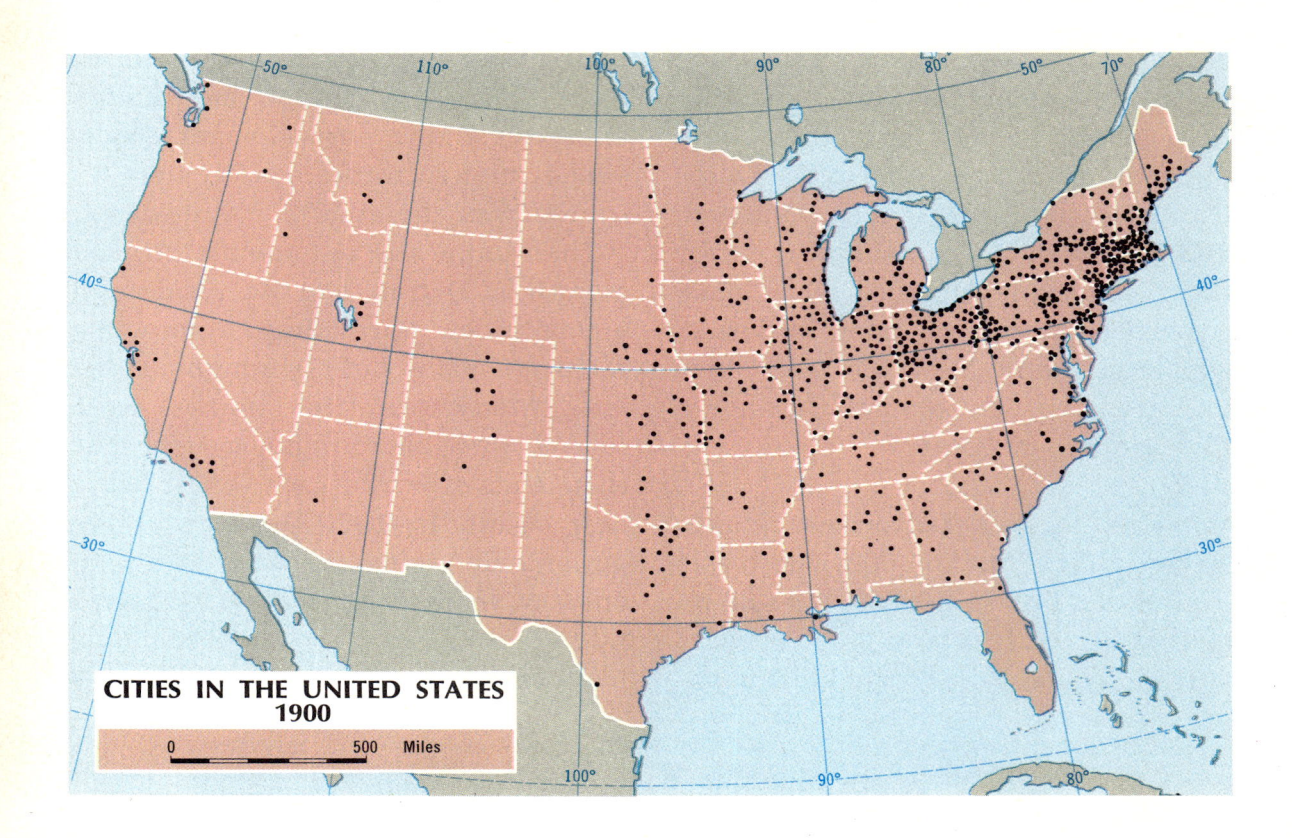

City, make or assemble automobiles, but no city is more closely identified with a product than Detroit is with the automobile.

Cities across the nation. By 1900, cities were spread throughout the entire nation. Almost every one of our present-day cities had been started by then, though of course many were still quite small. Millions of people from different countries in the world were coming to America. Many started farms, but many more were going to cities. American farmers produced more and more food, making it possible to support a large urban population. Manufacturing made new jobs, which in turn helped to make new cities and helped older ones grow bigger. The world's largest railroad system pushed farther into the West and the South. It carried the nation's goods and people and created new cities along its paths. The West was settled, and a flood of settlers poured into such new cities as Los Angeles, Seattle, and Portland.

Maps and charts show spread and growth. The maps about cities tell the story of the spread of American cities and of their increasing size. Look at these maps. Each dot on them represents a city in the United States. One of the maps shows the United States in 1870; the other, in 1900. Compare the 1870 map with the map on page 149 that shows America's cities at the time the United States became an independent nation. What differences do you see? Now compare the 1870 map with the one for 1900. What would you say are the important differences between these two maps? In what part of the nation are most of the larger cities located in 1870?

The table on this page will also tell you some things about the growth of American cities. It is a continuation of the one you have already studied on page 181. That one showed the population of America's largest cities in different years between 1800 and 1860. The table below shows the same thing for the years 1870 to 1900.

What would you say is the most important information this table gives you? Which city is the largest in 1900? Have there been any changes in rank between 1870 and 1900? What would you say has been happening in these cities?

Cities Push Outward

Transportation changes also made it possible for each urban center to spread out over more land and make

The population of some cities from 1870 to 1900

Cities	1870	1880	1890	1900
New York	1,478,000	1,912,000	2,507,000	3,437,000
Chicago	299,000	503,000	1,100,000	1,698,000
Philadelphia	674,000	847,000	1,047,000	1,294,000
St. Louis	311,000	350,000	452,000	575,000
Boston	251,000	363,000	448,000	561,000
Baltimore	267,000	332,000	434,000	509,000
Buffalo	118,000	155,000	256,000	352,000
Cincinnati	216,000	255,000	297,000	326,000
New Orleans	191,000	216,000	242,000	287,000
Detroit	79,000	116,000	206,000	286,000

room for its growing population. This is how it happened.

A city, you will remember, started out as a small settlement. When more people came to live there, the city spread out. After settlement reached about three miles in each direction from the center of the city, something happened. The city stopped spreading. Even though more people kept pouring into the city, the amount of space the city took up did not change much. It just became more crowded.

Inner city transportation. The reason cities stopped spreading is that until the middle of the nineteenth century, American cities were "walking cities." In other words, the main way to get from one place to another was to walk. There were plenty of horse-drawn coaches, of course—enough in some cities to cause traffic jams. Still, most people walked.

When people had to walk, they did not want to be too far from the center of town, for most of them worked and shopped there. A two- or three-mile walk was quite enough. Before the city could spread out farther, there had to be some way of transporting people from place to place faster than they could travel on foot.

The first important improvement in transportation within the city came in the 1830's. This was the horse-drawn street railway car, usually called the horsecar. The horsecar was a long, boxlike vehicle pulled along railway tracks by a team of horses. Each car could carry about fifty people. The tracks were set into the center of the main streets, level with the surface of the street.

Most big cities had horsecars by the 1850's. They could cover about six miles in an hour, while most people could walk only about three or four miles in that time.

The horsecar helped for a while, and soon people were building homes a little farther from the center of the city. But it usually did not take too long for these new areas to be filled with homes. To make room for the thousands of newcomers, the city would have to spread out still farther. This could not be done until some way was found to move people faster than the horsecar could.

Above, on, and under. Several ways were soon found. One new kind of city transportation was the elevated railway, which was nicknamed the "El." In New York, Chicago, and a few other large cities, railroad cars sped passengers along tracks that ran high above the busy streets. Supported by huge steel columns, the El looked like a long, thin bridge stretching for miles.

Els were very much faster than horsecars, but they were very costly to build. They were also noisy and dirty. Warned by the clacking of wheels that an El train was coming, pedes-

By the end of the 1800's, pedestrians in New York had to watch for horse-drawn wagons, trolleys, and soot from the El.

trians took cover to avoid being showered from above by oil or even hot ashes.

An even more important invention was the trolley car. The trolley was simply the old horsecar, using an electric motor instead of horses. It traveled nearly twice as fast as the horsecar. Trolleys were first used in cities in the 1880's. In a very few years, they had completely replaced the horsecar in large cities. They were the main form of passenger transportation in cities.

Just before 1900, engineers in Boston completed a short subway system, the first one in the United States. Soon other cities followed. So, with the subway, the El, and the trolley, passengers were able to move about more quickly under the ground, above the ground, and on the ground.

This allowed cities to spread out farther. Soon homes and apartment buildings were built in fields where corn and vegetables had grown a few years before. Homes eight or ten miles away from the center of the city were now more common.

Suburbs develop in America. These new forms of transportation made it possible for whole new communities to spring up outside the main city. These communities were called suburbs. In earlier years, and through most of the 1800's, only the wealthy could afford to live in the country. But with the improved public transportation, large numbers of people could live in the more open spaces and still be able to get to work, to the shops, and to the entertainment of the city.

These early suburbs did not have industry or commerce. They were places where people lived, not worked. People depended on the city almost entirely for jobs, shopping, entertainment, and nearly everything else.

ANOTHER INVENTION HELPS CITIES GROW TALL

While many inventions allowed the city to grow outward, another invention allowed the city to grow upward. That was the elevator. For some time, people had known how to build tall buildings. But there was not much sense building them if the only way to get to the upper floors was by climbing more stairs.

In 1857, men began experimenting with elevators. In 1889 a safe electric elevator for passengers was invented. Of course, those early elevators were not too comfortable. Here is how a passenger described his trip in one of the speedy new elevators in a Chicago office building in the 1890's.

"The slow-going stranger . . . feels himself loaded into one of those frail-looking baskets of steel netting, and then the next instant the elevator-boy touches the trigger, and up goes the whole load as a feather is caught up by a gale. The descent is more simple. Something lets go, and you fall from ten to twenty stories as it happens. There is sometimes a jolt, which makes the passenger seem to feel his stomach pass into his shoes. . . ."

But in spite of all the bumps and jolts, the elevator did its job. Beginning in the 1880's, tall buildings appeared in New York, Chicago, and a few other large American cities.

Working with Concepts and Generalizations

Identifying Concepts

Read the advertisement below. Then answer the questions that follow. Write the answers on paper.

LAND FOR SALE
in
NEW PARIS, AMERICA
Located where two rivers meet
Future TRADE AND
TRANSPORTATION CENTER
Plenty of GOOD FARMLAND
Perfect building sites for men of
BUSINESS AND INDUSTRY
Future site of RAILROADS AND CANALS
Land going fast — HURRY! HURRY! HURRY!

---

1. List the different kinds of people the advertisement is trying to attract to New Paris.
2. What does the advertisement promise New Paris will become?
3. Why does the advertisement say "Land going fast"?
4. Why does the advertisement point out that New Paris is "located where two rivers meet"?
5. Who is probably selling the land in New Paris?

Developing Concepts

Write the answers on paper.

1. You are a successful businessman. Three companies ask you to lend them money. One company builds canals; one builds steamships; one builds railroads. You can lend money to only one company. Which will you lend money to? Why?

2. You own three pieces of land shown in the sketch below as A, B, and C. You want to sell the land. Write an advertisement for each piece of land, pointing out its best features. Which piece of land will you be able to sell most easily? Why? Which piece of land will it be difficult to sell? Why?

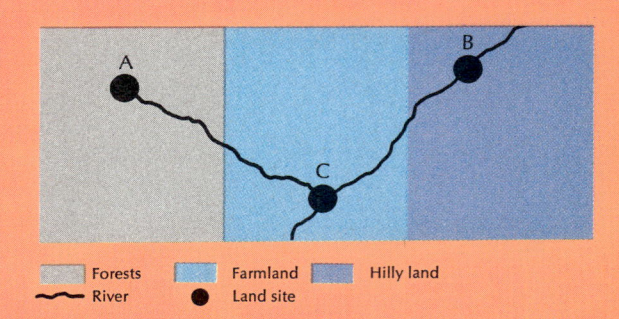

□ Forests　■ Farmland　■ Hilly land
〜 River　● Land site

3. List the improvements in transportation that helped cities grow. Write a brief description of each transportation improvement on your list or draw a simple sketch.

Generalizations

The statement below is taken from this chapter. Read the statement carefully. Think about what it tells you. Then write one generalization based on this statement. The generalization you write should tell something about man's use of technology.

"Harbors, rivers, and lakes were placed by nature, so that cities only existed where nature allowed them to. Railroads, however, could go almost anywhere that man chose. This meant that cities were now created by man's decisions more than by nature's."

My generalization based on this statement is _____

_____

WESTERN UNION TELEGRAPH CO.
JEWELRY
179
S.F. MYERS & CO.
LITH
WATCHES
JEWELERS
CO.
PETERSON & ROYCE DIAMONDS
189
PETERSON & ROYCE DIAMONDS
BIGLEY & CONWAY MERCHANT TAILORS
S.F. MYERS & CO. WATCHES 179
DUNLAP & CO. 181
ROGERS PEET & CO CLOTHIERS
HENRY L. SANDERS MERCHANT TAILOR 175
DELIVERY WAGON
BROADWAY
MARVIN SAFE CO.
MARVIN SAFE CO 265 BROADWAY
K. RADLER
GOLD RINGS & LOCKETS 179 BROADWAY
SOLID GOLD RINGS
FACTORY
HUDSON & FARNUM
196
THOS. F. ARNOLD SUCCESSOR TO ARNOLD & WEBSTER BAND RINGS
194
BLISS & MASON
INGRAM & CO.
THE S.A.L. BRO CO.
S.K. MERRILL
PLAINVILLE STOCK CO.
HAMILTON & HAMILTON JR 176
MARX & WEIS 180
ALFRED H. SMITH & CO. DIAMONDS LONDON
DENNISON
HAMILTON & HAMILTON JR
LINK & CONKLIN
POTTER & BUFFINTON
RICHMOND & CO.
FOSTER & BAILEY 178
176
BROAD WAY
CROUCH & FITZGERALD
TRUNKS SAMPLE CASES

10

Life in the City by 1900

In Chapter 9 you learned about the amazing growth and spread of cities throughout America in the 1800's. But the story of cities is more than the story of canals, railroads, factories, and trolley cars. It is also the story of people. This chapter tells their story—who came to the city and where they came from, why they moved to the city, and what kind of life they found there. It also tells of some of the many ways in which moving to the city changed their ways of living.

As you learn what life was like in an American city of 1900, compare it with what you know about life in a colonial city. In what ways was life similar, and in what ways different? Were city problems the same, or different? Later you will be able to compare cities and city life in the 1700's and in 1900 with cities of today. As you make these comparisons, you will be adding to your understanding of the idea of a city.

You will be reading from the letters and other writings of actual people of 1900 who moved to the cities. Some of these people were Americans, but many moved from other countries and became Americans. You will find out what they thought life in the city and in America would be like before they moved. You will also discover whether life in America was as they expected it to be.

People from the Farms

Why did so many Americans decide to leave the farms and villages to live in the cities? People often tell their reasons for doing something in letters and other writings like books or diaries. Because these writings are an important source of information to us, we call them *source material*. Let's read some source material written by people who moved to the city and find their reasons for moving.

USING SOURCE MATERIAL

The paragraphs below are from the life story of a writer named Hamlin Garland. As you read before, Hamlin grew up on a farm in the Midwest, but later moved to the city. There he became a famous author. In this part of his story, Hamlin tells about returning to his tiny village for a visit with his friends. He has just told them about his own life in the city. Now he writes about how they felt and what they said after listening to him.

Men who were growing bent in digging into the soil spoke to me of their desire to see something of the great eastern world before they died. Women whose eyes were faded and dim with tears, listened to me with almost breathless interest whilst I told them of the great cities I had seen, of the wonderful buildings, of theaters, of the music, of the sea. Young girls expressed to me their longing for a life which was better worth while, and lads, eager for adventure and excitement confided to me their secret intention to leave the farm at the earliest moment. "I don't intend to wear out my life drudging on this old place," said Wesley Fancher with a bitter oath.

What does this part of Hamlin Garland's autobiography tell us about why some people left the farm for the city?

Black farmers hoped to find opportunities in cities.

Southern Black Farmers

Among those who moved from the farms to the cities were many black

Americans. As slaves, most blacks lived in rural areas of the South. When slavery ended in the United States after the Civil War, they hoped that their conditions would improve. Most were disappointed.

Very few of the former slaves could afford to buy good land for farming. So they worked as laborers on other farms for low wages. They had few chances to go to school and learn other skills. Although many stayed on the farms, some began to move into the southern cities. Even there they found it hard to find well-paid jobs.

After 1900 many blacks tried to find a better life by moving to northern cities. There they joined others who had lived as freemen in northern cities for many years.

USING SOURCE MATERIAL

The following accounts give you some idea of what the southern blacks were thinking in the 1890's as they decided to move to northern cities. Here is what one man said.

I began to see that wages were better up North. Letters from friends caused me to ask myself the question: "Well, if they can do that well, why can't I?"

In the 1890's the wife of a former southern black farmer was asked how she felt about leaving the farm with her husband. She and her husband had lived on an island off the coast of South Carolina. They moved to Harlem in New York City. She had this to say:

People don't leave the Island because they want. It's because they can't make a living there. I would like to live down there, but to live down there now, you have to have some kind of a little business besides farming. . . . Naturally people are going to move. Then when they go back down there, everything seems so dull, they just don't like to stay there.

Would you say these farmers moved to a city for the same reasons as Garland's friends, or for different reasons?

Blacks had other reasons for moving to northern cities and away from southern farms. For example, few white farmers could have written the following letter. It is from a woman who left the South in 1895, and it tells quite a bit about the feelings of black people.

. . . since I moved away and had my eyes opened I've just got disgusted with the merciless treatment the folks get down there. They work hard, and get nothing for it. Of course, they get enough to eat, but people want to have a little extra. Of course the old people are used to their fare, and they never leave, but the children won't stand for the situation down there. One of them leaves and writes back about his job, his pay, the city. . . . I never could see why the white people in the South want to keep their feet on the necks of the blacks. They want the Negroes to stay down there, but they want them to stay down. They don't give a good man a chance.

Does this writer have a special reason for preferring the northern city to the southern farm?

Here is a letter written by a southern black who moved to Philadelphia in 1917.

Well, Dr., with the aid of God I am making very good. I make $75 per month. I am carrying enough insurance to pay me $20 per week if I am not able to be on duty. I don't have to work hard. Don't have to mister every little white boy that come along. . . . I can ride in the electric street and steam cars anywhere I get a seat. . . . If you are first in a place here shopping you don't have to wait until the white folks get through trading. Yet amid all this I shall ever love the good Old South and I am praying that God may give every well wisher a chance to be a man regardless of his color. . . . Well, Dr., when you find time I would be delighted to have a word from the good old home state.

If you had been a southern Negro and received this letter, would you be interested in moving north?

People Come from Other Lands

Millions of people poured into America's cities from other countries. Many immigrants, you will remember, moved right to the countryside, and took up farming on the rich land in the West. However, most settled in the cities, especially such large ones as New York, Boston, Philadelphia, and later, Chicago. Toward the end of the 1800's, they poured into the cities by the millions. In 1900, there were more Italians living in New York City than in any city in all of Italy except Rome, the capital. And more Irish than in any city in Ireland except Dublin. And more Germans than in any city in Germany except Berlin. And more Greeks than in any city in Greece except Athens. And more Jews than in any city anywhere in the world. All these people living in New York City at the very same time!

One of the most important reasons why immigrants came to the cities was jobs. Most immigrants were poor and needed jobs right away. Even though many were farmers and had no special skills, the city had all sorts of jobs for them. Other immigrants had lived in cities and towns in Europe. When they reached America, they wanted to follow the same kind of life.

USING SOURCE MATERIAL

Here is part of a letter from an immigrant to his friends back in Europe. It helps to explain another reason why immigrants stayed in cities. This man had traveled from

Norway with many other Norwegians, who were planning to become farmers in Minnesota. After landing in Canada and journeying as far as Chicago, the man tells what happened.

Late in the afternoon we arrived in Chicago, a very large city. Those who had no money could go no further. Almost half of them remained here.

Most immigrants arrived in the large seaport cities. Does this letter suggest to you one reason why many of them settled in those cities?

Sometimes the letters home told tall tales about what American cities were like. Many years after he came to America, a Polish immigrant recalled some of the stories he had heard about American cities while he was still in Poland.

The stories about America . . . were mostly fantastic. For instance, all one had to do was to walk along the streets with a shovel in one's hands and gather as much money as one pleased. The streets were covered with plush rugs.

Do you think you might have believed a story like this about another country somewhere in this world? Could you believe there might be a little truth in it?

Here is another reason why many immigrants decided to live in the crowded cities of America. Perhaps you will understand it, as you read

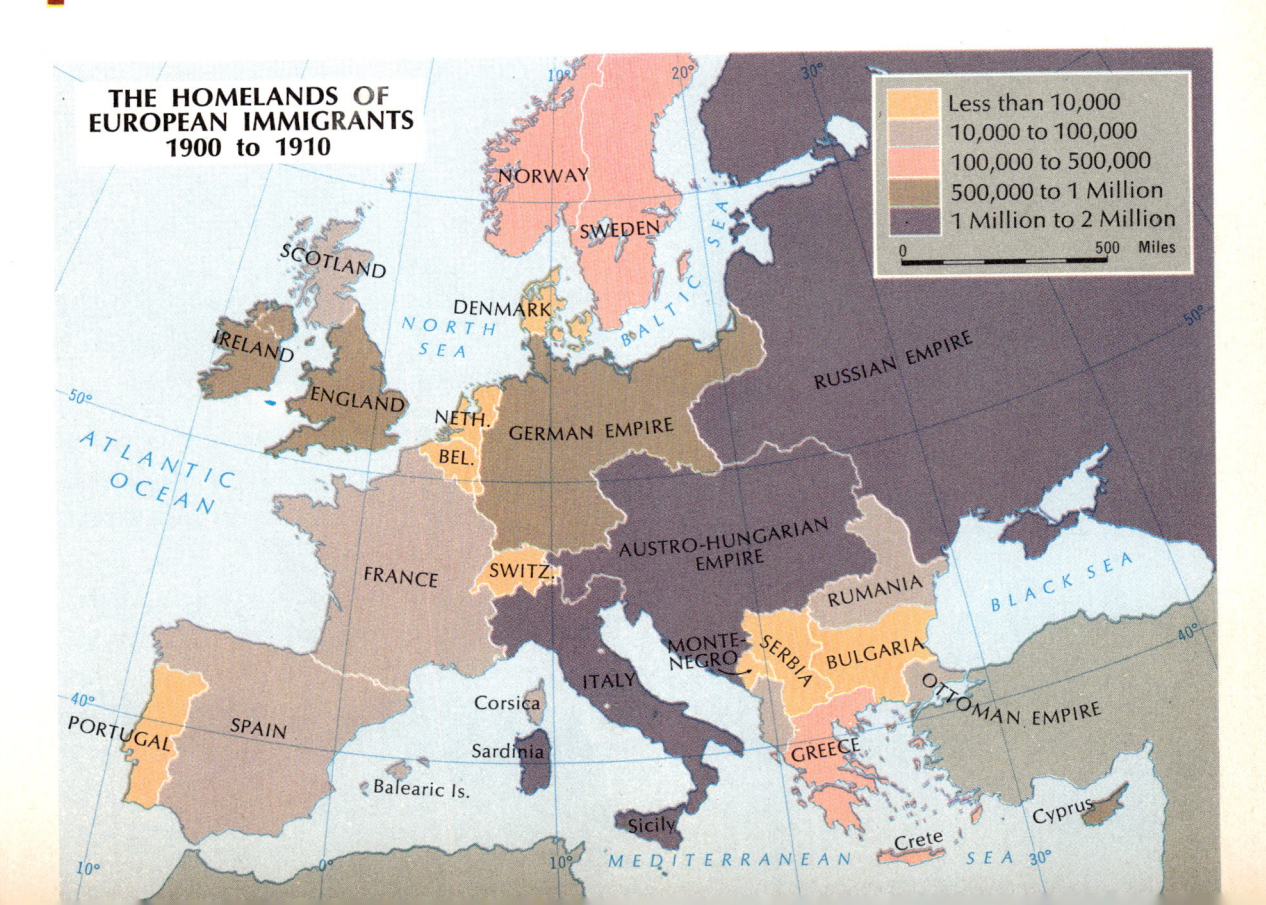

THE HOMELANDS OF EUROPEAN IMMIGRANTS 1900 to 1910

Less than 10,000
10,000 to 100,000
100,000 to 500,000
500,000 to 1 Million
1 Million to 2 Million

Many Italian immigrants came to Mulberry Street in New York.

what one Italian immigrant remembered about his youth in Rochester.

Most of my relatives lived in one neighborhood, not more than five or six blocks from each other. That was about as far apart as they could live without feeling that America was a desolate and lonely place. If it could have been managed, they probably would have lived under one roof.

What do you think he meant when he said that unless his relatives lived close together they would feel America was a lonely place? Does this fit in with what you already know about how people cling to their familiar cultures? Does this help you to explain why American cities had neighborhoods made up mostly of Italians, or Irishmen, or Germans, or Jews, or Poles?

There were other reasons why whole neighborhoods of immigrants developed. For one thing, most immigrants were poor, as you have seen. They could not afford very good housing, and so they clustered together in the poorer sections of town. But even when they could afford better housing, immigrants often found that people in the other parts of the city refused to rent to them. These people did not want to live near others they regarded as "different" and "strange."

A Changing Way of Life

Whether farmers came from parts of America or from European countries, they found that living in a city was different from rural living. Of course, by now you know many of these differences. Newcomers to the city found there were many more laws that told them what they must and must not do. There were laws about traffic, about building houses, about preventing fire, about getting rid of garbage, about using public buildings and parks. Why must cities have such laws?

People also found that city governments did many jobs that people in rural areas did for themselves. Cities provided for protection against fire by hiring and training firemen and supplying them with fire-fighting equipment. City governments had water brought into the city from distant points and made sure that it was clean. They provided for disposing of trash and garbage.

Change in daily living. People who moved from farm to city found their daily life changed in many important ways. For women, life in the city was not quite so hard as life on a farm. A mother found that many of her tasks could be done by walking to neighborhood stores. There she could buy meats, canned goods, baked goods, and ready-to-wear clothing. Water faucets and gas stoves meant no more hauling of water and firewood. After 1900 many inventions like washing machines, electric irons, and vacuum cleaners made housework easier. Women had more time to talk with neighbors, visit shops, or join clubs. There were many more places of worship in cities, and mothers had no great difficulty in getting their families off to services. Women could get jobs outside the home and help the family income.

The other members of the family found their lives changed also. Fathers and sons had different jobs, often at opposite ends of the city. Children made new friends in the neighborhood and spent less time with their brothers and sisters. They went to different schools and had different teachers.

The only time the family was together was perhaps at a hurried breakfast or at the evening meal after the long workday. Even then they were not always together for long. In the evening there was always some activity or form of entertainment in the city. Often the members of the family stayed home just long enough to eat dinner, before boarding a trolley or walking downtown.

Days were longer in the city. You may recall that on the farm, nature played

Central Park in New York gave residents the opportunity to relax and enjoy the company of friends.

a big role in deciding what people did and when they did it. Darkness and light were very important. In the city, nature still counted, but it counted far less. Do you think, for instance, that the different seasons would change the kind of work done by a factory worker, or a clerk, or a secretary?

At first, sunrise and sunset marked the beginning and the end of a city workday. Then factories, shops, and offices began to use man-made light. First came the gas light. Later, toward the end of the nineteenth century, came electric light, which was even better. Now the lives of the people in a city did not depend so much on sunup and sundown. Of course, on rainy and snowy days, people in the city were still very much aware of nature.

Many more people. Another difference between life on the farm and life in the city was the number of people one dealt with every day. On a farm a person might not see people outside his own family for days or weeks at a time. Those he did see were farmers like himself. City dwellers came into daily contact with dozens of people who did many kinds of work. They might be from the same neighborhood or from the same factory. Some might be wealthy, others poor. Some might be well educated, some not so well educated.

Of course, that did not mean everyone in the city had all those friends. Things were not the same as in a small village, where people usually knew each other from childhood and shared many experiences. Many of those who moved to cities found that although they saw dozens of people each day, they really did not know many of them. They discovered it was possible to be surrounded by people all day and yet be very lonely.

Remember, we said another word for "way of living" was culture. We can say that farmers left a rural culture and now had to change their ways to live in an urban culture.

What the Newcomers Found in Cities

To some newcomers, the city offered much of what they were looking for. They found they still had to work hard, but the rewards were worth it. For others the city offered more of the poverty, misery, and ugliness they had tried to escape.

Opportunities and excitement for some. Some of those who moved to cities found jobs, opportunities, excitement, and even wealth. Very few became rich, but many earned a fairly good income, especially those whose skills were needed. Those people found it easier to get used to the way of living in a city.

There was much about life in a city to make it pleasant, exciting, and comfortable. Throughout the cities there were fine residential sections a short distance from the commercial or industrial centers. Many beautiful homes or apartments were not too expensive to rent. Many homes had a special style of architecture (är′ kə tek′ chər) that is still admired today.

All cities had busy main streets lined with large stores, shops, places of business, hotels, restaurants, and places of entertainment. It was always fun to walk down the streets and window-shop.

Special points of interest, particularly in large cities, were often set off in little parks or on squares. Fine-looking City Halls and public buildings were the pride of these cities. Only in cities could so many magnificent places of worship be seen just a short distance from each other. And just about every city had its museums (myü zē′ əmz), art galleries (gal′ ərēz), concert halls, and fancy theaters. Only in a city were there enough people to visit or use such buildings.

Newcomers found the city offered many forms of entertainment or enjoyment. Where else but in a city could one watch great sporting events?

Even school hours were more interesting and pleasant for most city children. City schools were large and well built. Some had their own playgrounds and gymnasiums (jim nā′ zē əmz). City schools introduced new subjects and new methods of teaching. City colleges were available for the older youths.

Many of the immigrants and newcomers from the farms contributed to the development of the city. Neighborhoods adopted immigrant customs and holiday celebrations, which gave variety to the city. Hardworking immigrants opened shops and restaurants that attracted people from all over the city. Artists, sculptors (skulp′ tərz), and architects from other countries helped make cities more interesting and beautiful by their paintings, statues and monuments, and architecture.

Not so attractive for others. For many others, the way of living in a city was difficult. Some of the farmers who came to cities found they could not get jobs after all. Southern blacks found only the lowest-paid jobs open to them. They had received little education in the South and only a few had the skills that brought good wages. Those who had the skills were often not hired anyway. Very few, rich or poor, could rent decent homes.

Immigrants met different problems. They found it difficult to get jobs when they did not know the language. Many walked the streets for weeks looking for work and sometimes looking for a home.

Most of the newcomers, both white and black, increased the number of the city's poor. They made up a large part of the city's population. For them, the city was not a place of excitement, opportunity, and hope, but a place of hard work and bad living conditions. They could afford few of the pleasures of city living. Usually the only side of city life they knew was the noise, the traffic, and above all, the crumbling, crowded housing.

Housing for the poor. The population of American cities grew so fast that it was difficult for new housing to keep up with it. The poor, of course, had the worst housing. They crowded into the center of the city because they had to be within walking distance of their jobs.

Some of the poor looked for empty lots near the center of the city. They put together crude dwellings made of pieces of wood, cardboard, and any other material they could find. These shelters were called *shanties* (shan′ tēz). Nearly every American city in the nineteenth century had at least one shantytown. On page 201 is a picture of one of New York's shantytowns in the 1870's.

Other poor people crowded into unused warehouses. Most, however, lived in the old run-down apartments that no one else wanted to rent anymore. Areas crowded with these buildings came to be called *slums*.

The people in these shanties near Central Park in New York had few comforts and little time for relaxation.

People Describe Slums

There is much good source material that tells us how the poor lived in America's cities in the nineteenth century. For instance, here is part of a report written by a group of people who investigated New York City's slum conditions in 1857.

> We could tell of one room, twelve feet by twelve, in which were five resident families comprising twenty persons of both sexes, and all ages, with only two beds, without partition or screen, or chair or table; ... of another apartment, still smaller, ... inhabited by a man, a woman, two girls, and a boy: ... of another, an attic room, seven feet by five, containing scarcely an article of furniture but a bed, on which lay a fine-looking man in a raging fever, without medicine, drink, or suitable food, his toil-worn wife, ... and his little child asleep on a bundle of rags in the corner.

This same group of investigators described the buildings they visited. They saw

> ... dark, narrow stairways, decayed with age, reeking with filth, overrun with vermin; the rotted floors, ceilings begrimed, and often too low to permit you to stand upright, the windows stuffed with rags.

The living room in a slum tenement served many purposes.

Living conditions for the poor were not much different in other cities. Stories have come down to us about very bad conditions in almost every large city. Some even told of cows and pigs sharing the same shanty with families.

Little improvement by 1900. Conditions were no better by 1900 than they were in 1850. They may even have been worse. Look at this report about Boston's poor in the 1890's:

> Among the places we visited were a number of cellars or burrows. We descended several steps into dark, narrow passageways, leading to cold, damp rooms, in many of which no direct ray of sunshine ever creeps. We entered one room . . . we found a mother and seven boys and girls, some of them quite large, *all sleeping in two medium sized beds in one room;* this apartment is also their kitchen.

Jacob Riis (rēs) wrote a book in 1890 that described the life of the poor in New York City. In one part, he wrote about their homes. He wrote as though he were taking you, the reader, on a visit through the slum building with him. Here is his description:

> Be a little careful, please! The hall is dark and you might stumble over the children pitching pennies back there. . . . Here where the hall turns and dives into utter darkness is a step, and another, and another. A flight of stairs. You can feel your way if you cannot see it. Close? Yes! What would you have? All the fresh air that ever enters these stairs comes from the halldoor that is forever slamming, and from the windows of dark bedrooms. . . . That was a woman filling her pail by the hydrant you just bumped against. The sinks are in the hallway. . . . Here is a door. Listen! That short hacking cough, that tiny, helpless wail—what do they mean? . . . The child is dying with measles. With half a chance it might have lived. But it had none. That dark bedroom killed it.

Poor Conditions Help Spread Disease

It is not surprising that poor people, living in such dreadful conditions, often fell victim to disease. Many died, especially infants. In Holyoke (hōl′-yōk), Massachusetts, in the 1870's, one out of every three babies born did not live to see its first birthday. In one very poor section of Chicago some years later, more than half the babies died in their first year of life.

The problem of disease was especially serious for the poor, but it was shared by other residents of the city also. Germs did not care whether they struck the rich or the poor.

Poor sanitation. A big reason for the disease and many early deaths was the unsanitary conditions of the city. Most cities did not have any sewer systems for disposing of human wastes until late in the 1800's. Cities that had systems had poor ones. Usually they simply carried the sewage into a stream, where it polluted the water.

In the little city of Holyoke, Massachusetts, where so many infants died, the main sewer pipe dumped waste into the river near the pipe that drew the city's water supply. Little wonder that tragedy visited the city so often.

Garbage was another problem that few cities dealt with properly. Most still relied on hogs and dogs to get rid of garbage. In Charleston, South Carolina, vultures—large birds that feed on dead animals—were so important for getting rid of garbage that the city passed a law forbidding hunters to shoot them.

New York City, the nation's largest city, was no better. The filth in its streets made a fine feeding ground for rats that roamed the city and sometimes attacked people. A man who had once served as mayor of New York wrote that his city was one big pigsty. In fact, he said, a wise farmer would not let his pigs on the streets of New York, for fear thay might become diseased!

Dealing with the problems. In the 1870's, most cities realized that they had to do something about the unhealthy conditions. More of them began to build sewer lines. They also provided for regular garbage collection. To pay for these services, residents of the city paid taxes to the city government.

Poverty, unemployment, poor housing, sick and dying children are not problems of the city alone. These problems are sometimes worse on run-down farms or in villages. But in crowded cities, poor conditions are more noticeable. There are also more people who might become concerned.

Some people tried to find out what could be done about the problems. Some, like Jacob Riis, whose report you read, wrote books criticizing the poor conditions in slums. Others formed committees that investigated some of the serious situations and sent reports to city and state governments. Some cities began to take steps to correct the most serious problems.

Sanitation was improved; some slums were torn down. But most of the cities' problems remained. As we shall see, many of them have continued into our own day.

Slums, such as this one in Cincinnati, were widespread in the early 1900's.

Working with Concepts and Generalizations

Identifying Concepts

Read each statement below. Write C if the statement tells something about city life; write F if the statement tells something about farm life. Write the answers on paper.

1. Many newcomers could not afford very good housing, and so they clustered together in the poorest sections of town.
2. Children spent most of their time with members of their family and rarely saw strangers.
3. Many neighborhoods adopted immigrant customs and holiday celebrations.
4. The population grew so fast that it was difficult to build enough houses.
5. The day ended at sundown and the family usually went to bed early.
6. There were many more places of worship, and families could get to services easily.
7. Nature played a very important part in daily life.
8. In the evenings, family members often stayed home just long enough to eat dinner before going downtown.
9. Women could get jobs outside the home and add to the family income.
10. Newcomers found there were many more laws that told them what they must and must not do.

Developing Concepts

Write the answers on paper.

1. The year is 1900. You live with your family on a farm. Your father is thinking of selling the farm and moving to the city. He asks you to help him make the decision. You have never been in the city but you have heard stories about it. You know what farm life is like. List the reasons you would like to move to the city. Then list the reasons you would like to stay on the farm. Compare your lists. Will you decide to move, or to stay?
2. You are an immigrant and have just arrived in the United States. You find yourself in a large city. In which part of the city do you want to live? Why?
3. You are a black farm worker living in the South. You decide to move to a northern city? Why?
4. As more and more people moved into cities, city government was faced with more and more problems. List some of the problems city government had. For each problem on your list, write one way that city government tried to solve it.
5. You and your family have just moved to the United States from Europe. As immigrants, what problems will you face everyday?

Generalizations

Read the generalizations listed below. Find proof to support each generalization. Tell what the proof is and the page on which you found it. Write on paper.

1. Immigrants attempt to preserve their native culture in their new homeland.
2. City living often requires members of a family to make significant changes in the way they live and work.
3. In cities, government performs many services that people living in rural areas either do for themselves or do not need to have done.

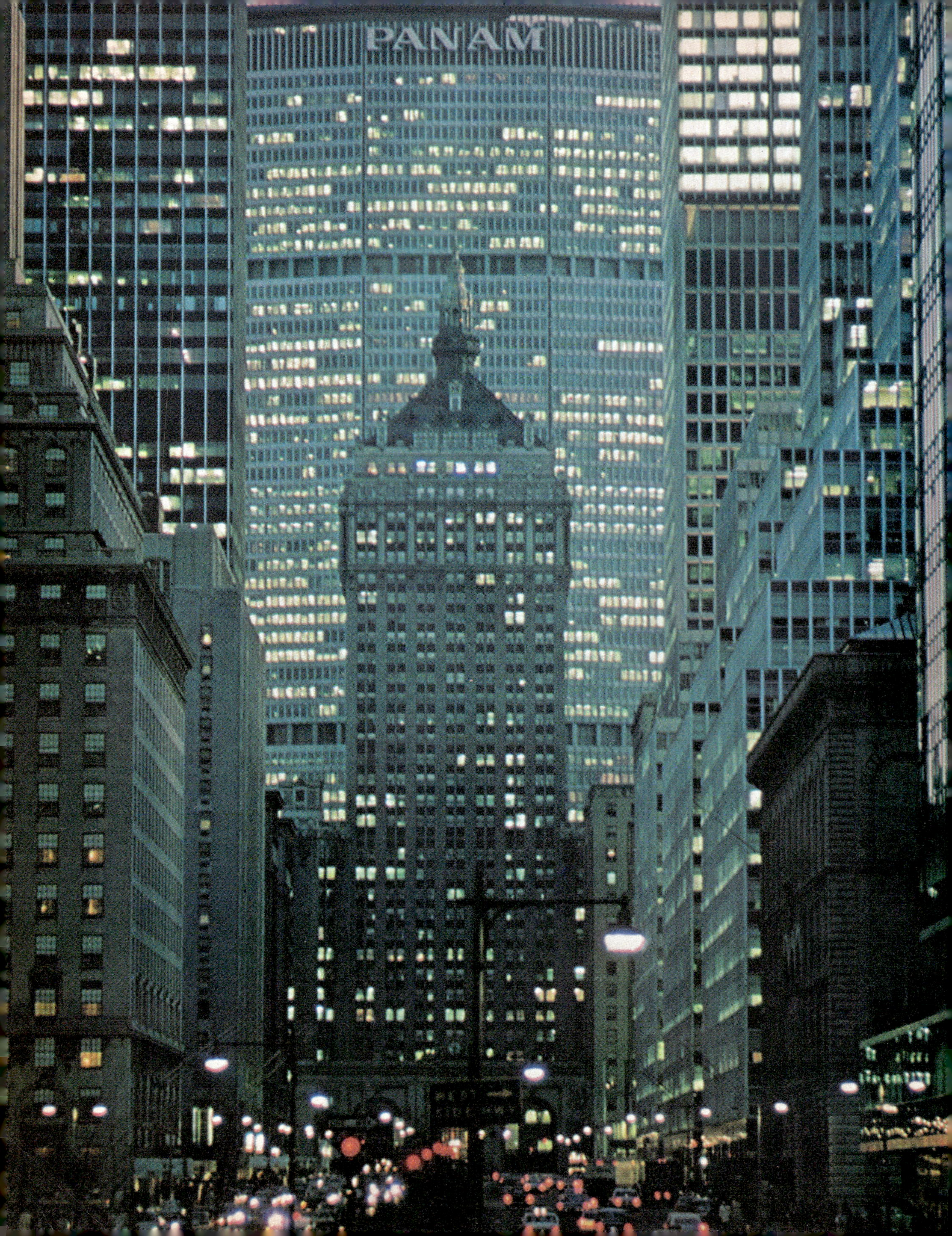
PANAM

11

City Life in Our Time

Knowing the history of American cities—how they grew, where their population came from, what their problems were—has given us a good understanding of much of our past. Now we will want to bring our knowledge of cities up-to-date. You know why cities grew in America in earlier days. Do cities grow for the same reasons today, or are there other reasons besides commerce and manufacturing? You know that much of the population of American cities in the past came from other lands. Do immigrants still come to the cities today?

Has life in today's city changed from what it was seventy years ago? Have the conditions of the poor improved? You also know how trolleys and subways helped cities to spread out. Have cities continued to spread out in our own day? You will also remember many of the problems of earlier American cities. Have our modern cities solved these problems? Do they face new problems today?

In other words—what is the American city like today?

People Still Move to Cities

The graph on this page shows the number of Americans living in urban areas, on farms, and in small rural communities with less than 2,500 people. What does it show about urban growth? Is it continuing? What has happened to the farm population? By what date did more of our people live in urban areas than on farms? During which period was there the greatest change in farm population? How many people were living in urban areas in 1970?

New city dwellers. As you see, the movement of people into urban areas has continued into the 1900's. However, there are some differences that the graph on immigrants shows. For one thing, about sixty years ago 1,200,000 immigrants entered our nation in a single year and most of them were from Europe. Nowadays fewer of the newcomers are European immigrants. This is because the Congress of the United States has passed laws that limit the number who may enter our country and especially those from lands outside of the Western Hemi-

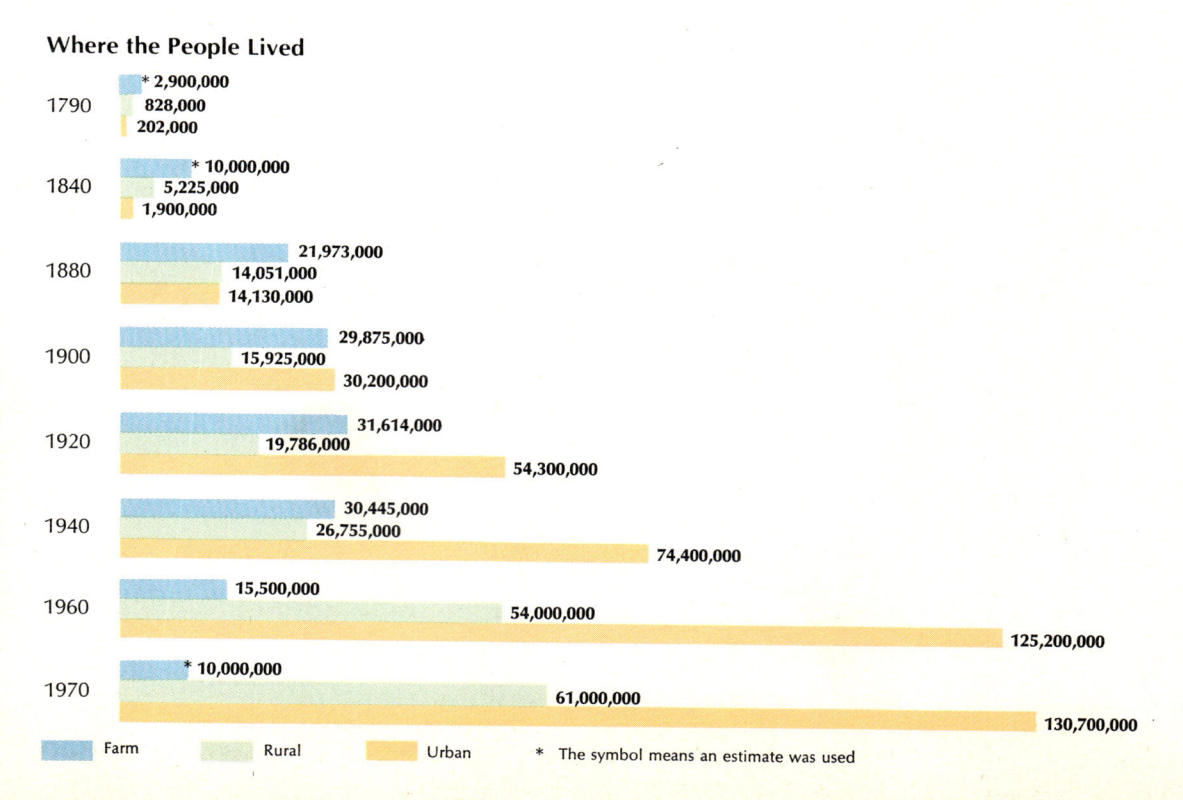

Where the People Lived

Year	Farm	Rural	Urban
1790	*2,900,000	828,000	202,000
1840	*10,000,000	5,225,000	1,900,000
1880	21,973,000	14,051,000	14,130,000
1900	29,875,000	15,925,000	30,200,000
1920	31,614,000	19,786,000	54,300,000
1940	30,445,000	26,755,000	74,400,000
1960	15,500,000	54,000,000	125,200,000
1970	*10,000,000	61,000,000	130,700,000

* The symbol means an estimate was used

Immigration from Europe and the Western Hemisphere

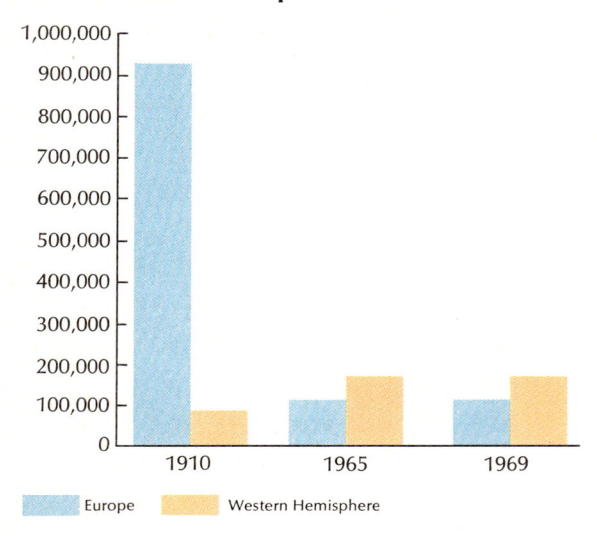

	1910	1965	1969
Europe	~930,000	~110,000	~115,000
Western Hemisphere	~85,000	~170,000	~170,000

sphere. Since cities kept growing, where did the new city dwellers come from?

People from the Western Hemisphere

People from countries in the Western Hemisphere can still come to the United States, and do. A great many Canadians moved to cities such as Boston, Detroit, New York, and Los Angeles. A large number of Mexicans came to Chicago, Los Angeles, and San Francisco. In recent years a number have come to us from Cuba. Many fled their country because they did not like the government there. Most Cubans settled in Miami, Florida.

There have also been many new arrivals from Puerto Rico. They have come to the mainland cities to make a better living than they could make on their island. Most Puerto Ricans have settled in New York City. In fact, that city is now the home of so many Puerto Ricans that Spanish is the city's second language. Puerto Ricans have also moved to other northern cities, including Chicago, Cleveland, Philadelphia, and Bridgeport, Connecticut.

Movement from rural areas. By far the most newcomers to our cities come from America's own rural areas. With today's modern farm machinery, new methods of farming, and the help of scientists, more food crops can be raised by fewer farmers. Men who used to farm are now without jobs. So are many of the men who used to earn a living digging coal in the hills of Pennsylvania, Kentucky, and West Virginia. Many coal pits have been mined out. In others, men have been replaced by huge machines. These miners are among the rural people who are now going to midwestern cities in search of jobs.

Others who have moved from rural areas to the cities are Mexican-Americans. Although most Mexican-Americans were born in the United States, many have clung to their Mexican culture. Many Mexican-Americans moved to cities in the southwestern states of Texas, New Mexico, Arizona, and southern California. In some cases a city grew up around an old Mexican-American town.

Black Population in Major Cities

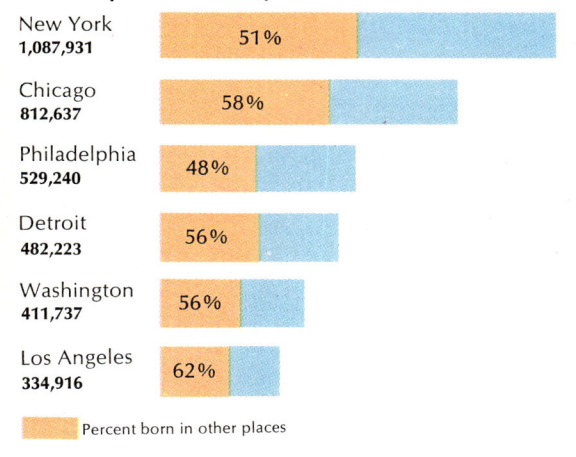

City		
New York 1,087,931	51%	
Chicago 812,637	58%	
Philadelphia 529,240	48%	
Detroit 482,223	56%	
Washington 411,737	56%	
Los Angeles 334,916	62%	

Percent born in other places

USING SOURCE MATERIAL

The graphs on these pages tell a very important part of the history of black Americans. In a brief period of time, as you can see from the graphs, a large percentage of the blacks moved into *metropolitan* (met′ rə pol′ ə tən) *areas* throughout the country—that is, the large central cities and the suburbs, towns, and small cities around them. Most blacks moved into the largest urban areas. The graphs also point out which part of the metropolitan area they moved to. Here they hoped to begin a new life. Does one of the graphs show any movement of white people into or out of central cities?

Black Migration Continues

As you recall, with little hope for their future in the South, blacks continued to move to northern and western cities. This great migration created special problems for blacks and for cities. Black farmers, like white farmers, were not prepared for city life. As you have learned, one of their greatest problems was education. They had not been prepared for the kind of employment city life offers. And, of course, another problem was race. Blacks were often denied opportunities simply because they were black. Lack of education and lack of employment made it difficult for blacks to take an active part in the life of the city.

The urban ghetto. Where do most black migrants to the city live? On page 211 is a map of one of America's large cities. What does this map tell you?

Percent of the Total Black and White Populations Living in Metropolitan Areas and Central Cities

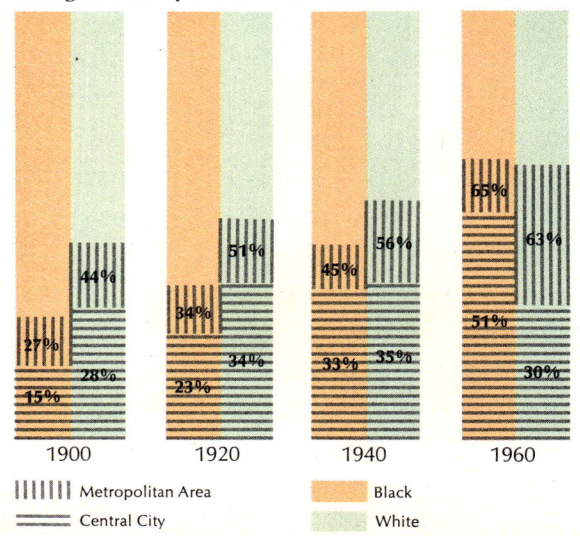

	1900	1920	1940	1960
Metropolitan Area Black	27%	34%	45%	65%
Metropolitan Area White	44%	51%	56%	63%
Central City Black	15%	23%	33%	51%
Central City White	28%	34%	35%	30%

Metropolitan Area — Black
Central City — White

210

Are most blacks scattered throughout the city, or are they concentrated in one or two places? This map shows only one of our cities, but a map of any of our cities would tell much the same story.

A section of a city where people of one racial or cultural group live very close together is called a *ghetto* (get′ ō). A hundred years ago, the European immigrants to our cities lived in ghettos. Many still do. But today it is usually Negroes, Puerto Ricans, and Mexican-Americans who are ghetto dwellers.

How a black ghetto develops. Let us see how a black ghetto develops. At first, a few blacks move into one area of a city—usually an area of older apartments. Other blacks looking for housing find that such a neighborhood is the only place they are welcome. They, too, move in.

What about the people who lived in these sections before the Negroes arrived? Do they stay, or do they leave? The map on page 212 tells us what happens. In 1920 this area had mostly white people. What has happened by 1940? by 1960?

As you see, the area has become an all-black neighborhood. But why do we call it a black ghetto? After all, in 1920, when whites lived there, no one called the neighborhood a "white ghetto." The reason is that white people were not forced to live there. When they wanted to move out, there were other places to which they could move and feel welcome. They felt they were a part of the city.

In a black ghetto the residents do feel separated from the rest of the city. Whites do not move into a black ghetto, and usually blacks cannot move out. Many do not want to, for they feel comfortable with their own people. Many others cannot afford to. Those who want to and can afford to usually find that apartment owners in other

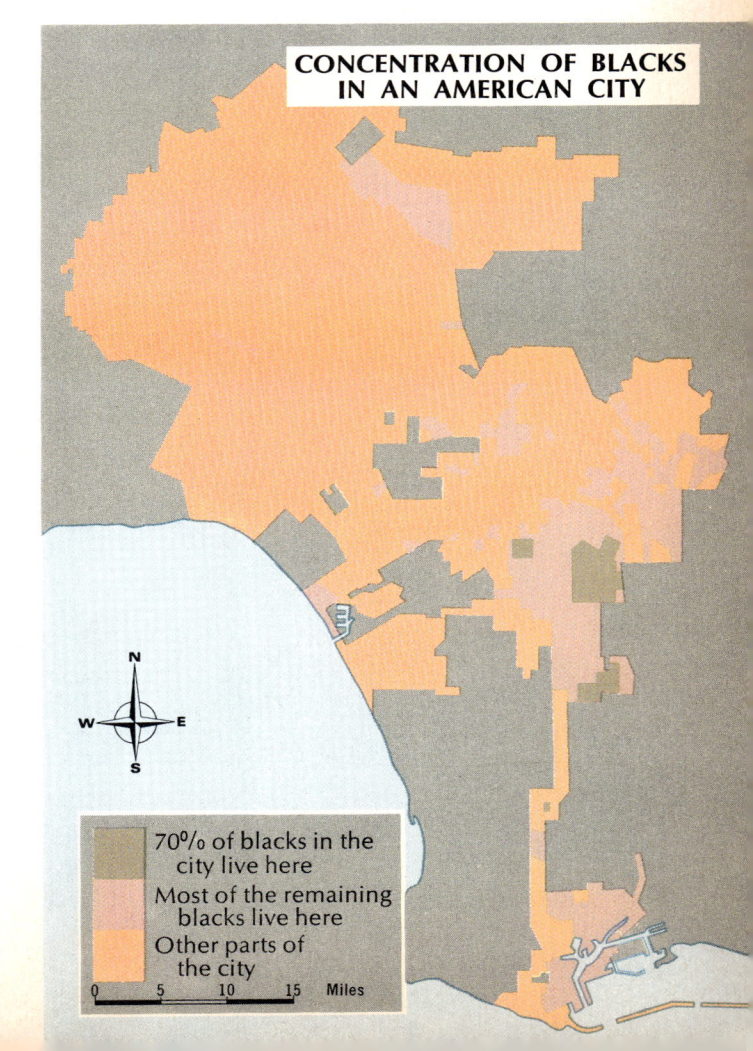

CONCENTRATION OF BLACKS IN AN AMERICAN CITY

70% of blacks in the city live here
Most of the remaining blacks live here
Other parts of the city

0   5   10   15   Miles

parts of the city refuse to rent to them. These owners do not want to let blacks into their neighborhood.

This makes black people despair of or give up any hope of ever leaving the ghettos. There is no wall around the ghetto, but there might as well be. Many of the residents feel locked in.

Do you see what really makes a neighborhood a ghetto? Is there a ghetto in your city or town? Is it a black ghetto?

USING SOURCE MATERIAL

Let us read the statements of people now living in a ghetto in New York to find out what living there is like. Below are some statements by black citizens describing some of their hardships.

. . . The main thing, we can't get a decent place to live, the rent is so high and the poor people working . . . the salary . . . where we live, we got to live where the rent is cheap, and make a living.

Woman, age 30

. . . Now, they had been complaining to the Department of Health about conditions in the buildings, about all the violations; no lights in the hall, the rats and roaches literally moving the tenants out of the building, and about six months ago the plumbing in the basement got jammed up somehow or other and there has been standing water in the basement, and the flies and maggots and everything else have been breeding there. Now, yesterday, I understand something happened in one apartment; rats forced the woman out of her apart-

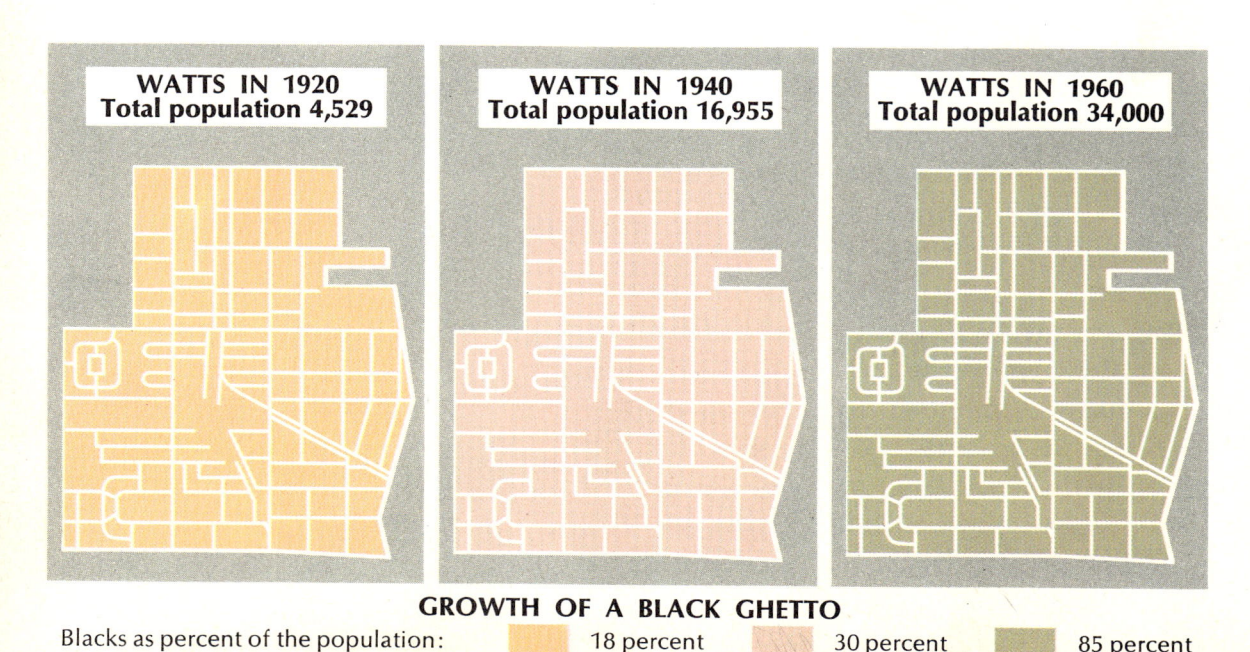

WATTS IN 1920
Total population 4,529

WATTS IN 1940
Total population 16,955

WATTS IN 1960
Total population 34,000

GROWTH OF A BLACK GHETTO

Blacks as percent of the population: 18 percent   30 percent   85 percent

ment. She couldn't at all control the rats; they were running all over the kitchen and all throughout the house and everything. . . .

Yeah, well, one woman said that the rats had chewed the clothes off her baby.

Girl, age 15

. . . They need to get rid of these slummy buildings. The children can't live in these buildings . . . not to be brought up right. There's filth! They need better schools, they need better playgrounds, more community centers. They need a whole lot!

Woman, age about 28

What are the main injustices these people complain of? What have the people done to get aid? Do you think good jobs and good wages would solve all their problems?

A way of life in the ghetto. As you study the city, especially the inner city, you come to realize that life is hard for most black Americans. It would be a mistake, however, to think that everything in the life of people in a ghetto is unhappy. For in spite of the ugliness and hopeless conditions of the ghetto, blacks have created a way of living that holds them together. Of course every ghetto is different, but each demonstrates something that is special to black culture.

One of the first things you notice in the ghetto are signs in restaurant and food store windows advertising "Black food" or "Soul food." This is food that blacks learned to prepare years ago in the South. It is simply inexpensive meats, vegetables, sauces, and fish. Because of his low income, the black American has little money to spend on food. Moreover, in many cases the price of food is often higher in black neighborhoods. The signs in store windows advertise chitterlings (chit' ər-lingz), fatback, pigs' knuckles, pigs' feet, collard (kol' ərd) greens or kale, cornbread, and fish dishes of many kinds. Blacks have learned to make these foods tender and delicious.

Religion in the ghetto. Another important part of the black culture that you would quickly notice in the ghetto is the great interest in religion. The harsh conditions of slavery encouraged strong religious feelings among black Americans. Life was so cold and hopeless that they found it necessary to look to a better world after death. Blacks also found that they could express protest through churches.

These feelings did not die after slavery ended. As a result of *segregation* (seg' rə gā' shən) and *discrimination*, black citizens had few opportunities to take part in the social life and entertainment of their cities. So they turned to their churches for these activities, too.

In some ghettos there are beautiful churches designed by black architects.

But there are not enough to care for the large population. So in every ghetto, ministers have simply rented unused stores to carry out their work. On many of the main streets, you can see *storefront churches*. Any day of the week, people passing these churches can hear the stirring spirituals, the music of protest and hope.

Strangely enough, despite the harsh conditions of ghetto living, there is a great deal of laughter, fun, and play on the ghetto streets. The ghetto sometimes sounds like a happier place than it really is. This is part of the black way of life, for, like most people, they are better able to face their misery together than by themselves. But there are times when the laughter fades, and the anger of blacks at their unjust conditions replaces it. At times this anger has exploded into violent riots.

People Leave the City, Too

Even though many people still move into the cities, the total population of many of our big cities is not increasing. In fact, if you look at the table, you will see that in some large cities it is decreasing. How is this possible?

The answer is that while many are entering our cities, others are leaving

Population of the ten largest cities in the United States, 1950-1970

Cities	1950	1960	1970*
1 New York	7,892,000	7,782,000	7,780,000
2 Chicago	3,621,000	3,550,000	3,325,000
3 Los Angeles	1,970,000	2,479,000	2,782,000
4 Philadelphia	2,072,000	2,003,000	1,927,000
5 Detroit	1,850,000	1,670,000	1,493,000
6 Baltimore	950,000	939,000	895,000
7 Houston	596,000	938,000	1,213,000
8 Cleveland	915,000	876,000	739,000
9 Washington	802,000	764,000	764,000
10 St. Louis	857,000	750,026	607,000

* Preliminary census report.
  Cities among the top ten in 1970: Dallas 836,000, Indianapolis, 743,000.

Poor children in slums play wherever they find the space.

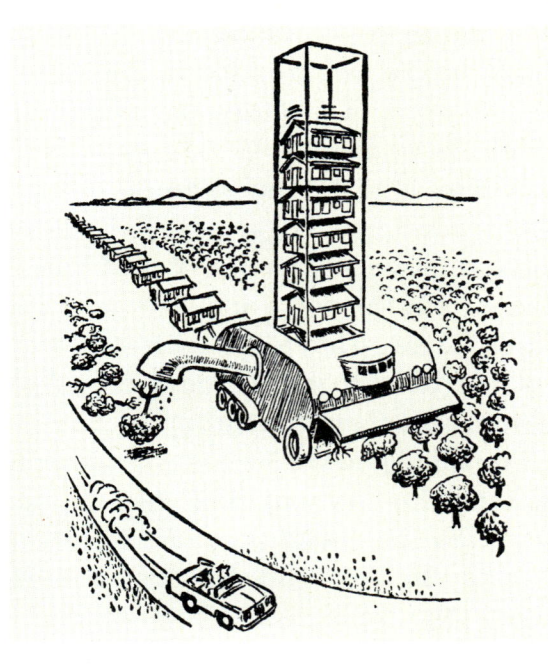

This cartoon presents the growth of suburbs in a humorous way.

them. These people are not moving to rural areas. They are staying in metropolitan areas, that is, the villages and towns that surround central cities. So the metropolitan area is still growing, but the growth is mainly in the suburbs.

Movement to the suburbs. Do you remember how the trolley car made it possible for people to move to the suburbs about eighty years ago? Today the trolley car has been replaced by automobiles, modern expressways, and *commuter* trains. Such modern transportation allows more people who work in the cities to live in the suburbs. In fact, they can live even farther away from the cities than before and not take too long getting to work. New suburban towns have grown up as far as twenty-five miles away from large cities.

Every day, land on which cows used to graze becomes the site of a large housing development. Each year thousands of acres of woodlands and orchards fall before the bulldozer to make way for more suburban homes. The cartoon on this page shows one man's idea of what has happened to many of California's orange groves as the suburbs have spread. Suburbs have grown so fast that today there are more Americans living in them than in the cities they surround.

Why do people leave the city? People move to the suburbs for many different reasons. Certainly some people today move for the same reason that others moved to the suburbs a hundred years ago. These people want to own a home near the countryside, away from the noise and crowds of the cities. Often they feel their children will be able to attend less crowded, newer schools in the suburbs.

For some people the main reason for leaving the city was that they did not want to be neighbors of Negroes, Puerto Ricans, and Mexican-Americans. Not many members of these three groups live in the suburbs, for most of them cannot afford to. Even those who can, usually find it hard to get a house in the suburbs. Many builders and owners refuse to sell or rent to Negroes, Puerto Ricans, Mexican-Americans, and sometimes other minority groups.

In 1968 the United States government passed a law that forbids discrimination, or unfair treatment, in housing. Now a person cannot refuse to sell or rent certain kinds of homes to another just because of his color, religion, or *nationality* (nash′ ə nal′-ə tē). Many states also have such laws. But many people do not obey these laws and it is hard to force them to. So far these laws have not done much good.

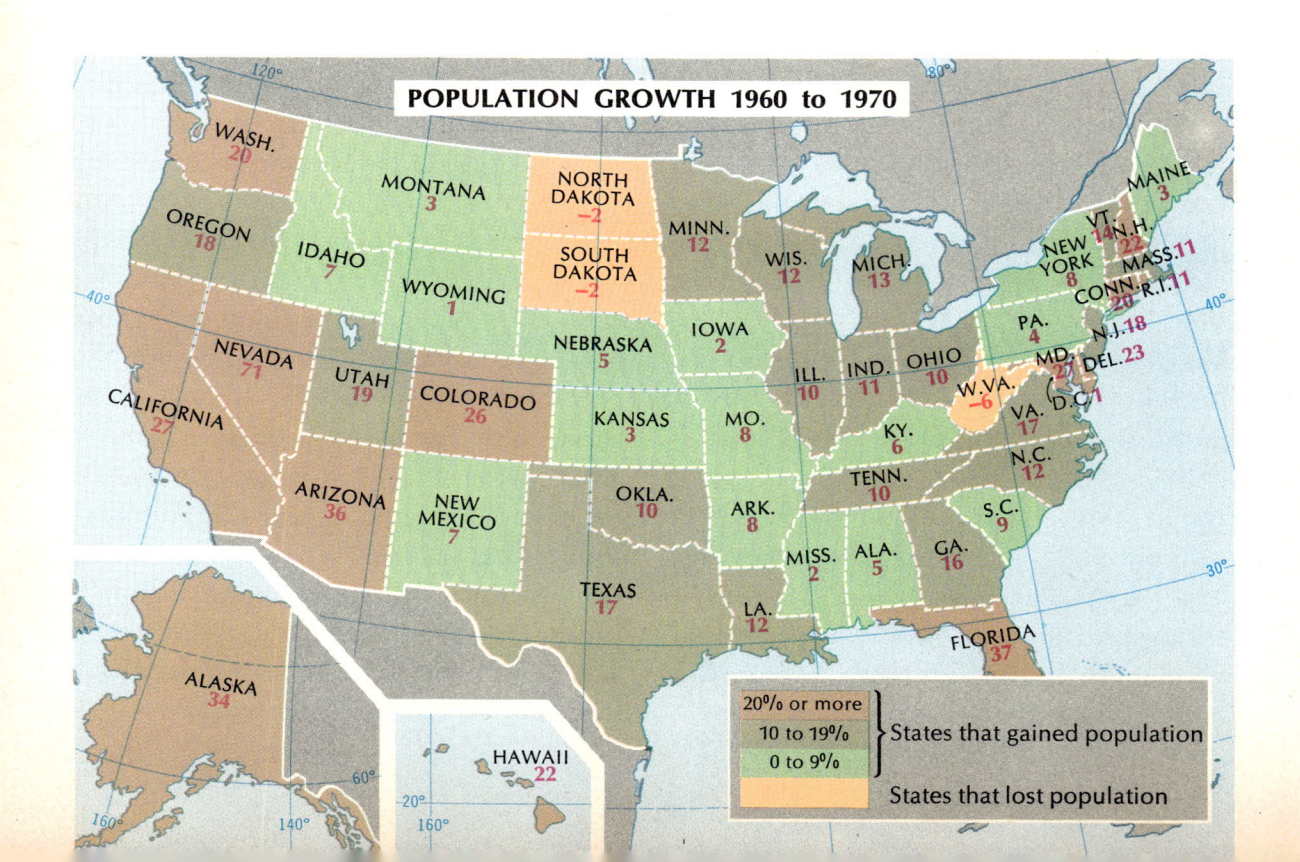

POPULATION GROWTH 1960 to 1970

State	%
WASH.	20
MONTANA	3
NORTH DAKOTA	-2
MAINE	3
OREGON	18
IDAHO	7
MINN.	12
VT.	14
N.H.	22
SOUTH DAKOTA	-2
WIS.	12
MICH.	13
NEW YORK	8
MASS.	11
WYOMING	1
CONN.	20
R.I.	11
NEVADA	71
NEBRASKA	5
IOWA	2
PA.	4
N.J.	18
UTAH	19
ILL.	10
IND.	11
OHIO	10
MD.	27
DEL.	23
CALIFORNIA	27
COLORADO	26
KANSAS	3
MO.	8
W.VA.	-6
VA.	17
D.C.	-1
KY.	6
TENN.	10
N.C.	12
ARIZONA	36
NEW MEXICO	7
OKLA.	10
ARK.	8
S.C.	9
MISS.	2
ALA.	5
GA.	16
TEXAS	17
LA.	12
FLORIDA	37
ALASKA	34
HAWAII	22

20% or more
10 to 19% } States that gained population
0 to 9%

States that lost population

Industry moves to the suburbs. Our suburbs are still mostly residential, but the number of factories and office buildings in them is increasing. Some companies have moved from crowded areas in large cities and have built new plants in the suburbs. The plants are often located in *industrial parks.* These are large sections of land that have been set aside for industrial use. They are usually near important highways. Large shopping centers with plenty of parking space have also opened in the suburbs. Residents nearby find these centers very convenient.

Many industries are attracted to the suburbs by well-planned industrial parks.

Megalopolis

The changes in the suburbs around the large cities and the continued growth of the suburbs have had some interesting effects on some parts of the country. Very long stretches of urban and suburban areas have developed. Let us look briefly at one such area.

Northeastern United States. United States Route 1 is one of the nation's oldest highways. It runs along the eastern coast from northern Maine to southern Florida. For many years U.S. 1 was the main highway connecting the cities along the Atlantic coast. But if you were to drive today from Portland, Maine, to Washington, D.C., you would almost certainly decide not to use U.S. 1. Driving on U.S. 1 between Portland and Washington today means slow, stop-and-go driving through city after city, large and small. Away from the highway, you would find vegetable and dairy farms, orchards, large areas of woodland, and state parks. There are miles of sandy beaches and plenty of hilly countryside. But on the highway, you pass housing developments, shopping centers, factories, restaurants, and motels. They seem to line the route from one end to the other. An area like this is called a *megalopolis* (meg′ ə lop′ ə lis). This word is used to mean a cluster, or group, of metropolitan areas close to one another. Some metropolitan areas have spread so far that they have run into one another almost like one endless city.

The urban strip along the eastern coast is only one of our megalopolises.

This stretch may not be the richest one in natural resources, and it may not have the most delightful climate. Yet it is one of the most important areas in the world. The deep harbors and navigable rivers have helped seaports here become the busiest trade centers in the world. Some of the most important industries are found here. Thousands of miles of railroads bring products from all over the country to eastern cities. Airplanes carry people from all over the world to this megalopolis.

The problems of a megalopolis. The megalopolis has created problems. The automobile has played a large part in the spreading out of cities. It has also brought many huge traffic jams to towns and cities between Portland and Washington. Some of the smaller towns have suddenly found themselves on busy highways. The sky overhead has become crowded with planes. Railroads are having a difficult time keeping up with their traffic. And the megalopolis has spread air pollution for many more miles and water pollution through hundreds of miles of streams.

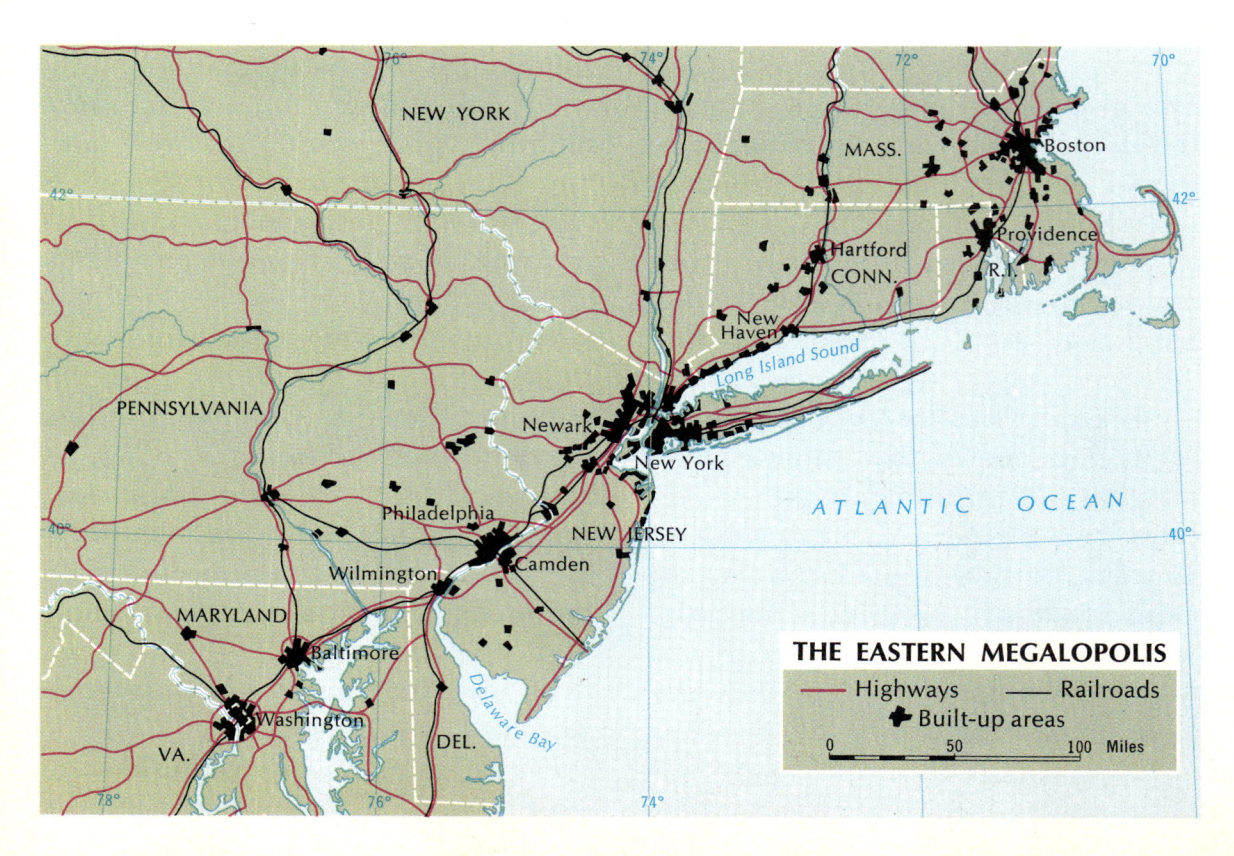

The megalopolis is here to stay. There are other sections of the country where megalopolises have begun. Look at a map of the United States and see if you can find these places.

Other Kinds of Cities Grow

Industrial cities and commercial cities have continued to grow. But not all of our cities are mainly commercial and industrial centers.

The nation's capital. An example of another kind of city is one that you all have heard about, Washington, D.C. Washington has no large harbor. It is not a manufacturing or railroad center. Yet Washington is the ninth-largest city in the nation.

What kind of city would you call Washington? Who would you suppose is the largest employer in our nation's capital? Can you think of any other city in our country, perhaps in your own state, where people do the same kind of work that the residents of Washington do?

Resort cities. You will recall that some cities grew and became important because they specialized in manufacturing one or two products. Another kind of city grew because it specialized in entertaining people. Miami Beach in Florida, Palm Springs in California, and Las Vegas in Nevada are three such cities. You will not find much, if any, manufacturing or commerce in these cities. A large part of the popula-

Resort cities, such as Miami, attract thousands of tourists each year. Many tourists decide to stay and make their homes there. Above you can see some of the things that attract tourists.

tion makes a living by serving those people who come to visit for a few weeks. This is the industry of these *resort cities*.

Centers of learning. There is another kind of city that is becoming more and more important. Universities and scientific research centers are increasing in number and size today. In some cities—such as Ithaca (ith′ i kə), New York, Ann Arbor, Michigan, and Cambridge, Massachusetts—the universities and research laboratories provide many jobs. They also make new scientific discoveries and inventions. Often these are the beginning of important new industries that provide many more new jobs. Manufacturers are attracted to these *university cities* because they can hire many of the scientists, engineers, and other specially trained people who graduate from the universities.

Climate helps cities grow. Weather and climate also play a bigger part than ever before in helping cities to grow. Many people want to live in warm, sunny climates and are moving to the southeastern and southwestern parts of the country. The Southwest—that is, Texas, New Mexico, Arizona, and southern California—is the fastest-growing section of the country. Albuquerque (al′ bə kər′ kē), New Mexico, Phoenix (fē′ niks), Arizona, and El Paso, Texas—once small towns—are now major cities.

Los Angeles, a City Made by Climate

Los Angeles, California, is a fine example of how an excellent climate has helped to create a great city. The temperature in Los Angeles is comfortable all year round. Rarely is it hotter than 85°, and even in the winter the daytime temperature is a pleasant 65° or 70°. Except during the rainy season in the wintertime, the sun shines most of the year.

A sleepy town awakes. Until the railroads arrived about a hundred years ago, Los Angeles was a sleepy little town of a few thousand people. Then, in the 1880's, some people began to move there from the Midwest, attracted by the mild climate. Most of these residents farmed for a living. Some raised oranges and lemons, for which California became famous.

Soon more people came to the area, and by 1900, Los Angeles had become a city of 100,000. Los Angeles had grown without the help of manufac-

In area, Los Angeles is larger than New York City, Chicago, and Pittsburgh combined.

turing and without a harbor. Although it is near the Pacific Ocean, the city has no natural harbor. Only after Los Angeles started to grow did the United States government build a harbor for the city. Today it has the largest man-made harbor in the world.

As the population of Los Angeles increased, industries came to the city. Among the important industries there today are aircraft, aerospace (ãr′ ə spās), automobile, and electronics (i lek′ tron′ iks).

Modern Los Angeles is a sprawling city. Suburbs have grown rapidly, and Los Angeles also has annexed, or joined to itself, little neighboring towns. Today the area of Los Angeles is twice that of Chicago and ten times that of San Francisco. This spread has been made possible by the automobile and by a fine network of highways.

With a population of three million people, Los Angeles is the third largest city in the United States. Its metropolitan area includes seven million people.

Los Angeles has its ghetto, too. Large numbers of Negroes have moved into the city in the last twenty years in search of jobs. Look back at the map on page 211. The city in that map is Los Angeles. The ghetto area you see there is named Watts. The housing in Watts is bad, but it is not so poor as in the ghettos of other large cities. But Watts is still a ghetto, because it is cut off from the rest of the city. Its residents feel locked in. Do you remember what this means?

The section is almost cut off from the life of the city by poor transportation. It is difficult for Negroes in Watts to get to downtown areas, or to get across town to industrial sections.

As in all ghettos, blacks who want to move find it very hard to get housing in other parts of the city. Not everyone wants to leave Watts, but all should have the freedom to decide that for themselves.

In the eastern section of Los Angeles another ghetto has developed. This ghetto could also be called a slum. In it live thousands of Mexican-Americans. At one time they worked on nearby farms. Now a large number of them are without work of any kind. Their living conditions are even worse than those of the blacks in Watts. Their houses remind us of the shanties of a hundred years ago.

Compared to other cities in the United States, Los Angeles has grown rapidly in a few years. But if it were not for its fine climate, Los Angeles might still be little more than the sleepy town it was a hundred years ago.

Life in Our Cities Today

The main reasons people moved to cities were the opportunities, the excitement, and the variety the city offered. Does the city still offer these things?

Take a look at the pictures. For many people the city *is* a place of opportunity, excitement, and variety. What do these pictures tell you of life in the city for some people? Have you ever been to places like those shown? Which of the pictures give you an idea of the opportunity and variety in a city?

But for many people life in the city is without joy and excitement. For them there are still few opportunities. Do the pictures on page 223 make you think that the people in them enjoy living where they do? Have they many things to do?

The city's poor. The people in the last set of pictures are the city's poor. Who are they? They are not one group. They are black, and they are white. They are immigrants, and they are also native-

223

born. Some speak English, some Spanish, some are new to the city, and some have lived there all their lives. They are young, they are middle-aged, and they are elderly.

A number of the city's poor are unemployed. Most do have jobs, but they are paid very low wages. One of the main reasons for this is that the poor often do not have a good education or special skills. Machines are doing many of the simpler jobs. So it becomes harder and harder to get a well-paying job without education.

Discrimination, or unfair treatment, against Negroes, Mexicans, Puerto Ricans, and other *minority groups* often keeps them from being hired for many kinds of work. Not many years ago, it was hard for a Negro to get any kind of job except one of the lowest-paid ones. Today things have improved a great deal, but the unfair treatment is not yet ended.

Same problems for all. Even for those who are not poor, living in the modern city is not so pleasant as it could be. Smoke, soot, and poisonous fumes pour out of factory, office, and apartment chimneys, polluting the air that city dwellers breathe. Automobiles add their exhaust to the pollution. Traffic becomes so tangled that goods

Artists in Chicago hide slum decay with a "Wall of Respect."

and people are moved about the city's streets at a snail's pace. Recently a bus and a pedestrian had a race across Manhattan Island at rush hour, and the walker won! Crime is increasing, and people are afraid to walk the streets at night.

In many cities, housing conditions are poor and getting worse, even for people with a good income. New York City is an example of this. Most builders in New York are constructing expensive apartment buildings, far too costly for the average New Yorker to rent. Only one out of fifteen residents in the city can afford these new apartments. Meanwhile many of the apartments that the other New Yorkers live in are wearing out. New York City already has so much worn-out housing that the entire population of Arizona could fit into it!

The government does try to help. It builds apartments that it rents for less money to low-income families. This is called *public housing*. There are many, many people who want to rent such apartments. But only a few are built each year. Those who apply for public housing are put on a waiting list, and the list is very long. If the government builds only as many apartments in future years as it is building now, a person applying today would have to wait *51 years* for an apartment!

Urban decay. Drive through any American city and you will see sights like

Urban decay spreads rapidly.

the building pictured above. Once it was new, and this part of the city was alive with activity. Today it has grown ugly with abandoned warehouses and factory buildings, run-down stores, decaying houses, and shabby schools. This is *urban decay*.

When a part of the city decays, many jobs are lost. Decay hurts the city in another way as well. Owners of buildings and businesses pay taxes to the city. These taxes help pay for the services the city provides, such as schools, police and fire protection, playgrounds, garbage collection, and street repair. When businesses move out of the city and old homes are run-down and abandoned, the city loses taxes. It has less money to spend for its services. Many of our cities are having trouble paying their expenses today. Schools that should be built are not, and this results in crowded classrooms in many parts of the city. This may lead to poor education, and poor education means low-paid jobs.

Injustice leads to riots. Cities have been the scenes of recent riots by the disappointed and angry people of the black ghettos. For years they asked for better jobs, improved housing conditions, and fairer treatment. Little was done. Across the nation there were many signs of great progress and increasing wealth. But in the ghettos there was just decay. Changes came slowly or not at all.

During the 1960's, violent riots broke out in the ghettos of city after city. Many people were killed or injured. Fires destroyed whole blocks of houses and stores. Transportation stopped, and businesses shut down.

Many people felt that the rioting was wrong. A number of whites decided to move out of the city because of them. But the riots also brought the many problems of black Americans to the nation's attention.

In recent years some important changes have come about in the way

HOW DOES URBAN DECAY HAPPEN?

Often it happens this way: This large home is built, many years ago, by Mr. and Mrs. Wealthy, who want to live near the center of town. As the city becomes busier, the Wealthies are annoyed by the increasing traffic and noise, and decide to move. They sell their home to the Comfortable family, who live there for twenty years before they, too, decide to move.

The Comfortables sell to Mr. Landlord, who makes the home over into five small apartments. These he rents to people like Mr. and Mrs. Poor and their family, who have recently moved to the city and cannot afford a larger apartment. When the Poors move in, neighbors decide to move out, and Mr. Landlord buys their homes, too.

After a while the houses begin to get run-down. Mr. Landlord blames the Poors, who, he says, never take care of things. The Poors say Mr. Landlord is at fault. All he does is collect the rent; he never makes repairs.

Meanwhile the buildings become more shabby, and the whole neighborhood begins to look run-down. Other peo-

blacks are treated. Even more important are the changes in black communities themselves. Blacks began to take a more active part in the life of the cities. They started new businesses. They formed theater groups. They wrote books and plays. They were elected to public office. Blacks began to take pride in being black. Some blacks took the words of a popular song as their motto: "Say it loud, I'm black and I'm proud!"

Today every black community shows some signs of change. There is greater emphasis on education, and greater interest in how the city is governed. Most important, black Americans have made all Americans aware of their problems and their pride. America can no longer ignore either.

City problems are suburb problems. Many of the problems of the cities are really problems of the entire metropolitan area. For example, polluted air from city factories and cars does not stop at the boundary line between the city and the suburbs. In fact, autos in the suburbs also pollute the air. The traffic problem is a headache for the suburban resident as much as for the city dweller. Suburbs pollute the rivers with their sewage as much as cities do. Crime is increasing in the suburbs.

Of course the suburbs are newer than the cities, and so there is less

ple in nearby areas see that this neighborhood is going downhill. Will theirs be next? Perhaps they had better move out now. Meanwhile Mr. Builder is looking for a place to put up a new apartment house. He decides against spending money to build in an area that is getting more run-down.

The same thing happens in the factory area and the downtown shopping center. Mr. Manufacturer decides that his old factory building near the downtown area is not modern enough. It is also too difficult for trucks to carry goods to and from his factory through the slow-moving city traffic. He decides to move to the new industrial park in the suburbs. His factory building and his warehouse now stand empty.

Mr. Storekeeper finds he is not selling as much as he used to. Many of his best customers have moved to the suburbs. So he decides to close his downtown store and open a shop in the suburbs. Soon there are many other empty stores on the downtown streets.

In cities across the country, there are children who are determined to make their neighborhood a better place in which to live.

decay there, and fewer slums. But many people are discovering that suburbs, too, can become crowded and ugly. In many areas, billboards, neon signs, and ugliness have replaced the trees and beauty of the countryside. These are some of the reasons why the suburban resident as well as the city dweller must help to solve the problems of modern urban living.

There is another reason why people who live in suburbs must help the city solve its problems. The city is very important to them. About one third of these people still work in the city, and the downtown area continues to serve many suburban shoppers. The city provides entertainment and pleasant life not only for its own residents, but for those of the suburbs. In the evenings and on weekends, suburban residents ride the highways into the city to take advantage of sporting events, symphony orchestras, theaters, museums, art galleries, and libraries. The big city remains the most important part of the whole metropolitan area.

Working with Concepts and Generalizations

Identifying Concepts

Choose the ending that correctly completes each sentence. Write on paper.

1. Today most newcomers to American cities come from (a) other cities, (b) rural areas, (c) the suburbs.
2. Two conditions often found in a ghetto are (a) full employment and good housing, (b) unemployment and urban decay, (c) integrated neighborhoods and industrial development.
3. Two large groups of newcomers to American cities today are (a) Eastern Europeans and blacks, (b) blacks and Puerto Ricans, (c) Puerto Ricans and northern Europeans.

Write T if the statement is true; write F if it is false.

4. A megalopolis is a cluster of metropolitan areas.
5. The problems of the city affect only those who live in the city.

Developing Concepts

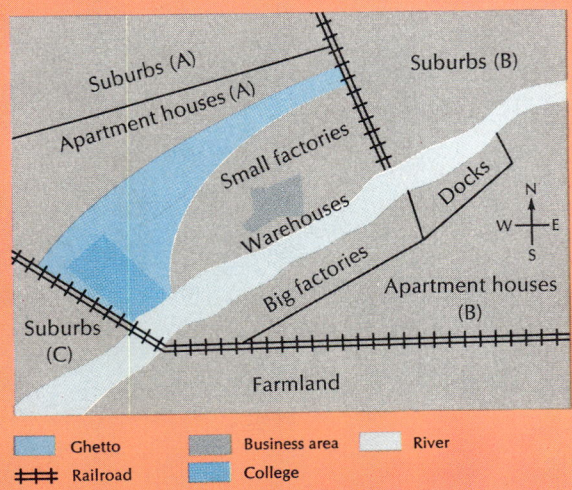

The map on this page shows City X. Use the map to answer these questions:

1. You work at the docks. Where are you likely to live? Why?
2. You teach history at the city college. Where are you likely to live? Why?
3. You work in a small factory. Where are you likely to live? Why?
4. You are a wealthy businessman. You work in the Business Area. Where are you likely to live? Why?
5. What type of people are likely to live in Suburb A? Why do you think so?
6. Where do you think most black people in City X live? Why?
7. You plan to build a shopping center northwest of the Business Area. Where will you build it? Why?
8. Where would you build low-cost public housing? Why?
9. Where would you build a city park? Why?
10. The city has purchased the land shown on the map as farmland. What should the land be used for? Why?

Generalizations

Important words are missing from each statement below. When you have filled in the missing words in each statement, you will have completed a generalization. Write on paper.

1. Modern _____ enables more people to live in the _____ and work in the city.
2. As a result of new methods of _____ and modern equipment, fewer _____ can grow more _____.

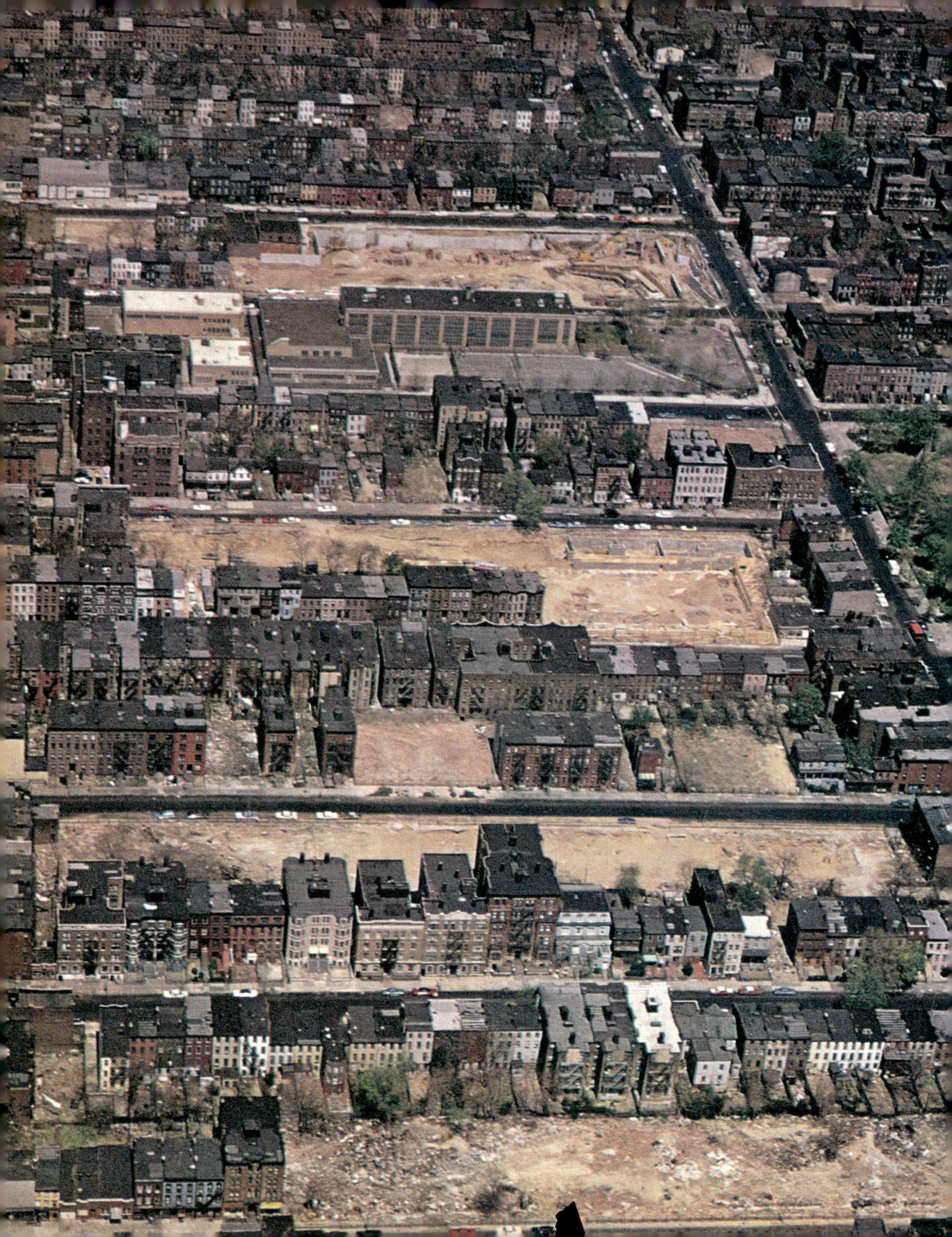

12 Improving Our Cities

In every library there is a card catalog. The cards give the name of each book and its author, and tell something about the book. In your next visit to your local library, check this catalog under the word *Cities*. Just a glimpse at some of the titles will tell you much about our cities today. Here are some of the books you may find: *Cities in a Race with Time* by Jeanne Lowe, *Sick Cities* by Mitchell Gordon, *Boston: The Job Ahead* by Martin Myerson and Edward Banfield, *New York City in Crisis* by The Staff of the New York Herald Tribune, and *A City Destroys Itself* by Richard Whalen.

What do these titles suggest about our cities? In this chapter you will learn about three cities that are doing something to win their "race with time." These cities have many similar problems. However, some problems may be more serious in one city than in another. You will find out how each city is trying to solve a particular problem or group of problems.

One of the cities, New Haven, is very old— it was settled while the American colonies belonged to Great Britain. Later in the chapter you will learn about cities that are very new— only about ten years old. They have been planned very carefully to avoid, or at least reduce, some of the problems that older cities have had.

New Haven Rebuilds Itself

New Haven, Connecticut, is an industrial city of about 150,000 people. The metropolitan area of New Haven has about 320,000 people. It was one of the first English settlements in America and is the home of one of the nation's great universities, Yale.

Taking a long, hard look. About twenty years ago, the citizens of New Haven took a long, hard look at their city. They did not like what they saw. Houses were aging, and few new ones were being built. Slums were spreading. In large sections of the city, rundown *tenement* (ten' ə mənt) *houses* stood side by side with old factories. The downtown shopping area, old and tired-looking, was losing customers to suburban shopping centers. Public schools were old and badly crowded. Some business companies that had been in New Haven for many years were talking about leaving the city. As the residents looked about them, they saw a city that was slowly dying.

The decision to act. The leaders and the citizens of New Haven decided to do something. They began to ask questions and to plan for the future. How could they save their city? How could they improve life there? What would be the best way to use the land in the city? What would have to be done to make the downtown area attractive to new stores and new customers? How could the spreading slums be stopped?

One person who became very important to New Haven's future was Richard Lee. Mr. Lee had run for mayor twice, and lost both times—once by only two votes! In 1953 Richard Lee ran for mayor again, promising to lead the way in rebuilding New Haven. This time the citizens elected Mr. Lee. In later years they would elect him seven more times. During the sixteen years he served as mayor, Richard Lee kept his word. He helped his city rebuild itself.

Mayor Lee first appointed several officials to be in charge of the rebuilding program. He also formed a Citizens Action Committee, made up of several hundred business and community leaders in New Haven. Night after night he presented his ideas to groups of citizens meeting in churches, schools, and clubs. Soon he won the support of all these groups for his plans to rebuild New Haven.

Such support is very important if city leaders are to carry out their plans. For there are always people who oppose change even when it would benefit the whole city. Some owners of private homes do not care to improve them because of the expense. Some landlords would like nothing better than to sit back and collect rents from slum dwellers and do nothing to repair their tenements. Some businessmen object to the cost of doing away with air pollution or water pollution from the factories. And some people just do not like changes of any kind. They prefer to leave things as they are.

Rebuilding downtown. The first part of the plan called for tearing down the city's worst slum. The slum covered several blocks not far from the downtown shops. Here, leather factories, junk yards, and shabby tenements were all jumbled together. More than half the apartments in this section did not have their own baths. Next, the plan called for completely rebuilding several blocks in the downtown shopping district. The long string of old stores would be replaced by modern ones. The map of New Haven shows you the Oak Street and Church Street Projects, where this rebuilding took place.

Clearing away all these buildings took a lot of money. Most of it was given by the federal government. The federal government tries to encourage cities to improve themselves and often provides funds to help them. This improvement program is called *urban renewal.*

The rest of the money came from the city. Once the land was cleared, private companies would be willing to spend their money to put up the new buildings.

After many years of work, residents began to see a new downtown rising.

Shown above is part of the business center of New Haven before urban renewal. When the renewal started, some old buildings were torn down and streets were redesigned. The results of the changes are shown below.

Each year new office buildings, banks, department stores, hotels, or restaurants were completed. Today New Haven has a beautiful downtown center that is alive with shoppers. In place of the slums and old factories stand three tall apartment buildings. Many of the people who live in them probably would have moved to the suburbs if the apartments had not been built. Shoppers from miles around can easily enter the city by a wide road that connects the main highway to the downtown area. There is plenty of parking space in a huge garage.

Shoppers can walk directly from the garage to two department stores and then to a long block of small stores, without ever stepping outdoors. The stores are in an enclosed mall. Traffic on the streets outside flows smoothly, for trucks no longer block the streets. Trucks making deliveries to the stores use a special road underneath the main street. A new hotel and an office building are also part of this rebuilt area.

Keeping industries and jobs. Keeping industries in the city and getting new ones to build there were two other parts of New Haven's renewal program. Industries provide jobs for the people and pay taxes to the city. Why

URBAN RENEWAL, OR NEGRO REMOVAL?

Does urban renewal always work well for all the residents of a city? When a city decides to begin urban renewal, its first project is usually the downtown area. Old factories and slum tenements are knocked down. The new buildings that are built often include fine apartment houses. Many times, however, they rent for much more than the residents of the old slum can pay. The people who used to live there have to find new housing elsewhere in the city. This is why some people say that urban renewal is often "poor family removal," or "Negro removal."

Some city governments have tried to help the former slum residents find other places to live. New Haven's government found housing for each of the 881 families who had lived in the slums that were torn down. Other city governments have not done so well in taking care of the residents who are forced to leave their slum homes.

Where do these people move to? Will it be to a newer neighborhood with houses in good condition? Or one that has older homes that are getting worn-out? Is there any way we can have urban renewal without creating new slums in other parts of the city?

The Long Wharf section of New Haven was a low-lying area of little benefit to the people.

Drained of water and filled in, Long Wharf is now the site of several factories.

is that important? There were many old factories still in *residential areas* in New Haven. The city needed to set aside some places where these companies could build new factories. Such an area should be near good transportation.

There was just such an area in New Haven. It was close to the railroad, to the harbor, and to the new highway. The only problem was that it was a swamp. The area was called Long Wharf.

"We will create industrial land where now there is only swamp," said Mayor Lee. Millions of tons of mud, dug up from the harbor bottom, were dumped into the swamp at Long Wharf. Thousands of truckloads of sand and gravel were added until the land was solid. Today, just as Mayor Lee said, new industries are locating on the land at Long Wharf.

Rebuilding Residential Areas

The mayor and his planning experts knew that the downtown section, the shopping areas, and the industrial parks are only parts of the city. Just as important are the places where people live. Rebuilding residential areas was one of New Haven's important needs.

Reclaiming Wooster Square. One of the first areas to be rebuilt was Wooster (wus' tər) Square. This area, which was only a short walk from downtown,

235

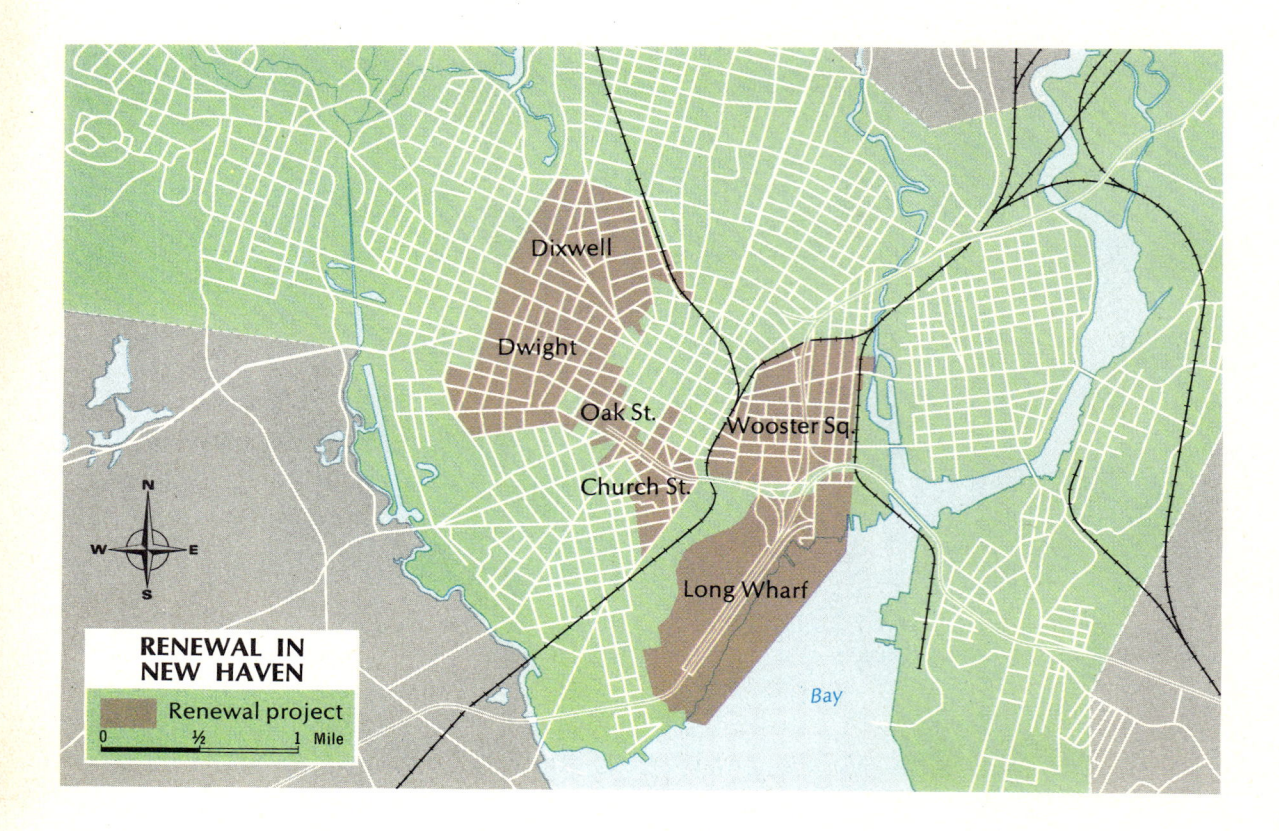

covered about thirty blocks. Wooster Square was once the finest section of New Haven. In the early 1800's, wealthy Southerners from New Orleans and Charleston, South Carolina, built large summer homes along the waterfront. Shade trees and flower gardens lined the area.

Late in the 1800's, industry came to Wooster Square. Starting first at the edges, then spreading across the whole area, came the factories—a rubber factory, a clock factory, breweries (brü′ ər ēz), bakeries, and a dozen others. Soon the smoke and noise of the industries drove out the older residents. The old homes were divided into small apartments. Tenement buildings were hastily built to house the immigrants who came to New Haven to work in the factories. Even when they were brand-new, these tenements were poor places to live. After fifty years of wear and neglect, they were dreadful. By the time New Haven woke up, much of Wooster Square was a slum.

A time to act. About the time that citizens were becoming aware of the poor conditions, the city was planning to build a new highway through Wooster Square. Some buildings would have to come down to make room for it. Where should the road be put? Instead of just deciding about the road, the residents and the city government realized that this was the time to plan for a better neighborhood in Wooster Square.

Together the city's planning experts and the neighborhood residents worked out a plan. The road would run through a corner of Wooster Square instead of through the middle. All the old buildings on one side of the new highway would be cleared away. This land would become an industrial park. Industries now in old buildings next to houses could build modern plants in this park.

The rest of Wooster Square would become a pleasant residential area of homes and apartments, with a few neighborhood shops and restaurants. The old factories, no longer needed, would be torn down. So would the rotting tenements. In their place would be built apartments for low-income and middle-income families. An apartment house for elderly people would also be built. A new school would replace the old ones that had been serving the neighborhood, and playgrounds would also be provided.

Putting this plan into effect would cost a lot of money. A little more than half of it would come from the federal government, and the city would provide the rest.

Rehabilitation. Not all the buildings in the neighborhood would be torn down. Many of the old houses could become very good places to live in if they were repaired. Fixing up old homes so that they can be lived in again is called *rehabilitation* (rē′ hə bil′ ə tā′ shən). About half the houses in Wooster Square could be rehabilitated. But first, the owners had to agree to do this.

City officials visited each homeowner in the neighborhood. New Haven had strict new safety laws for homes, and the officials told each homeowner what he would have to repair to make the house a safe place. They did more than that. A city architect drew plans for each homeowner, free of charge, to show how he could improve his home's appearance. The architect also showed how this would help improve the appearance of all of Wooster Square.

Homeowners did not have to make these changes, but after studying the drawings, most decided to accept many of the architect's suggestions. The picture on page 250 shows some of these houses, and the improvements made. Owners had to spend their own money to rehabilitate their houses, but they decided it was worth it.

Soon Wooster Square was a beehive of activity as the plan was carried out. People saw that Wooster Square was no longer a decaying neighborhood. They decided to *invest*, or put their money, in businesses in this area. Private builders built an apartment house. Banks loaned money to homeowners for remodeling work. Store-owners fixed up their shops with loans from the federal government. Businesses built modern plants in the industrial park section.

Today the people of Wooster Square are proud of their neighborhood. Wooster Square is once again a good place to live, because the residents, the city government, and the federal government all worked together to make it so.

Rebuilding a black ghetto. Wooster Square was only one of many neighborhoods in New Haven that needed help badly. Another was a section called Dixwell. Dixwell is a black ghetto. Conditions there were even worse than in Wooster Square.

Much decay in the Dixwell area was replaced by new housing units.

Mayor Lee, the city-planning experts, and the people who lived in the neighborhood worked together to decide how to improve Dixwell. Rebuilding this entire section would cost a great deal of money. Even though the federal government provided some, there was not enough money to do the whole job. The city and the neighborhood then had to decide how to use what money they could get. Some money was used to restore old homes. The rest was used to get rid of the worst slums and to build some new housing.

Today there is still much that must be done to make Dixwell a good place to live for all its residents. As the pictures show, an important start has been made to make it a better neighborhood.

The changes that have been made in New Haven since Richard Lee became mayor are very great. Of course there still is much to do. Many neighborhoods are still old and run-down, and most of the city's slums have not been removed. Yet New Haven is one of the most improved cities in America, and its people are justly proud of how much progress has been made.

Our Urban Traffic Problem

The traffic problem is a familiar one to people in every large city in the United States. The problem is easy to describe. There are just too many automobiles and trucks using city streets. New wide superhighways speed more cars and trucks into the city and dump them into narrow downtown streets. The cartoon on this page shows what happens.

Traffic delays hurt business. Drivers who struggle through all this traffic to get downtown must then hunt for parking spaces. Traffic and parking problems discourage shoppers from coming into the city. They prefer to use suburban shopping centers. Downtown stores lose business, and some of them close. Traffic delay is also one reason why offices and factories are being moved to the suburbs.

Traffic experts in many cities have been studying the problem. Some of them believe we need more highways, wider city streets, and more parking spaces. Others disagree. They say that in order to widen old streets or build new ones, buildings or parks have to

This cartoon hints at what may happen when there are just too many cars.

be removed. By the time we make more room for cars to get to the city, there will not be much left in the city worth getting to! Besides, these experts say, every time we solve the traffic problem with more roads, more people decide to drive into the city. Soon the new roads are just as clogged as the old ones.

The Bay Area tackles the problem. Below is a map of the area around San Francisco Bay, California. You will notice two very large cities next to each other. The map also shows you many of the suburban communities nearby. The whole area is usually called the San Francisco Bay Area, or the Bay Area.

Many people who live in the suburbs work in the big cities of San Francisco and Oakland. They drive into these cities every day. During rush hours the streets and bridges are very crowded. The population in the Bay Area has grown very rapidly, and each year more cars are added to the traffic. Soon the roads and bridges will not be able to handle all this extra traffic.

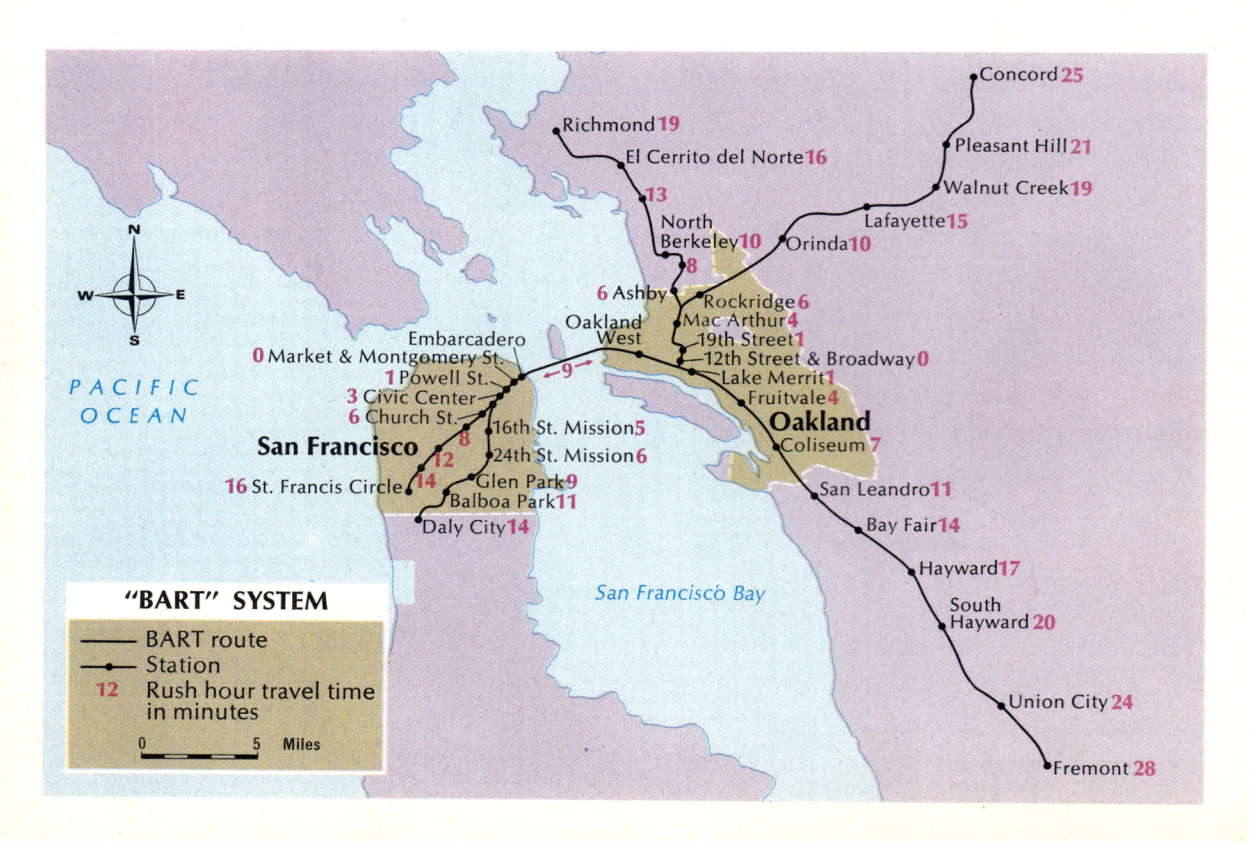

Several years ago, officials of San Francisco, Oakland, and the nearby communities realized something had to be done. They called in traffic experts to study the problem and recommend a plan. The experts decided the best answer was not more bridges and roads. Instead, they proposed a speedy public-railway system that would cover the entire Bay Area. The city and town governments agreed. They presented the idea to the voters of their communities. In 1962 the people voted in favor of building the *mass-transportation system*. Work was soon begun on a 75-mile-long stretch. One section of the railway system is now open. In time many more miles will be added.

BART. Since the transportation system will serve all the communities around San Francisco Bay, it is called the *Bay Area Rapid Transit*, or BART for short. The map shows the route that BART will follow. Each community along the BART line will have a well-designed, well-lighted BART station with plenty of parking space nearby. BART trains, traveling at almost a mile a minute, will speed passengers into the city. Already, a passenger can step into a train in Fremont, at the end of one BART line, and walk out onto the streets of San Francisco only 37 minutes later. Instead of driving through heavy traffic, he can relax and read his morning newspaper along the way. He does not have to worry about parking a car when he gets there. During busy rush hours, trains will run every ninety seconds. BART will be able to carry up to thirty thousand people every hour. BART will also help people to get from one suburb to another. These people will not have to use their cars for the trip.

Help for the people in ghettos. BART will also be a big help to poorer people living in the two big cities of San Francisco and Oakland, especially those in the black ghettos. Without a good public transportation system, the only way for city people to get to some of the well-paid jobs in the suburbs is to drive. But since poor people often do not have cars, they are cut off from these jobs. There are several BART stations in the black ghettos of San Francisco. When BART is completed, residents of those ghettos will be able to travel to a suburb twenty miles away quickly and cheaply. This will open up more jobs for them in suburban offices, factories, and stores.

BART will not solve all the traffic problems of San Francisco, Oakland, and the suburban communities. Many people will still want to drive their cars into the city and to drive them from one suburb to another. But BART will allow a great many people to leave their cars at home, and this will reduce the very heavy auto traffic that sometimes threatens to strangle the city. BART will also help to keep the air a little cleaner.

Fresno Makes Some Changes

An interesting plan for solving the traffic problems of downtown shopping

A Plan for Downtown Areas

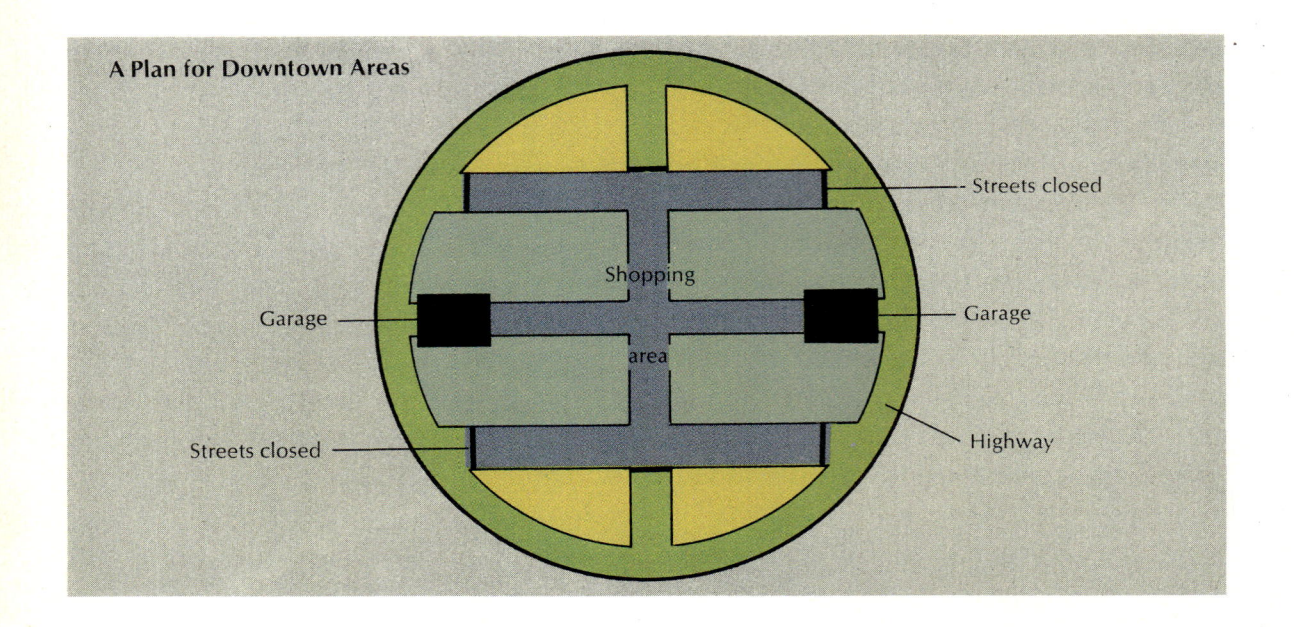

areas has been proposed by an architect and *city planner* named Victor Gruen. The first step in Mr. Gruen's plan is very simple: Keep cars out! The sketch on this page shows in a simple way how Mr. Gruen's plan would work. A wide highway circles the downtown shopping area. Drivers exit from this highway into large parking garages that stretch like long fingers into the shopping area. Each parking garage is only a three- or four-minute walk from the center of the shopping area. The downtown streets would be completely closed to auto, truck, and bus traffic. Streets would be turned into pedestrian malls lined with trees, shrubs, and flowers. There would be no honking horns, no traffic lights, no poisonous auto fumes. Downtown streets would belong to the pedestrian.

Fresno adopts the Gruen Plan. The city of Fresno, California, has begun to put Mr. Gruen's ideas into operation. Fresno is about the size of New Haven, Connecticut, and their metropolitan populations are about the same.

Fresno's downtown stores, like those in many other cities, were slowly losing business to the suburbs. Downtown businessmen decided to do something about it. They formed a group called the Downtown Association of Fresno. This group worked closely with officials in Fresno's city government. They had heard of Mr. Gruen's idea. Together they decided to hire Mr. Gruen to draw up a bold, new plan for downtown Fresno.

The first step in Mr. Gruen's plan was to close the main downtown street, Fulton Street. Instead of being the main street for cars, Fulton Street would become the main street for pedestrians.

The people of Fresno liked the idea and decided to adopt the plan. In the spring of 1964, Fulton Street was closed, and construction began. Five months later, on the day Fulton Mall was opened, a newspaper reported with pride, "Downtown Fresno was returned to the pedestrian today." So it was. The pictures on this page show the changes that came to Fulton Street. Instead of dodging between cars, pedestrians can now have a leisurely walk among shrubbery, fountains, and beautiful pieces of sculpture. Shoppers are returning to downtown Fresno, and storeowners are pleased with the change.

The Superblock. Fulton Mall was the first step in Mr. Gruen's entire plan for the shopping area. When the whole

This is Fulton Street before the renewal. Many of the stores were losing business.

After the renewal, business on the Fulton Mall began to prosper.

243

project is completed, a large part of downtown Fresno will be clear of cars. Fresno calls this area the *Superblock*. People will still be able to drive downtown in cars or buses; trucks will still bring goods to the downtown area. But motor traffic will be separated from pedestrian traffic.

On this page is a sketch of the Superblock. Locate the road around the Superblock. Find the parking garages. Next, find the service roads. What do you suppose the service roads are for? Why won't the service roads interfere with the pedestrian malls?

What are some of the differences between this plan for downtown Fresno and the sketch on page 242 that shows Mr. Gruen's general idea? Why do you think there are differences between the two?

The Superblock is one part of the plan for rebuilding the whole downtown area of Fresno. Mr. Gruen and

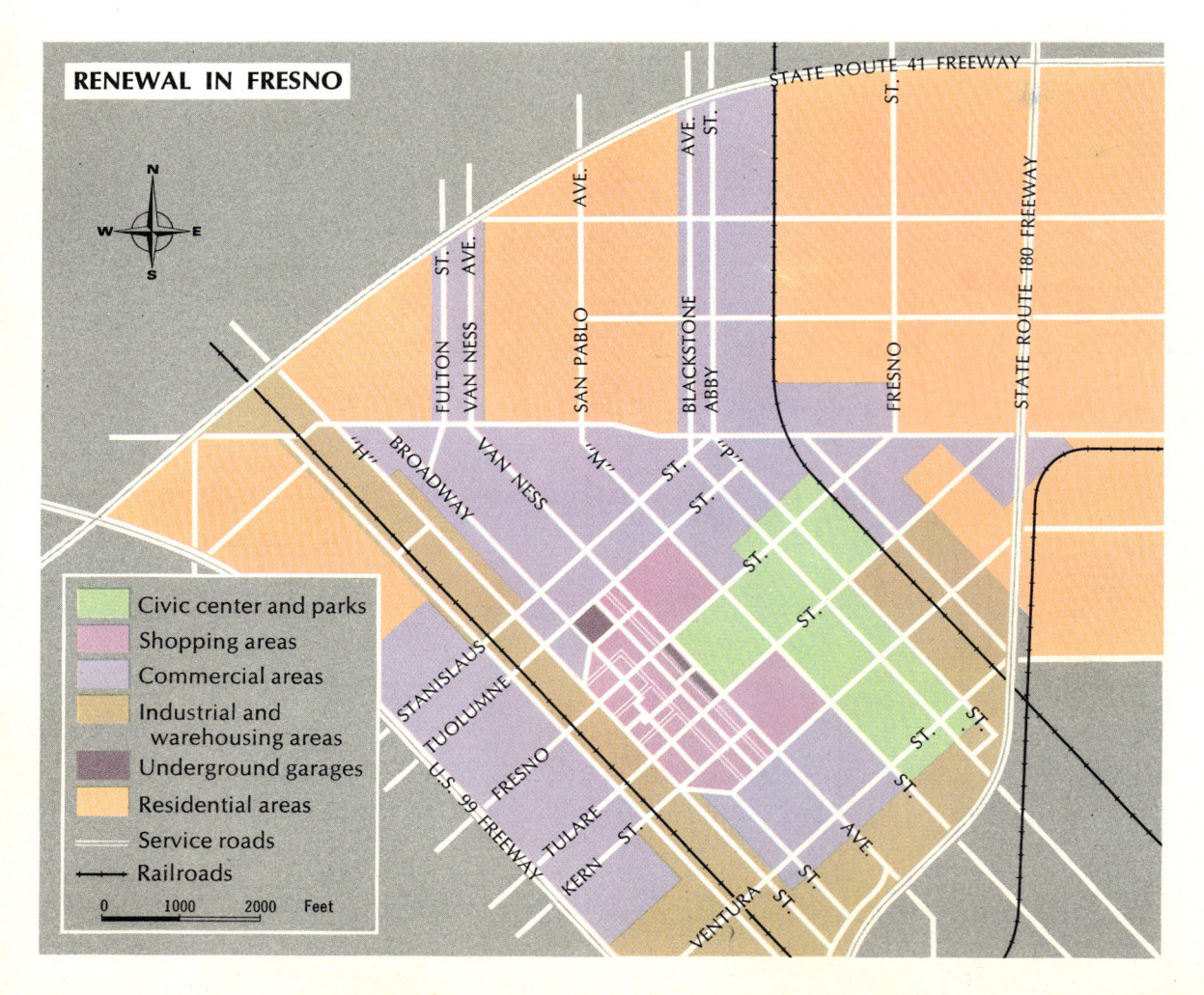

244

the city officials not only want to make downtown Fresno a shopping area again; they also want to make it the center of many activities for the whole urban area. The plans for the rest of downtown Fresno include a new convention hall, where theater and sporting events can be held, a new office building, a new hotel, and many other buildings. Many of these buildings are already completed. Also, large sections of the downtown area are being set aside for special purposes. Thus, industries will be located in one area, warehouses in another, downtown residences in still another. Auto and truck traffic will be permitted in these areas, and they will have wide roads to travel on. Only in the Superblock, set aside for shopping, are motor vehicles prohibited.

As a result of the cooperation of many groups and the support of its citizens, Fresno's downtown is being rebuilt to serve the needs of its people.

Building New Cities

In the 1960's some expert planners decided to build new cities on empty land. They were able to choose the location and shape of the land on which to build. They hoped to put everything in the right place—roads, homes, schools, stores, places for industries, and recreation areas. One very important part of the plans for the new cities is that the planners and the local governments will be able to guide the future development of the cities. In this way the new cities may avoid many of the problems that older ones have.

Reston and Columbia. One of the planned cities is Reston, Virginia, about twenty miles from Washington, D.C. Another is Columbia, Maryland, about fifteen miles from Baltimore. Both cities are in the megalopolis of the East, and both are in large metropolitan areas. Many of the people who live in these new cities travel over new expressways to their jobs in Washington or Baltimore.

Neither new city has been completed yet, but enough has been done to give us some idea of what they will look like someday. There are differences between the two cities, but in many ways they are alike. The plans for both cities call for a mixture of the urban life and the suburban life.

Clusters of villages. When they are completed, Reston and Columbia will have from thirty thousand to seventy thousand people. Each city will be made up of a number of villages built for about five thousand people. The villages will be set apart from one another by woodlands and parks. In each village there will be a center for small shops, churches, schools, and libraries. Homes will also be built in the village centers, as well as around them. All

Reston was built to provide people with the advantages of city life and a chance to enjoy natural surroundings.

homes will be within walking distance of the center.

In the village centers, high-rise apartments will stand close to one-family houses. Some homes will be built above storefronts as in many other cities. This is to give the village an urban look and satisfy people who like living in cities. At the same time there will be enough malls, greens, and wide walkways to leave the centers uncrowded.

Each village will be a short distance from the main city center. That way residents can enjoy the beauties of nature and still get downtown quickly and easily. This center will have buildings and provide services that the villages do not have—large office buildings, hospitals, tall apartments, hotels, theaters, large stores, restaurants, and transportation centers. One section of the center will be set aside for homes. These will be located on malls and squares. Here one will see more of the city life.

Will new cities help? These model cities will take some time to complete. After a while, problems will develop, and planners may have to change their ideas. Both cities are experiments and show what men can do to control their living conditions.

On the other hand, the model cities will not help the older cities solve their most pressing problems. These model cities are not being built for the poor. The price of the apartments and the homes will be too high for the poor.

Steps in Solving Urban Problems

It would be nice if we could plan all our cities from the very beginning on empty ground, as Reston and Columbia were planned. Then we could put everything in just the right places and even help solve some of the problems of the poor. There are some places where we can still do that. But most of us already live in cities that have existed for years. The problems of these cities must be taken care of as soon as possible. We must plan to improve what we already have. This kind of planning is very difficult. If we think about the improvements in New Haven, about BART, and about Fresno's Superblock, we will see why.

The importance of getting information. Let's begin with BART. We can be pretty certain that someone did not just wake up one morning and say, "Let's spend a billion dollars and build a rapid transit system in the Bay Area." Before deciding to build BART, officials had to do a great deal of studying, gathering information, and planning. All of that required a lot of skill. For example, the most important thing they needed to know was whether people would be willing to use BART instead of driving their cars. It would be silly to build an expensive system and then find out no one wanted to use it.

To find out if people were interested in the new plan, the officials carried out a *survey* (sər′ vā). People were hired to ask car drivers how they felt about using public transportation. The results showed that most drivers would use BART—if BART would get them to work as fast as a car, and if they did not have to wait too long for a BART train, and if the fare was not too high. Since engineers and traffic experts said they could build such a system, the city officials decided to go ahead. They drew up a plan and the voters approved it in an election.

There were other important questions. Where should the BART lines be located? Through which communities should its tracks run? Since BART should serve the largest number of people possible, that may seem to be an easy question to answer. BART should run through all the large suburban communities. But when you look at your map on page 240, you will see that these communities are not all in one straight line. BART trains could not go through every one of them. Choices had to be made.

Extending BART under San Francisco Bay required much engineering skill.

Looking to the future. Also, the people who planned the route for BART had to remember that BART would be used for many years. They were planning the route in the 1950's, but BART would have to serve the population in the 1970's and 1980's. Where would most of the population be by then? Remembering how quickly suburbs grow and populations shift, you can imagine how difficult it was to predict that. But after gathering information and making many studies, the experts were able to make a prediction (pri-dik′ shən).

As you can see, the people who designed and built BART had to make many studies, answer many questions, and plan very carefully before they began. They knew their plan would bother some people, but they had to decide in favor of what was good for the city as a whole.

Planning urban renewal. The people who rebuilt Wooster Square in New Haven also had to know many things before they began their work. What kind of place should Wooster Square be? What would be the best way to use the land in this part of the city? Would it be best to turn the whole area into an industrial park? After all, it was right near the railroad, the harbor, and a brand-new highway. Maybe all the old buildings should be torn down and luxury apartments be built to replace them. Possibly the whole area should be set aside for apartments for low-income families.

Wooster Square had some old, historic homes. Should these be saved and fixed up, or would it be better to clear away the whole area and put up new apartment buildings? Or maybe one-family houses, each with a small yard? Should an area for older people be built, or one where families with young children would want to live? As you see, there were some very important decisions to make.

Now think about Fresno. What do you suppose were some of the questions the officials and the people of that city had to ask themselves before they started to build their Superblock and plan the rebuilding of the whole downtown?

What did these three projects have in common? Of course, to begin with, the people had to decide they wanted to do something about their problems. Then they had to gather a great deal of information and make many decisions about what they wanted before they could begin. In other words, they had to plan very carefully.

To help them with their planning, each community called on experts. The planning expert has several jobs. First, he must gather information that will be needed to make a wise decision. Next, the city planner must show how to make the best use of the land in the city.

How Would You Decide?

Planning for urban renewal is more difficult than planning a new city. Nearly all the land in cities is already being used for something. Suppose it is very important to build a new highway into a downtown area. Where should it be placed? If you are starting a new city on empty ground, that will be an easy decision. You will put the highway wherever you think it will do its job best. However, in a city that already exists, you can almost be certain there will be something else occupying that ground.

Three choices. Perhaps you will have a choice of three possible routes. One leads through a quiet neighborhood of one-family houses. Should the highway go there? Not too many people will have to move to make way for the road. But certainly the noise and traffic will ruin a pleasant neighborhood.

Another route leads through an area of older apartment houses where many poor people live. If you knock down these buildings to make room for your road, where will these people go to live? Is it fair to destroy *their* homes?

A third possible route leads through the city park. This one will cost less to build than the other two, for the city already owns the land. No buildings will have to be bought and destroyed; no one will have to move out of his home. On the other hand, if you take this park away for a road now, the park will be lost forever—for you, for your children, and for everyone else who lives in the city.

Which route should be chosen? It will not be an easy decision. You can see why city planners, the city government, and the people who live in the city all have to take part in making such decisions. Planning means making choices. Good planning means making good choices.

Rebuilding Cities Costs Money

It will take a great deal of planning to make our cities better places to live.

But it will also take a great deal of money. Slums must be cleared. Downtown areas must be rebuilt. We need new housing that people can afford; we need roads, sewage-treatment plants, schools, and playgrounds.

Where will the money come from? Some will have to come from private investors—people who build homes, apartment buildings, offices, stores, and factories and sell or rent them. But private investors do not pay for schools, or clearing slums, or building sewage-treatment plants. Over the years, cities have taken these duties upon themselves. They pay for these things from the taxes they collect. Most cities today are short of money. After paying for their regular expenses, they do not have enough money left to do these jobs. Programs to save the cities will cost billions of dollars. Cities have had to turn to the United States government for help.

The United States government has provided some funds for clearing slum areas, for building new housing, and for restoring old housing. It was money from the United States government that enabled New Haven to do much of its rebuilding. If New Haven had been able to get more money, it could have rebuilt more of its neighborhoods.

An important choice. The United States government must spend money for many other things besides rebuilding cities. Some of these other programs are very important to the welfare of the country. Here again, the government and people of the United States are going to have to make choices. Are we ready to spend more money to help our cities? And if we are, where will the money come from? Will we spend less for other programs? If we do not, then we must be willing to pay higher taxes to raise the extra money.

Whatever we decide to do, we cannot afford to delay our decision. Do you recall the list of books given in the beginning of this chapter? One title was *Cities in a Race with Time*. Whether cities win the race or not will be decided by all the people of the United States.

Rehabilitation restored much of the original beauty of Wooster Square.

Working with Concepts and Generalizations

Identifying Concepts

Choose the ending that correctly completes each statement. Write on paper.

1. BART is a plan to (a) tear down tenements and eliminate slums, (b) move people into village-type units in a city, (c) provide a mass transportation system, (d) end traffic problems by creating pedestrian malls.
2. A city planner (a) decides which urban renewal plan a city will use, (b) helps the mayor please the most important voters in the city, (c) gathers information and suggests ways a city can be improved, (d) finds a plan to change cities to suburbs.
3. If urban renewal results in Negro removal, (a) black children will get the chance to live in the suburbs, (b) the needs of one group of citizens will be ignored, (c) city apartments will be eliminated, (d) city slums will be eliminated.

Complete each sentence.

4. Much of the money used to improve cities comes from the _____.
5. A program designed to improve cities is called _____.

Developing Concepts

Write the answers on paper.

1. You are an urban businessman. For several years you have been losing business to suburban shopping centers. Your city government is discussing an urban renewal plan. Do you want urban renewal? Why?
2. You are a landlord. As part of its urban renewal program, the city has demanded that you improve the apartments you rent. You must pay for the improvements yourself. Will you make improvements, or will you sell the property? If you decide to make improvements, will you charge more rent for the apartments? Explain.
3. You are a member of a tenement family. Your family has been ordered to move to make room for new industry. You can't afford to live in a more expensive apartment. What suggestions will you make to the city government?
4. You are a ghetto resident. The entire ghetto will be torn down during urban renewal. New, expensive apartment buildings will be put up where the ghetto now stands. Write to the mayor and explain the problems this will cause for you and others like you.
5. You are mayor of a city. The landlord, tenement dweller, ghetto resident, and businessman described above live in your city. What will you do to try to be fair to each of them? Will you favor the needs of one more than the needs of others? Would your decisions be the same if this were an election year? Explain.

Generalizations

Read the generalizations listed below. Find proof to support each one. Tell what the proof is and the page on which you found it.

1. Most urban centers have developed without careful planning.
2. Urban renewal affects those who live in cities as well as those who depend on the cities for goods, services, and employment.

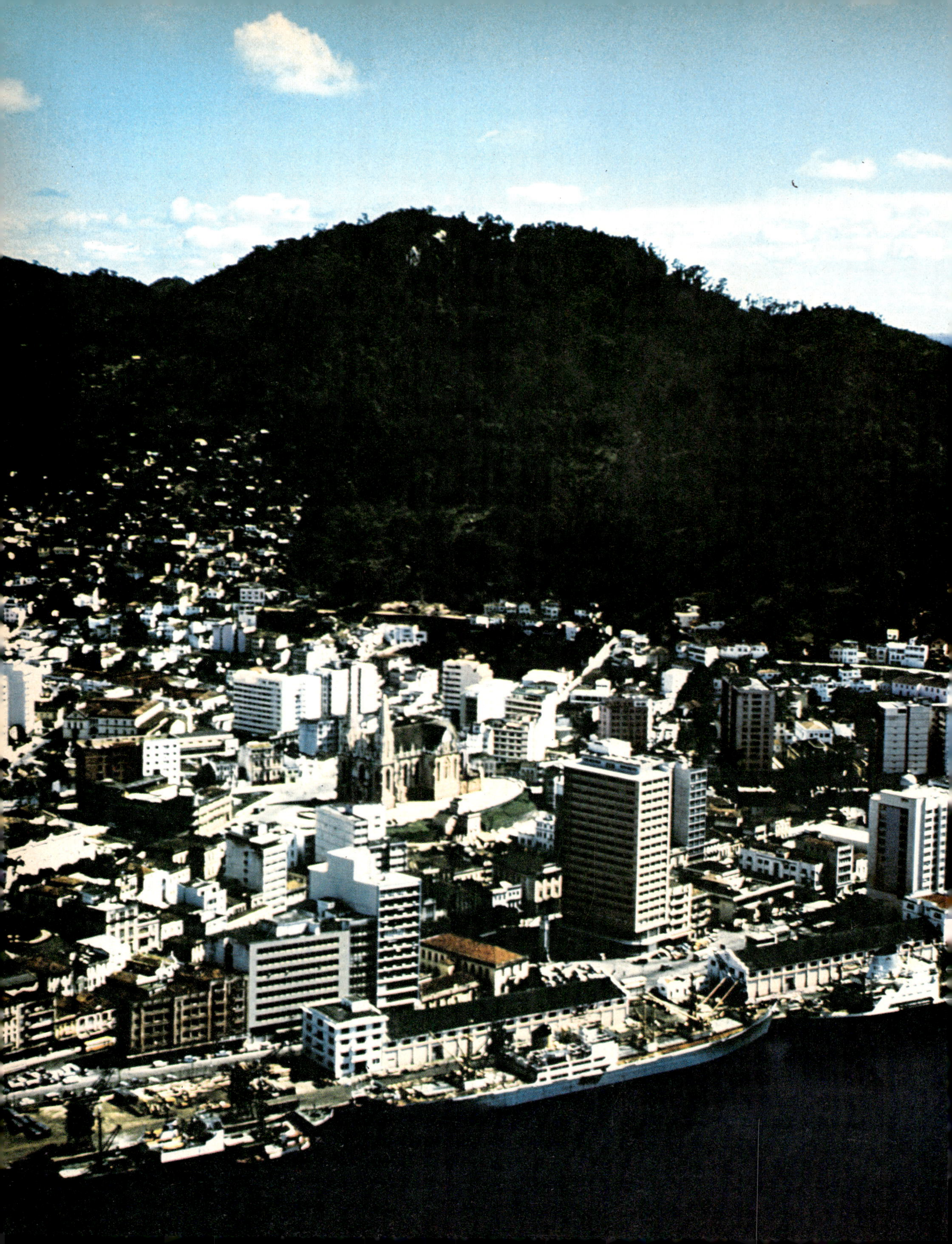

Cities in South America and Canada

13

The movement of people to urban centers is happening not only in the United States, but in other parts of the world as well. People everywhere are finding that cities are centers for many opportunities. To take advantage of these opportunities, millions of people throughout the world are willing to give up old, familiar ways of living. This is true in South America and Canada, where many cities are growing quite rapidly.

To learn more about South American cities, and why they grew up where they did, you will learn about the South American continent. Then you will be able to decide whether South American cities grew for the same reasons that the cities of the United States did. Finally, you will visit several important South American cities and see what life in them is like. You will also see how their problems compare with those of our own cities.

Then you will study the cities of Canada. The climate in much of Canada is very cold throughout the entire year. You will try to figure out whether this will influence the location of cities. In earlier chapters, you studied the importance of rivers to the location of cities. In this chapter, you will have a chance to examine that idea again.

Introducing the South American Continent

The map on this page shows that South America has the shape of a triangle. A study of *latitude* tells us that about two thirds of the continent lies in the *tropics*, that is, between 23½ degrees north and 23½ degrees south of the equator. The southern tip is close to the Antarctic (ant ärk′ tik) Circle. This leaves only a small part of South America in the middle latitudes. If latitude were all there were to consider, you would say that most of this land must be an uncomfortable place in which to live.

A rugged land. The landforms of South America give it a rugged appearance. This is especially true in the West, where the Andes extend four thousand miles along the Pacific coast. At least twenty peaks are about four miles high. Even at the equator some peaks are snow-capped all year round.

The Andes seem to rise straight up from the Pacific Ocean. They leave only a narrow strip of coastland, with very few good natural inlets for harbors. People who live along this narrow coastline are separated from the rest of the continent, for the Andes have few natural passes through which people can cross. Those who live in the high mountains are isolated even from people of their own country.

Mountain valleys. In Bolivia and southern Peru, the Andes form two ranges. Between them is a high, broad plateau called the *altiplano* (äl′ ti plä′ nō). This highland is twelve thousand feet above sea level, and yet there are mountains around it much higher. The climate on the altiplano is fine for farming. Although most of the people farm in this high mountain valley, the area is also important for mineral resources.

Many other mountain valleys in the countries of the Andes are very important as farmland. In most places the soil was formed by volcanoes and is very fertile. Even though these valleys are near the equator, the climate is made comfortable by the altitude. In fact, altitude in this region often affects the climate more than latitude does.

Climate in the Andes. The Spanish-speaking people living near these mountainous areas have named the land according to the climate. They have called the lowlands *tierra caliente* (tyer′ə ka lyen′ tə), or hot land. From such lands come cacao, bananas, cotton, rice, sugar, and tropical fruits. The highlands, such as the altiplano, are called *tierra fría* (frē′ ə), or cold land. There the altitude is from about one mile to two miles. Wheat and potatoes can be grown there. Many Indians raise herds of llamas and alpacas for work animals or for wool. Between the lowlands and the highlands is the *tierra templada* (tem-plä′ də), or temperate land. At this altitude the temperature ranges from 65° to 75° all year round. This is usually coffee-growing country in South America.

Eastern highlands. South America also has highlands to the east. They are older than the Andes and much lower in elevation. In most cases they are wide plateaus, or rolling hills about one thousand feet to three thousand feet high.

The northern part of the highlands is in Venezuela and the Guianas (gē-an′ əz). In fact it occupies about one

This dam in the highlands of Venezuela provides hydroelectric power for much of the country.

half of Venezuela. This part of the highlands is called the Guiana Highlands. As you see on the map, this area is south of the Orinoco (ōr ə nō′ kō) River and reaches almost to the Atlantic coast. The highlands make it difficult to travel into the interior of Venezuela. Parts of the Guiana Highlands are covered with forests, while other sections are treeless grasslands.

Farther south the Brazilian Highlands cover an area of about one million square miles. They run north and south from the Amazon valley to the southern part of Brazil. In the north the highlands are generally very dry. Many scrub, or dwarf, trees cover parts of the area, but the grass is very sparse.

Farther south the highlands make up one of the richest areas in Brazil.

Brazilian highways in the highlands require many bridges and tunnels.

There are miles of good grazing land, fertile soils for farming, and rich reserves of minerals. At one point, as you see on the map, the highlands crowd close to the coast. For many miles they rise so suddenly and so high, they seem to form a separate range of mountains.

Far to the south lie the highlands of Patagonia (pat ə gō′ nyə). For the most part, Patagonia is a cold, windy plateau squeezed between the Andes and the Atlantic Ocean. The small amount of vegetation in the area is chiefly used for grazing sheep.

Lowlands of South America. The Andes on the west and the highlands to the east enclose most of the lowlands of South America. The lowland areas follow the principal river systems of South America—the Amazon, the Orinoco, and the Paraná-Paraguay (par-ə nä′ par′ ə gwā). The lowlands run through the central part of South America, until they meet the Patagonia plateau.

The Amazon lowlands are the largest, and, as you can see on the map, they occupy much of Brazil. To the east along the Amazon, these lowlands are often wet and marshy. Dense jungles with thick underbrush lie along the banks. Indian farmers wage a daily battle to keep the fast-growing plants from covering the soil. In the western part of these lowlands, the land is a bit higher and less likely to be flooded. This is the rain forest, or the *selva*. The selva receives up to a hundred inches of rain in a year. Here the trees are so tall and so full that little sunlight reaches the ground. So, despite the rainfall, the selva is mostly free of the undergrowth you find in jungle areas.

The Amazon lowlands seem to join with those along the Orinoco River. Here the lowlands become a huge grassland, called the *llanos* (la′ nōz), the Spanish word for "plains." Early settlers expected the llanos to be very good pastureland. That has not happened, because the long, extremely dry season that follows the heavy rains leaves the land unfit for year-round grazing.

South of the selvas of the Amazon valley and stretching along the Paraná and Paraguay rivers is the Gran Chaco (grän chäk′ ō). This is a low-lying plain that seems to slope away from the Andes foothills. In July, during the winter, the Chaco is a dry area of scrub forest. During the summer much of the area is flooded. In some parts of the Chaco, the forest is too thick to move through.

To the south of the Gran Chaco lies the pampa, the continuation of the lowland. *Pampa* is an Indian word that means "vast, treeless plain." It extends for miles along the Paraná-Paraguay and the Río de la Plata (rē′ ō də-lə plät′ ə). The pampa is one of the richest farming and grazing lands in South America. Rainfall is even throughout the year. As your population map on page 261 shows, this land is far more heavily settled than the lowlands of the Amazon valley or the Gran Chaco.

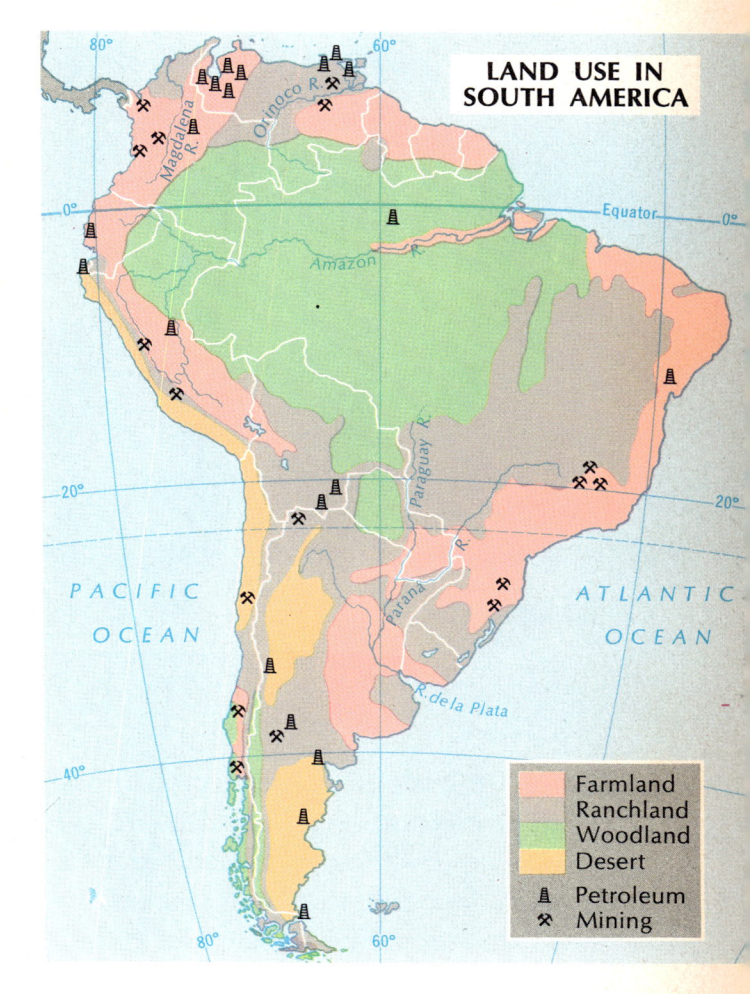

Coastal lands. Along much of the coast of South America, the mountains and highlands reach almost to the ocean and leave little room for coastal lands. Moreover, climate and rainfall make

Much of western Chile, on the Pacific Ocean, is desert.

living difficult in many parts of the South American coastal lands. In the north and northeast, the climate is extremely hot and wet. It is a very uncomfortable area in which to live or work. Only the cool breezes from the Atlantic prevent the same conditions from hurting much of the Brazilian coast.

On the western coast, in Peru and northern Chile, cool ocean winds keep any moisture from reaching the land. As a result, much of this coastal strip is desert land in which life is found only along strips of land irrigated by mountain streams. Yet some of the most pleasant land in South America is found south of this desert along the coast.

Looking at the mountains, lowlands, and wet and dry coastlands, you would say geography has made much of South America a difficult place in which to live. Yet the population of South America is close to 200 million people today. Look at the population map on page 261. Do the people avoid the more difficult locations you have read about above? Are any areas more densely populated than you expected?

Choosing Sites for Cities

In the next part of this chapter, you will have a chance to make use of your new information about South American geography. You will also use what you already know about why cities are

HIGHWAYS OF SOUTH AMERICA

RAILROADS OF SOUTH AMERICA

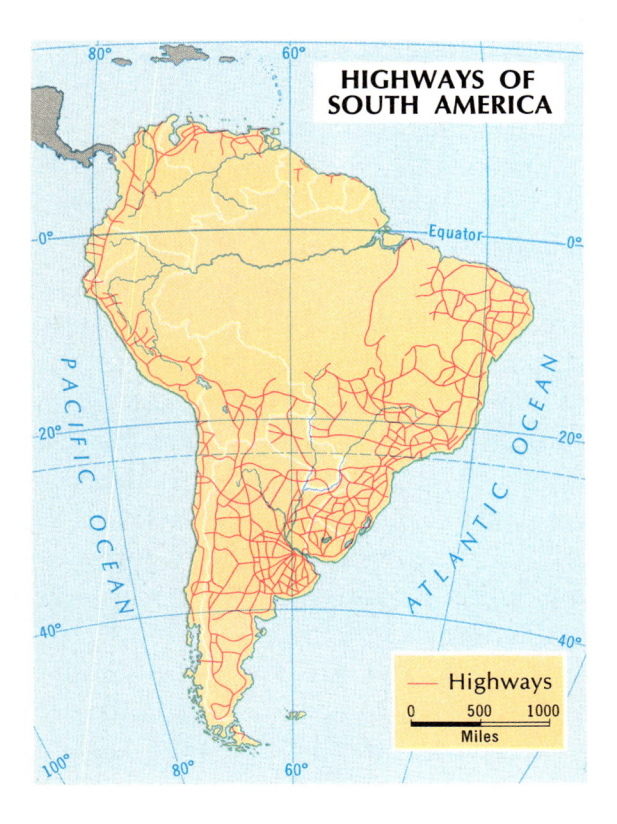

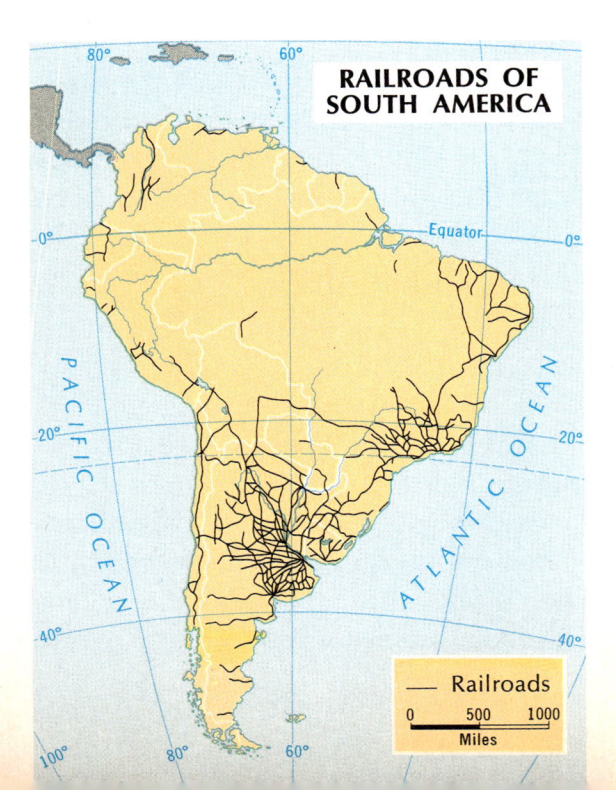

located where they are. You are going to try to decide where South American cities are located.

Study the maps of South America. These maps show the location of the main rivers, roads, and railroads on that continent. Now, using information from the maps along with all your other knowledge about geography and cities, where would you expect to find large commercial cities in South America? Later on, you will have a chance to check all of your choices. But for now, let us just look at two places you probably selected.

A splendid location. First, find the Río de la Plata. Did you name this as one of the areas where there would probably be a city? If you did, you were right. That is where the city of Buenos Aires (bwā nə sar′ ēz), in the country of Argentina, is located. It is a city of four million people, about as large as Chicago. The metropolitan area of Buenos Aires has about seven million people.

Look at the splendid location this is for a commercial city. The Río de la Plata (whose name is Spanish for "river of silver") is not a river at all, but an arm of the ocean that reaches 170 miles inland. A body of water such as this, at the mouth of a river where the tide meets the current, is called an *estuary* (es′ chủ er′ ē). The rivers that flow into this estuary have run through the pampa, the rich grazing and farming area you read about. In this backcountry, twenty million farmers, ranchers, and lumbermen live. Even more important than the rivers for traffic into Buenos Aires are the railroads. Look at your map and see how many railroads bring people and goods into Buenos Aires.

Large amounts of wheat, meat, and hides are sent from surrounding areas to Buenos Aires. There they are loaded on ocean-going ships and carried to the rest of the world. Meanwhile, factories in Buenos Aires send manufactured goods to the little towns in the backcountry.

Along the Amazon. For our second location, find the Amazon River on your map. The Amazon flows across almost the entire width of South America and is one of the world's deepest and widest rivers. Many smaller rivers and streams, called *tributaries*, flow into the Amazon. The Amazon carries twice as much water to the sea as the great Mississippi does. Because water transportation was cheaper and quicker years ago, you might expect that trading centers would have started along the Amazon. Today you might expect to find many commercial cities along this river.

Well, there are a few. At its mouth is a city named Belém (bə lem'). Its population is about 400,000. It is a good-sized city, but it is less than one tenth the size of Buenos Aires. This is hardly the great city you might expect to find where the world's largest river empties into the ocean.

A thousand miles upriver, where the Río Negro (nā' grō) joins the Amazon, is another city of about 300,000, called Manaus (mə naús'). Oceangoing ships can load and unload here. At one time Manaus was the chief center of the rubber trade.

On the whole 3,200 miles of the Amazon River, Belém and Manaus are the only large cities. Doesn't that seem strange? At first it does. But now you can use your information about the geography of this region.

What do you know about the climate and the land along the Amazon River? How is the land in the selva used? Look at your population map and see whether the population in that whole area is dense. How does it compare to the population along the Paraná River, on the pampa that makes up the backcountry for Buenos Aires? You already know the importance of a well-settled backcountry to a commercial city. Now does it seem so strange that there are only two large commercial cities on the Amazon?

Along two other rivers. Let us find another place where we can use our new information. Find the Orinoco River on your map. Did you choose the mouth of the Orinoco, or perhaps somewhere else along that river, as the place where a commercial center would develop? Now look at the physical map to see what kind of land there is along the route of this river. Now check your land-use map. How is the land near the river used? Finally, check your population map to see if the area along the Orinoco River is densely settled. Now, with all this information, you will be able to make a better guess about whether there will be a commercial city on the Orinoco River today.

A little farther west of the Orinoco is another important river system with a very different story. This is the Magdalena (mag də lā' nə) River and its tributaries. It runs north through the country of Colombia. Compared to the mighty Amazon, the Magdalena is not a large river. Still, it is deep enough for river barges to carry goods back and forth. After you have checked the physical map, the land-use map, and the population map again, would you expect to find a large commercial city somewhere along the Magdalena?

Check your choices. If you look carefully at the map that shows the rivers, railroads, and roads in South America, you should have no trouble choosing a few port cities on the coast of South America. You may have found a few already. They will be places with a good harbor, usually a harbor protected by a little hook-shaped piece of land. Of course, rivers, railroads, or roads, or all three, will connect the

Manaus, near the junction of the Amazon River and the Río Negro, is an important port.

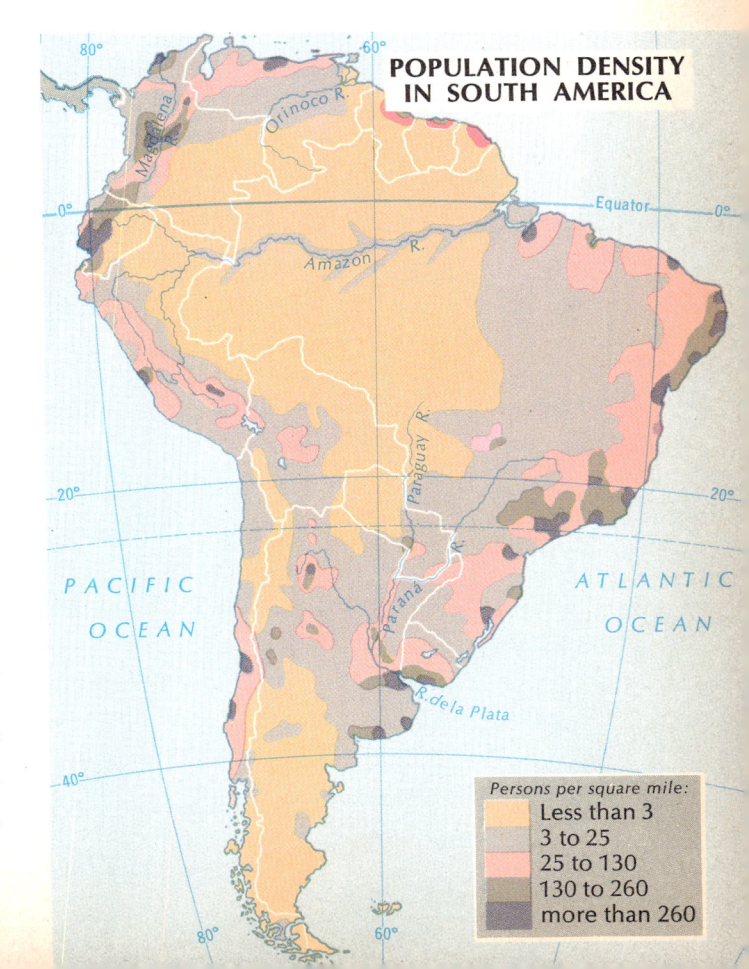

POPULATION DENSITY IN SOUTH AMERICA

Persons per square mile:
Less than 3
3 to 25
25 to 130
130 to 260
more than 260

Another Town of America. Do you remember the Town of America, which was discussed in an earlier chapter? You might be interested to know that South America had its own Town of America. It is called Ciudad Bolívar (sē´ ü thä bə lē´ vär), or Bolivar City, and is in Venezuela. The city was named after a great military leader, Simón Bolívar. He helped South Americans win their independence from the Spanish in the early 1800's. Like the Town of America in the United States, the city was "certain" to become great. At least that is what the people of the area said. How could it not become great? It was located about 250 miles up the Orinoco River, right at the edge of the llanos, or plains, of Venezuela. Everyone predicted that settlers would soon fill up those plains raising cattle and growing grain. They would then ship all their products to Ciudad Bolívar, which would become an important meat-packing and grain-milling center. Ciudad Bolívar—the whole world would soon know of this city as it became the great supplier of meat and grain.

Only it did not happen that way. Very few people ever heard of Ciudad Bolívar. Those who had predicted it would become great thought European immigrants would take up farming and ranching on these plains. Immigrants came, but they were too few to make a difference. There was some cattle raising, but most of it was on

port to the interior. You can check the locations you choose by looking at the population map. Is the population dense at the spot you picked for a city?

Now, as we promised at the beginning of this chapter, here is a map showing the principal cities of South America. The commercial cities are marked in a special way. How many of them did you pick out? Do your choices have anything in common? How many were in the interior?

Buenos Aires is an important manufacturing and port city in Argentina.

the part of the plains far away from Ciudad Bolívar. The cattle were shipped to other cities for packing. The government did not build good roads for the farmers and ranchers to get their products to Ciudad Bolívar. So, one hundred years after Ciudad Bolívar was supposed to be a great city, it was still a very small town. Unless people moved into the backcountry and produced goods for sale in the city, Ciudad Bolívar would not become a great commercial center.

A discovery brings a happy ending. The story of Ciudad Bolívar has a happier ending than the story of the Town of America. About twenty-five years ago, it was discovered that the nearby mountain, named Cerro Bolívar, was rich in iron ore. At the same time, some large ore deposits in the United States began to be used up. Two steel companies from the United States decided to start mining in Venezuela. They built roads and railroads to Cerro Bolívar. They also deepened the river channels so that ships with heavy ore cargoes could navigate them. Soon the mining industry developed, and Ciudad Bolívar became an important mining city of sixty thousand people. Instead of shipping meat down the Orinoco River to the rest of the world, the city is shipping iron ore. But it still did not become the great city that people hoped for.

Government Cities in South America

Let us now look at another kind of city—the government city. Do you remember what government cities are? Do government cities require harbors, docks, railroads in the way that commercial cities do?

There are eleven independent nations in South America and each of them has a capital city. A few of these capitals are great commercial centers or manufacturing centers, like Buenos Aires. Most of them are simply government cities.

We are going to look at two government cities that are very different from each other. One is the ancient city of Bogotá in Colombia; the other is Brasília (brə zil′ yə), the new capital city of Brazil.

263

Caracas, Venezuela, is an old city with many modern buildings.

Bogotá. The city of Bogotá lies in a long, green valley high in the Andes. As you can see on your map, it is near the equator, where the temperature at sea level is high the year round. But Bogotá is one and a half miles above sea level. Rarely does the temperature go above 80° or below 40°. That makes this city a very comfortable place to live.

Long before the Spanish ever heard of South America, Indian tribes had built a town on this spot. The comfortable climate was one of the reasons why they selected a valley in the mountains for their town. Another reason was that the mountains on all four sides protected them from attack by other Indian tribes. Also, the land in the valley was fertile and produced abundant food.

When the Spanish came to South America and conquered the Indians, they took over Bogotá. They liked it for the same reasons that the Indians did—the pleasant climate, the fertile land, and the protection of the mountains. The Spanish had still another reason for choosing it. Many of them were city people—they had enjoyed city living in Spain and wanted to enjoy it in America, too.

The Spanish rebuilt Bogotá to make it look like the towns they had known in Spain. In the center of the town was the great square, which the Spanish called a *plaza*. Facing the plaza were such government buildings as the governor's palace, the town council building where the local rulers made laws, and the jail for those who broke them. The largest church was also here. All the main streets of the town led into the plaza.

Bogotá could never become a great commercial city, for the same mountains that gave it protection cut it off from the rest of the world. The only way to move goods and people across the mountains was by muleback. The Spanish turned Bogotá into a government city. During almost three hundred years of Spanish rule, it grew steadily.

The city changes and grows. When Colombia won its independence from Spain in 1819, the new nation kept Bogotá as its capital. Today Bogotá is one of the largest cities in the Western Hemisphere. The population of metropolitan Bogotá is about two million, which is almost the size of the population of metropolitan St. Louis.

The original Spanish town with its large plaza is still there. Now it is just

Bogotá, a very modern city, was the site of an Indian town.

one section of the growing city. Beyond the city lie its suburbs, and farther into the valley are the villages and farms that produce the food for the capital.

Today Bogotá is a mixture of the old and the new. Along its streets one sees churches and homes built by the Spanish more than two hundred years ago. Next to some of these stand modern office buildings, tall apartment houses, and hotels. Some of these buildings are twenty stories high. One has fifty stories.

Bogotá is becoming a manufacturing center also. Its factories produce textiles, leather goods, radios, home appliances, paint, glass, cement, and many other products. They also prepare the food that is grown in the nearby valley. Several small automobile plants have opened in Bogotá.

Brasília. Set back almost six hundred miles from the Atlantic coast, in the thinly populated western plains of Brazil, is the city of Brasília. It is a government city, as is Bogotá, but it is different from Bogotá in almost every other way. While Bogotá is ancient, Brasília is new. Bogotá grew, without very much planning, from a small Indian town into a very large city, but every inch of Brasília was carefully planned before it was built. Bogotá grew slowly, but less than twenty years ago there was not a single building where Brasília now stands.

To understand why Brasília was built, we have to know something about Brazil's history. You will remember that the Portuguese first came to Brazil in the 1500's. Early Portuguese arrivals settled along the Atlantic coast. The population of Brazil increased steadily over the next 350 years. In the United States, much of the population moved west in search of new lands and new opportunities. In Brazil, almost all the population stayed where it was, in a narrow strip of land along the coast. Until 1900 the only Brazilians who moved west were miners searching for precious metals, cattle ranchers hoping to use vast grazing lands in the interior, and a few farmers. Ninety percent of the population remained within the narrow coastal strip.

In the last hundred years, many immigrants from Portugal, Italy, Germany, and Japan came to Brazil. Many were attracted to the south of Brazil, where the great coffee crop is grown. Brazil produces one half of the world's supply of coffee. Some immigrants started farms of their own; others worked on the large coffee plantations. When most of the land near the coast was already being used, immigrants moved farther west. The government of Brazil invited more and more immigrants to its country. Even though many people came and moved to the west, the area is still thinly settled.

These pictures are all of Brasília, the capital city of Brazil. It is a carefully planned city. Above is an overview of the city. To the left is Superblock West, a section of high-rise apartments and one of the main residential areas of the city. Below is the official government area. The buildings in the center house the Brazilian Congress and other government officials.

267

For many years the government was concerned about this problem. Only through more western settlement could the country become wealthier. How could more settlers be attracted to the west? How could the government make Brazilians aware of the vast unused riches of this area? One way the government could do this and surely impress the people would be to move the capital from Rio de Janeiro to the interior. Government workers would have to go there to live. This would attract merchants, manufacturers, teachers, and people of all kinds. In this way the government would show everyone that it had faith in the future of the western area.

A planned city. The idea of building a new capital city in the interior of Brazil was talked about for more than a hundred years, but it remained just a dream. Then, in 1956, Brazilians began to make the dream come true. Plans for the new city and designs for its buildings were drawn up by experts. Workers were brought from the coastal cities to clear the site. The project was under way.

The first thing to be built was an airport, for there were no roads and railroads into Brasília. Most supplies for construction had to be flown in. Soon roads and railroads also were built, connecting the future city with other parts of the nation. Meanwhile, buildings were rising where only months before there had been nothing but grass and trees. Each building was a piece of one great master plan.

After four years of work, enough of the city was completed for the government to move some of its offices from Rio de Janeiro to Brasília. Since then much progress has been made, but at a slower pace.

The plan of Brasília is in the shape of an airplane. The main body of the plane is reserved for government buildings and other public places. The wings of the plane are the residential areas. These residential areas will someday house about 500,000 people. The areas are divided into superblocks. Each superblock has its own school, a supermarket, a health center, a social center, and a playground area. At the front of the airplane design is a man-made lake, nineteen miles long. This will supply fresh water as well as beach and swimming areas.

What the people think. Most Brazilians are proud of their planned city. It showed the world what they could create. Some of the buildings are among the most beautiful in South America and the world. In ten years Brasília's population rose from zero to 350,000. Many factories have opened in the capital, and people who do not work for the government may find jobs in them. Roads to the coast give the people the chance to visit the older cities of Brazil. Brasília's airport is already a very busy one.

On the other hand, there are those who feel that Brasília is not doing what it is supposed to do. They say that the new capital is not attracting others to move west. They feel that the city will remain cut off from the life of Brazil. Some complain that the capital lacks the excitement of older cities.

Those who planned Brasília at the beginning are now disappointed because the government did not always keep to the plans. The government has not done enough to complete the housing plans. Slums have already developed around the city. When the city was being built, laborers lived in wooden houses in shantytowns or "free cities" outside the city limits. As the construction went on, these shacks were to be torn down. They were not, and they have since become slums. At the present time the population of these shantytowns is increasing more rapidly than that of Brasília itself.

Three Important Cities

As you can see on the map on page 262, South America has many other large cities. We are going to take a

Sugar Loaf Mountain is seen at the left in this view of Rio.

close look at three of the most interesting ones. The three we shall study are Rio de Janeiro and São Paulo (saù paù′ lü) in Brazil, and Caracas, the capital of Venezuela.

Rio de Janeiro, port and playground. The Portuguese word *rio* means "river," but Rio de Janeiro was misnamed, for it has no river at all. Rio is located on the Atlantic coast, and what it does have is one of the largest and finest harbors in the world. Even without a river, Rio has always been an important commercial city. At first sight the city seems to be cut off from the backcountry by a line of mountains. However, a number of valleys form narrow avenues to the interior of the country. In early days, farm goods and minerals were carried by mule down these valleys to the ships in Rio's harbor. Today railroads and highways wind through these same valleys into the backcountry.

Rio was the capital of Brazil until Brasília was built. Some government offices have not yet moved to the new capital. Of course, being a government city helped Rio to become a large city as much as its fine harbor did.

More than anything else, Rio is probably best known as one of the world's truly beautiful cities. A look at the picture on page 269 will help you to see why. The line of mountains makes a wonderful background for the miles of fine, curving beaches that form the shoreline. At the entrance to the harbor stands Sugarloaf Mountain. The sunny climate added to scenes like this makes Rio a tourist's paradise. The tourist business in this city of beaches provides many jobs for its residents.

In recent years manufacturing has also increased in Rio. Hundreds of factories produce clothing, leather goods, wood products, and such modern goods as cameras, tape recorders, and television sets. Rio also has some heavy industry that manufactures metal products, refines petroleum (pə trō′ lē əm), assembles automobiles,

Slum residents in Rio dry their laundry.

and turns out electrical equipment. Rio is also the money and banking center of Brazil.

The growth of manufacturing has brought many more people to Rio. New suburbs are spreading down the valleys like huge fingers. To ease the traffic problem of people in the suburbs, the government has built new highways. Many tunnels and bridges had to be built for some of the highways to reach the coastal lowland. Hundreds of narrow streets built in colonial days still cause traffic problems within the city.

Part commercial, part government, part resort, and part manufacturing, Rio is one of the continent's most interesting cities.

São Paulo—a city built by coffee. About two hundred miles from beautiful Rio is a city of a very different kind. This is the busy city of São Paulo. São Paulo was founded about four hundred years ago. For the first three hundred years, it was a small trading center for farms in the area. The farming population nearby grew slowly, and so did São Paulo.

Then, about a hundred years ago, many European immigrants began to come to Brazil, just as they were coming to the United States. The Brazilian government offered them cheap land if they would settle in farming areas. Many did, starting coffee farms and cotton farms. The

Coffee is being loaded in Santos, Brazil.

agricultural region grew, and São Paulo grew with it, supplying the farmers with the goods and services they needed—farm machinery, burlap bags for shipping coffee beans, and of course building materials, clothing, and food.

As you see on your map, São Paulo is not a port city. The port city from which coffee is shipped to the world is Santos (sant' əs), about thirty miles from São Paulo. Santos is right at sea level, and its climate is uncomfortably moist and hot. It is also plagued with mosquitoes and other insects. Because São Paulo is nearly three thousand feet above sea level, its temperature is much pleasanter, ranging from 50° to 80°. Therefore, people prefer to live in São Paulo rather than Santos.

271

(Top) Oil derricks rise from Lake Maracaibo. (Center) In these buildings the Venezuelan Congress meets. (Bottom) Caracas has a mixture of old and new architecture.

A great commercial center. Today São Paulo continues to serve the coffee growers. As a great banking center, it provides loans to them. As a transportation center, it furnishes trucks to move the coffee and warehouses to store it. It also sells the chemical sprays used by coffee and cotton growers to protect crops against insects.

But São Paulo is far more than a coffee center today. It is also the largest manufacturing center in Brazil. There are more factories in this Brazilian city than there are in such United States cities as Chicago and Pittsburgh. More people make their living in the factories of São Paulo than in the factories of most large American manufacturing cities.

São Paulo is the largest city in all of South America. In fact, it is the second-largest city in the entire Western Hemisphere. Only New York City is larger. And São Paulo continues to grow. Every eight minutes another house is built in São Paulo, and still this does not keep up with the demand in this booming city.

The rapid growth of São Paulo has brought other urban problems. Traffic in the city moves at a snail's pace. Someone discovered that cars could travel only six miles an hour during rush hours. Travel to and from work takes from four to six hours a day for some workmen.

About one third of the population of São Paulo lives in homes without running water, and about one half of the houses are not connected to sewers. So, like any other large city, São Paulo has problems that have come with its growth.

Caracas — a city made modern by oil. As you can see on your map, Caracas is not very far from the equator. Still the climate there is not uncomfortable, for the city is more than three thousand feet above sea level. It is located in a valley between high mountain peaks. Do you remember any other city near the equator that is comfortable because it is high above sea level?

Caracas is about ten miles inland from the Caribbean Sea. Like São Paulo, it has a port city nearby, named La Guaira (lə gwī′ rə). La Guaira is located near the sea in the lowlands. A new superhighway, which goes across and through the mountains, allows goods to be shipped easily and quickly between Caracas and its port city. La Guaira is a busy port, but the city is not nearly so large as Caracas. Why do you suppose people settled in Caracas instead of La Guaira?

Like so many cities in South America, Caracas became large partly because it was a government city. It is the capital of Venezuela. For many years, however, Caracas was only a quiet, medium-sized city, with no tall buildings or anything else very modern about it. Oil changed this ordinary city into the large, modern city it is.

About thirty years ago, rich oil fields were discovered in Venezuela, especially in Lake Maracaibo near the coast. Oil derricks sprouted up like trees in a forest, and before long, oil became Venezuela's most important product. The companies that actually explore for oil and recover it are not owned by Venezuelans. Most of them are American-owned companies. Under Venezuelan law, they must pay one half of their profits from Venezuelan oil to the government. It is the money from oil that has built the new offices, factories, and apartment buildings that make Caracas one of the most modern of all cities. Oil also pays for public services such as schools, recreation areas, and art museums.

A city of the past and present. Caracas is the most modern of the old cities on the continent. Its new buildings gleam in the sunshine and give the city a beautiful skyline. Its busy streets tell everyone that it is a city on wheels. In fact, Caracas has more taxicabs than even New York City. Its shops sell modern goods, and modern art decorates the city. Yet, in spite of all that, there are many interesting reminders of the past. Many of its nearly two million people cling to ways they knew when the city was smaller and quieter. Thousands of downtown office workers, for example, still follow the old custom of going home for lunch instead of eating at the office or a restaurant.

One result is that Caracas' streets have to handle four rush hours a day instead of the usual two!

Some Problems of South American Cities

Look at the pictures of South American cities in this chapter again. Do the pictures on page 270 and page 275 show that cities in South America have problems very much like those of our own cities?

Water and air. Though the problems of our own cities are serious, many problems are even worse in South America.

Urban Water Supply in the Americas

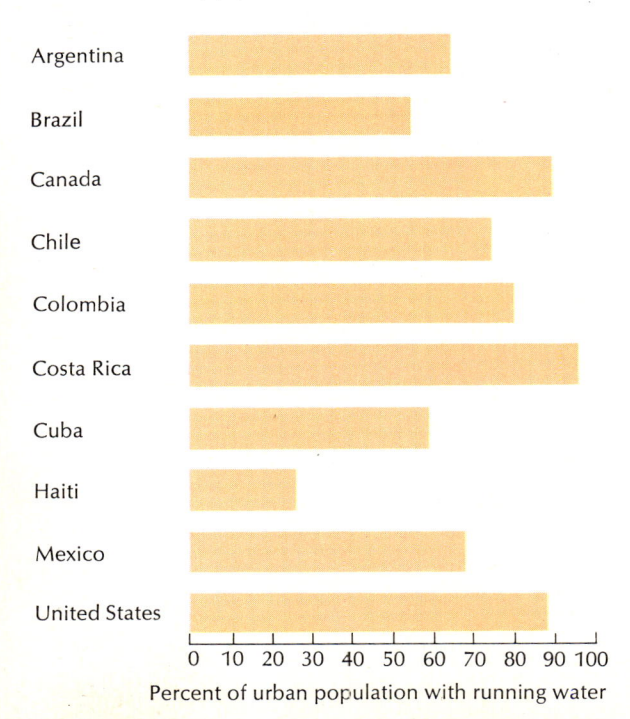

Argentina	▬▬▬▬▬▬
Brazil	▬▬▬▬▬
Canada	▬▬▬▬▬▬▬▬
Chile	▬▬▬▬▬▬▬
Colombia	▬▬▬▬▬▬▬
Costa Rica	▬▬▬▬▬▬▬▬▬
Cuba	▬▬▬▬▬
Haiti	▬▬
Mexico	▬▬▬▬▬▬
United States	▬▬▬▬▬▬▬▬

0 10 20 30 40 50 60 70 80 90 100
Percent of urban population with running water

For instance, all cities in the United States provide water pure enough to drink. Few South American cities do. Lack of pure water has caused much sickness. The water that comes out of faucets may be used for washing clothes and dishes, but not always for drinking. Residents in parts of many cities purchase their water in barrels or buckets. There are times when even the supply of impure water runs out. Then, for a day or so, no water comes out of the faucets at all.

The air pollution problem is also bad. Few South American cities have as many factories, apartment houses, and cars pouring smoke into the air as United States cities have. But the buses and cars burn a low-grade fuel that pours more dirt and poisonous gas into the air than the fuel we use.

Housing needs—a growing problem. Perhaps the worst problem for South American cities is a shortage of housing. Millions of people have recently moved from the rural areas to the cities all over the continent. These rural people have few skills they can use in city jobs, and so they must take the lowest-paid jobs or stay unemployed. They crowd into run-down housing in the oldest parts of the city. Sometimes they move in with relatives or friends. Often two or three families live in one crowded flat. Three and four children sleep in one bed, walls are crumbling, and rats and insects move freely through the rooms. Courtyards separating some buildings were once gardens, but now are covered with garbage or strung with clotheslines. Such slums are the scene of many crimes. People who live there simply try to keep alive. They spend their lives cut off from the rest of the city. One writer has called the areas "the slums of despair." What do you think the writer meant?

The barriada. There is another kind of slum in South American cities that also is unlike any found in the United States. This second type of slum is a shantytown that grows up on vacant land in the city or more often on the edges of the city. Nearly every South American city has slums of this sort. They appear on the hillsides near Rio, Caracas, and Bogotá. They even rise on the plains outside the brand-new city of Brasília.

We can learn something about these shantytown slums by studying those in Lima (lē′ mə), a city that has the largest slums of all. Find Lima on the map. It is the capital of Peru and has a population of more than 1,700,000, about the same size as Detroit's. Almost half of Lima's population lives in slums.

Each slum is not one large area, but really a number of shanty settlements. In Lima each such settlement is called a *barriada* (bär ē ä′ dä). Each barriada has hundreds of shacks in it. Though

Slum families live in poverty near this luxurious apartment building in Caracas.

called by different names in other South American cities, barriadas are all very much alike.

How a barriada develops. This is the way a barriada comes about. A number of rural families who are moving into Lima find no decent housing that they can afford. Many times there are no vacancies in the slums inside the city. Sometimes the rural families have lived in slums for some years and can no longer stand it. Groups of such families will wander through the city and around its limits until they find some empty land.

A number of them, perhaps a hundred families, get together and decide to take a piece of land and make their houses there. Sometimes the vacant land is owned by the government and sometimes by private citizens. It makes little difference to people who are desperate for houses of their own.

The people usually wait until the city is asleep. Then they move in quickly. When the city awakes, it finds dozens of shacks made of old scraps of wood, cardboard, tin, straw matting, and anything else that was lying around.

That is the beginning of a barriada. Soon hundreds of people join the settlement, and it grows rapidly. One barriada in Lima has over 35,000 people in it. Living conditions are dreadful. For years there is no running water, no garbage collection, no sewerage. Houses have no kitchens and little furniture.

You may wonder why people would rather live there than return to the country. As hard as life is in the barriada, it is even worse in the country. The land is worn thin, and the farmer cannot make a living. There are no jobs, no schools, no doctors, and no hospitals.

Slums of hope. After a few years, conditions in the barriada often begin to improve. Many of the squatters (skwot′ ərz) have been able to get jobs in Lima. They have been spending as much as they can of their small incomes on their houses. In time, the one-room straw hut has been replaced by a three- or four-room house made

New homes replace a slum in Caracas.

Shacks cover a hillside in this slum in Rio.

of wood. Beds, tables, and chairs have been brought in from time to time. One day they may build a new four-room house made of concrete or concrete blocks. Other families in the barriada may help them to construct the new house.

By this time, ten years may have passed since the families first took over the land. By now they have formed a little community. If they are fortunate, the city officials of Lima may decide to bring in running water, sewers, and electricity. They may even build an elementary school for the barriada.

Of course no one would mistake even the best barriada or any other such settlement for a comfortable housing development. Yet there are some benefits. The people pay no rent, since they just squatted there and built their own shacks. That means a little extra money for other needs. They also enjoy the friendliness of the community and receive help without charge. The governments of South American countries are beginning to see some advantages in these settlements. Barriadas are serving as waiting stations until public housing is put up. And without barriadas, the slums of the city would be terribly overcrowded.

In a great many ways, barriadas are like the slums we know in our cities. In fact, in the beginning, they are much worse than our slums. But you may have noticed an interesting difference between our slums and the barriadas. What usually happens as the years go by in a slum in the United States? What happens in a barriada that led someone to call them "the slums of hope"?

Cities in Canada

Let us look now at the cities of our neighbor to the north, Canada. We will start by studying a map of that land, for as in South America, geography and climate help explain much about the location of Canada's urban centers.

First, look at the latitude of Canada. What does it tell you about the climate? Do you think there will be farming in the northern part? As you see, much of the land area of Canada, like that of South América, is extremely difficult to make a living on. The farms of Canada are all in the southern part of the country, where there is at least a short growing season.

Next, look at the waterways throughout Canada. Find the St. Lawrence River. This river is also in the southern part of the country. Notice where it connects with the Great Lakes. Together they form a water highway, a thousand miles long, into the middle of North America.

Because of what you know about where cities are located, you have surely figured out by now that all

Canada's leading cities are located in the south, where the farming population is. And in eastern Canada every city is on the great water highway or on a river that flows into it.

Many kinds of cities. Like the cities of the United States and South America, Canada's cities are of many different kinds. Many of them began as commercial cities, and commerce is still a very important part of their activities. Montreal is a good example. Just beyond Montreal the St. Lawrence has rapids that prevent vessels from sailing farther inland. You may remember that this was why the explorer Jacques Cartier stopped where he did in 1535. Because ocean ships could not go beyond Montreal, it became an important seaport. Many years later a small canal was built to get around the rapids. This allowed small boats with their furs and farm products from the West to reach Montreal by water, increasing that city's trade.

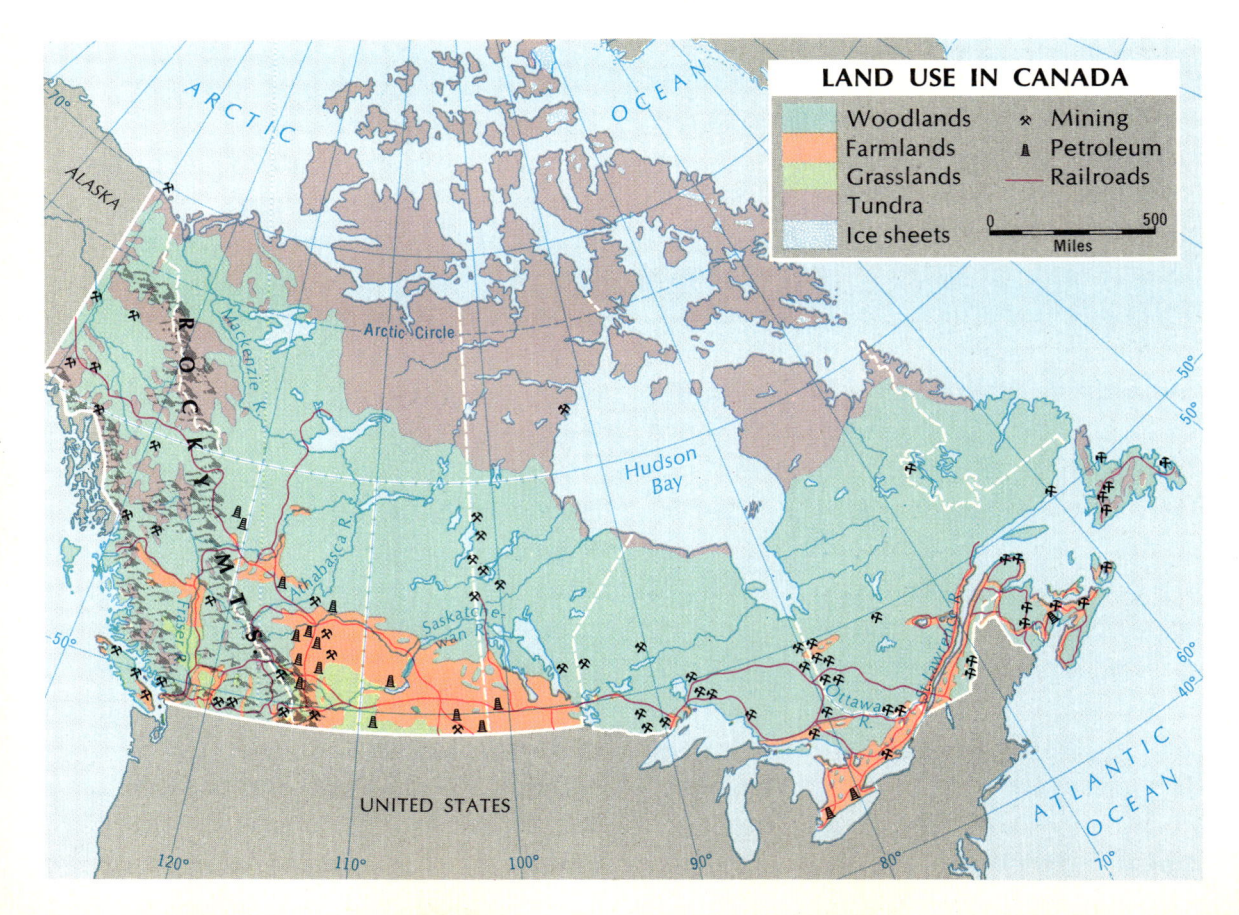

Today metropolitan Montreal has grown to more than two million people. It has many industries and offices and is also an important transportation center. As in most large cities, there are many ways that people make a living in Montreal today. But it was as a seaport that Montreal got its start, and it remains today Canada's leading commercial city.

Toronto, Canada's second largest city, also had its beginnings as a port city. It is still Canada's most important port on the Great Lakes. But today it is also a manufacturing center for cars and farm machinery, as well as the publishing center for all of Canada.

Canada's leading government city is Ottawa, where the Canadian Parliament meets. You can figure out the main activities of two other Canadian cities by their nicknames. Hamilton is known as the Pittsburgh of Canada and Windsor as the Detroit of Canada. Although the city of Quebec is important as a port and as a manufacturer of paper, shoes, and clothing, it is also one of the nation's leading tourist cities. Many people from the United States visit Quebec each year.

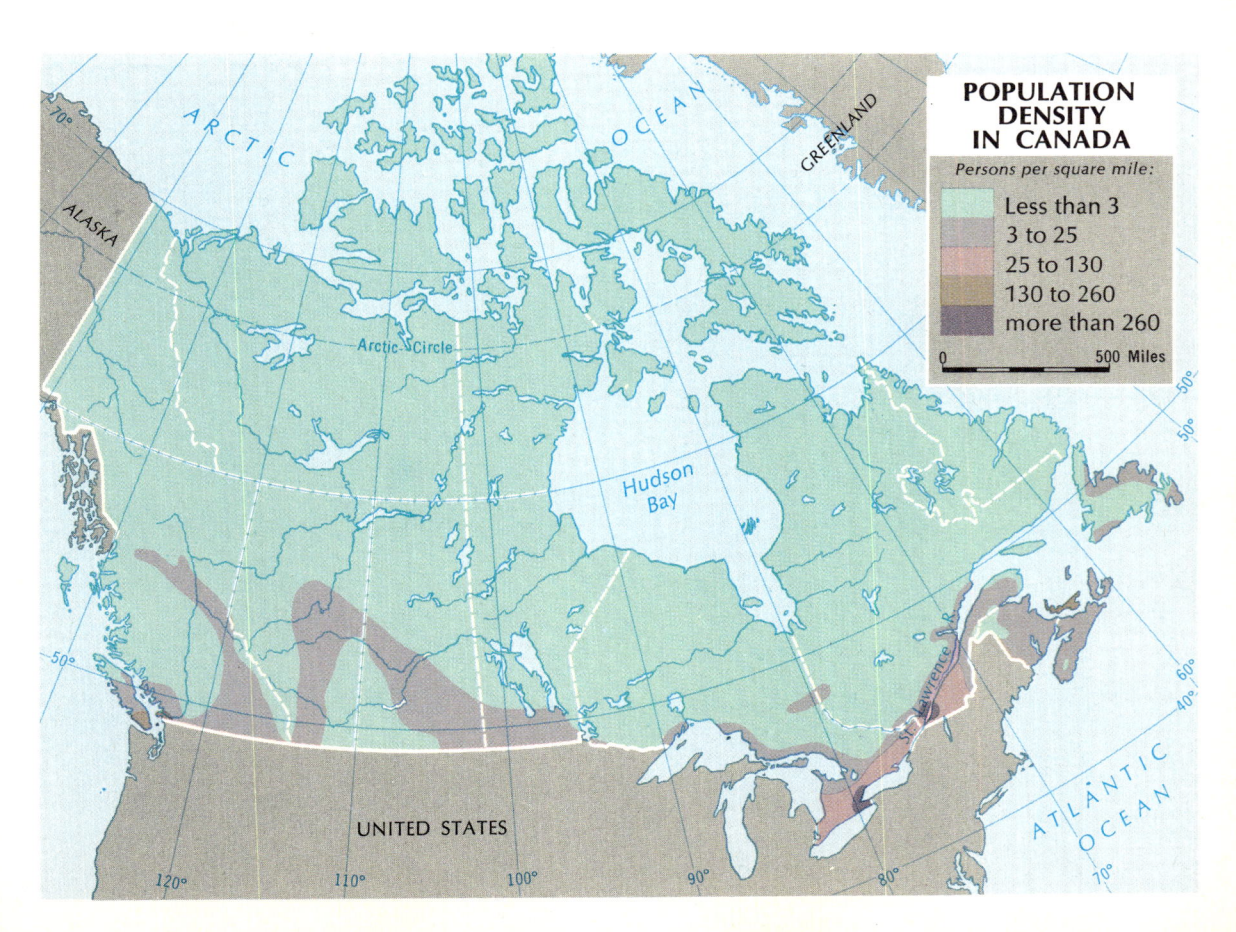

POPULATION DENSITY IN CANADA

Persons per square mile:
- Less than 3
- 3 to 25
- 25 to 130
- 130 to 260
- more than 260

Improving the water highway. For many years, men in Canada and the United states dreamed of improving the water highway of the St. Lawrence and the Great Lakes. What was needed was a canal around the St. Lawrence rapids big enough to allow ocean ships to sail directly into the lakes. In 1954, the United States and Canadian governments agreed to make that dream come true. Five years later, the St. Lawrence Seaway, a wide, deep canal, was opened. Ships can now sail from London, England, and other ports around the world directly into the middle of the North American continent — to such cities as Toronto and Windsor in Canada, and Chicago, Detroit, and Cleveland in the United States. Iron ore from eastern Canada now goes directly to the great steel plants along the Great Lakes, and wheat from the farms of the United States and Canada can be loaded at lake ports such as Port Arthur, Fort William, Chicago, and Cleveland for the voyage abroad. Even though the Seaway is frozen over five months of the year, it has brought a great deal of traffic to the port cities along the Great Lakes. In time the in-increasing trade should bring more wealth to these cities.

Montreal, a very modern city, is the major port of Canada.

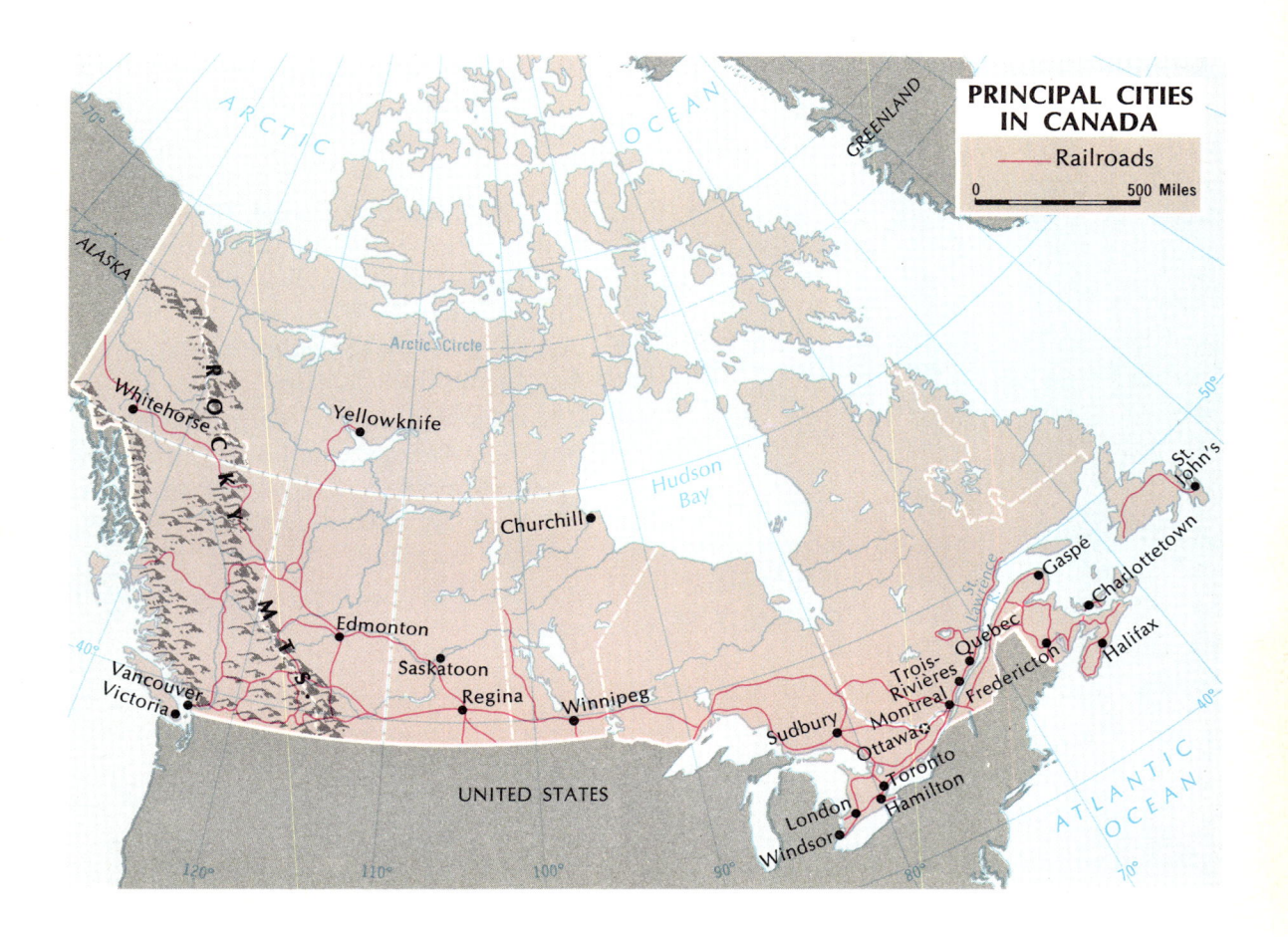

Cities in the West. As the population of Canada has spread westward, cities have grown with it—not along rivers, for there are few in this part of the country, but along railroad lines. A good example is Winnipeg, in the province of Manitoba. All transcontinental railroad trains pass through Winnipeg, and it has become an important transportation center. It is also a leading meat-packing city. As a result of the railroads, metropolitan Winnipeg now has more than half a million people.

One of the loveliest and most modern cities in Canada is Vancouver, in the province of British Columbia. Vancouver, with its excellent harbor on the Pacific Ocean, is the port of western Canada and the Pacific terminal for railroads. Vancouver is also an important manufacturing center. To its factories and mills come minerals, oil, wheat, and timber from as far east as the Great Plains and the Prairie Provinces. Today Vancouver is the third largest city in Canada with a population of about 500,000.

Working with Concepts and Generalizations

Identifying Concepts

In the left-hand column below is a list of cities in South America and in Canada. In the right-hand column is a list of descriptive phrases. Match each city with the phrase that best describes it. Write on paper.

1. Bolivar City
2. Montreal
3. Bogotá
4. Rio de Janeiro
5. Toronto
6. Caracas
7. Brasília
8. Ottawa
9. São Paulo
10. Winnipeg

a. Canada's most important Great Lakes port
b. A city made modern by oil
c. All transcontinental trains go through this Canadian city
d. The capital city of Colombia
e. Another "Town of America"
f. Where the Canadian Parliament meets
g. The largest city in South America
h. Once the capital of Brazil
i. Canada's leading commercial city
j. A carefully planned South American city

Developing Concepts

Write the answers on paper.

1. Your father tells you that your family is going to move to South America. He has not decided exactly where, but he wants to live in a city. He gives you a list of the cities he is considering. You discover that the list is made up of all the South American cities you have studied in this chapter. Based on what you have learned, which city will you ask your father to move to? Why?
2. You have learned that it is important to plan cities before building them. You know that the city of Brasília was carefully planned. Why are those who helped plan Brasília beginning to be disappointed in the city?
3. What is the St. Lawrence Seaway? Which two governments built the seaway? Why was the seaway built? What are its advantages? Does it have any disadvantages?
4. Bolivar City was supposed to become a great commercial city. It never did. Explain why.
5. You have learned that the cities of eastern Canada are located on the great water highway or on a river that flows into it. Where are the cities of western Canada located?
6. Explain this statement: "Today Bogotá is a mixture of the old and the new."

Generalizations

Read the generalizations below. Find proof to support each generalization. Tell what the proof is and the page on which you found it.

1. By studying maps and climate information, we are often able to understand why cities develop where they do.
2. Man often moves from rural areas to urban centers in an effort to improve his standard of living.
3. The location of natural resources often determines the location of urban centers.

Applying Concepts

1. You now know a great deal about cities. You have studied old cities and new cities. You have studied cities that were carefully planned and cities that were not planned at all. You have studied how cities can be improved and the problems involved in improving them. Take advantage of all you have learned. PLAN A CITY! You may draw plans of your city, showing what it will look like. (It will be helpful to look at the maps in Chapter 7 to see how some other cities were planned.) Or you may describe what your city will be like by writing a story, a poem, or even a song about it. Just make sure you communicate your ideas as clearly as possible.

2. You have learned that advancements in transportation aided in the development and growth of cities. Choose a form of transportation that interests you. There are many to choose from. Find out all you can about it. Then prepare a report to share with your class. If you like, prepare a picture report, using your own drawings or others. Your work, when added to that of your classmates, will make an impressive story of transportation.

3. You have learned that slavery in the United States ended after the Civil War. Use an encyclopedia or other reference book to answer the following questions about the abolition of slavery.
   a. What document freed some slaves *during* the Civil War?
   b. Which slaves did this document free?
   c. Who wrote the document?
   d. What is the date of the document?
   e. Which amendment to the Constitution abolished slavery?
   f. When was this amendment added to the Constitution?

4. You are to take part in a study to find out how your town can be improved. To do this, you must find out as much as you can about your town. Write *one* of the letters listed below. Ask specific questions so that you will get specific answers! The replies you and your classmates receive will help you suggest ways your town can be improved.
   a. Write a letter to the Town Clerk. Ask for a land-use map. This will show you how the land in your town is being used now.
   b. Write a letter to the President of the Board of Education. Ask some questions about school facilities and needs.
   c. Write a letter to the Chief of Police. Ask some questions about traffic problems.
   d. Write a letter to the President of the Chamber of Commerce. Ask some questions about the growth of industry and commerce in your town.
   e. Write a letter to the head of the Recreation Commission. Ask some questions about recreational facilities in your town.
   f. Write a letter to the head of the Sanitation Department. Ask some questions about the disposal of wastes in your town.
   g. Write a letter to the Tax Collector. Ask some questions about the use of tax money.
   h. Write a letter to the head of the Water Department. Ask some questions about the quality of the water supply in your town.

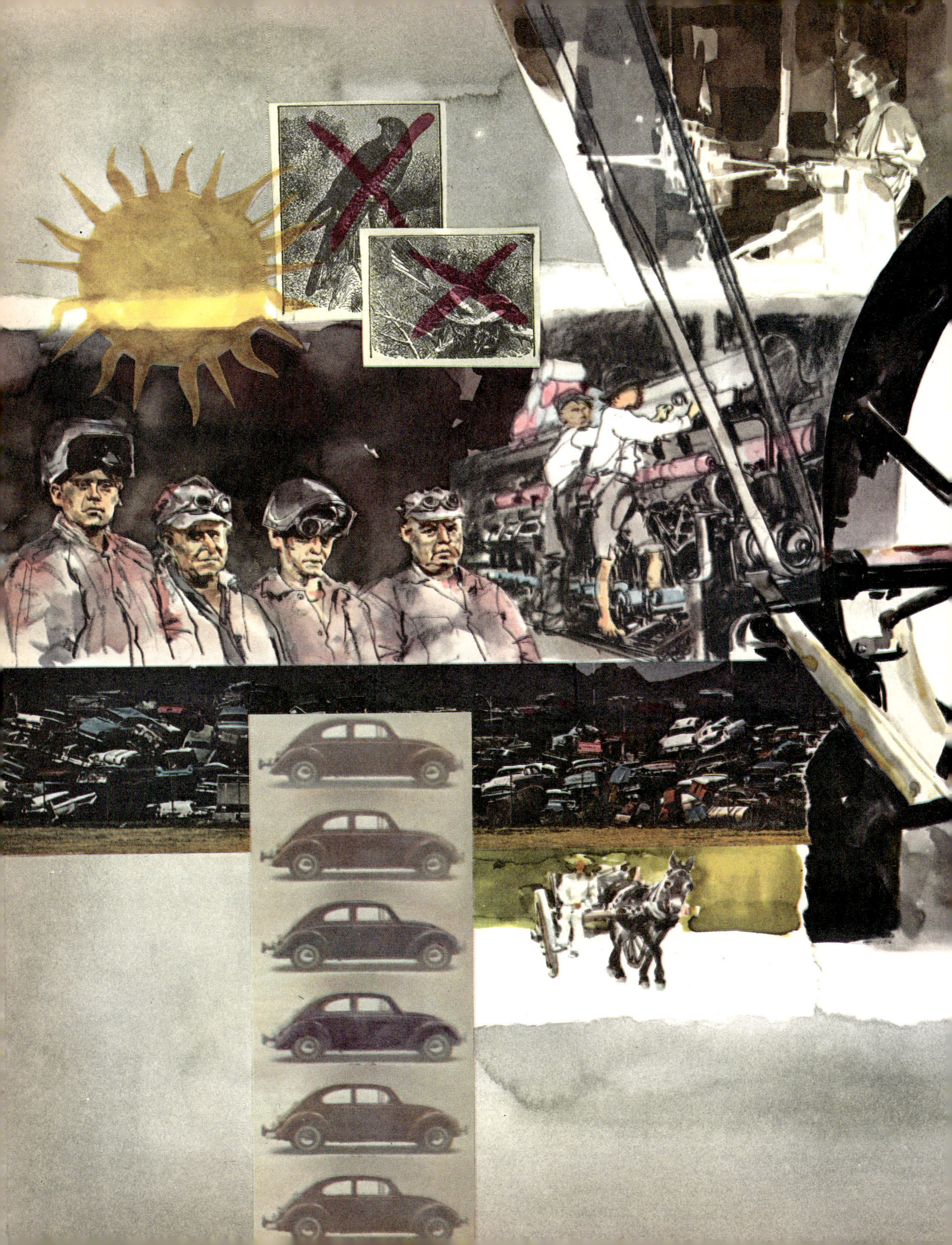

unit three
INVESTIGATING INDUSTRIALISM

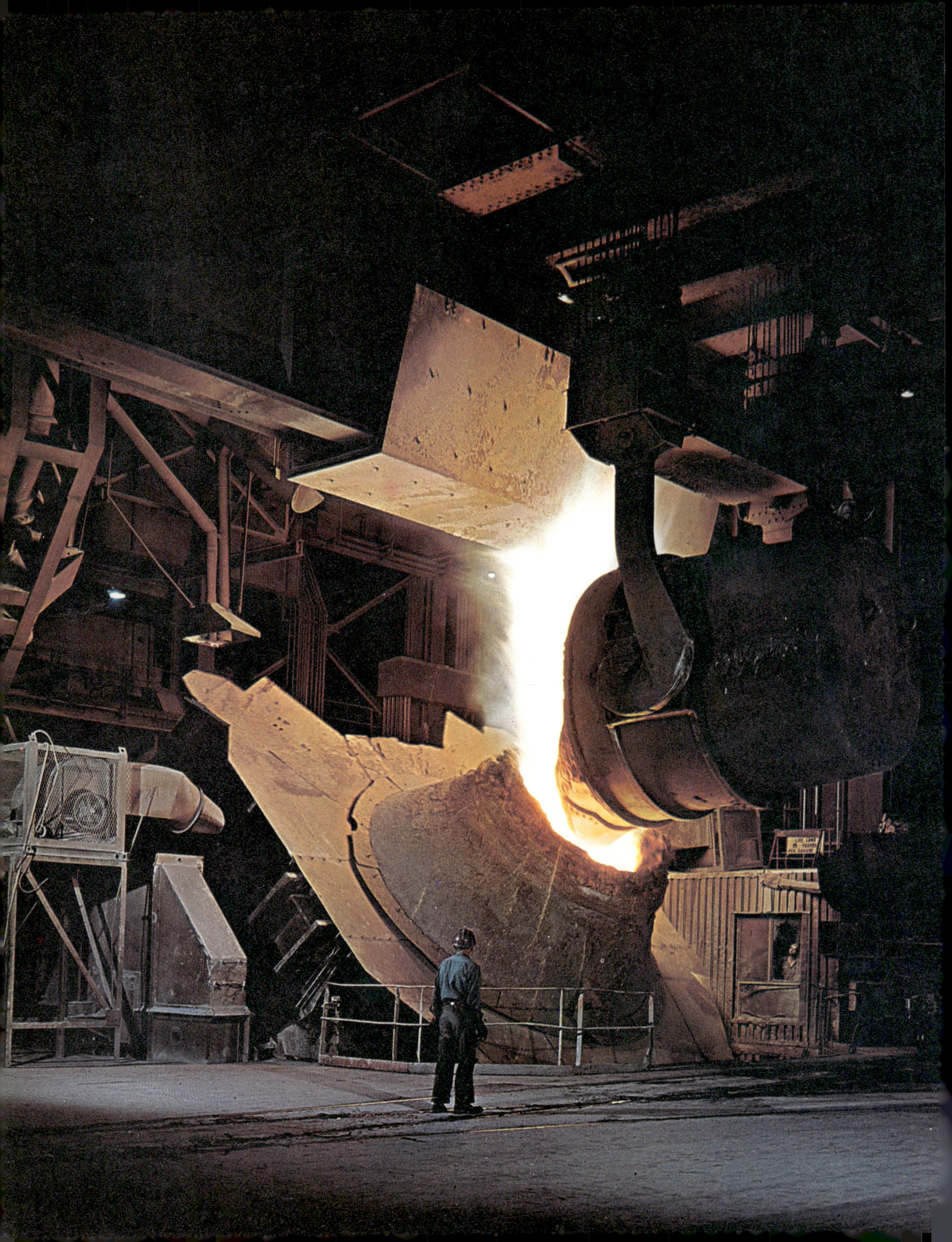

Learning About Industrialism

14

You have probably heard or read that the United States today is an industrial society. What does this mean? What is industrialism and what is an industrial society?

In this chapter you will begin to discover what industrialism is, just as earlier you discovered about that other important "ism" — urbanism. You will study how three products — iron, flour, and cloth — were made several hundred years ago, *before* industrialism, and how those same products are made in an industrial society. As you read about each product, ask yourself, what are the main differences between past and present ways of making this product?

Later, when you have read about all three of these goods, you will ask, what did the ways of manufacturing these three different goods in the past have in common? And you will ask, what do the present ways of manufacturing these three goods have in common? By answering these questions, you will begin your discovery of industrialism.

Producing Iron in Colonial Days

Let's begin by comparing ironmaking in the American colonies in the 1750's with ironmaking in the United States today.

Iron is never found in its pure form in nature. It is always mixed with soil and rock. This mixture is called iron ore. The iron is locked into the ore, and the only way to get it out is to heat the ore to a very high temperature. The iron, which melts at a lower temperature than the rock, becomes a liquid and is separated from the rest of the ore, which remains solid. This method of separating minerals from ore is called *smelting*. Men have made iron this way for thousands of years. It is the way we still make iron today.

The recipe. The recipe for ironmaking also has not changed over the years. This recipe calls for three ingredients, or raw materials. One, of course, is iron ore. Another is a fuel that can make a fire hot enough to melt iron. The third ingredient is a mineral called limestone. When iron ore is smelted, certain impurities are mixed in with the melted iron. The limestone, which melts along with the iron, mixes with these impurities and floats them to the top in a sort of scum, called slag. When this slag is skimmed off, pure iron remains.

Even though the smelters of 1750 used the same recipe that is used today, there are many differences between past and present ways of ironmaking. As you read about them, see if you can pick out the important ones.

Where were ironworks built? In 1750 the American colonies had several hundred ironworks, often called iron foundries or forges. There iron was forged, or hammered and formed into its final shape. Do you know of any place-name that contains the word forge? Almost certainly there was once an ironworks in that place.

In those days a great many people could afford to go into the ironmaking

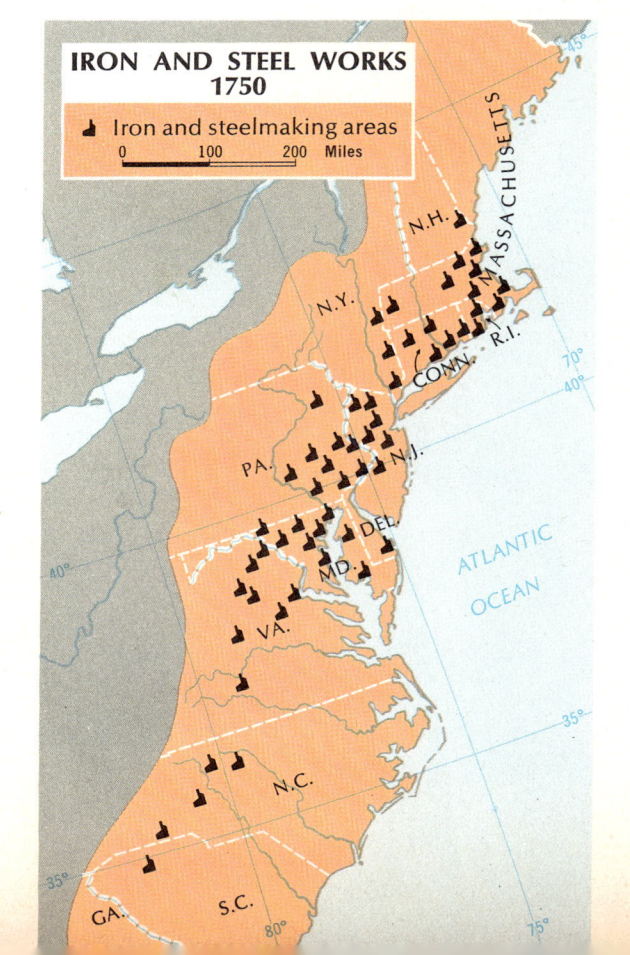

IRON AND STEEL WORKS
1750
Iron and steelmaking areas
0   100   200 Miles

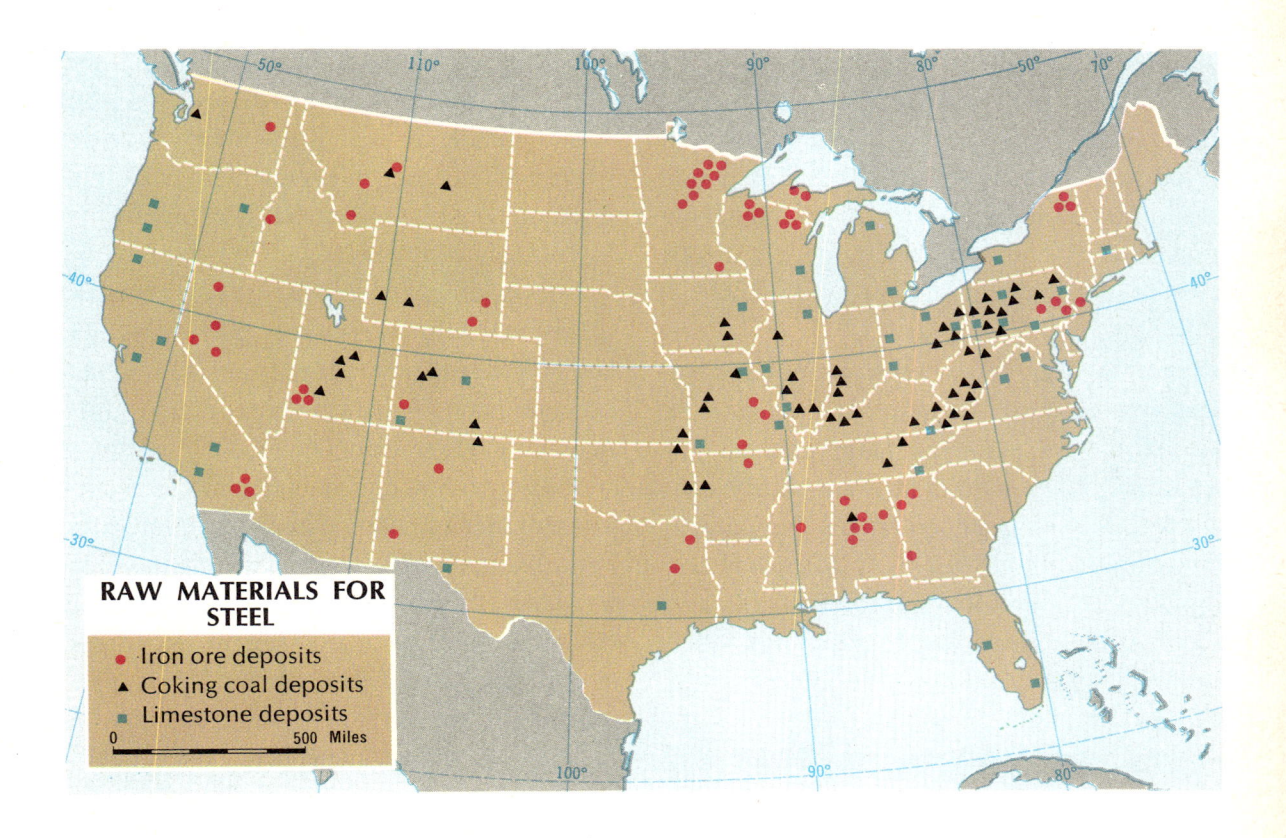

RAW MATERIALS FOR STEEL
- Iron ore deposits
- Coking coal deposits
- Limestone deposits

0   500 Miles

business, for there was not much costly machinery to buy, except for the furnace itself. Nearly all the work, as you shall see, was done by hand, so the main expense was the wages of workers. Of course, none of these foundries were very large. Iron was not used for many things in those days and the population of the colonies was small, so not much iron was needed.

An ironmaker could build his foundry only in certain locations. First, it had to be very close to the ore deposits. Iron ore is very heavy, and transporting it for long distances in horse-drawn wagons was both difficult and expensive. Second, the foundry had to be located near several thousand acres of forest, in order to have a supply of fuel.

Before building an iron foundry, then, the ironmaker's first step was to find iron ore. Actually, iron is a very common mineral. It is found in many parts of the earth, and in every state in the United States. Chances are the earth in your own neighborhood contains iron. However, the amount of iron is probably very small. It would not be worth the effort and expense to smelt that earth just to get a thimbleful of iron. Ironmaking is profitable only when the ore contains a lot of iron.

The iron manufacturers of 1750 found deposits of rich ore in Massachusetts, New Jersey, Virginia, and especially Pennsylvania. Most of these deposits were not very large, but they contained enough ore for the small needs of those days.

Preparing the ingredients. Once found, the ore had to be mined. Sometimes the iron was in rocks lying right on the ground. Then the miners simply collected the rock ore. At times they could rake up the rich ore they found at the bottom of a shallow pond. But usually the miners had to dig for the iron. With only a pickax and a shovel, they could not gather very much in a day.

The second ingredient, limestone, is common in many parts of the eastern United States. Unlike iron, limestone is not locked in an ore; usually it is found in its pure form. Miners chopped hunks of limestone from the earth and sent them to the foundry in animal-drawn carts.

For fuel, iron manufacturers used charcoal. Charcoal was made by partially burning wooden logs. The charcoal makes a much hotter fire than ordinary logs do. To make charcoal, woodsmen using axes and handsaws cut dozens of trees into logs about four feet long. Skilled workers called colliers then piled several hundred of these logs in a huge, round mound— as tall as a man and about thirty feet across at the bottom, which is perhaps as long as your classroom.

They left a small opening for air, down the center of the mound from top to bottom. Then they covered the whole mound with a layer of mud. The mud kept air from getting into the pile through any place except the narrow opening in the center. The idea was to let in just enough air to keep the logs smoldering, but not enough to let them catch fire and burn up.

Then the chief collier lit the fire. For the next four days, the colliers watched the mound day and night, checking the mud and the air hole to make sure the fire did not go out or flare up. Three or four colliers took turns working, eating, and sleeping right next to the smoking pile. As you might imagine, that was not the healthiest kind of

In earlier days in America charcoal for ironmaking was made in mounds like this.

work. When the logs were charred just right, the colliers closed the air hole, putting out the fire.

Smelting the ore. Then the ironmakers were ready to start smelting. The large stone furnace had a stack about thirty or forty feet tall. The furnace was usually built against the side of a hill that was about as high as the stack. The reason is that an iron furnace is loaded by dumping the ingredients down the top of the stack. The only way of getting the ingredients to the top of a thirty-foot stack was to wheel them up the hill and then across a small wooden bridge, which ran from the hilltop to the stack.

When the furnace was hot enough, workers called fillers moved their carts to the edge of the stack and emptied them into the fire below—first a layer of charcoal, then the iron ore, and then a thin layer of limestone. The three ingredients together were called the charge. To make the fire extra hot, an instrument called a bellows blew blasts of air through several openings near the bottom of the furnace. In small foundries a workman operated the bellows by hand. In larger foundries a waterwheel supplied the power.

The first ironworks in America was at Saugus, Massachusetts.

The finished product. After about fifty minutes the charge melted, and the liquid iron trickled down to form a pool at the bottom of the furnace. Workers then removed a plug from the furnace, and the iron ran out into a narrow channel, or gutter. As it did, a worker called a gutterman skimmed off the top layer of slag with a hoe. Another ironworker, known as a molder, filled a long-handled ladle with the liquid iron and poured it into molds made of sand. The molds were shaped in the form of pots, pans, and other goods.

Meanwhile, guttermen pushed the rest of the iron along the ground into other channels, where it cooled and hardened into bars about three feet long. Most of the bars were taken to the part of the foundry called the forge. There other workers hammered the bars into nails, hinges, horseshoes, or whatever product was desired. Most forges made dozens of different products and did not specialize in any one product.

Ironworks also sold bars to nearby blacksmiths, who made finished products on their own forges. Occasionally, if the workmen at the forge or the blacksmith knew the special methods, they might turn the iron into an improved form called steel. Swords, knives, and certain tools were made of steel.

A single furnace like the one described above could produce about three hundred or four hundred tons of iron a year. It took the labor of a great many workmen to produce that amount — woodsmen, colliers, miners, fillers, molders, guttermen, and others. All the American colonies together produced less than twenty thousand tons of iron in the year 1750.

Iron and Steel Today

Today, iron — and especially iron in its improved form, steel — is one of the most important products of the modern world. Buildings, bridges, cars, machines, home appliances, tools — in fact, hundreds of products — depend heavily upon steel. To make these goods for America's more than 200 million people, steel factories turn out more than 140 million tons of steel each year — more than any other nation in the world. More than 800,000 Americans have jobs connected with the steel industry.

Modern steel plants. Although about two hundred companies in America make this steel, most of it comes from the five or six largest companies. One company alone, the United States Steel Corporation, makes about 35 million tons of steel each year.

This steel is produced in huge plants, some of them covering several square miles. The largest steel plant in the United States is the Bethlehem Steel Company plant at Sparrow Point, Maryland. The furnaces there turn out

The steel mill at Sparrow Point enjoys the advantages of water, rail, and highway transportation.

24,000 tons of steel *in a single day*—more than all the iron produced *in a year* in all the colonial furnaces put together.

Plants as huge as these, with all their machinery and equipment, cost a great deal to build. Their owners must invest many millions of dollars in the buildings, machinery, and equipment before they begin to make any steel.

Gathering the raw materials. How are iron and steel made today for our modern industrial society?

Let's begin with the iron ore. Much of the ore comes from the Great Lakes states, where the richest deposits in the United States are found. The Mesabi Range in Minnesota, site of one of the world's most famous iron-ore deposits, has provided ore for the nation's mills since iron was discovered there more than a hundred years ago. Ore is also mined in seventeen other states.

In recent years much iron ore has been imported from other countries. Do you remember Cerro Bolívar, that iron mountain near Ciudad Bolívar in Venezuela? American steel companies use millions of tons of its ore every year. Ore is also brought from Chile, Mexico, and Canada.

Huge steam shovels do the mining today. Some of the newest shovels are as tall as twenty-story buildings and have dippers as large as two-car garages. With a single bite, they can scoop up two hundred tons of ore. Can you imagine how long it would have taken a miner of 1750 to dig that much ore?

Unlike the early foundries, modern steel plants are not located right next to the iron deposits. Steel mills in Pittsburgh, Pennsylvania, Gary, Indiana, and Birmingham, Alabama, are several hundred miles away from the nearest ore deposits. And certainly the ore in Venezuela and Chile is not very close to our steel mills. Instead, the plants are located near good transportation facilities—a main railroad line or, especially, a large port.

Ships, carrying 25,000 tons on a single voyage, bring ore from the mines to the steel plants quite inexpensively. The largest ore ship can carry 52,000 tons of iron ore. On one single voyage, this ship carries more ore than was mined in a year in the American colonies two hundred years ago.

For fuel, steel mills use coke, which is made from coal. Coal is turned into coke for the same reason logs were turned into charcoal by the earlier ironmakers—to make a hotter fire. The coal is mined in such states as Pennsylvania, West Virginia, Kentucky, Illinois, and Alabama. Then it is shipped by railroad to the steel plants. There it is converted into coke inside rows of high, narrow ovens.

Specially equipped railroad cars filled with coal move along tracks at the top of the coking ovens. At each oven, the car stops and dumps just the right amount of coal into the top. The oven is then sealed to keep out the air so the coal cannot burn up. The temperature in the oven is raised to more

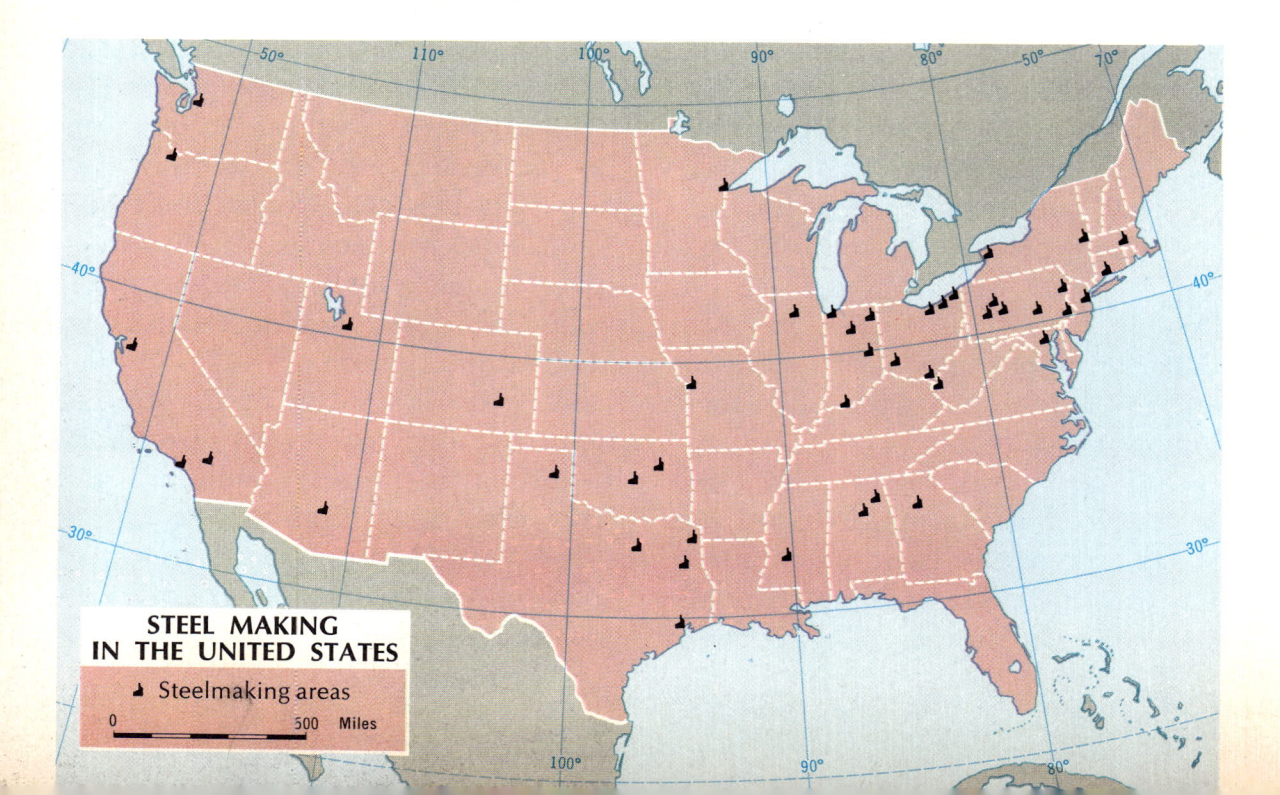

STEEL MAKING IN THE UNITED STATES

▲ Steelmaking areas

0　　　500 Miles

than 2,000°F for about eighteen hours. This baking forces certain gases to escape from the coal. What is left is coke.

Like the coal, limestone is also mined by huge machines and shipped by rail to the steel plants.

The blast furnace. All the ingredients are now ready for making iron. Iron is made in an enormous *blast furnace*, whose stack reaches about two hundred feet into the sky. This furnace, made of steel on the outside, is lined with special brick inside to withstand the great heat.

The charge is brought to the top of the furnace by cars, called skip cars, that are raised by cables. These little skip cars make regular trips up the steep incline and dump their loads of coke, ore, and limestone into the roaring furnace.

In modern plants, the air that is blown into the furnace to increase the heat is first passed through heating ovens. By the time the air enters the blast furnace, it is already about 2,000°F. Inside the furnace, where the iron is melting, the temperature often reaches 3,500°F. Engineers and scientists are constantly developing new ways of raising the temperature even higher to make better iron faster.

In a separate room, away from the blast furnace, a trained engineer guides the work. He watches the temperature gauges and other instruments that

(Above) As this furnace is tapped, molten iron gushes into a submarine car on a lower level. A blast furnace is usually about 200 feet high. (Below) Electric skip cars run up and down the ramp. They carry the charge to the top of the furnace.

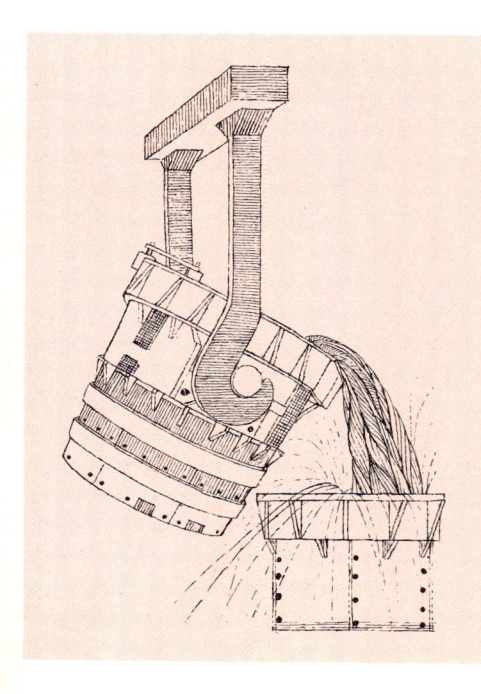

THE RECIPE FOR STEEL

Steel is made by adding other materials to the iron. By changing the recipe—adding a little more of one thing and a little less of another—scientists have invented more than three thousand different kinds of steel.

They can produce steel that is firm enough to support skyscrapers or steel that will bend like a willow branch. They can make steel that resists heat or steel that resists cold, superstrength steel or extra-soft steel. Do you want superstrength steel? Add a substance called manganese. Is it stainless steel you wish? You will need a little chromium.

These other materials that are added to the iron are brought to the steel plants from every part of the United States and the world. In addition, a great deal of scrap, or used steel, is melted down and mixed together with the liquid iron. Just about all the steel we use today contains large amounts of scrap metal.

tell him when the iron is melted. At the right moment, a valve is opened and the slag is drawn off the molten iron. Then, through another pipe, the iron is drawn off. Often the furnace will produce as much as three hundred tons of iron at a time. One modern furnace produces five thousand tons of iron in a day.

As the iron leaves the blast furnace, it may be emptied into a huge steel ladle, or bucket, which then pours the white-hot liquid into molds to cool as iron bars. More often, the iron is poured directly into a waiting, bottle-shaped railroad car called a hot iron car. The hot iron car, powered by electricity, then speeds its cargo to other furnaces, where it will be turned into steel.

Steel has many uses. Once again, men operating huge furnaces, great machines powered by electricity, and enormous ladles do their work. In an hour, tons of molten steel are ready for the rolling mill. There the hot steel is passed through huge rollers and pressed into many different shapes for later use—narrow strips, wide bars, rails for railroads, girders for bridges, sheets for automobile roofs and fenders.

Most plants specialize in making certain kinds and shapes of steel. One produces steel sheets thinner than a piece of paper. Another will make steel wire narrower than a human hair. Still others specialize in steel nuts and bolts, steel for tin cans (tin cans are really 99 percent steel), and steel for making tools and machines that will produce still other goods. What is the advantage of having steel plants specialize in this way?

The finished steel is loaded onto railroad cars, ships, and trucks, and transported to those who will use it. Sometimes it will be ready for immediate use, like the railroad rails and the girders for bridges and skyscrapers. More often, the manufacturer who buys it will change its form to suit his own special purposes. The auto manufacturer, for instance, will press the sheet steel into the form of a car roof, or the toolmaker will mold the steel into hammers and wrenches, and so on.

Steel is produced in many forms. Here you see a coil of steel, 80 inches wide, coming from a mill.

Thinking about the differences. Now that you have read both the past and the present stories of ironmaking and steelmaking, what are some of the main differences? Are raw materials still gathered in the same way? Is transportation different now? Is the smelting done in the same way? Was human labor used more in the past? Was a different kind of power used in the past to get work done? Would you say there was more specialization before industrialism or after it?

As you think about the answers to these questions, and find other differences, you will begin to understand more about industrialism.

Milling Wheat — Past and Present

For our second product, we are going to study the manufacture of flour — that is, the milling of flour — in 1700 and today. Once again, as you read you will ask yourself about the differences.

Also, as you read about milling wheat in 1700, think back to how iron was made in those years before industrialism. Of course, iron and flour are very different products. Still, see if you can find any similarities in the old ways of making these products. If you can, the similarities may give you some clues about how all goods were manufactured in the days before industrialism. If you can find things that modern steelmaking and flour milling have in common, would this also give

297

you some clues to the meaning of industrialism?

Raising wheat in colonial days. Wheat has been one of man's chief foods for thousands of years. In ancient times, men chewed wheat kernels whole, right from the stalk. Later, men learned they could grind the wheat and bake bread. Using flat stones, they ground their wheat by hand. Later still, men built special mills to grind wheat and other grains.

The first European settlers in America knew how to build grinding mills. However, since there were not enough people to support a mill, they ground their wheat by hand as the ancients had done. As the population grew, a few people were able to specialize as grain millers. It was not long before nearly every small community had at least one mill, where the local farmers could pay to have their wheat milled, or ground.

Most farmers in those days raised several different crops on their small farms, for their land had to supply everything the family needed. They generally raised, and brought to the mill, just enough wheat for their family's needs. In fact, quite a few farm families continued to grind their grain by hand. Those farmers who did have a surplus sold it to townspeople, or to merchants who milled it and traded it for the goods of other colonies and even other lands.

The mill in 1700. Let us look at a flour mill in about 1700 and see how milling was done. The first step in milling was to clean the wheat. The miller did that by placing it in a coarse cloth or a piece of burlap and shaking it to sift out the impurities. Then the wheat was ready to be ground in the millhouse.

The millhouse was usually a stone or wooden building about forty or fifty feet on each side—probably somewhat larger than your classroom—and twenty feet tall. Inside the building were two huge circular stones, each about five or six feet across, one on top of the other. The lower stone was fixed in place and did not move. The upper stone, which did turn, had a large hole in the center. Into this center hole the miller poured the wheat.

As the top stone turned, the wheat kernels spread out between the stones and were ground into a coarse flour. The turning of the wheel pushed the flour out to the edge of the stone, where the miller collected it in a trough or in pails. Meanwhile he kept refilling the center hole with more wheat kernels, repeating the process.

Power for the mills. In most mills the power for turning the heavy stone was supplied by falling water. The millhouse was built next to a stream, which was dammed up to create a small waterfall. A large wheel with paddles was put on the other side of the dam. As the water spilled over the top of the dam and fell below, it struck the paddles of the wheel, causing it to turn. The waterwheel was connected to the grinding stone inside the millhouse, so that as the wheel turned, it turned the grindstone.

In other mills, a horse walking in a circular track outside the mill supplied the power. Attached to the horse was a long pole, which was connected to a series of gears inside the building, which made the stone wheel turn. Fuel was simple—a little hay and oats. Other mills of the time were powered by wind. As long as the wind did not die down, or the horse did not get sick, or the stream did not go dry in the summer or freeze in the winter, the mills of 1700 could operate. A mill could grind about a hundred bushels of wheat a day—enough to fill about two hundred large shopping bags from our supermarkets.

The Wheat Industry Today

Today only a very small part of our population raises wheat. Unlike colonial farmers, these farmers do not raise a little wheat, a little corn, a few vegetables, and some beef and a few hogs to feed their family throughout the year. They specialize in wheat. They raise nothing else, buying whatever they need with the money they get for selling their wheat.

Throughout the country there are many old flour mills still standing. This one was powered by water.

Even though there are not many wheat farmers, they raise enough to feed our population of 200 million and still have a great deal left over to sell to other countries.

Our farmers raise so much today because of modern farm machinery and scientific agriculture. The farmer of 1700, harvesting by hand, could gather only seven or eight bushels of wheat in a full day's work. It took him three days to harvest one acre. Today's wheat farmer can harvest nearly a hundred acres in the same time. And the acres are richer in wheat, too, because of fertilizer and improved seed. In colonial days one wheat seed would produce a single stalk with a few kernels on it. Today's seed often yields fifty stalks, each with from thirty to fifty kernels.

Modern mills. After the harvest, the wheat is sent to enormous *grain elevators* to await shipment to the mills. The wheat may end up in a mill several hundred miles from the farm on which it was raised. You will no longer find a mill in every small community. Today about 225 mills, all powered by electricity, grind flour for the entire country. One hundred years ago, there were more than 22,000 mills—about a hundred times as many as today—and they did not grind nearly as much wheat.

Look at the map that shows where wheat is grown today. It also shows the cities where most of the milling is done. How is it possible for Buffalo, which is so far from where most wheat is raised, to be the largest miller of wheat? Why don't we need mills in every community now?

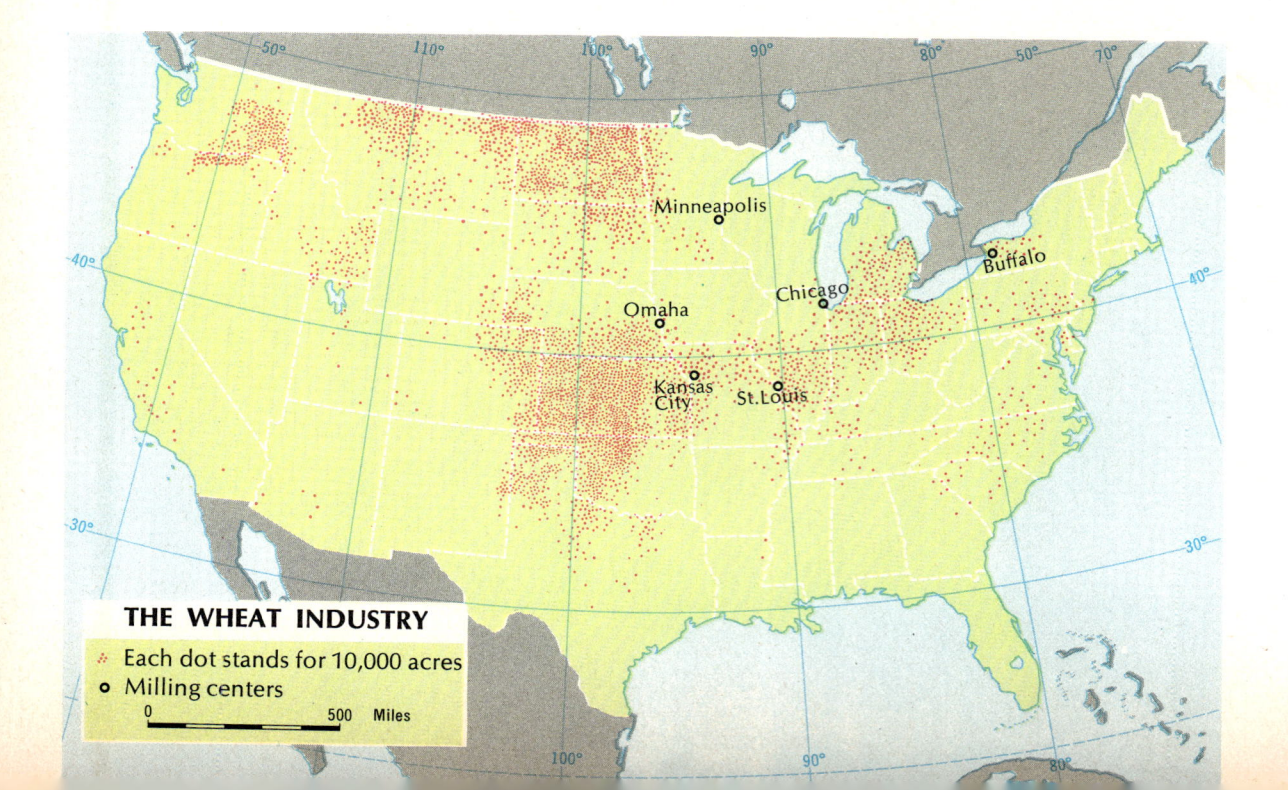

THE WHEAT INDUSTRY
- Each dot stands for 10,000 acres
- Milling centers

The milling process today. The first step in milling, just as it was in 1700, is cleaning the wheat. Today, the wheat is sent through several different machines that remove impurities. One sifts the kernels through self-moving screens, another blows away lightweight impurities like straw, a third removes any bits of iron and steel with powerful magnets, and a fourth washes out small stones and pebbles.

The cleaned wheat kernels are not ground right away. Instead, they are fed into a grinding bin where they pass through several sets of steel rollers and sifters. The first set of rollers separates the bran, which is the brownish outside cover of the kernel, from the *endosperm* (en' do sperm), which is the rest of the kernel.

The endosperm makes the white flour you are familiar with. Most Americans seem to prefer white flour to the brownish whole wheat flour, which contains the bran as well. The endosperm then passes through the rest of the rollers and sifters until the milling is complete. At that point, the mills add various vitamins to the white flour to enrich it, making up for the vitamins that were lost when the bran was removed.

A single modern wheat mill can handle about twelve million bushels of wheat in a year. In one day a modern mill can grind about forty thousand bushels—enough to fill a line of shopping bags about eighty miles long!

Grain is stored in these huge elevators until it can be transported to mills for processing.

From the mill, the flour is shipped to market. Some of it is packaged into small sacks, the sort you have seen on the shelves of your food market. Most of the flour, though, is loaded onto large trucks or railroad cars and shipped directly to bakeries. There it is baked into breads, cakes, and pastries in large ovens. The ovens that bake our familiar breads produce 2,800 loaves every twenty minutes.

Adding to our understanding. Now let's see what we can add to our understanding of industrialism from our story of milling in these two different times. Go back to page 297 to the questions you answered after reading about ironmaking, and ask the questions again about the milling of wheat.

Also, now that you have had a chance to see how two different products were manufactured in the 1700's, think about the things their manufacture had in common. In what ways were the manufacturing of iron in 1750 and the milling of wheat in 1700 alike? In what ways are the manufacturing of iron and the milling of wheat in today's industrial society alike?

The Textile Industry

Let's look at our third story, the making of textiles, or cloth. We are going to ask ourselves about the differences between making textiles in 1700 and making them in an industrial society. We will also ask how the making of textiles today is similar to the making of steel and the milling of wheat.

Preparing the raw materials. In 1700 making cloth was one of women's many jobs. It did not require very expensive tools or even very special skills. The women made cloth in their own homes. This was called household manufacture. In fact, a lot of goods were made by household manufacture in those days—shoes, candles, foodstuffs, and furniture, for example.

Nature supplied the raw material for making cloth. One could make cloth out of linen, which comes from the flax plant; or from wool, which is the hair of animals, chiefly sheep; or out of cotton, the fluffy product of the cotton plant.

There were several steps in making cloth. The first step was the preparation of the raw material. If cotton was used, the seeds that clung to the cotton were removed. That had to be done by hand, which was very slow. If wool was used, it first needed a thorough handwashing to remove all dirt. Once the wool was washed, or the cotton picked clean, it was drawn through a card, a tool that looked like a wire hairbrush. That separated the fibers into long strands.

The next step was spinning. In this step the ends of the strands were twisted together to make one continuous thread. The spinner operated the spinning wheel by pumping a foot treadle. Even for an experienced spinner, the work went very slowly. Working a full day, she might be able to convert barely a pound or two of raw cotton or wool into thread or yarn.

Weaving the thread. After she finished spinning, the woman of the house was ready to weave cloth on her loom. Weaving is not a very difficult job. You may have tried it yourself at some time. But although it is easy enough to weave, it is quite difficult to weave well. And it takes a long time to weave a large piece of cloth.

Most housewives, of course, were not expert weavers, and although the cloth they made was certainly usable, it was usually rough and uneven. It took countless hours to complete a job. As with spinning, weaving was only one of a woman's chores, and she rarely could spend a whole day at it. Even if she could, however, she could hardly hope to complete more than a yard or two in that time.

If one wanted high quality weaving for a special piece of cloth, he would take his yarn to an expert weaver. The weaver might have his own shop, but it was just as likely that he worked at a loom in his home. Some weavers produced very fine fabrics of beautiful design, but of course, since they worked by hand, their output was quite small. Often weavers bought their own thread or yarn and made textiles for sale.

As this shuttle moves back and forth, it carries new thread across those set already.

One could also buy manufactured cloth in shops. Very often, the merchant who sold the cloth was also the manufacturer. What he did was to buy the raw materials—cotton, wool, or flax—and hire people to work on them. These people worked at home, for there were no factories then.

To one home, he took the raw material for carding and spinning, paying a certain amount for this work. Then he took the finished yarn to the home of another person to have it woven into cloth. The finished cloth was then sold in his store—hopefully for more money than he had paid for the raw material and the labor of making the cloth.

Textile Manufacturing Today

As you surely have guessed, textile making today is very different from textile making in colonial days. Many changes have taken place in every part of the process, from the gathering of the raw material to the making of finished cloth. In fact, you probably know by now what some of the differences are.

Machines, materials, and men. Machines are used in every step of production. Although cotton is still picked by hand in some places, mechanical cotton pickers harvest most of the crops. Machines pick the seeds out of the raw cotton. They spin the cotton into thread and weave the thread into cloth.

303

Often the cleaning, spinning, and weaving are done in one factory.

There are hundreds of such factories today, mostly in our southern states. In some, as many as five hundred power-driven looms are at work at once, each one producing more than a hundred yards of cloth a day. Because machines make cloth inexpensively, most people can afford to buy it.

Men have not only invented machines to make cloth, but they have even invented new materials to make cloth from. Raw materials no longer come only from nature. New materials have been produced in laboratories. Today, such man-made fibers as nylon, rayon, Dacron, and polyester are familiar to shoppers.

Although machines do much of the work, textile companies employ thousands of people. Some operate the machines. Many others work in the offices where so much of the work of a modern business is done. Some of these people make the important decisions about the business—how much cloth the factory should produce, what styles or colors they should make, how much cotton or other material they should buy. Salesmen take orders for the goods. Designers plan new styles, secretaries type letters and reports, and bookkeepers keep track of the business the company does.

Adding up the differences. Do you see any differences between textile manufacturing in 1700 and the textile industry today? Are these differences like the ones you already noticed in wheat milling and in ironmaking? Do you think you can now make some general statements about how goods were manufactured in the 1700's, and how they are manufactured today? If you can, you have already discovered a good deal about industrialism.

Few people are needed to operate modern textile machinery.

Working with Concepts and Generalizations

Identifying Concepts

Read each statement below. Write BI *if the statement is about manufacturing as it was before industrialism; write* IS *if the statement is about manufacturing in an industrial society; write* BOTH *if the statement is about manufacturing before industrialism and manufacturing in an industrial society. Write on paper.*

1. An ironmaker had to build his foundry very close to ore deposits.
2. One could buy manufactured cloth in shops.
3. The first step in milling is cleaning the wheat.
4. Steel plants are near good transportation facilities.
5. Raw materials are used in the making of iron.
6. Most flour is shipped directly to bakeries.
7. Wheat was ground in more than 22,000 mills.
8. All cloth was made from materials supplied by nature.
9. Most iron forges made dozens of different products and did not specialize in any one product.
10. The millhouse was built next to a stream.

Developing Concepts

Write the answers on paper.

1. Use the map on page 300 to answer these questions:
   a. List the milling centers shown on the map.
   b. Which of these milling centers is closest to your hometown?
   c. Would you have more flour if a local miller ground wheat for your family in his millhouse?
   d. In which areas of the country is most of the wheat grown?
   e. How does wheat get from the wheat-growing areas to the milling centers? Was this true before industrialism?
   f. Is it better for a few farmers to spend most of their times growing wheat or for most farmers to spend some of their time growing wheat? Explain.
2. It is April 11, 1750. Your father is an ironmaker. He has discovered a deposit of iron ore quite close to his foundry. He says he will start men digging for it in the morning. Write a brief description of the work that will go on from the time the men dig up the iron ore until the iron is sent to the forge.
3. List the steps involved in making cloth in 1750. Draw a simple sketch showing one of the steps on your list. Give the sketch a title. Are any steps on your list used in the making of cloth today? Which ones?

Generalizations

An important word is missing from each statement below. By completing each statement, you will be stating a generalization. When your generalizations are complete, find proof to support each one. Tell what the proof is and the page on which you found it.

1. In a highly industrialized society, even very large plants and factories may _____ in the production of a single product.
2. Advancement in _____ facilities has made it possible for plants and factories to be located far from sources of raw materials.

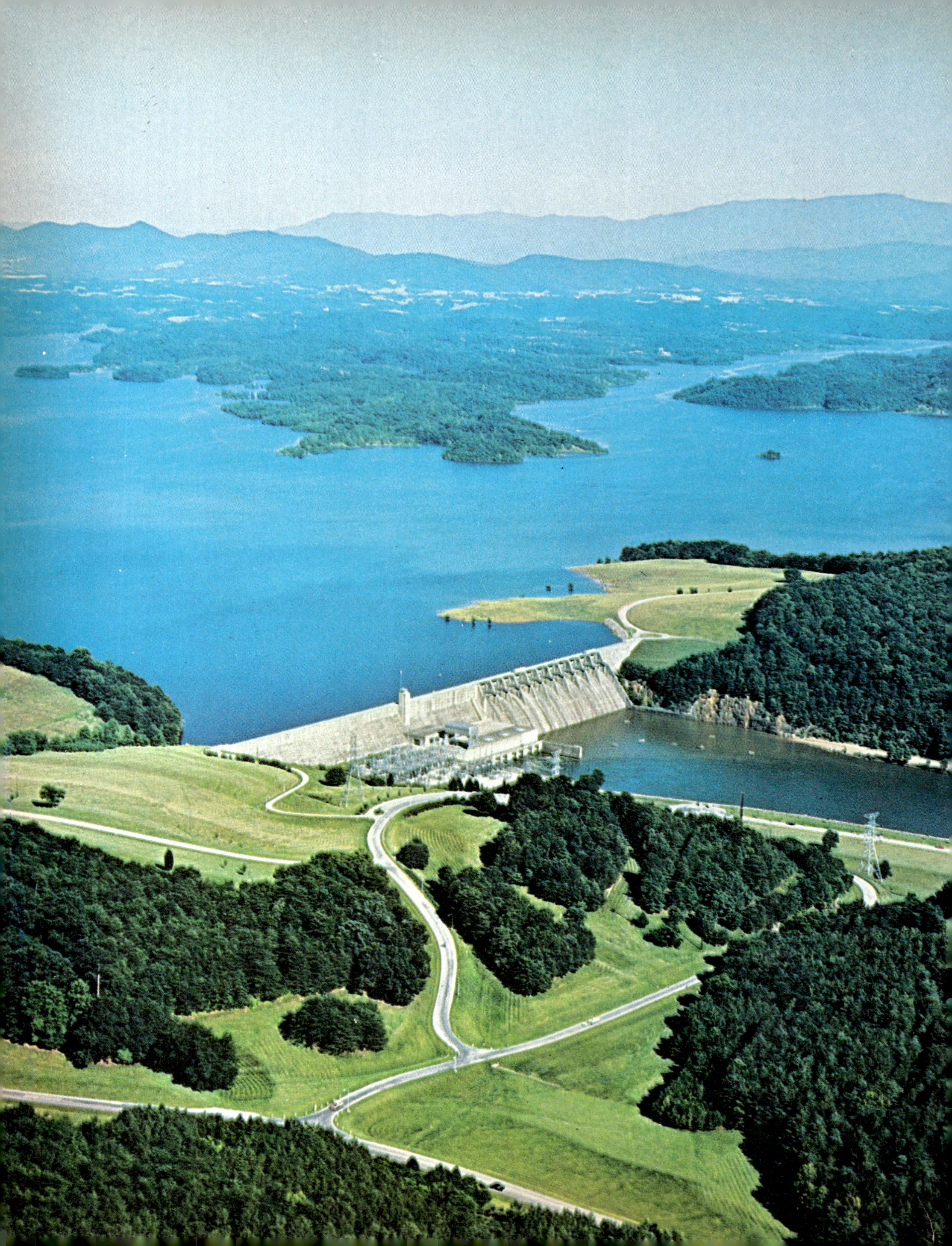

Main Features of Industrialism

15

One of the very first things you noticed in our stories of manufacturing was that far more goods are produced in an industrial society. And they are produced in far less time than they were in the days before industrialization. Do you remember the iron and steel industry? The amount of steel produced in an hour by a single blast furnace today is more than the amount of iron produced in one year by a furnace of 1750.

How many acres of wheat could a farmer manage in 1700? How many acres can today's farmer manage? How many bushels of wheat did a flour mill of 1700 handle in a day, and how many does a modern mill handle? Certainly our textile factories produce thousands of times more cloth than the American colonies produced in 1700.

How can we explain this great increase in production? Why is so much more produced in our industrial society today? In this chapter you will learn answers to these questions, as we study further the main features of industrialism.

Reasons for the Increase

One reason that our industrial society produces so much more is simply that our country is much bigger today. The population of the United States is about two hundred times as large as it was in 1750. There are many more people to buy goods. Another way of saying that is to say there is a larger market for the goods. Even if nothing else had changed, we would be producing a lot more goods to satisfy the needs of the larger market.

Our large population also means there are many more people to make these goods. That is very important, for manufacturing goods requires skilled human labor. If there are plenty of people to supply the labor, a lot of goods can be made. With a small supply of labor, fewer goods can be made.

For example, there were about a thousand people employed in making iron and steel in 1750. Suppose only the same number of people were available to work in our steel industry today. Could steel factories still produce the 141 million tons of steel they now produce every year?

So the large population of today is one reason our industrial society can produce so many goods. The large population provides a market for the goods and the labor to make them.

But there is more to it than population. With a market two hundred times larger and a labor supply two hundred times larger, we should expect to produce just two hundred times more of everything. But the iron and steel industry produces nearly *six thousand* times as much. Our textile factories also produce many thousand times as much cloth as was made in 1700.

Importance of machines. What are the other explanations for this great in-

This huge stripping shovel lifts 200 tons of earth at one time. The machine dwarfs the truck.

crease in production? Let us think back to Chapter 14 for the answers. One thing you certainly noticed is that machines do much of the work in an industrial society. There are machines that prepare raw cotton, spin it, dye it, and weave it. Huge machines mine and transport ore and coal, load the furnaces, and shape the hot steel. Machines produce the great quantities of goods in our society.

What is a machine? A machine is a kind of tool, but it is a little more complicated than ordinary tools. Machines have moving parts, while some simpler tools, such as hammers and saws, do not. Some machines, like pulleys, are simple. Some, like automobile engines, are very complicated. But even the most complicated machines of modern times have one important thing in common with the simplest stone ax of ten thousand years ago. Let's think about what that is.

You know that man needs food, shelter, and clothing to survive. Tools and machines are none of these. Man cannot eat a stone arrow, a hoe, a tractor, or an oven. He cannot wear a spinning wheel or a sewing machine. A hammer or an electric saw will not protect him from rain and cold. Why is man willing to spend his time, energy, and money to make these things?

Of course you know the answer to that. Tools and machines help him make the things he does want and need—his food, shelter, clothing, and many other things as well. They help him produce goods with less hard work, and they help him produce more goods than he could without the tools and machines.

We might think of tools and machines as "in-order-to" goods, or "roundabout" goods. Man makes them in order to help make other goods he needs. Making tools and machines first is a roundabout way of making other goods.

Machinery requires savings. Let's think a bit more about these "in-order-to" or "roundabout" goods. Suppose you have a job delivering newspapers. You have fifty customers and earn $2 a week. You could get fifty more customers and earn twice as much, but these people live quite a few blocks away. To deliver papers to them, you would need a bicycle, which costs $20. What will you do?

You could have the enjoyment of spending your whole $2 earnings every week on candy, comic books, toys, or whatever else you might want. There would be nothing left over from your earnings, but you would have had a good time spending them. Or you could postpone the enjoyment of spending, and save your earnings instead. After you save enough and buy your bike, you will have even more pleasure, for you will be earning twice as much and can buy twice as much.

"The Big Wheel" removes 5,250 tons of earth an hour.

The bicycle, in other words, is one of those "in-order-to" goods, for you buy it in order to produce more income. In the same roundabout way, a baker will save for a good oven that makes more bread, and a weaver will save for a machine that weaves cloth faster.

As you see, before we can buy "in-order-to" goods, we must first have savings. We call these savings *capital*. The "in-order-to" goods we buy with this capital we call *capital goods*. Capital goods are still savings. All we have done is change our savings from the form of money into the form of a machine that will help us produce more goods or more income.

Is there any other way to get capital goods without first saving up yourself?

Yes, there is. You can borrow the money from someone else. But then you are simply borrowing someone else's savings. Either way, somebody has to save before there is capital, and there must be capital in order to have capital goods.

Just as you wanted a capital good — a bicycle — to increase your earnings, so whole societies want capital goods. They would like textile machines, steel mills, automobile plants, and fertilizer factories to produce more goods for their people. In other words, they want to industrialize. But of course they will need savings to buy these capital goods.

A society can only have savings by using up less goods than it produces. That is very hard to do in many countries, where people can barely raise enough food to live on. Still, if they could only get the capital goods, they would then be able to increase their production. That is why today many such countries are trying to industrialize by borrowing capital from wealthier nations.

Changes in technology. Earlier we said that man invents machines and discovers new ways of doing things. How do inventions and discoveries happen?

Some inventions and discoveries have come about as a result of a lucky accident. Rubber is a good example. For years, Charles Goodyear tried to change soft, sticky natural rubber into a hard material that could be used for many products. He had mixed one chemical after another with the natural rubber, but all his efforts were fruitless.

For several months in 1839, he had been trying mixtures of sulfur and the gummy rubber. Goodyear thought he had failed again. Then one day he dropped some of his mixture on a stove. The heat turned the mixture into a leatherlike material.

Because of the accident, Goodyear discovered an important fact. If he applied just the right amount of heat to his mixture, he could make the kind of rubber he wanted.

Probably a few other discoveries and some inventions happened in the same lucky way. But the man who invented the steamboat did not do it by accident. He worked step by step to invent it. So did the people who invented the radio, television, automobile, airplane, and toaster. Nearly all inventions, in fact, have come about as men worked step by step to invent them.

One invention leads to another. Very often, the invention of one machine leads to the invention of another. You can see a good example of this in the inventions made in the textile industry in England during the 1700's. Before then, cloth was produced in England just as it was in the American colonies.

Spinners, working their own spinning wheels in their own homes, turned wool or cotton into yarn. Weavers, working their own looms in their homes, made the yarn into cloth. The spinners were able to make enough yarn to meet the weavers' needs. In other words, the supply of yarn and the demand for it were well balanced. Things had gone along just that way for many years. Of course, not much cloth was produced.

Then in 1733 a weaver named John Kay invented an improved loom, which he called a flying shuttle. With this machine a weaver could make much more cloth in a day. Naturally, he used more yarn. As more of Kay's flying shuttles were built, the demand for yarn increased. The spinners could not produce much more, no matter how hard they worked.

The great demand for yarn set some people to figuring out how to make it faster. In 1764 James Hargreaves invented a machine called a spinning jenny that did the job. Only a few years later, another Englishman, named Richard Arkwright, invented a machine called a water frame. This made yarn better and faster than the spinning jenny. And just ten years later, a third machine was invented to speed up the spinning of yarn.

As a result of these three inventions, there was soon plenty of yarn. In fact, there was more than the weavers could use, even with their flying shuttles. One spinner complained that with the new spinning machines there would soon be so much yarn that there would never be enough weavers to use it all.

Now it was the weaving that was slowing down production. People turned their attention to figuring out ways to speed up weaving. In 1785 an English minister named Edmund Cartwright invented a new weaving machine that was run by a steam engine. He called it a power loom. This loom made ten times as much cloth in a day as could a weaver with a hand-operated loom. Soon there were thousands of power looms in England, and yarn was once again being used as fast as it was made.

That is the way it is with inventions. One invention speeds up one step in the making of a product. This makes it necessary to invent a way of speeding up the other steps. A result of all these inventions, as you see, is the production of far more goods than ever before.

Machines — Past and Present

We have said that machines are a feature of industrial societies. But weren't there machines before industrialism? Some simple machines, like the pulley, existed for many centuries. Wasn't the spinning wheel of the colonial household a machine? It was a tool with moving parts that helped men — or usually women — produce more with the same amount of effort. We may think the spinning wheel was slow; however, the people who used it made more yarn than they could have without it. The grindstone in the flour mill of 1700 was another such machine.

A very important difference. If there were machines before industrialism, what is so different about machines in an industrial society? There are two main differences. One is that an industrial society has many more machines that do many more jobs.

Think of how flour is produced, starting with the planting of wheat and ending with the marketing of the flour. In 1700, the actual grinding of wheat was done by a machine. But every other step in producing the flour was done without machines. Only a few simple hand tools were used. Compare that to milling flour today. Are machines used in planting wheat, raising it, and harvesting it? Are they used in preparing the wheat for grinding? in grinding? in packaging? In fact, can you recall any step in which a machine is not used?

The story of flour milling is the story of almost every product. It is not that there were no machines at all before industrialism, but that there are so many more of them in an industrial society.

You can get an idea of the differences by looking at the records of inventions. The United States government has an office called the Patent Office, where inventors register their inventions. They do this so no one else can claim the invention as his own. By looking at the records we can tell how many inventions there were during any year in our history.

In 1790, industrialism had not yet come to the United States. In that year, only three inventions were registered. Seventy years later, when the United States was becoming industrialized, 4,357 inventions were registered at the Patent Office in a single year. In the year this book was written, people registered about 400,000 inventions.

Many of the inventions were machines, or improvements on machines, that enable each worker to produce more. That is why one worker today produces so much more iron and steel than a worker in 1750. And he does

A conveyor belt speeds up the work of picking and loading on this California farm.

not work as hard doing it. We could say, then, that before industrialism, most work was done without the aid of machines, and after industrialism, most is done with them.

A second great difference. So one difference is that, after industrialism, more machines were doing more jobs than before industrialism. Another important difference is in the kinds of power used to run the machines. All machines must have a source of power in order to work. What was the source of power for the spinning wheel? What supplied the power to turn the grindstones in the flour mills of 1700?

Many of the machines of early days, such as the spinning wheel, were run by human muscle power. Some used animal power. Two other sources of power were supplied in nature—wind and water. You may remember that some colonial mills were windmills, and others were operated by waterpower from an adjoining stream.

These four sources of power were the same ones man had used for a thousand years or more.

New Sources of Power

The great changeover to industrialism came when men found new sources of power to run machines. These new sources of power were also found in nature. The most important of them was coal.

Here you can readily see the changes in sources of power. The nuclear plant on the Hudson River supplies power for a large part of New York.

How did the change come about? For more than three thousand years, men knew that great amounts of energy were locked in coal. When coal is burned, energy is released in the form of heat. But how could this heat energy be made to turn wheels and operate machines? Was there some way the energy in a lump of coal could be made to spin yarn, or weave cloth, or move a ship?

The steam engine. In the 1700's, an Englishman invented a machine that eventually did all those things. The man was James Watt, and his invention was the steam engine. In this machine the heat from a coal fire turned water into steam. When water becomes steam, it expands tremendously. One quart of water turns into 1,700 quarts of steam. As water expands into steam, it is powerful enough to bend or even explode steel. Watt's machine controlled that great power and put it to work running machines such as Edmund Cartwright's power loom. The invention of the steam engine also made possible other inventions, such as the railroad.

The steam engine was the first machine to make use of a new source of power. Later, other sources of energy, such as oil and gas, were widely used to run machines. Later still, men learned how to use electricity, and even nuclear power, to run their machines.

Because of its power and its ability to move around the field, this tractor serves many different purposes for farmers.

New sources of power affect machines. Why is it important that machines use new sources of power? It means men can make bigger, more powerful machines that do much more work than ever before. Think of what that means to the farmer in the picture on this page. This wheat farmer uses a powerful tractor to do many jobs.

The motor in the tractor is rated at about 400 horsepower. That means it produces the same amount of pulling

One tractor has more power than all these mules.

power as four hundred horses. Suppose the farmer had all the same equipment for harvesting his wheat, but *not* the 400-horsepower engine. To get the same power, he would need about four lines of horses, with a hundred in each line.

Try to picture what that would look like—a line of horses nearly a quarter of a mile long! On some smaller farms, the line of horses might stretch from one side of the farm to the other.

Now of course most farmers would not own four hundred horses. And even if one farmer did, he would never hitch them all up at once, for that way he could not operate a harvester on his field. Instead, he would use a few of them, perhaps sixteen or twenty or so. That would be only about one twentieth as much power as the tractor gives him, and he would be able to do only about one twentieth as much work in the same time. To put it another way, using horses, the farmer would have to spend twenty days doing what the tractor could do in one.

Raw Materials

So far we have considered the importance of capital goods and new kinds of energy in creating an industrial society. But blast furnaces would not be of any use without the coal, iron ore, and limestone that they turn into iron and steel; and weaving machines would lie idle without the cotton, wool, or other fiber that they turn into cloth. As important as the machines are, they are useless without raw materials.

A need can lead to trade. Not every part of the world is blessed with fertile soil for growing some raw materials or with vast deposits of important minerals lying under the earth's surface. Does that mean such lands can never become industrialized? No, it does not. It is not necessary to have raw materials in your own country, as long as you can get them somewhere.

There are two main ways of getting these resources from other lands. One is to take them. Throughout history, strong nations have helped themselves to the natural resources and raw materials of weaker peoples—just as the Spanish did with the property of the Aztecs and Incas. This has led to many wars, and many deaths. Fortunately, most of the time, nations get raw materials in the second way, by trading for them. No nation in the world has every raw material it needs, so all nations trade.

Large Factories and Markets

You may also have noticed that industrialism brought another change. In colonial America, where did the carding and spinning of cotton and wool take place? Where was the cloth woven? Is it manufactured in the same kind of place today?

Why did manufacturing move out of the home when the country became industrialized?

Why did factories develop? One reason was that the new machinery was just too big for the home. There was room in a house for a small spinning wheel. But a power loom, complete with a steam engine, would never fit. It became necessary to build special buildings to house the machinery.

Also, the machines were very expensive. Before industrialism, spinners owned their spinning wheels, and weavers owned their looms. But the new machines were far too expensive for most workers to own. Only people with more money could buy them. These people usually bought a number of machines and built the factory to house them. People who used to manufacture goods in their homes with simple machines now worked in the

After machines were introduced, textile workers had little to do but change the spindles.

factories, with machines owned by others.

There is another reason why factories grew. Unlike the old, simpler machines such as the spinning wheel, the new machines did not run on human power. Some were run by waterpower, but more often they were run by steam. It was much more efficient, and less expensive, to assemble all the machines in one building. There, one large furnace could produce enough steam power to run all the machines. Can you see why keeping fifty machines in fifty separate homes (even if they could fit) would be less efficient?

How does transportation affect manufacturing? As you read Chapter 14, you noticed that past methods of transportation differed from present methods. How were goods moved in the past? How are they moved today? Do you remember why the ironworks had to be located right next to the iron-ore deposits, the limestone, and the woodlands? Why is it possible for modern steel companies to use ore from thousands of miles away?

Moving iron ore on the horse-drawn wagons of the colonial days was very costly. So was transporting finished iron products to market. These costs had to be added to the price of the goods. If either the ore or the finished product had to be shipped very far, the goods would become too expensive for many people to buy.

That is one reason there were so many iron furnaces in the early days. In the years just before industrialism came to America, there were several hundred iron furnaces in the state of Pennsylvania alone! Each one could only make small amounts, and each one could not sell very far away because of the cost of transportation.

Transportation in an industrial society also costs money, but it is much cheaper than in earlier days. Raw materials and finished products can be transported long distances quickly and

Lumber companies had to depend on animal power to drag the logs to nearby streams.

inexpensively by train, plane, truck, and steamboat. Therefore, many manufactured products can be sold cheaply, hundreds of miles away from the factory that made them.

That means factories have a very large market. Some factories in Los Angeles can sell their products in New York and Boston, on the other side of the continent. With the whole nation for a market, companies can manufacture a large amount of goods. That is another reason why factories today can be much larger.

Ships such as this carry 25,000 or more tons of ore on one voyage.

Cultural Values and Industrialism

There is still another important factor connected with industrialism. This one has nothing to do with raw materials, capital, machines, coal, or markets. It has to do with how people feel about change—in other words, with their values.

Suppose all the people in a society say, we don't want anything to change; we wish to do things exactly as our grandfathers did before us. Would you say such a society encourages inventions? Do you think it will use new scientific knowledge or new machinery or new sources of energy to raise its food and make its goods? Even if such a society has plenty of raw materials, capital, labor, and everything else that is needed, industrialism will come to such a land very, very slowly.

There are many such societies today. The leaders want very much to industrialize, but most of the people do not want to change their ways of doing things. Industrialism could be adopted much more quickly if a large number of the people believed industrialism was a better way of doing things.

These, then, are some of the features of an industrial society. In another chapter we will study how people live in an industrial society and how industrialism affects people. First, however, we are going to see how the United States changed from a farming country into the greatest industrial nation.

Working with Concepts and Generalizations

Identifying Concepts

Below is a list of the sources of power man has used to run machines. On paper, make two columns. At the top of the first column, write Before Industrialism. *At the top of the second column, write* Industrial Society. *Then place each item on the list in the correct column.*

1. Power supplied by man's muscle
2. Power supplied by nuclear energy
3. Power supplied by coal
4. Power supplied by animals
5. Power supplied by water
6. Power supplied by electricity
7. Power supplied by oil
8. Power supplied by gas
9. Power supplied by wind

Complete each sentence. Write on paper.

10. _____ do most of the work in an industrial society.
11. Nations have been able to get the natural resources they do not have by conquest and by _____.
12. A society can have savings only by using less goods than it _____.
13. When the United States became an industrial nation, manufacuring moved from homes to _____.
14. Textile machines, steel mills, and automobile plants are examples of _____ goods.
15. The _____ was invented by James Watt.

Developing Concepts

Write the answers on paper.

1. You decide to start a small business. You think you will need about ten dollars to get started. Name two ways that you, a fifth-grade student, can get the capital you need.
2. Look around you. List all the things you see in your classroom that you think were made in a factory or in a plant. Next to each item, write whether you think it has a large market or a small market and explain why you think so.
3. List some machines you use that will work only if *you* supply all the power. (Do you use a pencil sharpener?)
4. You and your classmates have decided to make and sell cookies and punch in the school cafeteria. You have been given permission to sell your goods during the lunch period.
   a. What is the market for the cookies and punch?
   b. What supplies and equipment will you need? How will you get them?
   c. Will everyone be responsible for just one job, or will everyone do part of every job?
   d. How will you get your goods to the cafeteria?
   e. Will everyone sell cookies and punch, or will just a few sell them? Why?
   f. What arrangements will you make for handling the money you earn?

Generalizations

Read the generalizations listed below. Find proof to support each generalization. Tell what the proof is and the page on which you found it.

1. Many nations acquire the raw materials they need by trading with other nations.
2. A society can have savings only by using fewer goods than it produces.
3. A nation cannot industrialize unless it is able to get the raw materials it needs for industrialization.

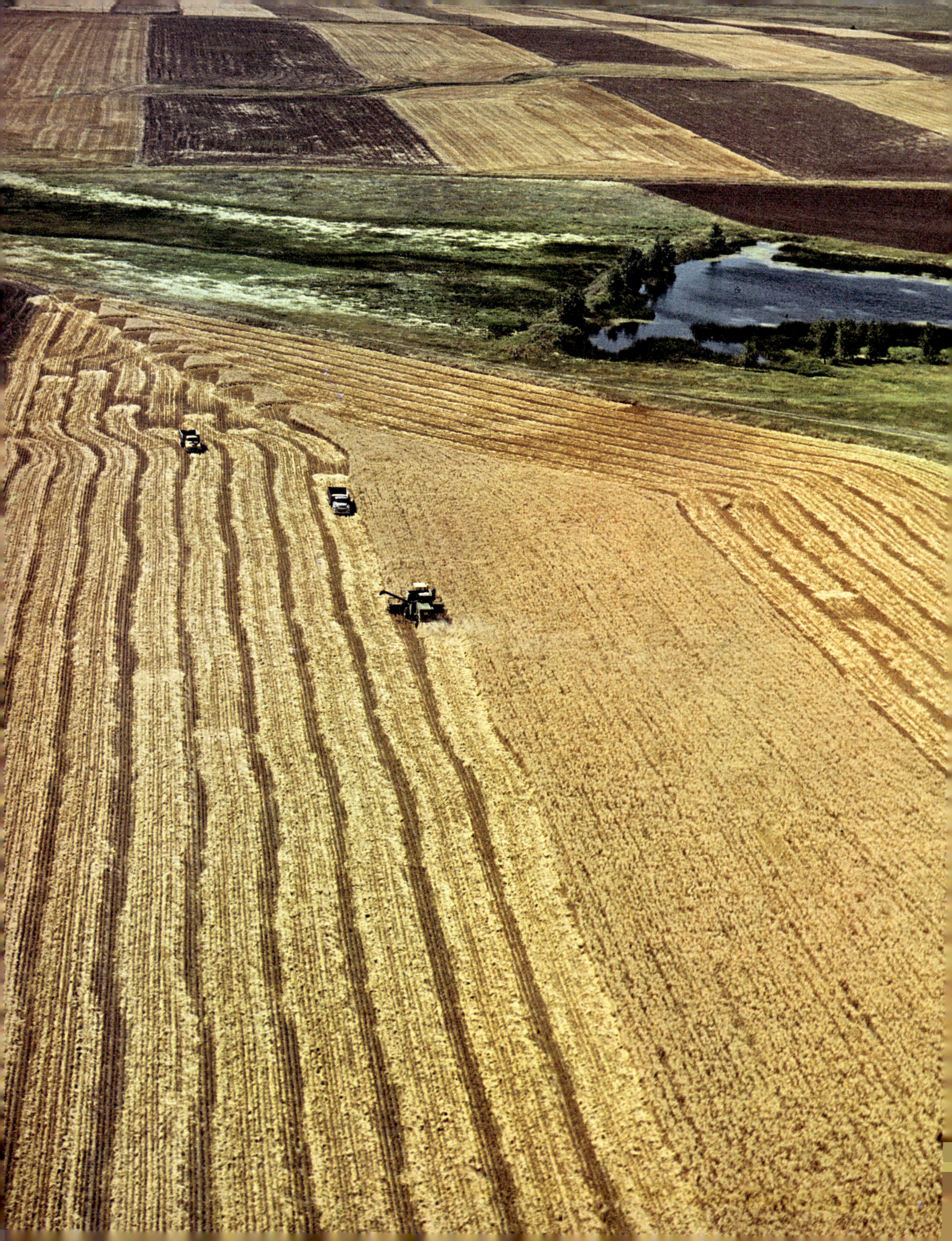

The United States Becomes an Industrial Nation

16

The United States today is the most industrialized nation in the world. It produces more manufactured goods, makes more steel, and uses more energy from coal, oil, gas, and electricity than any other nation. Yet less than two hundred years ago, the United States was a farming nation. Although skilled workmen made various goods by hand in their homes and shops, there was not a single factory in the entire country.

This chapter tells the story of the great change from a farming nation to an industrial giant. As you read it, keep in mind the things we decided nations must have in order to become industrialized. Ask yourself if the United States had such things as raw materials, capital, and new sources of energy. Did it have machines and a large number of inventions? Did it have enough labor and a growing market for goods? If the United States did not have all these things, was it able to get them elsewhere? Is industrialization increasing in the United States today?

Beginnings in England

The story of America's industrialization begins in England in the last half of the eighteenth century. There, many changes in the manufacturing of goods were happening, especially in the making of cotton textiles. Englishmen had invented new machines that made yarn and wove cloth much faster than before. You read about those machines in Chapter 15. The most important invention of all was the steam engine. It provided a new kind of power to run machines and do man's work. Soon there were machines to make still other goods. All were powered by coal and steam.

The Industrial Revolution. These changes took place over a period of about sixty years. Does that seem like a long time? It probably does—until you realize that before these changes, man had made most goods in the same old way for thousands of years. When you realize what a great change was brought about by industrialization, sixty years does not seem like such a long time after all. In fact, it is such a short time that we

In England the Industrial Revolution first affected the textile industry.
Barfoot; Progress of Cotton, No. 6: Spinning, Yale University Art Gallery, Mabel Brady Garvin Collection

call this changeover to an industrial society the *Industrial Revolution.* The word revolution means "a very big change in a very short time."

Although England made cotton textiles, she did not grow cotton herself. She got it from other lands by trading. But England did have the two most important raw materials needed to industrialize. The first was iron, which was needed to make tools, machinery, and many other goods. The second was coal, which supplied the energy for running machines.

English businessmen were quick to make use of the new inventions and to take advantage of the raw materials. They built hundreds of machines and put up factories to house them. They hired thousands of people to operate the machines. Soon factories turned out unheard-of amounts of cloth.

The machines made a cloth of good quality and made it far more cheaply than a weaver could by hand. This meant more Englishmen could afford to buy the cloth. In other words, we can say that machines made the market for textiles larger by lowering the cost of the textiles.

Also, people in other countries bought these English goods. It was cheaper to buy machine-made cloth from England than handmade cloth produced in their own countries. That made the market for English cloth even larger and allowed English manufacturers to produce still more.

Closely guarded secrets. Soon England was the envy of the world, for her machines brought her great wealth. People in other countries did not know how to make such machines. This secret was the key to great wealth for England, and she guarded it closely. The English government passed a law that no one could take out of the country plans for building the machines. In fact, no one who had even worked on textile machines was allowed to leave England.

Secrets such as inventions are hard to keep for long, as the English soon found out. On a gray morning in September 1789, a twenty-one-year-old Englishman boarded a ship bound for America. His name was Samuel Slater, and in his head he carried the information that ended England's secret.

The Revolution Comes to America

Samuel Slater had worked in English cotton mills for seven years. During that time he had heard that Americans were anxious to have a textile industry. They believed it would mean great wealth and progress for their country. They even advertised in England, saying they would pay good wages to men who were experienced in making and operating textile machines.

Slater decided to go to America to make his fortune by building a textile factory. He studied Arkwright's spinning machine until he had memorized each part. Then, in disguise, Slater slipped past the English authorities and boarded a boat for America.

America's first factory. Shortly after Samuel Slater arrived, a Rhode Island company named Almy & Brown hired him to build a cotton spinning machine. It took about a year for Slater to make each piece and build the machine from memory. Then, in 1791, the first spinning machine in America began to produce cotton thread. The machine was so successful that Almy & Brown built several more. They also built a factory for the machines in Pawtucket, Rhode Island. This was America's first factory. It was built next to a stream, for the machines were run by waterpower. The steam engine had not yet come to America.

Samuel Slater was well rewarded for his work. With the opening of the factory in 1793, the firm of Almy & Brown added a partner and changed its name. From that time on, the firm was Almy, Brown & Slater.

An engine to clean cotton. In the same year that America's first factory opened, another important invention was made. This time it was an American, Eli Whitney, who invented the machine. His invention is another example of how one invention so often leads to another.

With the new spinning and weaving machines in England, the textile factories needed more raw cotton. It was easy to grow more cotton, but the problem was to prepare it for spinning. Before cotton could be spun, the seeds that clung to the fluffy ball had to be removed. This was a very slow job. A single worker could only clean about a pound of cotton in a whole day's work. What was needed was a machine that would separate the seeds from the cotton fibers more quickly.

That is what Eli Whitney invented. He called his machine a cotton engine, or *cotton gin*. It was a simple little boxlike machine with a hand crank. Eli excitedly wrote to his father:

> One man [using this machine] will clean ten times as much cotton as he can in any other way before known. This machine may also be turned by water or with a horse. One man and a horse will do more than fifty men working the old way.

The importance of one machine. Over the years, larger and improved cotton gins were built. Soon men could clean a thousand times as much cotton in a day. This meant that one man using this machine could clean more cotton in a single *day* than he could clean in almost three *years* without it.

Would someone else have invented a machine for cleaning cotton if Eli Whitney had not? Probably yes. For the need was there, and men were bound to set their minds to find an answer to the problem. When that happens, inventions usually follow just as

This painting shows Slater's cotton-spinning mill in Pawtucket, Rhode Island. The mill drew its power from the falls.

Whitney's cotton gin made cotton profitable.

they did in England when men tried to find ways of speeding up spinning and weaving. Of course, we do not know how much longer it might have taken before someone else invented a similar machine. Perhaps it might have been many years.

Now that cotton could be cleaned quickly, it became a very profitable crop. Southern farmers planted more and more of it. At first, almost all the cotton was shipped to English factories from southern ports such as Charleston, South Carolina, and New Orleans, Louisiana. Later, after more mills like Slater's were built, much of the cotton went to American factories in the North.

An industry grows. Machines for manufacturing cotton cloth soon followed machines for manufacturing cotton thread. In the early 1800's, Francis Lowell, a wealthy Boston merchant, visited England's textile factories. There he saw the power looms, run by steam, turning out hundreds of yards of cotton cloth each day.

Why should America buy cotton cloth from England when she could make her own, Lowell wondered? Of course, it would be expensive to build such machines and factories. But Lowell had made a lot of money as a merchant, and he was willing to risk some of his capital to build a weaving mill. Certainly it could be a very profitable business. It would also be a good thing for America to start manufacturing more of her own goods. Then people would not have to depend on England for the manufactured goods they needed.

On his return, Francis Lowell built a factory in Waltham, Massachusetts. In the factory were machines copied from those in England and improved by Lowell and a helper. There, the first machine-made cotton cloth was woven in America. The factory turned out to be very profitable. Lowell persuaded some of his merchant friends to join him and invest enough capital to build more mills. They selected a site for their new mills along the Merrimack River in Massachusetts and named it after their leader. Lowell, Massachusetts, soon became famous for its textile mills.

More machines, more industries. Soon machinery was invented to manufacture other goods, and more factories were opened. Boots and shoes, woolen cloth, tools, and finished lumber were some of the goods turned out by these new factories.

Often a single invention created a whole new industry. The invention of the sewing machine in 1846 made it possible for many factories to manufacture ready-made clothes.

There was plenty of labor to run these machines. Women, and very often small children, could operate the machines as easily as men could. Most of the new factory workers came from the farms nearby. They were attracted to the towns by the jobs. Later, immigrants supplied much of the needed labor. The growing population of the nation provided not only a labor supply to make the goods, but also a large market to buy them.

New England becomes an industrial area. Most of these early factories were located in the northeastern part of the United States, especially in New England. There were two reasons for that. One was that the capital goods were expensive. Ordinary workers could not afford these things. But in New England there were men who did have enough capital. Merchants like Francis Lowell or Almy and Brown, the people who hired Samuel Slater, had already

The swiftness of New England's rivers made their banks excellent sites for factories such as this one in South Windham, Maine.

made fortunes in trade—the business of *selling* goods. Some of them now decided to take a chance and invest their money in manufacturing—the business of *making* goods.

Sometimes the factories and machines were too expensive for one merchant. Then a number of merchants got together and became partners, as the Boston merchants did when they built the mills at Lowell. These wealthy New England merchants built the factories in towns near their homes. There they could watch over the new and risky businesses.

A second reason for locating the early factories in New England had to do with the geography of that region. New England has many rivers and streams. Factories needed the running water to provide the power to run their machines. Soon the riverbanks were crowded with factories. For example, on one small river between Worcester, Massachusetts, and Providence, Rhode Island—a distance of forty miles—there were 150 mills and shops using waterpower.

A new source of power. By the 1840's, factories were beginning to appear in other parts of the nation. Wealth was being created in those areas, too, and people there were willing to invest their capital in manufacturing. Also, it was no longer so important to be near New England's streams. By this time, machines were run by steam engines, as in England. For fuel, these engines used a different source of energy—coal.

There are huge coal deposits in the United States, especially along the Appalachian Mountains. In many areas, chunks of coal could even be found on the surface of the ground. People had long known about this coal, but except for some blacksmiths who used it to heat their forges, few people seemed to want it. Most of them preferred to burn logs instead of "black stones" in their fireplaces.

The steam engine greatly increased the demand for coal. Mine fields were opened in Pennsylvania, West Virginia, and later on in Illinois and Kentucky. Mining companies hired thousands of men to dig the coal from the earth. Most of the men were immigrants who had recently come to America. The work was very hard, for these were the

Production of Coal, Crude Petroleum, and Pig Iron in the United States

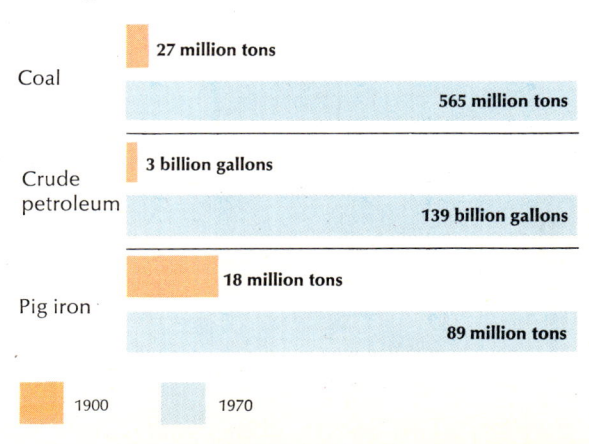

	1900	1970
Coal	27 million tons	565 million tons
Crude petroleum	3 billion gallons	139 billion gallons
Pig iron	18 million tons	89 million tons

Steel plants depend on railroads for their raw materials.

years before modern mining machinery was invented.

Railroads and Industries

Coal provided power for another important invention that helped America become industrialized. That invention was the railroad train. The railroad locomotive was itself a huge steam engine that provided the power to move the train along the tracks.

The importance of railroads. You have already read how railroads helped open up new parts of the country to settlers, and how they helped cities grow. Railroads also helped industries grow. They brought raw materials long distances to the factories, and carried the finished products to distant markets. And they did it cheaply. That meant the cost of transportation did not add too much to the price of goods. People living far from the factory could still buy its products.

Do you see why we say railroads created a greater market for manufacturers? Would that lead the manufacturer to produce more, or less? Do you think he might invest in more machines for his factory? Why?

STEELMAKING IN THE GREAT LAKES REGION

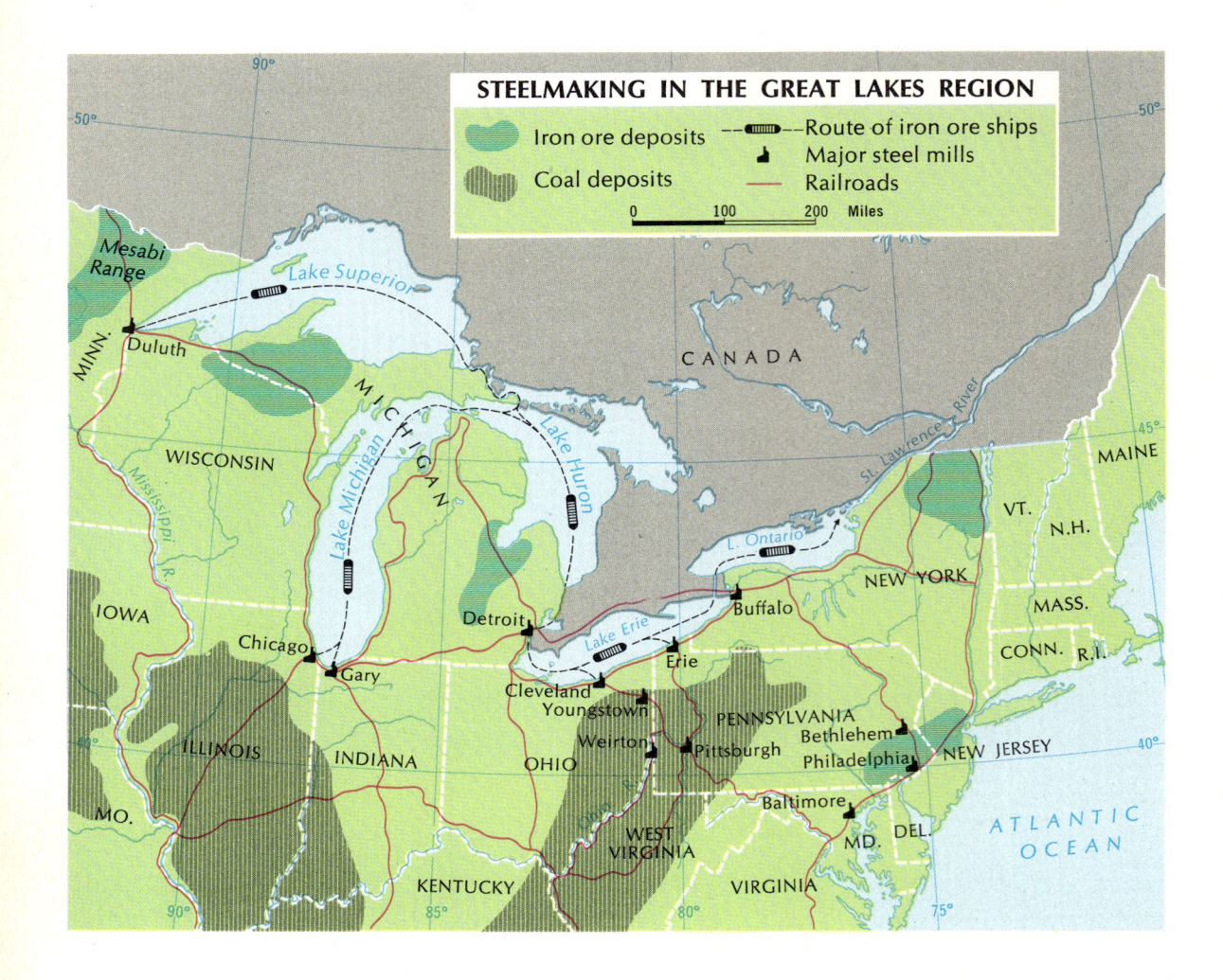

Railroads were very expensive to build. They required far more capital than building a factory or two. Where did this capital come from? Part of it came from wealthy Americans, who invested in this business just as they had earlier invested in the textile business. State governments and the United States government also provided some of the capital, because our government leaders believed having more railroads was good for the country. In addition, a large amount of capital came from people in other countries, especially England. They thought investing in a railroad in a growing country might be very profitable. It took capital from all these sources to build America's railroads.

Railroads create a demand for steel. The growth of railroads created a great demand for steel. Steel was needed to build locomotives and track. When the railroad first appeared in the 1830's, there were several hundred small iron foundries in Pennsylvania. About a hundred more were scattered among the other states. These ironworks still operated as they had a hundred years earlier. Each one made a small amount of iron from the ore in its own neighborhood.

Then, in the 1850's, a way of making large quantities of steel quickly and cheaply was invented. Within ten years, iron manufacturers built huge new furnaces to make steel this new way. To make the millions of tons of steel, companies hired thousands of workers. Most of them were European immigrants, but there were also many from within the United States who had left their farms for jobs in the city.

With the great new demand for steel, steel mills required more iron ore. Rich ore deposits had earlier been found in the states of Michigan, Wisconsin, and Minnesota. However, they were of no use to the Pennsylvania furnaces, because there was no way of getting the ore to Pennsylvania.

Railroads solved that problem. They carried the ore from the new mines to the shores of the Great Lakes. From there, the ore was shipped by boat to a port on Lake Erie. Railroads carried it the rest of the way to the mills at Pittsburgh, which had become a big iron and steel center. Railroads also carried coal and limestone from the mines to the steel mills. The demand for those minerals also increased greatly as the furnaces turned out ever more steel.

Huge blast furnaces at Cleveland turn out tons of steel daily.

Charts tell us about industrialization. As you read the stories of railroads, coal, and iron and steel, do you see how each helped the other to grow? Could coal mining have become so important without railroads to ship the coal to the markets? Could steel have been made without large amounts of coal? Could the railroads have spanned the country without steel? And could they have run without coal? Could large amounts of steel have been made without a railroad to carry the ore and the finished steel products?

That is the way it is in an industrial society. Each product depends on the making of other products. Look at the table that shows coal production, iron production, and the number of miles of railroad track in the United States during different years of our history. Does the table show any connection between the three products?

You remember that the amount of coal and steel a nation produces is a sign of how industrialized it is. What does this table tell you about how industrialized America was between 1810 and 1830? between 1830 and 1860? between 1860 and 1890? Does the number of miles of railroad track also tell you something about industrialization in each period? Why?

Another way of seeing how industrialized a nation is becoming is to see how many people make their living by

Coal, iron, and railroad track
1810–1900

Year	Tons of coal	Tons of pig iron	Miles of railroad track
1900	212,300,000	15,500,000	21,500
1890	111,000,000	10,300,000	17,000
1880	51,000,000	4,300,000	14,000
1870	21,000,000	1,900,000	9,000
1860	9,000,000	900,000	3,500
1850	4,000,000	600,000	1,800
1840	1,300,000	300,000	531
1830	646,000	185,000	
1820	330,000	22,000	
1810	176,000	60,000	

farming and how many by manufacturing. Look at the graph that shows this. Can you tell from the graph how industrialized America was from 1800 to 1830? from 1830 to 1860? from 1860 to 1890?

Does the information from this graph fit in with the information from the table you studied above? How can you account for the fact that there are more people in farming *and* more people in manufacturing? What does this tell you about the population of the country? Does this give you information about the labor supply? about the market for goods?

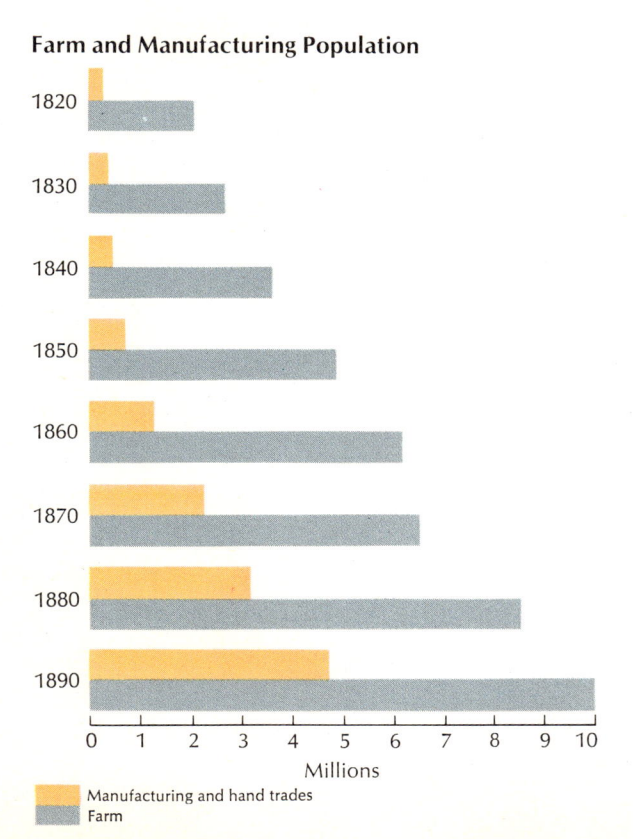

Farm and Manufacturing Population

1820	
1830	
1840	
1850	
1860	
1870	
1880	
1890	

Millions (0–10)

Manufacturing and hand trades
Farm

New Sources of Energy

As you have seen, new sources of energy play a large part in industrializing. After 1850, several new sources of energy were developed in the United States. One important source was oil.

Black gold. Oil, or petroleum, was long known to many people. In some places, such as in parts of Pennsylvania, it seeped from the ground and lay in shallow pools and under rocks. But few people paid much attention, even those who thought the oil could be useful. Unless a way could be found of getting large amounts of it from the ground, it was not worth the bother.

Then, in 1859, the first oil well was drilled in Titusville, Pennsylvania. The discovery that oil could be pumped from the ground set off a wild rush for the *black gold*. Soon there was a forest of oil derricks in the rolling fields of Pennsylvania. In later years oil was found in other states. After 1900, drillers discovered huge deposits in the southwestern states of Texas, Oklahoma, and California.

At first most of the thick, black fluid was used to make kerosene, a clear, thin oil used in oil lamps. In making kerosene, another product, called gasoline, was produced. However, none of the companies knew of any use for it, so they threw it away.

They stopped throwing it away after 1895. That was the year Henry Ford

335

first drove his horseless carriage, or automobile, down the streets of Detroit. Ford's automobile was powered by an engine that used gasoline for fuel. Several inventors in different countries had been trying to make a gasoline engine powerful enough to pull a vehicle. Henry Ford, working nights in the shed behind his Detroit home, was one of the first to succeed.

At first, people thought Ford's invention was an amusing toy and not much more. His own father was embarrassed that a grown man like Henry would waste his time tinkering with such a silly contraption. But in a few years, people stopped thinking that Ford's automobile was so silly. In time, this new form of transportation changed the face of America.

The invention of the automobile created a whole new industry. Henry Ford started a factory that produced thousands of cars a year. Others followed. The automobile in turn helped other industries to grow. Oil companies produced more in order to supply cars with gasoline, which was now the companies' most important product. Automobile makers used large amounts of steel. Their great need for rubber tires created a whole new industry.

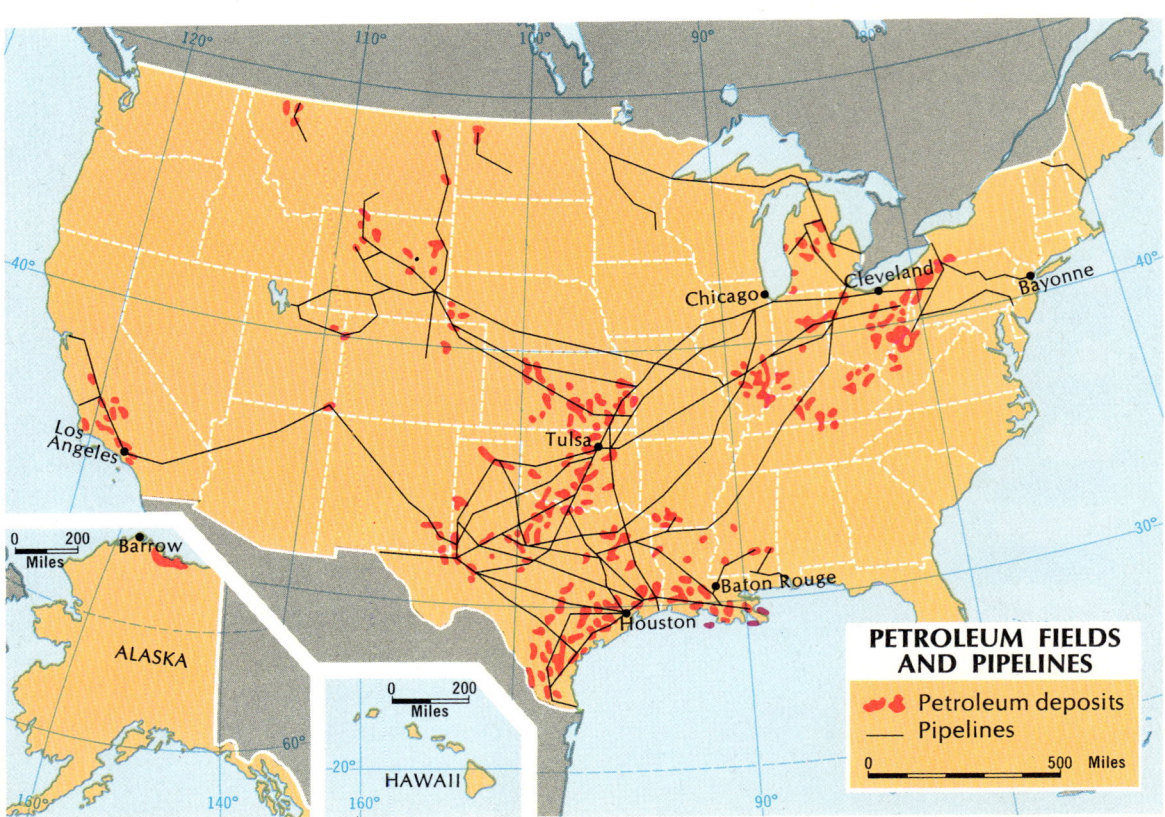

PETROLEUM FIELDS AND PIPELINES
- Petroleum deposits
- Pipelines

Henry Ford's first assembly line looks quite simple compared to those used today; yet it completely changed the way of making automobiles. Above is an early Ford plant.

Petroleum refineries multiplied after the invention of the automobile.

The cement manufacturers produced more, as more roads were built. You can probably think of other industries that have grown because of the automobile.

Electricity. Electricity was a second important source of power developed in the late 1800's. Machines called generators were built to convert the power of rushing water into electricity. Other generators converted steam power to electricity. In the 1880's, an inventor named Thomas Edison built a generator that created enough electricity to light several buildings in New York City. That was the beginning. In a few years, larger generators were sending electricity over power lines to distant cities.

Today, electricity lights our homes and offices and runs nearly all the machines in our factories. The machines in the modern flour mill and the textile factory that you read about in Chapter 14 were all run by electricity.

Industrialization Comes to the Farm

When we think of industrialization, we usually think of the city, for that is where most machines and factories are. But machines made it possible to produce more farm goods, too.

Machinery for the wheat farmer. Industrialization came to the farm in the 1830's. That was about forty years after America's first factory began to produce cotton thread. Industrialization came first in wheat farming.

One of the big problems for wheat farmers is harvesting the crop. When wheat ripens, the crop must be harvested within two weeks. If the wheat is not cut and gathered, the grain falls to the earth and is lost to the farmer.

In 1830 the farmer harvested wheat in the same way that his ancestors did. He used a long-handled tool with a blade at the bottom, called a scythe (sīTH). Swinging it from side to side, he walked through the field cutting the stalks of wheat. Later he tied the stalks into bundles and brought them into his barn. There he threshed the stalks; that is, he beat them with a whiplike tool until the wheat kernels fell to the dirt floor.

Harvesting with a scythe was tiring work, and it was also slow. Working alone, a farmer could harvest less than half an acre in a day, or about five or six acres in the two-week harvest period. Unless he had extra helpers, he would not plant more than five or six acres. After all, there would be no sense in planting more than he could harvest.

In 1832 a young Virginian named Cyrus McCormick invented a machine to harvest wheat. He called it a *reaper*. McCormick's reaper, a clumsy-looking wooden machine drawn by a team of horses, reaped as much wheat in one hour as a man could in three or four days. McCormick moved to Chicago and opened a factory to manufacture his reapers. Soon he was selling thousands of these machines to farmers every year. These farmers now could plant many more acres than ever before, because the reaper made it possible to harvest more.

Inventions increase production. The reaper was only one of the important inventions that helped the farmer. Soon there were machines to help him with all the other farm operations—

Harvesting with a scythe and cradle, as this farmer is doing, was long and tiring.

plowing, planting, binding, and threshing. Meanwhile, scientists studied ways of making the earth yield larger crops. They developed fertilizers, special seeds, and new methods of farming for different soils. In 1900 a farmer who used machinery and scientific methods could produce nearly twenty times as much as his grandfather had.

In later years the steam engine and then the gasoline motor replaced the horse. That allowed the farmer to produce even more. With today's modern machinery, farmers can reap, thresh, and bag forty bushels of wheat in thirty minutes. That is more than a farmer of 1830 was able to do in about three days.

Industrialism Continues to Expand

In 1894, the year before Henry Ford drove his horseless carriage on Detroit's streets, the United States passed England as the greatest manufacturing nation in the world. In the space of a single lifetime, the country had changed from a land of very few factories, to the giant of the industrial world.

With modern machinery, farmers can perform several operations at the same time.

Very few Americans of 1894 could even begin to imagine how much more industrialized their nation would become. Today, more than seventy-five years later, we can look back and see how industrialism has continued to expand. The graph on page 330 gives you some idea of how great the change has been. It shows the amount of coal, crude petroleum, and pig iron produced in 1900, and how much of each is produced now.

Look at the graph that shows how much of our work in 1900 was still being done by human and animal muscles. This was even after we had become the greatest industrial nation. Compare that with the amount of work being done this way in 1960.

The pace of industrialism quickens. Even as we are using more coal and oil than ever before, modern science is finding still newer ways of getting energy from nature. Scientists have found a way of harnessing the enormous energy of the nucleus of the tiny atom. The atom is the basic building block in nature. *Nuclear energy* is already being turned into electrical power in many parts of the United States, and nuclear energy will be used much more in the future. Scientists have also found ways of converting the energy of the sun into electrical energy through solar batteries.

All this use of energy has lightened man's work greatly, and has allowed

Manpower Production Hourly Output

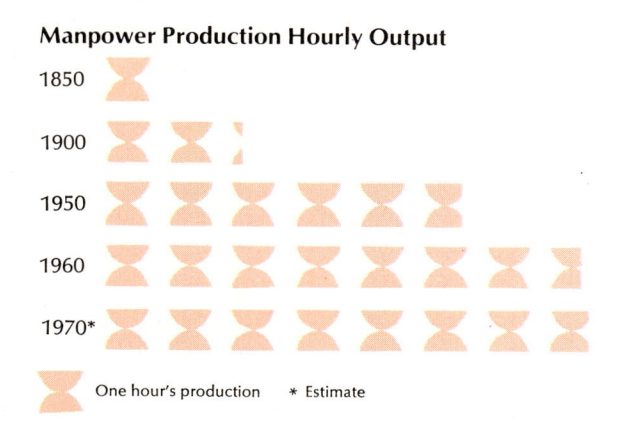

1850
1900
1950
1960
1970*

⧗ One hour's production   * Estimate

Man, Animal, and Machine Power

1860
1880
1900
1920
1940
1950

0 10 20 30 40 50 60 70 80 90 100
Percent

☐ Machine power
☐ Animal power
☐ Man power

him to produce more goods than ever. One common way of expressing how much a country produces is to say that it produces so much per hour, or so much per worker. The graph on this page shows how new machines and new sources of energy have made our workers much more productive than ever before.

These graphs tell only part of the story of industrialism in America today. They do not tell of the millions of autos and trucks, the thousands of miles of highways, or the growth of a whole new form of transportation with the invention of the airplane. And they do not tell of the amazing new machinery in certain industries.

Some modern factories use such advanced machines that they do not even need humans to operate them. In fact, machines operate other machines. A computer "tells" the machines what to do, checks the quality of the goods they make, and stops the machines or adjusts them if it finds something

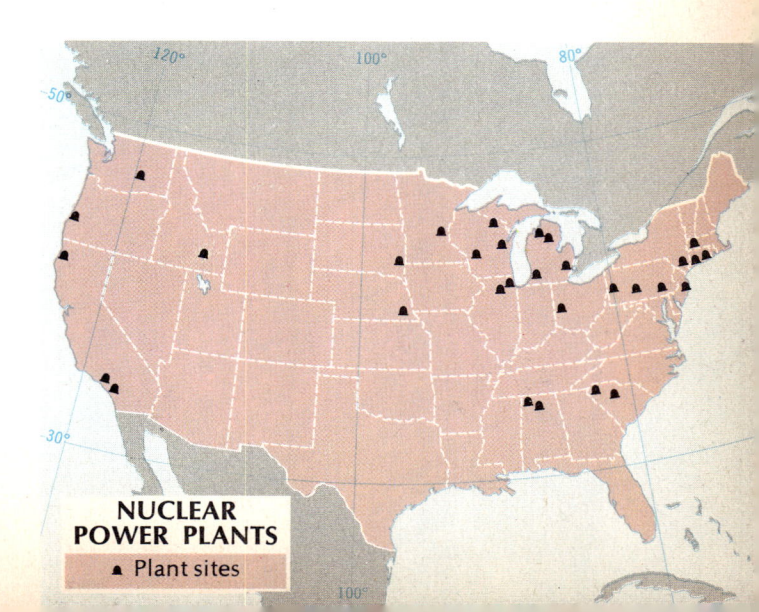

NUCLEAR POWER PLANTS
▲ Plant sites

341

wrong. Using machines to run other machines is called *automation.* In automated factories, only a few men are needed to supervise the computers, or master machines.

Industrialism brings new products. Nor do the charts and graphs we studied tell us of the many new products of modern industrialism. Chemical factories product wonders undreamed of by our parents. They have created new fibers such as rayon, nylon, and polyester. These can be used not only in clothing, but in tires, in building, and in hundreds of products. Chemists have also given us plastic materials, which have a thousand uses. New household appliances have been invented.

Around each invention a new industry has grown. Forty years ago there was no television or television industry. Today thousands of people are employed in manufacturing television sets, and thousands more are engaged in producing television programs.

Certainly industrialization has made great changes by bringing us the many goods we now enjoy. But in what other ways has industrialism affected our lives? What other changes has it brought? Have they all been good? Those are the questions we will consider in the next chapter.

Automation enables this man to use television to guide and control several tasks at the same time.

Working with Concepts and Generalizations

Identifying Concepts

Complete each sentence. Write the answers on paper.

1. The Industrial Revolution began in _____.
2. The first area in the United States to become industrialized was _____.
3. The invention of the _____ made it profitable for southern farmers to plant more cotton.
4. The steam engine greatly increased the demand for _____.
5. The first factories in the United States used _____ as a source of power.
6. The invention of the _____ created a great demand for gasoline.
7. The invention of the _____ made it possible for factories to manufacture ready-made clothing.
8. Industrialization came to wheat farming with the invention of the _____.
9. Railroads created a demand for _____.
10. England had the two most important raw materials needed to industrialize: _____ and _____.

Developing Concepts

Write the answers on paper.

1. In this chapter you read about many inventions that were part of the Industrial Revolution. In your opinion, which invention was most important in making the United States an industrial nation? Give good reasons for your answer.
2. You know that if a nation wishes to industrialize it must have capital. Who supplied the capital to build the first textile mills in the United States? Who supplied the capital to build the first railroads?
3. Samuel Slater was able to build the first spinning machine in the United States because he remembered exactly what one looked like and how it worked. You will have a greater appreciation for what Samuel Slater did if you try to show what a machine looks like, relying only on your memory. You have used a pencil sharpener as long as you have been in school. You know what one looks like, how it works, and what it does. Draw a sketch showing a pencil sharpener. Label each part, tell what the part is made of, and what it does. Could someone build a pencil sharpener, using your sketch as a guide? Could you?
4. Why was the invention of the steam engine so important to the growth of industry in the United States outside the New England area?
5. Almost everything around you was invented by one person or a group of people. Which invention have you enjoyed most? Which invention has been very important to the way you live?

Generalizations

Read the generalizations listed below. Find proof to support each generalization. Tell what the proof is and the page on which you found it.

1. In an industrial society, each product depends on the making of other products.
2. Raw materials become valuable only when man discovers a productive way of using them.
3. The price of a product helps determine the market for that product.

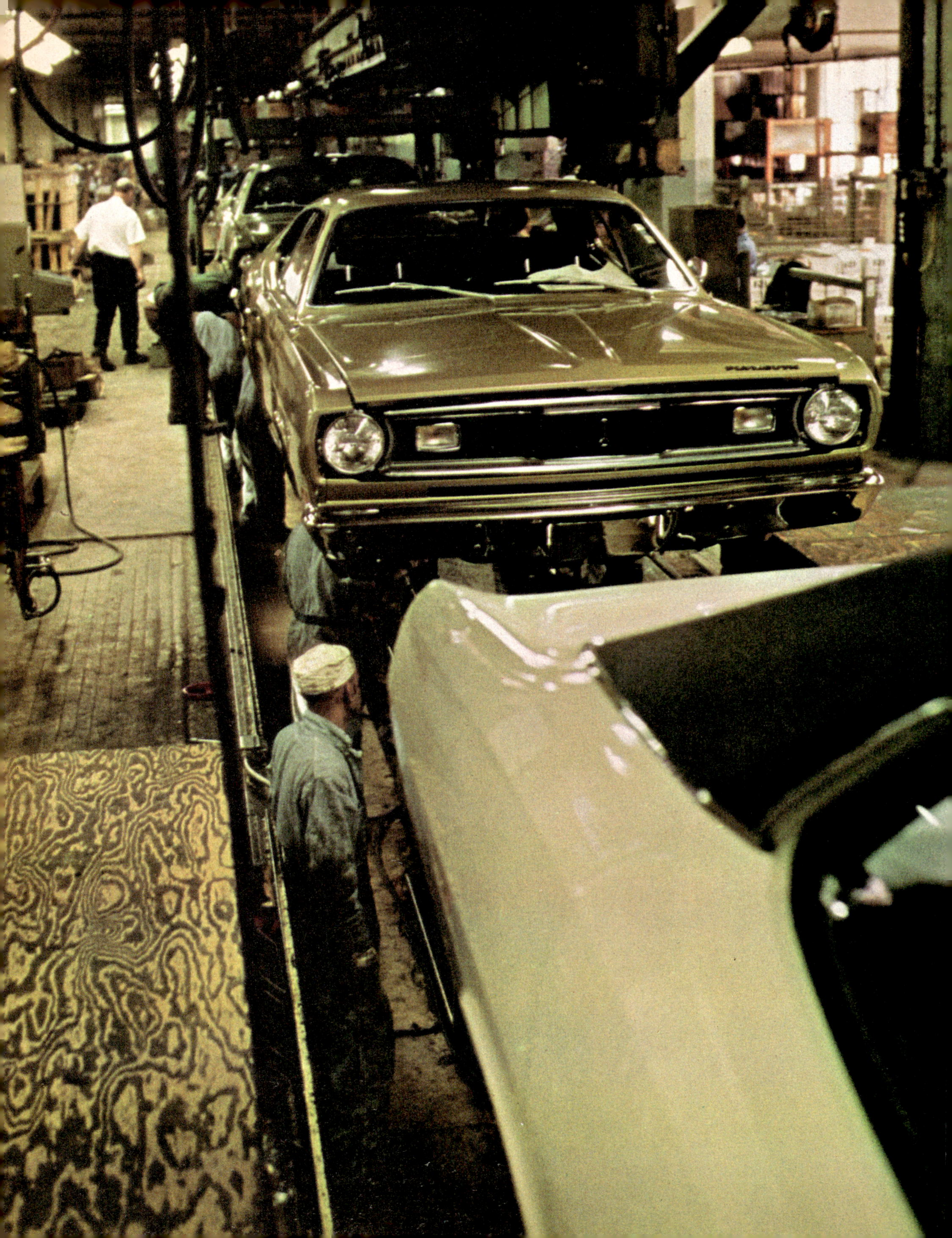

Industrialism Changes Our Ways of Living

17

As the United States changed from an agricultural society to an industrial society, great changes occurred in the ways of living in this country. Certainly many Americans benefited from industrialism. For them life was made easier and more enjoyable. But industrialism also brought hardship and pain to many people. It also brought new problems for society as a whole. Often the American people were not prepared for these problems. Years passed before any answers were found.

What are some of the ways in which industrialism has changed ways of working and living? How has our society tried to deal with the problems that industrialism brought with it? Have we been successful in this? Are there new and different problems that industrialism is creating today? If so, what are they, and what can we do to deal with them? These are some of the questions we shall answer in this chapter.

From the answers to these questions, you should obtain a deeper understanding of the meaning of industrialism. You should also realize how much of your life is affected by it.

Industrialism Changes Ways of Working

One of the biggest changes that industrialism made was in our ways of working. Below is the story of two workmen. One was a cloth weaver before industrialism came to America; the other wove cloth after industrialism had come. As you read their stories, see if you can find some of the changes that industrialism brought to our ways of working.

Mr. Weaver works at home. Nathaniel Weaver was starting his day a little later than usual. He liked to get started early, for the more cloth he wove, the more he could earn. But the family and the neighbors had stayed up quite late the night before.

Well, thought Mr. Weaver, he could always work a little longer to make up for his late start. Or perhaps not. He would decide that later. That was one good thing about being your own boss.

Not that making a living was easy. He had to work ten or twelve hours a day, and sometimes longer. But somehow working for himself made the long hours easier.

Right after breakfast, Nathaniel Weaver went into the front room of his house, where his loom was set up. It was a simple, inexpensive machine — a great many farm housewives owned looms just like it. But not everyone could produce fine cloth on it. That took skill and experience — the kind that Nathaniel Weaver had, that his father before him had had, and that someday his son, Samuel, would have.

As he settled at his loom, Mr. Weaver planned the work ahead of him. There was that special yarn Mr. Harold, the shipowner, had brought to be made into cloth for his elegant clothes. Better get to that right away. Then he could start on the cloth he would sell to shopkeepers.

Just about that time, Samuel entered the room. "Well," said the father, "shall we start with Mr. Harold's yarn? This would be a good time for you to learn how to use special material like this in weaving."

"Yes, sir," replied the son, and the two prepared the loom for the work ahead.

Mr. Carter works in a factory. It was still dark outside, but George Carter had already set out for the factory, about a mile away. He set out at this time every morning — never later, for it was important to be on the job before the factory whistle blew at 6:30. If not, he would lose part of his day's pay. In fact, George knew of some who had lost their jobs for being late a few times.

George had worked in this textile factory for two years. Before that, he worked at the docks. Making the change in jobs had not been difficult, for weaving cloth in the factory required no great skill. The factory owners decided what kind of cloth and how much cloth should be made. The power looms in the factory really did most of the work. Anyone could be taught to run them in a few days.

Machines like this were expensive. An ordinary worker like George Carter could never hope to own one himself — not on his low pay. It was hard enough to make a living for his family even in good times, when there was plenty of work. Then there were those other times, like last winter, when business slowed down and there was work enough for only two or three days a week. Those months had been hard on the Carter family. Still, he knew he had been one of the luckier ones, for there were many who were told not to report to work at all.

By now George Carter and several hundred other employees had entered the factory and taken their places. "Whooee!" the whistle shrieked. It was 6:30. The machines started. Another workday was beginning at the factory.

Comparing the two workmen. Why could Mr. Weaver start his working day later than usual? Did Mr. Weaver, or Mr. Carter, require more skill to do his job? Who had to do more planning, Mr. Weaver or Mr. Carter? Do you think Mr. Carter could set up a shop in his own home as Mr. Weaver did? Do you think Mr. Carter could do the special jobs that Mr. Weaver did?

Pride in one's work. After industrialism, there was an important change in the way the worker felt about his product and in the way people felt about the worker. For example, before industrialism, shoes were made by a skilled worker. He cut the leather, hammered it, shaped it, and stitched it. From the first step to the last, he made the shoes himself. At the end of his work, he could look at his product and say, "There is no one anywhere who makes finer shoes than I." Others in his town respected him for the quality of his work.

How did industrialism change this? In factories, shoemaking was divided

The cobbler of years ago took pride in his skill.

When machines were used in shoemaking, each step in production was done by a different worker.

into sixty-four separate steps—cutting the sole, stitching it, attaching the heel, punching the shoelace holes, and so on. Each step was done by a different worker. One man might do nothing except punch holes for shoelaces, day after day. Many found their work boring.

It was hard for any worker to feel proud of the finished product. A factory worker did not say, "I am proud of that shoe. I punched out the holes for the laces." In his town he was not highly respected for his skill, for almost any other man, woman, or even child could easily learn to run the same machine he used.

Craftsmen such as the shoemaker were doomed to disappear. Doing each step himself and using only simple hand tools, the shoemaker could not produce many shoes in a day. He had to charge a high price for them. Because of machines and specialization of labor, factories produced shoes far more cheaply than the skilled shoemaker could. People no longer bought his product, so he had to find another way of making a living. Often he entered the factory—perhaps to become a puncher of holes for laces.

Who decides, machines or men? Machines were invented to help men do their work. But there were times when machines seemed to be the masters of men rather than the servants.

For example, the machine decided how long the workday should be. The owner wanted to produce as much as he could from his expensive machines, so he ran them as long as possible. In those days before electric lights, that meant from sunup to sundown. During the longer summer days, that might be thirteen or fourteen hours. So factory workers worked thirteen or fourteen hours a day, not because they wanted to, but because it was the way of getting the most out of the machines.

Steel furnaces could be operated most cheaply if the furnaces were kept hot twenty-four hours a day. So the day was divided into two parts, each twelve hours long. Men worked twelve hours a day in the intense heat of a steel mill, not because it was good for them or because they wanted to, but because 24 divided by 2 equals 12. In those days, few people would have suggested dividing the 24-hour day into 3 shifts of workers working 8 hours each.

Some Evils of Industrialism

When Samuel Slater opened the first textile factory in America, the first nine people he hired to run his machines were all less than twelve years of age. He could hire them because no great skill or experience was needed to operate his machines. He paid children much less than he would have had to pay a grown man.

Child labor was a common practice in early textile mills. The owners hoped to save on wages.

349

As other factories were opened, their owners also hired children or women. Often a man could get a job only if he would work for the same low wages the children and women received. It was very hard to earn enough to provide for a family. Usually the only way of making ends meet was for everybody in the family—husband, wife, daughters, and sons—to work.

Industrialism encourages child labor. Child labor was very common in industrial America. Many children your age—and some even younger, only seven or eight years old—worked ten hours a day. Often their working conditions were very poor, and sometimes they were unsafe.

Little butchers. Here is how one investigator described what she saw in Chicago's slaughterhouses.

> Some of the children are boys who cut up the animals as soon as the hide is removed, little butchers working directly in the slaughter house, at the most revolting part of the labor performed in the stockyards. These children stand, ankle deep, in water [which was] used for flooding the floor [to carry] off blood and refuse into the drains; they breathe air so sickening that a man not accustomed to it can stay in the place but a few minutes.

The investigator added that we would never dream of punishing criminals by making them stay in such horrible conditions, but we allowed our children to work in them!

Breaker boys would sit for hours picking pieces of slate from the coal.

Breaker boys in coal mines. A common job for children working in the coal mines was that of breaker boy. Coal came out of the mines in large chunks. Heavy rollers, or breakers, crushed these chunks into smaller lumps and poured them onto a long table in the "screen room." Here the breaker boys screened, or picked out, the pieces of slate and threw them away. Here is an eyewitness description of working conditions. Remember, the breaker boy is just about your age.

At seven o'clock in the morning.... The whistle screams, the ... machinery is set in motion ... then the black, shallow streams of broken coal start ... down the shutes to be screened. The work is monotonous. The boy must sit on his bench all day, bending over constantly to look down on the coal that is passing beneath him. His tender hands must become toughened by long and constant contact with sharp pieces of slate and coal. Many cuts and bruises have left marks and scars on them for a lifetime. He must breathe an atmosphere thick with the dust of coal, so thick that one can barely see across the screen room....

It is no wonder that ... his lungs are liable to suffer from the disease known as "miner's consumption."

In the hot days of summer the screen room is a stifling place. The sun pours its rays upon the broad, sloping roof ... the dust-laden atmosphere is never cleared or freshened by so much as a breath of pure, sweet air.... Yet even this is not so bad as it is to work here in the cold days of winter. It is almost impossible to heat.... The boys on the benches shiver at their tasks, and pick ... slate with numb fingers.

Other children worked in the underground mines, driving the mules that hauled the coal-filled carts out of the mines. During the shorter winter days, they never saw daylight except on Sundays, when the mines were closed.

Mining coal was a dangerous occupation. The miners' safety often depended on makeshift beams such as those shown.

Working children like these did not go to school. They never had the chance to learn about anything except what they were already doing—butchering animals, driving mules, or sorting useless pieces of slate from the broken coal.

Poor working conditions. Industrialism also brought unsafe and unhealthful working conditions to many people. Coal mining was one of the most dangerous jobs created by industrialism. A man writing about his childhood in an Alabama mining town remembered the dangers of mining this way.

> One day there was excitement. "Black damp" had gotten into the mine—men were dead. At the mine entrance, a hushed, awed, resentful crowd gathered, waiting the bringing up of the bodies to the surface. Most of all I wanted to know what "black damp" might be, but I didn't have the courage to ask. Someone else did. "It is a poisonous mine gas," a spokesman replied.

Other conditions also made mining a dangerous occupation. Men could be crushed or trapped alive by the sudden collapse of a mine roof. Fires and explosions took the lives of still others. In the late 1800's, not a year went by without a thousand miners being killed and another fifty thousand being injured, some of them too seriously ever to work again.

Even coal miners who were not in accidents usually did not live as long as other people. Breathing in coal dust day after day, many got "black lung," which was something like lung cancer.

Conditions in early factories. Many factories, too, were unsafe. In some, dangerous machinery was left unprotected. A child working in a string factory explained how she and her sister both lost fingers while working with a dangerous machine.

> You mustn't talk or look off a minute. My sister was just like me. She forgot and talked, and just that minute her finger was off, and she didn't even cry till she picked it up.

One slip could cost an arm, a leg, or a life. In one single year, 25,000 Americans were killed in such industrial accidents.

Although people did not realize it at the time, many jobs were bad for the health of factory workers. People who worked in match factories often became mysteriously ill. After many years, doctors found out why. The chemicals used in matches were causing the jawbones to decay.

When a worker was injured or became ill while working, it was simply considered his bad luck. He received no income to feed his family while he was out. In fact, if his injury kept him out too long, he usually lost his job. The families of those who were killed were left with nothing at all.

Industrialism affects employment. In 1894, thousands of blacksmiths made a liv-

Few factory owners took any steps to protect children from accidents.

ing shoeing horses. The next year the automobile was invented. It was not long before blacksmiths had to look for new ways of making a living. So did the manufacturers of saddles and of horse-drawn carriages.

Actually, new inventions such as the automobile created far more jobs than they took away. Thousands of people found jobs in the new automobile factories. New businesses grew up to make tires, batteries, glass, paint, and many other things needed for cars. The oil industry grew larger. Men got jobs constructing roads, selling gasoline, and repairing cars. So, in the end, industrialism always created more jobs. But for the man who lost his business, like the blacksmith and the carriage maker, the swift changes of industrial society were not very pleasant.

Industrialism created another kind of unemployment, too. Sometimes when companies found they were not selling all their goods, they would decide to make less for a while. As a result, fewer workers were needed. When many companies lowered production at the same time, large numbers of people became unemployed. Without their weekly wage, their families went through hard times.

Another price of industrialism. In time, people found that there was another price they were paying for industrialism. See whether you can find what it was as you read this description of the coal-mining district of Shenandoah, Pennsylvania, fifty years ago.

> The streams are black with soot and there are black piles of refuse . . . and the men returning from work wear masks of coal dust. Trees have been cut down for mine timber so that only stumps and scrubby bush, saplings, or misshaped trees are left. The earth mixed with the slate and coal dust is for the most part bare. . . . Throughout the region are . . . cave-ins where the props in the mines have given way.

Shenandoah was once described as a beautiful place, where the mountains sloped down to meet the green

Coal mining left ugly scars across the countryside.

valleys. Would you say that Shenandoah is still beautiful? What has happened to it?

As industrialism spread, there were hundreds of places like Shenandoah. The city factories that provided jobs and goods poured a thick film of soot over everything. America the Beautiful was becoming America the Ugly.

Early Steps to Control Industrialism

By the end of the nineteenth century, America had become the greatest industrial nation in the world. No one could doubt that industrialism was bringing more goods and a better life to many people. But the price of industrialism was high. The swift changes it brought to America caused pain and hardship for many people. Many Americans realized that something would have to be done.

Workers form labor unions. Workers themselves sought ways of improving their conditions. They knew that one worker alone could not get better wages or shorter hours or safer conditions just by asking his employer. Big companies employed thousands of men. How important was just one man? If he did not like his wage, he was told he was always free to quit. Others were waiting to take his place. The worker knew he would be lucky to find a job that paid any better. He might not find one at all. To many workers, the freedom to quit their jobs did not seem like much of a freedom.

Some decided they would have a better chance to improve their conditions if they banded together. They joined organizations called *labor unions.* In a labor union, a few people are chosen to speak for all the members. They ask the employer for better pay, better hours, and better working conditions for the employees. The employer may agree to some demands, or he may refuse.

A hundred years ago violence was common in labor disputes.

If the members think the employer has not offered them enough, they may decide to stop work all together. This is called a *strike*. Workers do not earn any pay during a strike, of course, but neither does the employer. By striking, the workers hope to make their employers give in more.

Opposition to unions. It was not easy to start a union, for at the beginning most employers were opposed to unions. Some owners would not hire a person until he signed a statement promising he would never join a union. If the worker later joined one, he was fired. Employers often refused even to talk to union leaders. Many times, workers had to go on strike just to make the owner agree that they could have a union. Another thing that led to many strikes was that employers sometimes tried to lower wages.

Sometimes strikes were successful, and the employers gave in to the union. But often the strike failed, and workers went back to work without having gained anything. When that happened, many discouraged workers decided the union was not able to do much for them, and they stopped being members.

You can see why union membership grew very slowly in the late 1800's. Still, by the start of the twentieth century, a large number of workers had joined unions. Unions were becoming a little stronger and were beginning to win better pay and shorter working days for their members.

Laws to protect workers. Americans also turned to their government to deal with the problems of industrialism. Many states passed laws to make working conditions safer. These laws said that owners must protect workers from dangerous machinery. They also dealt with other dangers, such as fires. After 106 women were trapped in a fire in a New York City shirt factory, a number of states said that factory owners had to put in fire escapes and other protections.

Some states required employers to set aside money to pay workers who were injured on the job. These workers would receive a part of their regular pay until they could return to work.

Not everyone agreed that such laws should be passed. Some said the government had no right to interfere in business. But others said it was up to the government to protect people from the problems caused by industrialism.

People even disagreed about whether states should prohibit child labor. Those who wanted to end child labor said that long hours of work damaged the health of young children and prevented them from going to school.

Other people believed the government had no right to tell employers whom they could hire. They said that work helped children form good habits and learn useful jobs. Besides, said some, the families of these children needed the wages they earned.

Enforcing the laws. In the end, most states passed laws saying that children under fourteen could not work in factories or mines, but they were still allowed to do many other kinds of work.

Unfortunately, many of these laws were often disobeyed. Many states appointed too few inspectors to check up on the thousands of factories. Therefore many owners paid no attention to the law, because they knew they would not be caught. Even if they were caught, they knew the punishment was very small.

Even though some of these early laws were poorly enforced, they were still very important. The laws showed that the American people were ready to use their government to help those who were hurt by the changes industrialism brought.

The American Worker in Modern Times

Working conditions for most Americans are far different in modern times than they were seventy years ago. Factory workers then could hardly make ends meet. Today millions of these workers own their own homes and cars and can afford many of the modern conveniences. The living standard of the American worker is the highest in the world.

Labor unions today. Labor unions have played an important part in improving the workingman's wages. Even though more than half of America's workers do not belong to unions, millions of others do. In such industries as steel, rubber, auto manufacturing, and trucking, nearly all the workers belong to a union. Skilled workers such as plumbers, electricians, and carpenters also have strong unions. Even some schoolteachers now belong to unions. Efforts are also being made to unionize farm workers.

Unions have done more than help members get better wages and shorter

Today unions vote on whether or not to strike. Union leaders are bound by the results.

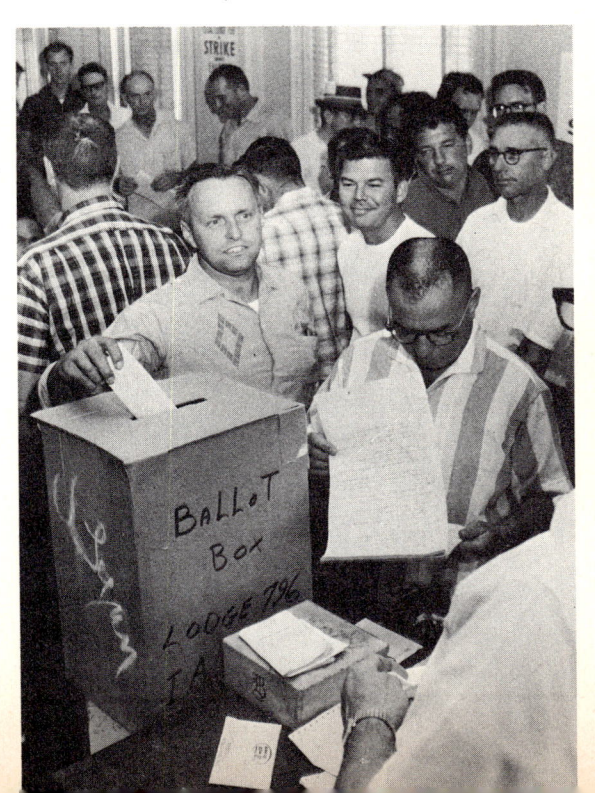

hours. Unions have bargained successfully for inexpensive medical care, vacations with pay, and pensions. A pension is a regular payment a worker receives after he retires.

Some people feel that labor unions may be too strong. They claim that some unions ask for too much and have too many strikes. These people believe certain employees, such as firemen, teachers, bus drivers, and hospital workers, should not be allowed to strike. When these workers strike, they cause hardship for the whole public, not just for their employer. Some people also say that certain unions do not let many members of minority groups into their membership.

Supporters of unions argue that there are still many workers who are paid poorly. America, they say, needs more strong unions to help them. As for striking, unions say that if the right to strike is taken away, they will no longer be able to win improvements in pay and working conditions. Many union people admit that a few unions have discriminated against minority groups. But they point out that others, like the steel workers and auto workers unions, have a large percentage of black members. Unions, they say, help both black workers and white workers.

Increased production helps workers. The work of unions is not the only reason that Americans have a high standard

These grape pickers refuse to work until their demands are met.

of living. The most important reason is that American industry is so productive. We can produce more goods today with fewer workers. This has created the wealth that allows companies to pay better wages.

Also, many companies that do not even have unions treat their employees well today. They know workers must earn a decent wage if they are to be able to buy the goods our factories make. Many companies provide safe working conditions, because they know injured workers cannot produce goods. Companies pay for medical care, vacations, and pensions because they know satisfied workers will produce more in the long run.

This does not mean all American workers are well off. Far too many still receive low wages, even though they work very hard. And some cannot find jobs at all. We shall be reading more about this later on.

Passing stronger laws. In modern times our government has also helped our people to live better lives in an industrial society. Child labor laws are strictly enforced. Today, it is far less dangerous to work in our factories than to ride on our highways. Even though coal mining still is not good for the health of miners, conditions are much better than they used to be. We have also improved the laws that provide payments for workers who are injured on the job.

In addition, we have many more laws to help workers in our modern industrial society. There is a *minimum wage law* for most workers. This law says that workers must be paid a certain amount of money for an hour of work. The minimum wage now is $1.60 an hour.

Under another law, the worker and his employer each contribute a small amount to a fund. Then when the worker retires, he receives a payment, similar to a pension, from this fund every month as long as he lives. This program is called *social security.* Another law allows unemployed workers to receive a small amount of money while they look for new jobs. These are some of the ways we have used our government to help millions of people living in our industrial society.

Those still unprotected. Not all Americans, however, have been helped. There are still many who are not protected by these laws. One such group is the migrant farm workers. These are people, usually entire families, who make a living harvesting fruits and vegetables on other people's farms. They move, or migrate, from one farm to another, and from one part of the country to another, wherever there is a crop to be harvested. Usually they earn very little pay, and the shacks that farm owners provide for them often have no toilets, running water, or lights.

Migrant workers move from field to field across much of the country.

The children of migrant workers do not have much opportunity for schooling and often grow up unable to read or write, Fortunately, Americans are becoming concerned about this problem. They have asked Congress to pass laws to help the migrant worker.

More Effects of Industrialism Today

In the first part of this chapter, we have seen some of the ways industrialism has affected jobs and workers. What are some other ways in which industrialism affects our way of living?

More goods per worker. You know that one of the features of an industrial society is a great increase in production. Before industrialism, one farmer raised just enough food to support his own family, with little left over to sell. Today, each American farmer produces enough food to feed more than twenty people. Today's miner produces six times as much as his grandfather did in 1900. An American factory worker produces more in one hour than his grandfather did in one day. So Americans produce more goods than ever before, and it takes fewer people to do so.

This frees people to do other kinds of work. More people can be repairmen, doctors, teachers, musicians, clerks, and architects. These people do not make goods, as a factory worker or farmer does, but they all do important work. Instead of producing goods, they produce or provide services. Their services make life more enjoyable, more convenient, and healthier. Actually, more people make a living by providing services than by producing goods.

Industrialism increases specialization. Industrialism has made it possible for people to specialize more than ever before, whether they are producing goods or providing services. In the early days of America, when most people were still farmers, there were probably no more than two hundred different kinds of jobs that people could specialize in. In 1937 a book called *A Dictionary of Occupational Titles* appeared. It listed the names of 17,500 different jobs in our industrial society. Thirty years later another edition of the book listed 22,000 separate jobs. People have more choice than ever before about the kind of of work they will do.

More leisure time. Industrialism has also affected the way we spend our time. American workers do not have to work nearly as many hours a week as their grandfathers did. In 1900 an American laborer worked an average of fifty-eight hours each week. His son only had to work forty-eight hours a week in 1930. But his grandson works only about thirty-seven hours a week today.

Because we work fewer hours each week, we have more spare time, or leisure time. How do we spend it? Here, too, industrialism has given us many choices. How are we able to have a more interesting and varied life than workers of a hundred years ago had?

You can find still another way industrialism affects our way of life by studying the charts on the value of goods produced and who produces them.

Industrialism reduces some differences. Industrialism in America has also

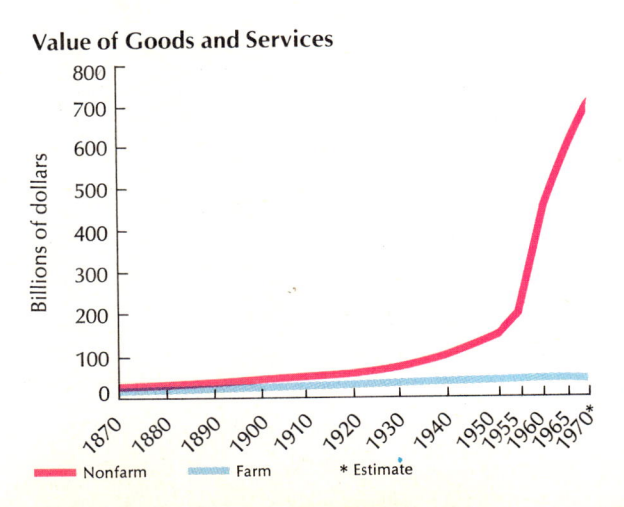

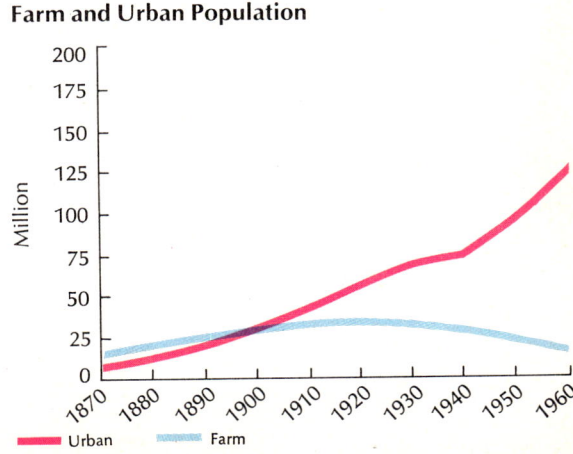

Value of Goods and Services

Farm and Urban Population

helped to erase many differences between urban and rural ways of living. Do you remember what some of those differences were? Today, most farm homes have all the modern electric and gas appliances that city homes have. Farm families see the same news reports, variety shows, and movies on television that city people see. Automobiles and good roads make it easy to get to town, where wives can buy the same kinds of clothes that city people wear. There are still differences between farm and city living of course, but Hamlin Garland would hardly recognize farm life today.

Here is still another way industrialism has affected our society. Look at the picture showing people on a street in a large city. Try to pick out the people in this picture who have very well-paid jobs and those whose pay is only fair. Which ones would you say are secretaries, and which ones shoppers from a wealthy suburb? Which men are bankers? Which ones are clerks in stores? Is this a picture of an eastern city, or a western one, or a southern one? Is it a very big city, or a smaller community? Can you answer any of these questions? What has the production of large amounts of goods by machine to do with this?

Problems Still Remain

Not all the effects of modern industrialism have been good. The two pictures about mining show one of the unhappy results. How are these two pictures connected? What has happened to the coal miner?

After work, people with many types of jobs start home.

Coal mining with a pick and shovel required great strength but little skill.

This rotating machine digs and loads eight tons of coal a minute.

Unemployment. In the early days of industrialism, men like this one found jobs digging iron ore and coal, laying railroad tracks, or doing other unskilled work. The work was hard and it paid very little, but with a strong back, a pickax, and a shovel, a man could get work without any special skills.

Today, however, machines like the giant coal digger in the picture are replacing unskilled laborers. Some of the workers leave these mining towns in search of other jobs. Others remain, hoping for at least a few days of work. They know that even if they move elsewhere, jobs will be hard to find, for they have no special skills to offer.

Even people who have skills often find their jobs disappearing—just as the carriage makers did when the automobile was invented. Many of the unemployed are young people who have never been able to get a job at all. Many have dropped out of school, and now they do not have the education they need for today's jobs.

Need for new skills. To get work, these people must learn new skills. Some of them go to special schools where they learn to work with modern machines, repair autos or television sets, bake, or do many other jobs that are needed. The United States government has several programs for helping the un-

New machines have made it necessary even for men with experience to undergo retraining.

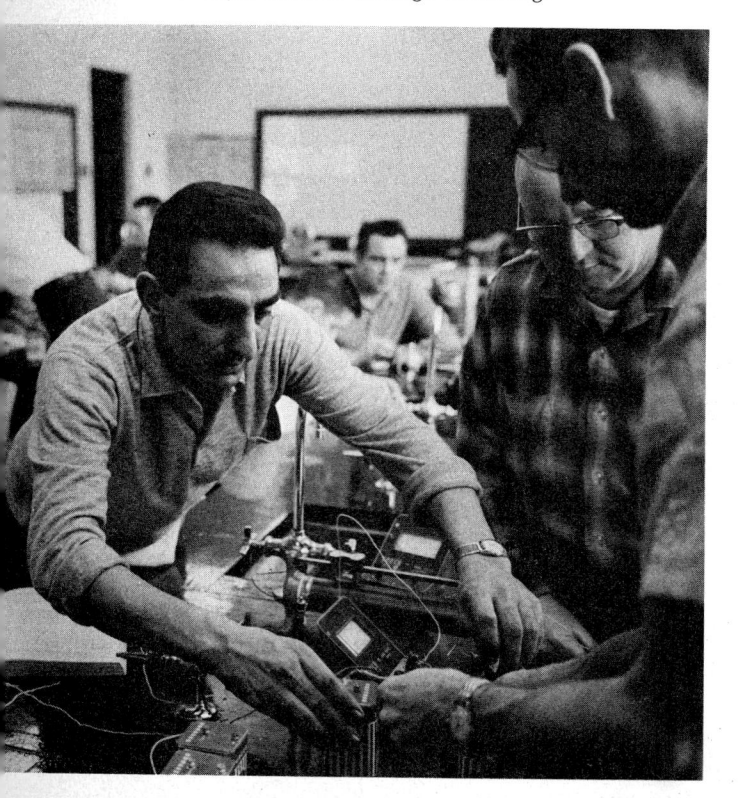

employed learn skills. In one of them the government even pays a small salary to people while they learn useful jobs in special training centers.

The government also pays some businesses to hire people and teach them new skills while they are working. This is called on-the-job training. In 1968 President Lyndon Johnson asked several leaders of American industry to help with this program. These men organized a group called the National Alliance of Businessmen. The group got businessmen in many cities to hire those people who had the biggest problem finding jobs. They were taught skills in on-the-job training. If they learned the skills well, the company promised to keep them on as regular workers.

In the first two years, the National Alliance of Businessmen found jobs for nearly 200,000 unemployed. This was a very good record, but of course the problem is a very big one, and our businesses and government and labor unions must all do much more to help solve it.

Pollution Grows Worse

Early in this chapter we saw how industrialism made many places in America ugly and unhealthful. Today pollution is worse than ever. It even threatens human life.

Pollution from fuels. Industrialism is connected with pollution in several

For hours without end, factories pour smoke into the air.

ways. First, our industrial society creates pollution by the fuels that it uses. We burn millions of tons of coal and billions of gallons of oil and gasoline every year to run our factories, heat our buildings, make our steel, and power our railroad trains, planes, trucks, and cars. Most of the electricity we use is produced by burning coal and oil. These fuels contain a chemical called sulfur. When sulfur is burned, it produces a gas that is poisonous to plant and animal life. Every day we add thousands of tons of this poison to the air.

The worst polluter of air is one of the most important products of our industrial society—the gasoline engine. The smog in most American cities is created mainly by the exhaust of our automobile and truck engines. The car has brought pollution even into such wilderness areas as Yellowstone National Park, which occupies part of Wyoming, Montana, and Idaho. On many summer days the exhaust from tourists' cars creates a blue haze that hangs over large areas of the park.

Products of industry create pollution. Many of the products that are made in our industrial society also cause pollution. Detergents are one such product. Detergents were invented about twenty-

365

Rivers and streams take many colors because of chemicals spilled into them.

five years ago. Because detergents clean better than ordinary soaps, people began to use them to wash their clothes, their dishes, their floors, and their cars.

Soon a strange thing began to happen. From various parts of the country came reports that mounds of foam were appearing in rivers. On the Rock River in Illinois, the foam reached a height of 40 feet. People in Wisconsin reported a wall of foam in the Mississippi River that was 35 feet wide, 15 feet high, and 300 feet long!

In another case, several men were fishing off a long dock, or pier, near Dubuque (də byük′), Iowa. When they turned around, they found their path back to land was blocked by a huge wall of foam that had crept down the river and rolled onto the dock behind them. People in several areas complained that foam instead of water was coming out of their faucets.

The problem was detergents. When waste water found its way back into rivers and streams, it carried the detergent with it. The rushing water of the river caused the detergents to suds up again.

A few years ago, detergent manufacturers changed the chemicals in the detergent and solved the foam problem. But another problem still remains, and this one is more serious than foam. Detergents contain chemicals called phosphates (fos′ fāts). Phosphates are very good for getting dirt out of clothes. They are also good for fertilizing plants. When phosphates are carried back into rivers and lakes with the waste water, they cause a form of plant life in the water, called algae (al′ jē), to grow much faster. Raw sewage, which also contains phosphates, does the same thing. Eventually these tiny plants die. As they decay, they use up oxygen. This leaves less oxygen for the fish, which need it to survive. Soon the fish die. How strange it is that a product used to *clean* our homes is polluting our waters!

Harmful sprays. Other industrial products that pollute our waters are insect killers, especially one called DDT. DDT is stored up in the bodies of the insects that eat it. When animals and birds eat these insects, the harmful DDT enters their bodies. DDT also works its way into the soil and eventually finds its way into our waters, killing many fish.

DDT has been found also in cattle, fish, and many other things that humans eat, which means that it is entering our bodies, too. So far it is not dangerous to humans. But it will become so if we take in DDT for a long time.

Disposing of wastes. Most products of industrial society are not harmful like DDT, but they add to our pollution problem anyway when the time comes to get rid of them. Every year we throw away millions of used-up television sets, washing machines, tires, stoves, and cars, as well as bottles and cans. The problem of finding a place to dispose of these wastes becomes more serious all the time. Too often, thoughtless people discard these items in the nearest empty lot or stream, adding to the growing ugliness of our surroundings.

Factories add to pollution. Factories create pollution while they produce the very products we all enjoy. Ride through an industrial area and you will

Even our most modern factories pollute both the air and the waterways.

see a sky of many colors. Black smoke, brown smoke, and tan smoke stream upward from power plants that make our electricity. Factories producing chemicals for wonderful new products pour brilliant orange, yellow, and purple smoke into the air. Cement factories making materials for roads and buildings add their white smoke to the combination, and from the oil refineries that make gasoline for our cars come large smudges of black smoke. All together, they make a colorful sky—and sickening air for breathing.

Our factories also add to water pollution. Great amounts of water are used in manufacturing certain goods. For example, it takes 150 tons of water to manufacture just one ton of paper. When this water is returned to the river or lake, it carries in it the waste from the raw materials, mainly the bark of logs. It also contains many chemicals—chemicals that are fine for making paper, but bad for fish, plant life, and humans.

Papermaking is only one of the many industries that pollute the waters in this way. Recently, scientists discovered that small amounts of a substance called mercury were escaping into the water from a number of factories. This is the same silvery substance that you find in thermometers. Mercury can be deadly to human beings who drink these waters, or who eat the fish taken from them.

Even factories that can our foods often add to pollution. Dirt and insect killers are washed off fruits and vegetables before they are canned. What happens to the water used to wash them?

A Great Lake is dying. One of the worst examples of what is happening to our lakes and rivers is Lake Erie. Lake Erie is one of the five Great Lakes. On its shores are more than a dozen large United States cities and three Canadian ones.

Lake Erie was once a beautiful lake. Gentle breezes blew over the sweet water and cooled the surrounding land. People enjoyed its lovely beaches and swam in its clear waters. A big fishing industry provided jobs for many people.

Over the years this beautiful lake has been turned into a dumping ground. Raw sewage from the cities, industrial chemicals and wastes, de-

This picture shows you why Lake Erie is dying. Polluted water and debris from factories near the Cuyahoga River float downstream into the lake.

tergents, and many other things that cause pollution have been poured into it.

Today the breezes still blow over the lake, but they carry an awful odor. A film of algae covers much of the lake, and a glass of water taken from its center looks like thin green paint. The beaches are often covered with sewage and, at times, dead fish. The few swimmers are coated with algae when they come out of the water. The fishing industry has been destroyed. In 1956, fishermen caught nearly *seven million* pounds of blue pike. Seven years later they caught only *two hundred* pounds! Lake Erie is dying.

Lake Erie is not alone. There is hardly a stream or river in all America that is completely free from pollution. Some are much worse than others. A few years ago, someone demonstrated how polluted the Willamette River in Oregon was. He put several healthy trout in a cage and lowered them into the river. The fish died almost immediately.

In the early 1960's there was a drought in the eastern part of the United States. New York City's residents were urged to save water by fixing dripping faucets, taking showers instead of baths, and not washing their cars. All this time, the Hudson River, with billions of gallons of water, flowed right past the city's door, but it was so polluted that the city did not dare to use it.

Action Against Pollution

Scientists and other concerned people have warned about pollution for years, but until recently few people paid attention. Now the whole country is finally listening. We realize that our choice is very simple. Either we clean up our earth, or it will be unfit for human life.

Cities pass laws. Many cities have passed laws to cut down on air pollution. Los Angeles has the strictest laws. All cars there must have a special attachment that reduces pollution from exhaust. Buildings may not burn fuels that have a high sulfur content. Homeowners are forbidden to burn trash, and factories must equip their chimneys with a device to trap soot and chemicals before they escape into the air.

Even with all these efforts, Los Angeles still has a serious smog problem. Other cities are not much better off than Los Angeles. They, too, are passing stronger air pollution laws. But often the cities do not enforce these laws very well, so pollution pours out of chimneys in spite of the laws. In fact, sometimes the city government itself is one of the chief lawbreakers, as its garbage-incinerating plants add their choking smoke to the city's air.

Cleaner fuels. We are also trying to do something about our worst polluter, the gasoline engine. Auto manufacturers have been looking for ways of cutting down the pollution. Also, Congress has passed a law ordering manufacturers to get rid of nearly all the pollution by 1975. To do this, the manufacturers will have to hire more scientists and spend more money on research.

Some people believe the gasoline engine can never be completely free of pollution. They feel it will be necessary to replace the gasoline engine with an electric one. Some inventors and manufacturers are now experimenting with electric motors powered by extra-large batteries. However, much work will have to be done before electric cars are ready for use.

In the meantime, oil companies are cooperating by developing gasolines that do not pollute so much. Some companies have stopped adding lead to their gasoline, since lead is one of the main polluting chemicals.

Saving the water. The United States government and our cities are now attacking water pollution, too. Cities and towns are building sewage treatment plants, and the federal government is helping pay for them. These plants treat raw sewage with chemicals and remove much of the waste materials from the water before returning the water to the river or lake. Some states also have laws that prohibit factories from dumping their wastes into our

Major automobile companies are taking important steps to control pollution.

waters. These laws are usually not well enforced, so they have not done much good so far. If the people insist, however, the laws will be enforced.

Even with all these efforts, we are not yet winning the battle against pollution. Much, much more must be done. This will be very expensive for our businesses and for all of us, the taxpayers. But there is no choice. Experts tell us there is not much time left. Some say that at the rate we are polluting our environment, the world will be unfit to live in by the year 2020. Others say 2000. In your lifetime, the problem must be solved, or there may not be anyone left to worry about it.

Working with Concepts and Generalizations

Identifying Concepts

In Set A is a list of titles. In Set B is a list of statements. Each statement belongs with one of the titles. Copy each title on paper. Under each title, write the statements that belong there.

Set A

1. Working at Home
2. Working in a Factory
3. Working in Coal Mines
4. Labor Unions
5. Pollution

Set B

a. Much of the smog in cities is created by exhaust from gasoline engines.
b. The worker began work at the same time each day.
c. Children had jobs as breaker boys.
d. Membership grew very slowly until the late 1880's.
e. The worker took pride in the product he made.
f. Small amounts of mercury are escaping into water.
g. Workers banded together to try to improve working conditions.
h. The worker could learn to run a machine in only a few days.
i. Workers suffered from "black lung."
j. The worker decided how long he would work each day.
k. These organizations helped workers get better pay and shorter hours.
l. Waste water on its way back to rivers carries detergents with it.
m. The worker owned the equipment he used.
n. Men could be crushed alive or trapped by the sudden collapse of a roof.
o. The worker did only one part of a job.

Developing Concepts

Write the answers on paper.

1. List the ways your life would be different if children your age were still permitted to work in factories, mines, and slaughter houses.
2. Explain this statement taken from the text: "After industrialism, there was an important change in the way the worker felt about his product and in the way people felt about the worker."
3. How did industrialism help erase the difference between urban and rural ways of living?
4. You have learned that industrialism made it possible for people to specialize. Name at least fifteen different jobs available in your town. Next to each, write whether the job provides a service or produces a product.
5. List the evidences of pollution in your town.

Generalizations

Important words are missing from the statements below. By completing each statement, you will be stating a generalization. When your generalizations are complete, find proof to support each one. Tell what the proof is and the page on which you found it.

1. Because of machines and specialization of _____, factories produce _____ more cheaply than the skilled _____ could.
2. One feature of an industrial society is a great increase in _____.
3. Industrialism makes it possible for more people to _____ in jobs, whether they are producing goods or providing _____.

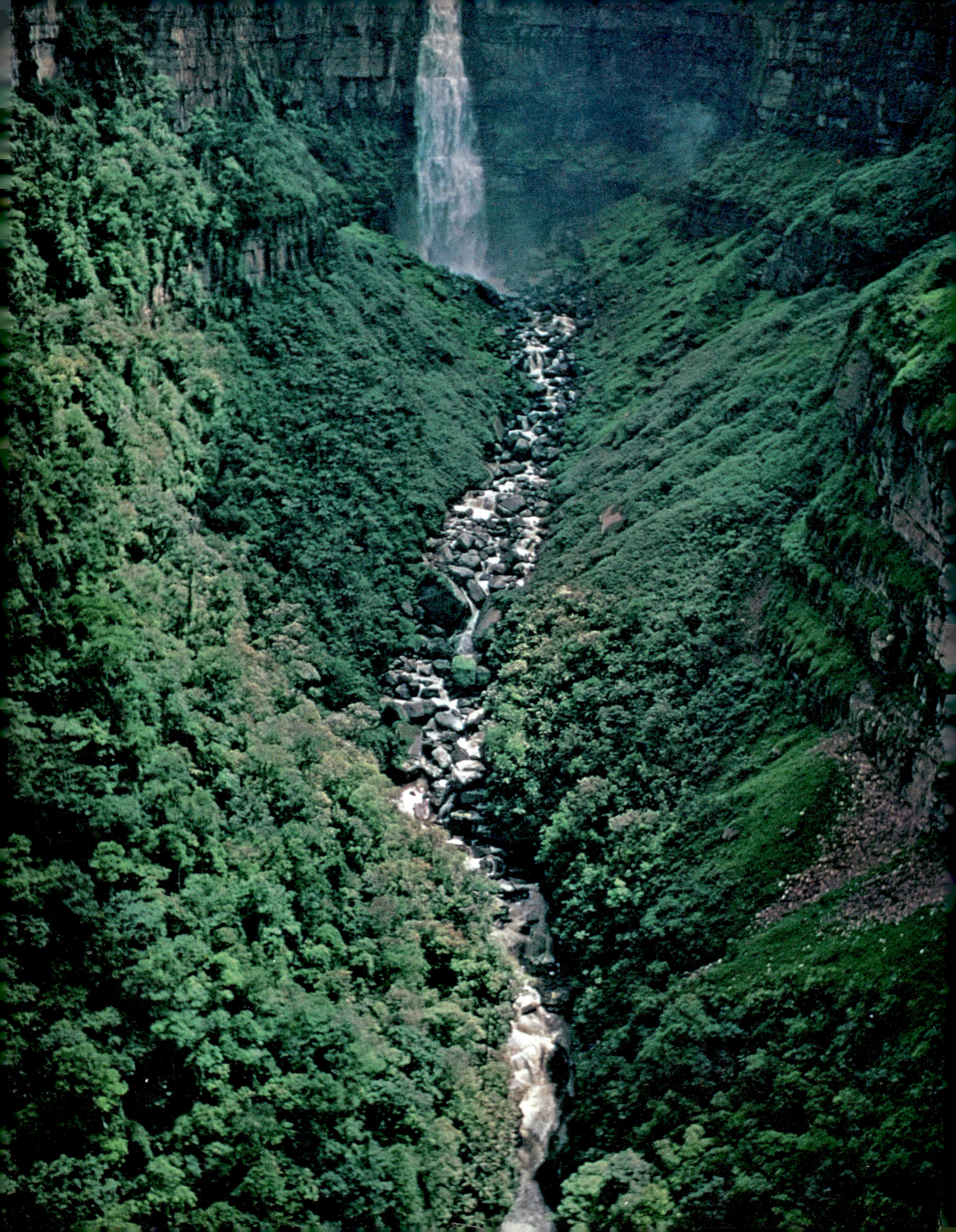

Western Hemisphere Neighbors Industrialize

18

Living in a nation that has so much industry, we might think all people live as we do. In fact, most of the world does not. In many lands, there are few factories. Many have only simple machines run by man's own muscles or by his oldest helpers—animals, wind, and water. Most manufacturing is still done by hand, and therefore not many goods are produced. Farm production is also small. The people in these lands have a low standard of living.

Many of these countries are now trying to develop more industry. They believe that is the path to a better life for their people. Some are just beginning; others have already made much progress. Most of these nations are in Africa and Asia, and in Middle and South America.

What problems do these countries face? Are they succeeding in their efforts to become industrial nations? In this chapter we shall examine one such country, Colombia. We shall also see how our neighbor to the north, Canada, has already succeeded in becoming industrialized.

The Land of Colombia

Colombia is located in the northwestern part of South America. It occupies an area about the size of Texas and California combined. The map shows the major land features of Colombia. Which two bodies of water lie off its coasts? Look at the eastern part of the country. This is flat lowland that reaches south to the Amazon rain forest. What do you know about the climate of the rain forest? Few Colombians live in the rain forest, because it is hard to make a living there.

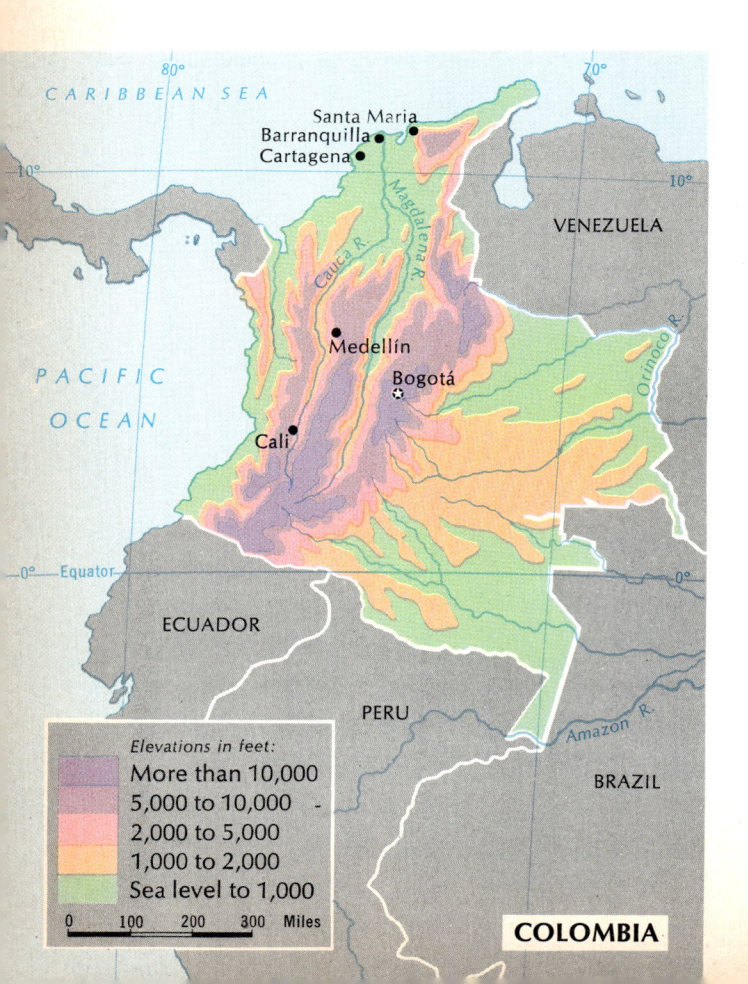

The rest of the eastern part of Colombia is the llanos, or plains. How close are the llanos to the equator? Are they at a high, or a low, altitude? What does that tell you about the temperature? During the dry season, everything on the llanos turns brown. The rainy season brings the green again, but it also brings floods and insects that make life miserable. The people who live on the llanos raise cattle.

How would you describe the western part of Colombia? In Colombia the Andes split into three ranges, the eastern, the central, and the western. Long, narrow valleys lie between these ranges, in the shadows of peaks rising three miles in the sky. The valleys are never more than fifty miles wide. Most of the country's population is clustered in these valleys and along the lower slopes of the mountains. The lower parts of the valleys are quite hot, but the higher altitudes are more comfortable.

Colombia has several rivers and many rushing mountain streams. The rivers that run down the eastern slopes of the mountains are often wide, but they are shallow enough to wade across. During the dry season they are only trickles.

The two main rivers of the country flow through the long valleys between the mountains. The most important river is the Magdalena. It flows through one valley and empties into the Caribbean Sea at the port city of Barranquilla (bar ən kē′ yə). The Cauca River flows northward through the other valley and joins the Magdalena.

The people of Colombia. About twenty million people live in Colombia. Half of them now live in the cities or in the slums that have sprung up around the cities. The slum dwellers have recently left the poverty of the countryside, hoping to make a living in the city. Some find jobs, but many are bitterly disappointed.

Of the half that still live in the rural areas, the largest group are poor peasants, called *campesinos* (käm pä sē′nōz). On his tiny plot of two or three acres, the campesino grows barely enough for his family. The family lives in a hut with dirt floors. There is no running water. Women carry water from the nearest stream, which is often a mile away.

The campesinos are almost always illiterate; that is, they cannot read or write. There are few schools to educate their children. They eat poorly, have little sanitation, and get little medical care. As a result, sickness and death are quite common. Of every five children born to these peasant families, two do not live through childhood.

Farming country. Colombia is chiefly a farming country. Because sections of Colombia are at different altitudes and have different temperatures, farmers

Farm Products at Different Altitudes

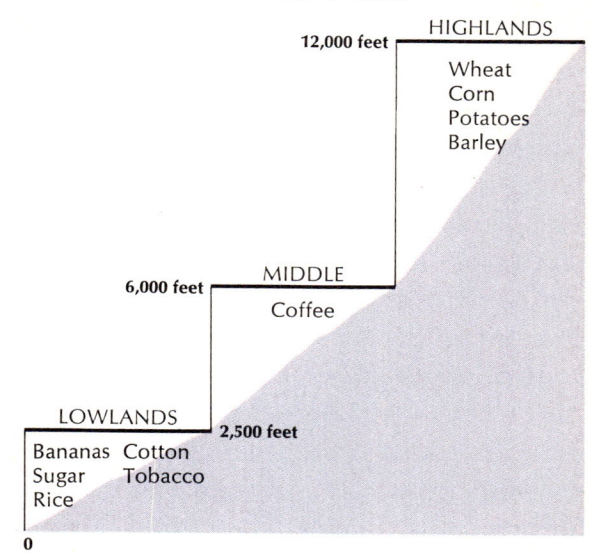

12,000 feet — HIGHLANDS
Wheat
Corn
Potatoes
Barley

6,000 feet — MIDDLE
Coffee

LOWLANDS
2,500 feet
Bananas Cotton
Sugar   Tobacco
Rice
0

grow a variety of crops. In the hot lowlands, bananas, cotton, tobacco, sugar, and rice are raised. In the high valleys and on the lower slopes of the mountains, the finest coffee in the world is grown. This coffee is Colombia's most important export.

At the higher, cooler elevations, wheat, corn, and potatoes are grown. Farmers also grow barley, from which they make beer, the favorite beverage of the people. Except for the coffee and the bananas, which are exported, nearly all this food is used by Colombians. In fact, Colombia has to import wheat from other nations.

On the larger farms in the valleys, more and more owners use modern farming methods. Machines and fertilizers are used in the growing and harvesting of wheat. Until ten years ago Colombia raised little cotton, and its textile factories had to import most of their raw cotton. Then farmers began to irrigate and fertilize the land in the Magdalena valley. They planted cotton and harvested it with modern machinery. Today these cotton growers raise enough for all the nation's textile factories. Moreover, they have a surplus left over to export to other South American countries.

But on most of Colombia's farms, the work is still done by hand. No one has invented machines to help the farmer grow and gather Colombia's biggest crop, coffee. The coffee farmer cultivates his bushes by hand, prunes them by hand, and picks the ripe berries by hand.

The millions of campesinos farm their tiny plots of land as their ancestors did. They know nothing of modern methods and use little more than a hoe to till the land. As a result, they produce small crops.

Another reason why Colombia's food production is not large is that much of the richest soil in the valleys is used for grazing cattle instead of for growing crops. In fact, ten times as much land is used for cattle as for crops. The cattle could graze just as easily on the poorer soil on the mountain slopes. That, however, is where the campesinos try to make a living by farming.

Steps Toward Industrialization

Natural resources. Look at the map that shows the location of some of the natural resources of Colombia. Does Colombia have any deposits of iron ore? Why are such deposits important for a nation that wishes to industrialize? Are there any coal deposits? Does Colombia have the other resources needed for making steel?

Oil is another very important resource in the modern world. How many locations do you see where there is oil in Colombia? Colombia now produces enough oil for her own needs, and exports some besides. Does Colombia have any other minerals? What are they?

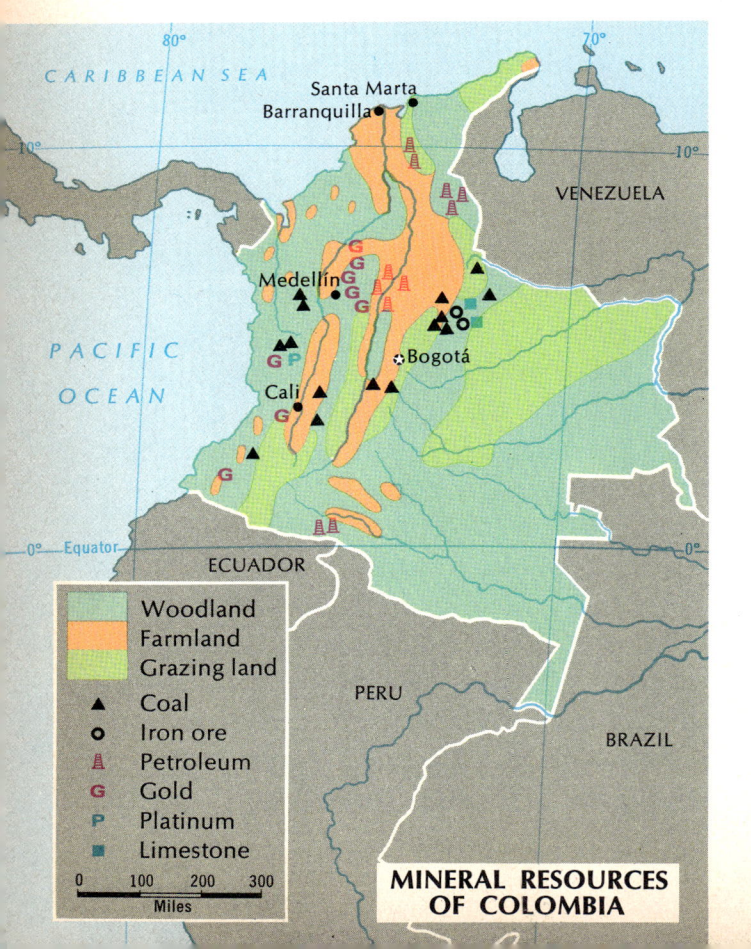

MINERAL RESOURCES OF COLOMBIA

Colombia has another important resource that does not appear on this map. That is the rushing water from her rivers and streams. Why might these be as important as coal and oil for an industrial nation?

Would you say that Colombia has many of the resources needed to become an industrial nation?

A factory comes to Colombia. In 1901 Pedro Nel Ospina (pā′ drō nəl os-pēn′ yə), the son of a coffee grower of Medellín, Colombia, took a trip to Mexico. While there, he studied that country's textile factories. Why could not the same kind of factory be built in Colombia, Pedro wondered?

When he returned to his home city of Medellín, he discussed the idea with other coffee growers. They agreed to take some of the money they had made in coffee growing and invest it in building a textile factory.

Machines were bought from England, but getting them to Medellín proved difficult. The machines were shipped up the Magdalena River and then loaded on mules for the journey across the mountain. The looms had to be taken apart to squeeze through the narrow mountain passes. After several weeks, the machines arrived in Medellín. The owners built their new factory next to a waterfall, which provided power to run the machines. In 1906 Colombia's first textile factory opened. How many years had passed since Slater started his factory in Rhode Island?

This salt mine near Bogotá is important to the food-processing industry in that city.

Cotton is grown in many South American countries. In some places, harvesting is still done by hand. The cotton is then made into cloth in textile factories such as this one in Medellín, Colombia.

Manufacturing increases. Until about thirty years ago, textile companies had the only factories in Colombia. Since then, a number of new industries have been started in such fast-growing cities as Bogotá, Cali, Medellín, and Barranquilla. Modern factories make flour, refine sugar, and brew beer. There are factories that make medical supplies, cigarettes, and tires. Colombia also has several oil refineries, chemical plants, and automobile factories.

In 1954 a steel mill was opened in a mountainous area about 120 miles from Bogotá. Using coal, iron, and

Natural Resources Production 1968

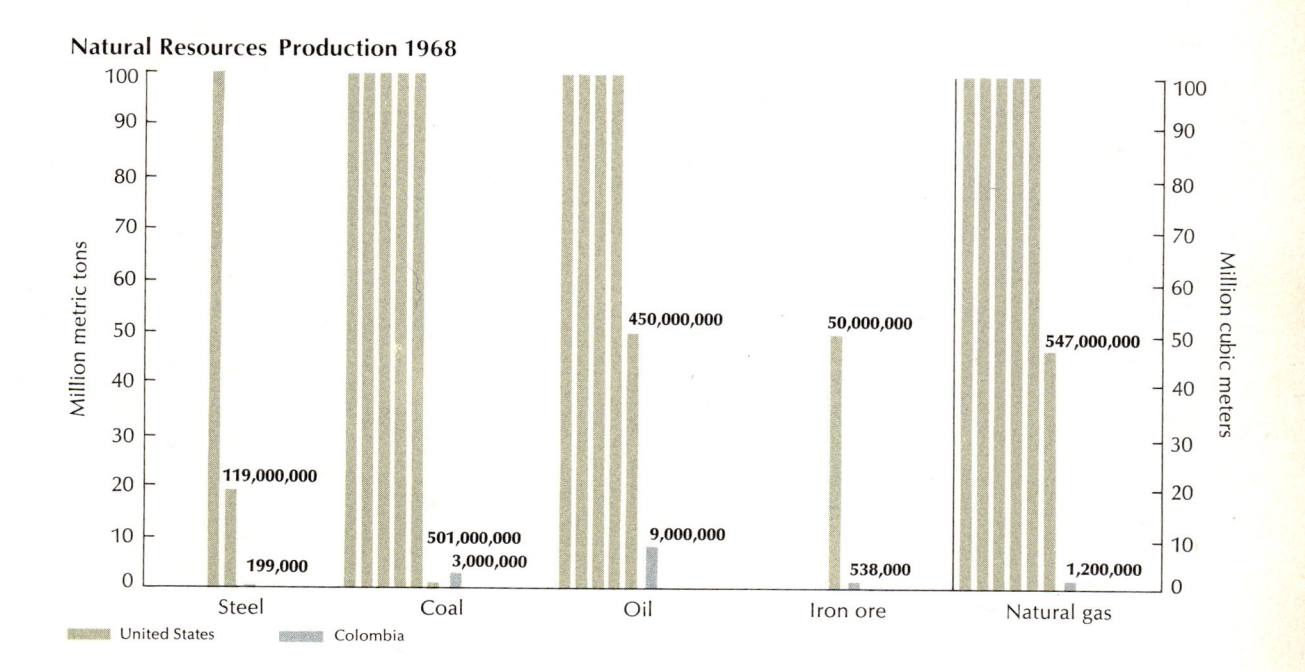

	Steel	Coal	Oil	Iron ore	Natural gas
United States	119,000,000	501,000,000	450,000,000	50,000,000	547,000,000
Colombia	199,000	3,000,000	9,000,000	538,000	1,200,000

(Steel, Coal, Iron ore: Million metric tons; Oil, Natural gas: Million cubic meters)

limestone from Colombia's own mines, the steel mill now makes a quarter of a million tons of steel a year.

Each year, Colombia increases its production of electric power. The most important electric power plant is on the Cauca River. Dams were built on the river in the 1950's to control flooding and to provide irrigation, as well as to produce electricity. As a result, the production of sugar, soybeans, and cotton on the farms in the Cauca valley was greatly increased. The dams also provided the industrial city of Cali with abundant, cheap electricity.

A long way to go. The new factories are a big step toward industrialization, but they do not produce nearly as much as Colombia needs. For instance, the steel mill makes only half the steel the nation uses. In 1967 the automobile factories made 1,300 cars and trucks, but Colombians needed 250,000. Colombia must import the steel and cars that she cannot make.

While some factories cannot make enough for Colombia's needs, others do not produce as much as they are able to. The reason is simple: they would not be able to sell the goods. The thousands of slum dwellers in their cardboard and tin huts cannot afford the goods. Neither can the poor campesinos. In other words, the market for manufactured goods in Colombia is small. Even with the new factories, most manufactured goods are still made by hand in small shops employing three or four people.

Colombian and United States Imports and Exports*

Colombian Imports from
$598,100,000

- Europe 32%
- United States 59%
- L.A. 4%
- Canada 2%
- Japan 3%

Colombian Exports to
$441,900,000

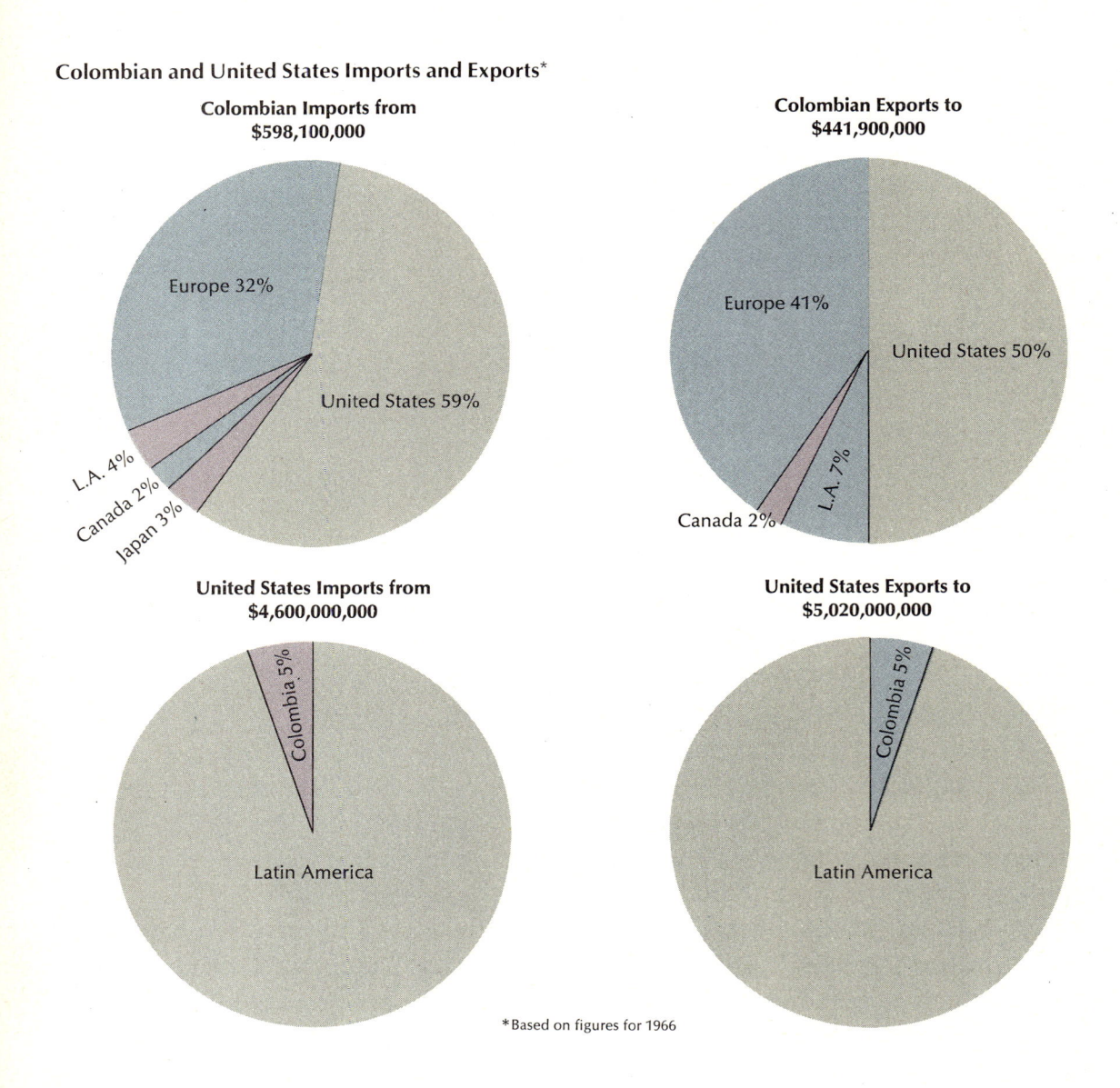

- Europe 41%
- United States 50%
- Canada 2%
- L.A. 7%

United States Imports from
$4,600,000,000

- Colombia 5%
- Latin America

United States Exports to
$5,020,000,000

- Colombia 5%
- Latin America

*Based on figures for 1966

Some Problems to Overcome

Colombia has made an encouraging start toward becoming an industrial nation, but it still has a long way to go. Let us see some of the problems Colombia must solve in order to become more industrialized. Let us also see what Colombia is doing about these problems. Keep in mind what you have already learned about our own nation's efforts to industrialize.

Moving goods to market. Pablo Emilio Ramirez (pab′ lō ə mē′ lēō ram ir′ əz) lives on a farm about 120 miles from Bogotá. When his crops are ready, Pablo sets out to sell them in the capital city. First he carries his produce through two miles of ankle-deep mud over a path cut in the jungle. He then loads the crops onto a small motorboat, and motors up the river to a landing two and a half hours away. The produce is then put in a jeep for a two hour ride over very rough roads. Then the crop is transferred to a truck for the nine-hour drive over the twisting mountain roads to Bogotá. Altogether, it takes sixteen hours to move Pablo Ramirez' goods from his small farm to the market only 120 miles away. Of course, it takes the same amount of time to bring goods from Bogotá to Pablo's farm.

The need for good transportation. The story of Pablo Ramirez tells you about one of Colombia's biggest problems, transportation. In this land of jungles, flooded llanos, and rugged mountain peaks, it is very hard to move goods from one place to another. It is most difficult to move them from one side of the mountain to another, for there are few good natural passes.

Colombia's rivers are important to farmers like Pablo Ramirez, who move small loads for short distances. But the Magdalena River is the only river that is deep enough for larger ships. Even the Magdalena is too shallow for modern oceangoing vessels. At the seaport of Barranquilla, cargo has to be transferred from these larger ships to smaller flat-bottom barges. These are pushed upstream by river tugboats. In very dry seasons, the river becomes too shallow for even these barges.

About six hundred miles upstream, there are rapids. Here the goods must be loaded onto railroad cars for the rest of the trip to Bogotá. The whole trip, covering about seven hundred miles, takes five or six days. Until recent years, the Magdalena provided the only way of shipping goods between the seaports and the cities of the interior.

In all of Colombia, there are only 2,500 miles of railway track. That is a very small amount for a country the size of Colombia. Often the railroads do not even connect important cities with each other. The map on page 382 shows the four main manufacturing cities of Bogotá, Medellín, Cali, and Barranquilla. See which are connected by rail, and which are not.

Efforts to improve transportation. Colombia has been trying to improve its transportation. It has built a new railroad line, connecting the seaport of Santa Marta to Bogotá. Several highways have been built for trucking goods between different areas of the country. One highway now connects Bogotá and Cali, and as your map shows, there are other important highways, too.

But many of the highways you see on the map are really dirt roads. Others are paved two-lane roads that twist and turn along mountainsides or squeeze through narrow passes. On most of Colombia's roads, traffic moves slowly. Also, these roads only connect main cities. Most towns and villages are still not connected to the highways. Village farm products sometimes rot before they can get to market.

The Colombian government knows this. It is already building new highways and planning many more. It has begun to pave some of the dirt roads.

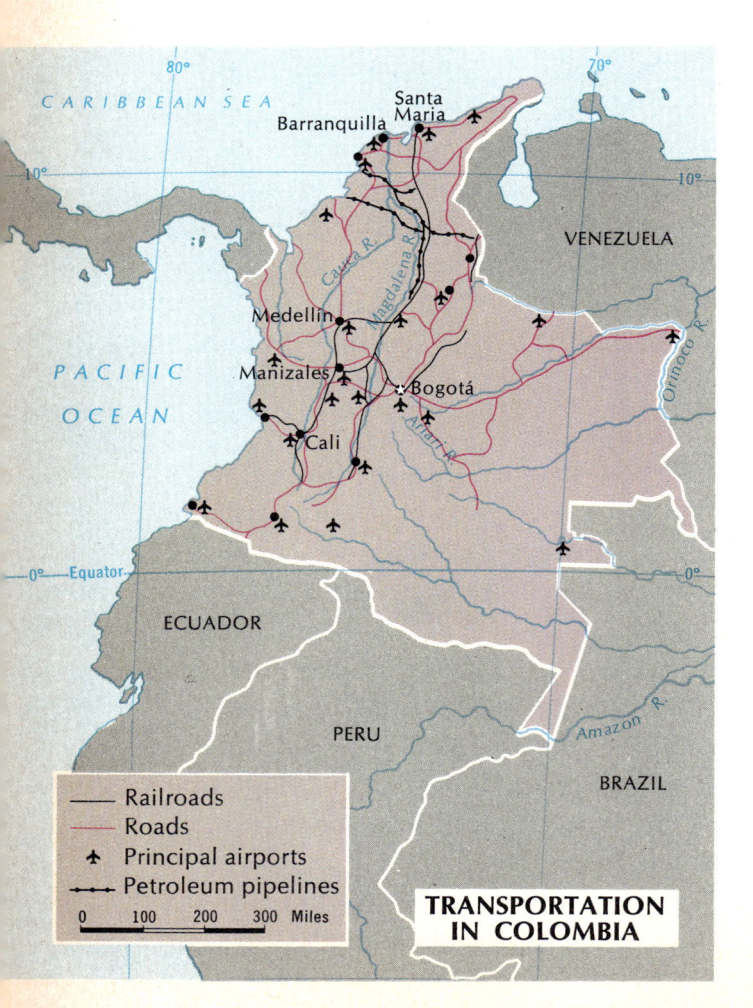

Transportation and Communication in Colombia in 1941 and 1968

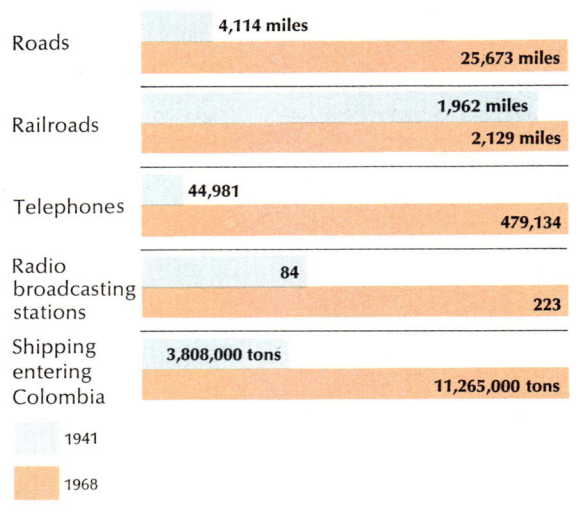

	1941	1968
Roads	4,114 miles	25,673 miles
Railroads	1,962 miles	2,129 miles
Telephones	44,981	479,134
Radio broadcasting stations	84	223
Shipping entering Colombia	3,808,000 tons	11,265,000 tons

But this will take time, and a great deal of money.

Because travel by highway and railroad in this rugged, mountainous country is difficult and expensive, the airplane is very important. Every small city has its own airport. Even when cities are not connected by railroads and highways, they are linked by airplanes. This has helped Colombia's transportation system a great deal. But it cannot completely make up for the poor railroad and highway systems.

The Government Takes Important Steps

About fifteen years ago, Carlos Ramos decided to give up his miserable life as a campesino and move to the city. He settled in the growing slum outside Cali. But there was no job in the city for Carlos. He had spent his last *peso* and was wondering whether to become a beggar or a thief to stay alive. Then he found out about a new government farm program.

The government had set aside an area for new farms along the Ariari (är′ ē är′ ē) River. The Ariari is in the southern part of Colombia, east of the mountains. The government would lend settlers money to buy 125 acres for a farm. It would also provide medical services, public schools for the children, and instruction in modern farming methods.

Carlos could hardly believe it. Was it true? he asked the government official in Cali. Yes, he was told, the government wanted to encourage people to settle on the land east of the mountains. Carlos signed up.

After several weeks of chopping and burning jungle trees, the land was cleared, and Carlos planted his first rice crop. Meanwhile, the government had sprayed the area with insect killers. In those first years on the Ariari, Carlos and other settlers sent crops to market by mule. Now they send crops by jeep to the market at San Martín, because the government has built a narrow dirt road.

Not everything has worked out just the way Carlos had hoped. There are few schools, and they are all far from his farm. The nearest doctor is in San Martín, three hours away. Still, Carlos has few complaints. He owns his land and is making a living. He plans to spend the rest of his life there.

Aid to farmers helps industry. Making more land available for farming is one of the ways Colombia is trying to help campesinos like Carlos Ramos live a better life. What do the campesinos have to do with industrializing Colombia? About half of the nation's inhabitants are campesinos. Right now most of them are extremely poor.

You will recall that some of the factories of Bogotá and Cali do not produce as much as they are able to because the market for their goods is too small. If the campesinos made more money, they could buy more goods. This would mean more production, more jobs for people, and more factories. Everyone in Colombia, on the farms and in the cities, would have a higher standard of living.

Increasing food production. Colombia's farms are connected to her industrialization in another important way. Every year the population increases; so more food must be raised. If the nation's farmers do not increase their production, Colombia will have to buy food from other countries. This will leave less money to buy the machines that Colombia needs to industrialize.

Because of Colombia's geography, only about a quarter of the land can be farmed. But if Colombia's farmers used modern farming methods and

Bogotá, a city surrounded by mountains, is the capital of Colombia and is also an important manufacturing center.

made wise use of the land, they could raise all the food the population needs. Moreover they could make a good living while doing it.

Colombia's government is trying hard to increase food production. We have seen how it has opened up farmland east of the mountains. It is also trying to increase production from the rest of the land. Government experts are teaching the campesino to use fertilizer and better seed on his small plot. This is very difficult, for the campesino is uneducated and often is unwilling to change his ways.

Most important, the government is trying to make the rich landowners in the valleys use their land for growing crops instead of for grazing cattle. Landowners have been warned that if they do not start farming the land, the government will give it to poor people who will. So far, only a few landowners have agreed to change from grazing to farming.

Colombia has also built several fertilizer factories. It is building more roads from farm villages to the market cities. It has forty agricultural colleges that train people in scientific farming.

These people then go out to the farming country and show the farmer how to improve his production. Also, money is loaned to farmers who want to buy farm machinery.

Colombia is making some progress in bringing industrialization to her farms, but as you can see, there are many problems. Complete industrialization will take a long time.

Education Plays a Big Part

To help plan its factories and run them, Colombia has had to call on many foreign experts. But now Colombia wants its own citizens to manage its factories. So the government sends promising students to schools in other countries to learn the necessary skills.

Training in new skills. As this book is being written, a 22-year-old Colombian named Rodrigo is completing his studies at the Philadelphia College of Textiles & Science in the United States. When you read this, Rodrigo will have returned to his home in Cali with his new skills. He may be managing a textile factory somewhere in Colombia right now.

Each year there are more people like Rodrigo in Colombia. To become an industrial nation, however, Colombia will have to do more than send a few people to schools in other lands. Many Colombians will have to learn to operate machines and to repair them, to manage factories, and to run offices. Also, as more people leave the farm for the city, they will need new skills to make a living. Farm children, too, must learn modern farming methods. They must change those ideas and beliefs that have kept farming methods the same for centuries.

Coffee is Colombia's biggest crop. Most of the work of coffee-growing is still done by hand, and everyone in the family helps. Above, the ripe berries are being picked from the coffee bushes. Below, they are being spread to dry in the sun.

Obstacles to education. Unfortunately, Colombia has not done so well in providing education for all her people. One half the population cannot read or write. Two fifths of the children do not even go to elementary school. Only about one out of ten goes to high school, and one out of a hundred goes to college.

Colombia has passed a law that all children must attend school, but the law is not obeyed. Some campesinos feel they need their children's help on the farm more than the children need school. But people could not obey the law even if they wanted to, for there are not enough schools in Colombia for all the children. The shortage is very great in rural areas.

Also, even if Colombia were to build tomorrow all the schools it needs, there would not be enough teachers. Many of the teachers now in Colombia's elementary schools have completed only the fifth grade themselves. Building schools takes money and time, but training good teachers takes even longer. Colombia must make a great effort to do these jobs before she can become fully industrialized.

Need For Investments

When Pedro Nel Ospina and the coffee growers of Medellín built Colombia's first factory seventy years ago, they paid for it with their earnings from the coffee business. With their earnings from this factory, they built others. By investing their money, these men provided the capital for Colombia to begin industrialization.

Unfortunately, not all of Colombia's wealthy people have been willing to follow the example of the coffee growers of Medellín. Some wealthy people do not want to risk their money by building a factory in their own country. They fear it may not succeed. They believe their money will earn more elsewhere, so they invest it in other countries.

Water from mountain streams is purified at this filtration plant in Medellín. Notice the pipeline.

Money from other nations. It would certainly be better for Colombia if her wealthy citizens would provide more capital to build up industries. But even if all of them did, Colombia would still not have enough capital.

This is always a big problem for a country that is just beginning to industrialize. Did the United States have this problem in the nineteenth century? Where did we get much of the capital that built our railroads?

Colombia depends on businesses and individuals from other nations to invest in Colombian industry. Belgian and French investors provided the money to build Colombia's only steel mill. English, United States, and Japanese companies invested the money to build new automobile factories. Foreign oil companies built new oil refineries.

Colombia is trying to increase its own capital in order to build new industries, roads, schools, and electric power plants. Already most of the money earned by exporting coffee is used to buy capital goods. In other words, Colombia is spending its wealth to buy goods that will make more goods. This is how a nation builds up capital.

But it takes a long time for a country to create new capital by itself. In the meantime, other nations can help by lending money. The United States government has loaned large amounts to the Colombian government for im-

The people are testing the water to be sure it is safe to drink. Part of the money for this laboratory came from the United States.

proving railroads and building highways. The railroad from Santa Marta to Bogotá was built with those funds.

Planning for the future. Recently Colombia began a ten-year plan for industrializing. Each year during that time, it plans to do certain projects. The United States is lending money to help with this work.

The Colombian government does not have all the money it would like. Therefore it must decide which projects are most necessary and should be done first. Should factories be built to make more goods? Or electric power plants to make more electric energy? Or roads for transporting goods? Or schools to educate the people who must run the factories and modernize the farms? Or fertilizer factories to increase farm production? The ten-year plan calls for making a little progress in each of these things each year, so they will grow at the same rate.

When this long-range plan is completed, Colombia will start another one. Again it will set certain goals for each year. And each year, it will move a little closer to an industrial society.

Industry in Canada

While most nations to the south are still struggling to industrialize, our northern neighbor has already become an industrial nation. In earlier chapters you learned some of the things a country needs in order to become industrialized. Can you list them now? Then we will see whether Canada has these things.

Natural resources. Let's begin with raw materials. Find the resources map of Canada. What would you say is Canada's greatest natural resource? Does Canada have many minerals? Which ones? Canada is the world's leading supplier of two important materials needed by industrial nations. One is nickel, which is used in making stainless steel. The other is asbestos,

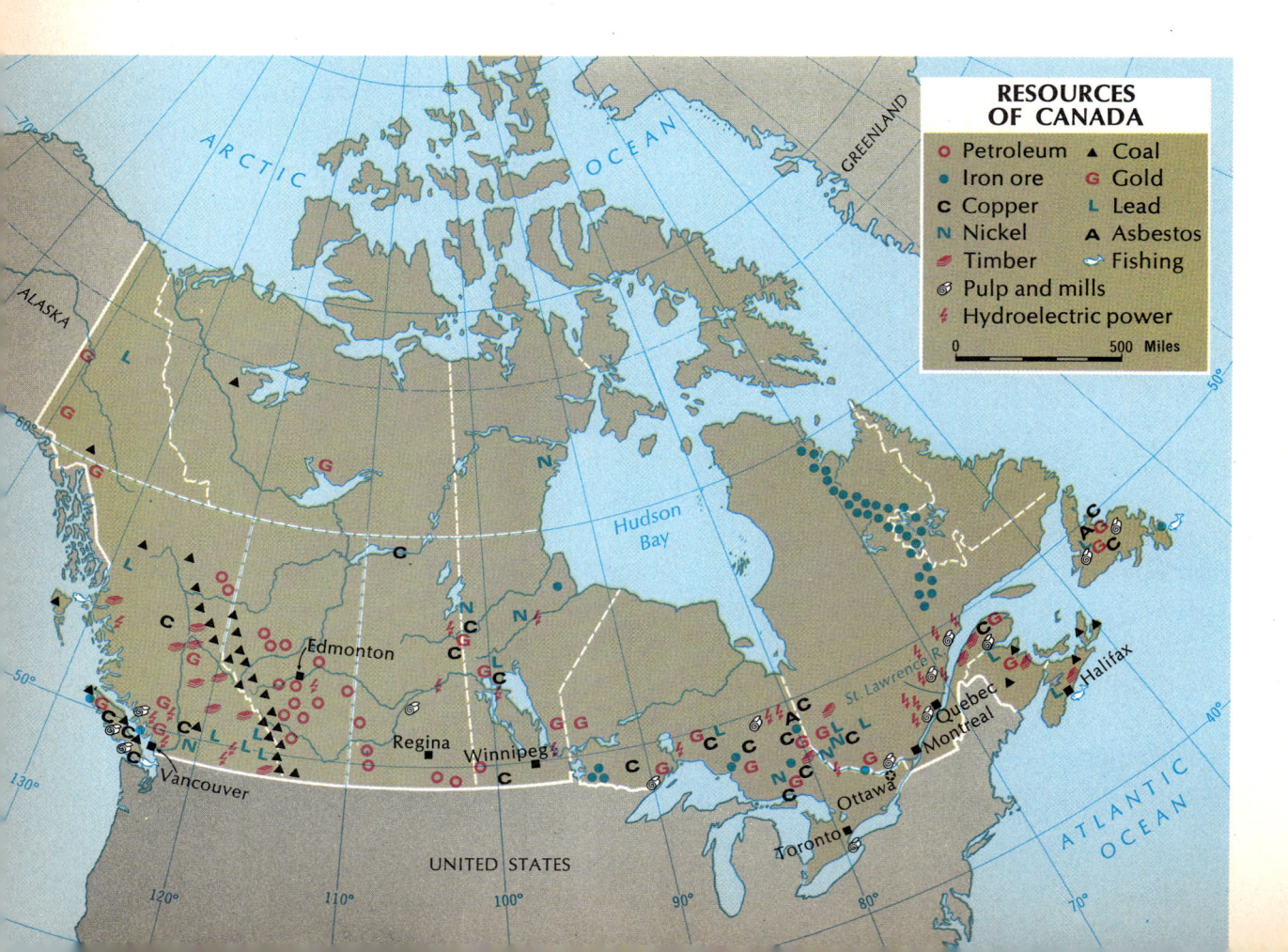

RESOURCES OF CANADA

- O Petroleum
- ▲ Coal
- • Iron ore
- G Gold
- C Copper
- L Lead
- N Nickel
- A Asbestos
- Timber
- Fishing
- Pulp and mills
- Hydroelectric power

0   500 Miles

a greenish rock fiber that does not burn. It is used to make fireproof building materials and special gloves and suits for fighting fires.

The huge iron-ore deposit that we see on the border of Quebec and Labrador was discovered only a few years ago. It is in a very cold part of Canada, which made it difficult to mine and ship the ore. Before any mining could be done, workers and supplies had to be flown in to build a town to live in. Workers then built a 360-mile railroad through the forest to the nearest river. Next they had to build a port where the ore could be loaded onto ships and sent along the great water highway to Canadian and United States steel mills near the Great Lakes. It took several years to complete the job, but now the mine produces millions of tons of rich ore each year.

The deposits of oil and natural gas that you noted in western Canada have also been discovered only recently. Many scientists believe that more mineral treasures are hidden in the frozen lands of northern Canada and that one day soon they will be discovered and mined.

Rich in natural resources as Canada is, she does not have all the things she needs. For these items, Canada trades with other nations. For example, in order to buy cotton raised in warmer countries, Canada sells wheat and forest products such as lumber, newsprint, and wood pulp.

Transportation. Industrial nations also need a good transportation system. Does Canada have one? We have already seen that Canada has a fine water highway that allows ocean ships to go directly to the middle of the continent. Canada also has excellent railways and roads. Most of them are in the south, which is the most populated and developed part of the nation. Canada's railway system, which carries wheat from the western prairies to Great Lakes ports, is among the finest in the world. One of Canada's highways, called the Trans-Canada Highway, runs from St. John's on the eastern coast to Victoria in the west, a distance of 5,000 miles. In addition, airlines connect many of the large and small cities of the nation.

Sources of power. Your resources map shows that Canada does not have very large coal deposits. There is some coal in Nova Scotia, but that is far from most markets, and not much is mined. Where does Canada get the power to run her machines? The source of power is in the fast-flowing water of her rivers. Canada has converted this rushing water into electricity. The rivers are one of the nation's greatest resources, and they have enabled Canada to produce great amounts of electricity cheaply.

This plentiful, cheap electricity powers Canada's machines. It has made possible an entirely new industry in Canada. Look at your resources map again and see if you can find bauxite. Bauxite is a reddish, claylike ore from which aluminum is made. Did you find any? Yet Canada is the world's third largest producer of aluminum! This seems odd until you understand certain facts. A great deal of electricity is needed to make aluminum. In fact, the electricity used in making a single pound of aluminum would light your home for ten years. But countries like Jamaica where bauxite is found, do not have the electric power to smelt the ore. They are anxious to export it. Canada with its abundance of power is happy to import the bauxite for its aluminum industry.

Capital for Canada's industries. Does Canada have the capital needed for getting capital goods—machines, factories, and electric power plants? Because Canada is a great trading nation, it is able to raise much of the capital it needs. Her main exports are forest products—lumber, wood pulp, and paper. Most of these are sold in the United States. Chances are that the newspaper you read is printed on paper that comes from Canadian forests.

Another very important export is wheat. Scientists have produced a special variety of wheat that grows well in the short growing season of the Canadian prairies. Aided by modern machinery and methods, Canada's farmers produce enough wheat to feed ninety million people—nearly five times as much as Canada needs. The surplus is sold to other nations in exchange for goods and money.

Canada also sells much of its iron ore to steel manufacturers in the United States. Recently she has begun to sell oil and natural gas as well. All these exports have helped Canada acquire the capital goods needed for more industrialization.

Even so, Canada has not been able to produce enough capital for all her needs. Some of the capital used in Canada's growing industries comes from the investments of United States businesses and banks, as well as private individuals.

A small population. One thing that Canada lacks is a large population. Do you remember the connection between population and the market for goods? between population and the supply of labor? Although Canada is a larger country than the United States, its population is only about one tenth as great, or about twenty million people. Most of the people live in the east.

The Canadian government realizes that a larger population would help Canada's economy to grow. That is why it has encouraged immigration. The government and the railway companies have placed advertisements in European newspapers offering free land in the west and free railroad passage to anyone who will move there.

Does this remind you of anything you have read about before?

Even though Canada's labor supply is not large, much of it is very skilled. All Canadian children attend school, and a great many continue on to get special training in colleges and universities. Canada has several outstanding universities. They produce many scientists, engineers, and people trained in managing factories and businesses. Canadian schools also produce doctors, teachers, and specialists of many other kinds, who provide the important services necessary to an industrial society.

Today Canada is an industrialized nation. This has brought many changes in the ways of living of the people. It has also brought some of the familiar problems of industrialism. Canada must now protect her rivers and lakes and keep them free of harmful chemicals. She must also take measures to protect her air. But along with these problems, industrialism has brought to Canadians one of the highest standards of living in the world.

Canadian-made tractors are being loaded at the docks in Montreal for shipment to other parts of Canada and to other countries.

Working with Concepts and Generalizations

Identifying Concepts

Complete each sentence. Write on paper.

1. Canada's main exports are _____ products.
2. Colombia is chiefly a _____ country.
3. Canada gets power to run machinery by converting water from its rivers into _____.
4. Much of the richest soil in Colombia is used for _____ _____.
5. Because travel by highway and railroad is difficult and expensive, every small city in Colombia has its own _____.

Developing Concepts

The map below shows a farming country that is planning to improve its transportation facilities. Copy the map. Then do the work in 1 through 5 below.

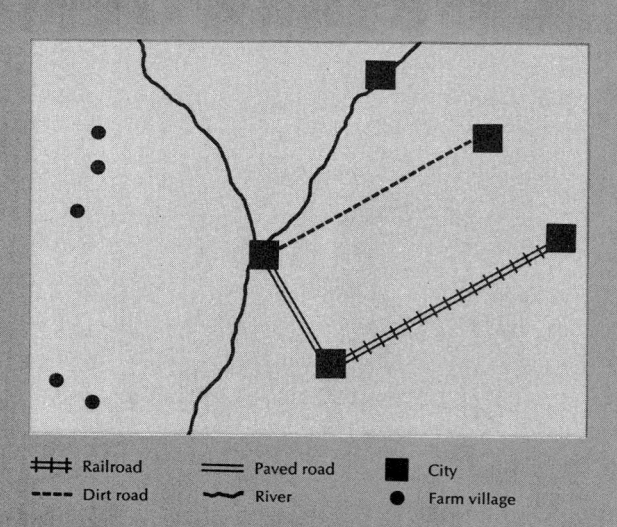

┼┼┼ Railroad   ═══ Paved road   ■ City
---- Dirt road   〜 River   ● Farm village

1. The country can afford to build only two railroad lines. Show where these should be built. Then, at the bottom of your paper, explain why.
2. The country can afford to build two paved roads. Show where these roads should be built and explain why.
3. The country can afford to make five dirt roads. Show where these roads should be made and explain why.
4. Now, using a different color, show where two railroad lines should be built when more money is available.
5. Using a different color, show where three paved roads should be built when more money is available.

Write the answers to these questions on paper.

6. Why is the Canadian government trying to get more people to move to Canada?
7. The Colombian government is helping farmers. How will this help industry in Colombia?

Generalizations

Read the generalizations listed below. Find proof to support each generalization. Tell what the proof is and the page on which you found it.

1. Farming nations often attempt to industrialize, hoping to improve the standard of living.
2. An inexpensive and efficient transportation system is an important feature of an industrial nation.
3. Before a country can industrialize, it must produce more that it uses.
4. The change from a farming to an industrial economy requires the investment of capital.

Applying Concepts

1. You have learned that before industrialism almost every product was made in the home. You have also learned that workers could take pride in their creations. Do you think you would be proud of something you made all by yourself? Here is a chance to find out. MAKE SOMETHING! Your product can be anything you choose. It can be made of anything. Perhaps you will create something from wood or cloth or metal. Perhaps you will make cookies or cake or bread. Use your imagination. Bring your finished product to class to share with your classmates and fellow craftsmen.

2. One of the greatest concerns in the United States today is the pollution of the environment. You are to help plan a "Save the Environment Day" for your school. You may do any *one* of the activities listed below. Each activity requires you to find information on an environmental problem. When you have found the information, suggest ways the problem can be solved. Your work, when added to that of your classmates, will provide ideas that *you* can use to help save the environment.
   a. Find out as much as you can about the forms of American wildlife that are in danger of extinction unless something is done to protect them from man and from the wastes of his industrial society.
   b. Find out as much as you can about the pollution of rivers, lakes, and streams caused by industrial wastes and by man's neglect.
   c. Find out as much as you can about the pollution of the land.
   d. Find out as much as you can about the destruction of our forests and wooded areas to make way for superhighways.
   e. Find out as much as you can about air pollution in cities and industrial areas.
   f. Find out as much as you can about the wastes created by the way food products are packaged for sale. (Just look at the items your mother brings home from the grocery store. How many of them are wrapped in paper? How many are in cans, bottles, and bags?)

3. Laws regulating child labor were passed before you were born. Yet these laws greatly affect your daily life. Go to the library. Find out as much as you can about child labor laws in the United States today. Prepare a report to share with the class.

4. Labor unions are an active force in American life today. Newspapers carry stories of labor negotiations nearly every day. Find some of these newspaper stories. Add them to those your classmates find and make a bulletin-board display.

5. You know that Eli Whitney invented the cotton gin. But he made another contribution to industrialism that had a great influence on the way many products are manufactured today. Go to the library. Find out as much as you can about Whitney's great idea of interchangeable parts. Prepare a report for the class on the importance of this idea and on how Whitney first demonstrated that his idea would work.

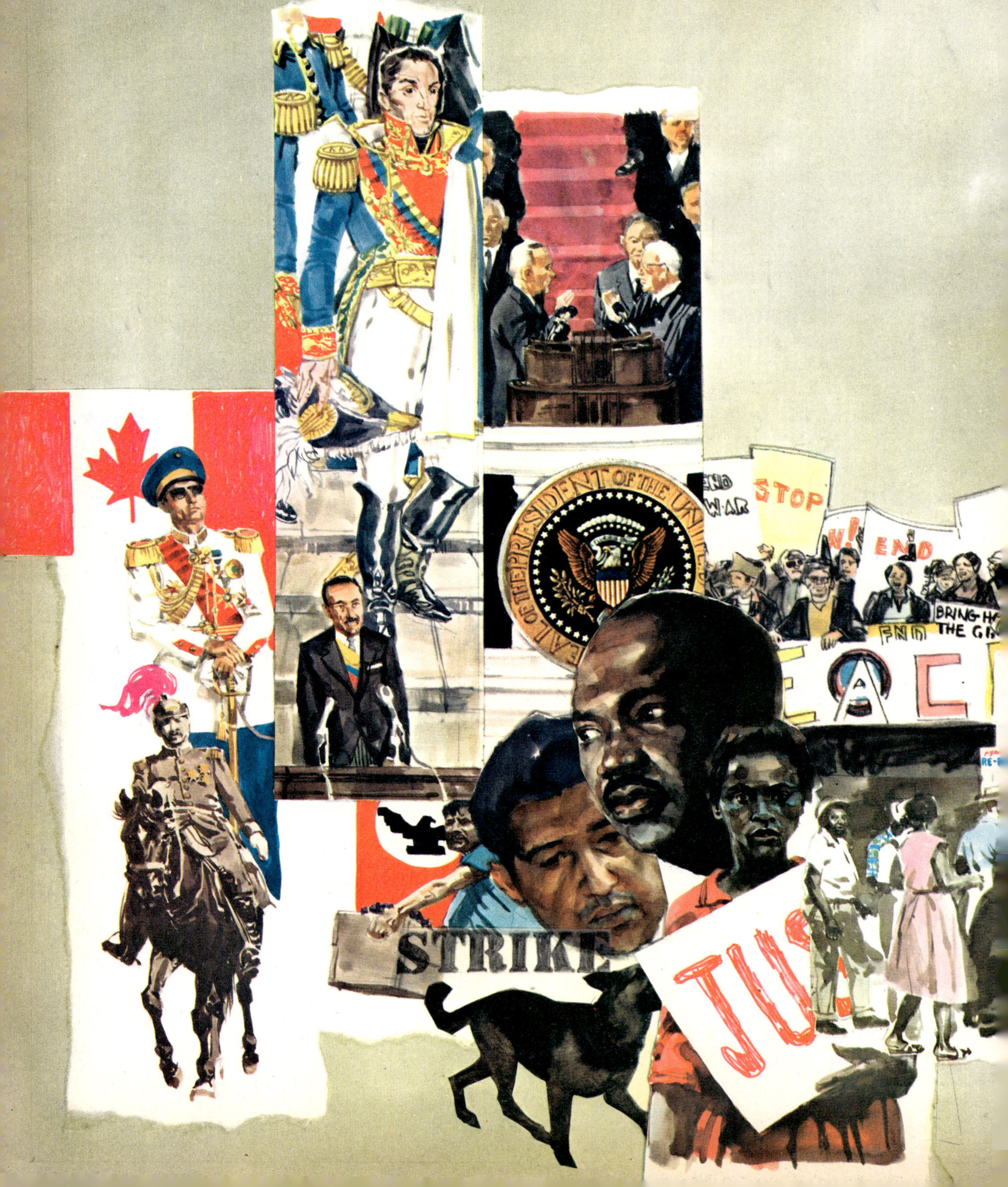
STOP
END
STRIKE

unit four

INVESTIGATING AMERICAN VALUES AND GOVERNMENT

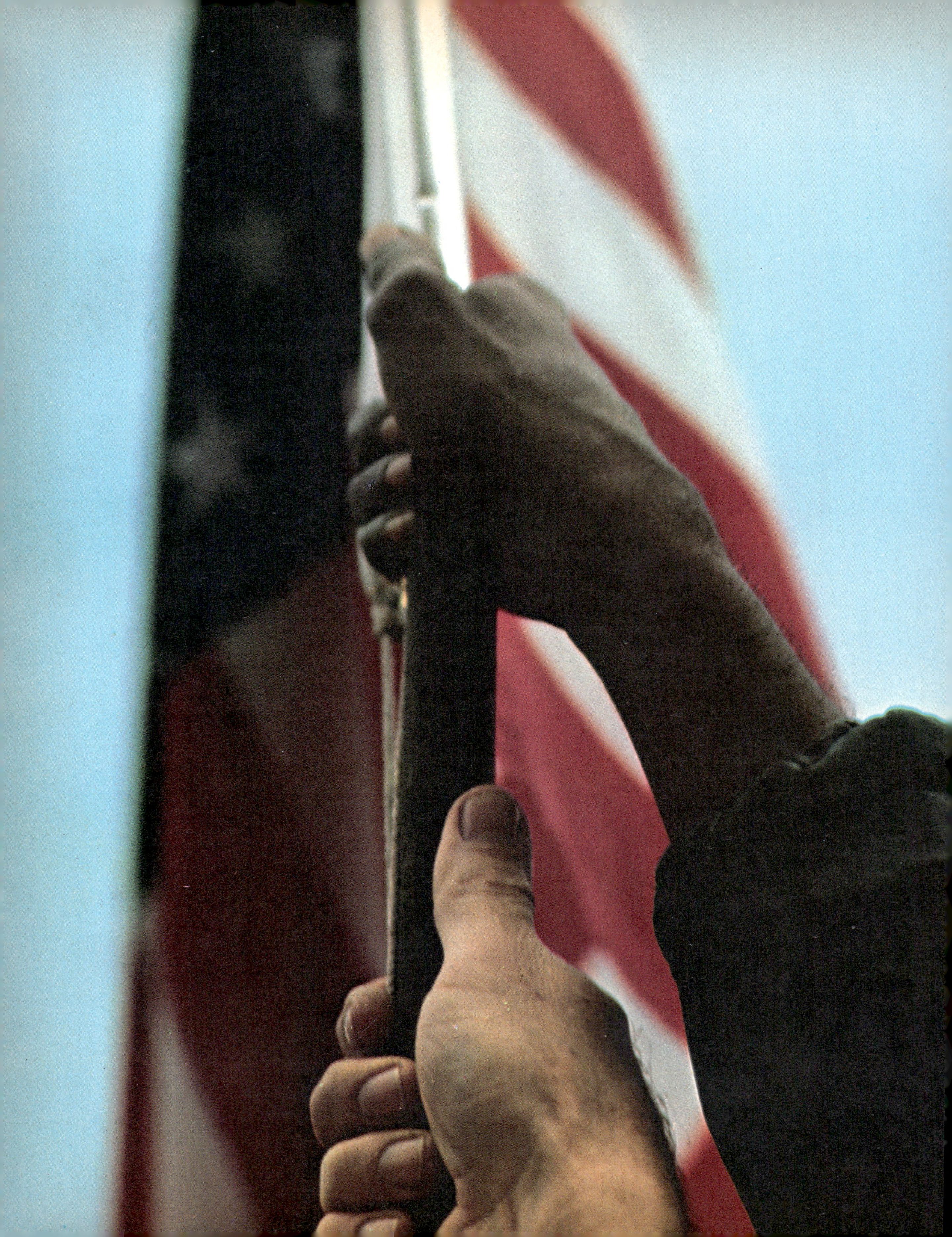

19 Equality

In June 1776, after a year of fighting between the colonists and the British troops, the American colonies decided to break away from the mother country, England. Colonial leaders believed they should explain to the world why the colonies had decided on this very serious step. They appointed a committee to write a statement about it.

Most of the writing was done by one member of the group. He was a young sandy-haired Virginian named Thomas Jefferson. The document was called the Declaration of Independence. It became the most famous document in our history.

In the Declaration of Independence, Jefferson included many of the beliefs that Americans of his day had about government and society. One of the most important statements that he wrote is this one.

"We hold these truths to be self-evident; that all men are created equal, that they are endowed by their Creator with certain unalienable rights, that among these are life, liberty, and the pursuit of happiness."

"All men are created equal." That simple phrase has been quoted and discussed many times since it was written. That phrase is what this chapter is about.

All Men Are Created Equal

Let's think a moment about Jefferson's famous phrase. Actually, it seems like a silly thing to say, doesn't it? Would you say that everybody in your class was created with an equal ability to do arithmetic? or to run fast? or to sing? Can everyone play basketball as well as Kareem Jabbar can? Was everyone created with equal abilities? Of course, everybody knows that all people are *not* created equal.

Certainly Thomas Jefferson knew that. In fact, though he was a modest man, he probably would have admitted that few people were created with the ability to write a great document like the Declaration of Independence. Then why did Jefferson use the phrase "all men are created equal"? What did he mean by it? And why did he say that all Americans agreed with the idea?

What Thomas Jefferson meant. What Jefferson meant is that all people have an equal right to be treated with fairness, dignity, and respect. They have this right because they are fellow human beings. This idea of equality was an important value to most Americans in Jefferson's time. It is still an important American value.

In the first chapter of this book, you were asked to decide how you felt

Thomas Jefferson finished his work on the Declaration of Independence. Congress studied it and approved it.

about certain statements. Do you remember this one: "Every person, no matter who he is, should be treated with the same fairness as every other person"? Did you and your classmates agree with that statement? If you did, you were really agreeing with Thomas Jefferson and the Declaration of Independence.

The value of equality affects almost everything in our society. In this chapter, we will be able to study only a few of those things. We will see what equality has to do with our laws, with our making a living, and with our taking part in government.

USING SOURCE MATERIAL

You may not realize it, but you already have many ideas about how the value of equality affects our laws. As you answer some questions about the three examples below, you will be able to bring out your ideas more clearly.

For the first example, we will go back to something you read earlier in this book. It is the case of the three indentured servants who were caught after running away from their master. They were brought to court and found guilty. Read again how the judge decided to punish each one.

The court does therefore order that the said three servants shall receive the punishment of whipping and to have thirty stripes apiece [.] One called Victor, a dutchman, the other a Scotchman called James Gregory, shall serve . . . one whole year apiece after the time of their service is expired . . . and after that service . . . to serve the colony for three whole years apiece, and that the third being a Negro named John Punch shall serve his said master . . . for the time of his natural life.

What do you think about the judge's decision? Why? What did the judge believe about people?

In the second example, imagine that you are a judge in your community. Three people have been arrested for speeding. Each was driving 50 miles an hour on a street where the speed limit is 25.

The first driver, Mr. Jones, is one of the most respected men in town. He owns a department store and is very active in raising funds for the local hospital and for playgrounds. Miss Brown, the second driver, is one of the most popular teachers in the school. You know she is a kind person and not one who usually breaks the law. The third driver is Mr. Hicks. He does not seem to be a very pleasant fellow. He certainly has never done much to help the community. He is out of work now and does not seem to be trying too hard to get another job.

To which of these three speeders would you give the heaviest punishment? To which would you give the

399

lightest punishment? Why did you decide as you did?

For the third example, we will look at a statement that has been part of the law of our country for about one hundred years. This is what it says.

> The right of citizens of the United States to vote shall not be denied . . . on account of race, color, or previous condition of servitude.

Does this seem to you to be a good law, or a bad one? Why?

Understanding equality under the law. How do you feel about the cases and laws you have just read? Take the case of John Punch first. Probably everyone in your class thought the judge's decision was not fair. Since all three runaways did exactly the same thing, shouldn't they have received the same punishment? They certainly were not treated equally.

In the second case, where you were the judge, did all the speeders get the same punishment? Most of us would agree that they should have, for all three broke the same law in the same way.

What about the law that deals with the right to vote? That is a good law because it treats all people equally. Certainly you would not agree with a law that said: It is all right to take away a person's right to vote because of his race or color.

Do you see how your ideas about equality helped you make up your mind about those three examples? The idea that laws should be the same for all people, and that all people should be treated the same if they break the laws, is an important one to most people in our country. That is what we mean by "equality under the law."

Equality for Many, but Not for All

Even in the early days of our country, Americans believed in equality under the law. However, they usually did not mean equality for *everybody*. They really meant equality for white men. Indians were not included. Neither were black slaves. Thomas Jefferson himself, the man who wrote that "all

Practices like using separate drinking fountains made blacks feel unequal for years.

men are created equal," owned dozens of slaves all his life. He believed black people were inferior and should not have the same rights as others.

Inequality by law. Even the free blacks in northern and southern states did not have the same rights as whites. They would almost certainly receive heavier punishments than whites for breaking the law. And the same was true for Mexican-Americans in the Southwest.

With the end of slavery in 1865, and for many years after, blacks did not receive equality under the law. They could not stay in the same hotels as white people. They could not use the same playgrounds, or attend the same schools, or use the same waiting rooms in railway stations. Blacks could not even drink water from the same fountains as whites. The laws that allowed this unequal treatment were called segregation laws. They were intended to segregate, or separate, whites and blacks in almost everything they did. The nickname for such laws is Jim Crow laws.

USING SOURCE MATERIAL

Does equality under the law mean there can never be different laws for different people? Certainly we can agree that traffic laws should be the same for all. But here is another case.

A family has two children, aged five and ten. Bedtime for the five-year-old is 7:00. The parents announce that in order to have equality under the rules, or law, both children must be in bed at the same time—7:00.

What do you think about this rule?
How do we decide when the rules should be the same for everybody and when they should be different? Does fairness have something to do with it? You know that when the five-year-old is ten, he too will be allowed to stay up later. So in this case, a different rule for each child was not unfair.

Some of our laws also treat different people differently. One example is the *income tax* law.

An income tax is a tax that people pay on the money they earn. Our federal government's income tax law requires that people who earn more must pay a larger share of their income than those who earn less. People who earn a very small amount pay little or no income tax. The United States has had income tax laws for about sixty years.

Is it a fair law? Our ideas about the fairness of this law have changed over the years. In the 1800's many people would have thought such a law very unfair. But nowadays most feel it is a fair law, as long as the poorer man understands that when he earns more, he too will have to pay more taxes to support the government.

The Jim Crow laws you have read about treated people differently. Have our ideas about their fairness changed also?

In some of our western states, the laws did not treat people born in Asia equally. One state did not allow Japanese immigrants to buy land, even though all other immigrants and citizens could.

In most places the words of the laws were fair enough, but members of minority groups were not treated equally under the laws. For instance, members of minority groups often did not receive fair trials, and usually they were given harsher punishments than others.

Equality under the law grows. By 1950, things had begun to change. Blacks insisted that they should have equal rights. So did members of other minority groups. Some Americans did not agree, but most did. If our country really believed in equality under the law, how could we allow unequal laws and unequal treatment? As a result, Jim Crow laws and other laws like them are no longer allowed anywhere in the United States.

Bringing equality under the law up-to-date. Many people thought that once Jim Crow laws were gone, all men would be treated with fairness, dignity, and respect. But soon we realized that was not so.

It was true that the laws no longer forbade blacks to eat in the same restaurants as whites. But often when blacks tried to eat in these restaurants, they were not served. Laws no longer prohibited blacks from using the same hotels and motels as whites. But when they tried to use them, they were often refused rooms. The laws had changed, but the people had not.

Americans realized that they could not end unfair treatment just by ending unequal laws. Unfortunately, many people accepted the value of equality in words but not in daily living. And too many other people had never accepted the value of equality, in spite of the laws. We needed laws to *make* these people treat others fairly.

The United States Congress passed such a law in 1964. It is called the Civil Rights Act. This law says that no person can be refused the use of restaurants, hotels, service stations, city parks, city swimming pools, and places of this kind just because of his color, his religion, or the country he was born in. Many states have also passed such laws. In most places in the country these laws are being obeyed.

In 1968 Congress passed another law that says a person cannot refuse to sell a house or rent an apartment to another person just because of his color, religion, or place of birth. Many states also have such laws.

But how well are these laws enforced? The following account from

The New York Times is a good example of what still takes place.

> The New York Chapter of the American Jewish Committee charged yesterday that Jews were being excluded from more than 100 cooperative apartment houses in Manhattan. . . .
>
> [The] president of the chapter said . . . that "several years" of work by the committee had produced evidence of discrimination by selection boards consisting of tenants. . . .
>
> [The leader of a special committee to investigate the problem said that] when Jews apply for vacant apartments they are usually told "You wouldn't be comfortable in this building," or "This is a church-going group of people," or "This is a clubby kind of place."

The same thing often happens to members of other minority groups when they try to find housing. Even these laws, as you see, have not brought complete equality under the law to all Americans. In fact, true equality cannot be brought about by laws alone. Men's minds must be changed too. But when you compare the present with Thomas Jefferson's time, you can see how this value—equality under the law—has been broadened to include more people. Do you see how this value has helped us decide the kind of laws we want our government to pass?

Equality of Opportunity

Most immigrants to America caught their first sight of their new homeland as their ships headed into the port of New York. For those who arrived after 1886, there was an added sight—the splendid Statue of Liberty. This statue was a gift from the people of France to the United States.

Even before the statue was put in place, it inspired Emma Lazarus to write a poem about it. Today a copy of that poem appears on the base of the statue. It is read by hundreds of thousands of visitors each year.

It will take many years to overcome the ill effects of segregating schools.

In her poem, Emma Lazarus has the statue, representing America, say to the European countries:

> Give me your tired, your poor,
> Your huddled masses, yearning to breathe free . . .

What do you think these words mean? Why did Miss Lazarus say that the United States would welcome Europe's tired and poor masses? Is it because we wanted to have a large number of poor people living in America? What did we believe would happen to the tired and poor when they came to America? Would they always remain poor?

An equal chance for a better life. Americans believed that in their country a person could try to become whatever he wanted to be. Why did Americans believe this? Not just because America was a rich land. There were other rich lands on the earth. But in most of them, the kind of family a person was born into was what counted. Children of poor, humble families could expect to stay poor and humble all their lives. That was the way it had always been, and that was the way many people thought it should be. But in America people believed every person *should* have an equal opportunity to make a better life for himself, no matter what his family's background was. Equality of opportunity was an important value to Americans.

An important footrace. In the early years, Americans liked to compare life in this nation to a footrace. Everyone, they said, no matter how humble, could enter the race. All would begin at the same starting line. No one would have any advantages over the others. When the race started, each person would be able to go just as fast as he could. And he could go as far as his abilities carried him.

How could Americans say that everyone started at the same starting line? Did the son of a poor farmer start life at the same starting line as the son of a wealthy merchant? Didn't one have many more advantages than the other all through the race? Who had a better chance to "train" for the race with good schooling? Could they both afford the same things? Saying that everyone started at the same line and had no advantages seems about as silly as saying that all men are created equal.

Certainly those who talked about the footrace knew that their example was not completely correct. They agreed that the rich man's son certainly had some advantages. But they pointed out that these advantages did not prevent millions of poor people from succeeding in America. Immigrants, and their children, did become lawyers, merchants, tradesmen, farmers, and even government leaders. Even if the race was not perfect, there really was more equality of opportunity in America than anywhere else on the earth.

Equality of opportunity means very little to the Hopi Indians living on these reservations in Arizona.

Equality of opportunity for some. Americans who said they believed in equality of opportunity in those early years usually did not mean equality for everybody. Again, Indians, blacks, Mexicans, and Asians were not included. Even some European immigrants did not find the equal opportunity that America boasted about.

In some cities Irish immigrants looking for jobs found signs reading, "No Irish need apply." Jews, Italians, Greeks, and others often found themselves targets of discrimination, too. Often these people could get only the low-paid jobs, and had little opportunity for advancing to better jobs.

In time, America's population increased greatly. No longer did an empty continent stretch before the settlers. The land was filling up. Newcomers could not count on as much opportunity as the earlier settlers had. Industrialism also seemed to bring changes in equality of opportunity. Do you remember the ten-year-old boys who worked all day in the coal mines for pitifully low wages? Do you think they would ever have much opportunity to find better jobs?

Some early steps toward equality. Many Americans began to wonder if equality of opportunity was disappearing. How could they bring it back again for people such as the children who worked in the factories and mines? The best answer seemed to be through education.

With an education, a person would have a chance to improve himself. But in those early years, schools were not free. Most poor families could not afford to send their children to school. Therefore, in the middle 1800's, most states opened free public elementary schools. Still later they added free public high schools. They also passed laws requiring children to attend school for a certain number of years. Before long, many more young people were finishing high school. They then had more opportunity to find better jobs.

In our own times we have also begun to do something about bringing equality of opportunity to those groups that were left out in earlier days. Our federal government and many of our states have passed laws to make sure that everyone, regardless of his color or religion, has an equal chance to be hired for a good job.

Many private businesses are helping in this effort to put our values into

Poor families in the Appalachians spend hours searching for coal.

practice. If you look in the "Help Wanted" advertisements in newspapers you will often see the words *An Equal Opportunity Employer*. This means the company that is advertising has promised to give all people an equal opportunity for its jobs.

As a result of all these efforts, blacks, Puerto Ricans, Mexican-Americans, and members of other minorities can be seen working as bank tellers, policemen, store managers, and in many other jobs once closed to them.

Some exceptions. But again, we must note that the problem is not completely ended. There are still many Americans who discriminate. Here is how one man describes the experience of some blacks who are looking for jobs.

> If a man qualifies, it should be first come, first serve[d]. You understand what I mean? Regardless of whether we're black or white, we all have families! It should be first come, first serve. But that's not how they do you! If you're black, you're automatically turned down on a lot of jobs. They'll take your application, but no sooner than you walk out of the office, or wherever it is, they take the application and put it in the wastebasket, and tell you they'll let you know in a couple of weeks. They have no opening, and things like that.
>
> Man, age about 24

Women, too, have pointed out that they are not always treated equally in employment. Employers often refuse to hire them. And even when they are hired, women often get paid less than men for doing the same job. Here, too, our federal government and many states are passing laws to try to end this kind of discrimination.

Pushing the starting line ahead. Are there things we must do today to give more meaning to equality of opportunity? America has its own tired, poor, and huddled masses "yearning to breathe free." It is much harder now for the poor to make a decent living and to improve themselves. This is partly because, as we have seen, many are members of groups that are still discriminated against when they look for jobs. But there are also a great many poor whites.

One of the most important reasons it is so hard for the poor to improve their position is that America is a very advanced industrial nation today. In factories, businesses, and offices, much more education and many more skills are needed than ever before. Even making a living by farming is not simple any more. Many skills and much money are needed.

If we think of the footrace again, we might say the starting line has been pushed ahead a long way. Most Americans realize that if we are to have equality of opportunity, we must find ways of getting everybody up to the new starting line.

What are some of the things you think our society should do to bring this about?

Equality and Government

The value of equality also has a lot to do with the way our country is governed. You know, of course, that in our country we believe everyone should have an equal right to take part in choosing the people who will run our government. But have you ever wondered why? After all, what would be wrong if we left the voting to the most intelligent people? What about leaving it to the people with the most experience, or to those who have been very successful in their careers? Would not each of these groups give us a wiser, better government?

An equal right to vote. Suppose your teacher announced, "Next week your parents will visit our school. We will have a special display to show what the pupils in our class are interested in. However, only students who do well in music will be allowed to serve on the committee that makes the display. They will decide what will be in the display."

What do you think of this way of choosing the committee? What subject do you think would be given a special place in the display? If people who do well in science, social studies, and athletics were also allowed to serve on the committee, do you think the display might be different? Suppose you wanted to be sure that the display would show more of the things the *entire* class is interested in. What would be the best way of choosing the committee? Suppose you wanted to make certain that everyone in the class cooperated in preparing for visiting night. What would be the best way of choosing the committee then?

But wait. Perhaps we have been unfair to that first committee of music students. After all, they might say, "Let's put things in our display that the other children in the class are interested in, too." They might do that, and that would be very fair. On the other hand—they might not. What would be the best way to be *sure* that everybody's interests would be represented in the display?

Now perhaps you can see why we say every person should have an equal

Children learn the meaning of equality in school.

right to vote. If we believe every person is equal, then the government should treat everyone equally. It should pass laws that look after everybody.

We *could* say, "Let's just allow one group of citizens to do all the voting — the rich, perhaps, or the most intelligent, or the members of one religion." We could then *hope* they would choose a government that would make laws that would be fair to all of us. But the best way to be *sure* that the government will be fair to all groups is to let everyone have an equal voice in choosing it. And that is also the best way to be sure that almost everyone will be willing to accept the laws that the government makes.

An Equal Voice in the Government

Like American ideas about equality in other areas, ideas about political equality in the early years of our country did not include everybody. Do you remember some who were left out? They were not the only ones. At the time our government was founded, many people believed that only those who owned property could be counted on to vote wisely. Government should be left in their hands. So men who did not own a certain amount of property did not have the right to vote. Women were also left out. After all, men said, they belonged in the home and did not know anything about running the government.

A long struggle. By the 1820's, the idea of equality had been expanded. If we are really equal, many asked, shouldn't all men have an equal voice in choosing the government? The government should work in the interest of all the people, whether they own property or not. Soon all adult white males were allowed to vote. But blacks were still left out, and so were women.

After the Civil War ended slavery, an important statement was added to our Constitution. It is the statement you read on page 400: "The right of citizens of the United States to vote shall not be denied . . . on account of race, color, or previous condition of servitude." The phrase "previous condition of servitude" refers to those who had once been slaves. This amendment was added to the Constitution to be sure that black people would have the right to vote. They did in the northern states, and for a while they also did in the southern states.

But many whites in the southern states did not want black people to have any voice in government. They soon found ways of keeping former slaves from voting. Blacks were often threatened that they would be harmed or would lose their jobs if they voted.

Some southern states passed laws to get around the amendment to the Constitution. One of these laws, passed in about 1900, said that a person could not vote unless his grandfather had been a voter in the state.

409

Since the grandfathers of nearly all black people in that state had been slaves, who were not allowed to vote, the grandsons could not vote either. The United States courts later said that states could not use such laws to keep blacks from voting. But most southern states found other ways, and for many years few blacks voted.

Extending the right to vote. After 1900, women began to demand more strongly the right to vote. How could we talk about valuing equality and mean only men, they asked? Since women have to obey the same laws, they should also have a voice in choosing the people who make the laws. To win attention to their cause, women held protest marches in many cities. Some women even chained themselves to the fence of the White House to show how they felt about their unequal position. These actions made more people think about the problem, and they realized that the inequality of women was wrong. In 1920, an amendment to the Constitution finally gave women the right to vote.

Despite the efforts by some people to stop them, black Americans in the southern states became more determined than ever to vote. Many white Americans agreed that it was wrong to deny any citizen his right to vote. The United States Congress passed an important law in 1965 that helps anyone who wants to vote to do so. As a result, several million blacks vote in our southern states today. They have elected some black citizens to serve in a number of local offices in their states. Now they feel more certain that their interests are represented in their local laws.

Today women are struggling to achieve equality of treatment in many fields. By using the vote, they, too, will see their interests and rights protected in the laws of the nation.

The United States has come a long way since those days when only white males, who owned property, could vote. Today there is no group of Americans that does not have the right to vote.

Only after a long struggle did women attain the right to vote in the United States.

Working with Concepts and Generalizations

Identifying Concepts

Read the poem below. Find the words and phrases that help explain what equality means to you. Write them on paper.

My Name Is Equality

My name is Equality.
It takes time for people to understand me.
In fact, many never do.
To some I am just a word, nothing more.
To others I am a dream come true.
To many I am a life-long friend.
To some, a promise that was broken.
Would you like to know who I really am?
I am a doorkeeper.
I stand beside a door called Opportunity.
I invite every man to make as much of his life as he can.
You see, I belong to everyone or I belong to no one.
You cannot claim my benefits for yourself and deny them to others.
If you close the door to schools, or to jobs, or to voting booths, or to housing,
You close the door on another man's opportunities, on his future.
My job is to keep that door open.
And all men must help.
For if you are strong enough to close the door on others,
Someone will be strong enough to close it on you.
Think well before you act.
Are you willing to live without Equality?

Developing Concepts

Write the answers on paper.

1. In your own words, explain the meaning of the last four lines of the poem above.

2. Explain this statement taken from this chapter: "We needed these laws to *make* people treat others fairly."

3. a. If the laws that guarantee equality to American citizens are strictly enforced, all Americans will be equal in certain ways. List as many of these ways as you can.
   b. No matter how many laws are passed to guarantee equality to all Americans, Americans will continue to be unequal in certain ways. List as many of these as you can.

4. You, and probably most of your classmates, are American citizens. Yet you are not permitted to vote. You are not permitted to drive a car. You must go to school, whether you want to or not. There are very few jobs that are available to you and these must not interfere with your education. Should laws be passed to give you an equal opportunity to vote on the things that affect your life? Give good reasons to support your answer.

Generalizations

Read the generalizations below. Find proof to support each one. Tell what the proof is and the page on which you found it. Write on paper.

1. If a government is to be fair to all groups, all groups must have an equal voice in choosing that government.

2. The passing of a law does not guarantee the result promised by that law.

3. Our ideals and values influence our behavior and our judgment of others.

ASBURY
I.U.E.
AFL-CIO
FOR
FULL
EMPLOYMENT
WE
MARCH
FOR
JOBS
FOR ALL
NOW!

Freedom

20

In July 1966, officers of the army and navy of Argentina took over the government of that country. They made a retired army general, Juan Onganía, president. The people of Argentina had nothing to say about this. When a magazine called *Tia Vicenta* criticized the new government, the army closed down the magazine.

A few days later, the military government announced it was taking over the national universities. University officials were given two days to pledge that they would do whatever the government ordered them to. If they did not pledge, they had to resign. The government sent armed policemen to the University of Buenos Aires. They beat students and professors who disagreed with the government. A hundred students were taken to the hospital, and another 150 were arrested and put in jail.

Most Americans believed what happened in Argentina was very wrong. Probably you do, too. But do you know why? The reason has to do with another value that is very important to Americans. That is the value of freedom. This value has a great effect on the way we live and on the way our government works. The value of freedom is what this chapter is about.

USING SOURCE MATERIAL

Everybody has some idea of what freedom is. What is your idea of the meaning of freedom?

Perhaps you can add to your understanding of freedom by studying four examples. Each example contains a different idea about freedom. As you read each one, decide whether you would include that idea in your own definition of freedom.

You have already read the first example — the story about Argentina at the opening of this chapter. What do you think about what happened in Argentina? Do you think the government should have forced the magazine to stop publishing? Why? Should the government have taken over the universities and beaten up people who disagreed with the government? Why?

The second example is a law of one of our states. This is what it says.

All persons shall be entitled to the full and equal enjoyment of the facilities and privileges of inns, restaurants, eating houses, barbershops, public means of travel, theaters and all other places of amusement in this state.

Do you see any idea of freedom in this law? Would you include this idea in your own definition of freedom? Why?

Here is a third example. You may be familiar with a situation like this in your school or local library.

You and your friends are reading in the library. It is quiet. Suddenly several people come in, yelling and making a great deal of noise. The librarian asks them to please be quiet so that people can read. The noisy ones reply, "Why should we? Isn't this a free country? If you force us to be quiet when we want to make noise, you are taking away our freedom."

What do you think of their idea of freedom? Do you agree with them?

In the fourth example we will imagine a case that is similar to many actual events.

One of your classmates decides that he would like to drive the family car. Of course he does not know how to drive, but he gets behind the wheel and starts the motor anyway. The car begins to move down a crowded street. It crashes into some people standing on a sidewalk, and seriously injures three of them. When asked why he was driving the car, your classmate says, "I wanted to, and if I am really free, I should be able to do whatever I want."

Do you agree with him? Why?

What is freedom? Earlier, each member of your class defined freedom. Probably someone in your class said something like this: "Freedom means being able to do anything you want, whenever you want to." After thinking about these four examples, do you want to add anything to your definition?

Let us see how your values and your ideas of freedom helped you decide about each example. Americans believe all peoples have certain rights. These include choosing their own government, saying and writing what they believe, and studying what they wish. If anyone interferes with these rights, he is taking away freedom. That was why you thought the military government in Argentina was wrong. When it refused to let people print a newspaper, and when it beat people who disagreed with the government, it was taking away their freedom. Governments, we believe, should never do this.

In fact, Americans believe one of the jobs of government is to make sure that no one takes away another's freedom. That is what the law in the second example is about. We can certainly agree that having the equal right to use restaurants, barbershops, and theaters is another thing we mean by freedom. As you see, the two values of equality and freedom are closely connected. If a person is not treated equally, has some of his freedom been taken away?

Now all this does not mean that a person is free to do just anything he wants to. Certainly you did not think that the visitors in the library should be free to make all the noise they felt like making. They were interfering with the right of other people to enjoy *their* freedom. And certainly no one has the "freedom" to injure others, as our eleven-year-old driver did.

Do laws keep us free? To make sure that people do not use their freedom in wrong ways, we make rules, or laws. You may think these laws take a little bit of everybody's freedom away, and you are right. But without these laws, no one could have any freedom.

For example, an adult is free to drive a car anywhere he wishes. But how free would he really be without the laws that make people obey stop signs, traffic lights, speeding laws, and parking laws? Imagine how far he could drive if there were no law against parking cars in the middle of the road!

When do we need these laws? If we must have such laws, do we need many of

For the good of all, freedom is often restricted.

415

them, or just a few? The answer to that depends on many conditions. You already know one condition. Remember what you learned about the differences between farm living and city living in early times. In the countryside, were there laws limiting a person's freedom to ride a horse as fast as he wanted? or to get rid of garbage any way he wanted? Why? Were there laws about these things in the city? Why?

As you see, the place where a person would have the freedom to do almost anything would be the South Pole! But if he wanted to live with other people, he would have to accept some laws limiting his freedom. That is the only way everyone can have freedom.

So far we have agreed that a person may use his freedom as he wishes as long as he does not interfere with the freedom of anyone else. Are there any exceptions to the rule?

Suppose one of your classmates announces, "From now on, I am not going to school anymore. I certainly have the freedom to do this, for I am not interfering with anyone else's freedom." Would you agree? There is a law that says your classmate must go to school, whether he wants to or not. Does this law take away his freedom? Do you think it is an unfair law?

There are many other laws that permit adults to do certain things but do not permit children to do the same things. Can you think of any? Are these laws unfair to children? Why? Does experience have anything to do with it?

People Without Freedom

If everyone favors freedom, why do we worry about it so much? The sad fact is that all through history there have been people who favored freedom for themselves, but not for others.

More than two thousand years ago, the Greeks built a great civilization. The Greek people enjoyed a great deal of freedom, but they made slaves of the people they conquered. Certainly the Spanish conquerors did not believe in freedom for the Aztecs.

In our own country, European settlers were concerned about freedom for themselves. Yet they did not worry much about freedom for the Indians they found here or for the Africans they brought here. Even today there are millions of people in lands all over the world who are denied freedom.

Haiti. Most of the time, people who take away the freedom of others use the power of government to do it. There are many governments in the world today that do not let their people live in freedom. The government of Haiti, here in the Western Hemisphere, is an example of one government that restricts freedom.

Haiti is a small nation on an island in the Caribbean Sea. It shares the

In countries like Haiti, where freedom is not respected, people live in fear.

island with another small country, the Dominican Republic. Haiti is a very poor country. It has no industry, and people farm their tiny patches of worn-out soil in primitive fashion. Most of them barely make enough to stay alive. In a year most Haitians earn only as much as most Americans earn in two days. Nearly 90 percent of the population cannot read or write. Most of the people know almost nothing about the world outside their tiny island.

Government by tyrants. The people of Haiti have never had very much freedom. Throughout most of their history their government has been controlled by tyrants. Tyrants are leaders who have complete power over the country. But Haiti has had no tyrant worse than the present ruler, François Duvalier.

In 1957, Duvalier was elected to the presidency of Haiti. Soon after, he dismissed most government officials and replaced them with his own followers. The president also encouraged organized gangs of hoodlums to roam through the countryside killing, robbing, and spreading terror. They took "contributions" from the people for the government. Many Haitians had to flee to other lands. Some came to the United States.

Then Duvalier got rid of the lawmakers and put his own men into power. They make any law he tells them to. After six years, Duvalier decided there would be no more elections. He announced that he would be president for life. Many in Haiti live in fear. They do not dare speak out against the government, for they know they will be beaten, tortured, jailed, or killed.

When kings had complete power. It is not just in our own time that governments have taken away freedoms from the people. In the days when the American colonies were being settled, most European nations were ruled by kings who had complete power over their people. Kings made their own laws, and broke them when they felt like it. They could demand new taxes, without anyone's consent. And the kings never had to explain to anyone how they spent the money. They could put people in jail for any reason at all. They could even execute people if they wished.

English ideas of freedom. That was no longer the case in England, however. When the kings of that country had tried to do such things, the English people had struggled against them. They had made the kings agree that a king no longer had the right to take certain freedoms away from the people.

By the time the colonies were being settled, a king could no longer order a new tax whenever he wanted to. He had to get permission from *Parliament* (pär′ lə ment), which is something like our Congress. In fact, only Parliament, not the king, could make laws for the country. No longer could the king force people to put up soldiers in their homes. No longer could he imprison people who had not broken laws. If an Englishman were accused of breaking the law, he would have a fair trial, and would be judged by other citizens like himself. These were some of the freedoms that Englishmen had won. They were proud of their rights.

Freedom Comes to America

The idea that people had certain rights and freedoms like those became a part of English culture. Freedom was an

The representatives of the colonists of Virginia met in the House of Burgesses to pass laws.

important value to Englishmen. The Englishmen who came to America brought this part of their culture with them, just as they brought their religious beliefs, their thatched roofs, and their wooden plows. The English settlers in America were proud of their rights as Englishmen. Even though they were three thousand miles from England, they felt they should still have those rights and freedoms.

Freedom in the colonies. America was fertile soil in which to plant the value of freedom. Not that all who came here were willing to give others the same freedom they claimed for themselves. Not at the beginning, anyway.

The Puritans, some of our first settlers, had been driven out of England because they did not share the king's religious beliefs. But no sooner had they settled in Massachusetts than they drove out all who did not share *their* religious beliefs. Peaceful Quakers were threatened with death if they did not leave, and Catholics and Jews would never have dreamed of setting foot in the Puritan colony.

But in wilderness America, there was always somewhere else to go. One of the people who fled for his life from Massachusetts was Roger Williams. He started the settlement that became Rhode Island. Williams believed in religious freedom, and in his colony every person was free to worship as he wished. Later, other colonies also had freedom of religion. Do you recall the Charter of Privileges that William Penn wrote for his colony?

If a person did not want to go to one of these colonies, he could always go off into the wilderness and carve out a farm for himself. There he could believe and do whatever he wanted.

How were the colonies governed? At first, the colonies were ruled either by the government in England or by their owners, such as William Penn. Parliament made laws for the colonies, even though the colonists had no voice in choosing the members of Parliament. The king or the owners sent men over to America to be governors of the colonies.

Soon people realized that Parliament could not possibly make all the laws the colonies might need. How could this group of men make laws for a land three thousand miles away that they had never even seen? Just getting a message across the ocean, perhaps telling the colonists of a new law, took six weeks!

Before long, most colonies developed their own lawmaking bodies, or *legislatures*. They were something like small parliaments, and the people in each colony had a chance to vote for the members of its legislature. The legislature made most of the laws for the colony, while Parliament now made just certain important ones.

All in all, the system did not work out badly for the colonists. In those early years, the colonies were quite weak. They depended on England for everything — including protection against other countries. It did not seem unreasonable that the English Parliament should make some laws for them. Often those laws worked out to the benefit of the colonists. Most of the ones that did not were not enforced very well anyway, and the colonists usually ignored them.

A change brings trouble. That arrangement worked smoothly for more than a hundred years. The colonists were satisfied that they still had all the rights and freedoms of Englishmen. Then, in 1764, the English Parliament made a big change in the system of governing the colonies. As it turned out for England, it was a very unwise change.

England had just fought a long war against France. The war was fought in many parts of the world, including the American colonies and Canada. Even though the fighting was at their own back door, the colonists did not give much help to the English. In fact, English soldiers did nearly all the fighting. In the end, England was victorious. She had won a great stretch of land from France. In the New World, she gained all the land between the Appalachian Mountains and the Mississippi River, as well as Canada.

But it had been a costly war. Parliament decided that since the English army and navy had defended the colonies, the colonists should help pay their cost. Therefore, Parliament passed a law requiring the colonists to pay a special tax. Another law required them to provide living quarters and some supplies for the troops who were being sent to America to maintain defense.

This seemed very fair to the English, but the colonists were outraged. The people of England, the colonists said, had struggled for years to win certain rights. Englishmen could only be taxed by Parliament. But because they elected representatives to Parliament, Englishmen had a voice in making the tax laws. Indirectly, then, they gave their consent to being taxed. They could not be forced to provide shelter for soldiers, or keep them in their own homes. Colonists felt that they too were Englishmen and should have all the rights of Englishmen. What right did Parliament have to tax the colonists? What gave Parliament the right to force them to shelter soldiers? The colonists were not represented in Parliament, so they certainly had not given their consent.

Besides, many colonists wondered, why was England sending so many troops to the colonies? The war with France was over. The troops were not needed—unless England was planning to take away the colonists' freedoms. England was not planning any such thing, of course, but the colonists came to believe she was.

Colonists often attacked English tax collectors.

The colonists refuse to obey. The colonists refused to obey the tax law. They decided to stop buying English goods unless the tax law was repealed, or taken back. This worked. Parliament repealed the law the next year. But it also insisted that it had the right to pass such a law again any time it wanted to. So even though things quieted down a bit, the argument between the colonists and the Parliament over colonial freedoms was not really settled.

Meanwhile, English troops remained in the colonies. Seeing the troops on their streets night and day angered the colonists and made them feel their freedoms were being threatened. One March day in 1770, a crowd of Bostonians taunted the British troops and threw snowballs at them. The troops lost their temper and fired into the crowd, killing five. This deed, which was soon called the Boston Massacre, angered the colonists still more. When England passed other tax laws, the colonists again refused to obey, insisting their English freedoms were being taken away.

England adopts strong measures. This time the English government tried to force the colonists to obey. It tried punishing some colonies by not allowing their legislatures to make laws or even to meet. It punished Massachusetts, which was the leader of the opposition, with several harsh laws. One law closed the harbor of Boston to all trade. Another said that the king would appoint that colony's lawmakers.

This proved to the colonists that the mother country really was trying to take away their freedom. Of course, they exaggerated, for Parliament certainly was not trying to make them slaves. But the English government did insist that Parliament, not the colonial legislatures, would keep making important laws for the colonies.

When the colonies had been young and weak, they had been willing to accept that, but not now. They said that only people elected by the colonial legislatures had the right to make laws for the colonies.

Before long, disagreements led to angry words, and angry words led to fighting. In 1775, British troops and colonists started firing on each other. After a year of fighting, the colonists finally decided to declare their independence. On July 4, 1776, the colonies adopted the Declaration of Independence, the famous document written by Thomas Jefferson. From then on, they were not merely fighting for their rights as Englishmen. They were fighting to be a free and independent nation.

Forming a New Government

After the American colonies won their independence, they had to set up a new national government of their own.

What kind of government should it be? How much power should the government have over the people? Certainly not *too* much, for then it might take away their freedoms. After all, hadn't the colonists just fought a long war to be free of such a government?

On the other hand, the government must have enough power to make the people obey its laws. If people do not obey laws, as we have seen, there will be *less* freedom for everybody instead of more.

Controlling the powers of the government. That was a difficult problem for the men who founded the government. They solved it in two ways. First, they decided to have a written constitution, or supreme law of the land. It said what the government would and would not be allowed to do.

For example, the writers of the Constitution of the United States would allow the government to raise an army, since an army might be needed someday to protect our nation. They also gave the new government the right to collect certain kinds of taxes. Without taxes, the government could not pay its expenses.

But they also wrote in the Constitution that the government cannot take away a person's property without paying a fair price for it. Neither could the government put anyone in jail during peacetime without a hearing by a court.

In other words, the men who wrote the Constitution said, "The government of the United States is being created to serve the people, not to be their master. These are the powers the people of the nation are willing to give to this government, but that is all." If any future leaders tried to take too much power, the people could always point to the Constitution and say, "You cannot."

The separation of powers. The second way the founders of our nation solved the problem of government control was to separate the powers of government into three parts, or branches, and put different people in charge of each.

One branch was the Presidency, or the executive. The second branch was the Congress, or the legislative. The third was the courts, or the judicial. The idea was that each branch would have power to do only certain things.

For example, Congress could make national laws, but it could not punish people for not obeying them. The President had the job of carrying out the laws, but he did not have the power to make them. The courts had the power of punishment if the national laws were broken. But they were not given the job of making laws.

If any one branch of government tried to take over the job of another branch, the other two would be able to stop it. It was like a door that needs three keys to open it. Each branch of

Separation of Powers

Executive Branch

THE PRESIDENT

Appoints Justices, grants pardons

Approves or vetoes bills, may call special sessions of Congress, may recommend legislation, heads a political party

Judicial Branch

SUPREME COURT AND OTHER FEDERAL COURTS

Interprets laws and treaties

Decides whether laws are constitutional

Legislative Branch

CONGRESS

Passes laws, may override vetos, confirms presidential appointments, approves treaties, may impeach President

Creates federal courts, approves appointments of justices, may impeach justices, may propose constitutional amendments to override decisions of Supreme Court

---

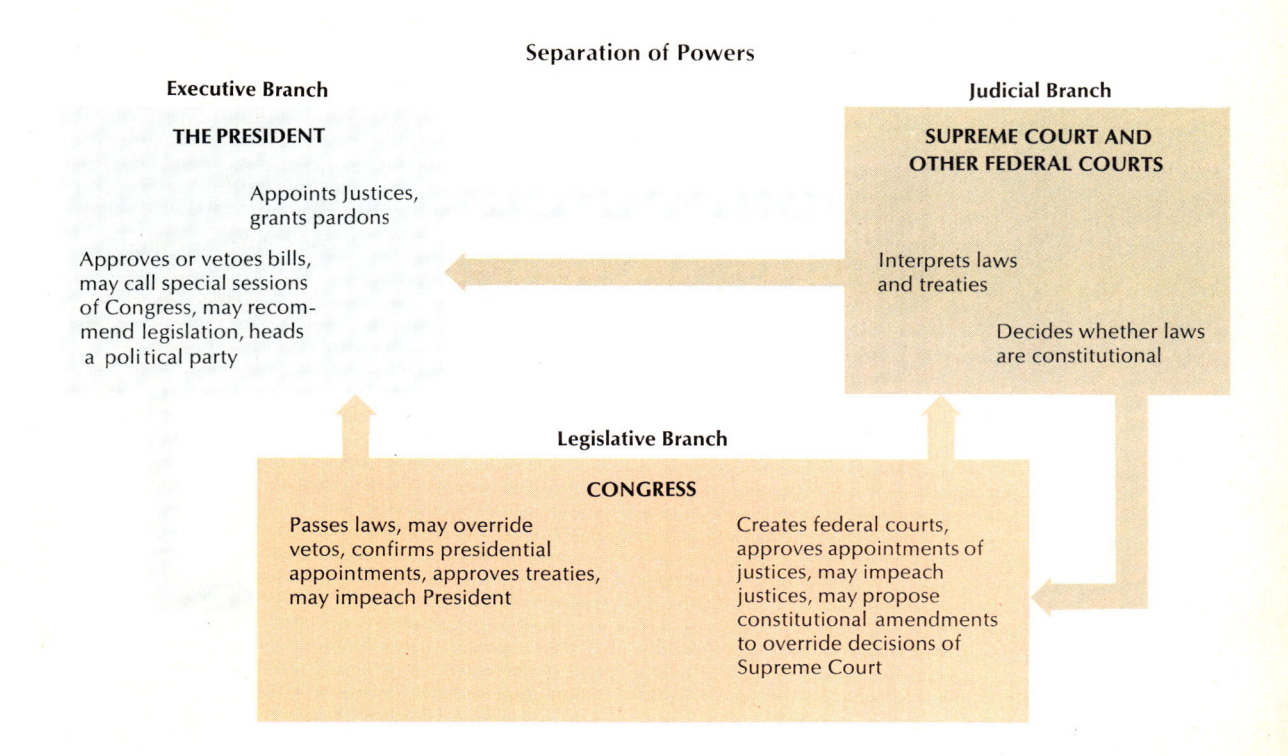

government was given only one key. None of the three could open the door without the other two. If the three cooperated, and one did not try to seize too much power from the other two, the door could be opened and government would work.

The Bill of Rights. With all this protection, you might think that Americans of that time felt safe enough. Many did, but not all. After the Constitution was written, some still feared that the government's power might someday be used to take away the freedoms of the people. They would not agree to this Constitution, they said, unless more safeguards for their freedoms were added to it.

The right of people to worship as they please should be guaranteed in writing, they insisted. The government must not interfere with a citizen's right to say or print what he wishes. People should be protected from having their homes broken into by the government and searched.

Because some men insisted, the guarantees of these other freedoms were added to the Constitution. Additions to the Constitution are called amendments. Ten of these amendments were added at the same time. Together they are known as the Bill of Rights.

The Constitution became official in 1789, and the Bill of Rights, two years later. They have served us well for nearly two hundred years. Time has proven how wise the authors were. They created a government that could work, but that did not take away freedom.

Of course, there have always been some Americans who would gladly deny others the right to speak freely or to have a fair trial. But the Constitution and the Bill of Rights, the great protectors of our freedom, stand in their way.

The Meaning of Freedom Grows

Americans of those years had good reason to be proud of their freedoms. For most of them, America was the freest country in all the world. But as we saw when we studied equality, the value of freedom did not include all Americans. In fact, you will remember that many lived their lives, not in freedom, but in its opposite—slavery.

Freedom for blacks. Earlier in this book you read the story of how Americans came to oppose slavery. You may remember the part that the abolitionists played. The abolitionists were a small group in the 1830's, and very few people agreed with them at first. In fact, some Americans disagreed so strongly that they tried to take away the freedom of the abolitionists to speak and write their beliefs. Some slaveholding states passed laws to jail any abolitionists who even entered the state!

Gradually, however, more and more white Americans came to agree with the abolitionists that the slavery of black Americans was wrong. The reason, of course, was the value of freedom. They realized that America could not boast of being a land of freedom so long as it permitted one man to own another. As you read in Chapter 5, slavery was finally ended in the United States in 1865, after the Civil War.

Limiting Freedom to Protect Our Rights

By the end of the Civil War, the two big "isms" you have studied, urbanism and industrialism, were rapidly coming to America. These "isms" caused Americans to change some of their ideas about freedom. Let us see how.

Why limit freedom? Try to recall some of the ways that an urban, industrial society is different from a rural, farming society. You will remember that one big difference is in the density of population. As you saw earlier in this chapter, the more closely people live together, the more rules and laws they need. Do you remember some of the laws passed by America's earliest cities and towns more than three hundred years ago? Why were these laws passed? As cities grew larger in the late 1800's, many more such laws had to be passed. These laws took away a person's freedom to do just anything he might want to, but everyone knew they were needed.

Another important reason that our urban, industrial societies are different is that we depend on others for so many things in our daily living. In fact, our health, our safety, and even our lives depend on many other people — usually people we do not even know or see. Is the canned food we buy free of germs? Our medicines — are we sure they are pure and safe to use? Are the tires on our cars built well enough so they will not blow out at high speeds? Do we know the person who packed our can of food, mixed our bottle of medicine, or built our tire?

Using the government to protect freedom. These changes in our way of living have caused Americans to think hard about what the job of their government should be. In the early days, remember, Americans felt their government should not make too many laws, for they might interfere with freedom. But because of urbanism and industrialism, people came to realize that certain laws were needed. In order to protect the rights, safety, and health of most, the laws would have to limit the freedom of some. In Chapter 17 you saw examples of such laws. Employers no longer had the "freedom" to use unsafe machinery in factories, to employ young children, or to pay lower wages than the law required.

Today we have many laws like these. Manufacturers of foods and medicines do not have the freedom to sell unhealthful products. Companies do not have the freedom to pollute the air and water. Sellers do not have the freedom to cheat customers by telling lies in their advertisements. None of us have the freedom to litter the highways, or to use poisons carelessly.

In the last chapter we saw that laws limiting a person's freedom are sometimes needed for another reason — to protect everyone's equal rights. For example, an apartment-house owner has the freedom to rent his apartments to anyone he wants, but our laws now

Government inspection of food protects people.

say he does not have the freedom to refuse to rent to people just because of their race or religion. If we did not limit the apartment owner's freedom this way, could we live by our value of equality?

Some people believe we now have too many such laws. They say we are protecting people too much, and the government is limiting our freedom too much. Others feel that these laws are necessary. In fact, many believe we need even more such laws in our modern society to protect people further.

USING SOURCE MATERIAL

Over the years, Americans have given newer meanings to the idea of freedom just as they have to the idea of equality. Today we believe freedom must mean more than not being a slave. Some say it must even mean more than having the right to speak freely. Here is how one person might explain his feelings about freedom.

You call me free? Sure, I'm no slave, and I can knock the government without going to jail. Big deal. What am I free to do? Take a ride in the country whenever I want to? I don't have a car. Go to the movies or a fancy restaurant? Who can afford that? They say I'm free to rent a decent place to live. Only trouble is there ain't a decent place to live in this whole city, that a man like me can afford. With the pay I get, I'm lucky to stay alive, never mind enjoying freedom.

This man seems to be saying that freedom to do many things does not mean anything if you cannot afford them. Would you agree, or disagree, with this man's idea of what freedom is? Why? Would you say his case is the same as, or different from, the case of the man who was "free" to quit his low-paid job in the mines or factories? If we are to give freedom new meaning today, what sorts of things do you think our society will have to do to make more freedom for all?

These words were spoken by a Mexican-American college student from Hidalgo, Texas. They show that the idea of freedom has still another meaning for him.

My ancestors came from one of the most civilized nations in the world. I'm not going to forget what they taught me. I'm proud of being an American but I won't become a gringo. Now they're offering us equality. That's fine. I want to be equal before the law and have a chance to make money if I choose. But the Anglos are denying me the right to be myself. They want me to be like them. I want the chance to be a Mexican-American and to be proud of that Mexican bit. The Anglos offer us equality but whatever happened to freedom?

What is this person's idea of freedom?

Working with Concepts and Generalizations

Identifying Concepts

Complete each sentence. Write on paper.

1. The first ten amendments to the United States Constitution are called the _____.
2. _____ are leaders who have complete control over a country.
3. In England the laws are made by _____.
4. Settlers in Rhode Island were guaranteed _____ freedom.
5. The three branches of the United States government are the _____, the _____, and the _____.

Write T if the statement is true; write F if the statement is false.

6. Industrialism and urbanism caused Americans to change some of their ideas about freedom.
7. Puritans were willing to give others the same freedom they claimed for themselves.
8. If all men are to be free, each must give up some of his freedom.
9. People who take away the freedom of others often use the power of government to do it.
10. The idea that all people have certain rights was part of the English culture.

Developing Concepts

Write the answers on paper.

1. List the measures that François Duvalier, ruler of Haiti, used to take away the freedoms of the Haitian people.
2. How did the growth of industrialism in the United States cause American citizens to change some of their ideas about freedom? List some of the kinds of laws that were passed as a result of industrialism.
3. You have learned that most of the people of Haiti know almost nothing about the world outside their tiny island. Does this fact help explain why Haiti is ruled the way it is? Explain your answer.
4. List five things you and your family are free to do because you are American citizens. Look at the list you have made. Write it again. This time, list first the freedom that is most important to you. List the second most important freedom next, and so on. Which freedom on your list would you be most unwilling to give up? Why?
5. Draw a picture or write a poem or a story that explains what freedom means to you. Be as creative as you can.
6. The idea that all men have certain rights was important to American colonists. How did this idea influence their decision to refuse to pay taxes to England and to fight a war for independence from England?

Generalizations

Read the generalizations listed below. Find proof to support each generalization. Tell what the proof is and the page on which you found it.

1. Ideas about freedom and equality change and develop as people change their ways of living and thinking.
2. When people live in groups, laws are necessary to protect the freedom of all members of the group.
3. A government must be given the power it needs to carry out its duties and it must accept the responsibility for use of that power.

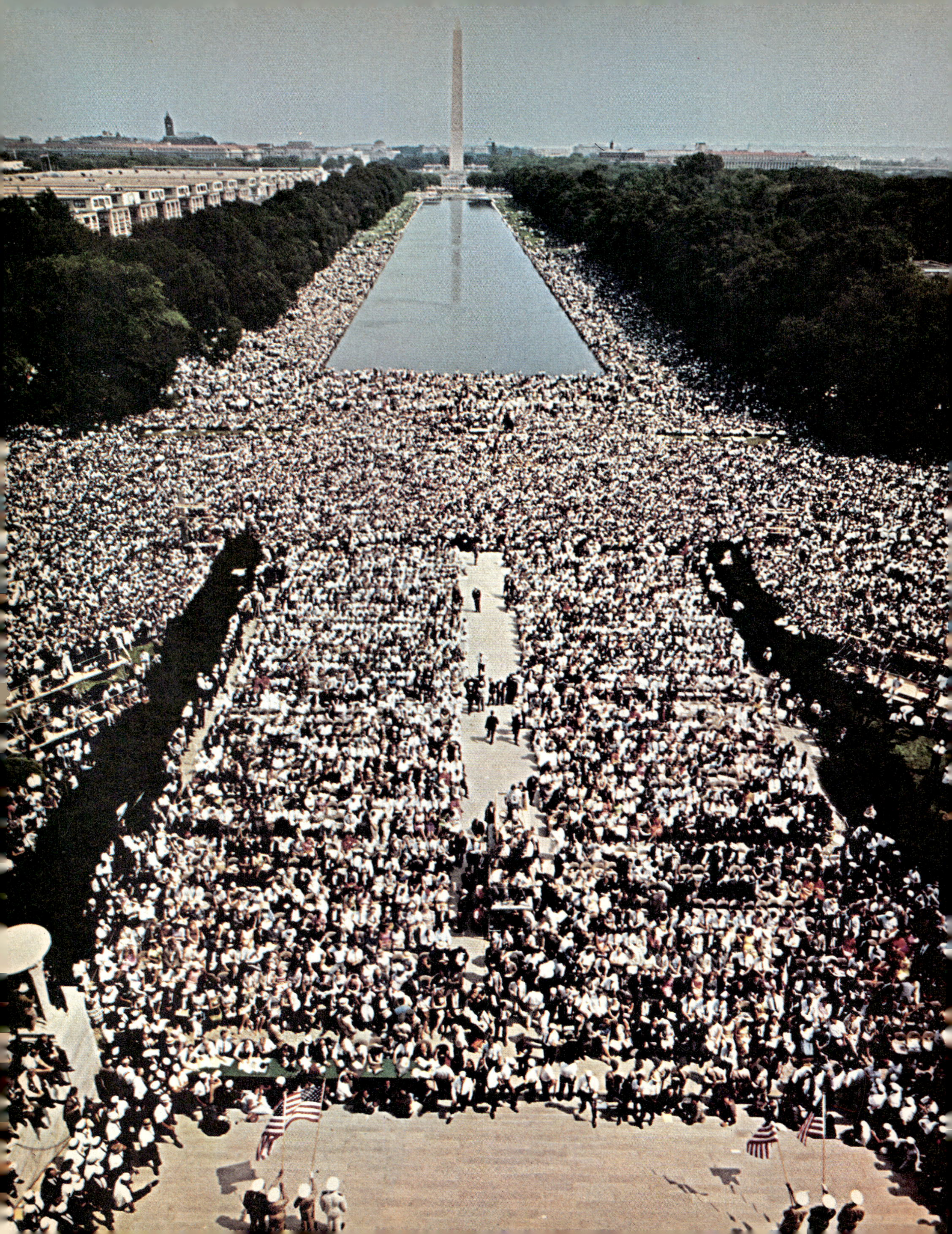

21

Democracy

In 1960 the people of the United States elected a President, just as they do every four years. The two major candidates were John F. Kennedy and Richard M. Nixon. Both men worked very hard to persuade people to vote for them. Thousands of their supporters gave a great deal of money to pay for television, billboard, and newspaper advertisements to win votes.

On November 8, 1960, more than 68 million Americans voted. John Kennedy won the election by a very small margin.

At noon on January 20, 1961, Mr. Kennedy officially took office as President. Everyone in the United States, including Mr. Nixon and the 34 million people who voted for him, agreed that Mr. Kennedy had won fairly and should take office.

This story about an election seems normal to us. Yet in most countries in the world this is not how governments are chosen at all. Many countries have no elections. In others, elections are held, and then the loser gets the army's help and seizes control of the government anyway.

Why don't these things happen in the United States? The reason can be found in another value that is important to Americans — democracy.

Making Laws in a Democracy

Earlier in the book you saw that we often needed laws in order to have equality. We need laws to provide education and job training, and laws to protect people against unfair treatment. Laws are also needed to allow people to enjoy their freedoms.

If laws are so important to us, then we must know who is going to make them. If a king of three hundred years ago or the present president of Haiti were to make them, would the laws protect our rights and our freedom?

Who should make our laws? What do Americans believe about the way laws should be made and who should make them? This example will show you.

Suppose your teacher announces that there are two possibilities for a class field trip. One is the zoo and the other is the art museum. How should the decision be made? You will almost certainly say that the members of the class should decide by voting. Whichever side gets the majority of the votes will win. Now you may have to think hard about *what* your decision will be, but you do not have to think at all about *how* the decision should be made.

You would not say that the school principal should decide, or that only the boys should vote, or that just the people with red hair should decide. *Of course* the class should decide. *Of course* everyone should vote. *Of course* the side with the majority should win. And *of course* the minority, the side with fewer votes, will accept the decision and go along with the majority.

Because of your values, you do not have to think about how the decision should be made. In our society we believe decisions should be made that way, and you have been brought up with that same value. That value is belief in democracy.

Democracy and equality go together. The two values of democracy and equality are closely related. When you said that the class should make the decision, you meant that everyone should be equal and have one vote. That is why you can accept a democratic decision, even if your side loses.

In a democracy everyone should be equal and have one vote. This man has just voted for his choice.

Suppose you lost because some of the children on your side were not allowed to vote, or because each person on the other side was allowed five votes while each person on your side had only one. The winning side would still have a majority of the votes, but would you say the decision was made fairly? Would you be willing to accept a decision made with this kind of voting?

You would say that people had not been treated with equality, and therefore, the decision was not really democratic. As you see, the idea that everyone should have an equal vote is one of the things we mean by democracy.

How Does Democracy Work?

In the United States we have a democratic government. It is much more difficult to run a country democratically than it is to decide where a class will go on a field trip. Your class has about thirty people in it, but there are more than 200 million people in the United States. And governing a country requires making many, many decisions, not just a single one. How can so many people take part in making so many decisions?

Choosing a few to speak for the many. The American colonies faced this same problem when the population was much smaller. At first it was possible for all the people of a community to

Town meetings in Boston were not always orderly affairs. The people felt free to express themselves on any matter discussed.

attend a town meeting. They could all help make their own laws. A number of towns, especially in New England, did this. Some small towns, in fact, do that today. But that could not be done when the towns grew into cities of many people. And even while the villages and towns were still small, an entire colony could not govern itself in this way. How could all the people in the colony of Virginia or New York be expected to travel hundreds of miles to gather in one place and make laws?

An idea the settlers brought with them from England solved this problem. It was the idea of *representative government.* In this form of government, people choose representatives to make laws and to govern for them. England had long used the representative idea to choose members of Parliament. The colonists adopted the same idea for choosing their colonial legislatures. We have had representative government in America ever since.

Just because the legislatures were representative, though, did not mean they were democratic. In those days, democracy was not held as an important value by many people in America. Few people were allowed to vote. Do you remember which groups were left out?

Today most Americans strongly believe in democracy. We elect our representatives democratically. Everyone over a certain age is allowed to vote. We call our government a *representative democracy.*

We elect representatives for many different offices in our government. We choose people to represent us on a city council or town council. They make laws for our community. We elect representatives to the state legislature to make laws for our state. We also elect a governor to lead the state. For our national government, we elect representatives to the House of Representatives and the Senate, which are the two parts of Congress. They make laws for the whole nation. And of course we also elect the President of the United States.

Representatives serve the people. In a representative democracy like ours, the men and women who are elected are expected to follow the wishes of the majority that elected them. But what if the representatives, once they are in office, ignore the people's wishes and make laws to suit themselves? In a democracy the majority is supposed to rule. But if the representatives re-

Representatives, such as Mrs. Chisholm of New York City, meet the people as often as possible.

fuse to do what the majority wants, then the majority is not ruling anymore, is it?

How do we make sure this does not happen? One way we make sure is by having new elections every few years. If your representative wants to serve another term of office, he must be elected again. He must try to persuade the voters that he deserves another term. Certainly he will not succeed if he has refused to pay attention to the voters' wishes. Regular elections are an important part of a representative democracy. If we voted only once for our representatives, and then they served for life, would we still have a representative democracy?

Making Your Voice Heard

Of course we do not have elections every week. Our Constitution says that every member of the House of Representatives serves for two years, and every member of the Senate for six years. The President of the United States serves for four years. That is a long time to have representatives vote against your wishes. Do the people in a democracy have any voice in government between elections? Is there any

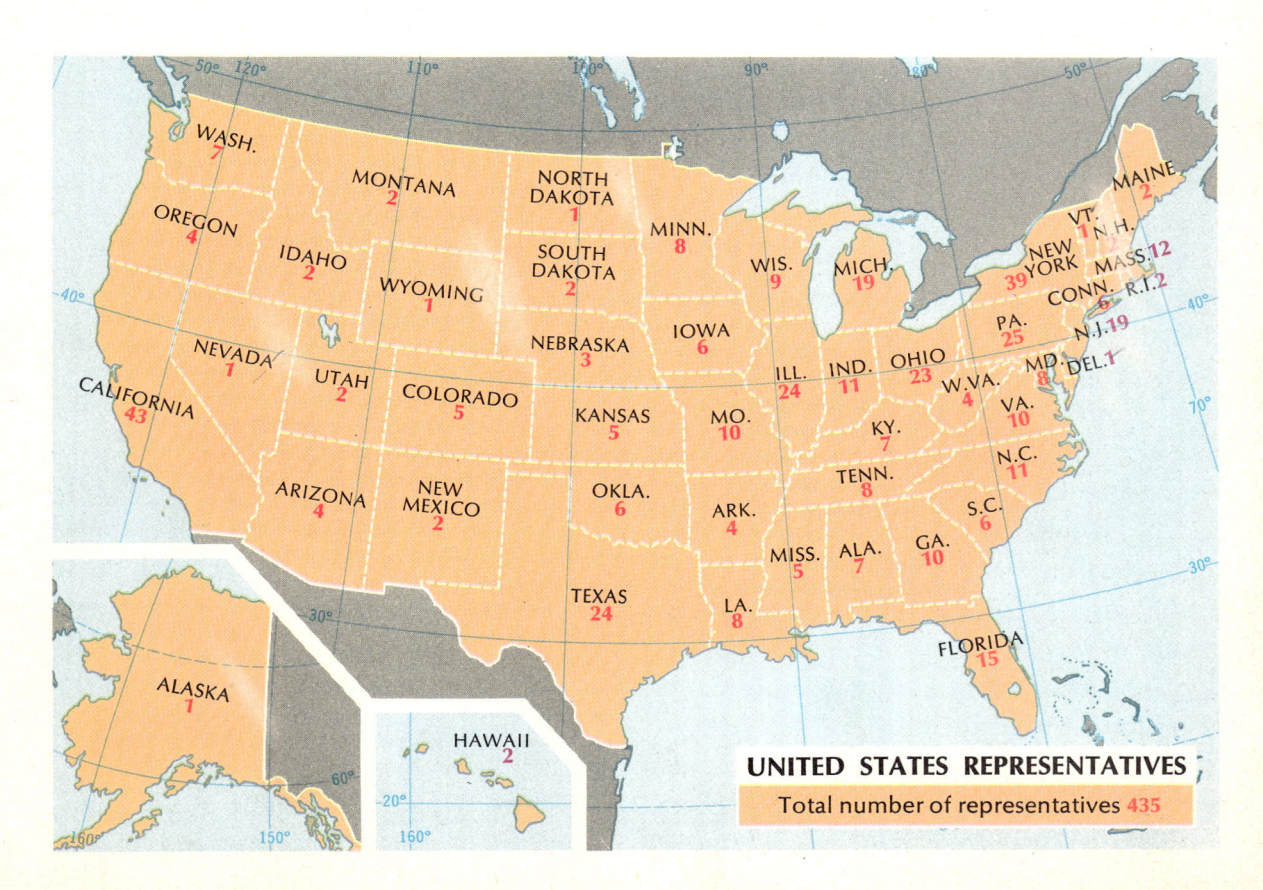

UNITED STATES REPRESENTATIVES
Total number of representatives 435

way they can influence the representatives to vote according to their wishes?

A citizen takes action. Here is an example of the way citizens can influence their representatives.

The government has announced a plan to build a new airport on land that is now set aside for wildlife. Mr. Jones is strongly opposed to this plan. The wildlife area has been a wonderful place to visit. There, away from the noise and hurry of modern city life, people have been able to relax and enjoy watching the many rare birds and small animals. The airport would mean the end of this relaxing spot and the end of the rare birds and animals. Mr. Jones reads in the newspapers that his representative in Congress is in favor of the plan.

Immediately, Mr. Jones writes to his congressman and urges him to oppose the airport plan. Mr. Jones knows that the congressman welcomes mail from the people he represents, for he wants to know what they think about the issues he has to vote on.

Mr. Jones also knows that if the congressman receives enough letters opposing the plan, he will think carefully before voting for it. If he goes against the wishes of a great many people, they might not vote for him in the next election. Mr. Jones also gets a number of other people who feel as he does to sign a petition, or statement, urging the congressman to oppose the airport.

Strength in numbers. Then Mr. Jones joins with other citizens to form a group to oppose the government's plan. The group calls itself the Citizens' Committee to Save the Wildlife Area. This group does many things that would be difficult for Mr. Jones to do by himself. It collects money for newspaper advertisements to inform other voters about the danger to the wildlife area. The group also holds public meetings for the same purpose. It even sponsors a peaceful protest march from the wildlife area to the city hall. The committee hopes that because of these activities, more citizens will oppose the airport plan.

The citizens' committee also makes a careful study showing that the airport could be located in several other places without destroying the wildlife area. It sends copies of this study to the newspaper and to the congressman.

By organizing with a group, Mr. Jones is able to make his own voice in government much louder. He is able to have more influence than he could have by himself. As a result of all these efforts by Mr. Jones and his friends, the congressman decides to vote against building the new airport in the wildlife area.

Is it fair? Another resident of the area, Mr. Smith, was in favor of the airport

Senator Brooke of Massachusetts discusses his views with voters.

plan. But he did not bother to write to his congressman or to join any groups. As he sees Mr. Jones doing all these things to oppose the airport, he complains, "That is not fair. Why should Jones be allowed to have more influence in government than I have? I am a voter, too, and should have an equal voice in government."

The answer to Mr. Smith is that if he cares about the airport, he has the right to do all he can to influence his representatives. If he does not care enough to do anything, he should not complain about Mr. Jones's actions. A healthy democracy depends on citizens, such as Mr. Jones, who take an active part in their community. If our representatives know what we are thinking, they are better able to represent us. It is fair for people to write letters, sign petitions, hold rallies, and organize into groups to influence their representatives, so long as everybody else has an equal right to do the same. There is our value of equality again.

The kind of organizing that Mr. Jones did takes place all the time in our democracy. Many organizations are active all year round. Airplane manufacturers, labor unions, railroads, schoolteachers, religious groups, and a thousand others have permanent organizations. These organizations have special groups called *lobbies*. Mr. Jones and his committee were trying to influence only their own representative, but lobbies try to influence many congressmen and other government officials. The big organizations hire many people to work all year round as lobbyists. Many lobbies have offices in the nations' capital as well as in many state capitals.

Democracy Needs Laws

As you have seen, democracy is an important value to Americans. Because it is, we have worked hard to make our government a democratic one. But just as with the other two values we have been studying, democracy can only work if people agree to certain rules.

The minority must follow the rules. What are some of these rules? The most important one is that everyone must accept the results of a vote. That is easy for the majority to do, of course. But the minority, the losers, must accept too—whether the vote is on a class field trip, a plan to build an airport, or the election of a president.

Why is this so? Is it because we think losers should be "good sports"? There are more important reasons than that. If losers do not accept the result of a fair vote and say they are going to have their way anyway, what is the sense of voting? Wouldn't it be silly to vote on where to go for a class trip if the vote did not decide anything? Why waste time on an election if the loser is going to take control of the government anyway? If we could not all agree that the loser must accept the result of a vote, democracy would soon be dead.

Democracy offers a second chance. There is another reason why losers in an election should accept the results. As long as there are more elections, losers will have another chance. If they can convince enough people to vote for them the next time, the minority can become the majority.

In Chapter 12 you read about Mayor Richard Lee of New Haven. Do you recall how many times Mr. Lee was defeated before he finally won election as mayor? The last defeat was by only two votes! But than Lee was elected and did such a good job that the people elected him seven more times! At the beginning of this chapter, you read about the election of 1960, when Richard Nixon was narrowly defeated for the Presidency. In 1968 Mr. Nixon ran for the Presidency again. Again the vote was close, but this time Richard Nixon was elected President of the United States.

Even if Mayor Lee and Richard Nixon had not won, they still would have had to accept the election results. Otherwise we could not have democracy.

Does this mean the minority must change its opinions? Not at all. The minority may still believe its candidate would have been a better representative, or believe the law the majority adopted is an unwise law, or believe the policy of the government is unjust. And the minority has the right to try to change the law or the policy.

In a democracy, we expect that people may disagree with their government. A person may disagree very strongly. He may make speeches criticizing his government, or march in protest, or do many other things, so long as he does not interfere with other people's freedoms. If people did not have these rights, democracy would not work very well.

The majority follows rules, too. So far we have looked at rules the minority must accept. Does the majority have to accept any rules, too? Let us see.

Television offers candidates an opportunity to reach millions of people.

Candidates encourage as many people as possible to vote. Here Mr. Nixon greets his supporters.

Suppose a high school class has saved money during the year and is now deciding how to spend it. There are more boys than girls in the class. All the boys vote together and, as the majority, decide to use the money to buy footballs and baseballs. Is this fair? Of course it is, say the boys. The vote was democratic — everyone had an equal vote — and the majority should rule.

That's true, the girls reply, but just because the boys are in the majority does not mean they can do whatever they want. Who is right?

The democratic rule was followed, it is true. But we certainly can agree that the result was very unfair to the girls. Why should they agree to a democracy if the result will always leave them with nothing at all?

You can see that if we expect democracy to work, the majority cannot do just anything it wishes. It has to govern for *all* the people, not just for itself. If it does not, the minority will have no reason to want to live by democratic rules. Can you think of some way of spending the money so that the boys could have pleased the girls?

USING SOURCE MATERIAL

One of the most precious rights of Americans is the right to vote. You might think that everybody would be sure to use this right. But the surprising fact is that in this country only about half the people who are entitled to vote ever do so. In some countries that have democratic elections, such as England, France, Belgium, and Italy, more than 80 percent of the people vote.

Why do so few Americans use this right? There are several answers. One is that, in some areas of the country, black Americans have just recently been allowed to vote, and it will take time before all of them do so. But probably the main reason for the small number who vote can be seen in the two quotations that follow. These are replies given by two different people to the question, why don't you vote in our elections?

The first man said:

I don't know. I guess I'm just too busy with other things. I never have paid much attention to government anyway, and I don't know much about what's going on. But it doesn't seem to make much difference, does it? I mean, I've got a good job and I'm doing fine, and the country is going all right too, and I haven't voted yet. So I don't see why I should start now, do you?

The second man said:

Why should I? What difference does it make who gets elected? They're all the same. Just a bunch of politicians. They spend a lot of time making laws to do this and do that and they blah blah blah a lot, but what do they care about folks like me? What did they ever do for me? Look at this rattrap I live in. What is the government doing about that? We got laws that say the owners of these buildings are supposed to keep them safe and keep the plumbing working. You just go in there and see how that plumbing works. You think the government will make the owners live up to the law and fix up these things? Are you kidding? They pass lots of fancy laws, but they don't mean a thing. It's all a big show. They care as much about me as the man in the moon.

What do you think of each person's reasons? Do you think one has better reasons than the other for not voting? Is there anything you might say to persuade either one of them that he should take part in government?

Why the need for rules? Are there any other rules majorities must accept? To answer this, think of all the things a majority might be able to do once it gained control of the government. It might pass a law that there would be no more elections. That way the minority would never get a chance to win. Or the majority might pass laws that would take away the property of the minority, or that would forbid them to practice their own religion, or that would forbid free speech. In other words, if there were no rules for the majority, majority rule could become as bad as rule by the worst kind of tyrant.

In our country, most of the rules the majority must accept are written in the United States Constitution and in the Bill of Rights. You will remember that these documents spell out what the government—which represents the majority—can and cannot do.

The government cannot call off elections. It cannot take away the right to vote. It cannot take away the right to hold property, or to have a fair trial.

Can you remember some of the other things the majority is not allowed to do?

Protecting the values we cherish. Someone once said that democracy is like a delicate plant. It must be planted in good soil, and then carefully cultivated if it is to stay healthy. Otherwise it will soon wither and die.

There are people in many lands who know how true that is. Some have never had a chance to take part in governing themselves. Others have had democracy in the past, but the delicate plant was not cultivated and it withered and died. In other lands the carefully cultivated plant has been crushed by the boots of a conqueror.

America, with its values of equality, freedom, and democracy, has provided good soil. The plant has been cultivated carefully, and it has produced a fine flower. But the job of cultivation never ends. We have to try to live by our values, and we must be sure our government lives by them, too. Then we can be reasonably sure that democratic government will work for all the people. And then, hopefully, all the people will work for democratic government.

Those people who appreciate the right to vote and use it are helping to safeguard democracy.

Working with Concepts and Generalizations

Identifying Concepts

Write T if the statement is true; write F if the statement is false.

1. The American colonists were the first to use the idea of representative government.
2. In a democracy, the government has the right to decide whether elections will be held.
3. In a democratic society, the minority has the right to try to change the law.
4. Lobbies are organized to try to influence congressmen and other government officials.
5. In a democracy, all citizens are expected to agree with the laws and policies of their government.
6. There are no rules that tell the majority what it can and cannot do.
7. In the United States, every citizen who is eligible to vote must vote in every local and national election.
8. The colonial legislatures were democratic.
9. Those elected to be representatives are expected to follow the wishes of the people they represent.
10. In a democracy, the government has the right to take away freedom of speech if the citizens criticize the government unfairly.

Developing Concepts

Write the answers on paper.

1. Explain this statement: "Regular elections are an important part of representative democracy."
2. Your class elects a representative to the student council. He will represent your class for the first half of the school year. At the beginning of the year, the student council announces it will vote on this question: Should members of the student body be allowed to decide how they will dress for school? Your class instructs its representative to vote Yes. The student council defeats the measure. There were 5 Yes votes and 6 No votes. Your representative voted No.
   a. What measures can the class take to make sure its representative follows its wishes in the future?
   b. Are these measures ones that should be taken in a democratic society?
3. List some of the rules a majority must follow if democracy is to work.
4. You have taken part in making democratic decisions. Perhaps you did this as a member of your family, as a member of your class, or as a member of an organization. Think of one situation in which you helped make a democratic decision. Tell what the situation was. What issue was being decided? How was the decision made? Were you willing to accept the decision? Were you a member of the majority, or the minority?

Generalizations

Read the generalizations below. Find proof to support each one. Tell what the proof is and the page on which you found it.

1. A democratic government receives its power from the people it governs.
2. Democracy can work only if people agree to obey certain rules.
3. In a large democratic nation, the work of government is best done by representatives elected by the people.

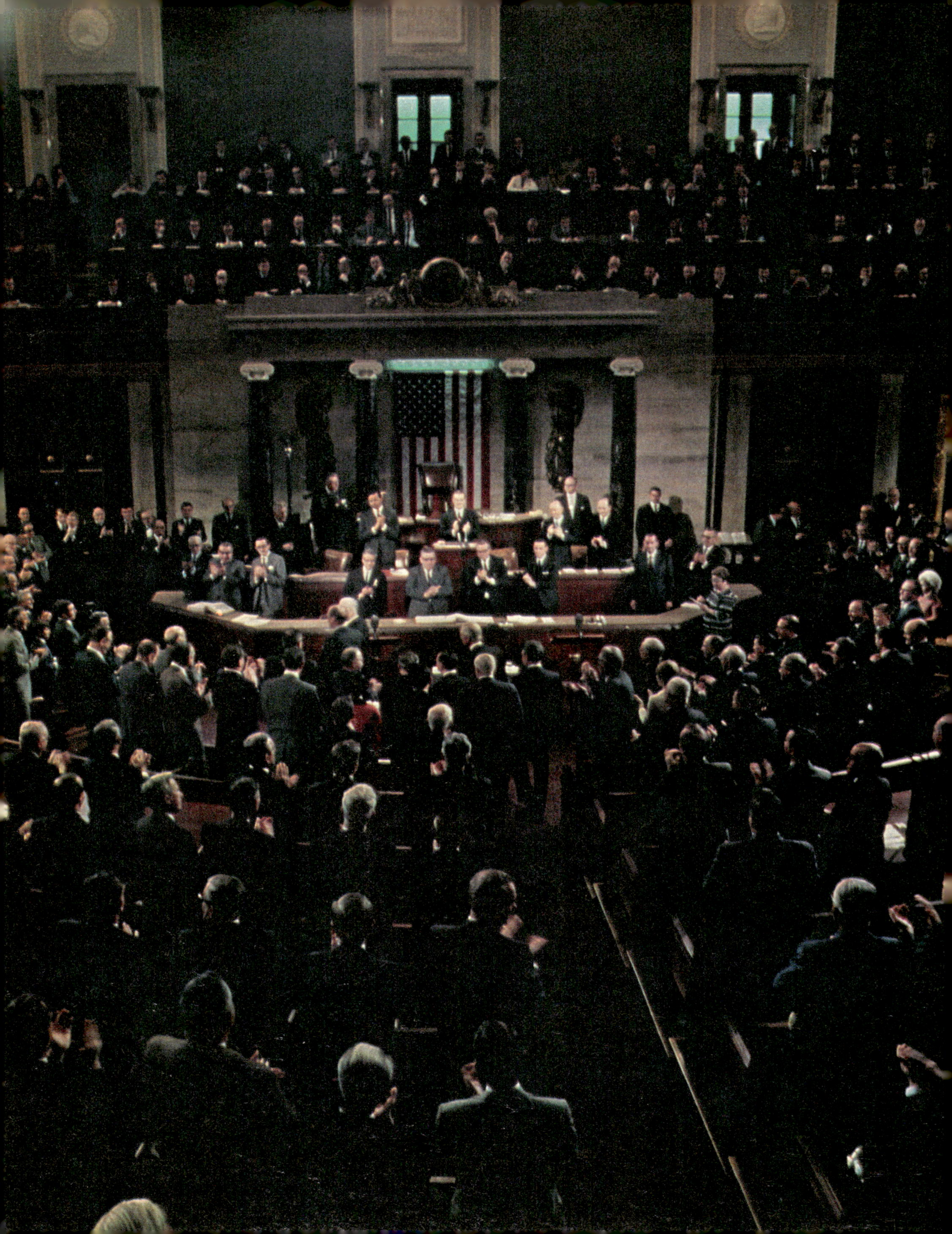

Making a Decision in a Democracy

22

In a democracy, the majority rules. This sounds quite simple. But often it is not. Sometimes it is difficult for lawmakers to know exactly what the majority wishes. And sometimes it is possible to have two "majorities."

For example, the majority of people in a city might favor a certain project, such as a new road. They honestly feel it is for the good of the entire city. But the road will bring hardship to the neighborhood in which it is to be built. The majority of people in that neighborhood oppose the road. Which majority does a leader follow in making a decision—the one in the neighborhood or the one in the entire city?

There are also times when a law does not help very many people at the time it is passed. In fact, it may cause hardship for some. However, it will help future generations. Should a lawmaker vote for this law?

We will study two cases in which lawmakers meet such problems in making a decision in a democracy. In one case it is the mayor of Philadelphia who had to make the decision. In the other it is the United States Congress.

Bringing Change to Philadelphia

In Chapter 7 of this book you read about the early years of the city of Philadelphia. You will remember that even by 1776 Philadelphia had changed greatly from the "green country town" that William Penn had planned many years before. Today, with a population of two million in the city and four million in the metropolitan area, Philadelphia ranks as the nation's fourth largest city.

Size is not the only change in Philadelphia. Over the years much of the downtown area had become old and run-down. The people of Philadelphia wanted to be proud of their city, so they decided to take action. They welcomed the urban renewal programs of their mayors. These programs restored much of the beauty of early Philadelphia. They also brought many modern buildings to the downtown area.

In most cases the people of Philadelphia agreed with their mayors. At such times decisions are not hard to make. But this was not always the case.

Philadelphia faces a traffic problem. William Penn's plan for his city called for streets fifty feet wide. In the early days these streets were thought to be very wide. But for today's cars, trucks, and buses, the streets are narrow and crowded. Like most other cities, Philadelphia has had to build newer highways to carry its traffic. The map on this page shows two of the highways that carry traffic in a north-south direction. Another expressway, north of the center of the city, carries traffic in an east-west direction.

For many years, some people said that another east-west expressway was needed. They thought this one should be built *south* of the center of the city, where traffic became clogged on the narrow streets, especially during rush hours. After many studies, engineers and city planners agreed that the city should build such an expressway. Because this highway would run across the city, it was to be called the Crosstown Expressway. The road would carry eight lanes of traffic.

The planners recommended that all the buildings and stores between South

THE PROPOSED CROSSTOWN EXPRESSWAY

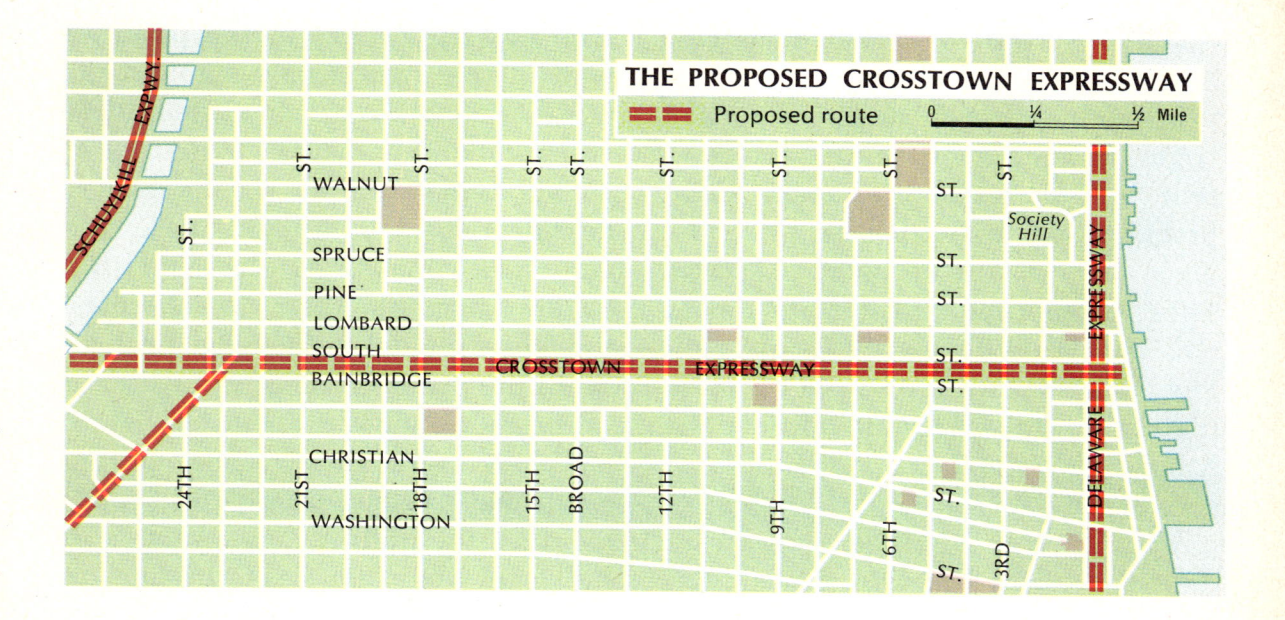

Street and Bainbridge Street be torn down in order to make a path straight across the city for the Crosstown Expressway. Why did they choose this area for the Crosstown? One reason was that many of the buildings were already old and decaying. As long as buildings had to come down, the planners felt it made more sense to knock down these decaying buildings than to tear down those in better condition in other areas.

It would also cost the government less to build the road through the older section. You will remember that under our Constitution, when the government needs land to build a road, it must pay for any land and buildings it takes. Do you see why building a road through this section would cost less than building it elsewhere?

The people speak. Up to this point, all the planning and decisions had been made by the city planners and the highway builders. The people of Philadelphia had not been asked how they felt about it. The next step was to explain the project to them.

In 1964, after completing their plans for the highway, city officials held a public hearing on the Crosstown Expressway. A *public hearing* is a meeting at which citizens are asked to tell government officials how they feel about plans for roads, proposed laws, and such things. Hundreds of citizens attended the hearing. Most of these people had supported urban renewal in the past. But now they opposed the decision to build the Crosstown.

They pointed out that new expressways had not always solved the traffic

445

problems of cities. These roads had only attracted more cars into the cities, they said, and soon traffic jams had begun all over again. In fact, they said that such roads had often made traffic problems worse, for there had been no place to park all the additional cars. These people said that the city should not encourage the use of cars in downtown areas. Instead of building more highways, the city should improve the subway, bus, and *commuter* railroad services.

Another group of citizens who were unhappy about the Crosstown Expressway lived in an old area of Philadelphia known as Society Hill. Society Hill was right next to the proposed path of the expressway. Many of the residents had bought homes built 150 years ago and had spent thousands of dollars fixing them up. Others lived in new apartment buildings. These residents all complained that the road would bring into their neighborhood the pollution and traffic noise of thousands of cars and trucks.

The people who were most unhappy, however, were those whose homes would have to be torn down to make room for the highway. One section of the road would go right through an area of historic old homes. The government would of course pay the owners, but Philadelphia, a city proud of its history, would never be able to replace these buildings.

Most of the people who would lose their homes, however, lived in run-down apartments between South Street and Bainbridge Street. Many of them were quite poor and elderly. The majority were black, but many were white. They had lived in this section for many years. This was their neighborhood, and now it was to be destroyed to make room for a highway.

Worst of all, they feared they would not be able to find other housing in Philadelphia for the same rent, and they could not afford to pay more. The owners of the buildings would be paid by the government for their property. They could buy other buildings elsewhere. But those who rented the apart-

The people of Society Hill had spent much money restoring their area to its original beauty and removing some run-down buildings. They believed the Crosstown Expressway was a threat.

ments would not be so lucky. They would have to move out, but they would get nothing. City governments do try to help people find housing they can afford when they must be relocated, but often the governments are not too successful.

Many people opposed the Crosstown because it would separate white people, who would be living on streets north of the expressway, from black people, who would be living south of it. Many people in both neighborhoods believed it was good for blacks and whites to be together as part of the same community. Many people of both races were working hard to encourage this. If the Crosstown were built, it would be a three-hundred-foot-wide barrier of speeding cars and trucks, which no one could cross. It would separate the black and white neighborhoods as completely as would a stone wall a hundred feet high.

Even though many people opposed the expressway plan, it did not seem that they could do anything about it. After all, the engineers and city planners said a highway was needed. The federal and state governments were ready to pay for building it. Philadelphia's mayor, James Tate, seemed to be in favor of the Crosstown. What could these individuals do to change the plans of the government? Some months after the hearings, it was announced that work would soon begin on the Crosstown Expressway.

Organizing the Opposition

Opponents of the Crosstown were very discouraged. But some of them believed there was still a chance. One of these people was George Dukes, a schoolteacher. He had lived in the neighborhood all his life, just a few blocks from where the expressway would be built. Mr. Dukes believed the mayor had heard only one side of the story. If all the people who opposed the expressway joined together, they would have one strong voice instead of many weak ones. Then the mayor would hear the other side and might change his mind. If the mayor did not give his approval, the Crosstown could not be built.

Another person who felt the same way as Mr. Dukes was Mrs. Alice Lipscomb. She too was a resident of the area that was in the path of the Crosstown. She had been a strong influence in her neighborhood already. Now she helped to start an organization that would try to stop the building of the highway.

Pulling together. Forming such an organization took a lot of time and hard work. Evening after evening, Mr. Dukes visited with neighborhood families. He explained about the plan to build the highway, because many people still had not heard about it. Mr. Dukes told them that if they did not act soon, they would be forced to move.

But if they pulled together, there was still a chance to save their neighborhood.

After many months of this work, Mr. Dukes, Mrs. Lipscomb, and others announced the formation of their new organization. This was in the spring of 1967. They named it the Citizens' Committee to Preserve and Develop the Crosstown Community. The citizens' committee believed that instead of tearing down their neighborhood for a highway, the city government should try to make it a better place to live. It could do this by repairing homes and building new recreational facilities for the residents.

Everybody who was interested in stopping the Crosstown and in improving the community was invited to join this committee. Blacks and whites were members. Poor people living on Bainbridge Street and those who were better off on Society Hill were members. People from other parts of Philadelphia who agreed with the ideas of the citizens' committee joined it or supported it.

Getting the facts. The leaders of the committee knew they would need a lot of facts and information if they were to be successful. For example, they wanted to show that the highway was not as necessary to Philadelphia as some people believed. This meant they had to learn about highways and talk to traffic and transportation experts. They found some experts who believed the highway really was needed, but they also found others who said the city could get along without it.

Then the leaders had to learn about housing. People who wanted the Crosstown Expressway said that there was plenty of inexpensive housing for the people to move to. Was this really so? To get definite information, the committee called upon the Philadelphia Housing Association. This association had been a leading organization in improving housing conditions in Philadelphia for more than sixty years.

The housing association made a special study to find out exactly how many people lived between South and Bainbridge Streets and how many would need inexpensive housing. It found that 6,500 people would have to move to make room for the Crosstown. It also learned that there was not enough good housing at low rentals in the city to take care of these people.

Informing the people. During the next few months, the citizens' committee held dozens of block meetings. These are meetings to which everyone on a certain block is invited. The committee also held public rallies. At these meetings and rallies, speakers explained the plan for the expressway and told the citizens what they could do about it.

The committee put stories about its activities in the Philadelphia newspapers. It persuaded other organizations in the city to give their support. Committee members wrote letters to city officials and met with several of the mayor's assistants to explain why the expressway should not be built. They even held a peaceful march around City Hall to call attention to their ideas.

The mayor makes a decision. Mayor James Tate had been elected in 1963. Many of the people who opposed the Crosstown had voted for him. The mayor knew they were supporting him for another term in the coming election. Of course he would like to make a decision that would please his supporters. But he also had to be sure his decision was the best one for the whole city. He carefully studied the facts and the arguments that had been presented to him.

In November 1967, Mayor Tate was reelected by a small margin. Shortly afterward, he announced his decision. He said he opposed the building of the Crosstown Expressway. The main reason was that there was not enough decent housing for the families that would have to move. He then instructed his assistants to start making plans to help rehabilitate the Crosstown neighborhood.

The mayor's announcement caught everyone by surprise. Some people said he decided against the highway to reward his supporters who lived in the area. Others said he really was concerned about the families who would have to move out of the area. Mayor Tate had grown up as a poor boy himself, they said, and he knew how these people felt. But no one, except the mayor himself, could be exactly sure why he decided against the highway.

Reviewing the Decision

The members of the Citizens' Committee to Preserve and Develop the Crosstown Community were overjoyed. They had shown that people really could influence their government by joining together.

But there were many others who were disappointed by the mayor's an-

These homes, in the path of the proposed Crosstown Expressway, will be torn down if the Expressway is built. The families in the neighborhood will have trouble finding housing they can afford.

nouncement. They believed the Crosstown was needed to solve Philadelphia's traffic problem. They felt sorry that 6,500 people would have to move, but they said that all the other people of Philadelphia should be considered, too. They would benefit from this road.

Another point of view. In a democracy, people have the right to try to change their government's decision. The people who opposed the Crosstown had done this. Now those who favored the Crosstown decided to try to change the mayor's mind again.

The leaders were a group called the Philadelphia *Chamber of Commerce.* There is a chamber of commerce in almost every city. It is an organization made up of merchants, businessmen, manufacturers, and others who are interested in increasing the commerce, or business, of the city. Its members believe more business is not only good for them, but good for the whole city.

The Philadelphia Chamber of Commerce urged the mayor to review his decision about the Crosstown Expressway. The members said they had not had a chance to present all the arguments in favor of an expressway. They also said they could show that there really was enough good housing for relocating the residents who had to move. They suggested that the expressway would not have to be a wall between whites and blacks if it were built differently. Perhaps the expressway could be built below ground level, with a special cover over it. This would allow pedestrians and automobile traffic to travel over it.

The Citizens' Committee to Preserve and Develop the Crosstown Community tried to arouse the people to action against the Expressway. Here is one of their posters.

Case reopened. Mayor Tate wanted to do what was best for the city. If there were other reasons for building the expressway, he wanted to know about them. Certainly, the leading merchants and businessmen of the city should have a chance to have their say.

Of course, the mayor of a big city is a very busy man. He cannot possibly look into every single problem himself. Instead, he appoints special committees made up of other government officials and private citizens to study each problem. These committees listen to all sides and then recommend what the mayor should do. So Mayor Tate appointed a special committee to study the Crosstown Expressway plan again. The members included some people who strongly favored the Crosstown and some who strongly opposed it.

The reasons for. The special committee held many hearings and listened to many arguments from those who believed the highway should be built. Downtown merchants told the committee that people found it difficult to drive to the city in slow-moving traffic. If the highway were not built, they warned, people would not come to the city to shop. This would be bad for the downtown stores and bad for the city also. Do you remember why?

The head of a large manufacturing company told the committee that industries would not locate in the city if there were no good highways over which trucks could move goods to and from the factories. Why should a city be concerned about this?

The port of Philadelphia, which is one of the largest ports in the nation, could benefit from a road that would allow goods to be carried to and from the docks more quickly. A new highway would make it easier to get to Philadelphia's busy airport. People driving from the suburbs to work or to shop wanted the new highway.

Other groups also favored the new highway. Can you think why trucking companies would? Why construction companies and cement companies would? Some of those who owned stores along Bainbridge Street and South Street favored the road. Over the years, business had declined in their area, and storeowners did not make as good a living as they used to. Why might the owner of such a store be glad to have it torn down to make room for a highway?

The arguments against. Opponents of the Crosstown also presented their arguments. A total of thirty-seven organizations, including church groups and and neighborhood groups—all of whom were interested in improving the city—opposed the expressway. They got together and sent one representative to tell the mayor's committee how they felt about the Crosstown. Housing experts repeated that there was not enough decent housing that Crosstown residents could afford elsewhere in the city.

A leading citizen cautioned that black people would no longer stand for being pushed out of their homes and neighborhoods to make room for highways, office buildings, and other things they got nothing out of. He said that if cities continued to do things like this, they could expect riots.

Others pointed out that a new highway near the middle of town would increase noise and air pollution in the city. Still other opponents claimed that if parking was prohibited on certain streets, there would be enough lanes to allow traffic to move smoothly, and an expressway would not be necessary. During the committee's hearings, it was also learned that the idea of a covered highway would have to be dropped because it would be too expensive.

Each side sincerely believed it was right. Each side included people who had the best interests of the city at heart. Each side also included people who were thinking only of their own interests.

At the time this book is being written, the committee has not completed its work. We do not know what it will recommend to Mayor Tate. We do not know whether the mayor will change his earlier decision. Mayor Tate is not going to run for reelection. He does not have to worry about the votes of people on either side of the Crosstown argument. He would certainly like to do what is best for the city, and he must make a decision soon.

What do you think the mayor's decision should be?

Congress Passes a Law

What about the laws that Congress makes for the 200 million people of the United States? How are these laws made? Do people have a say about these laws as they did about the decision in Philadelphia? To answer these questions and to see how our democratic government works, we are going to follow the important steps taken in making a proposal into a law. As we do, you can decide what part people or groups of people play when Congress makes a decision.

Shrinking heritage. In the northwestern corner of California stand the last giant *redwood trees* on the earth. Redwoods are very special trees. Some of them are the tallest living things, and some are the oldest.

The special qualities of the redwoods make them valuable to lumber companies and builders. The wood resists fire, rot, termites, and weather. It is soft and easy to cut and shape. Redwood lumber is in great demand for outdoor use. You may have seen porches, panels, patios, and patio furniture made of this wood.

About one hundred years ago, there were at least a million acres of redwood forests in the Far West. At that time most of the redwood forest land belonged to the national government. In the late 1800's, the government either gave away most of this land or sold it very cheaply to the lumber companies. These companies were in the business of cutting and selling the redwoods and did not pay much attention to preserving them. Storms and floods also destroyed many redwoods.

During those years a few people urged the government to protect these forests from destruction by man and nature, but little was done. Now there are only 300,000 acres of redwood forests left, and most of these are on land belonging to private owners.

Save the redwoods. About seventy-five years ago, a number of Americans became more concerned about our natural resources. They felt that we should start doing things to conserve our forests, our minerals, and our fertile soil. Conserve means "to use with care, to keep what we can, and to replace what we use." One of these natural resources was our redwood forests. *Conservationists* formed clubs such as Save-the-Redwoods League and tried to get a law passed to protect the trees. The Save-the-Redwoods League persuaded the government of California to join them in buying land that held the finest stands of redwoods. As a result, about 100,000 acres of redwood forest land were saved and turned into state parks.

In time, other conservationist organizations, such as the Sierra Club, the American Forestry Association, and the Garden Club of America, added their numbers to the drive to save the redwoods. Members of these groups wrote articles to newspapers and magazines about the need to preserve the trees.

Their main goal was to get the national government to buy back the redwood lands and turn them into a *national park.* In a national park no trees can be cut without special permission. Also, the government protects trees against flooding and other natural disasters. In a national park, these grand redwoods would be preserved for the enjoyment of future Americans.

Each year thousands of tourists view the giant trees of Prairie Creek Redwoods State Park.
David Muench

Conservationists wrote to their representatives in Congress and urged them to pass such a law, but only a few congressmen were interested. Meanwhile, storms, flooding, and lumber companies continued to reduce the number of redwoods. By the 1960's, the million acres we once had had shrunk to less than one third that amount.

Very often it takes a shock or a startling event to arouse the public to action. Such a shock came in 1963 when a report by a well-known national magazine was published. The report warned that because of lumbering operations and disasters such as floods and windstorms, the redwoods were in danger of disappearing. The report made the public more aware of the problem. Soon letters began to pour into Congress.

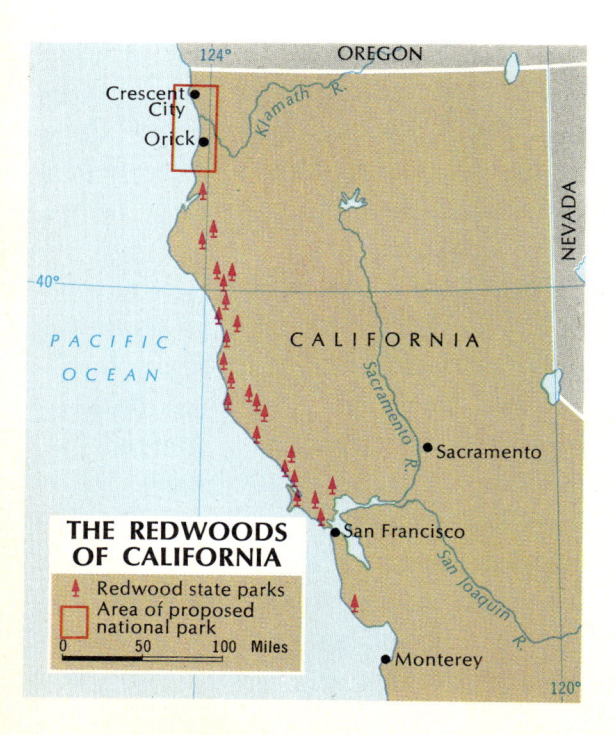

Congress Takes Action

In 1965, Lyndon Johnson was President of the United States. President Johnson was strongly in favor of conserving all our natural resources, including the redwoods. He urged Congress to pass a law that would preserve the redwoods. Conservationists were pleased, for they knew that when the President makes a recommendation to Congress, it has a good chance of becoming a law.

That year a number of representatives and senators wrote bills, or proposals for laws, to create national parks in the redwood forests of California. As you will see, it sometimes takes years before a bill becomes a law. The bill that we are going to follow on its way to becoming a law started in the United States Senate. Let us see what this bill recommended.

Some of the best groves of redwoods were already in two state parks in Del Norte County, California. The bill proposed that these two state parks become part of the new national park. For the rest of the national park, the government would buy some of the redwood land owned by lumber companies. Most of this land also was in Del Norte County, right next to the state parks. One additional area, called Tall Trees, was farther south, in Humboldt County. Find these areas on your map on page 457. Altogether, the national park would cover 43,000 acres. You will want to remember that number as we follow the bill along.

A Senate committee studies a bill. Each year thousands of bills on hundreds of subjects are proposed by our representatives and senators. It is impossible for the entire House and Senate to study each bill carefully. Therefore, Congress sets up a number of committees to study the bills. Each house of Congress has its own committees. Each committee specializes in certain kinds of bills—housing bills go to one committee, bills about agriculture go to another, and so on.

Usually about fifteen or twenty representatives or senators serve on each committee. The committee decides which bills are important, studies them, and makes changes in them. Then the committee presents each bill to the Senate or the House with a recommendation to pass it or not pass it.

In studying these bills, each committee usually holds special hearings. The committee often invites experts on the subject to come and give information. The committee also calls on people who might have a special interest in the bill, including lobbyists. After serving on the same committee and studying the same subjects for a number of years, many of the members themselves become experts.

Like all bills, our Senate bill to create a redwood national park was sent to a committee for study. The committee decided to hold special hearings to learn all it could about the plan. Some of the hearings were in Washington, D.C., where most committees hold their hearings. The committee also went to northern California for a number of hearings so that the residents who lived near the area that might become a park could be heard from.

Lumber companies speak. Lumber companies were very interested in this bill. If it became law, they would have to sell the government thousands of acres of lumber land for the national park. They opposed this. They also felt that many people criticized them unfairly for destroying redwoods.

It was true that many years ago some lumber companies had been greedy and had cut trees recklessly. But today's lumber companies, said their owners, believe in conservation. They are careful about which trees and how many trees they cut. These owners felt that they were being made to look like "bad guys."

The president of one lumber company told the committee that all the land of his company was in Del Norte County. His company had spent a lot of money to buy a new sawmill and other equipment. If this bill became law, the company's land would become part of the national park. "We don't want to be put out of business," he told the committee.

The lumber company president also said, "I owe it to my workers to continue logging in northern California." He meant that his company was the largest employer in that area. Without lumbering, many residents would be without jobs. Storekeepers and others would suffer, also. In addition, the lumber company paid over $400,000 in taxes to Del Norte County every year. That, too, would be lost if the company went out of business. The company had been planning to expand, which would have resulted in more than five hundred new jobs for residents in the next five years. The company would also be paying twice as much tax money in the future. "Would a national park do all that for Del Norte County and its residents?" asked the president of the lumber company.

The same man added that we did not need a national park anyway. His company was willing to do "all that a national park could do." It would open its land to visitors, make paths and picnic areas, and offer tours among the redwoods. Other speakers for the lumber companies said that a national park was not needed to preserve the redwoods, for the state parks were already doing this. It was true that there were not as many acres of trees being saved in the state parks, but after all, asked one opponent of the bill, "How many redwoods do you need for viewing?"

The governor speaks. One of the most important statements made to the committee came from the governor of California. Remember, the bill called for turning over two state parks to become part of a national park. The United States government could not force the state of California to do this. If the governor did not agree to it, it could not be done, and that would be the end of the bill.

The governor could not attend the hearings himself, but he sent an assistant to read his statement. The governor's statement said that the state of California was very concerned about the redwood forests. State parks already protected the oldest and best stands of trees.

The governor's statement also reminded the committee that lumber companies would lose a large investment if they had to stop their businesses. Jobs and taxes would be lost, too. If making a national park meant putting these companies out of business, the governor would oppose it.

The governor said that he would agree to turn over the two state parks on two conditions. He noted that the federal government owned forest lands elsewhere in California. So his first condition was that the government must allow the lumber companies to cut on these lands in exchange for selling the redwood lands to the government. By using this government land, companies could continue lumbering operations. The governor was determined about this. He told the committee, "No exchange—no national park."

The governor's second condition was that the federal government must pay the towns and counties to make up for the loss of taxes when lumber companies gave up their land. This seemed only fair to the governor.

The committee was disturbed by both of the governor's conditions. The federal government had never before exchanged its land for sites it wanted to acquire from states or private citizens. Also, paying the towns and counties might so increase the cost of making this national park that Congress might vote against it. Should the committee agree to the governor's conditions? If it did not, there could still be a national park, but it would be a much smaller one, for it would not include the state parks. This would be a difficult decision to make.

Hearing from the people. What about the people who lived in Del Norte County, where most of the national park would be? The park would affect them most of all. How did they feel about this proposal? To find out, the committee invited many citizens from nearby towns and farms to speak at the hearings. Many of the people who appeared said they did not want a national park. Where would lumbermen find jobs if companies stopped work?

"Things were bad enough since the tidal wave of 1962 hit our coast. We're still rebuilding," said a businessman from Crescent City. If the lumber companies closed now, he said, it would be bad for all the businesses in the area.

Another resident pointed out that most of the land in Del Norte County was already owned by either the national government or the state of California. Governments do not pay taxes on the lands they own. Businesses do, and this resident said that if lumber companies now turned over

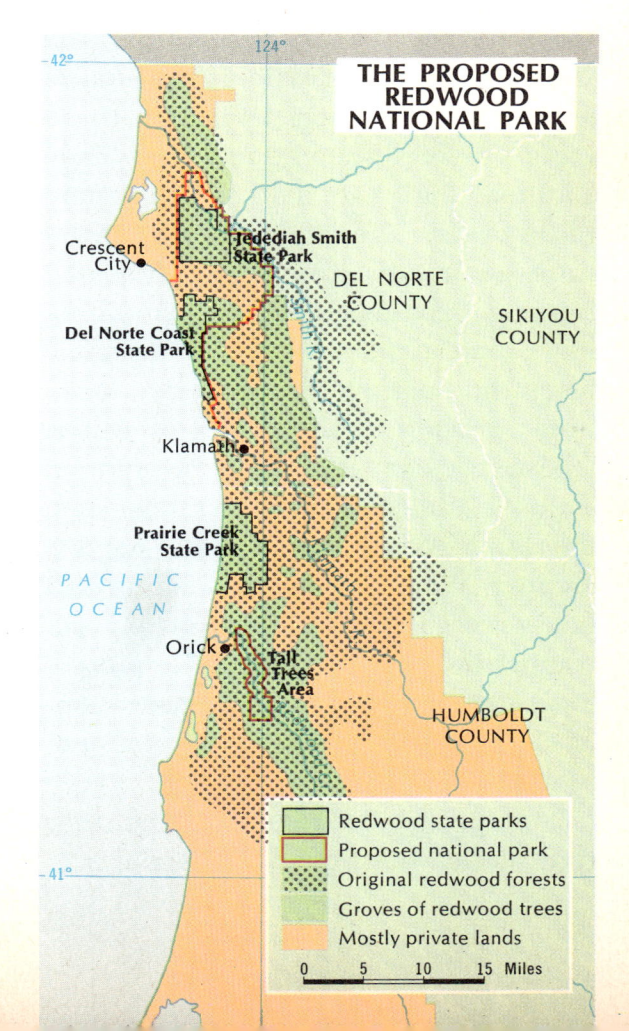

THE PROPOSED REDWOOD NATIONAL PARK

- Redwood state parks
- Proposed national park
- Original redwood forests
- Groves of redwood trees
- Mostly private lands

their land for a national park, there would be no more tax money from them to pay for schools and roads. It did not seem fair, said this person, for one county to have to give up so much.

Other residents said they wanted a national park so long as it was a small one. These were the owners of motels and restaurants. They agreed that a park would attract tourists during the summer. But for the rest of the year these businesses depended on businessmen connected with lumbering and lumber products. Nothing should be done to hurt the lumber business.

Those in favor of a park. The committee also invited conservationist groups to testify at the hearings. Of course, these groups favored the national park. They doubted that the state parks alone could protect the redwoods. Would the state put roads through the redwood forests? Frequently, roads leave ugly scars and expose trees. Sometimes, when not completed properly, roads cause erosion or the runoff of water.

Also, the conservationists wondered if they could count on the state to keep the land. What if the state needed money? Would it be tempted to sell more redwood forest land to private companies? The surest way to protect the redwoods, said the conservationists, was to put them into a national park.

Conservationists also warned that state parks were not large enough to protect the redwoods. They explained that the lumbering on private land near the state parks was already damaging the redwoods in the state parks. The leading conservation group, the Sierra Club, presented its own plan for a national park to the Senate committee.

The club said that only a very large national park would do any good. The park should be near a river drainage system and be able to control nearby slopes. This was the only way floods could be controlled and erosion prevented. Only in a large park might the

THE REDWOOD NATIONAL PARK

- Park boundary
- Redwood state park
- Federal land opened to lumber companies

0 5 10 15 Miles

federal government control all the damage that would otherwise be done by man. They argued that the Senate bill left out some of the finest redwood forests in the state.

In the Sierra Club's plan, the national park would include a state park in Humboldt County, in addition to the Tall Trees area of Humboldt County. It also called for the purchase of a large amount of private land surrounding a river drainage system. Altogether, the Sierra Club wanted a national park of 92,000 acres — more than twice as large as the one suggested in the Senate bill. It would cost about $200 million to buy the land for the park. The committee members were impressed by the Sierra Club's idea, but they wondered whether the Senate would be willing to spend that much money.

The main argument that people gave against the national park was the loss of jobs and taxes. Conservationists brought in experts to show that a national park would actually help the people of northern California. In a few years there would be more income from a national park than from lumbering. They advised the people to learn the tourist trade, to build motels, restaurants, and gift shops. Besides, said the experts, if the national park were not created, the redwoods on the lumber company lands would all be cut down in twenty years or so. Then companies would shut down and people would be without jobs.

The committee reports to the Senate. After the hearings, the committee still had much work to do. The members had listened to the people of Del Norte County, to the governor, to the lumber companies, and to the conservationists. Certainly the ideas of all these people were important. But the committee had to consider more than these opinions. A national park would be for all the people in the nation, now and in the future. Should the nearby residents and the lumber companies be the only ones to have a say about whether to have a national park? Who was there to speak for the future generations that might want one?

On the other hand, buying the land for a park would be costly. Should the committee recommend a large park or a smaller, less expensive one? Would a smaller park really protect the redwoods? The committee members had to consider all these things as they decided whether to make changes in the bill.

When the committee finished its work, the chairman offered the committee report to the Senate. Copies of the proposed law, along with the opinions of the members of the committee, were given to the members of the Senate to study. Committee members who opposed the bill made a separate report.

Then it was up to the senators to decide. The Senate does this by discussing, or debating, the bill. Any senator may give his arguments for or against it, and try to convince others. He may also suggest changes in the bill.

A few senators from eastern states claimed that their people were tired of hearing about money spent on parks and recreation areas in the West. Such money would be better spent solving the problems of the cities. What good would more national parks do for the people in slum areas? Other senators argued that the United States was fighting a war in Asia that was costing millions of dollars. How could the country afford money for a national park at a time like that?

Many other senators spoke strongly in favor of a national park. They thought it was time the nation gave consideration to its resources. Some senators criticized lumber companies for opposing a park that would serve the whole nation. They said that every American should take pride in this beautiful forest land. And Congress should delay no longer in passing the necessary law to create the park.

The Senate votes. When the Senate finally voted, it accepted some parts of the committee's recommendations and rejected others. The majority of senators voted in favor of a park of 64,000 acres. That was much larger than the size recommended in the original bill, but smaller than the Sierra Club had recommended. It would cost the fed-

This picture shows some of the destruction of the redwood forests caused by lumbering.

eral government $100 million. The bill accepted the demand of the governor of California that the federal government give up some of its land to private lumber companies. It also stated that Del Norte and Humboldt counties, the two counties in which the park would be located, would be given aid for five years for the taxes they might lose. So the Senate had completed its work.

But a bill does not become a law until it is approved by *both* houses of Congress. From the Senate, the bill went to the House of Representatives.

The House takes action. The House of Representatives had also been considering and studying the need for a national park to protect the redwoods. In fact, some representatives had introduced bills of their own for such a park. A committee of the House had held hearings similar to those held by the Senate committee.

However, after all the investigations and hearings, the members of the House committee had come to favor a national park of 28,000 acres. This was far smaller than the size recommended in the Senate bill. Conservationists were disappointed. If the two houses of Congress did not agree, there might not be a park at all.

Compromise in Congress. However, there was a way out. When both houses of Congress favor a certain type of law but disagree on details, they try to compromise. Representatives and senators know that only by compromising can they finally get a law passed. They form a special committee made up of a few senators and a few representatives to do this. This is called a conference committee.

This is what Congress did with the two different bills on the national park. A conference committee met and discussed the differences in the bills. Then they worked out a compromise. The compromise bill was then presented to both houses. It was voted on and passed. In October 1969, the President of the United States signed the bill and it became a law.

Here are some of the major parts of the law passed to protect the redwoods of California.

The law creates the Redwood National Park, with 58,000 acres. The map shows you the boundaries of the new park. The national park is to take control of three California state parks. Two of these state parks are in Del Norte County, but the third is in Humboldt County. About thirty thousand acres of private forest land is to be bought in both counties. Several lumber companies, not just the company whose largest holdings were in Del Norte County, will have to surrender land.

The largest amount of private land will be from companies operating in Humboldt County. The law allows the government to spend $92 million for the purchase of the private land.

The law also permits the government to exchange some of the forest land it owns for the private land it has to buy. The law also states that this exchange of land is not to apply in any future cases in which the federal government buys state or private land for parks.

Did Congress listen to any advice that its committee received? Did it listen to the conservationists? Did the committee pay heed to the governor of California? Do you think that the testimony of the people in northern California influenced the decision of Congress in any way? Would any of the interested groups of which we read be unhappy with the new law? Was the decision to save the redwoods a wise one?

Working with Concepts and Generalizations

Identifying Concepts

Read the poster below. Then answer the questions that follow.

CITIZENS OF LINWOOD
plan to attend a
PUBLIC HEARING
Which is more important
a new highway OR
THE HOMES WE LIVE IN?
Which is more important
room for more cars OR
ROOM FOR OUR CHILDREN?
Which is more important
saving business profits OR
SAVING OUR NEIGHBORHOOD?
City planners will destroy your homes!
The mayor will destroy your neighborhood!
DEFEAT THE NEW HIGHWAY PROPOSAL!
Prepared by the Citizen's Council to Save
the Linwood Area

---

1. According to the poster, who is in favor of the proposed highway?
2. According to the poster, who will benefit from the new highway?
3. Who is asked to attend the public hearing?
4. Who prepared the poster?
5. According to the poster, what will the new highway do to the Linwood area?
6. Do you believe the poster tells all the facts about the proposed highway?

Developing Concepts

Write the answers on paper.

1. You are a citizen of Linwood. All you know about the proposed highway is what the poster tells you. Write a list of questions you will ask at the public hearing.
2. You are a businessman who owns a store just outside of Linwood. You have been losing business because traffic gets tied up in the Linwood area. You know the new highway will help you get more business. You also know that more business will enable you to hire more people. Make a poster showing your point of view.
3. You are the mayor of Linwood. Make a list of all the things you will have to consider before you decide whether the proposed highway should be built.
4. In your own words, explain how a bill becomes law. You may use your textbook to help you answer this question.
5. Explain the following statement taken from this chapter: "In a democracy, people have the right to try to change their government's decision." Give examples of how this can be done.

Generalizations

You have been working with generalizations all year. By now you have learned two important facts about generalizations. The first fact is that a generalization is a statement that is usually true of all people or of all places. The second fact is that a generalization does not name any specific time, place, or group of people. Now you will have the chance to write three generalizations.

1. Write a generalization that tells something about the influence that groups and individuals have on government.
2. Write a generalization that tells something about why public opinion influences government leaders.
3. Write a generalization that tells something about conserving natural resources.

Applying Concepts

1. Find out what the voting requirements are in your state. Prepare a report to share with the class. Your report should include information that answers the following questions.
   a. How old must a voter be?
   b. How long must a voter live in the state? the community?
   c. Are there literacy requirements?
   d. Must a voter register before he can vote?

2. Prepare a short biography of the man who represents you in the United States House of Representatives. Much of the information you can get from writing directly to your congressman. The biography you prepare should include information that answers the following questions.
   a. How many years has he served in Congress?
   b. How old is the representative?
   c. Which political party does he belong to?
   d. What was his profession before he became a congressman?
   e. How has he voted on major issues?
   f. Which bills has he introduced in the Congress?
   g. Have any of these bills become law?

3. Read the Bill of Rights, the first ten amendments to the Constitution of the United States. First make a list of all the rights guaranteed by these amendments. Then draw sketches or find pictures that illustrate American citizens taking advantage of these rights. Give each sketch or picture a title.

4. You have learned that regular elections are an important part of representative democracy. You have also learned that many Americans do not exercise their right to vote. You are to plan a voting campaign for your community. The object of the campaign is to point out to all eligible voters how important the right to vote is. Work toward getting 100 percent of the voters in your community to vote in the next election. Here are some things you might like to do as part of your campaign. Add others you think might be effective.
   a. Choose a campaign theme. Make your theme one that will be easy to show and easy to talk about.
   b. Make posters for stores in your community. Tell when the next election will be and ask every registered voter to turn out.
   c. Make campaign buttons to hand out to residents of the community. You will want the buttons to say something about the importance of voting.
   d. Talk to your parents and neighbors. Ask them to vote. Tell them that it is very important to you.
   e. Make leaflets that other members of the student body can distribute in their neighborhoods.
   f. Write letters to officials in your community, asking their help in your campaign. Surely, a large voter turnout is important to them.
   g. Write a personal letter to several of your neighbors who can vote. Introduce yourself. Tell them you have been studying democracy in school. Tell them you have learned how important the right to vote is in this country. Ask them to be sure to vote in the next election.

Map Skills

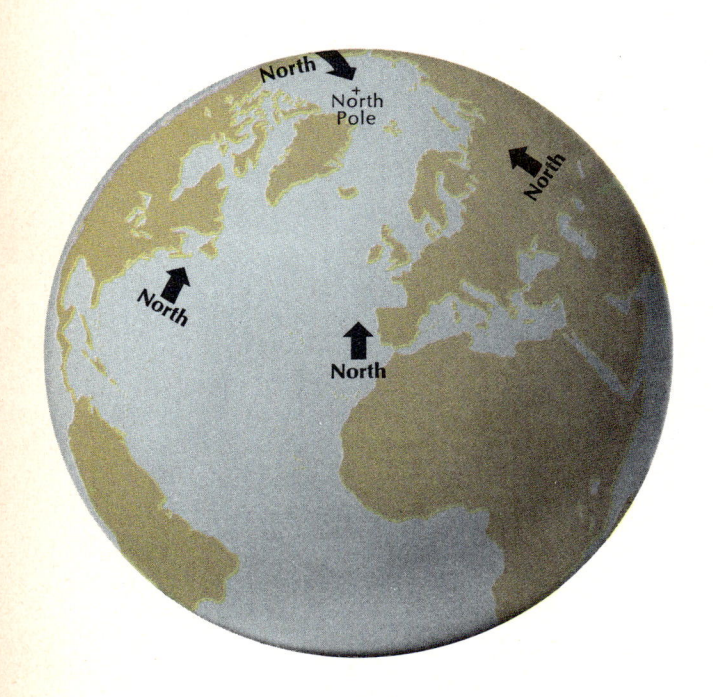

DIRECTIONS

The North Pole is a very special place. It is the most northern place on the earth. North is the direction toward the North Pole.

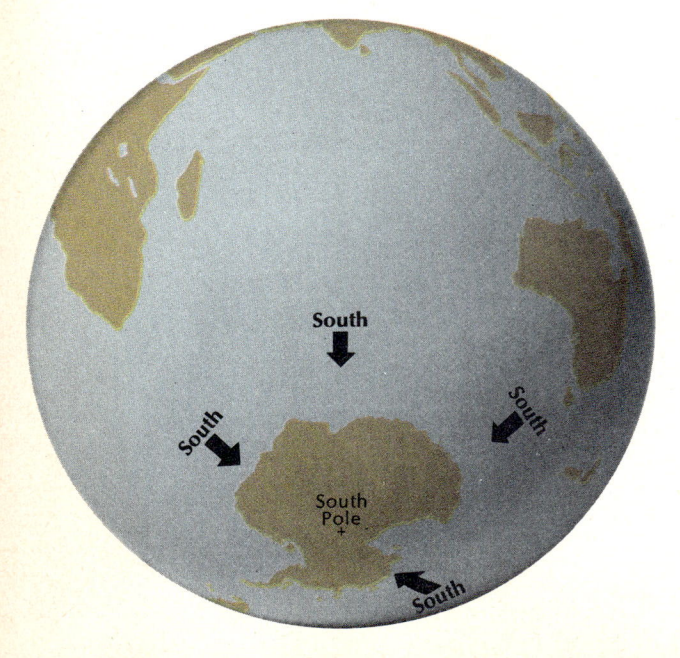

The South Pole is another very special place. It is the most southern place on the earth. South is the direction toward the South Pole. The South Pole is opposite the North Pole.

North and south are directions. Two other directions are east and west. The sun seems to rise in the east and to set in the west. When you face north, east is to your right and west is to your left. East and west are opposite each other.

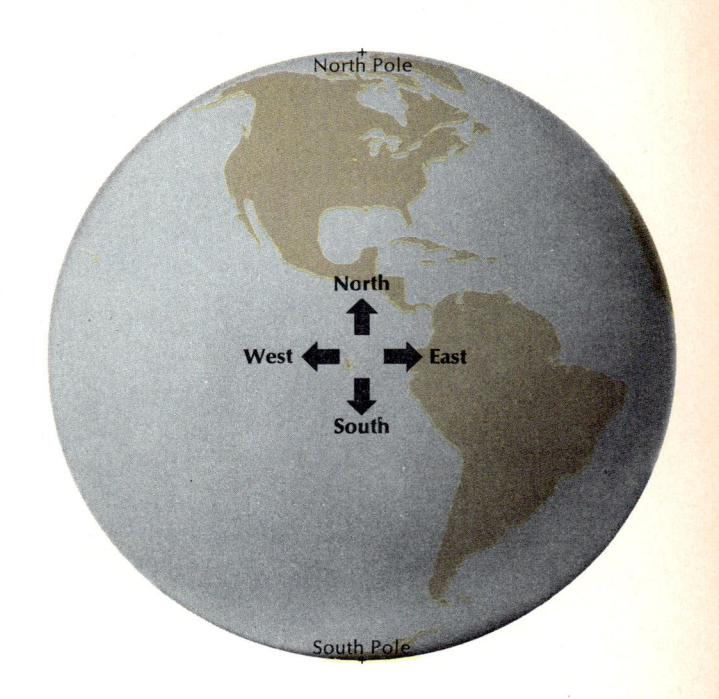

Directions help us to find places on maps and globes. Sometimes directions are shown by a small drawing on the map. This drawing is called a compass rose. Find the compass rose on this map.

In which direction would you travel to go from the state of Illinois to the state of Wisconsin? from Illinois to Indiana?

ILLINOIS and nearby states

465

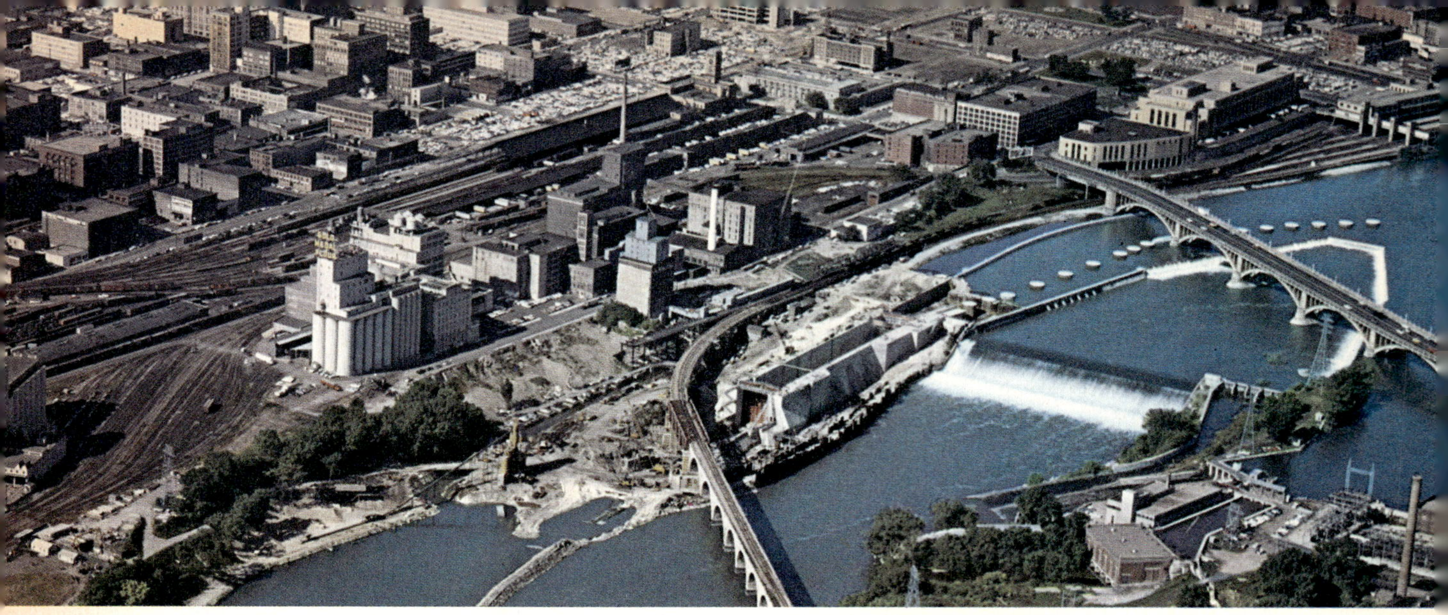

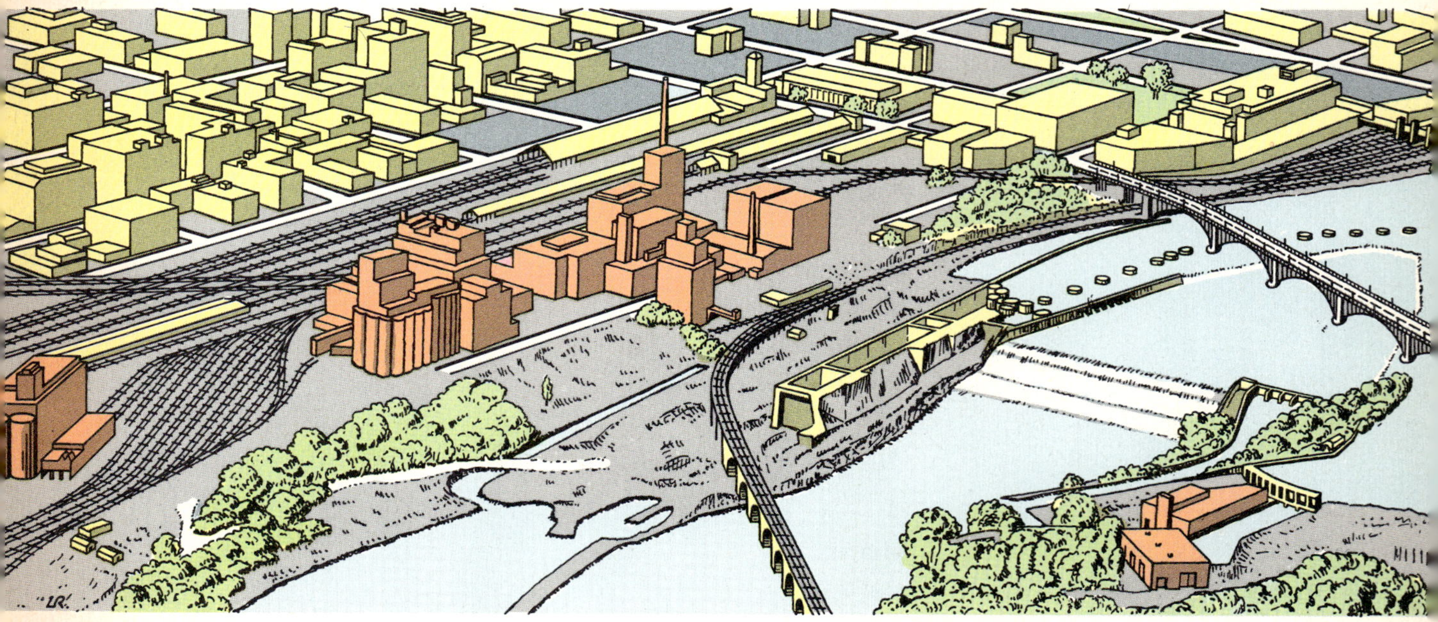

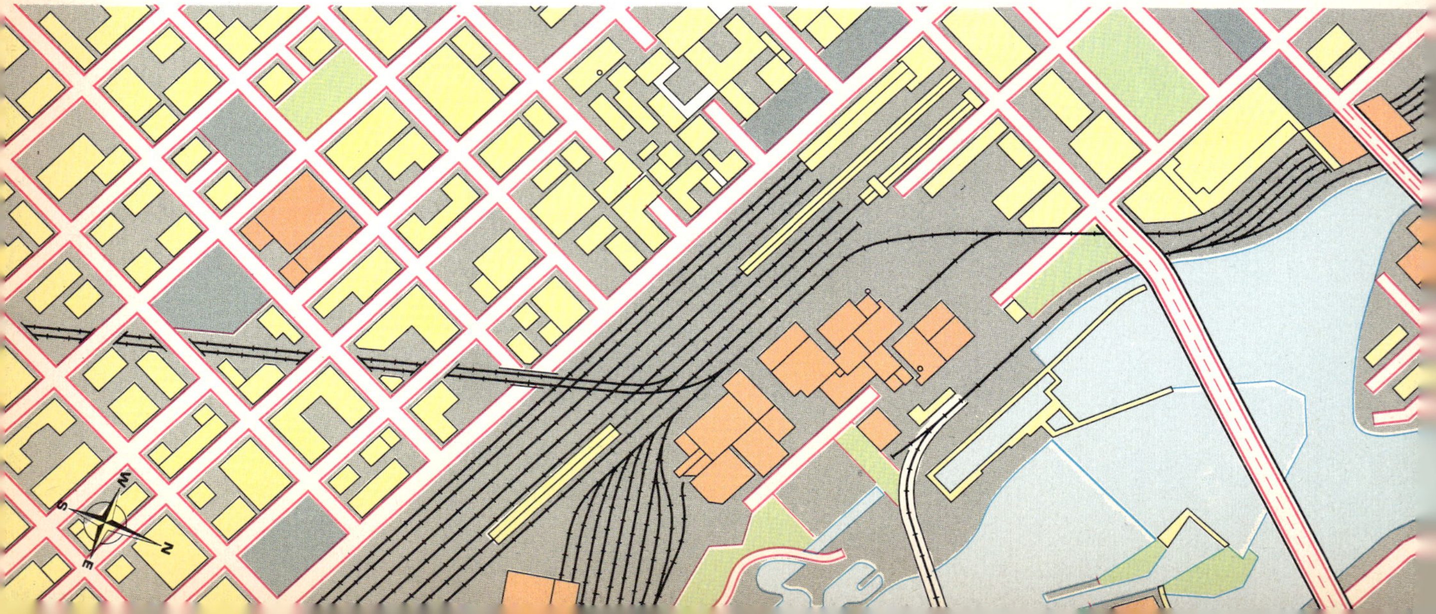

SYMBOLS

At the top of the page is a photograph. It shows a part of Minneapolis, Minnesota. This photograph was taken from an airplane.

Under the photograph is a drawing of the same part of Minneapolis. This is a special kind of drawing. It uses symbols. The symbols stand for real things and places in Minneapolis. The key shows what real things and places the symbols stand for. What symbol is used for bridges?

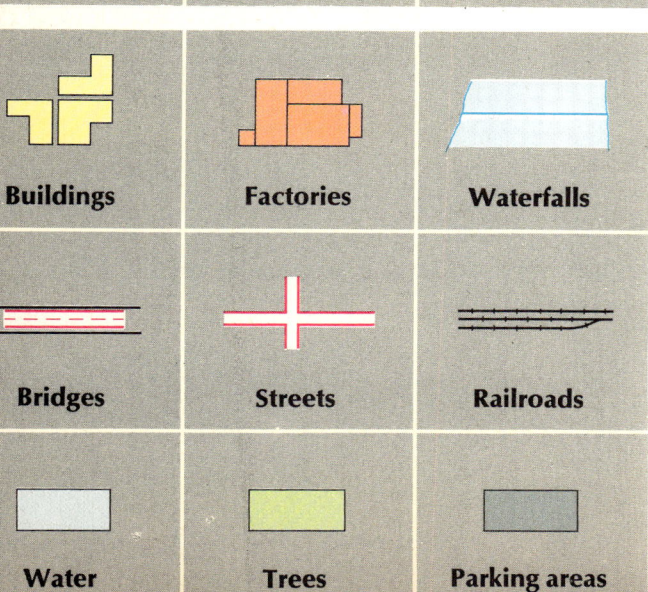

The map at the bottom of the page shows the same part of Minneapolis that the photograph and the drawing show. This map, like the special drawing, has a key. The symbols in the map key are different from those in the drawing. But they, too, stand for real things and places. What symbol is used for bridges?

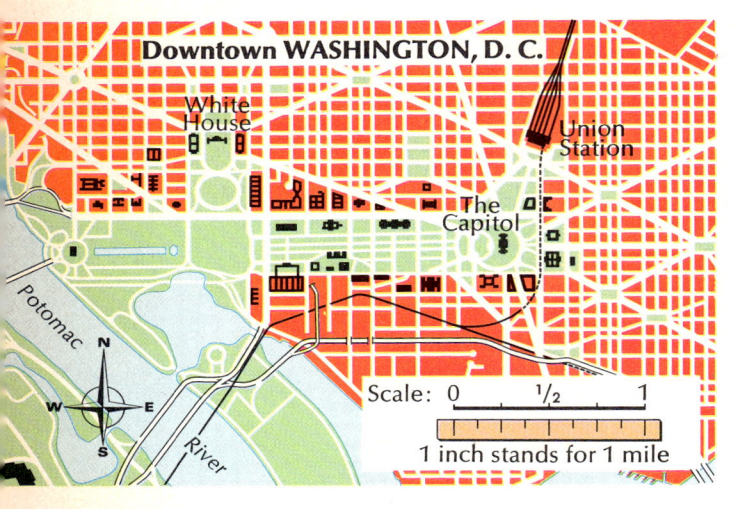

SCALE

The places and distances shown on maps must be smaller than their real size on the earth. So a certain number of inches on a map are used to show a certain number of miles on the earth. This way of showing size or distance on a map is called scale.

Each of these three maps has a different scale. The map at the top of the page has a scale of one inch to one mile. This means that a distance of one mile on the earth is shown on this map by a distance of one inch.

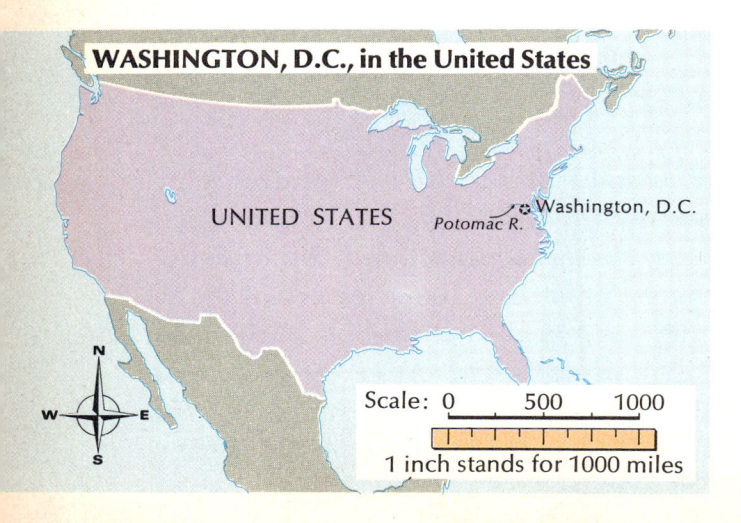

What are the scales on the other two maps? Which is the best map to use if you are in Washington, D.C.?

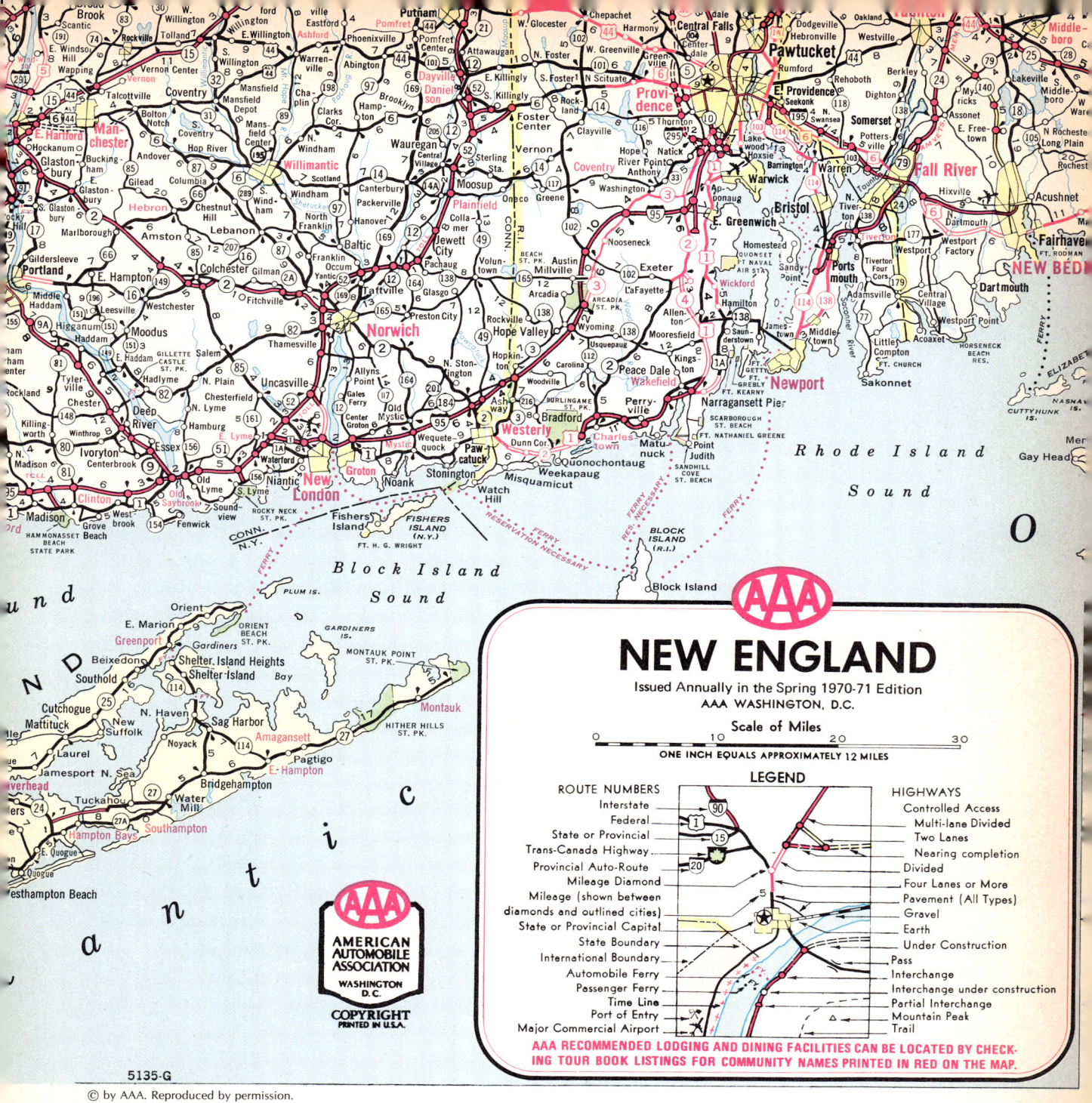

ROAD MAP

What is the scale of miles on the road map shown above? Look at the key to this map. What symbol is used to show a state capital? What symbol is used to show a state boundary?

What is the number of the route you would take if you were traveling from Fall River, Massachusetts, to Providence, Rhode Island? Why do people use road maps?

469

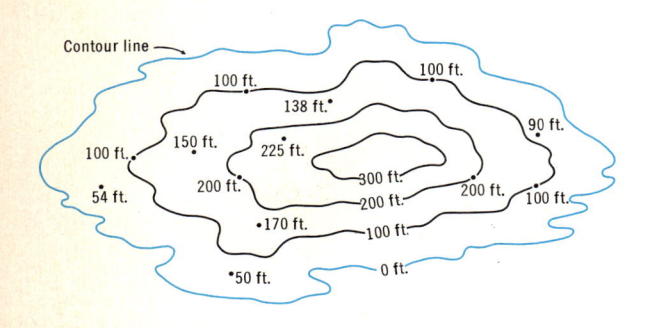

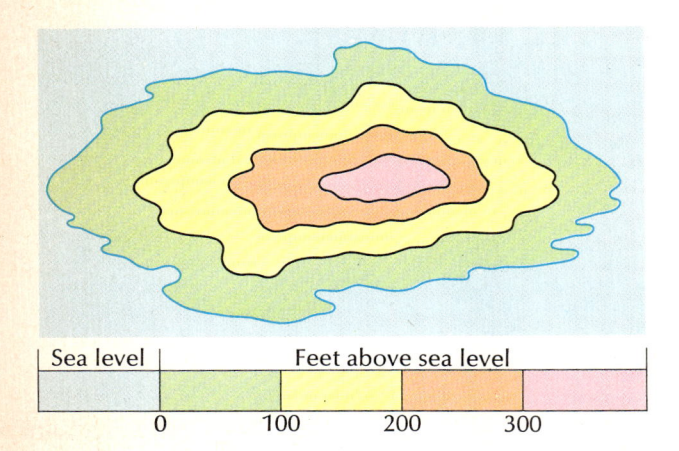

CONTOURS

To measure your height, you would measure the distance from the bottom of your feet to the top of your head. The bottom of your feet would be your *base*. The earth's hills and mountains are also measured from base to top. The base for all the earth's hills and mountains is sea level. Find sea level (0 feet) on the drawing of the mountain. Distance above sea level is called elevation. The lines on the drawing are contour lines.

Contour lines are a good way to show elevation. All points along one contour line are the same distance above sea level. Find the 200-foot contour line on the drawing. Now find it on the contour map of the mountain. What is the highest contour line shown on the drawing? What is the highest contour line shown on the map?

Sometimes color is added between contour lines. What does the yellow color stand for? What is the elevation of the green part? Find the orange part. Can you find the same part on the drawing at the top of the page?

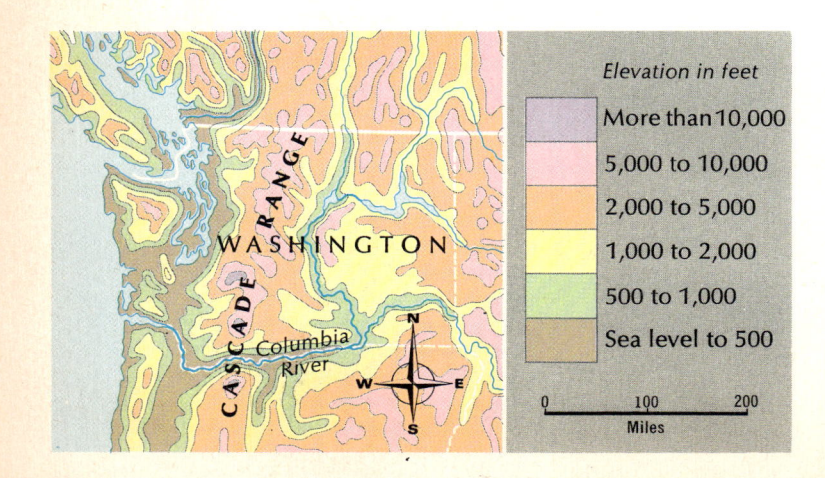

Elevation can be shown in this same way on maps of any part of the world. This is a map of part of the United States. What is the elevation of the land around the Columbia River? What is the elevation of the highest places in Washington?

LATITUDE AND LONGITUDE

The lines drawn on this map are called lines of latitude. The best known latitude line is the equator. The equator is halfway between the two Poles. Latitude lines measure distance north and south of the equator.

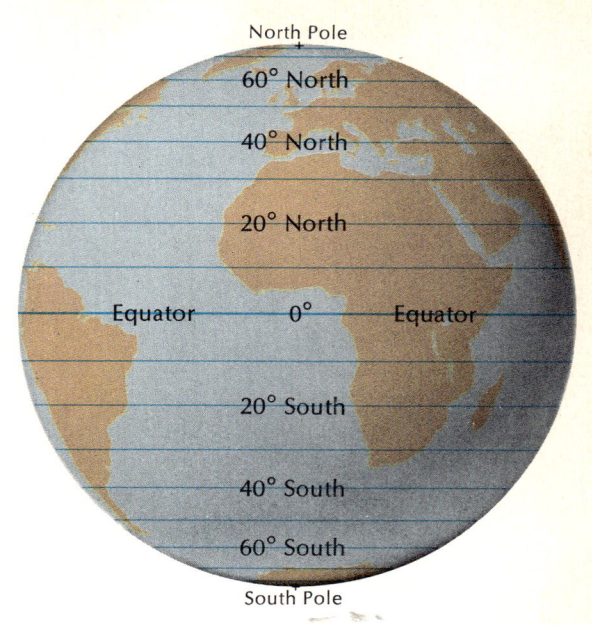

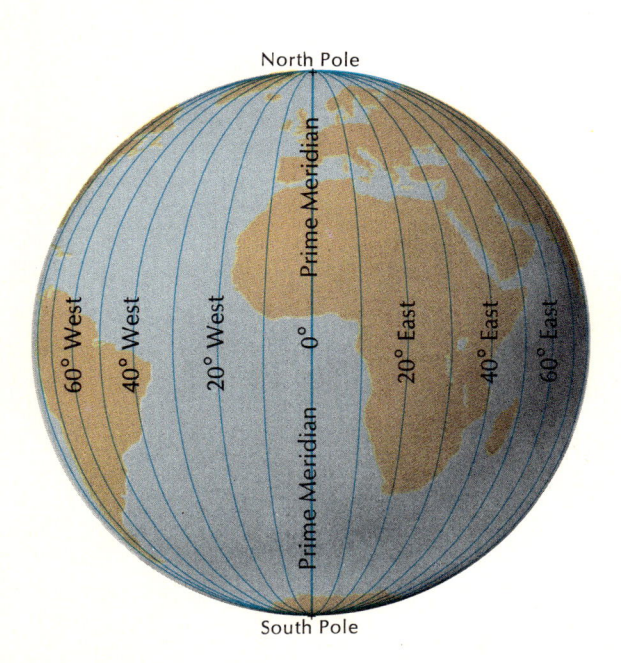

The lines drawn on this map are called lines of longitude, or meridians. The best known longitude line is the prime meridian. Longitude lines measure distance east and west of the prime meridian.

Latitude and longitude lines cross one another on maps and globes. If you know the longitude and latitude of a place, you can find it on a map or globe. Find the place where 20° south latitude and 20° west longitude cross. Find the place where 40° north latitude and 30° east longitude cross.

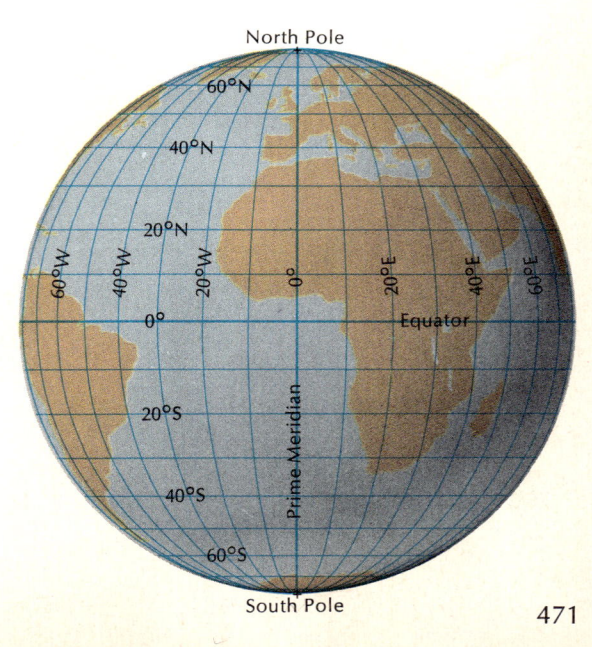

471

Atlas

THE WORLD (Political)

0 — 1000 — 2000 Miles

WEST INDIES

0 — 300 Miles

AFG.	—AFGHANISTAN	C.A.R.	—CENTRAL AFRICAN REPUBLIC
ALB.	—ALBANIA	CZECH.	—CZECHOSLOVAKIA
ALG.	—ALGERIA	DAH.	—DAHOMEY
AND.	—ANDORRA	EL SAL.	—EL SALVADOR
AUST.	—AUSTRIA	EQ.GUI.	—EQUATORIAL GUI
BEL.	—BELGIUM	GHA.	—GHANA
BHU.	—BHUTAN	GIB.	—GIBRALTAR (U.K.)
BOTS.	—BOTSWANA	HUN.	—HUNGARY
BR.HON.	—BR. HONDURAS	LEB.	—LEBANON
BUL.	—BULGARIA	LIECH.	—LIECHTENSTEIN
BUR.	—BURUNDI	LUX.	—LUXEMBOURG
CAMB.	—CAMBODIA	MAL.	—MALAWI
CAM.	—CAMEROON		

472

Austl. –AUSTRALIA
Braz. –BRAZIL
Den. –DENMARK
Ec. –ECUADOR
Fr. –FRANCE
Ind. –INDIA
It. –ITALY
Neth. –NETHERLANDS
N.Z. –NEW ZEALAND
Nor. –NORWAY
Port. –PORTUGAL
Sp. –SPAIN
U.K. –UNITED KINGDOM
U.S. –UNITED STATES
OCEAN
Spitsbergen (Nor.)
UNION OF SOVIET SOCIALIST REPUBLICS (SOVIET UNION)
E U R A S I A
EUROPE (see inset below)
MONGOLIA
JAPAN
N. KOREA
S.
PEOPLE'S REP. OF CHINA
PACIFIC OCEAN
TUN.
ISRAEL
IRAQ
IRAN
AFG.
LIBYA
U.A.R.
JORDAN
PAKISTAN
SIK.
NEP.
BHU.
Ryukyu Is. (Jap.)
SAUDI ARABIA
TR.ST.
PAK.
INDIA
BURMA
TAIWAN
Marcus I. (Jap.)
MUSCAT AND OMAN
LAOS
N. VIETNAM
S.
THAI.
CAMB.
PHILIPPINES
Wake I. (U.S.)
M I C R O N E S I A
NIGER
CHAD
SUDAN
YEM.
S. YEMEN
Laccadive Is. (Ind.)
Andaman Is. (Ind.)
NIGERIA
AFRICA
ETHIOPIA
Nicobar Is. (Ind.)
DAH.
C.A.R.
SOMALIA
CEYLON
MALDIVE IS.
BRUNEI (U.K.)
Terr. of the Pacific Islands (U.S.)
CAM.
MALAYSIA
UGA.
KENYA
REP. OF THE CONGO
GABON
DEM. REP. OF THE CONGO
SING.
Equator
Gilbert Is.
NAURU
Ellice Is.
RWA.
BUR.
TANZANIA
Seychelles (U.K.)
Chagos Arch. (U.K.)
I N D O N E S I A
Terr. of New Guinea (Austl.)
M E L A N E S I A
(U.K.)
Solomon Is.
ANGOLA (Port.)
ZAMBIA
MAL.
(Fr.)
Cocos I. (Austl.)
Christmas I. (Austl.)
Port. Timor
New Hebrides (U.K. & Fr.)
FIJI IS.
RHO.
MOZ. (Port.)
MALAGASY REP.
S.W. AFRICA (S.Afr.)
BOTS.
MAURITIUS
New Caledonia
AUSTRALIA
INDIAN OCEAN
SWAZILAND
SOUTH AFRICA
LESOTHO
Norfolk I. (Austl.)
Amsterdam I.
St. Paul I.
NEW ZEALAND
(Fr.)
Pr. Edward Is. (S. Afr.)
Crozet Is.
Kerguelen Is.
Tasmania
Auckland Is. (N.Z.)
Macquarie Is. (Austl.)
EUROPE
0 500
Miles
FINLAND
Helsinki
SWEDEN
Oslo
NORWAY
Stockholm
Moscow
North Sea
DENMARK
Copenhagen
UNION OF SOVIET SOCIALIST REPUBLICS (SOVIET UNION)
IRELAND
Dublin
UNITED KINGDOM
Amsterdam
Hague
NETH.
Berlin
E.
W. GERMANY
Warsaw
POLAND
London
Brussels
BEL.
Bonn
Prague
CZECH.
ATLANTIC OCEAN
Paris
LUX.
Vienna
Budapest
FRANCE
LIECH.
AUST.
HUN.
RUMANIA
Bern
SWITZ.
Bucharest
Black Sea
Belgrade
YUG.
BUL.
Sofia
MON.
S.M.
Ankara
Corsica (Fr.)
V.C.
Tirana
AND.
Madrid
Rome
ITALY
ALB.
TURKEY
PORTUGAL
Lisbon
SPAIN
Sardinia (It.)
GREECE
SYRIA
Balearic Is. (Sp.)
Athens
Mediterranean Sea
Sicily
Nicosia
LEB.
GIB.(U.K.)
MALTA
Crete
CYPRUS
ANTARCTICA
MON. –MONACO
MOR. –MOROCCO
MOZ. –MOZAMBIQUE (Port.)
NEP. –NEPAL
NETH. –NETHERLANDS
PAK. –PAKISTAN
PARA. –PARAGUAY
PORT.GUI. –PORT. GUINEA
RHO. –RHODESIA
RWA. –RWANDA
S.M. –SAN MARINO
SIK. –SIKKIM
SING. –SINGAPORE
SP.SAH. –SP. SAHARA
SWITZ. –SWITZERLAND
THAI. –THAILAND
TR.ST. –TRUCIAL STATES
TUN. –TUNISIA
U.A.R. –UNITED ARAB REPUBLIC
UGA. –UGANDA
URU. –URUGUAY
U. VOL. –UPPER VOLTA
V.C. –VATICAN CITY
YEM. –YEMEN
YUG. –YUGOSLAVIA

NORTH AMERICA (Physical)

Elevations in feet
- More than 10,000
- 5,000 to 10,000
- 2,000 to 5,000
- 1,000 to 2,000
- Sea level to 1,000

0 — 500 Miles

Arch. — Archipelago
C. — Cape
G. — Gulf
Mt. — Mountain
Pen. — Peninsula
Pt. — Point
RA. — Range
Str. — Strait

474

NORTH AMERICA
(Political)
International boundaries
National capitals
Other cities
0
500
Miles
Den. —DENMARK
Fr. —FRANCE
Neth. —NETHERLANDS
Mex. —MEXICO
U.K. —UNITED KINGDOM
U.S. —UNITED STATES
ASIA
Bering Sea
ARCTIC OCEAN
Beaufort Sea
Barrow
ALASKA (U.S.)
Fairbanks
Anchorage
Dawson
Gulf of Alaska
Arctic Circle
Juneau
Port Radium
Great Bear Lake
Great Slave Lake
Thule
GREENLAND (Den.)
ICELAND
Pond Inlet
Baffin Bay
Godthaab
Hudson Bay
Labrador Sea
Churchill
PACIFIC OCEAN
Edmonton
CANADA
Calgary
Victoria
Vancouver
Seattle
Portland
Spokane
Regina
Lake Winnipeg
Winnipeg
Goose Bay
Gander
St. John's
Seven Islands
Quebec
Montreal
Ottawa
Halifax
Great Lakes
Missouri R.
San Francisco
Great Salt L.
Salt Lake City
UNITED STATES OF AMERICA
Minneapolis
St.Paul
Milwaukee
Toronto
Buffalo
Boston
Omaha
Chicago
Detroit
Cleveland
New York
Los Angeles
Colorado R.
Denver
Kansas City
St.Louis
Cincinnati
Pittsburgh
Philadelphia
Baltimore
Washington
San Diego
Phoenix
Ohio R.
Arkansas R.
Norfolk
Guadalupe I. (Mex.)
El Paso
Dallas
Mississippi R.
Memphis
Atlanta
Bermuda Is. (U.K.)
Tropic of Cancer
G. of California
Rio Grande
San Antonio
Houston
New Orleans
ATLANTIC OCEAN
Monterrey
GULF OF MEXICO
BAHAMA IS. (U.K.)
Grand Bahama I.
Great Abaco I.
Miami
Nassau
Eleuthera I.
Andros I.
Cat I.
Gr. Exuma I.
Long I.
MEXICO
Guadalajara
Havana
CUBA
Acklins I.
Mayaguana I.
Gr. Inagua I.
Mexico City
Orizaba
Santiago-de-Cuba
JAMAICA
HAITI
DOMINICAN REPUBLIC
(U.S.)
Virgin Is.
(U.K.)
Kingston
Port au-Prince
Santo Domingo
PUERTO RICO
Belmopan
BR. HOND. (U.K.)
Guadeloupe (Fr.)
Dominica (U.K.)
Martinique (Fr.)
St. Lucia
St. Vincent (U.K.)
GUATEMALA
Guatemala
HONDURAS
Tegucigalpa
San Salvador
EL SALVADOR
CARIBBEAN SEA
NICARAGUA
Neth. Antilles
Managua
Grenada
San José
COSTA RICA
CANAL ZONE (U.S.)
Panamá
PANAMA
TRINIDAD AND TOBAGO
SOUTH AMERICA
West longitude

Vancouver
C. Flattery
WASHINGTON
Seattle
Olympia
Tacoma
Mt. Rainier 14,410 ft.
Spokane
Portland
Salem
Eugene
OREGON
C. Blanco
C. Mendocino
Great Falls
Helena
MONTANA
Missouri R.
Yellowstone R.
Billings
NORTH DAKOTA
Bismarck
Fargo
IDAHO
Boise
Snake R.
Grand Teton 13,766 ft.
Idaho Falls
WYOMING
BLACK HILLS
Pierre
SOUTH DAKOTA
Sioux Falls
Cheyenne R.
ROCKY MOUNTAINS
GREAT PLAINS
Columbia Plateau
Great Salt Lake
Ogden
Salt Lake City
UTAH
Great Basin
NEVADA
Reno
Carson City
SIERRA NEVADA
Central Valley
COAST RANGES
CASCADE RA.
Sacramento
San Francisco
Berkeley
Oakland
San Jose
Fresno
Mt. Whitney 14,495 ft.
CALIFORNIA
Bakersfield
Pt. Conception
Mojave Desert
Las Vegas
Death Valley
Los Angeles
Pasadena
Long Beach
San Bernardino
Riverside
Anaheim
San Diego
PACIFIC OCEAN
Cheyenne
N. Platte R.
S. Platte R.
NEBRASKA
Omaha
Lincoln
Longs Pk. 14,256 ft.
Denver
COLORADO
Mt. Elbert 14,433 ft.
Pikes Pk. 14,110 ft.
Pueblo
Blanca Pk. 14,317 ft.
Colorado Plateau
KANSAS
Wichita
Arkansas R.
ARIZONA
Phoenix
Tucson
Santa Fe
Albuquerque
NEW MEXICO
Amarillo
OKLAHOMA
Oklahoma City
Lubbock
Llano Estacado
El Paso
Fort Worth
Dallas
TEXAS
Waco
Austin
San Antonio
Laredo
Corpus Christi
Coastal Plain
Rio Grande
MEXICO
ASIA
SOVIET UNION
Arctic Circle
Bering Strait
Barrow
BROOKS RA.
ALASKA
Nome
Fairbanks
Yukon R.
St. Lawrence I.
St. Matthew I.
ALASKA RANGE
Mt. McKinley 20,320 ft.
Anchorage
CANADA
Monday International Date Line Sunday
BERING SEA
Nunivak I.
Kenai Pen.
Gulf of Alaska
Juneau
Alexander Arch.
Kodiak I.
ALEUTIAN ISLANDS
Near Is.
Rat Is.
Andreanof Is.
Fox Is.
Unimak I.
0 300 Miles
West longitude

UNITED STATES OF AMERICA
(Physical-Political)

——	International boundaries
– – –	State boundaries
⊛	National capitals
★	State capitals
•	Other cities

Elevations in feet
- More than 10,000
- 5,000 to 10,000
- 2,000 to 5,000
- 1,000 to 2,000
- Sea level to 1,000

0 100 200 300
Miles

CONN. — CONNECTICUT
D.C. — DISTRICT OF COLUMBIA
MASS. — MASSACHUSETTS
MD. — MARYLAND
N.H. — NEW HAMPSHIRE
R.I. — RHODE ISLAND
VT. — VERMONT
W.VA. — WEST VIRGINIA

C. — Cape
Mt. — Mountain
Pen. — Peninsula
Pk. — Peak

477

SOUTH AMERICA
(Physical)
Elevations in feet
More than 10,000
5,000 to 10,000
2,000 to 5,000
1,000 to 2,000
Sea level to 1,000
0
500
Miles
Arch. –Archipelago
C. –Cape
G. –Gulf
Mt. –Mountain
Pen. –Peninsula
Pt. –Point
CARIBBEAN SEA
PACIFIC OCEAN
ATLANTIC OCEAN
Guajira Pen.
Maracaibo
Caracas
Margarita I.
Tobago
Trinidad
Orinoco R. Delta
Orinoco R.
G. of Panama
Malpelo I.
Mt. Tolima 19,049 ft.
Bogotá
Meta R.
Llanos
Angel Falls
GUIANA HIGHLANDS
Devils I.
C. Orange
Amazon R. Delta
Rio Negro
Caquetá R.
AMAZON
BASIN
Japurá
Amazon
Marajó I.
Equator
Mt. Chimborazo 20,561 ft.
Gulf of Guayaquil
Marañon R.
Juruá R.
Purus R.
Madeira R.
Tapajoz R.
Xingu R.
Tocantins R.
Aguja Pt.
Ucayali R.
Mt. Huascarán 22,205 ft.
C. São Roque
Parnaíba R.
Araguaia R.
Tocantins R.
São Francisco R.
Lima
Beni R.
Mamoré R.
Mato Grosso Plateau
Brasília
BRAZILIAN HIGHLANDS
ANDES MOUNTAINS
Mt. Ancohuma 21,490 ft.
Lake Titicaca
Poopó
Paraguay R.
Pilcomayo R.
Gran Chaco
Paraná R.
Mt. Bandeira 9,462 ft.
São Paulo
C. Frio
Rio de Janeiro
Tropic of Capricorn
San Felix I.
San Ambrosio I.
Salado R.
Uruguay R.
Mt. Aconcagua 22,834 ft.
Santiago
Juan Fernández Is.
Buenos Aires
Montevideo
Rio de la Plata
Pampas
Colorado R.
Blanca Bay
San Matías Gulf
Valdés Pen.
Chiloé I.
Chonos Arch.
Taitao Pen.
Patagonia
Gulf of San Jorge
C. Tres Puntas
Grande Bay
Strait of Magellan
Strait of Magellan
Falkland Is.
Tierra del Fuego
Cape Horn
West longitude
80°
60°
50°
40°
30°
20°
90°
10°
0°
10°
20°
30°
40°
50°

SOUTH AMERICA (Political)

- International boundaries
- ⊛ National capitals
- • Other cities

Col. — COLOMBIA
Fr. — FRANCE
Neth. — NETHERLANDS
U.K. — UNITED KINGDOM

AFRICA (Physical)

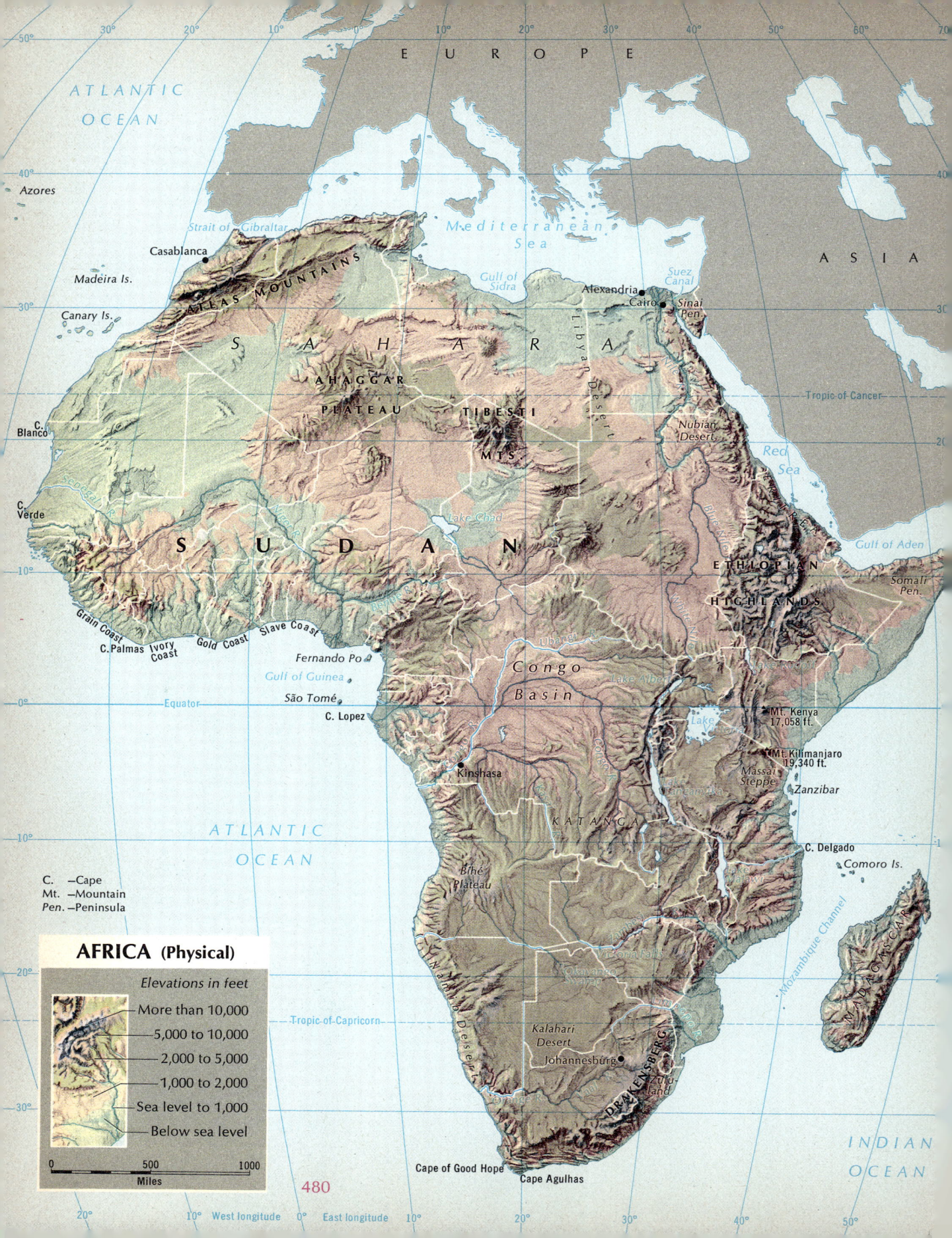

Elevations in feet
- More than 10,000
- 5,000 to 10,000
- 2,000 to 5,000
- 1,000 to 2,000
- Sea level to 1,000
- Below sea level

C. — Cape
Mt. — Mountain
Pen. — Peninsula

480

EURASIA (Physical)

Elevations in feet
- More than 10,000
- 5,000 to 10,000
- 2,000 to 5,000
- 1,000 to 2,000
- Sea level to 1,000
- Below sea level

Mt. — Mountain
Pen. — Peninsula
RA. — Range
Str. — Strait

BHU. –BHUTAN
BUL. –BULGARIA
CAM. –CAMBODIA
DEN. –DENMARK
GER. –GERMANY
IRE. –IRELAND
JOR. –JORDAN
NEP. –NEPAL
PAK. –PAKISTAN
RUM. –RUMANIA
YUG. –YUGOSLAVIA
1–ALBANIA
2–ANDORRA
3–AUSTRIA
4–BAHREIN
5–BELGIUM
6–BRUNEI (U.K.)
7–CZECHOSLOVAKIA
8–HUNGARY
9–KUWAIT
10–LEBANON
11–LIECHTENSTEIN
12–LUXEMBOURG
13–MONACO
14–NETHERLANDS
15–QUATAR
16–SAN MARINO
17–SIKKIM
18–SINGAPORE
19–SWITZERLAND
ATLANTIC OCEAN
ARCTIC OCEAN
INDIAN OCEAN
EUROPE
ASIA
AFRICA
UNION OF SOVIE
(SOVIET UNIO
PORTUGAL
SPAIN
FRANCE
UNITED KINGDOM
IRE.
NORWAY
SWEDEN
FINLAND
DEN.
POLAND
ITALY
YUG.
RUM.
BUL.
GREECE
TURKEY
SYRIA
IRAQ
ISRAEL
JOR.
CYPRUS
MALTA
IRAN (PERSIA)
AFGHANISTAN
PAKISTAN
INDIA
CEYLON
SAUDI ARABIA
YEMEN
SOUTHERN YEMEN
MUSCAT AND OMAN
TRUCIAL STATES
NEP.
TURKESTAN
SINKIAN
TIBE
HINDUSTA
UKRAINIA
Jammu and Kashmir
North Sea
Black Sea
Mediterranean Sea
Caspian Sea
Aral Sea
Red Sea
Arabian Sea
Barents Sea
Empty Quarter
Neutral Zones
Madeira Is. (Port.)
Balearic Is. (Sp.)
Spitsbergen (Nor.)
Novaya Zemlya
North Land
Socotra (S.Yemen)
Laccadive Is. (Ind.)
MALDIVE ISLANDS
Lisbon
Madrid
Valencia
Barcelona
Bordeaux
Paris
Marseilles
Nice
Corsica
Sardinia
Sicily
Valetta
Palermo
Naples
Rome
Milan
Bern
Munich
Vienna
Prague
Berlin
Warsaw
Wroclaw
Budapest
Belgrade
Bucharest
Sofia
Tirana
Athens
Crete (Gr.)
Istanbul (Constantinople)
Ankara
Izmir
Nicosia
Beirut
Damascus
Jerusalem
Amman
Baghdad
Basra
Abadan
Kuwait
Al Manamah
Doha
Dubai
Muscat
Riyadh
Mecca
San'a
Aden
Madinat ash Sha'b
Tehran
Kabul
Islamabad
Lahore
Karachi
Hyderabad
Delhi
New Delhi
Katmand
Ahmadabad
Bombay
Madras
Colombo
Male
Tashkent
Baku
Krasnodar
Volgograd
Saratov
Kuibyshev
Orenburg
Magnitogorsk
Chelyabinsk
Sverdlovsk
Ufa
Kazan
Perm
Omsk
Tomsk
Novosibirs
Urumc
Moscow
Kiev
Kharkov
Odessa
Leningrad
Tallinn
Riga
Kaliningrad
Helsinki
Stockholm
Oslo
Bergen
Narvik
Murmansk
Archangel
Göteborg
Copenhagen
Hamburg
Hanover
Amsterdam
Hague
Brussels
Bonn
London
Dublin
Glasgow
Ob R.
Volga R.
Euphrates R.
Tigris R.
Indus R.
Ganges
Sinai Pen.
East longitude

EURASIA (Political)

Legend:
- Austl. — AUSTRALIA
- Gr. — GREECE
- Ind. — INDIA
- Indo. — INDONESIA
- Jap. — JAPANESE
- Nor. — NORWAY
- Pen. — Peninsula
- Port. — PORTUGAL
- TERR. — TERRITORY
- Trust. — Trusteeship
- U.K. — UNITED KINGDOM
- U.S. — UNITED STATES
- U.S.S.R. — SOVIET UNION

- ⎯⎯⎯ International boundaries
- ⎯ ⎯ ⎯ Indefinite or temporary boundaries
- ⊛ National capitals
- • Other cities

Scale: 0 — 500 — 1000 Miles

AUSTRALIA AND OCEANIA
(Physical-Political)

- International boundaries
- ⊛ National capitals
- • Other cities

Elevations in feet
- 5,000 to 10,000
- 2,000 to 5,000
- 1,000 to 2,000
- Sea level to 1,000

0 500 1000 1500 Miles

Labels on map

EURASIA

Sea of Okhotsk
Sea of Japan
East China Sea
JAPAN — Tokyo
Ryukyu Is. (Jap.) — Okinawa
BONIN IS. (Jap.)
VOLCANO IS. (Jap.)
Marcus I. (U.S.)
Taipei, TAIWAN
Philippine Sea
MARIANA IS.
Quezon City, PHILIPPINES
South China Sea
Guam (U.S.)
Eniwetok Atoll
Yap Is.
Palau Is.
CAROLINE ISLANDS
Truk
TERRITORY OF THE PACIFIC ISLANDS (U.S.)
Arabian Sea
Socotra (S.Yemen)
Bay of Bengal
Laccadive Is. (Ind.)
Andaman Is. (Ind.)
Colombo, CEYLON
Nicobar Is. (Ind.)
MALDIVE ISLANDS — Male
AFRICA
Equator
SEYCHELLES (U.K.)
Amirante Is.
Cosmoledo Group
Farquhar Group
Agalega Is.
CHAGOS ARCH. (U.K.)
INDIAN OCEAN
INDONESIA
Djakarta
Christmas I. (Austl.)
Cocos I. (Austl.)
Port. Timor
Timor Sea
Bismarck Arch.
TERR. OF NEW GUINEA (Austl.)
WEST IRIAN (Indo.)
PAPUA (Austl.)
BR. SOLOMON IS.
COMORO IS. (Fr.)
Tananarive
MALAGASY REP.
St. Brandon
Port Louis
Rodrigues
La Réunion
MAURITIUS
Tropic of Capricorn
Arnhem Land
Cape York Pen.
Great Barrier Reef
Coral Sea
Great Sandy Desert
Western Plateau
Great Artesian Basin
Central Lowlands
GREAT DIVIDING RANGE
Brisbane
Lord Howe (Aus.)
Great Victoria Desert
Nullarbor Plain
Perth
Darling
Adelaide
Sydney
Botany Bay
Canberra
Mt. Kosciusko 7,316 ft.
Melbourne
AUSTRALIA
King I.
Flinders I.
Tasman
Tasmania
Amsterdam I. (Fr.)
St. Paul I. (Fr.)
Kerguelen I. (Fr.)
Heard I. (Austl.)
Macquarie Is. (Austl.)

Tropic of Cancer
Equator
East Longitude

Bering Sea
Gulf of Alaska
NORTH AMERICA
NORTH PACIFIC OCEAN
Midway Is. (U.S.)
HAWAIIAN ISLANDS
HAWAII (U.S.)
Oahu
Honolulu
Maui
Hawaii
Tropic of Cancer
Guadalupe I. (Mex.)
Wake I. (U.S.)
Johnston Atoll (U.S.)
Revilla Gigedo Is. (Mex.)
Sunday
International Date Line
Monday
POLYNESIA
MARSHALL ISLANDS
Clipperton (Fr.)
Palmyra I. (U.S.)
Washington I. (U.K.)
Fanning I. (U.K.)
Gilbert Is.
Howland I. (U.S.)
Baker I. (U.S.)
Christmas I.
(U.S.&U.K.)
Equator
GALAPAGOS IS. (Ec.)
GILBERT AND ELLICE IS. (U.K.)
Ellice Is.
PHOENIX IS. (U.K.&U.S.)
Malden I.
Starbuck I.
TOKELAU IS. (N.Z.)
MARQUESAS IS.
Santa Cruz Is.
W. SAMOA
Pago Pago
Manihiki
Flint I.
SOUTH AMERICA
Wallis I. (Fr.)
Apia
Suvorov I.
AMERICAN SAMOA (U.S.)
SOCIETY IS.
TUAMOTU ARCH.
FIJI IS.
Suva
NEW HEBRIDES
(U.K.)
Niue
(N.Z.)
COOK IS.
Tahiti
FRENCH POLYNESIA
TONGA IS.
Rarotonga
EDONIA
Tropic of Capricorn
TUBUAI IS.
Gambier Is.
(U.K.)
Pitcairn I.
Rapa
San Felix I. (Chile)
San Ambrosio I. (Chile)
Easter I. (Chile)
Norfolk I. (Austl.)
Kermadec Is. (N.Z.)
SOUTH PACIFIC OCEAN
Juan Fernández I. (Chile)
Auckland
North Island
NEW ZEALAND
Wellington
Christchurch
Chatham Is. (N.Z.)
Bounty Is. (N.Z.)
Antipodes Is. (N.Z.)
Campbell I. (N.Z.)
Austl. —AUSTRALIA
Ec. —ECUADOR
Fr. —FRANCE
Ind. —INDIA
Indo. —INDONESIA
Mex. —MEXICO
N.Z. —NEW ZEALAND
U.K. —UNITED KINGDOM
U.S. —UNITED STATES
180°
160°
140°
120°
100°
80°
60°
40°
West longitude
60°
40°
20°
0°
20°
40°

The Constitution of the United States

The Constitution is adapted and presented here in a form in which pupils should be able to understand its fundamental ideas and principles. However, the actual words of the Constitution have been used to demonstrate certain important parts.

PREAMBLE

We the People of the United States, in order to form a more perfect Union, establish justice, insure domestic tranquility, provide for the common defense, promote the general welfare, and secure the blessings of liberty to ourselves and our posterity, do ordain and establish this Constitution for the United States of America.

ARTICLE 1: THE LEGISLATURE
(Congress and Its Powers)

All legislative powers herein granted shall be vested in a Congress of the United States which shall consist of a Senate and a House of Representatives.

Section 1. All laws are made by a Congress of the United States, made up of a Senate and a House of Representatives.

Section 2. (How the House of Representatives is chosen) Members of the House of Representatives are elected every 2 years. To be eligible for election, a person must be at least 25 years old, a citizen of the United States for at least 7 years, and must live in the State where he is elected. The number of representatives from each state depends on the size of its population. Every 10 years there is a census, or counting of the population, to determine how many representatives each state has.

Section 3. (How the Senate is chosen) The Senate of the United States is made up of two senators from each state. Each senator serves for 6 years. To be eligible for election, a person must be at least 30 years old, a citizen of the United States for at least 9 years, and must live in the state that elects him.

The Vice-President of the United States presides over the Senate, but he does not have a vote unless there is a tie. An official of the United States government may be removed from office in the following way: The House of Representatives impeaches him, or accuses him of wrongdoing. The Senate, acting as a court, then tries him on the charges brought by the House. A $2/3$ vote of the senators is required to convict him. If found guilty, the convicted person is removed from office.

The times, places, and manner of holding elections for Senators and Representatives shall be prescribed in each state by the legislature thereof; but the Congress may at any time by law make or alter such regulations, except as to the places of choosing Senators.

Section 4. (The election of Congress) Each state decides when and where to hold the election for senators and representatives, but Congress may pass a law to decide this itself, if it wishes.

Section 5. (Rules of Congress) At least half the members must be present for each house of Congress to do its business. Each house may make its own rules for carrying on its business. It also keeps a record of what it does, including how the members vote, and publishes this record.

Section 6. (Privileges of congressmen) The senators and representatives are paid for their work by the United States government. They may not be arrested while attending a meeting of Congress, or while traveling to or from Congress. Also, they cannot be punished for anything they might say in a meeting of Congress.

No senator or representative can hold any other office that receives pay from the United States government.

All bills for raising revenue shall originate in the House of Representatives; but the Senate may propose or concur with amendments as on other bills.

Section 7. (Making federal laws) All bills for raising money must begin in the House of Representatives, but the Senate may propose changes in such bills. Other bills may begin in either house.

When a bill has passed the House of Representatives and the Senate, it is presented to the

President of the United States. If he approves, he signs it and the bill becomes law. If he does not approve, he returns it to Congress and explains why he does not approve it. If ⅔ of each house again votes to pass it, the bill becomes law without the President's signature. If the President does not return a bill to Congress within 10 days after he receives it, the bill becomes law without his signature. But if Congress adjourns before these 10 days are up, the bill does not become law unless the President signs it.

Section 8. (The powers of Congress) Congress has the power to collect taxes, to pay the debts of the government, to provide for the defense of the United States, and to provide for the general welfare of the country; to borrow money; to make laws about commerce with other nations and commerce among the states; to make laws about citizenship; to coin money; to punish counterfeiters; to establish post offices; to issue copyrights and patents to authors and inventors in order to keep their writings and discoveries from being copied by others without their permission; to set up courts; to punish pirates; to declare war; to raise armies; to maintain a navy; to make rules for governing the army and navy personnel; to put down rebellions and fight off invasions; to govern the District of Columbia; to make all laws necessary for carrying out all the powers of Congress listed above, and for carrying out the powers of the United States government in general.

Section 9. (Powers the federal government does not have) Only in special emergencies may the federal government hold a person in prison without a court hearing.

Congress may not tax articles exported from any state, and all trade regulations must be the same for every part of the country.

No official or department of the federal government may obtain money from the United States Treasury before Congress enacts a law permitting the withdrawal. As a republic the United States is forbidden to establish a class of noblemen. Federal officers may not accept foreign honors without congressional approval.

Section 10. (Powers the state governments do not have) States may not make treaties, coin money, or interfere with the obligations of people to carry out their contracts. States may not levy taxes on imports or exports. They must not have troops or naval vessels in peacetime, or make agreements with other states or with another country, unless Congress gives its approval.

ARTICLE II: THE EXECUTIVE
(The President and Vice-President)

The executive power shall be vested in a President of the United States of America. He shall hold his office during the term of 4 years, and, together with the Vice-President, chosen for the same term, be elected as follows:

Section 1. The power to carry out the laws belongs to the President of the United States. He and the Vice-President serve for 4 years. They are chosen as follows: Each state chooses a number of electors, equal to the total number of senators and representatives of that state. These electors vote for two persons. The person receiving the highest number is elected President, provided he has a majority of all the votes cast. The one with the next highest number is elected Vice-President. If no one has a majority, then the House of Representatives chooses from the five highest people on the list. If the House chooses the President, the vote is taken by states. That is, each state has one vote, and the representatives from that state decide how it is to be cast. The person getting a majority of these votes is elected President. The person with the next highest becomes Vice-President.

No person except a natural-born citizen, or a citizen of the United States at the time of the adoption of this Constitution, shall be eligible to the office of President; neither shall any person be eligible to that office who shall not have attained to the age of thirty-five years, and been fourteen years a resident within the United States.

To be eligible for election, a person must be born in the United States and be at least 35 years old.

If the President dies, resigns, becomes unable to carry out his duties, or is removed from office, the Vice-President becomes President.

The President takes the following oath:

"I do solemnly swear (or affirm) that I will faithfully execute the office of President of the United States, and will, to the best of my ability, preserve, protect, and defend the Constitution of the United States."

Section 2. The President is Commander in Chief of the Army and Navy of the United States. He may also pardon those who are convicted of offenses against the United States.

With the approval of ⅔ of the senators, the President has the power to make treaties. With the approval of a majority of the senators, he can appoint ambassadors, Supreme Court judges, and many other officials of the United States.

Section 3. The President must make reports to Congress on the condition of the country, and recommend to Congress laws that he thinks should be passed. He is responsible for seeing that all laws are carried out. He also commissions all officers of the United States.

Section 4. The President, Vice-President, and all other officers of the United States are removed from office if they are impeached and convicted of treason, bribery, or other crimes.

ARTICLE III: THE JUDICIARY
(The Federal Courts and Judges)

The judicial power of the United States shall be vested in one Supreme Court, and in such inferior courts as the Congress may from time to time ordain and establish.

Section 1. There is a Supreme Court of the United States; and Congress may also create other federal courts. All federal judges hold their offices for life, unless they are impeached and convicted.

Section 2. The federal courts deal with cases that involve the Constitution, or federal laws, or treaties with other countries. They also deal with cases between two or more states, or between citizens of different states. Congress decides which kinds of cases may be appealed from the federal courts to the Supreme Court.

The trial of all crimes, except in cases of impeachment, must be by jury.

Treason against the United States shall consist only in levying war against them, or in adhering to their enemies, giving them aid and comfort. No person shall be convicted of treason unless on the testimony of two witnesses to the same overt act, or on confession in open court.

Section 3. The definition of treason is making war against the United States, or joining its enemies, or giving them aid. No person can be convicted of treason unless there are at least two witnesses to his act, or unless he confesses to treason in court. Congress sets the penalty for treason.

ARTICLE IV: RELATIONS AMONG THE STATES

Full faith and credit shall be given in each state to the public acts, records, and judicial proceedings of every other state. And the Congress may by general laws prescribe the manner in which such acts, records, and proceedings shall be proved, and the effect thereof.

Section 1. Each state must recognize the laws of every other state.

Section 2. The citizens of each state are equal before the law to the citizens of all the other states.

A person who is wanted for a serious crime in one state and is found in another state must be sent back to the state where he is wanted, if the governor requests it.

Section 3. New states may be admitted to the Union by Congress. Congress makes rules about the territory or other property belonging to the United States.

Section 4. The United States must protect the states from invasion and domestic violence.

ARTICLE V: PROVISION FOR AMENDMENTS

The Constitution may be amended, or changed as follows:

1. First, the amendments must be proposed to the states. One way is for each house of Congress to pass the proposed amendment by a ⅔ vote. Another way is for ⅔ of all the states to ask Congress to call a special convention or meeting, during which amendments can be proposed.

2. Second, the amendments must be ratified, or approved, by ¾ of all the states. This can be done by the legislatures of the states, or by special conventions in each state; Congress decides which method is used in each case.

The only part of the Constitution that cannot be changed is that each state is guaranteed two votes in the Senate as long as it wants to have them.

ARTICLE VI: GENERAL PROVISIONS

This Constitution, and the laws of the United States which shall be made in pursuance thereof, and all treaties made, or which shall be made, under the authority of the United States, shall be the supreme law of the land; and the judges in every state shall be bound thereby, any thing in the constitution or laws of any state to the contrary notwithstanding.

The Constitution, the laws of the United States, and the treaties made by the United States, are the supreme law of the land.

Senators, representatives, members of state legislatures, and all other officers of the United States government and of the states take an oath to support this Constitution.

ARTICLE VII

This Constitution shall go into effect when nine states approve it.

AMENDMENTS

Amendment I Congress may not interfere with freedom of religion, freedom of speech, freedom of the press, or the right of people to assemble peaceably or send petitions to their government.

Amendment II The right of the people to keep and bear arms may not be interfered with.

Amendment III During peacetime, the government cannot require citizens to put up soldiers in their homes.

Amendment IV The government may not search people or their homes unreasonably.

Amendment V Persons accused of serious crimes are entitled to a jury trial. They may not be forced to give evidence against themselves. Their lives, freedom, and property may not be taken from them unfairly. If the government takes a person's property for public use, it must pay the owner for it.

Amendment VI A person accused of a serious crime is entitled to a speedy and public trial. He must be told what he is accused of. He is entitled to have a lawyer. He has the right to see and question those who accuse him.

Amendment VII In most cases, there must be a right to a jury trial.

Amendment VIII Punishment may not be cruel and unusual.

Amendments IX and X If the constitution does not give a certain right to the United States government, and also does not forbid a state government to have that right, then the states and the people have it.

Amendment XI The power of the judicial branch is limited to certain kinds of cases.

Amendment XII Electors vote for President and Vice-President separately.

Amendment XIII Slavery may not exist in the United States.

Amendment XIV People born in the United States or naturalized here are citizens of the United States. They are also citizens of the states they live in.

States may not make laws that limit the rights of citizens of the United States. They may not take away a person's life or freedom or property unfairly. They must treat all people equally under the law.

Amendment XV No citizen may be denied the right to vote because of his race.

Amendment XVI Congress is allowed to pass an income tax law.

Amendment XVII United States senators are elected by the people.

Amendment XVIII Liquor may no longer be manufactured or sold in the United States. (This amendment was repealed by the 21st amendment.)

Amendment XIX No citizen may be denied the right to vote because of sex.

Amendment XX Presidents start their new terms on January 20; Congress starts its new term on January 3.

Amendment XXI The 18th amendment to this Constitution is repealed, or taken back.

Amendment XXII Presidents are limited to two terms in office.

Amendment XXIII Residents of Washington, D. C., have the right to vote for President.

Amendment XXIV Citizens may not be required to pay a tax in order to vote for President, senators, or congressmen.

Amendment XXV In case the President becomes too ill to carry on his job, the Vice-President will take over as Acting President until the President is better.

Glossary

abolitionist. A person who actively opposed slavery.

adobe. Clay or mud mixed with straw and shaped into blocks, and dried in the sun.

altiplano. A large, high plateau lying between two ranges of the Andes in Bolivia.

aqueduct. A man-made channel that carries flowing water. The channel might be made of cement, clay, or other material.

archaeologist. A scientist who studies the history of people through the things they made and left behind. These things include items as small as needles and as large as cities.

artifact. An object made by man, such as a piece of pottery, a tool, or an ornament. These objects are studied by archaeologists.

astronomy. The science that studies the sun, moon, stars, and planets.

autobiography. The life story of a person, written or told by that person.

automation. The use of machines to operate other machines in the manufacture of a product.

Aztecs. The Indians who founded the Mexican empire conquered by Cortes.

barriada. A slum settlement made up of shacks or shanties, built on vacant land near the edges of cities in Peru.

barter. To exchange goods, instead of money, for other goods.

Bay Area Rapid Transit. A modern railway system to help move people in the San Francisco area into and out of that city.

Bering Strait. The waterway separating North America from Asia.

blacksmith. A person who shapes iron into various objects by forging, or heating and hammering, the iron.

blast furnace. A huge furnace, or smelter, in which iron is separated from its ore by forcing tremendous blasts of air into the lower part of the furnace.

bucket brigade. A method of fire fighting used in eighteenth-century American cities. People stood in lines and passed buckets of water from a well or other water supply to the fire.

canal. A man-made waterway that is used sometimes for travel and sometimes to channel water to dry areas.

capital. Wealth in the form of savings invested in factories, machines, or any other business adventures.

capital goods. Goods or machines used to produce other goods that will be sold.

caulker. A skilled worker who makes certain that wooden ships are watertight by filling the seams with a waterproof material.

causeway. A raised road or path across shallow water or marshland.

chamber of commerce. A private organization of merchants, businessmen, manufacturers, and others who are interested in increasing the commerce, or business, of a city.

chinampa. A small floating island, made by the Aztecs to increase the land area of Tenochtitlán.

Chinatown. A section of a city in which most of the residents are Chinese.

cholo (or *mestizo*). A Spanish word for a person of Indian and European descent.

city planner. A person, usually an engineer, who studies the physical problems of cities—such as housing, layout of streets, transportation, water and sewage systems—and designs remedies.

civil war. A war between two groups of people of the same nation or country.

civilization. The culture and ways of living of a people or nation.

climate. The average condition of the weather in one place over a period of years, as shown by temperature, rainfall, and prevailing winds.

coastal plain. A low, nearly flat land once covered by the sea.

colony. A settlement in a new land whose people remain subjects of the land from which they came.

commerce. The buying and selling of goods on a large scale. Commerce usually involves transportation.

commercial city. A city in which the principal business activity is trade.

commuter. A person who travels back and forth regularly by train, bus, or automobile, especially from the suburbs to the city.

conquistadores. The Spaniards who conquered the Aztecs in Mexico and the Incas in Peru in the sixteenth century.

conservationist. A person who supports the conservation, or preservation and careful use, of natural resources.

continent. A great landmass. North America, South America, Europe, Asia, Africa, Australia, and Antarctica are *continents*.

cooper. A person who makes or repairs barrels, tubs, or casks.

cotton gin. A machine that removes the seeds from the cotton fibers. It was invented by Eli Whitney in 1793.

cultivate. To prepare and use the soil for the growing of crops.

cultural pluralism. The presence of many different cultures in one nation.

culture. The way of living of a group, which includes their customs, traditions, values, and level of technology.

custom. A practice that is special to one people or a special way of doing something that is common to many people.

desert. A region with little or no rainfall.

discrimination. The making of a distinction in favor of or against certain persons based on the group or class to which they belong rather than on individual merit.

division of labor. A system by which each person in an economy specializes in a particular kind of work.

drought. A period of time, at least two weeks in length, during which little or no rain falls in an area.

economy. The way the people of a culture or country make their living—that is, how they make and use goods and services.

encomienda. A system by which the Spanish conquerors were to take care of the Indians in exchange for their services.

endosperm. The inner part of the kernel of wheat, from which white flour is made.

environment. The surroundings in which a person lives.

epidemic. The spread of a disease to a large number of people in a short time.

estuary. An arm of the sea at the mouth of a great river, where the tide meets the current of the river.

fertilizer. A substance used to enrich soil.

frontier. A sparsely settled area lying between a civilized, populated area and the wilderness.

fuel. A material that is used to produce heat or power.

ghetto. A neighborhood where members of minority groups are forced to live because they cannot afford or are refused homes in other parts of the city.

glacier. A large field or body of ice moving slowly down a mountain slope or valley; formed where snowfall exceeds melting.

grain elevator. A tall storage building for grain. It contains machinery for loading, unloading, cleaning, and mixing grain.

Great Plains. A large, mostly level area that stretches from the Rocky Mountains almost to the Mississippi River and from central Canada to the Gulf of Mexico.

hacienda. A large estate, especially in Middle or South America.

high population density. Many people living in a given area as compared to the number living in other areas of the same size.

historical records. All the available writings and symbolic markings that tell of past important events.

humidity. The amount of moisture in the air.

Inca. The ruler of the Incan Indians who, the people believed, was a descendant of the sun-god.

income tax. A method of taxation used by the federal government and by many states. Each person is taxed according to his income.

indentured servant. A person who sold his services for a certain period of time in exchange for free passage to America.

Indies. The name given to India, China, the East Indies, and Japan at the time of Christopher Columbus.

industrial park. An area in the suburbs set aside for use by industries.

Industrial Revolution. The period of great change in the way we work and live that was brought about by power-driven machines.

irrigation. A method of bringing water from a river or well to dry land.

isthmus. A narrow strip of land connecting two larger bodies of land.

labor union. An organization of workers that represents its members in disputes with employers.

latitude. The distance north or south of the equator, measured in degrees.

legislature. A group of people with the power to make laws for a state or nation.

literature. The writings of a people or nation.

llanos. A large plain in Spanish America.

lobby. A person or group of people, who represent a particular interest group and try to influence lawmakers.

longhouse. A long, loaf-shaped dwelling made of poles covered with bark, branches, or leaves and used by the Woodland Indians of North America to house several families.

manta. A small piece of cloth used by the Aztecs to express the worth of an object they wished to buy.

mass-transportation system. A system of commuter trains or buses built to move large numbers of people into, through, and out of a city.

Mayan Indians. The Indians of Central America and Mexico. Their ancestors founded a great empire in Yucatán.

megalopolis. A cluster, or group, of metropolitan areas, so close to one another that they seem to form a continuous urban area.

mestizo (or *cholo*). A Spanish word for a person of Indian and European descent.

metropolitan area. An area that contains at least one large city and many smaller cities and towns, which center on that city.

Mexican-American. An American of Mexican descent.

Middle America. The region consisting of the mainland and the islands between the United States and South America.

minimum wage law. A federal or state law that sets the minimum amount of money workers must receive for an hour of work.

minority group. A group, within a country, that differs from the majority of the population in national, racial, or religious background.

mita. The system by which the Inca Indians paid taxes by working for the government for a certain number of days each year.

mountain basin. A valley or large area of level land found high in mountainous areas. The basins are surrounded by mountain peaks.

national park. A large area of land of natural beauty or historical interest set aside by the government for the use and enjoyment of the people of the nation.

nationality. A person's status, or condition, as a member of a particular country. A child receives either the *nationality* of his parents, most often that of his father, or that of the country in which he is born.

People are also said to be of a certain *nationality* because they hold onto the habits, customs, and even the language of their native land.

New Amsterdam. The Dutch settlement that later became New York City.

New France. The French possessions in North America before 1763.

New Sweden. The Swedish colony in North America from 1638 to 1655, situated on the Delaware River.

nuclear energy. The energy that is produced by changing the matter of the nucleus, or central part, of an atom.

pampa. A large grass-covered plain that extends for miles along the Paraná-Paraguay and the Río de la Plata. It is one of the richest farming and grazing lands in South America.

Parliament. The lawmaking body of Great Britain or those of several other nations.

Pilgrim. A member of the group that crossed the Atlantic on the *Mayflower* and founded Plymouth Colony.

plantation. A large farm, with many workers, on which a crop such as cotton, sugar, tobacco, or coffee is grown.

plaza. A large public square or open area, found in towns or cities.

pollution. The condition of the air, of rivers, and of bodies of water when wastes such as fumes, smoke, garbage, and detergents are emptied into them.

public hearing. A meeting at which citizens tell government officials their opinions on proposed laws or public activities.

public housing. The housing projects, or groups of apartment buildings, that are constructed with the help of the government.

public well. A well provided by a government to enable people to get water.

Pueblo. A member of a group of Indians living in the American Southwest in what today is Arizona and New Mexico.

Quechua. The language of the Incas. It is spoken by many Indians in Peru, and also in parts of Bolivia, Ecuador, Chile, and Argentina.

race prejudice. An opinion or judgment about a person based on the color of his skin and not on the person himself.

reaper. A machine that cuts stalks of ripe grain while moving across a field.

redwood. A giant evergreen tree found in the western United States. Some *redwoods* grow more than 500 feet tall and live two or three thousand years.

rehabilitation. The remodeling of old homes so that they may be lived in again.

representative democracy. A form of government in which political power belongs to the people and is exercised with their consent.

representative government. A government in which people choose other people, or representatives, to make laws.

reservoir. A man-made lake that usually serves as a source of water for a city or other settled area.

residential area. An area consisting mostly of homes, with little or no commerce or industry.

resort city. A city whose principal industry is to offer entertainment and relaxation to people who come there on vacation.

Revolutionary War. The war of 1775–1781, in which the thirteen American colonies won their independence from Britain.

sanitation. The acts or processes necessary to make sure that unhealthful conditions are prevented or done away with.

segregation. The deliberate separation of groups, such as people of different races, from one another.

selva. A rain forest, or an area of tall trees so close together that sunlight rarely reaches the ground.

shanty. A small, shabby building made of cardboard, tin, or pieces of wood.

slash-and-burn. A system of forest clearing used by certain American Indian groups.

slave-trade center. A city or town to which slaves were brought to be sold.

slum. A neighborhood, or section of a neighborhood, in which the housing conditions are poor.

smelting. Heating ores and certain other materials to a high temperature in order to separate the metal from the ore.

social scientist. A person who studies the way individuals and groups of people live in society.

social security. A program carried out by federal and state governments to provide insurance payments to unemployed workers and to the handicapped, and to provide pensions to the aged. The program relies on taxes collected by federal and state governments.

source material. The important documents, written or unwritten records, and other facts containing information that is necessary to social scientists.

Spanish Harlem. A section of New York City in which most of the residents are Puerto Rican.

specialize. To concentrate one's efforts on a particular branch of an activity.

speculator. A person who buys something at a low price, hoping its value will rise. If the value rises, he sells the object.

steamboat. A boat or ship that uses the pressure from steam for its power to move.

storefront church. A store in a low-income area, usually a black ghetto, that is converted into a church.

strike. A work stoppage carried out by workers, usually union members, to force an employer to agree to their demands.

stucco. A material made by mixing sand, lime, and cement. It is applied to the outside of buildings in a soft form, but it soon hardens.

suburb. An area just outside the limits of a central city.

superblock. A section of a city enclosing several streets and designed for a special purpose.

survey. A sampling, or a partial collection, of facts, figures, or opinions. A *survey* is used to indicate what a complete collection might reveal.

surveyor. A person trained in the use of instruments that help him locate, position, measure, and mark definite areas of land.

tax. The money paid by people to cover the cost of running the government.

technology. The amount of scientific knowledge and the kinds of tools a people have.

tenement house. An apartment building in very poor and sometimes unsafe condition, in which many families live. Usually such houses are built in rows, close to each other.

tepee. The tent home of Plains Indians.

terracing. A method of farming in which the fields are like giant steps—each step a block of soil supported by walls.

thresh. To separate the tiny grains of wheat, oats, etc., from the straw.

tierra caliente. "Hot land." A term used in Middle and South America for the hot lowlands.

tierra fria. "Cold land." A term used in Middle and South America for the zone of low temperatures in mountainous land from above 6,000 feet up to 11,000 feet.

tierra templada. "Temperate land." A term used for the zone of mild temperatures found in mountainous regions of Latin America. The zone extends from about 2,000 up to 6,000 feet.

trade. To exchange goods by barter or sale.

tradition. The passing on of customs from one generation to another.

travois. A device, made of two trailing poles with a platform between, used by the Plains Indians to drag loads along the ground.

treaty. A signed agreement between two or more nations.

tributary. A small river that flows into a large river.

tropics. The area lying between $23\frac{1}{2}°$ north of the equator and $23\frac{1}{2}°$ south of the equator.

university city. A city that develops around a university.

urban decay. The decline in a part of a city brought about when buildings fall into ruin and are abandoned.

urban renewal. A program that cities undertake in order to improve living conditions.

value. A person's belief about what is good, desirable, and worth holding to.

volcano. A large hole in the crust of the earth, through which erupts or gushes hot molten rock, gases, and steam. Over the centuries a conelike peak builds up around the opening.

Western Hemisphere. The half of the earth that includes North and South America and the surrounding waters.

wharf. A long platform built along a shoreline, or into a body of water, so that ships can load and unload cargo.

wigwam. A small, dome-shaped hut made of poles and covered with bark, branches, or leaves, used by American Indians.

Yucatán Peninsula. The geographic area that includes southeastern Mexico, British Honduras, and part of Guatemala.

INDEX

Key to Pronunciation

a hat, cap	i it, pin	ou house, out	zh measure, seizure
ā age, face	ī ice, five	sh she, rush	ə represents:
ã care, air	ng long, bring	th thin, both	a in about
ä father, far	o hot, rock	ŦH then, smooth	e in taken
ch child, much	ō open, go	u cup, butter	i in pencil
e let, best	ô order, all	ù full, put	o in lemon
ē equal, see	oi oil, voice	ü rule, move	u in circus
ėr term, learn			

The Key to Pronunciation above is from *The World Book Dictionary* copyright © 1970, by Doubleday & Company, Inc. Reprinted by permission of the publisher. The respellings for pronunciation of words in this book are based on this Key to Pronunciation.

A

Abolitionists, 100–101
Adobe, 33, 127, 128
Africans
  achievements of, 57
  in Brazil, 70–72
  coming to America of, 56, 57–60, 85–86
  cultures of, 56–57, 111
  See also Blacks; Slavery.
Agriculture
  in Canada, 390
  in Colombia, 375–376, 382–385
  in English colonies, 91–92
  of Indians of North America, 25, 28, 32, 54, 79
  of Indians of South America, 36, 40, 64
  industrialization and, 209, 338–340
  and migrant farm workers, 359–360
  in South America today, 66, 69–70, 255, 256, 271–272, 375–376, 382–385
  transportation and, 172–175
  See also Farm life.
Amazon River, 256, 260
America, coming of man to, 22–24
Andes Mountains, 65, 254–255, 374
Animals, use of, 31, 34, 54, 298, 314, 316–317
Archaeologists, 125
Artifacts, 125
Automation, 341–342
Automobiles
  and growth of cities, 183–184, 218
  invention of, 335–337
  and new industries, 335–336, 353
  and pollution, 224, 227
  and traffic problem, 239–241
Aztec Indians, 37–39, 50, 55
  capital city of, 124–133
  defeat of, 48–49, 124–125
  division of labor among, 54
  level of technology of, 48–49

B

Bahia, 71–72
Barriada, 275–277
BART (Bay Area Rapid Transit), 241, 247–248
Bering Strait, 22
Bill of Rights, 423, 424
Blacks
  in Brazil, 70–72
  coming to America of, 56, 57–60, 84–86
  and equality, 400–401, 405
  freedom for, 424
  in ghettos, 210–214, 221, 238–239, 241
  movement to cities of, 192–194, 210–211
  poor, city life of, 222, 224, 226–227
  and right to vote, 100, 409–410, 438–439
  riots by, 226
  slavery of, 56–60, 99–101
  in Watts, 221
  See also Africans; Slavery.
Blast furnaces, 295
Bogotá, Colombia, 264–266
Bolívar, Simón, 60
Boston, Massachusetts, 149, 162
Brasília, Brazil, 266–269
Brazil
  African influence in, 70–72
  cultures in, 70–72
  geography of, 256
  Portugal and, 52, 60
Bucket brigades, 158–159
Buenos Aires, Argentina, 259–260
Buffalo, use by Plains Indians, 31

C

Calendars, 36, 38
California, redwoods in, 452–461
Campesinos, 375, 382–384
Canada
  agriculture in, 390
  cities in, 277–281
  different cultures in, 113–117
  education in, 391
  French Canadians in, 115–117
  history of, 113
  industry in, 388–391
  natural resources of, 388–389
  people of, 114, 390
  pollution in, 391
  transportation in, 389
Capital, 310, 311, 390
Capital goods, 310, 311
Caracas, Venezuela, 273–274
Carnaval, 71
Charcoal, 290–291
Chicago, Illinois, 182–183
Child labor, 329, 349–352, 356–357, 359
Chinampas, 132
Chinatown, 110–111
Chinese-Americans, 110–111
Cholos, 66
Cincinnati, Ohio, 169, 180
Cities
  advantages of, 140, 199–200, 222
  advertisements for, 167–

498

168
  of Aztecs (Tenochtitlán), 124–133
  building of new, 245–247, 266–269
  in Canada, 277–281
  colonial, 133–141, 148–162
  development in the West of, 166–171
  different kinds of, 219–220
  ghettos in, 210–214, 221, 238–239, 241
  on Great Plains, 176–179
  growth of, along Great Lakes, 171–175
  immigrants in, 194–197
  improvement of, 231–250
  location and growth of, 161, 166–170
  manufacturing and growth of, 179–184
  of Mayas, 35, 36
  movement from, 214–217
  movement to, 192–194, 209, 210–211
  nineteenth-century growth of, 165–188
  planned, 245–246, 266–269
  problems of, 224–228, 274–277
  railroads and growth of, 175–179
  rivers and growth of, 168–169, 170–171
  sanitation in, 156–157, 160–161, 197, 203–204
  solving problems of, 227–228, 239–241
  in South America, 258–277
  specialization in, 150–152, 180, 181–184
  steamboat and growth of, 170–171
  and suburbs, 188, 214–217
  transportation within, 186–188
  urban decay in, 225–227
  See also Urban renewal; Slums.
Citizens, influence of, on representatives, 434
Citizens Action Committee, 232
Citizens' Committee to Preserve and Develop the Crosstown Community, 448–449
City life
  advantages of, 140, 199–200, 222
  differs from farm life, 197–198

  disadvantages of, 222–228
  today, 208–228
  See also Cities.
City planning, 133–134, 241–245, 249
Civil Rights Act of 1964, 402
Civil War, 101
Coal mining, 294, 330, 334, 350–354, 359
Coffee growing, 255, 271, 375
Colombia
  education in, 384, 385–386
  farming in, 375–376
  geography of, 374–375
  natural resources of, 376–377
  need for investments in, 386–387
  problems of industrializing in, 380–387
  steps toward industrialization in, 376–379
Colonies
  Dutch, 77–78
  English, 78–80, 84–86, 113, 419, 432
  freedom in, 418–419
  French, 76–77, 113
  government of, 51–52, 419–420, 432
  manufacturing in, 317–318
  Spanish, 51–52, 60
  Swedish, 78
Columbia, Maryland, 245–246
Columbus, Christopher, 48
Commerce, 149–150, 170–171
  See also Trade.
Congress, and redwoods, 454, 455–461
Conquistadores, 50
Conservationists, 453–454, 458–459
Co-parents (compadres), 110
Cotton, 99, 302–303
Cotton gin, 326
Crosstown Expressway
  opposition to, 445–449, 451–452
  reasons for, 444–445, 449–451
Cultural borrowing, 18
  in Brazil, 70–72
  between colonists and North American Indians, 79, 87, 91
  between Europeans and Indians of Latin America, 54, 65
Cultural pluralism, 112
Culture
  of Africans, 56–57

  of black Americans, 111
  in Brazil today, 70–72
  in Canada, 113–117
  changes in, 18
  and customs, 13
  different meanings of, 3
  of immigrants to U.S., 104–105
  of Indians of Middle America, 34–39
  of Indians of North America, 24–34
  of Indians of South America, 39–43, 64, 66–67, 69–70
  learning a, 15–16
  in North American colonies, 88–91
  in Peru today, 64–70
  Spanish, 50, 52
  technology and, 14, 18
  values and, 12–13
Culture groups, 13–18
Customs, 13
Cuzco, as Incan capital, 43

D

Declaration of Independence, 397, 398
Democracy
  elections in, 429, 433
  failure to vote in, 438–439
  making decisions in, 443–461
  making laws in, 430, 436
  majority in, 437–438
  minority in, 436, 437
  opposition in, 437
  representative, 432
  voting in, 430–431, 438–439
Denver, Colorado, 177
Detroit, Michigan, 175, 183–184
Discrimination, 405
  against blacks, 213, 224
  against French Canadians, 116–117
  against Indians in Peru, 67–68
  laws against, 216, 402
  against women, 407
Division of labor, 36, 54, 131
Dixwell, rebuilding of, 238–239
Duvalier, François, 417
Dukes, George, 447–448

E

Earthquake, in Peru, 68–69
Eastern Woodland Indians, 27–30
Economy, simple, 54
Edison, Thomas, 338

Education
  in Canada, 391
  in Colombia, 384, 385–386
  and equality of opportunity, 406
  lack of, and unemployment, 210, 224
  by on-the-job training, 364
  of Peruvian Indians, today, 68, 69–70
Elections, 429, 433
  See also Voting.
Elevators, and growth of cities, 188
Encomienda system, 50–51
Energy, sources of, 330, 335–336, 338, 340–341
Environment, 8
  of English colonies, 91, 92
  of Incas, 40
  of Indians of North America, 27, 30–33
  of Mayas, 35–36
  and way of life, 25
Epidemics, 140
Equality
  and freedom, 415
  for French Canadians, 116–117
  and government, 408–410
  Jefferson's meaning of, 397–399
  lack of, 400–401
  laws to bring about, 402–403
  of opportunity, 403–407
  steps toward, 402–403, 406–407
  under the law, 400–403
Erie Canal, 172–175
Europeans
  coming to North America of, 76–84
  coming to South America of, 48–52

F

Factories
  in Colombia, 376
  development of, 317–318
  first, in America, 325–326
  and growth of cities, 180–184
  See also Industrialism.
Farm life
  differs from city life, 142–144, 197–198
  effects of industrialism on, 362
  See also Agriculture.
Farms, movement of people from, 192–194, 209, 210–211

Federal government, and urban renewal, 238–239, 249–250
Fire fighting, in colonial cities, 157–159
Flour milling. *See* Wheat industry.
Flying shuttle, 311, 312
Ford, Henry, 335–336
Freedom
 for blacks, 424
 English ideas of, 418
 equality and, 415
 laws and, 415–416
 limits on, 424–426
 meaning of, 414–415
 people without, 416–418
 value of, 415, 418
French Canadians, 115–117
Fresno, California, 241–245
Fulton Mall, 242–244

G

Garbage
 in colonial cities, 136–137, 156–157
 in nineteenth-century cities, 197, 203–204
 in Tenochtitlán, 132, 133
Garland, Hamlin, 142–143, 192
Ghettos, 210–214, 221, 241
 rebuilding of, 238–239
 riots in, 226
 See also Slums.
Goodyear, Charles, 311
Government, representative, 432
Government cities, 219
 in Canada, 279
 in South America, 263–269
Grain elevators, 300
Great Lakes, 389
 growth of cities along, 171–175
 pollution of, 369
 and St. Lawrence Seaway, 280–281
Great Plains, 30–31, 176–179
Gruen Plan, 242–245

H

Hacendado, 52
Haciendas, 52, 67
Haiti, 416–417
Hidalgo County, Texas, 108–110
High population density, 131
Historical records, 125
Housing
 discrimination in, 216, 402
 minority groups and, 403

problems of, in South America, 274–277
public, 225
See also Slums, Urban renewal.
Human sacrifice, 37, 38–39

I

Ice ages, 22
Immigrants, 200, 202–203, 330, 403–404
 from China, 101, 102
 from Europe, 96–98
 from Japan, 101, 102, 402
 limiting number of, 208
 movement to cities of, 194–196
 reasons for coming, 96–98
 from Western Hemisphere, 103, 209
Inca, the, 43, 49
Incan Indians, 39–44, 49–50, 54
Indentured servants, 84
Indians, 48–52
 and equality, 400, 405
 and ideas of private ownership, 28, 43, 55, 87–88
 of Middle America, 34–39
 of North America, 24–34
 religious beliefs of, 56
 of South America, 39–43, 66, 69–70
Indies, 48
Industrial parks, 217
Industrial Revolution, 324–325
Industrialism
 and agriculture, 338–340
 and child labor, 356–357, 359
 control of, 354–357
 and cultural values, 320
 effects of today, 360–369
 and employment, 352–353
 evils of, 349–354
 and growth of cities, 179–184
 inventions and, 311–312
 and labor supply, 308
 and labor unions, 354–356
 machinery and, 308–311
 main features of, 307–319
 and need for new skills, 363–364
 railroads and, 331–335
 raw materials and, 317
 and specialization, 360
 technology and, 311–312
 and ways of working, 346–349

and workers today, 357–359
 and working conditions, 351–352, 356–359
Industry
 in Canada, 388–391
 creation of, 353
 and growth of cities, 179–184, 221
 movement to suburbs of, 217
 and urban renewal, 234–235
 See also Industrialism.
Inventions, and industrialism, 311–313, 324–325, 326
Ironmaking
 in colonial times, 288–292
 today, 292–297
Irrigation, 32, 40

J

Jamestown, Virginia, 78–79, 84, 87, 90
Jefferson, Thomas, 397, 398, 399, 400–401
Jews, 111, 419
Jim Crow laws, 401, 402

K

Kansas City, Missouri, 178
Kennedy, John F., 429

L

Labor
 division of, 36, 54, 131
 and industrialism, 308
Labor unions, 354–356, 357–358
Lake Erie, pollution of, 368–369
Lake Maracaibo, 273
Laws
 in colonial cities, 161
 in democracy, 430, 436
 and freedom, 415–416
 Jim Crow, 401, 402
 need for, 8, 436, 439
Lazarus, Emma, 403–404
Lee, Mayor Richard, 232, 235, 239
Legislatures, 419, 432
Level of technology
 of Africans, 57
 of Aztecs, 48–49
 definition of, 9
 differences in, 53–54, 104
 and environment, 25
 of Incas, 40, 42
 of Indians of North America, 26–27, 31
Lima, Peru, 275–276
Limestone, 36, 295

Lipscomb, Alice, 447, 448
Llama, 40, 54, 255
Lobbies, 436
Long Wharf, 235
Longhouse, 29
Los Angeles, California, 220–221
Lowell, Francis, 328, 329–330, 349

M

McCormick, Cyrus, 339
Machinery
 farm, 338–340
 and industrialism, 308–311
 before industrialism, 312–313
 and new sources of power, 315–316
Magdalena River, 261, 374–375, 381
Maize, 25
Mantas, 130–131
Manufacturing
 in colonial America, 317–318
 and growth of cities, 179–184
 of iron, in colonial times, 288–292
 and markets, 308
 in South America, 270–271, 272, 378–379, 387
 of steel today, 292–297
 of textiles, 302–304, 311–312, 324–325, 328–330
 and transportation, 318–319, 378–379
 See also Industrialism.
Mass-transportation system, 241
Mayan Indians, 34–36
 division of labor among, 54
 picture language of, 55
 religious beliefs of, 37
Megalopolis, 217–219
Mestizos, 66, 67, 68
Metropolitan areas, 210
Mexican-Americans, 103
 discrimination against, 224
 and equality, 401, 407
 in ghettos, 211
 in Hidalgo County, Texas, 108–110
 movement to cities of, 209
 values of, 109–110
Middle America, 24
Migrant workers, 359–360
Milling. *See* Wheat industry.
Minimum wage law, 359
Mining
 of coal, 294, 330, 334,

500

350–354, 359
industrialism and, 359, 363
of iron ore, 290, 293–294
of limestone, 290
in South America, 263
Minority groups, 224, 403
   See also Negroes; Mexican-Americans; Puerto Ricans.
Missionaries
   in New France, 77
   in South America, 50
Mita, of Incas, 43
Montreal, Canada, 278–279
Motilones, culture of, 64

N

"Negro removal," 234
Negroes
   and African culture, 56–57, 111
   in Brazil, 70–72
   city life of poor, 222, 224, 226–227
   coming to America of, 56–60, 84–86
   and equality, 400–401, 405
   freedom for, 424
   and ghettos, 210–214, 221, 238–239, 241
   movement to cities of, 192–194, 210–211
   and right to vote, 100, 409–410, 438–439
   riots by, 226
   slavery of, 56–60, 99–101
   in Watts, 221
   See also Africans.
New Amsterdam, 78, 89
New England, industrialization of, 329–330
New France, 76–77
New Haven, Connecticut, urban renewal in, 232–239
New Orleans, Louisiana, 169, 171
New Sweden, 78, 89
New World
   coming of Africans to, 56–60, 84–86
   coming of Europeans to, 48–52, 76–84
   discovery of, 48
New York City
   in colonial period, 149, 152, 154, 156, 162
   in nineteenth century, 194, 200, 202–203, 204
Newport, Rhode Island, 149, 162
Nixon, Richard M., 429, 437
North America
   coming of Africans to, 56–60, 84–86
   coming of Europeans to, 76–84
   Indians of, 24–34

O

Oil industry
   automobile and development of, 335–336, 353
   in Canada, 389
   at Lake Maracaibo, 273
   in South America, 273, 276
On-the-job training, 364
Orinoco River, 256, 260–261
Orphans, sending to America of, 83–84
Ottawa, Canada, 279

P

Parliament, 418, 419, 420, 421
Patent Office, 313
Penn, William
   colony of, 82
   and Pennsylvania Charter of Privileges, 82
   planning Philadelphia by, 133–134
Pennsylvania, colony of, 82, 89
Pennsylvania Charter of Privileges, 82, 419
Peru
   cultures in, today, 64–70
   geography of, 64–65
   Incas in, 39–43, 44, 49–50, 54
Philadelphia (colonial), 135, 141, 149
   city services in, 137, 140
   industry and trade in, 137–139
   planning of, 133–134, 444
   sanitation in, 136–137
   social life in, 140
Philadelphia (today)
   and proposed Crosstown Expressway, 445–452
   traffic problems in, 444–445
Pilgrims, coming to America of, 79
Pittsburgh, Pennsylvania, 168
Plains Indians, 30–31, 87
Planned cities
   Brasília, 266–269
   colonial Philadelphia, 133–134, 444
   Columbia and Reston, 245–246
Plantations
   in Brazil, 52
   slavery on, 85–86
Plymouth, Massachusetts, 79

Police, in early cities, 161–162
Pollution
   action against, 369–370
   air, 224, 365, 367
   in Canada, 391
   from fuels, 364–365
   in South America, 274
   in suburbs, 227
   in Tenochtitlán, 133
   water, 365–367, 368–369
Population
   and growth of cities, 181, 185
   and industrialism, 308
   in U.S. today, 214
Population density, 131
Portugal, 52, 60
Power (industrial), 298–299, 313–317, 330
Public housing, 225
Pueblo Indians, 32–33
Puerto Ricans, 103, 209, 407
   discrimination against, 224
   in ghettos, 211
   values and customs of, 107–108
Puritans, 418–419

Q

Quebec, Canada, 76–77, 113, 279
Quechua language, 67, 70

R

Race prejudice, 72
   See also Discrimination.
Railroads
   advertisements of, 98
   building of, 102, 103
   and growth of cities, 175–179
   and industries, 181, 294, 331–335
Raw materials, and industrialism, 317
Reaper, invention of, 339
Redwood National Park
   creation of, 461
   lumber companies and, 452, 453, 455–456, 457–458, 460, 461
   opposition to, 455–458
   proposals for, 453, 454–455, 459–461
Redwoods, 452–461
Rehabilitation, of Wooster Square, 237–238
Religion, 56
   of Aztecs, 38–39
   in Brazil, 71
   in Canada, 115, 116
   in ghetto, 213–214
   of Incas, 41, 42, 49

of Mayas, 37
   in United States, 111, 213–214, 418–419
Representative government, 432
Representatives, 432–433, 434
Residential areas, rebuilding of, 235–239
Resort cities, 219, 270–271
Reston, Virginia, 245–246
Revolutionary War, 99
Riis, Jacob, 203–204
Rio de Janeiro, Brazil, 270–271
Riots, 214, 226
Rivers, and growth of cities, 168–169, 170–171
Roads, in colonial cities, 153–154
Rubber, discovery of, 311
Rural areas, movement to cities from, 209

S

St. Lawrence River, 77, 277, 280
St. Lawrence Seaway, 279
Sanitation
   in colonial cities, 136–137, 156–157, 160–161
   in nineteenth-century cities, 197, 203–204
   and spread of disease, 203–204
   in Tenochtitlán, 132, 133
São Paulo, Brazil, 271–273
Save-the-Redwoods League, 453
Scientific knowledge, 8, 9
   and environment, 25
   of Plains Indians, 31
Scotch-Irish, 80, 92
Segregation, 213
   See also Discrimination.
Selva, 257
Separation of powers, 422
Shanties, in nineteenth-century cities, 201
Sierra Club, and redwoods, 453, 459
Simple economy, 54, 66
Slash-and-burn, 28
Slater, Samuel, 325–326, 349
Slave trade, 56, 57–58, 149
Slavery
   abolitionists and, 100–101
   of Africans, 56, 57–60, 84–86, 90
   end of, 101
   of Indians, 50–51
   steps against, 99–101
   See also Slave trade; Slaves.

501

Slaves
    after Civil War, 193
    coming to America of, 56, 57–60, 84–86
    inhumane treatment of, 50, 58–60
    See also Slave trade; Slavery.
Slums
    disease in, 202, 203–204
    in nineteenth-century cities, 200, 202–203
    rebuilding of, 233, 238–239
    in South America, 274–277
    See also Housing; Urban renewal.
Smallpox, 50, 160
Smelting, 288, 291
Social scientists, 3
Social security, 359
South America
    agriculture in, 255, 256, 271–272, 375–376, 383–385
    cities in, 258–277
    coming of Europeans to, 48–52
    geography of, 254–258
    urban problems in, 269, 271, 272–273, 274–277
Spaniards
    colonies of, 60, 76
    and Indians of Middle and South America, 48–52
Spanish Harlem, 107–108
Sparrow Point, Maryland, 292–293
Specialization, 54
    by Aztecs, 131
    and growth of cities, 148–149, 150–152, 180, 181–184
    industrialism and, 360
    by Mayas, 36–37
Speculators, and growth of cities, 166
Spinning jenny, 312
Statue of Liberty, 403–404
Steam engine, 315, 330
Steamboat, 170–171, 175
Steel
    production of, 292–297, 334, 378–379
    railroads and, 332–334
    raw materials for manufacture of, 293–294
    recipe for, 296
    uses of, 296–297
    See also Ironmaking.
Storefront churches, 214
Strikes, 356
Suburbs
    cities and growth of, 140–141, 188
    movement of industry to, 217
    movement of people to, 215–217
    and problems of cities, 227–228
    transportation and, 240–241
Subways, 187–188

T

Tate, Mayor James, 449, 450–451, 452
Technology
    and culture, 14, 18
    definition of, 9
    and industrialism, 311–312
    and ways of living, 10
Tenements, 232
    See also Slums; Urban decay; Urban renewal.
Tenochtitlán, 37–38, 124–125, 128–131
    building of, 126–127
    sanitation in, 132, 133
    water supply in, 132
Tepee, 31
Terracing, by Incas, 40
Textile industry
    in colonial times, 302–303
    growth of, 328–330
    Industrial Revolution and, 324–325
    inventions and, 311–312
    today, 303–304
Tierra caliente, 255
Tierra fria, 255
Tierra templada, 255
Timbuktu, 57
Tools, 91, 312
    of European conquerors, 53–54
    of Indians of Middle and South America, 34, 35, 66
    of Indians of North America, 26, 87
    and level of technology, 9–10
Town meetings, 431
Town of America, 167–168, 170
Trade, 166, 179
    by Aztecs, 130–131
    in early Philadelphia, 137–139
    effect of Erie Canal on, 172–175
    and growth of cities, 148–150
    and raw materials, 317
Tradition, definition of, 13
Traffic problems, 224–225, 227
    and proposed Crosstown Expressway, 444–452
    solving of, 239–241
    See also BART.
Transportation
    in Canada, 389
    in Colombia, 380–382
    in ghettos, 221, 241
    and growth of cities, 170–171, 185–188
    and industrialism, 181, 289, 294, 318–319
    and movement to the suburbs, 215
    within cities, 186–188
Travois, 31
Treaties, between Indians and colonists, 87–88
Trolley car, 187
Tyrants, 417

U

Unemployment
    industrialism and, 352–353
    lack of education and, 210, 224
    and need for new skills, 363–364
United States
    constitution of, 422–424
    immigrants to, 96–98
    industrialization of, 323–342
    President of, 433
University cities, 220
Urban decay, 225–227
Urban problems
    solving of, 247–250
    in South America, 269, 271, 272–277
    See also Slums; Traffic; Urban decay; Urban renewal.
Urban renewal
    cost of, 249–250
    in New Haven, 232–239
    planning of, 248–249
Urbanism
    of Aztecs (Tenochtitlán), 124–133
    in Canada, 277–281
    in colonies, 133–141, 148–162
    industrialism and growth of, 179–184
    of Mayas, 35, 36
    in nineteenth century, 165–188
    problems of, 224–228, 274–277
    railroads and spread of, 175–179
    rivers and spread of, 168–169, 170–171
    in South America, 258–277
    and suburbs, 140–141, 188, 214–217
    transportation and spread of, 172–179, 185–188

V

Values, 14–15, 18
    of Aztecs, 38–39
    of Chinese-Americans, 110
    and culture, 12–13
    definition of, 10
    differences in, 11–12, 87–88
    of equality, 399
    of freedom, 414–415
    of Incas, 43
    and industrialism, 320
    of Mayas, 37
    of Mexican-Americans, 109–110
    protection of, 440
    of Puerto Ricans, 107–108
    understanding of, 11–12
Venezuela
    geography of, 255–256
    Motilones in, 64
    oil industry in, 273
Vicos, Peru, 69–70
Vote, equal right to, 408–410, 438–439
Voting
    and blacks, 100, 408–410
    in democracy, 430–431

W

Water supply
    in colonial cities, 136, 159
    in South American cities, 274
    in Tenochtitlán, 132
Watt, James, 315
Watts, 221
Wheat industry
    in colonial days, 297–299
    today, 299–301
Whitney, Eli, 326
Wigwam, 29
Women
    discrimination against, 407
    and right to vote, 410
    work in early factories by, 329, 350
Wooster Square, rehabilitation of, 235–238, 248
Work, specialization of, 36, 54, 131, 150–152
Workers
    labor unions formed by, 354–356
    laws for protection of, 356–357

Y

Yellow fever, 160
Yucatán Peninsula, 35–36